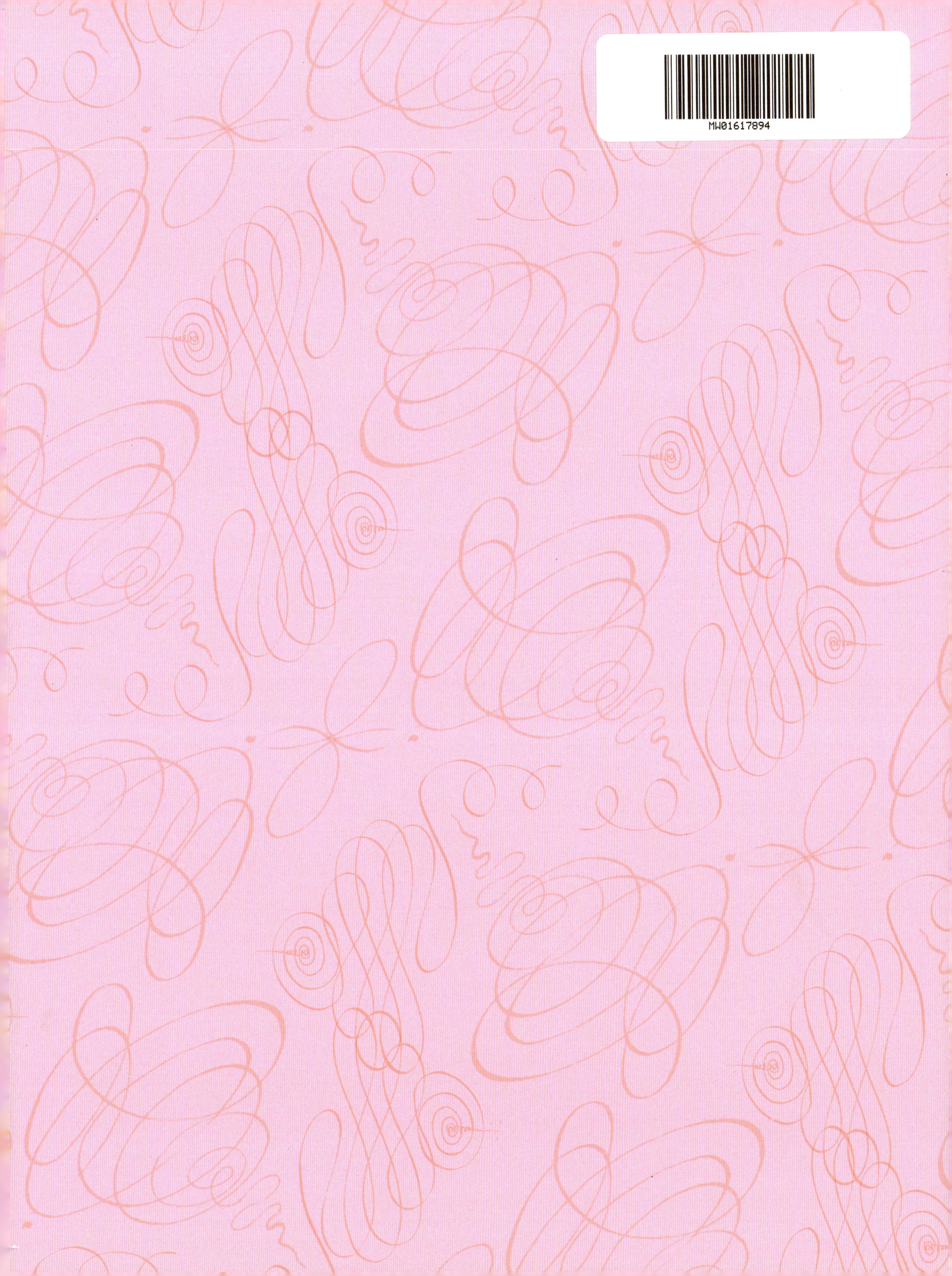

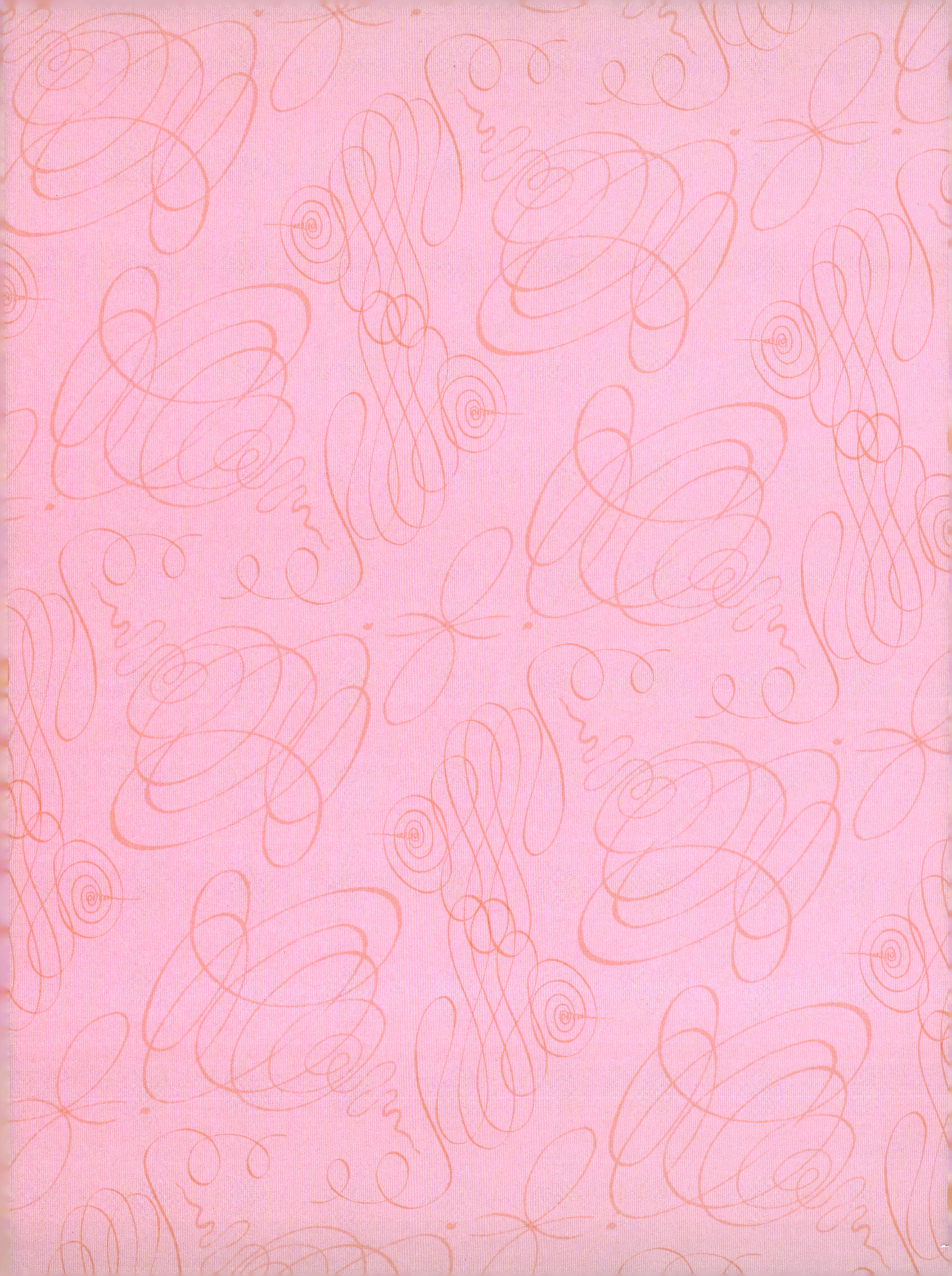

HENDRICK GOLTZIUS

PETER PAUL RUBENS

HIRMER

STAATLICHE
GRAPHISCHE
SAMMLUNG
MÜNCHEN

HENDRICK GOLTZIUS

PETER PAUL RUBENS

Careers by design

HERAUSGEGEBEN VON / EDITED BY NINA SCHLEIF

MICHAEL HERING & NINA SCHLEIF

Ehre und Gold

VORWORT

Honor and Gold

FOREWORD

Die Sehnsucht nach Ruhm und Ehre spornt bis heute den Erfindergeist gefeierter Künstler an. Im aufblühenden Barock um 1600 mit seinen um Renommee wetteifernden europäischen Höfen und einem vermehrt nach Prestige strebenden finanzkräftigen Bürgertum empfahl sich die Strategie, über lokale Grenzen hinweg ferne Kunstmärkte und neue Käuferschichten zu erreichen, um das eigene Werk gewinnbringend bekannt zu machen. Sperrige Skulpturen und fragile Gemälde waren für diese vielfältigen Transaktionen wenig geeignet. Vielmehr sollte die Druckgraphik zum perfekten Gesandten im kunstdiplomatischen Dienst der eigenen Sache werden. Mit graphisch hinreißenden Kupferstichen versuchten die Künstler, das Publikum zu betören und es auf dem Laufenden über die eigenen Neuschöpfungen zu halten. Die in dieser Hinsicht erfolgreichsten Virtuosen um 1600 waren Hendrick Goltzius (1558–1617) und Peter Paul Rubens (1577–1640).

Exemplarisch präsentieren wir aus dem reichen, erst jüngst wissenschaftlich vollständig bearbeiteten Bestand der Staatlichen Graphischen Sammlung München eine prononcierte Auswahl von 140 Druckgraphiken unter thematischen Schwerpunkten wie dem Vorbild Antike oder der Rolle von Widmungen, um die jeweiligen künstlerischen Strategien, die die Karrieren von Goltzius und Rubens beflügelten, sichtbar zu machen.

Dieser Ausstellung ging eine mehrjährige Bearbeitung der Druckgraphikbestände beider Künstler voraus. Die Werke mit den dazugehörigen Datensätzen können von nun an online eingesehen und recherchiert werden. Dank der großzügigen Unterstützung der Kulturstiftung der Länder war es möglich, alle Werke

The longing for fame and glory has kindled the inventive spirit of celebrated artists right up to the present day. During the blossoming Baroque period around 1600, as European courts were vying for renown and an increasingly affluent middle class was striving for prestige, it became common to adopt a strategy of reaching out to distant art markets and new groups of buyers across local borders in order to promote one's own work profitably. Bulky sculptures and fragile paintings were less than suitable for these transactions. Instead, the print was to become the perfect envoy in the diplomatic service of the artist's agenda. With graphically captivating engravings, artists attempted to beguile the public and keep it up to date on their new creations. In this respect, the most successful virtuosos around 1600 were Hendrick Goltzius (1558–1617) and Peter Paul Rubens (1577–1640).

This exhibition presents a distinctive selection of 140 prints from the rich collection of the Staatliche Graphische Sammlung München, which has only recently been fully researched. Focusing on themes such as the paragon of antiquity and the role of dedications allows us to reveal the artistic strategies that inspired the careers of both Goltzius and Rubens.

The exhibition was preceded by several years of work on our holdings in prints by both artists. The works and corresponding records can now be viewed and researched online. Thanks to the generous support of the Kulturstiftung der Länder, it was possible to place all the works of the collection in acid-free mounts so that the originals are close at hand and can be presented to visitors in the study hall. For the exhibition,

in säurefreie Passepartouts zu verbringen, sodass die Originale im Studiensaal griffbereit sind und vorgelegt werden können. In Hinblick auf die Ausstellung mussten 140 Werke gerahmt und gehängt werden. Für diese Teamleistung bedanken wir uns ausdrücklich bei den Mitarbeiterinnen und Mitarbeitern der Staatlichen Graphischen Sammlung München. Unterstützung für die Ausstellung erhielten wir vom Königreich der Niederlande.

Den Autorinnen und Autoren des Katalogs gilt ein ganz besonderer Dank. Sie alle waren unmittelbar bereit, ihre Expertise in die hier versammelten Texte einfließen zu lassen. Nachdem Karolien De Clippel (Direktorin am Modemuseum Hasselt) und Filip Vermeylen (Professor für Global Art Markets in Rotterdam) 2012 in einem Aufsatz auf den wichtigen künstlerischen und kulturellen Austausch zwischen den nördlichen und südlichen Niederlanden, insbesondere zwischen Goltzius und Rubens, hingewiesen hatten, greifen sie diesen Ansatz sehr passend für unser Projekt wieder auf. Nadine M. Orenstein, Drue Heinz Curator in Charge of the Department of Drawings and Prints am New Yorker Metropolitan Museum of Art, verdankt die Kunstgeschichte Grundlagenforschung zum niederländischen Verlegerwesen im 16. und 17. Jahrhundert und auch zu Hendrick Goltzius. So war es uns eine besondere Freude, dass wir sie für einen Beitrag zu diesem Künstler gewinnen konnten. Nils Büttner, Vorsitzender des Centrum Rubenianum vzw in Antwerpen und Professor für Kunstgeschichte an der Kunstakademie Stuttgart, krempelte vor einigen Jahren mit Quellenforschung zu Rubens unser Denken über diesen Künstler um und zeigte, dass dieser außer seinem künstlerischen Genie und seinem politisch-diplomatischen Engagement auch über einen ausgeprägten Geschäftssinn und einen systematischen Ansatz zum

140 works had to be framed and hung. We would like to expressly thank the staff of the Staatliche Graphische Sammlung München for this team effort. Support for the exhibition came from the Kingdom of the Netherlands.

Special thanks go to the authors of the texts in this catalog, who were all immediately enthusiastic about contributing their expertise. In a 2012 essay, Karolien De Clippel (Director of the Hasselt Fashion Museum) and Filip Vermeylen (Professor of Global Art Markets in Rotterdam) had pointed out the important artistic and cultural exchange between the Northern and Southern Netherlands, and especially between Goltzius and Rubens. The authors revisited this intriguing approach for our project. Art history is indebted to Nadine M. Orenstein, Drue Heinz Curator in Charge of the Department of Drawings and Prints at the Metropolitan Museum of Art in New York, for her foundational research on Netherlandish publishers in the sixteenth and seventeenth centuries and on Hendrick Goltzius. It was therefore a special pleasure for us to win her over for a contribution on this artist. A few years ago, Nils Büttner, Chairman of the Centrum Rubenianum vzw in Antwerp and Professor for Art History at the State Academy of Fine Arts Stuttgart, changed the way we think about Rubens by uncovering new sources on the artist and showing that, in addition to his artistic genius and his political and diplomatic commitment, he also had a keen business sense and a systematic approach to developing his artistic career. All of this research has been incorporated into the concept of the exhibition.

Ausbau seiner künstlerischen Karriere verfügte. All diese Forschungen sind in das Konzept der Ausstellung eingeflossen.

Die Finanzierung dieses Ausstellungskatalogs ermöglichten die Tavolozza Foundation sowie die Ernst von Siemens Kunststiftung. Dafür bedanken wir uns sehr. Für die Gestaltung dieses Bandes fand Sarah Nöllenheidt, Buero Noc, Berlin, die richtige Form.

Schließlich möchten wir das Entgegenkommen unserer Leihgeber würdigen, die uns fantastische Zeichnungen von Goltzius beziehungsweise Rubens für die Laufzeit der Ausstellung anvertraut haben: Unser herzlicher Dank geht an das Städel Museum in Frankfurt am Main mit seinem Direktor Philipp Demandt und der Kuratorin Astrid Reuter, an das Museum der bildenden Künste Leipzig mit seinem Direktor Stefan Weppelmann und der Kuratorin Jeannette Stoschek sowie an Mon Müllerschön für eine Privatsammlung in München.

„Eer boven golt" – Ehre *vor* Gold, so lautete das persönliche Motto von Hendrick Goltzius, das auch ein Wortspiel auf seinen Namen enthielt. So nobel dieser Wahlspruch, so zutreffend war sicher für beide Künstler, Goltzius und Rubens, auch die leicht abgewandelte Fassung, welche zugleich thematischer Leitfaden unserer Ausstellung ist: „Eer en golt" – Ehre *und* Gold!

We are very grateful that the financing of this exhibition catalog was made possible by the Tavolozza Foundation and the Ernst von Siemens Kunststiftung. Sarah Nöllenheidt of Buero Noc, Berlin, has superbly designed this volume.

Finally, we would like to acknowledge the kindness of our lenders, who have entrusted us with fantastic drawings by Goltzius and Rubens for the duration of the exhibition: our heartfelt thanks go to the Städel Museum in Frankfurt with its director Philipp Demandt and curator Astrid Reuter; to the Museum der bildenden Künste Leipzig with its director Stefan Weppelmann and curator Jeannette Stoschek; and to Mon Muellerschoen for a private collection in Munich.

"Eer boven golt"—honor *before* gold—was Hendrick Goltzius's personal motto, as well as a pun on his name. As noble as this motto was, a slightly modified version, one which thematically guides our exhibition, was certainly just as appropriate for Goltzius and Rubens: "Eer en golt"—honor *and* gold!

MICHAEL HERING
DIREKTOR / DIRECTOR

NINA SCHLEIF
KURATORIN / CURATOR

STAATLICHE GRAPHISCHE SAMMLUNG MÜNCHEN

Förderung der Restaurierung der Goltzius- und Rubens-Bestände durch die /
Support for conservational treatment of the print holdings by Goltzius and Rubens from the
KULTURSTIFTUNG DER LÄNDER

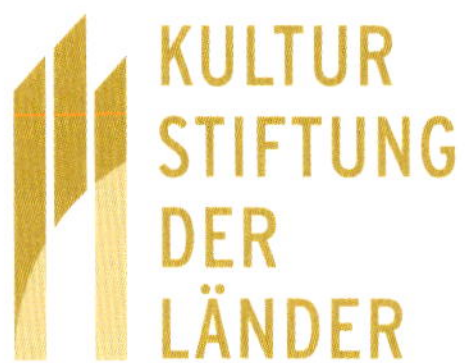

Die Veröffentlichung dieses Katalogs wurde ermöglicht durch die /
Publication of this catalog is made possible by the
ERNST VON SIEMENS KUNSTSTIFTUNG & TAVOLOZZA FOUNDATION

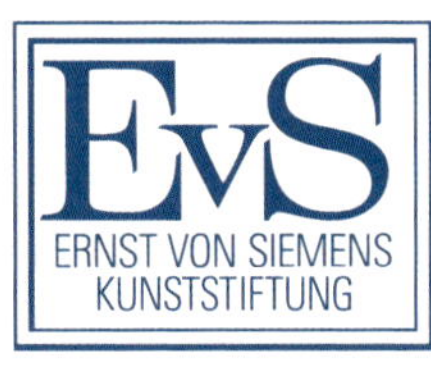

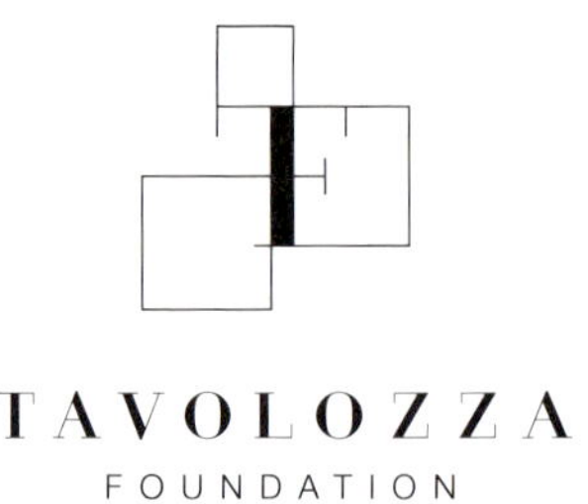

Weitere Unterstützung durch das Königreich der Niederlande /
Additional support by the Kingdom of the Netherlands

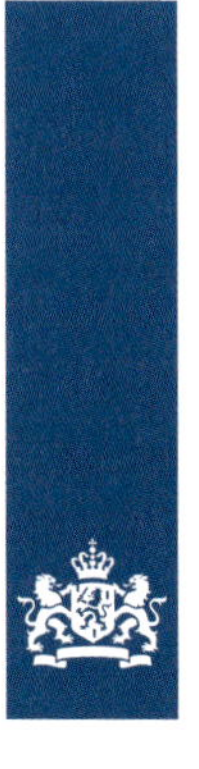
Königreich der Niederlande

BESONDERER DANK AN / SPECIAL THANKS TO

Saskia van Altena

Jens Burk

Wolfgang Holzapfel

Michaela Lechner

Jan Nicolaisen

Uta Piereth

Ulrike-Claudia Pulzer

Anna Rühl

Jaco Rutgers

Moritz Schueler

Joanna Seidenstein

Simon Turner

Marius Wittke

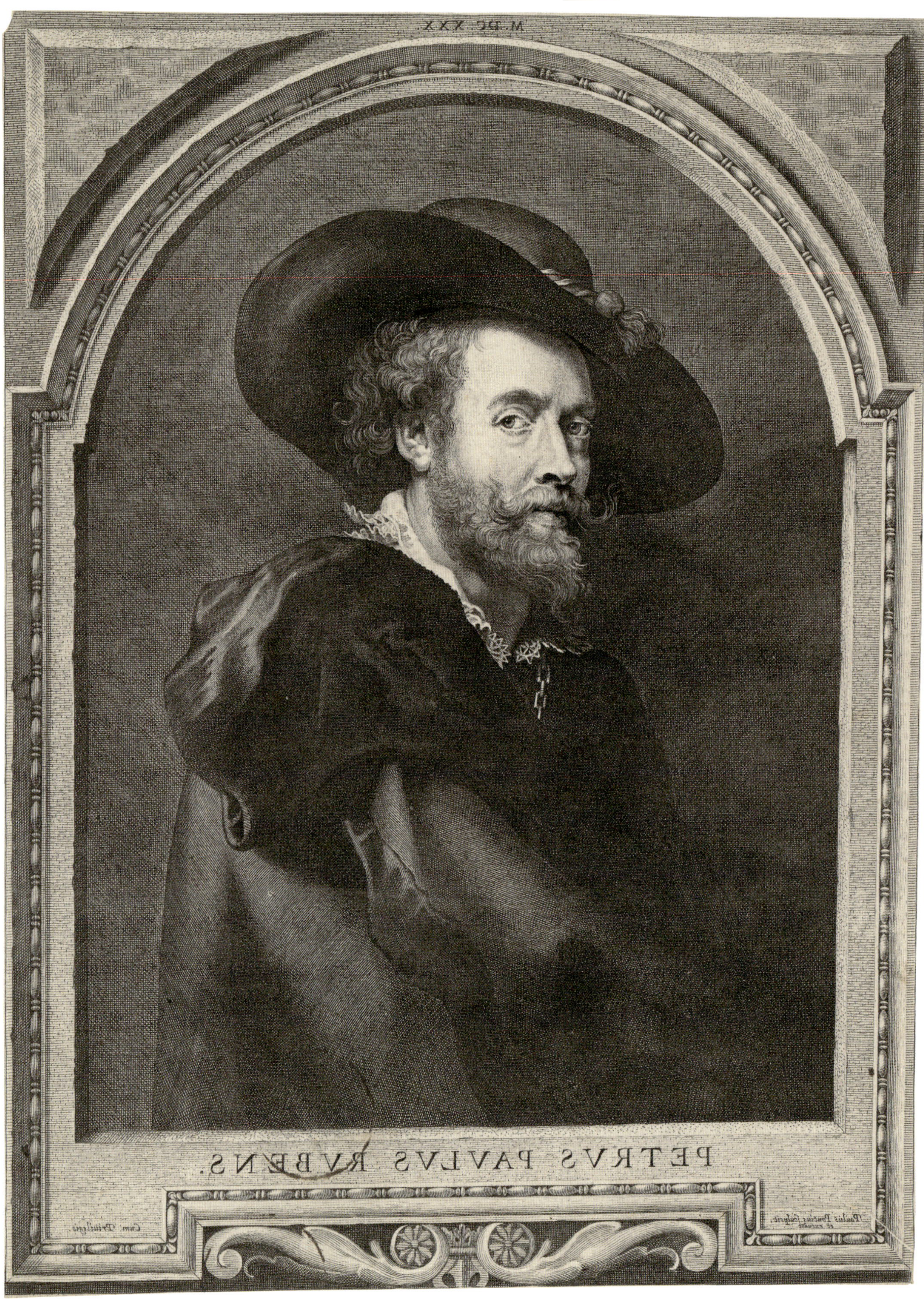

Paulus Pontius (Stecher, Verleger / engraver, publisher), nach / after Rubens
Selbstbildnis des / Self-Portrait of Peter Paul Rubens, ca. 1630
Umdruck / counterproof, Kupferstich / engraving SGSM, Inv. 30286 D

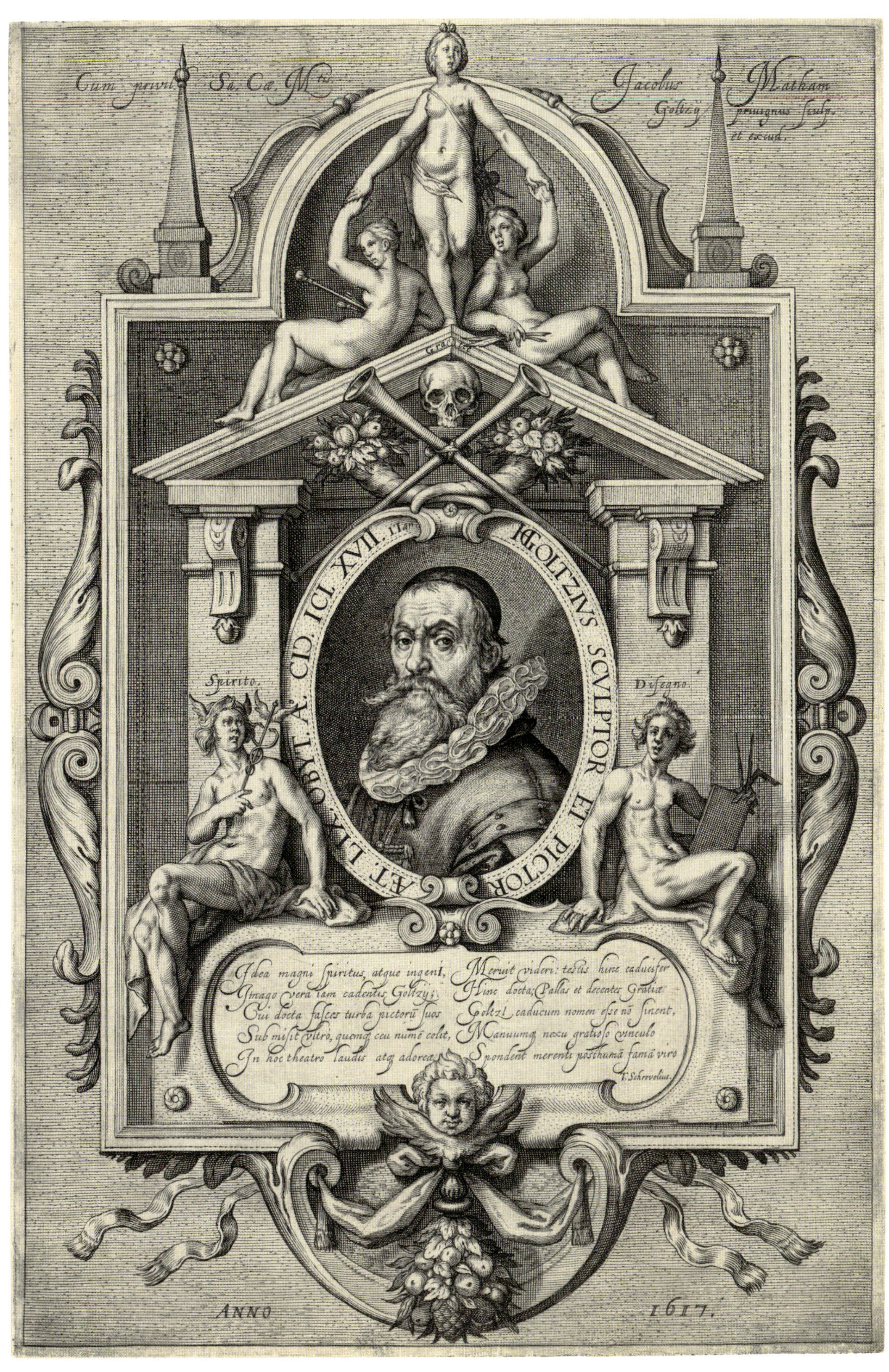

Jacob Matham (Stecher, Verleger / engraver, publisher), nach / after Goltzius
Bildnis des / Portrait of Hendrick Goltzius, 1617
Kupferstich / engraving SGSM, Inv. 38293 D

NINA SCHLEIF

Careers by Design

Hendrick Goltzius & Peter Paul Rubens

Was verbindet die Heroen dieser Ausstellung? Bei der Begegnung mit ihren Druckgraphiken muss die Antwort lauten: die Wucht, die ihre Werke bei Erscheinen entfalteten und auch heute noch haben! Aus diesem Grund zeigt die Staatliche Graphische Sammlung München die beeindruckende Zahl von 140 Arbeiten von Hendrick Goltzius (1558–1617) und Peter Paul Rubens (1577–1640) aus ihrem Bestand, der immerhin mehr als zehnfach so groß ist. Mit dieser Auswahl ist zugleich der Wunsch verbunden, dass das Interesse, noch mehr zu sehen, wachsen möge.[1]

Diese Ausstellung hat aber gleichzeitig ein thematisches Anliegen. Sie richtet den Blick auf die Strategien des Manieristen Goltzius (Abb. S. 13) und des Barockkünstlers Rubens (Abb. S.12), zeigt deren Mechanismen auf und stellt folgende Fragen: Wie haben sie ihre druckgraphischen Werke geplant, umgesetzt und vertrieben und wie wurden sie dadurch zu den berühmtesten Künstlern im Europa ihrer Zeit? Der Titel ist folglich doppelsinnig zu lesen: „Design" meint zum einen die Ideen und Entwürfe für Stiche, also den Produktionsprozess, zum anderen aber auch die systematische Planung der Wirkung dieser Stiche, um beide Künstler berühmt(er) zu machen. In viel stärkerem Maße als an den Gemälden von Goltzius und Rubens lassen sich an den Stichen viele ihrer Strategien aufzeigen und sind für das Publikum nachvollziehbar.

Der Fokus auf das Systematische ihres Vorgehens richtet unser Augenmerk auf das Ziel, das die beiden verfolgten und in dem sie übereinstimmten, und auf ihre teils vergleichbaren, teils unterschiedlichen Konzeptionen, um dieses Ziel zu erreichen. „Eer boven golt" – Ehre vor Gold – lautete Goltzius' Motto, aber natürlich brachten ihm wie Rubens die Ehre und der Ruhm auch Wohlstand.

What do the heroes of this exhibition have in common? As we encounter their prints, the answer must be: the force that their works unfurled when they first appeared, and that they still have today! This is why the Staatliche Graphische Sammlung München is showing an impressive 140 original works by Hendrick Goltzius (1558–1617) and Peter Paul Rubens (1577–1640) from its holdings of more than ten times as many works by these artists (figs. pp. 13,12). These works were chosen in hopes that they will spark a desire to see more.[1]

In addition, our exhibition has a thematic focus. It highlights the artistic strategies of the Mannerist Goltzius and the Baroque artist Rubens, revealing their methods and posing the following questions: how did they plan, realize, and distribute their prints, and how did they become the most famous artists of their time in Europe as a result? The title of the exhibition therefore has a two-fold meaning: "Design" refers to the ideas and designs for engravings—the production process. But it also refers to the systematic planning of the impact these engravings should have in order to make both artists (more) famous. Many of Goltzius's and Rubens's strategies are much more discernible in their engravings than in their paintings, and they can be readily perceived by visitors.

The focus on the systematic nature of their approach directs our attention to the shared goal that the two pursued, as well as to their approaches, some similar, some different, to achieving this goal. "Eer boven golt"—honor before gold—was Goltzius's motto, but of course honor and fame brought him prosperity as well, just as they did Rubens.

Es ist nicht das vorderste Ziel der Ausstellung, motivische oder stilistische „Einflüsse“ aufzuzeigen, insofern geht es nicht um ein Kernanliegen der Kunstgeschichte, das vergleichende Sehen. Für Goltzius' Gemälde sind verschiedentlich Anregungen oder Anleihen aus Rubens' Bildern geltend gemacht worden, der ältere Künstler – Goltzius – schaute bewundernd auf die Gemälde des fast zwanzig Jahre jüngeren Rubens und lernte von dessen Frühstil.[2] Aber beim Vergleich der druckgraphischen Werke treten solche Anleihen nach meiner Beobachtung nur in Ausnahmen auf. Einer der ersten Goltzius-Forscher, Otto Hirschmann, benannte das Erbe und damit den Bezug zwischen beiden Œuvres: „So baut sich also das in seiner Gesamtheit wahrhaft imponierende Werk der Rubensstecher ganz und gar auf dem von Goltzius auf.“[3] Daher spielt das Angehören der Künstler zu unterschiedlichen Generationen in unserer Ausstellung nur eine untergeordnete Rolle. Ein Trauergedicht auf Goltzius von 1618/20 beschreibt Rubens als den Anführer eines allegorischen Trauerzugs.[4] Damit war Letzterer bereits damals als wichtigster Erbe des Haarlemer Meisters benannt, ohne dass ein Aufzeigen von motivischen Anleihen nötig gewesen wäre.

Zudem ist es für unsere Fragestellung kaum zielführend, kunsthistorische Kategorien aufzunehmen, die Hendrick Goltzius als *peintre-graveur*, als erfindenden Stecher bezeichnen, Rubens hingegen als Auftraggeber von Reproduktionsgraphik, der diese Art der Vervielfältigung seiner Gemälde anderen überließ. Diese Denkweise verunklärt und verkürzt spannende Sachverhalte. Auch Goltzius hat Kunstwerke anderer Künstler reproduziert, aber mehr noch war ihm daran gelegen, in Technik und Stil in den Wettbewerb mit großen Vorläufern zu treten. *imitatio* und *aemulatio* waren die Schlagworte der damaligen Gelehrten, um dieses verbreitete künstlerische Anliegen zu beschreiben.[5] Es blieb Goltzius ein

The exhibition's primary aim is not to demonstrate "influences" in motifs or style, and thus it is not about that core concern of art history, comparative viewing. Various impulses or borrowings from Rubens's paintings have been cited in Goltzius's paintings: the older artist, Goltzius, admired the works of Rubens, who was almost twenty years younger, and studied Rubens's early style.[2] However, when it comes to the prints, such borrowings occur only in exceptional cases. One of the first scholars on Goltzius's work, Otto Hirschmann, identified the legacy and thus the relationship between the two oeuvres as follows: "Thus the work of the Rubens engravers, truly impressive as a whole, is built entirely on that of Goltzius."[3] The fact that the artists belonged to different generations therefore only plays a subordinate role in our exhibition. A commemorative poem of 1618/20 dedicated to Goltzius describes Rubens as the leader of an allegorical funeral procession.[4] This in itself early on designated the latter as the Haarlem master's most important heir, without it being necessary to point out iconographic borrowings.

Moreover, for the questions we pose, it is hardly useful to adopt art-historical categories that describe Hendrick Goltzius as a *peintre-graveur*, an inventive engraver, and Rubens as a commissioner of reproductive prints who left this type of replication of his paintings to others. This mode of thought shortsightedly obscures fascinating issues. Goltzius also reproduced works of art by other artists, though he was even keener to compete with his great precursors in terms of technique and style. *Imitatio* and *aemulatio* were the keywords used by scholars at the time to describe this widespread artistic goal.[5] It remained a lifelong objective for Goltzius, one from which he hoped to achieve financial success and,

lebenslanges Anliegen, von dem er sich finanziellen Erfolg und, mehr noch, Bewunderung erhoffte. Und auch bei Rubens muss man differenzieren: In den meisten Fällen hat er seine Gemälde nicht unverändert in Graphik übersetzen lassen, sondern seine eigenen Kompositionen weiterentwickelt und abgewandelt.

Als ich erstmals über ein Konzept für diese Ausstellung nachdachte, fiel mir ein Text in die Hände, den Karolien De Clippel und Filip Vermeylen 2012 veröffentlicht hatten und der im vorliegenden Katalog in einer aktualisierten Fassung abgedruckt ist (S. 24–49).[6] In ihrem Aufsatz erwähnten sie Rubens' erste Reise 1612 in die nördlichen Niederlande und seinen Besuch in Haarlem, bei dem der damals in Antwerpen lebende Flame auf Hendrick Goltzius traf. Zu dieser Begegnung kennen wir bislang nur zwei schriftliche historische Quellen, die keinen Aufschluss über die Gründe für Rubens' Reise nennen.[7] Allerdings kam er in Begleitung der beiden Maler Jan Brueghel I (1568–1625) und Hendrick van Balen (1573/75–1632) und traf in Haarlem auf eine ganze Reihe von Künstlern, allen voran Goltzius, daneben sicher auch Cornelis Cornelisz. van Haarlem (1562–1638) und Jacob Matham (1571–1631), womöglich auch Hendrik Vroom (1562/63–1640), Frans Badens (1571–1618) und andere. Daraus kann man schließen, dass der Abstecher des Flamen nach Holland und insbesondere zum Wohnort von Goltzius künstlerisch motiviert war. Wollte Rubens den damals berühmtesten und besten Stecher Europas gewinnen, damit er für ihn eine Druckwerkstatt einrichtete und führte? Vermutlich wusste Rubens, dass Goltzius um 1600 die Druckgraphik zugunsten der Ölmalerei aufgegeben hatte, und erhoffte sich lediglich einen Einblick in die Struktur der überaus produktiven Druckwerkstatt, die inzwischen von Goltzius' Stiefsohn Jacob Matham geführt wurde. Doch inwiefern unterschied sich eine solche auf Einzelblätter spezialisierte Werkstatt von

still more, admiration. In the case of Rubens, too, we must differentiate: in most instances, he did not have his paintings simply translated unchanged into prints, but rather further developed and modified his own compositions.

When I was first thinking about a concept for this exhibition, I came across a text published by Karolien De Clippel and Filip Vermeylen in 2012, which they have graciously allowed us to include in this catalog in an updated form (pp. 24–49).[6] In their essay, they discuss Rubens's first trip to the Northern Netherlands in 1612, during which the Fleming, who was living in Antwerp at the time, met Hendrick Goltzius in Haarlem. So far, we know of only two written historical sources about this encounter, neither of which provides information about the reasons for Rubens's journey.[7] However, we know that he came in the company of the painters Jan Brueghel I (1568–1625) and Hendrick van Balen (1573/75–1632), and that he met a whole host of artists in Haarlem: above all Goltzius, but certainly also Cornelis Cornelisz. van Haarlem (1562–1638) and Jacob Matham (1571–1631), and possibly Hendrik Vroom (1562/63–1640), Frans Badens (1571–1618), and others as well. From this we can conclude that the Fleming's trip to Holland, and in particular to Goltzius's place of residence, was artistically motivated. Did Rubens want to attract the most famous and best engraver in Europe at the time to set up and run a printing workshop for him? Rubens likely knew that Goltzius had given up printmaking around 1600 in favor of oil painting and was simply hoping to gain insight into the structure of his extremely productive print workshop, which was now run by Goltzius's stepson Jacob Matham. In what way, however, did such a workshop, which

der Officina Plantiniana, der führenden Buchdruckerei Antwerpens, für die Rubens bereits seit 1608 Buchillustrationen und später auch Buchtitel entwarf? In einem Brief schreibt Rubens einmal, er bevorzuge es, einen jungen, formbaren Stecher für sich arbeiten zu lassen, nicht ein angesehenes Genie.[8] Machte er in dieser Formulierung aus der Not eine Tugend, weil er den Meister selbst nicht gewinnen konnte, und begnügte sich mit Goltzius' Schülern und Assistenten? Wahrscheinlich suchte Rubens in Haarlem nach Kupferstechern, die technisch auf höchstem Niveau arbeiteten und vertraut waren mit einem professionellen, auf europaweite Verbreitung abzielenden Werkstattbetrieb. Wie im Katalogteil gezeigt wird, traf er solche Spezialisten im Norden an und konnte einige von ihnen, vor allem aus der Goltzius-Schule, dazu bringen, ihm später nach Antwerpen zu folgen.

De Clippel und Vermeylen richteten in ihrem Essay den Fokus auf den kulturellen Austausch zwischen den südlichen und nördlichen Niederlanden in der Zeit um 1600. Sie beschrieben, wie rege dieser Austausch war trotz der schwierigen oder sogar gefährlichen politischen Situation in Gebieten, die ganz unmittelbar vom Spanisch-Niederländischen Krieg betroffen waren. Ihre Untersuchung zeigt, dass es Künstlern durchaus möglich war, zwischen dem Norden und dem Süden hin- und herzureisen und sogar umzuziehen. Auch manche der Stecher, mit denen Goltzius und Rubens arbeiteten, waren solch örtlich flexible Künstler. Sie gingen dorthin, wo interessante und gut bezahlte Arbeit auf sie wartete. Dieser kunstsoziologische Blick der beiden Autoren scheint mir ein überzeugender und spannender Ansatz, um auch die Druckgraphik von Goltzius und Rubens unter erweiterten Parametern im Nebeneinander zu betrachten.

specialized in single sheets, differ from the Officina Plantiniana, Antwerp's leading book printshop, for which Rubens had been designing book illustrations since 1608 and later also designed book titles? In a letter, Rubens once wrote that he preferred to have a young, malleable engraver work for him rather than a renowned genius.[8] Was he making a virtue of necessity in this formulation because he had been unable to recruit the master himself and instead had to make do with Goltzius's pupils and assistants? Rubens was probably looking for engravers in Haarlem who worked at the highest technical level and were familiar with the operations of a professional workshop that aimed for Europe-wide distribution. As shown in the catalog section, he met such specialists in the North and was able to persuade some of them, especially engravers from the Goltzius school, to later follow him to Antwerp.

In their essay, De Clippel and Vermeylen focus on the cultural exchange between the Southern and Northern Netherlands in the period around 1600, describing how lively this exchange was despite the difficult, even dangerous political situation in areas directly affected by the Eighty Years' War. Their research shows that it was perfectly possible for artists to travel between the North and the South, and even to relocate. Some of the engravers with whom Goltzius and Rubens worked were just such geographically flexible artists who went wherever interesting and well-paid work awaited them. This sociological view of art taken by the two authors struck me as a convincing and exciting approach for looking at the prints of Goltzius and Rubens side by side from a broader perspective.

DER ENTWURFSPROZESS

Einige Vorbemerkungen zu Gemeinsamkeiten und Besonderheiten der beiden Künstler seien noch erlaubt. In den vergangenen Jahrzehnten hat sich die Forschung vermehrt auch mit dem Produktionsprozess von Druckgraphik auseinandergesetzt. So wurde die Bedeutung von Vorzeichnungen und Probedrucken deutlicher. Für Goltzius wie Rubens darf man annehmen, dass so gut wie keine Kupferplatte in Angriff genommen wurde, ohne dass vorher eine Zeichnung die Komposition und die Licht- und Schattenverhältnisse geklärt hatte. Eine solche Zeichnung konnte der Künstler selbst (Goltzius) oder der spezialisierte Stecher (Goltzius, die Stecher von Goltzius und Rubens) umsetzen. Im nächsten Schritt wurden ein oder mehrere Probedrucke (manchmal auch Umdrucke) angefertigt, um die Wirkung zu prüfen und gegebenenfalls Korrekturen auf diesen Proben zu vermerken, die dann auf der Platte selbst noch abgeändert wurden. Für Goltzius sind wenige dieser Probedrucke erhalten, für Rubens dagegen sehr viele.[9] In Rubens' Fall sind die Probedrucke für uns ein Hinweis, an welchen Druckgraphiken er aktiv mitgewirkt hat und welche unter seiner Ägide geschaffen wurden. Denn für beide Künstler gilt, dass bereits zu ihren Lebzeiten Blätter entstanden, die nicht von ihnen autorisiert und die qualitativ oft minderwertig waren. Ein weiteres Indiz dafür, welche Stiche unter Rubens' Aufsicht entstanden, ist die Privilegsformel, die in seinem Fall (als einzigem Künstler in Europa) Privilegien aus drei Ländern umfasste: das der niederländischen Generalstaaten, das der südlichen Niederlande und schließlich jenes von Frankreich (siehe das Kapitel „Privilegien", S. 116–127).

Zwei Besonderheiten stechen im reifen Werk von Hendrick Goltzius (und den Stechern seiner Schule) heraus, die auch Nadine M. Orenstein in ihrem Essay hervorhebt (S. 50–66): Als herausragender

THE DESIGN PROCESS

I would like to make a few preliminary remarks on the similarities and peculiarities of the two artists. In recent decades, research has increasingly dealt with the production process of prints, leading to a clearer understanding of the importance of preparatory drawings and proof impressions. For both Goltzius and Rubens, it can be assumed that virtually no copperplate was commenced without a drawing first clarifying the composition and the light and shadow conditions. Such a drawing could be executed by the artist himself (Goltzius) or by the specialized engraver (Goltzius, the engravers of Goltzius and Rubens). In the next step, one or more proof impressions (sometimes also counterproofs) were made to check the effect. If necessary, corrections were noted on these samples and the plate itself was then altered. Few of these trial prints have survived for Goltzius, but many exist for Rubens.[9] These proof impressions provide us with evidence as to which prints Rubens actively contributed to or were created under his aegis, as unauthorized prints, often of inferior quality, were attributed to both artists even during their lifetimes. A further indication of which engravings were created under Rubens's supervision are his print privileges. Rubens was the only artist in Europe to receive privileges from three countries: the States General of the Netherlands, the Southern Netherlands, and finally France (see the chapter "Privileges," pp. 116–127).

Two special features stand out in the later work of Hendrick Goltzius (and the engravers of his school), which Nadine M. Orenstein also emphasizes in her essay (pp. 50–66): As an outstanding technician, Goltzius led the swelling line—first mastered by Cornelis Cort (1533–1578)—to new

Techniker führte Goltzius die von Cornelis Cort (1533–1578) erstmals erprobte schwellende Linie zu neuen Höhen und verlieh seinen Figuren dadurch eine Plastizität und Bewegung, wie sie die Druckgraphik vor ihm nicht gekannt hatte.[10] Er setzte den Stichel schmal an, ließ ihn breiter werden, um ihn zum Ende der Linie wieder zu verjüngen. Solche bis dahin nur in der Kalligraphie geführten Linien veränderten die Optik der Druckgraphik unwiderruflich.[11] Doch Goltzius nutzte seine Virtuosität auch in eine rückwärtsgewandte Richtung, indem er die Stechstile von Albrecht Dürer (1471–1528) und Lucas van Leyden (1494–1533) imitierte. Laut seinem Biographen Karel van Mander (1548–1606) legte er es tatsächlich auf eine Verwechselung mit den Werken der Vorgänger an, denn sie galten als die Leitsterne nordeuropäischer Druckkunst (siehe die Kapitel „Meisterdrucke", S. 186–217, und „Vorbilder", S. 234–247). In der Ausstellung zeigen wir mehrere Werke, die diese Art der ambitionierten Nachahmung, auch *aemulatio* genannt, betreiben (Abb. S. 122, 198 f., 235).[12] Dem Künstler brachte dieses Können den Beinamen „Proteus" – ein Meeresgott mit der Gabe zur Gestaltverwandlung – ein.[13]

Peter Paul Rubens selbst hatte nicht den Ehrgeiz, als Kupferstecher tätig zu werden, die Malerei war sein Metier. Jedoch wurde ihm wohl früh bewusst, dass seine Gemälde erst durch die Druckgraphik die Reichweite haben würden, die er sich wünschte. Nils Büttner führt das in seinem Beitrag im vorliegenden Katalog aus (S. 68–93). Zwar ließ Rubens etliche Assistenten in seinem Atelier von den meisten Gemälden auch gleich Repliken anfertigen, jedoch schwebten ihm offensichtlich höhere Zahlen und größere Märkte vor.[14] In den ersten Jahren nach seiner Rückkehr 1608 aus Italien nach Antwerpen entschloss sich der „Apelles seiner Zeit",[15] wie Rubens nach dem bedeutendsten Künstler der griechischen

heights, lending his figures a plasticity and movement unknown to printmaking before him.[10] This was accomplished by allowing the initially narrow stroke of the burin to widen in the middle and then taper off again toward the end of the line. Such lines, which until then had only been used in calligraphy, irrevocably changed the look of printmaking.[11] However, Goltzius also used his virtuosity in a purposely retrospective manner by imitating the engraving styles of Albrecht Dürer (1471–1528) and Lucas van Leyden (1494–1533). According to his biographer Karel van Mander (1548–1606), he was in fact aiming for his works to be confused with those of his predecessors, as they were regarded as the leading stars of northern European printmaking (see the chapters "Masterprints," pp. 186–217, and "Models," pp. 234–247). In the exhibition, we show several works that engage in this kind of ambitious imitation, also known as *aemulatio* (figs. pp. 122, 198–199, 235).[12] This skill earned the artist the nickname "Proteus," from the sea god with the gift of shape-shifting.[13]

Peter Paul Rubens had no ambition to become an engraver himself; painting was his profession. However, he probably realized early on that his paintings could only gain the reach he desired through printmaking. Nils Büttner explains how Rubens organized his print production in a new and highly efficient manner in his contribution to this catalog (pp. 68–93). Although Rubens had several assistants in his studio immediately make replicas of most of his paintings, he obviously had higher numbers and larger markets in mind.[14] In the first few years after his return to Antwerp from Italy in 1608, the "Apelles of his time,"[15] as Rubens was called after the most important artist of Greek antiquity, decided to add engraving

Antike bezeichnet wurde, seiner Gemäldeproduktion auch eine Kupferstichproduktion anzugliedern. Hierfür testete er die Zusammenarbeit mit mehreren Stechern, aber schließlich blieb es bei einer Handvoll, mit deren Arbeit er zufrieden war und mit denen er länger zusammenarbeitete – die meisten davon aus dem Umkreis und der Nachfolge von Goltzius. Die Vorzeichnungen ließ er von Assistenten seiner Malwerkstatt nach ausgewählten Gemälden anfertigen und überarbeitete sie selbst erst, kurz bevor sie als Stichvorlagen (auch Modelli, teils auf Papier, teils auf Holztafeln) an den Stecher gingen. Dies geschah oft erst Jahre nach der Fertigstellung der Gemälde. Aufgrund der erhaltenen Probedrucke mit Rubens' Korrekturen wissen wir, dass er die Tätigkeit seiner Stecher streng überwachte.[16]

DIE STRATEGIEN

Im Mittelpunkt dieser Ausstellung stehen Fragen, die jeden Künstler heute noch umtreiben: Wie werde ich berühmt? Wie bleibe ich berühmt? Wie kann ich diesen Ruhm vermehren und auch finanziell nutzen? Sowohl Hendrick Goltzius als auch Peter Paul Rubens haben sich diese Fragen gestellt und wie wenigen ihrer Zeitgenossen gelang es beiden, die richtigen (und oft auch heute aktuellen) Antworten für sich zu finden und diese in ihrer Kunstproduktion umzusetzen.

Die für diese Ausstellung ausgewählten Themen orientieren sich daran, was anhand der Werke selbst sichtbar und nachvollziehbar gemacht werden kann. Besondere Merkmale der Druckgraphiken, die zwar bei Hendrick Goltzius wie Peter Paul Rubens auch eine Rolle spielen, wie etwa die von namhaften Intellektuellen ihrer Zeit verfassten lateinischen Bildunterschriften oder die Beschäftigung

production to his painting output. To this end, he tested collaboration with a number of engravers but eventually settled on just a handful with whose work he was satisfied and with whom he worked for a longer period of time—most of them from the circle and succession of Goltzius. He had preparatory drawings after selected paintings made by assistants in his painting workshop and revised them himself shortly before they were sent to the engraver as engraving designs (also called *modelli*, some of them on paper, some on wooden panels). This often happened years after the paintings had been completed. Based on the surviving proof impressions with Rubens's corrections, we know that he strictly supervised the work of his engravers.[16]

THE STRATEGIES

At the center of this exhibition are questions that still occupy every artist today: How do I become famous? How do I stay famous? How can I increase this fame and use it financially? Both Hendrick Goltzius and Peter Paul Rubens asked themselves these questions and, more than most of their contemporaries, both succeeded in finding the right (and often still relevant) answers and implementing them in their art production.

The themes selected for this exhibition have been drawn up keeping in mind what can be made visible and comprehensible on the basis of the works themselves. Special features of the prints, which admittedly play a role in the work of both Hendrick Goltzius and Peter Paul Rubens, such as the Latin

herausragender Kalligraphen für deren Ausführung, wurden im Rahmen dieser Ausstellung hintangestellt, sind jedoch erwiesenermaßen wertvolle Forschungsgebiete für die Kunstgeschichte.[17] Stattdessen stehen elf Bereiche im Vordergrund, die teils Aspekte des Herstellungsprozesses (I. Werkstattbetrieb und Stecher, IV. Verleger, V. Druckgraphik und Zeichnungen, VI. Technische Experimente), teils inhaltliche Themensetzungen (VIII. Antike, IX. Vorbilder, X. Porträts) und teils Instrumente systematischer Markenbildung aufzeigen (II. Widmungen, III. Privilegien, VII. Meisterdrucke). Eine Überprüfung der Ausstellungsthese, dass beide Künstler die Produktion ihrer Druckgraphik mit Kalkül angingen und betrieben und nicht zuletzt deshalb langen Nachruhm genossen, erfolgt im Kapitel „XI. Nachbilder" anhand von Graphiken der folgenden Jahrhunderte.

Die Werkauswahl für jedes Kapitel zu treffen, war angesichts der vielen in der Staatlichen Graphischen Sammlung München vorhandenen Schätze nicht leicht und ist an manchen Stellen persönlichen Vorlieben geschuldet. Bei Rubens fiel die Auswahl oft auf Werke, die einen Bezug zum Gemäldebestand der Alten Pinakothek haben (so *Der sterbende Seneca*, *Die Nilpferdjagd*, *Das Kleine Jüngste Gericht* und das *Martyrium des hl. Laurentius*). Besucherinnen und Besucher, die ihr Lieblingswerk nicht in der Auswahl finden oder Lust auf mehr haben, sind herzlich eingeladen, sich auf unserer Homepage unter „SGSM online" unseren Bestand digital anzuschauen oder sich Originale im Studiensaal der Staatlichen Graphischen Sammlung vorlegen zu lassen.

captions written by renowned intellectuals of their time or the employment of outstanding calligraphers for their realization, have a lesser role in this exhibition, although these have proven to be valuable areas of research for art history.[17] Instead, the focus is on eleven areas, some of them dealing with aspects of the production process (I. Workshop Operation and Engravers, IV. Publishers, V. Prints and Drawings, VI. Technical Experiments), some with thematic content (VIII. Antiquity, IX. Models, X. Portraits), and some with instruments of systematic branding (II. Dedications, III. Privileges, VII. Masterprints). The proposition of the exhibition—that both artists approached and practiced the production of their prints with careful calculation, and that it is not least for this reason that they enjoyed long-lasting fame—is tested in the chapter "XI. Afterimages" on the basis of prints from the following centuries.

Given the many treasures in the Staatliche Graphische Sammlung München, it was not easy to select the works for each chapter, and in some instances the choice came down to personal preference. In the case of Rubens, works were often selected that have a connection to the Alte Pinakothek's collection of paintings (such as *The Death of Seneca*, *Hippopotamus Hunt*, *The Small Last Judgment*, and *The Martyrdom of St. Lawrence*). Visitors who cannot find their favorite work in the selection or who would like to see more works by the artists are cordially invited to research at "SGSM online" on our website or to have the originals presented to them in the study hall of the Staatliche Graphische Sammlung München.

Ich danke Michael Hering, Konrad Renger und Nils Büttner für die kritische Durchsicht meiner Beiträge in einer frühen Fassung.

1 Mehr zum Münchner Bestand an Werken von Hendrick Goltzius und Peter Paul Rubens sowie zur Sammlungsgeschichte siehe im vorliegenden Katalog S. 290–294.
2 Vgl. De Clippel/Vermeylen, bes. S. 42–46, in diesem Katalog sowie Nichols 2013, bes. S. 58–61, weitere Literatur dort in Anm. 61; Amsterdam/New York/Toledo 2003, S. 6; Juntunen 2004. Martin Kirves (Kirves 2017) hat Rubens' Skulpturentheorie für Goltzius' Herkulesdarstellungen herangezogen.
3 Hirschmann 1920a, S. 158.
4 Vgl. Hymans 1892, Stechow 1927, bes. Hirschmann 1920b, Smet 1977. Autor des Gedichts, das 1618 verfasst und 1620 gedruckt wurde, war Balthazar Gerbier (1591–1663), der anscheinend mit beiden Künstlern bekannt war. 1627 war er Rubens bei Vorbereitungen zu seiner zweiten Holland-Reise behilflich (vgl. Magurn 1955, S. 161–240, zum Briefwechsel zwischen Rubens und Gerbier sowie Büttner 2023a). Gerbier umschmeichelte Rubens in diesem Gedicht als „een cloecken Gheest", einen klugen Geist (Hirschmann 1920b, S. 108).
5 Vgl. Müller/Pfisterer 2011, S. 1–32, bes. S. 1–15, für eine griffige Definition sowie zeitliche und kulturelle Kontextualisierung. Beide Konzepte in Bezug auf Goltzius und Rubens werden in den Kapiteln „Antike", S. 218–233, und „Vorbilder", S. 234–247, im Katalogteil behandelt.
6 De Clippel/Vermeylen 2012.
7 Vgl. Hymans 1892, Hirschmann 1920b, Smet 1977.
8 Rooses/Ruelens 1887–1909, Bd. 2 (1898), S. 199. In dtsch. Übers. vgl. Zoff 1918, S. 95.
9 Zu Goltzius' Probedrucken vgl. Filedt Kok 1991/92. – Die meisten von Rubens' Probedrucken werden in der Bibliothèque nationale de France in Paris aufbewahrt. Konrad Renger (Renger 1974a und 1975) hat sie als Erster systematisch herangezogen, um den Produktionsprozess von Rubens-Graphiken zu rekonstruieren. Zuletzt umfangreich diskutiert und abgebildet hat sie Meier 2020a.
10 Vgl. die sehr guten Ausführungen in Peters 2009 und Pollack 2020 sowie ebenso Melion 1993, S. 63f.
11 Vgl. Namowitz Worthen 1991/92 und Peters 2009 sowie Roettig 2002.
12 Weitere Ausführungen zu diesem Konzept in den Kapiteln „Antike", S. 218–233, und „Vorbilder", S. 234–247, im vorliegenden Katalog.
13 Vgl. das Kapitel „Widmungen" im vorliegenden Katalog, S. 106–115.
14 Vgl. z. B. Büttner 2017a und Büttner 2017b.
15 Bei Büttner 2006, S. 83, findet sich eine Zusammenfassung der Erwähnungen dieses Beinamens.
16 Eine gute Übersicht über erhaltene Probedrucke samt Abbildungen bietet Meier 2020a. Auf die Bedeutung der Probedrucke hat zuerst Konrad Renger in seinen grundlegenden Beiträgen hingewiesen (Renger 1974a und Renger 1975).
17 Zu den Bildunterschriften siehe Wolkenhauer 2006, Schmidt-Clausen 2016, Leesberg 2017a, Arbeitsgruppe Estius 2017, Venne 2017 sowie zuletzt Arnulf 2020.

I would like to thank Michael Hering, Konrad Renger, and Nils Büttner for their critical review of early versions of my texts.

1 For more on the Munich collection of works by Hendrick Goltzius and Peter Paul Rubens, and on the history of the collection, see pp. 290–294 in this catalog.
2 See De Clippel/Vermeylen, pp. 42–46, in the present catalog. See also Nichols 2013, esp. pp. 58–61, further literature on this in note 61; Amsterdam/New York/Toledo 2003, p. 6; Juntunen 2004. Martin Kirves (Kirves 2017) has used Rubens's theory of sculpture for Goltzius's depictions of Hercules.
3 Hirschmann 1920a, p. 158. Translation by Julian Jain.
4 See Hymans 1892, Stechow 1927, esp. Hirschmann 1920b, Smet 1977, Büttner 2023a. The author of the poem, which was written in 1618 and printed in 1620, was Balthazar Gerbier (1591–1663), who was apparently acquainted with both artists. In 1627, he helped Rubens with preparations for his second trip to Holland (see Magurn 1955, pp. 161–240, on the correspondence between Rubens and Gerbier). In this poem, Gerbier flattered Rubens by describing him as "een cloecken Gheest," a bright mind (Hirschmann 1920b, p. 108).
5 See Müller/Pfisterer 2011, pp. 1–32, esp. pp. 1–15, for a concise definition as well as temporal and cultural contextualization. Both concepts are dealt with in relation to Goltzius and Rubens in the chapters "Antiquity," pp. 218–233, and "Models," pp. 234–247, in the catalog section.
6 De Clippel/Vermeylen 2012.
7 See Hymans 1892, Hirschmann 1920b, Smet 1977.
8 Rooses/Ruelens 1887–1909, vol. 2 (1898), p. 199. English translation in Magurn 1955, p. 69.
9 On Goltzius's sample prints, see Filedt Kok 1991/92. Most of Rubens's sample prints are kept in the Bibliothèque nationale de France in Paris. Konrad Renger (Renger 1974a and 1975) was the first to use them systematically in order to reconstruct the production process of Rubens's prints. They were most recently discussed and illustrated in detail in Meier 2020a.
10 See the excellent explanations in Peters 2009 and Pollack 2020, as well as Melion 1993, pp. 63–64.
11 See Namowitz Worthen 1991/92 and Peters 2009, as well as Roettig 2002.
12 Further details on this concept can be found in the chapters "Antiquity," pp. 218–233, and "Models," pp. 234–247, in this catalog.
13 See the chapter "Dedications" in this catalog, pp. 106–115.
14 See e.g. Büttner 2017a and Büttner 2017b.
15 Büttner 2006, p. 83, contains a summary of the mentions of this byname.
16 Meier 2020a provides a good overview of surviving sample prints, including illustrations. Konrad Renger first pointed out the importance of the proof impressions in his seminal contributions (Renger 1974a and Renger 1975).
17 On the captions, see Wolkenhauer 2006, Schmidt-Clausen 2016, Leesberg 2017a, Arbeitsgruppe Estius 2017, Venne 2017, and, most recently, Arnulf 2020.

FILIP VERMEYLEN & KAROLIEN DE CLIPPEL

Rubens und Goltzius im Dialog

Der künstlerische Austausch zwischen Antwerpen und Haarlem während der Revolte

Rubens and Goltzius in Dialogue

Artistic Exchanges between Antwerp and Haarlem during the Revolt

Seit Langem wird Haarlem von einem Teil der Kunstwissenschaft als Archetyp einer holländischen Stadt angesehen, in der sich eine spezifische Malerschule herausgebildet hat. Von den berühmten Landschaften, Stadtansichten und Genrebildern Haarlems soll ein ganz besonderer holländischer Charakter (*Dutchness*) ausgehen.[1] In der Tat gilt die sogenannte Haarlemer Malerschule als Musterbeispiel für eine lokale Schule mit erkennbaren und typisch „holländischen" Merkmalen.[2] Wir möchten diese vermeintliche Autonomie der Haarlemer Schule durch eine Bestandsaufnahme der (künstlerischen) Beziehungen der Stadt mit Antwerpen im letzten Drittel des 16. und in den ersten Jahrzehnten des 17. Jahrhunderts infrage stellen. Anfang des 17. Jahrhunderts erlebte Antwerpen einen bemerkenswerten Aufschwung, der durch die Rückkehr von Peter Paul Rubens im Jahr 1608 eingeleitet wurde, und dank des florierenden Kunstmarkts blieb die Stadt lange Nettoexporteur von Gemälden.[3]

In unserem Beitrag werden wir zeigen, dass Künstler, Kunstwerke und künstlerisches Know-how während des größten Teils des 17. Jahrhunderts zwischen den südlichen Niederlanden, die unter katholisch-spanischer Herrschaft standen, und den nördlichen, vornehmlich protestantischen Niederlanden, zu denen auch die Provinz Holland gehörte, frei verkehrten und ein kultureller Austausch in vielerlei Gestalt möglich war – trotz der jahrzehntelangen kriegerischen Auseinandersetzungen von 1568 bis 1648, die nur von einem zwölfjährigen Waffenstillstand ab 1609 unterbrochen wurden.[4] Durch eine eingehende Untersuchung des künstlerischen Dialogs zwischen Hendrick Goltzius und Peter Paul Rubens wollen wir die faszinierende Beziehung zwischen dem holländischen Haarlem und dem südniederländischen Antwerpen – zwei der führenden niederländischen Kunstzentren im 17. Jahrhundert – beleuchten.

Haarlem has long been considered the archetype of a Dutch city school by many art historians. A quintessential *Dutchness* is said to emanate from its famous landscapes, cityscapes, and genre paintings.[1] Indeed, the so-called Haarlem school of painting has been deemed a prime example of a local school with recognizable and typical "Dutch" characteristics.[2] We wish to challenge this perceived autonomy of the Haarlem school by taking stock of the (artistic) relationships the city maintained with Antwerp during the latter third of the sixteenth and the first decades of the seventeenth centuries. At the beginning of the seventeenth century Antwerp enjoyed a remarkable resurgence, inaugurated by the return of Peter Paul Rubens in 1608, and thanks to the booming art market, the city continued to be a net exporter of paintings.[3]

In our contribution, we will emphasize that throughout most of the seventeenth century, artists, artworks, and artistic know-how moved freely between the Southern Netherlands (under Catholic-Spanish rule) and the (mainly Protestant) Northern Netherlands, to which the province of Holland belonged. This artistic circulation allowed for cultural transmission in many guises, despite the decades of war between 1568 and 1648, interrupted only by a twelve-year truce beginning in 1609.[4] Through a close reading of the artistic dialogue that occurred between Hendrick Goltzius and Peter Paul Rubens, we aim to shed light on the fascinating relationship between two of the leading Netherlandish art centers of the seventeenth century: Haarlem, in the Northern province of Holland, and Antwerp, in the Southern Netherlands. Since this is a rather vast area of research, we will limit ourselves as follows: In the first part

Da es sich hierbei um ein recht umfangreiches Forschungsgebiet handelt, werden wir uns auf folgende Punkte beschränken: Im ersten Teil möchten wir eine allgemeine Einführung in den Aufstieg des Haarlemer Kunstmarkts in Verbindung mit Antwerpen geben und dabei die Migration einer beträchtlichen Zahl von Künstlern und die stark verbesserte Verkehrsinfrastruktur des 17. Jahrhunderts berücksichtigen, welche das Reisen zwischen den beiden Kunstzentren erheblich erleichterte. Anschließend wird die Bedeutung der persönlichen Beziehungen, die Künstler in Antwerpen und Haarlem in der ersten Hälfte des 17. Jahrhunderts zueinander unterhielten, hervorgehoben, indem wir die engen Verflechtungen zwischen Goltzius und Rubens in den 1610er-Jahren und die gegenseitige künstlerische Befruchtung untersuchen, welche sich aus solchen Kontakten ergeben haben könnte.

DIE FLÄMISCHE MIGRATION NACH HAARLEM

Der Grundstein für die engen Beziehungen zwischen den Städten Haarlem und Antwerpen wurde zur Zeit der großen Migration gelegt, die mit dem Ausbruch des niederländischen Aufstands zwischen 1566 und 1568 begann, als sich die niederländischen Provinzen gegen die Herrschaft der spanischen Habsburger erhoben.[5] Die Fakten sind bekannt, und es ist ein interessanter Zufall, dass beide Städte in der Anfangsphase des Aufstands viel zu leiden hatten. Antwerpen wurde durch den Bildersturm, die sogenannte spanische Furie, in deren Zuge die Stadt tagelang geplündert und niedergebrannt wurde, und eine lange Belagerung verwüstet, die 1585 in der Kapitulation gipfelte und die Stadt wirtschaftlich isolierte. Auch Haarlem hatte mit einer langen und katastrophalen spanischen Belagerung zu kämpfen, welche die

we will give a general introduction to the rise of the Haarlem art market in connection to Antwerp, taking into account the migration of substantial numbers of artists and the vastly improved transportation infrastructure of the seventeenth century, which greatly facilitated travel between the two art centers. We will then highlight the importance of the personal relationships that artists in Antwerp and Haarlem maintained with each other in the first half of the seventeenth century, by examining the close ties that existed between Goltzius and Rubens during the 1610s and the artistic cross-fertilization that may have resulted from such contacts.

FLEMISH MIGRATION INTO HAARLEM

The basis of the strong ties between the cities of Haarlem and Antwerp was forged at the time of the great migration which started with the outbreak of the Dutch Revolt between 1566 and 1568, when the Dutch provinces rose up against the rule of the Spanish Habsburgs.[5] The facts are well known, and it is an interesting coincidence that both cities suffered much in the early phases of the Revolt. Antwerp was ravaged by iconoclasm; the so-called Spanish Fury, in the course of which the city was looted and burned for days; and a long siege culminating in surrender in 1585 that left the city economically isolated. Haarlem also had to contend with a lengthy and disastrous Spanish siege which brought the town to its knees, a cataclysmic event which would later claim its place in the Dutch canon of patriotic bravery. To make matters worse, a devastating fire laid waste to major sections of Haarlem in October 1576.[6]

Stadt in die Knie zwang – ein traumatisches Ereignis, das später einen festen Platz im niederländischen Kanon patriotischen Heldenmuts finden sollte. Zu allem Überfluss verwüstete ein verheerender Brand im Oktober 1576 große Teile Haarlems.[6]

Da die meisten Kämpfe in den südlichen Provinzen stattfanden und die Spanier in Flandern und Brabant Fuß fassten, wanderten viele Menschen in den Norden aus. Das schließlich vom spanischen Joch befreite Haarlem war eine erschöpfte Stadt, die Ende der 1570er-Jahre ihre Tore für flämische Flüchtlinge öffnete. Und diese wanderten in großer Zahl ein. Sie kamen aus allen Teilen des Südens, jedoch überwiegend aus der Grafschaft Flandern. Die meisten von ihnen waren in der Leinen- und Tuchindustrie tätig und stammten aus Städten wie Kortrijk und Gent, aber auch Angehörige vieler anderer Berufe strömten nach 1578 nach Haarlem. Das führte dazu, dass die Stadt in den Jahrzehnten vor und nach der Jahrhundertwende ein exponentielles Wachstum erlebte. Zwischen 1580 und 1622 verdoppelte sich die Bevölkerung, was vor allem auf die starke Zuwanderung aus den südlichen Provinzen zurückzuführen ist. Man schätzt, dass 1622 etwa 20 000 der 39 500 Einwohner – mehr als fünfzig Prozent der Gesamtbevölkerung – flämische Einwanderer und deren Nachkommen waren. Bis zum Ende des zwölfjährigen Friedens im Jahr 1621 hatten die flämischen Einwanderer alle Schichten der Zivilgesellschaft (mit Ausnahme des politischen Establishments) durchdrungen und die Morphologie der Stadt geprägt. Sie trugen wesentlich zur Wirtschaft und zum kulturellen Leben Haarlems bei. So wurde beispielsweise eine eigene flämische Rhetorikerkammer mit dem Namen *De witten angieren* eingerichtet, die an öffentlichen Ritualen und Veranstaltungen wie dem *Landjuweel* von 1606 teilnahm.[7]

Still, with most of the fighting taking place in the Southern provinces and with the Spanish acquiring a stronghold in Flanders and Brabant, significant numbers of people began to migrate north. Freed at last from the Spanish yoke, Haarlem was an exhausted city which opened its gates in the late 1570s to Flemish refugees. And they migrated in great numbers. They came from all parts of the South, but notably from the county of Flanders. Most of the immigrants were active in the linen and cloth industries, originating from towns such as Kortrijk and Ghent, but members of many other professions also flocked to Haarlem after 1578. As a result, the city witnessed an exponential growth during the decades preceding and following the turn of the century. The population doubled between 1580 and 1622, principally due to the vast immigration from the Southern provinces. In fact, it has been estimated that by 1622, some 20,000 souls out of a population of 39,500—more than 50 percent of the total population—were Flemish immigrants and their descendants. By the end of the Twelve Years' Truce in 1621, Flemish migrants had infiltrated all layers of civil society (with the exception of the political establishment) and left their mark on the morphology of the city. They contributed substantially to Haarlem's economy and cultural life. For instance, a separate Flemish chamber of rhetoric was established, named *De witten angieren*, which participated in public rituals and events such as the 1606 *Landjuweel*.[7]

Jan Briels and Pieter Biesboer in particular have elaborated extensively on the general causes of the town of Haarlem's attractiveness for immigrants.[8] There were many push and pull factors, some of them unique to Haarlem. For instance, a historical accident helped to create the physical space needed to house

Insbesondere Jan Briels und Pieter Biesboer haben sich ausführlich mit den allgemeinen Ursachen für die Attraktivität der Stadt Haarlem für Einwanderer befasst.[8] Es gab viele Push- und Pull-Faktoren, von denen einige einzigartig für Haarlem waren. So trug etwa ein historischer Unfall dazu bei, den für die Unterbringung der Neuankömmlinge erforderlichen Raum zu schaffen: Der Brand von 1576 zerstörte mindestens vierhundert Häuser und schuf auf diese Weise Platz für flämische Flüchtlinge. Eine Karte aus dem Jahr 1578 zeigt deutlich die leeren Flächen im Südwesten der Stadt (Abb. 1). Darüber hinaus konnte Haarlem ab 1581 aufgrund des Vertrags zwischen den Vereinigten Provinzen und Wilhelm dem Schweiger die Grundstücke ehemaliger Klöster als Bauplätze erschließen und sie an Einwanderer aus dem Süden verkaufen oder zur Verfügung stellen. Haarlem empfing die Neuankömmlinge also mit offenen Armen. Der Magistrat der Stadt bot Subventionen und andere Vergünstigungen an, um zugewanderte Weber und andere Fachleute anzulocken, damit sie ihre Webstühle sozusagen innerhalb der Stadtmauern aufstellten, was sie mit großem Erfolg taten.

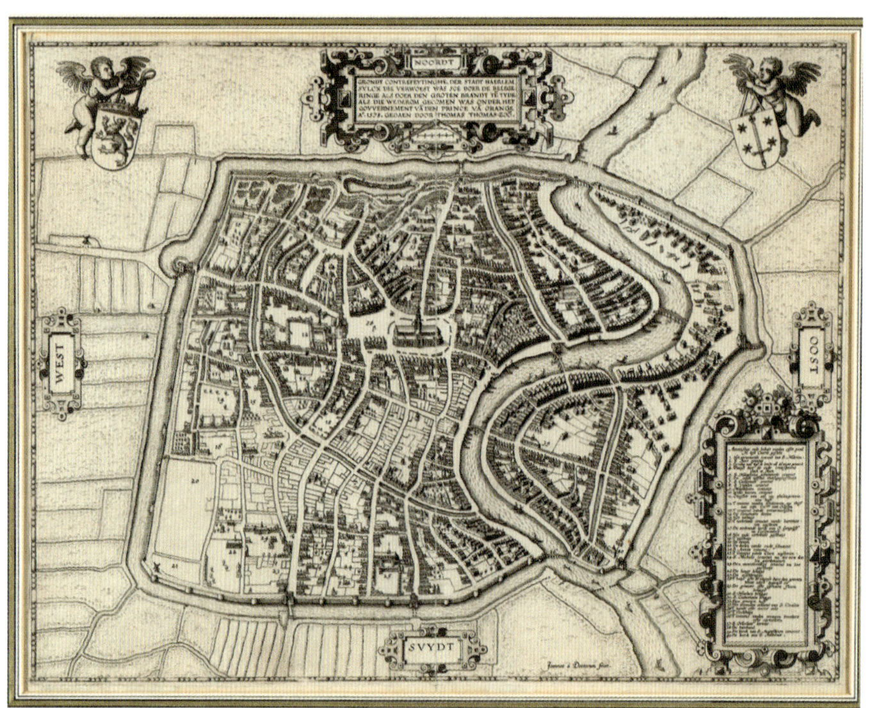

1 Joannes van Doetecum I (Stecher / engraver), nach / after Thomas Thomasz. *Stadtplan von / Map of Haarlem*, 1578 Kupferstich / engraving
Haarlem, Noord-Hollands Archief, Inv. 51872

new arrivals: The fire of 1576 destroyed at least four hundred houses and thus made space in the city for Flemish refugees. A map dating from 1578 clearly shows the empty areas in the southwestern part of the city (fig. 1). Moreover, starting in 1581, as a result of the treaty between the States of Holland and William the Silent, the city was able to develop the properties of former monasteries as building sites, and sell or make them available to immigrants from the South. Haarlem thus welcomed the new arrivals with open arms. In fact, the city's magistrate offered subsidies and other perks to lure immigrant-weavers and other professionals to set up their looms within the city walls, so to speak, and they did so most successfully.

Along with scores of textile workers, many Flemish artists were among the myriad of professionals who found their way to Haarlem. Up until the eve of iconoclasm, Antwerp had been a highly commercial

Neben zahlreichen Textilarbeitern gehörten auch viele flämische Künstler zu den unzähligen Fachleuten, die ihren Weg nach Haarlem fanden. Bis zum Vorabend des Bildersturms war Antwerpen ein kommerziell äußerst erfolgreicher Markt für Gemälde gewesen – einer der internationalsten und innovativsten in Europa. Doch die Welle des Bildersturms, die im Sommer 1566 über die Niederlande hinwegrollte, brachte schwierige Zeiten für die große Künstlergemeinde in Antwerpen. Viele packten ihr Hab und Gut zusammen und suchten einen sicheren Zufluchtsort, wobei sich die meisten in holländischen Städten wie Amsterdam, Middelburg und Haarlem niederließen.

Die ECARTICO-Datenbank enthält die Namen von 56 Malermeistern, die vom Ausbruch der Revolte bis 1630 in Haarlem tätig waren (Tabelle 1).[9] Von den vierzig Künstlern, deren Herkunft bekannt ist, wurde etwa ein Drittel in den südlichen Niederlanden geboren, wobei die meisten aus Antwerpen stammten. Zu den heute bekannteren Malern gehören Jacques de Gheyn II (1565–1629), Jan Porcellis (1584–1632), der junge Frans Hals (1582/83–1666) und Pieter Soutman (1593/1601–1657). Darüber hinaus

***Tabelle / Table 1:* Geburtsorte von Malern, die von 1565 bis 1630 in Haarlem tätig waren / Place of birth of painters active in Haarlem from 1565 to 1630**

GEBURTSORT / PLACE OF BIRTH	ANZAHL DER MALER / NUMBER OF PAINTERS	% DER GESAMTZAHL / % OF TOTAL
Haarlem	11	19.6
Antwerpen	10	17.8
Amsterdam	4	7.1
Kortrijk	3	5.4
Middelburg	2	3.6
Republik der Vereinigten Niederlande, andere / Dutch Republic, other	5	8.9
Südliche Niederlande, andere / Southern Netherlands, other	3	5.4
Ausländische Herkunft / Foreign origin	2	3.6
Unbekannt / Unknown	16	28.6
Total	56	100.0

Quelle / Source: ECARTICO database, Huygens Instituut (https://ecartico.org/)

market for paintings—indeed, one of the most international and innovative markets in Europe. But the iconoclastic wave that swept the Low Countries in the summer of 1566 introduced challenging times for Antwerp's extensive artistic community. Many packed up their belongings and headed for safer havens, with the majority settling in Dutch towns such as Amsterdam, Middelburg, and Haarlem.

The ECARTICO database supplies the names of fifty-six master painters who were active in Haarlem from the outbreak of the Revolt until 1630 (table 1).[9] Of the forty artists whose origin is known, about a third were born in the Southern Netherlands, with the majority coming from Antwerp. Among the more well-known painters to this day are Jacques de Gheyn II (1565–1629), Jan Porcellis (1584–1632), the young Frans Hals (1582/83–1666), and Pieter Soutman (1593/1601–1657). In addition, a cluster of

gab es eine Reihe von Künstlern aus der Grafschaft Flandern, vor allem aus Kortrijk, Gent und Brügge. Der berühmteste von ihnen ist der Maler und Autor von *Het schilder-boeck*, Karel van Mander (1548–1606), der in Meulebeke bei Kortrijk geboren wurde.

Unabhängig von ihrem genauen Herkunftsort führte diese Zuwanderung von Künstlern zu einem regelrechten Angebotsschock. Mit anderen Worten: Der beträchtliche Zustrom von Humankapital nach Haarlem trug dazu bei, den lokalen Kunstmarkt in Schwung zu bringen. Diese qualifizierten und erfahrenen Künstler brachten neue Gattungen mit und machten die Einheimischen mit der Landschaftsmalerei sowie mit Genrebildern und Seestücken bekannt. Sie richteten auch Werkstätten in ihrer Wahlheimat ein und bildeten vor allem dort ansässige begabte junge Leute aus. Es ist bemerkenswert, dass diese im Wesentlichen kriegsbedingte Abwanderung künstlerischer Talente es Haarlem ermöglichte, sich zu einem bedeutenden Kunstzentrum zu entwickeln.

Die Tatsache, dass Haarlem eine solche Anziehungskraft auf flämische Künstler ausübte, sollte uns nicht völlig überraschen. Schließlich wies die Stadt eine lange künstlerische Tradition auf und bedeutende Künstler wie Jan Mostaert (1475–1552/53), Jan van Scorel (1495–1562), Maarten van Heemskerck (1498–1574) und natürlich Hendrick Goltzius waren dort ansässig. Van Mander gab zu, dass er sehr erstaunt war, „solche Maler [in Haarlem] zu finden".[10] Außerdem gibt es Hinweise darauf, dass auch die Mundpropaganda zu dem anhaltenden Zustrom südniederländischer Künstler nach Haarlem beitrug. Kein Wunder also, dass van Mander meinte, er genieße es, das ganze Jahr über die flämische Sprache zu hören.

artists came from the county of Flanders, notably Kortrijk, Ghent, and Brugge. The most famous of these is the painter and author of *Het schilder-boeck*, Karel van Mander (1548–1606), who was born in Meulebeke near Kortrijk.

Irrespective of their exact place of origin, this immigration of artists resulted in a veritable supply shock. In other words, the significant influx of human capital into Haarlem helped to jump-start the local art market. These skilled, experienced artists brought with them new genres and exposed the locals to landscape painting and genre and naval scenes. They also set up workshops in their adopted hometowns and, most importantly, trained talented local youths. It is noteworthy that this displacement of artistic talent, in essence caused by war, allowed Haarlem to emerge as a major art center.

The fact that Haarlem exercised such a pull on Flemish artists should not entirely surprise us. After all, the town had a long tradition in the arts, with important artists such as Jan Mostaert (1475–1552/53), Jan van Scorel (1495–1562), Maarten van Heemskerck (1498–1574), and of course Hendrick Goltzius residing there. Van Mander admitted that he was quite astonished "to find such painters [in Haarlem]."[10] Furthermore, there are indications that word of mouth also contributed to the sustained influx of Southern artists into Haarlem. No wonder, then, that Van Mander commented that he enjoyed hearing the Flemish language all year round.

DAS WACHSTUM DES HAARLEMER KUNSTMARKTS

Mit einer solchen kritischen Masse an künstlerischem Kapital in der Stadt wuchs der Haarlemer Kunstmarkt schnell und entwickelte sich zu einer reifen und innovativen Szene, die in vielerlei Hinsicht nur von Amsterdam übertroffen wurde. Die in Haarlem lebenden Maler und Kupferstecher entwickelten ihre eigenen Stile und Spezialisierungen, unter anderem in der Landschafts- und Marinemalerei (exemplarisch hierfür sind Esaias van de Velde, 1587–1630, und Pieter de Molijn, 1595–1661) sowie in der Genremalerei, wenngleich auch behauptet wird, dass diese auf malerische Innovationen aus Antwerpen zurückgingen.[11]

Bald spezialisierten sich weitere Künstler. Die Nachfrage wuchs nicht nur, sondern wurde auch komplexer und vielfältiger, und ab Mitte der 1620er-Jahre traten professionelle Kunsthändler auf den Plan. In ihrer Dissertation stellte Marion Boers-Goossens fest, dass alle Kunsthändler, die zu dieser Zeit in Haarlem tätig waren, entweder erst kurz zuvor eingewandert oder direkte Nachkommen von Eingewanderten waren.[12] Diese Einwanderer importierten auch Techniken der Kunstvermarktung aus Antwerpen. Lotterien, Auktionen und Verlosungen wurden zwar nicht in Antwerpen erfunden, aber sie wurden dort in großem Umfang eingesetzt, um den Markt für Gemälde zu erweitern und die Nachfrage zu steigern. Die Anwendung der gleichen Strategien in Haarlem – wo sie oft auf Widerstand stießen – deutet auf eine Kommerzialisierung und Professionalisierung des Kunstmarkts hin, der sich an Antwerpen orientierte.[13] Und es gibt noch weitere auffällige Ähnlichkeiten. Die Tatsache, dass viele Haarlemer Kunsthändler – und auch Maler – nicht der Gilde angehörten (und sich daher nicht an deren Regeln und

THE GROWTH OF THE HAARLEM ART MARKET

With such a critical mass of artistic capital in the city, Haarlem's art market grew quickly, developing into a mature and innovative scene that was in many ways surpassed only by Amsterdam. Haarlem painters and engravers developed their own styles and specializations, including in landscape and marine painting (exemplified by Esaias van de Velde, 1587–1630, and Pieter de Molijn, 1595–1661) and genre painting, although it has been argued that these were indebted to painterly innovations that originated in Antwerp.[11]

Soon, more artists were specializing. Demand not only grew but also became more complex and diverse, with professional art dealers appearing on the scene in the mid-1620s. In her dissertation, Marion Boers-Goossens determined that all of the art dealers active in Haarlem at this time were either recent immigrants or the direct descendants of immigrants.[12] These immigrants also imported art-marketing techniques from Antwerp. While lotteries, auctions, and raffles may not have been invented in Antwerp, they were employed there on a large scale to widen the market for paintings and stimulate demand. The implementation of the same strategies in Haarlem—where they often met with resistance—points to a commercialization and professionalization of the art market that was modeled on Antwerp.[13] And there are other striking similarities as well. The fact that many Haarlem art dealers—and painters, for that matter—did not belong to the guild (and therefore did not abide by its rules and restrictions) may have been a *bad* habit imported from Antwerp.[14] At any rate, by the 1610s, Haarlem had

Beschränkungen hielten), könnte eine aus Antwerpen importierte *Un*sitte gewesen sein.[14] Auf jeden Fall hatte sich Haarlem um 1610 zu einem sehr wettbewerbsfähigen und führenden Markt für Gemälde und Stiche entwickelt, der keineswegs von der Welt abgeschottet war. Diese „Offenheit“ verschwand auch nach dem Abflauen der Migration nicht, und der Austausch fand nicht nur in materieller Hinsicht durch den Kunsthandel statt, sondern auch auf der Ebene der persönlichen Kontakte zwischen den Künstlern selbst.

REISENDE KÜNSTLER

Allgemein herrschte unter den Künstlern der frühen Neuzeit eine große Mobilität, mehr als wir heute wahrscheinlich annehmen. Viele Künstler reisten nach Italien, um ihre Ausbildung zu vervollständigen, wanderten im Gefolge militärischer Konflikte und wirtschaftlicher Not aus, zogen aus religiösen Gründen um oder wurden von besseren Möglichkeiten in anderen Ländern angelockt. Darüber hinaus zögerten die Künstler nicht, vorübergehend große Entfernungen zurückzulegen, um einen Auftrag auszuführen oder Kollegen, Freunde oder die Familie zu besuchen. Die Künstler scheinen besonders gern zwischen den Städten der Niederlande hin- und hergezogen zu sein. Dafür gab es viele Gründe, doch die verbesserten Transportmöglichkeiten wirkten zweifellos als Katalysator.

Die Provinz Holland verfügte über eine unübertroffene Infrastruktur in Form von Straßen und Kanälen, die ein relativ günstiges und sicheres Reisen ermöglichten. Die Republik der Vereinigten Niederlande war dank ihres verzweigten Netzes von Kanälen und Überland-Kutschenverbindungen überhaupt ein Land, in dem man leicht herumreisen konnte.[15] Vor allem die Lastkähne waren ein

grown into a very competitive and leading market for paintings and engravings, one that was by no means closed off from the world. This “openness” did not disappear after migration tapered off, and exchanges took place not only from a material perspective, through the art trade, but also on the level of personal contacts between artists themselves.

TRAVELING ARTISTS

In general, a great mobility existed among early modern artists, more than we probably assume today. Many artists traveled to Italy to complete their training, migrated in the wake of military conflict and economic hardship, relocated for reasons of religion, or were lured by better opportunities elsewhere. In addition, artists did not hesitate to travel great distances on a temporary basis to complete a commission or visit with colleagues, friends, or family. Artists appear to have been particularly eager to move between towns in the Low Countries. There were many reasons for this, but improved transportation facilities without a doubt acted as a catalyst.

The province of Holland could offer unrivaled infrastructure in terms of roads and canals, facilitating relatively cheap and safe travel. The Dutch Republic overall was an easy place to get around in as well, thanks to its intricate network of canals and overland coach connections.[15] Barges in particular provided a comfortable and reliable mode of transportation with regular service between the major cities, and this network would be developed in the course of the seventeenth century. The digging of canals

bequemes und zuverlässiges Verkehrsmittel, das regelmäßig zwischen den großen Städten verkehrte, und dieses Netzwerk wurde im Lauf des 17. Jahrhunderts noch ausgebaut. Das Anlegen von Kanälen von Haarlem nach Leiden und Amsterdam in den 1630er- und 1640er-Jahren verbesserte die Erreichbarkeit der Stadt erheblich, aber gute Verbindungen nach Antwerpen hatte es bereits zuvor gegeben.[16]

Die relative Leichtigkeit, mit der die Menschen innerhalb der gesamten Niederlande reisten, geht aus den Reisebüchern hervor. In ihnen sind Fahrpläne, Kosten und Häufigkeit von Land- und Wasserstraßenverbindungen, geeignete Gasthäuser zum Übernachten und sogar Sehenswürdigkeiten in den jeweiligen Städten aufgeführt. Die frühneuzeitlichen Reiseführer fanden weite Verbreitung und ermöglichten es, Reisen auf zweckmäßige Weise zu planen. Anhand dieser und anderer Quellen haben Jan De Vries und in jüngerer Zeit Gerrit Verhoeven festgestellt, dass das Reisen auf Lastkähnen besonders bequem war.[17] Verhoevens Untersuchungen zeigen, dass Reisen in der Republik der Vereinigten Niederlande im Vergleich zu anderen europäischen Ländern pro Kilometer am günstigsten waren. Außerdem herrschte in den Niederlanden ein hohes Maß an gefühlter Sicherheit, sprich Reisende hatten weit weniger Angst, Opfer von Raubüberfällen zu werden als anderswo.

Abgesehen davon, dass Reisen immer zeitaufwendig, mühsam und mit Kosten verbunden war, gab es noch andere Hindernisse. Nach der Wiederaufnahme der Feindseligkeiten im Jahr 1621 wurden wieder Pässe benötigt, um die Frontlinie zu überqueren, aber selbst dann dokumentieren die Archive viele Fälle, in denen Künstler von Süden nach Norden und umgekehrt reisten. So beantragten etwa Jacob Jordaens (1593–1678) und Mitglieder der Familie Teniers in den 1630er- und 1640er-Jahren Pässe für Reisen in die Republik.[18]

from Haarlem to Leiden and Amsterdam in the 1630s and 1640s respectively greatly enhanced the city's accessibility, but good connections with Antwerp had already existed prior to that.[16]

The relative ease with which people traveled within the whole of the Low Countries emanates from travel books, which mention the timetables, cost, and frequency of both overland connections and those via waterways, as well as detailing suitable inns where travelers could spend the night, and even places of interest to visit in the respective towns. The early modern travel guides were widely disseminated and allowed travelers to plan their trips in an expedient manner. Using these and other sources, Jan De Vries and more recently Gerrit Verhoeven have established that travel on barges was particularly convenient.[17] Verhoeven's research shows that compared to other European countries, travel in the Dutch Republic was the cheapest per kilometer. Furthermore, there was a high degree of perceived safety in the Low Countries—in other words, travelers were far less worried that they would fall victim to robbers compared to elsewhere.

Other impediments to travel existed apart from the fact that it was time-consuming and cumbersome, and always involved a cost. After the reopening of hostilities in 1621, passports were once again required to cross the front line, but even then, the archives document many instances of artists traveling from South to North and vice versa. For instance, Jacob Jordaens (1593–1678) and members of the Teniers family requested passports to travel to the Republic in the 1630s and 1640s.[18]

PERSÖNLICHE BEZIEHUNGEN UND KULTURELLE ÜBERLIEFERUNG

Der zweite Teil dieses Aufsatzes befasst sich mit der Bedeutung der künstlerischen Beziehungen zwischen Antwerpen und Haarlem, die sich nach der Ausrufung des zwölfjährigen Waffenstillstands offenbar intensivierten. Der künstlerische Austausch zwischen den beiden Städten hatte nie aufgehört, auch nicht in den finstersten Jahren des niederländischen Aufstands. Doch es versteht sich fast von selbst, dass sich die Künstler aus den südlichen und nördlichen Niederlanden ab 1609, als der Waffenstillstand begann und der Frieden vorübergehend wiederhergestellt wurde, viel leichter gegenseitig besuchen konnten. Unter Nutzung der bereits erwähnten außergewöhnlichen Transportmöglichkeiten zu Lande und zu Wasser reisten Antwerpener Künstler nach Haarlem und ihre Haarlemer Kollegen in die Stadt an der Schelde, und diese Praxis hielt auch nach der Wiederaufnahme der kriegerischen Auseinandersetzung im Jahr 1621 an. Die Reise von Rubens und einigen seiner Kollegen 1612 nach Haarlem ist gut dokumentiert (mehr hierzu unten), und wenn Arnold Houbraken Recht hat, traf Anthonis van Dyck (1599–1641) zu Beginn der 1630er-Jahre in Haarlem mit Frans Hals zusammen.[19] Zu den namhaften Haarlemer Malern, die sich wiederum in Antwerpen aufhielten, gehörten Pieter Soutman,[20] Frans Hals,[21] Frans Pietersz. de Grebber (1573–1649) und Pieter de Grebber (1600–1652/53).[22] In

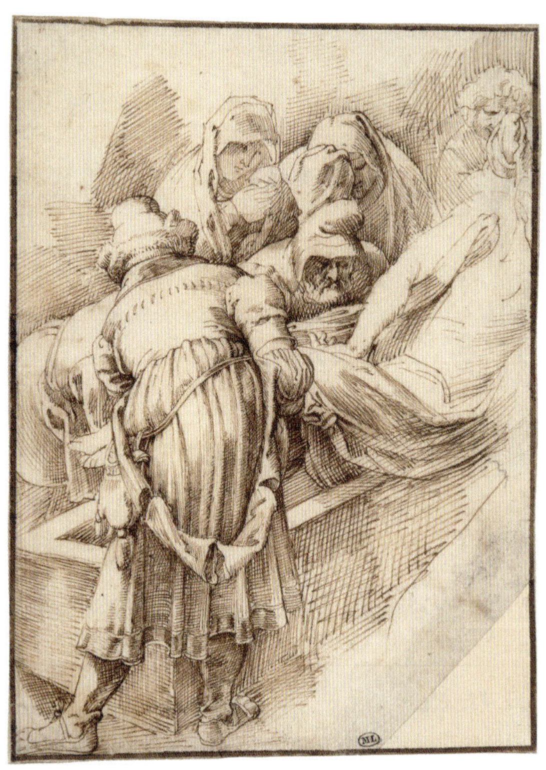

2 Rubens, nach / after Goltzius
Grablegung / Entombment, nach / after 1596/97
Feder / ink
Paris, Louvre, Département des Arts graphiques, Inv. 22602, recto

PERSONAL RELATIONSHIPS AND CULTURAL TRANSMISSION

The second part of this essay elaborates on the significance of the artistic ties between Antwerp and Haarlem, which appear to have intensified after the proclamation of the Twelve Years' Truce. Artistic exchanges between the cities had never ceased, not even during the darkest years of the Dutch Revolt. But it is almost a matter of course that from 1609 onward, when the truce was declared and peace restored, artists from the Southern and Northern Netherlands were able to visit with each other much more easily. Making use of the earlier mentioned extraordinary transportation facilities over land and water, Antwerp artists traveled to Haarlem and their Haarlem counterparts went to the city on the River Scheldt, and this practice persisted even after hostilities resumed in 1621. The trip Rubens and some of his colleagues made to Haarlem in 1612 is well documented (see below), and if Arnold Houbraken is right, Anthony van Dyck (1599–1641) met with Frans Hals in Haarlem at the beginning of the 1630s.[19] Notable Haarlem-based painters who spent time in Antwerp include Pieter Soutman,[20] Frans Hals,[21] Frans Pietersz. de Grebber (1573–1649), and Pieter de Grebber (1600–1652/53).[22] In the following paragraphs, we will draw attention to how

den folgenden Abschnitten soll aufgezeigt werden, wie solche „Auslandsreisen" und die damit verbundenen persönlichen Kontakte zu einer Art Assimilation von Stilen und Motiven über geographische Grenzen hinweg führten und insbesondere für den fortlaufenden künstlerischen Dialog zwischen Antwerpen und Haarlem von entscheidender Bedeutung waren.

RUBENS UND GOLTZIUS

Einige der intensivsten und wichtigsten dieser Interaktionen fanden zwischen Peter Paul Rubens und Hendrick Goltzius und seinem Umfeld statt. Schon sehr früh in seiner Karriere, in den 1590er-Jahren, richtete Rubens seinen Blick auf Goltzius, dessen gestochene Serie *Die Passion Christi* (1596–1598) er kopierte.[23] Kristin Lohse Belkin zufolge wurden Rubens' Kopien kurz nach der Veröffentlichung der Serie angefertigt, sodass die Originale für ihn fast unmittelbar zugänglich gewesen sein müssen. Ein wunderbares Beispiel für diese Reproduktionspraxis ist die Teilkopie nach Goltzius' *Grablegung* (1596; Abb. 2, 3).[24] Rubens konzentrierte sich auf die zentrale Gruppe, ließ einige Figuren weg und ordnete andere neu an. Maria Magdalena und eine der drei weiteren Frauen wurden entfernt, Johannes wurde an einen anderen Ort versetzt und der Kopf Christi

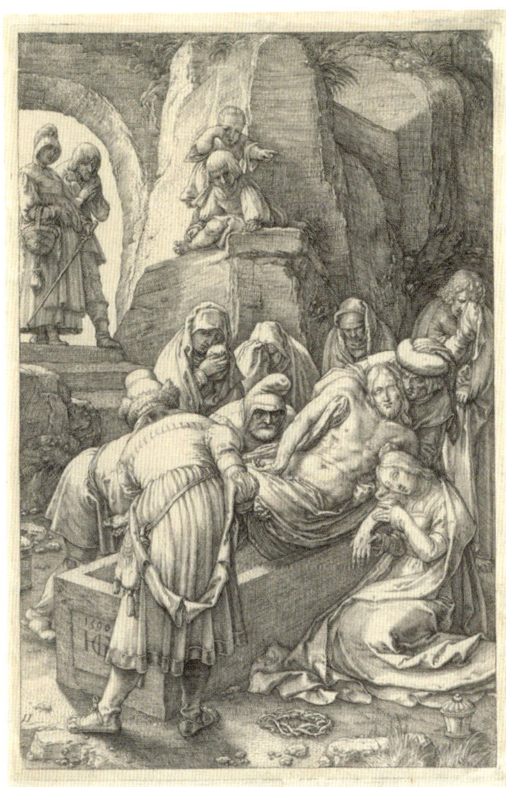

3 Goltzius (Inventor, Stecher / designer, engraver)
Grablegung / Entombment, 1596
Aus der Serie *Die Passion Christi* /
from the series *The Passion of Christ*, 1596–1598
Kupferstich / engraving SGSM, Inv. 30916 D

such journeys "abroad"—and the personal contacts they fostered—led to a kind of assimilation of styles and motifs across geographical borders and were, more specifically, of critical importance for the ongoing artistic dialogue between Antwerp and Haarlem.

RUBENS AND GOLTZIUS

Some of the most intensive and important of these interactions took place between Peter Paul Rubens and Hendrick Goltzius and his entourage. Very early in his career, during the 1590s, Rubens turned his gaze to Goltzius, whose engraved *Passion of Christ* series (1596–1598) he copied.[23] According to Kristin Lohse Belkin, Rubens's copies were made shortly after the publication of the series, which means that the originals must have been almost immediately accessible to him. A wonderful example of this reproduction practice is the partial copy after Goltzius's *Entombment* (1596; figs. 2–3).[24] Rubens concentrated on the central group, omitting certain figures and rearranging others. Mary Magdalene and one of the other three women are removed, John has been relocated, and the head of Christ and the figure of Joseph of Arimathea are cut off. Lohse Belkin contends that two aspects in particular attracted the young Rubens to Goltzius's engravings:

und die Figur des Josef von Arimathäa wurden abgeschnitten. Lohse Belkin schließt, dass der junge Rubens vor allem von zwei Aspekten von Goltzius' Stichen angezogen wurde: von ihrer kompositorischen Stärke und insbesondere von ihrem archaisierenden Stil, dessen Hauptbestandteil die Kostüme aus dem frühen 16. Jahrhundert sind.[25] Darüber hinaus zeichnet sich die *Passions*-Serie auch durch den virtuosen Einsatz des Stichels aus, mit dem Goltzius überraschende koloristische Hell-Dunkel-Effekte erzielte.[26] Folglich vertreten wir die These, dass diese auffällige Bildtechnik ein zusätzlicher Anziehungspunkt für Rubens in seiner Eigenschaft als Maler gewesen sein könnte.

Außerdem sollte man Goltzius' Rolle als Entwerfer nicht vergessen, zumindest in der Zeit nach seiner Rückkehr aus Italien. In den Jahren 1592 bis 1600 schuf er seine einfallsreichsten Drucke und er spielte eine entscheidende Rolle bei der Verbreitung der mythologischen Ikonographie – vor allem bei jenen Themen, die die Darstellung aufreizender Akte erlauben.[27] Damit stand er in offener Konkurrenz zu seinen Zeitgenossen in Italien und andernorts.[28] Sollte es da überraschen, dass dieser Aspekt von Goltzius' Kunst eine besondere Faszination auf Rubens ausübte?

Sein Interesse an Goltzius' Stichen scheint mehr gewesen zu sein als nur die Laune eines Anfängers. Etwa 15 Jahre später, im Juni 1612, reiste Rubens nach Haarlem, um sein großes Vorbild persönlich zu treffen. Dabei war er nicht allein, sondern wurde von anderen Antwerpener Malern wie Jan Brueghel I (1568–1625) und Hendrick van Balen (1573/75–1632) begleitet.[29] Es ist schwierig, den genauen Grund für Rubens' Besuch zu ermitteln. Wir können nur einige Hypothesen aufstellen. Es scheint recht plausibel, dass seine erste und wichtigste Motivation künstlerischer Natur war. Wie bereits oben

their compositional strength and, most of all, their archaizing style, of which the early sixteenth-century costumes form a main component.[25] In addition, Goltzius's *Passion* series also distinguishes itself by its virtuosic use of the burin to attain surprising coloristic chiaroscuro effects.[26] Consequently, we argue that this striking pictorial technique could have been an additional pull factor for Rubens in his capacity as a painter.

Moreover, one should not forget Goltzius's role as a designer, certainly in the period after his return from Italy. It was in the years 1592 to 1600 that he made his most inventive prints. He played a crucial role in the dissemination of mythological iconography—especially of those subjects allowing the representation of titillating nudes.[27] He hereby openly competed with his contemporaries in Italy and elsewhere.[28] Should it be any surprise that this aspect of Goltzius's art held a special fascination for Rubens?

His interest in Goltzius's engravings appears to have been more than just a beginner's fancy. About fifteen years later, in June 1612, Rubens traveled to Haarlem to meet his great role model in person. He did not go on his own, but was accompanied by other Antwerp painters including Jan Brueghel I (1568–1625) and Hendrick van Balen (1573/75–1632).[29] It is difficult to ascertain the precise reason for Rubens's visit. We can do no more than formulate some hypotheses. It seems quite plausible that his first and main motivation was artistic. As suggested above, Rubens would have seen in Goltzius a kindred spirit and a giant in the creative sphere.

angedeutet, erkannte Rubens in Goltzius sicherlich einen verwandten Geist und einen Riesen auf dem Gebiet der Erfindungskraft.

Ein zweiter interessanter Punkt waren wahrscheinlich Goltzius' besondere Arbeitsmethoden und die Art, wie er sein Druckgeschäft organisierte. Zu dieser Zeit hatte Goltzius in den Niederlanden ein Alleinstellungsmerkmal, da er alle Teile des Produktionsprozesses – vom Konzept über den Entwurf bis hin zur Veröffentlichung – persönlich kontrollierte, wobei er sowohl technisch als auch künstlerisch die höchstmögliche Qualität anstrebte und sich an ein internationales Publikum wandte. Obwohl das Atelier anfangs auch Werke nach anderen Meistern reproduzierte, verbreitete es nach und nach nur noch Goltzius' eigene Arbeiten.[30] Da Rubens auch in seiner Gemäldeproduktion eine stark hierarchische Organisation anstrebte,[31] muss er sich von Goltzius' Vorgehensweise bei der Druckgraphik inspiriert haben lassen. Als Rubens selbst ernsthaft in die Druckgraphik einstieg, scheint er auf ähnliche Weise gearbeitet zu haben wie Goltzius, und er stellte offenbar schließlich auch Stecher an, die in der Lage und willens waren, unter seiner Aufsicht nach hohen Standards zu arbeiten.[32]

Die häufig formulierte Hypothese, dass Rubens nach Haarlem ging, weil er aufgrund der zunehmenden Verfügbarkeit von Raubdrucken auf dem Markt die Kontrolle über die Reproduktion seiner Kompositionen zurückerlangen wollte,[33] wurde von Kerry Barrett – unserer Meinung nach zu Recht – in ihrer Dissertation über Pieter Soutman bestritten. Sie argumentierte, dass Rubens frühestens sechs Jahre nach seinem Besuch 1612 Privilegien beantragte und eine echte Druckproduktion begann.[34] Dennoch ist es bemerkenswert, dass in den Jahren nach dem Besuch in Haarlem einige hervorragende Kupferstecher

A second point of interest was probably Goltzius's special working methods and the way he organized his print business. At the time Goltzius was unique in the Netherlands in that he personally controlled all parts of the production process—concept, design, and publication—thereby aiming at the highest possible quality, both technically and artistically, and targeting an international audience. Although the studio initially also produced work after other masters, it gradually came to disseminate only Goltzius's own work.[30] As Rubens also aimed at a strongly hierarchical organization in his painting business,[31] he must have been inspired by Goltzius's approach to printmaking. Once Rubens seriously took up printmaking himself, he seems to have worked analogously, ultimately also hiring engravers who were able and willing to work to high standards and under his supervision.[32]

The frequently formulated hypothesis that Rubens went to Haarlem out of a desire to exert control over the reproduction of his compositions, due to the increasing availability of pirate prints on the market,[33] was contested by Kerry Barrett—in our opinion correctly—in her dissertation on Pieter Soutman. She argued that Rubens did not apply for privileges and start a real print production for at least six years after his visit in 1612.[34] This being said, it remains striking that during the years following the visit to Haarlem, some excellent engravers from Goltzius's circle created prints of Rubens's works. One of these was Goltzius's pupil and stepson Jacob Matham (1571–1631). Matham made a wonderful engraving after Rubens's famous composition of *Samson and Delilah*, painted around 1609 for Nicolaas Rockox, the burgomaster of Antwerp (figs. 4–5). Some details in the print suggest that it was made not after the final

aus Goltzius' Kreis Drucke nach Rubens' Werken anfertigten. Einer von ihnen war Goltzius' Schüler und Stiefsohn Jacob Matham (1571–1631). Matham schuf einen wunderbaren Stich nach Rubens' berühmter Komposition *Samson und Delilah*, die der Flame um 1609 für Nicolaas Rockox, den Bürgermeister von Antwerpen, gemalt hatte (Abb. 4, 5). Einige Details des Drucks lassen vermuten, dass er nicht nach dem vollendeten Gemälde entstanden ist, das sich heute in der Londoner National Gallery befindet, sondern nach Rubens' Ölskizze oder Modell, das heute im Cincinnati Art Museum aufbewahrt wird (Abb. 6).[35] Der bartlose Barbier, die Anordnung der Krüge auf dem Wandregal, der Teppich und die Anzahl der Soldaten in der Türöffnung entsprechen eher der Ölskizze (*modello*) als dem fertigen Gemälde. Über die genaue Datierung des Drucks herrscht keine Einigkeit, doch es scheint plausibel, dass er um 1613 entstanden ist.[36] Daher könnte man sich vorstellen, dass Rubens die Ölskizze entweder mitbrachte, als er im Juni 1612 Haarlem besuchte, oder sie danach dorthin schicken ließ, um sie als Stich reproduzieren zu lassen.

Bei diesem Besuch lernte Rubens wahrscheinlich auch einige Kollegen von Jacob Matham kennen. Einer von ihnen war Willem Buytewech I (1591/92–1624), der um die Zeit des Besuchs oder kurz danach ebenfalls mehrere Reproduktionen von Rubens' Werken anfertigte. Um 1612/13 schuf er etwa einen Stich nach Rubens' *Kain erschlägt Abel* (um 1608; Abb. 7, 8).[37] Die Quelle für diesen Stich, wie auch für die anderen, ist schwer zu ermitteln, und die Frage, ob diese

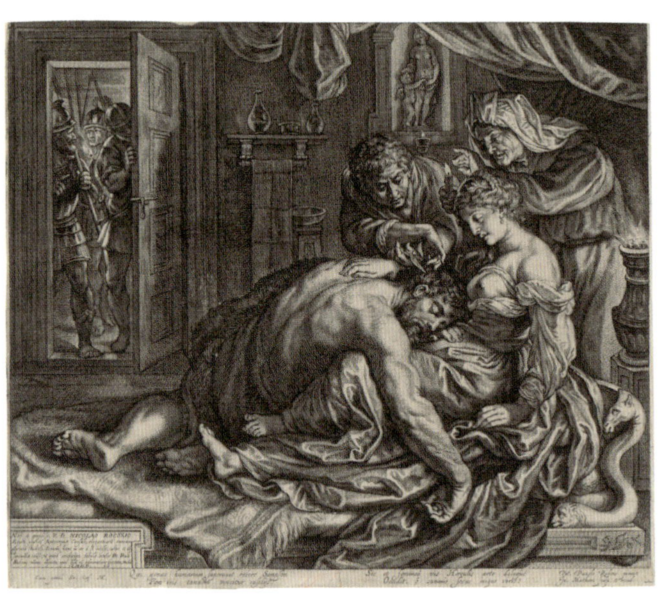

4 Jacob Matham (Stecher / engraver), nach / after Rubens
Samson und / and Delilah, ca. 1613
Kupferstich / engraving SGSM, Inv. 29987 D

painting, which is now in London's National Gallery, but after Rubens's oil sketch or *modello* now held at the Cincinnati Art Museum (fig. 6).[35] The beardless barber, the arrangement of jars on the wall shelf, the tapestry, and the number of soldiers in the doorway correspond more closely to the *modello* than to the finished painting. There is no consensus on the precise dating of the print, but it seems plausible that it was made around 1613.[36] Therefore, one could imagine that Rubens either brought the oil sketch with him when he visited Haarlem in June 1612 or had it sent there afterward to be reproduced.

During this same visit Rubens probably also met some of Jacob Matham's colleagues. One of these was Willem Buytewech I (1591/92–1624), who also made several reproductions of Rubens's works around the time of the visit or shortly thereafter. Around 1612/13, for example, he produced an engraving after Rubens's *Cain Slaying Abel* (ca. 1608; figs. 7–8).[37] The source for this engraving, as for the others, is difficult to ascertain and the question as to whether these etchings were made after existing paintings or after drawings or oil sketches cannot be resolved at this point in time. But the dating is such that their creation almost has to be linked to Rubens's visit to Haarlem.

Radierungen nach vorhandenen Gemälden oder nach Zeichnungen oder Ölskizzen angefertigt wurden, kann zum jetzigen Zeitpunkt nicht geklärt werden. Doch die Datierung ist so, dass ihre Entstehung fast zwangsläufig mit dem Besuch Rubens' in Haarlem in Verbindung gebracht werden muss.

Ein weiterer Künstler, den Rubens bei dieser Gelegenheit kennengelernt haben muss, ist Pieter Soutman. Diese Begegnung war von großer Bedeutung, denn kurz darauf, im Jahr 1616, überzeugte Rubens Soutman, in seinem Atelier in Antwerpen als Graphiker und Maler zu arbeiten. Viel zu lange blieb Soutman in der Kunstgeschichtsschreibung eine geheimnisvolle Figur, was zum Teil auf seine Tätigkeit in zwei Regionen, den südlichen und den nördlichen Niederlanden, zurückzuführen ist. Dank der Dissertation von Kerry Barrett 2012 hat er jedoch endlich seinen wohlverdienten Platz in der Kunstgeschichte erhalten.[38]

Bisher haben wir gesehen, in welchem Maße Rubens' Schaffen der Haarlemer Kunstszene verpflichtet war, und zwar von Beginn seiner Karriere an. Daher scheint es nicht allzu weit hergeholt zu sein zu behaupten, dass Goltzius als eine Art Lehrer für den jungen Künstler fungierte, da Rubens sein Werk als Teil seiner künstlerischen Ausbildung sorgfältig studierte. Zum Zeitpunkt ihrer Begegnung im Jahr

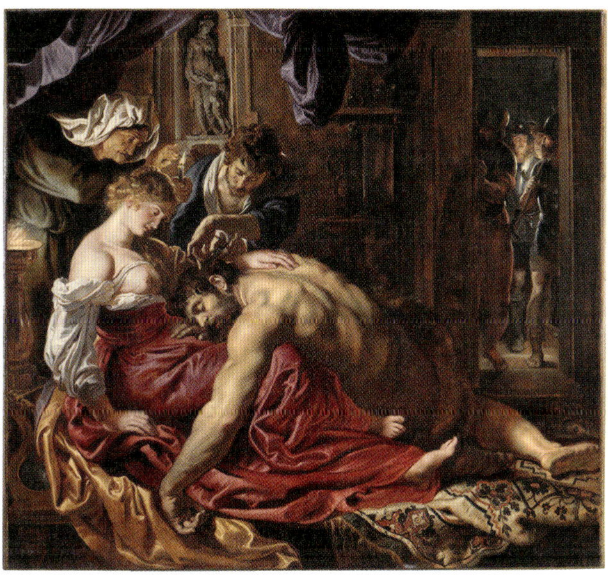

5 Peter Paul Rubens
Samson und / and Delilah, ca. 1609
Öl auf Holz / oil on panel London, National Gallery, Inv. 6461

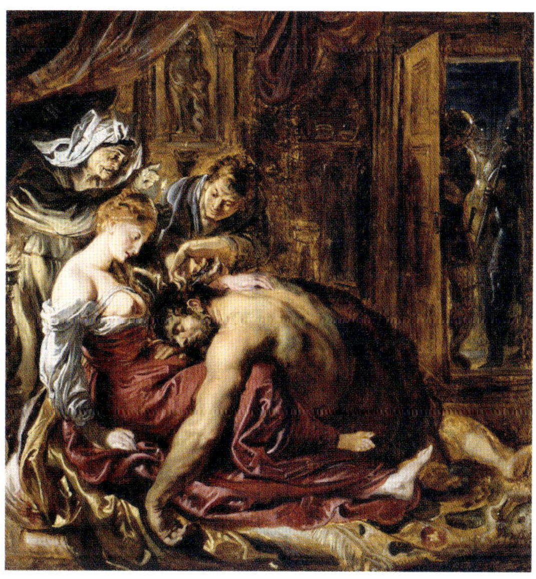

6 Peter Paul Rubens
Samson und / and Delilah, ca. 1609
Öl auf Holz / oil on panel Cincinnati Art Museum, Mr. and Mrs. Harry S. Leyman Endowment, Inv. 1972.459

Another artist Rubens must have met on this occasion is Pieter Soutman. This encounter had significant implications since shortly afterward, in 1616, Rubens convinced Soutman to come work in his studio in Antwerp as a printmaker and painter. For far too long Soutman remained a mysterious figure in art historiography, partly due to his activities in two regions, the Southern and the Northern Netherlands. Thanks to Kerry Barrett's 2012 dissertation, however, he has finally received his richly deserved place in art history.[38]

So far we have established the extent to which Rubens's production was indebted to the Haarlem art scene, from the very beginning of his career. Therefore, it does not seem too far-fetched to argue that Goltzius acted as a kind of teacher for the young artist as Rubens carefully studied his work as part of his artistic education. At the moment of their meeting in 1612, the Dutch master had already exchanged the

1612 hatte der holländische Meister bereits den Stichel gegen den Pinsel getauscht und arbeitete in der von Rubens geschätzten Disziplin. Goltzius wurde zu dieser Zeit für sein malerisches Talent hoch gelobt, insbesondere für sein außergewöhnliches Geschick bei der Darstellung menschlicher Haut.[39]

Auch wenn man keine Gelegenheit hatte, seine Werke zu sehen, konnte man in van Manders *Schilder-boeck* nachlesen, wie Goltzius sich nach seiner Rückkehr aus Italien der Darstellung dessen, was van Mander „glühende" Haut nannte, widmete, zunächst in seinen Arbeiten mit der Feder und später in einer Disziplin, die viel naturgetreuere Schattierungen erlaubt: der Malerei.[40] Der Effekt des unter der Oberfläche glühenden Inkarnats, der vor allem durch die Verwendung von Rot und Ocker erreicht wurde, kommt in Goltzius' *Die schlafende Danaë* (Abb. 9) wunderschön zum Vorschein: Er lässt sich nicht nur an Danaës Körper und den roten Wangen beobachten, sondern auch im Gesicht der alten Frau,

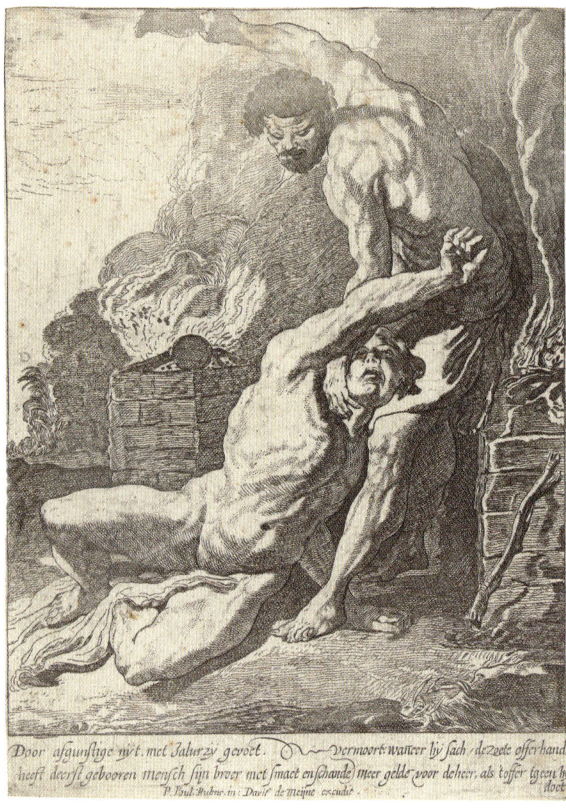

7 Willem Buytewech I (Radierer / etcher), nach / after Rubens
Kain erschlägt Abel / Cain Slaying Abel, ca. 1612/13
Radierung / etching Amsterdam, Rijksprentenkabinet, Inv. RP-P-BI-5323

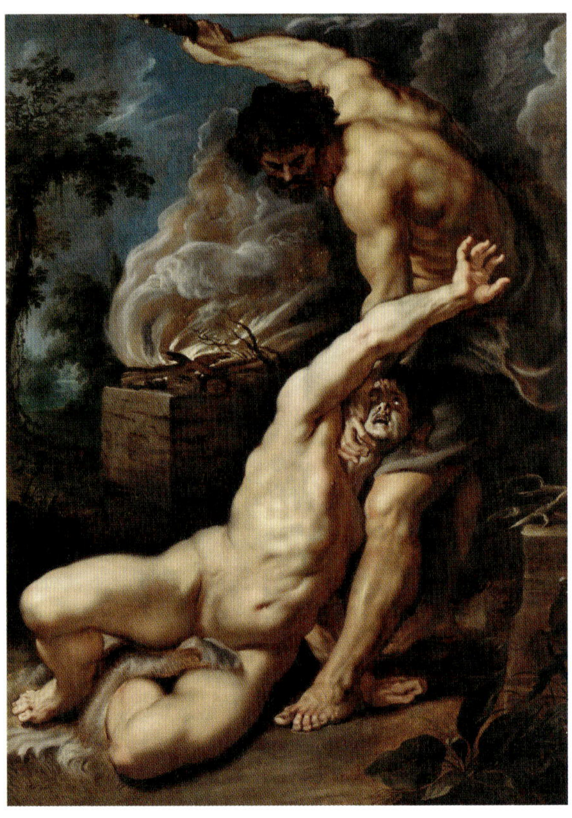

8 Peter Paul Rubens
Kain erschlägt Abel / Cain Slaying Abel, ca. 1608
Öl auf Holz / oil on panel
London, The Courtauld, Inv. P.1978.PG.353

burin for the brush and was working in Rubens's cherished discipline. Moreover, by that time Goltzius was highly praised for his painting talent, especially for his exceptional skillfulness in the representation of human skin.[39]

Even if one did not have the opportunity to see his works, one could still read in Van Mander's *Schilder-boeck* how Goltzius had applied himself, following his return from Italy, to the depiction of what

das buchstäblich glüht. Wie van Mander erzählte, war diese Herangehensweise zu Beginn des Jahrhunderts in den Niederlanden einzigartig und steht in starkem Kontrast zu dem steinernen Grau oder der „blassen, fischartigen, kalten Farbe", den „harten Schatten" und den „scharfkantigen Lichtern", die für die nördlichen Akte so typisch waren. Goltzius' besonderes Talent und sein innovativer Beitrag auf diesem Gebiet müssen Rubens sehr beeindruckt haben. Und wer weiß, vielleicht stellte das für ihn einen zusätzlichen Anreiz dar, nach Haarlem zu gehen. Aber wie dem auch sei: In Goltzius muss er eine verwandte Seele gefunden haben, die nicht nur ein einzigartiges Interesse an der Aktmalerei und der menschlichen Haut hatte, sondern sich auch von den nordischen Meistern sowie von der antiken Tradition und der italienischen Renaissance inspirieren ließ. Der besondere Respekt und die Bewunderung des flämischen Künstlers für seinen holländischen Kollegen wird nirgendwo deutlicher als in Balthazar Gerbiers 1618 verfasster und 1620 veröffentlichter Totenklage für Goltzius, bei der Rubens unter allen Künstlern der Niederlande auserwählt wurde, den Trauerzug anzuführen.[41]

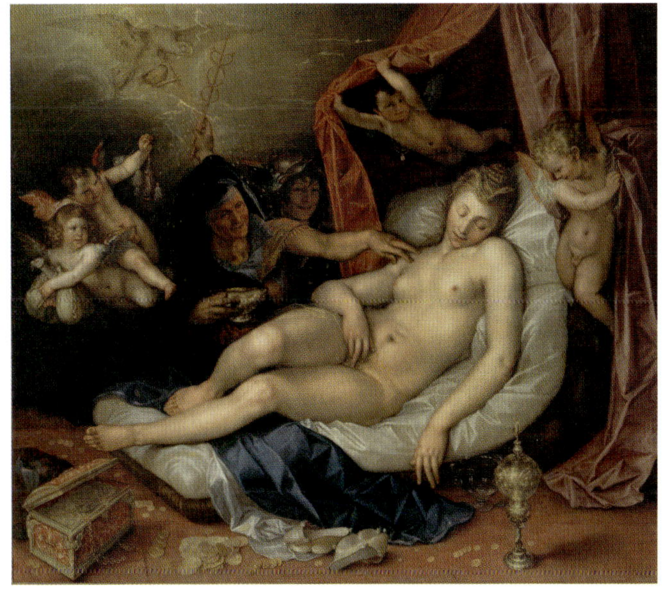

9 Hendrick Goltzius
Die schlafende Danaë / The Sleeping Danaë, 1603
Öl auf Leinwand / oil on canvas
Los Angeles County Museum of Art, Gift of The Ahmanson Foundation, Inv. M.84.191

he called "glowing" skin, first in his works with pen and later in a discipline allowing much more lifelike shades: painting.[40] The effect of an incarnate glowing from beneath the surface, which was mainly reached through the use of red and ocher, is beautifully seen in Goltzius's *Sleeping Danaë* (fig. 9): it can be observed not only in Danaë's body and red cheeks, but also in the face of the old woman, which is literally glowing. As Van Mander pointed out, this working method was unique in the Netherlands at the turn of the seventeenth century and contrasted strongly with the stony grayness or "pale, fishy, coldish color," "hard shadows," and "sharp-edged highlights" which were so typical of the northern nudes. Goltzius's special talent and innovative contribution in this field must have been a delight to Rubens. And who knows? Perhaps it gave him an extra incentive to go to Haarlem. Whatever the case may be, in Goltzius he must have found a kindred soul who not only had a unique interest in the painting of the nude and of human skin, but who also drew inspiration from the northern masters as well as from the antique tradition and the Italian Renaissance. The special respect and admiration of the Flemish artist for his Dutch colleague is nowhere more poignantly illustrated than in Balthazar Gerbier's lament on the death of Goltzius, written in 1618 and published in 1620, in which Rubens was chosen from all the artists in the Low Countries to lead the funeral procession.[41]

GOLTZIUS UND RUBENS

Rubens wird in Gerbiers Huldigung an Goltzius nicht nur eine herausragende Stellung eingeräumt, das Gedicht verleiht ihm sogar den Titel des größten Künstlers der Niederlande. Es ist daher vorstellbar, dass der verstorbene Künstler diese Meinung teilte. Und tatsächlich gibt es Anzeichen für gegenseitige Sympathie und Respekt. Besonders nach der persönlichen Begegnung zwischen den Künstlern 1612 scheint der ältere Meister von seinem jüngeren Kollegen fasziniert gewesen zu sein.[42] Am deutlichsten wird dies in den Szenen, die Rubens nach seiner Rückkehr aus Italien 1608 gemalt hatte und die sich durch eine begrenzte Anzahl von Figuren und ein hohes Maß an Sinnlichkeit auszeichnen, wobei der Akt im Vordergrund steht.[43] Mindestens sechs Gemälde, die Goltzius zwischen 1613 und 1616 schuf, ähneln früheren Bildern von Rubens, die in Holland entweder in ihrer authentischen, gemalten Form oder als Stich präsent waren, oder sind ihnen zu verdanken. Ein Gemälde, das einen tiefen Eindruck auf Goltzius gemacht haben muss, ist Rubens' *Jupiter und Kallisto* von 1613 (Abb. 10).

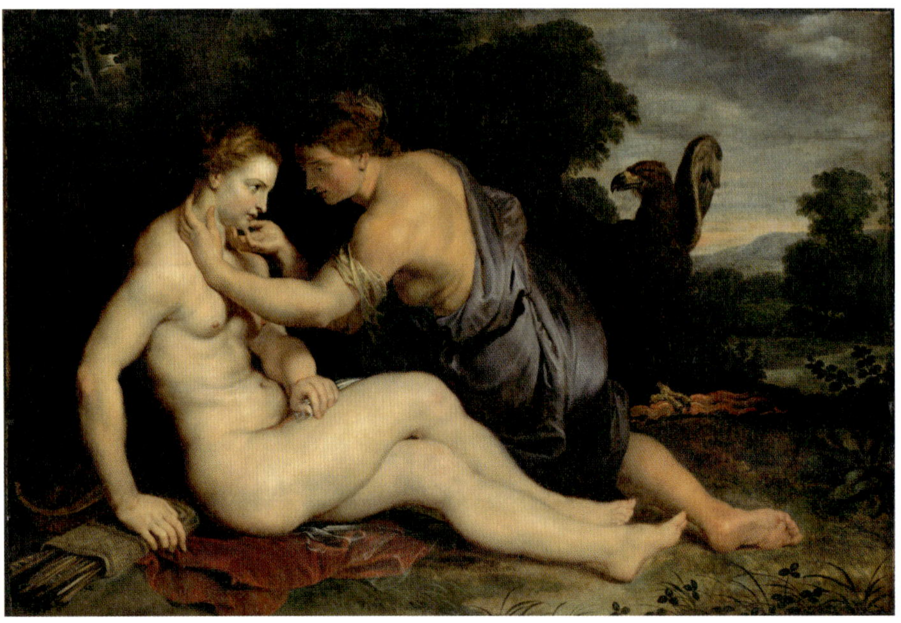

GOLTZIUS AND RUBENS

Rubens was granted a prominent position in Gerbier's homage to Goltzius—indeed, the poem bestowed on him the title of the greatest artist in the Netherlands. This makes it conceivable that this opinion was shared by the deceased artist. And indeed, there are signs of mutual sympathy and respect. Especially after the personal meeting between the artists in 1612, the older master appears to have become fascinated by his younger colleague.[42] This is most evident from the scenes Rubens had made after his return from Italy in 1608, characterized by a limited number of figures and a high degree of sensuality, with the nude prominently featured.[43] At least six paintings Goltzius made between 1613 and 1616 bear resemblance to or are indebted to earlier pictures by Rubens which were available in Holland either in their authentic, painted form or in the form of an engraving. A painting which must have made a profound impression on Goltzius is Rubens's *Jupiter and Callisto* from 1613 (fig. 10).

Es handelt sich um eines der typischen klassizistischen Gemälde von Rubens, bei dem die Handlung von einer begrenzten Anzahl von Figuren im Vordergrund ausgeführt wird, die deutlich hervorgehoben sind und dem Gemälde eine fast reliefartige Anmutung verleihen. Das Thema des Gemäldes ist Ovids *Metamorphosen* entnommen. Rubens zeigt uns hier, wie Kallisto, eine der Nymphen Dianas, von Jupiter verführt wird, der sich als Diana verkleidet hat, um sich der Nymphe zu nähern, dessen Identität dem Betrachter jedoch durch den Adler neben ihm verraten wird. Nur zwei Jahre später malte Hendrick Goltzius *Vertumnus und Pomona*, das eine sehr ähnliche Geschichte aus Ovids Erzählungen darstellt: Ein männlicher Gott verkleidet sich als Frau, um sich der Dame zu nähern, die er liebt. Die Inszenierung der beiden skulpturalen Figuren im Vordergrund, die natürliche Umgebung hinter ihnen, mit einem Baum auf der linken Seite und einer Aussicht auf eine Landschaft auf der rechten Seite, der glatte Farbauftrag und die hellen Hautpartien – all diese Elemente erinnern an Rubens' *Jupiter und Kallisto*. Leider ist die frühe

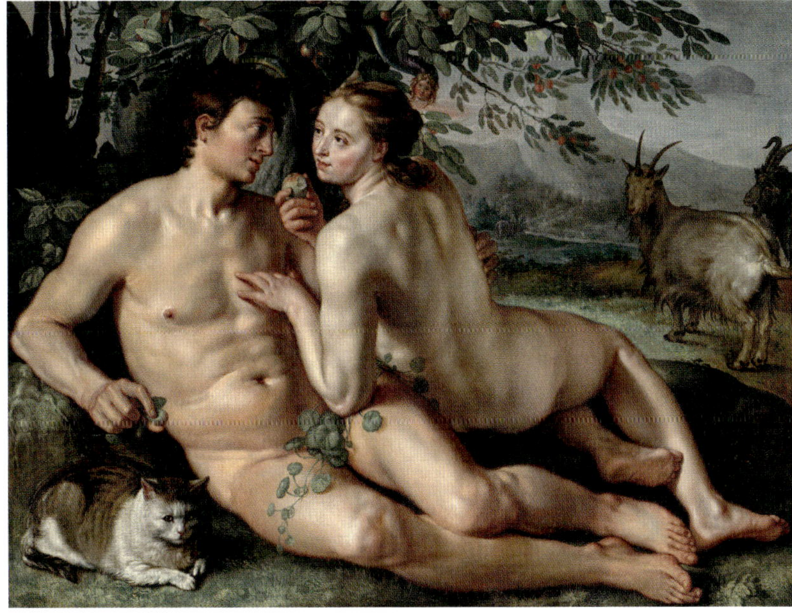

LINKE SEITE / LEFT PAGE

10 Peter Paul Rubens
Jupiter und Kallisto / and Callisto, 1613
Öl auf Holz / oil on panel
Kassel, Gemäldegalerie Alte Meister, MHK, Inv. GK86

11 Hendrick Goltzius
Der Sündenfall / The Fall of Man, 1616
Öl auf Leinwand / oil on canvas
Washington, DC, National Gallery of Art, Inv. 1996.34.1

This is one of Rubens's typical classicist paintings in which the action is carried out by a limited number of figures in the foreground that are clearly highlighted, giving the painting an almost relief-like appearance. The subject of the painting is taken from Ovid's *Metamorphoses*. Rubens shows us here how Callisto, one of Diana's nymphs, is being seduced by Jupiter, who has disguised himself as Diana in order to approach the nymph, but whose identity is betrayed to the viewer by the eagle next to him. Only two years later, Hendrick Goltzius painted *Vertumnus and Pomona*, which depicts a very similar Ovidian story, with a male god disguising himself as a woman in order to gain access to the woman he loves. The staging of the two sculptural figures in the foreground; the natural setting behind them, with a tree on the left and a view to the right; the smooth coat of paint and the bright parts of the skin: all these elements remind us of Rubens's *Jupiter and Callisto*. Unfortunately, the early provenance of Rubens's picture is not known, meaning that we do not know where and when Goltzius might have seen it.[44] However, the fact remains that it had a

Provenienz von Rubens' Bild nicht bekannt, sodass wir nicht wissen, wo und wann Goltzius es gesehen haben könnte.[44] Unstrittig aber ist, dass es einen bleibenden Eindruck auf ihn machte, da ein anderes Werk aus dem Jahr 1616 ebenfalls deutliche Bezüge zu diesem Bild aufweist, wie Eric Jan Sluijter festgestellt hat.[45] Es handelt sich um den *Sündenfall* (Abb. 11). Auch hier sehen wir zwei ineinander verschlungene Figuren inmitten einer Landschaft; und auch hier versucht die rechte Figur, die linke mit einer Handbewegung und einem durchdringenden Blick zu verführen. Dies sind nur zwei Beispiele für Goltzius' Zitierpraxis, doch es gibt noch viele weitere.

Goltzius' Verbindung zu Rubens wurde von seinen talentiertesten Schülern Pieter de Grebber und Salomon de Bray (1597–1664) fortgesetzt. Beide Künstler zeichneten sich als Historienmaler aus und griffen, wie Xander van Eck in seinem sehr anregenden Buch über die katholische Historienmalerei in den nördlichen Niederlanden feststellt und anschaulich illustriert, immer wieder auf Kompositionsschemata, Figuren und Stilelemente von Rubens und Anthonis van Dyck zurück, deren Werke sie vor allem dank der verbreiteten Drucke kannten.[46] In jüngerer Zeit hat Marloes Hemmer gezeigt, wie de Grebber sich die künstlerischen Ideen von Rubens aneignete und damit eine innovative Bildsprache schuf, die einen wesentlichen Beitrag zur Historienmalerei in den nördlichen Niederlanden leistete.[47] Pieter de Grebber hatte wahrscheinlich einen zusätzlichen Anreiz bei seiner Vorliebe für Rubens' Kunst. Im Alter von 18 Jahren lernte er den flämischen Meister anlässlich der berühmten Verhandlung mit Sir Dudley Carleton im Jahr 1618 kennen. In dieser Angelegenheit fungierte sein Vater, Frans Pietersz. de Grebber, als Agent für Rubens, und Pieter begleitete seinen Vater auf dessen Reise nach Antwerpen.[48] Während ihres

lasting impression on him, since another composition, dated 1616, shows clear references to it, as has been pointed out by Eric Jan Sluijter.[45] This is *The Fall of Man* (fig. 11). Here too we see two intertwined figures against a natural background; here too the right figure tries to seduce the left one with a sweep of the hand and a penetrating gaze. These are only two examples of Goltzius's quoting practice. There are many more.

Goltzius's link with Rubens was continued by his most talented pupils, Pieter de Grebber and Salomon de Bray (1597–1664). Both artists distinguished themselves as history painters and, as has been noted and clearly illustrated by Xander van Eck in his very stimulating book on Catholic history painting in the Northern Netherlands, both repeatedly fell back on composition schemes, figures, and stylistic elements from Peter Paul Rubens and Anthony van Dyck, whose works they knew mostly thanks to widespread print production.[46] More recently, Marloes Hemmer demonstrated how De Grebber appropriated Rubens's artistic ideas and thus created an innovative imagery which constituted a vital contribution to history painting in the Northern Netherlands.[47] Pieter de Grebber likely had an additional incentive for his Rubensian inclination. At the age of eighteen, he met the Flemish master on the occasion of the famous negotiation with Sir Dudley Carleton in 1618. In this matter his father, Frans Pietersz. de Grebber, acted as an agent for Rubens, and Pieter accompanied his father on his trip to Antwerp.[48] During their stay in the city on the River Scheldt, De Grebber junior must have seen a fair number of paintings by Rubens, and probably also by other masters such as the young Van Dyck. These impressions had a lasting effect on the precocious Catholic artist, who would develop into a specialist of monumental history scenes

Aufenthalts in der Stadt an der Schelde muss der jüngere de Grebber eine ganze Reihe von Gemälden von Rubens und wahrscheinlich auch von anderen Meistern wie dem jungen van Dyck gesehen haben. Diese Eindrücke prägten den frühreifen katholischen Künstler nachhaltig, der sich zu einem Spezialisten für monumentale Historienszenen und religiöse Altarbilder entwickeln sollte. Außerdem nutzte er das große katholische Netzwerk seines Vaters und baute es weiter aus, nicht nur in den nördlichen, sondern auch in den südlichen Niederlanden. In der Tat scheint es recht plausibel, dass es de Grebber trotz der Präsenz berühmter Historienmaler im Süden gelang, Aufträge von flämischen Klöstern und Kirchen zu erhalten.[49] Es wäre sehr interessant, mehr über die Aktivitäten von dem älteren de Grebber als Händler und Vermittler zwischen den Kunstgemeinschaften von Antwerpen und Haarlem zu erfahren und auch über die Bedeutung katholischer Netzwerke für die grenzüberschreitende Weitergabe des künstlerischen Erbes.

Die vielfältigen Interaktionen zwischen Goltzius und seinen Schülern und Nachfolgern einerseits und Rubens und den seinen andererseits – sowohl in der Welt der Druckgraphik als auch in der Welt der Malerei – haben hoffentlich deutlich gemacht, dass es schwierig ist, den Ursprung und die Entwicklung der Haarlemer und der Antwerpener Malerschule als unabhängige Phänomene zu betrachten. In diesem Aufsatz haben wir uns auf ein einziges Beispiel konzentriert, doch im Zusammenhang mit den zahlreichen Spezialisierungen, die sich in den ersten Jahren des 17. Jahrhunderts herausbildeten, können noch viele weitere grenzüberschreitende Austauschbeziehungen erwähnt werden. Man denke nur an Jan Porcellis, der im Süden geboren wurde, in Haarlem ein führender Spezialist für Marinemalerei wurde und einen Teil seiner Karriere in Antwerpen verbrachte.[50] Ein weiteres bemerkenswertes Beispiel ist

and religious altarpieces. Moreover, he would make good use of his father's vast Catholic network and further expand it, not only in the Northern Netherlands but in the Southern Netherlands as well. Indeed, it seems quite plausible that despite the presence of famous history painters in the South, De Grebber managed to acquire commissions from Flemish cloisters and churches.[49] It would be very interesting to learn more about De Grebber senior's activities as a dealer and intermediary between the Antwerp and Haarlem artistic communities, and also about the importance of Catholic networks in the transmission of artistic patrimony across the borders.

The varied interactions between Goltzius and his followers on the one hand and Rubens and his followers on the other—in the worlds of both printing and painting—have hopefully illustrated that it is difficult to consider the origin and development of the Haarlem and Antwerp schools of painting as independent phenomena. In this essay, we have focused on one example only, but many more cross-border exchanges can be mentioned in the context of the numerous specializations which were taking shape during those early years of the seventeenth century. We need only think of Jan Porcellis, who was born in the South, became a leading specialist in marine painting in Haarlem, and spent part of his career in Antwerp.[50] Another noteworthy example is Adriaen Brouwer (1603/05–1638), who through his travels between Antwerp and Haarlem had an important impact on the development of genre painting in both cities.[51] Or think of the still-life painter Pieter Claesz. (1597/98–1660/61), who originated in Antwerp and in 1620 imported an Antwerp style to Haarlem, where it in turn underwent significant changes.[52]

Adriaen Brouwer (1603/05–1638), der durch seine Reisen zwischen Antwerpen und Haarlem einen wichtigen Einfluss auf die Entwicklung der Genremalerei in beiden Städten ausübte.[51] Interessant ist auch der Stilllebenmaler Pieter Claesz. (1596/97–1660/61), der aus Antwerpen stammte und um 1620 einen lokalen Stil aus seiner Heimat nach Haarlem importierte, der dort seinerseits bedeutende Veränderungen erfuhr.[52]

Wir hoffen, mit diesen Beispielen veranschaulicht zu haben, dass die grenzüberschreitende Migration sowohl im Norden als auch im Süden einen entscheidenden Einfluss auf die ikonographischen Traditionen hatte. Weitere Untersuchungen sind erforderlich, um das Wesen des gemeinsamen Erbes und die erkennbaren Unterschiede auf beiden Seiten der Grenze zu erfassen. Darüber hinaus ist es wichtig zu untersuchen, wie sich diese Wechselwirkungen gegen Ende des 17. Jahrhunderts entwickelten, als die Antwerpener Malerschule einen Großteil ihres Glanzes verlor und auch die Haarlemer Malerschule viel von ihrer Innovationskraft einbüßte.

SCHLUSSBEMERKUNGEN

Der Haarlemer Kunstmarkt ist weitgehend durch externe Faktoren entstanden. Haarlem nahm nicht nur flämische Künstler auf, die vor Gewalt und religiöser Verfolgung flohen oder nach neuen Möglichkeiten suchten, sondern importierte auch die Antwerpener Sammelsucht und innovative Vermarktungstechniken. Haarlem wurde, wie Amsterdam, zur neuen Heimat der Antwerpener Szene. Doch die Geschichte endet nicht mit der Integration flämischer Künstler in nördlichen Städten. Ein einfacher, preiswerter, sicherer

We hope to have illustrated by these examples that cross-border migration had a critical influence on the iconographic traditions in both the North and South. Further research is needed to grasp the essence of the shared patrimony and the discernible differences on both sides of the border. Furthermore, it is important to explore how these interactions developed toward the end of the seventeenth century, when the Antwerp school of painting had lost most of its brilliance and the Haarlem school of painting was also losing much of its innovative power.

CONCLUSIONS

The Haarlem art market emerged to a large extent as the result of external factors. Haarlem not only welcomed Flemish artists who were fleeing from violence and religious persecution or were seeking opportunities, but also imported the Antwerp addiction of collecting pictures, along with new marketing techniques. Haarlem—like Amsterdam—in effect became the new home of the Antwerp scene. But the story does not end with the integration of Flemish artists into Northern towns. Easy, inexpensive, safe, and reliable passenger transport proved essential for continued exchanges between artists in the Southern Netherlands and the Dutch Republic. Family ties played a crucial role, as did the networks artists belonged to. Through the art trade, a shared visual culture was both maintained and further developed, not least by the dissemination of prints. All of this facilitated artistic crossovers and cross-fertilization in the visual arts. Despite the tendency of Haarlem artists to specialize in certain genres, they did not operate in a vacuum

und zuverlässiger Personenverkehr erwies sich als wesentlich für den weiteren Austausch zwischen Künstlern in den südlichen Niederlanden und jenen in den nördlichen Vereinigten Provinzen. Familienbande spielten eine entscheidende Rolle, ebenso wie die Netzwerke, denen die Künstler angehörten. Durch den Kunsthandel wurde eine gemeinsame visuelle Kultur aufrechterhalten und weiterentwickelt, nicht zuletzt durch die Verbreitung von Druckgraphiken. All dies ermöglichte künstlerische Überschneidungen und eine gegenseitige Befruchtung in der bildenden Kunst. Obwohl die Haarlemer Künstler dazu neigten, sich auf bestimmte Gattungen zu spezialisieren, agierten sie nicht im luftleeren Raum und verdankten auch viel den Entwicklungen in anderen niederländischen Städten.[53] Rubens' Exkursion nach Haarlem zeigt, dass persönliche Kontakte zwischen Künstlern in den Niederlanden – ob gelegentlich oder dauerhaft – zur Verbreitung künstlerischer Kenntnisse beitrugen. Wir möchten bei dieser Gelegenheit noch einmal betonen, dass dieser Austausch keineswegs eine Einbahnstraße war.

Zusammenfassend lässt sich sagen, dass man die Autonomie und die Identität der nach Städten unterschiedenen Schulen kritisch beleuchten muss, wenn man einen umfassenden Einblick in die künstlerischen Entwicklungen und den Wandel der Bildtraditionen gewinnen will, auch wenn dies bedeutet, Grenzen zu überschreiten und althergebrachte kunsthistorische Paradigmen infrage zu stellen. Um es noch deutlicher zu sagen: Indem wir die Aufmerksamkeit auf das Flämische der Haarlemer Schule lenken, möchten wir dafür plädieren, die holländische Malerei aus einem internationaleren Blickwinkel heraus zu betrachten.

and were indebted to influences from developments in other Netherlandish towns.[53] Rubens's excursion to Haarlem demonstrates that personal contact—whether casual or more sustained—between artists of the Low Countries contributed to the spread of artistic expertise. We want to take this opportunity to once again stress that these exchanges were by no means a one-way street.

In conclusion, if we wish to gain full insight into artistic developments and changes in pictorial traditions, we need to question the autonomy and identity of city schools, even if this means crossing borders and challenging time-honored art-historical paradigms. To put it more bluntly, by drawing attention to the Flemishness of the Haarlem school, we wish to make the case for a more international approach to studying Dutch painting.

Dies ist eine leicht überarbeitete und aktualisierte Fassung eines Artikels, der im Dezember 2012 in *De Zeventiende Eeuw* veröffentlicht wurde. Wir danken Anna Tummers für ihre Ermutigung und ihr Feedback.

1 So bezeichnete der renommierte Kunsthistoriker Christopher Brown in seiner bemerkenswerten Antrittsvorlesung am Centre for the Study of the Golden Age in Amsterdam im Jahr 2002 Haarlem als den Archetyp einer holländischen Stadtschule in Bezug auf die Malerei. Brown 2002.
2 Biesboer 2008. Auf der Ebene der nationalen Schulen war die Divergenz zwischen der holländischen Schule und ihrem flämischen Pendant Thema eines Aufsatzes von Theodore Rabb; siehe Rabb 2011, S. 78 und 83.
3 De Marchi/Miegroet 2006; Vermeylen 2004.
4 Über den kulturellen Austausch in den Niederlanden allgemein siehe De Clippel/Vermeylen 2012.
5 Zu den Ursachen der massenhaften Auswanderung flämischer Künstler während der niederländischen Revolte siehe Vermeylen 2014.
6 Marnef 1996; Biesboer 2002, S. 1f.
7 Biesboer 2002, S. 2f.; Biesboer et al. 1996, S. 10.
8 Vgl. hier und in diesem Absatz ebd.
9 Diese Datenbank ist im Wesentlichen eine Online-Version von Groenendijk 2008.
10 „[…] hier sulcken schilders te vinden", zit. in Briels 1976, S. 150.
11 Bok 2001.
12 Boers-Goossens 2001.
13 Boers-Goossens 1999.
14 Vermeylen 2003, S. 127–139; Biesboer 2002, S. 18.
15 De Vries 1981; Verhoeven 2009b; Verhoeven 2009a.
16 In den 1620er-Jahren nahmen die Reisenden von Antwerpen nach Haarlem mit Sicherheit eine Kutsche in Richtung Dordrecht (über Breda), von wo aus sie mit einem Lastkahn nach Leiden fuhren und dann entweder mit einer Kutsche oder einem Schiff nach Haarlem weiterreisten. Wir danken Gerrit Verhoeven für diese Informationen; Biesboer 2002, S. 5.
17 Wie Anm. 15.
18 De Clippel 2006, S. 22.
19 Houbraken 1718–1721, Bd. 1, S. 90f.
20 Barrett 2012, S. 24–51.
21 Thiel-Stroman 1989b, S. 19; Thiel-Stroman 1989a, S. 377, Dok. 17; S. 378, Dok. 22.
22 Thiel-Stroman 2006, S. 163f., 168.
23 Lohse Belkin 2009, Bd. 1, S. 36; S. 164f., Kat. 72; S. 218f., Kat. 108.
24 Ebd., S. 218f., Kat. 108.
25 Ebd., S. 36, 219.
26 Amsterdam/New York/Toledo 2003, S. 266.
27 Ebd., S. 203f.
28 Ebd., S. 205f.
29 Zu dieser Reise siehe Gelder 1950/51, S. 119f.; Smet 1977.
30 Amsterdam/New York/Toledo 2003, S. 33–39, 203–209.
31 Balis 1993; Balis 2007.
32 Renger 1974a; Renger 1975; siehe auch Huvenne 2004.
33 Siehe beispielsweise Huvenne 2004, S. 13.
34 Barrett 2012, S. 18–23. Rubens erhielt sein erstes Druckprivileg im Jahr 1619. Siehe Van Hout 2004.
35 Siehe Greenwich/Berkeley/Cincinnati 2004, S. 92.
36 Die vorgeschlagenen Daten reichen von 1611 bis 1614. Siehe Held 1980, S. 432, und McGrath 1997, Bd. 1, S. 50 (beide 1614); Peter Sutton, in: Greenwich/Berkeley/Cincinnati 2004, S. 92 (um 1613); David Jaffé, in: London 2005, S. 161 (1611).
37 Gelder 1931, S. 52; D'Hulst/Vandenven 1989, Kat. 4 (Kopie 2); London 2005, S. 171.
38 Barrett 2012, Kat. 20.
39 Sluijter 2005.
40 Mander (1604) 1916, fol. 285v23, 286r21, und Mander (1604) 2000, S. 341; siehe auch Taylor 1998.
41 Der Teil von Gerbiers Gedicht, in dem Rubens die Szene betritt, wird von David Freedberg kommentiert. Siehe Freedberg 1983; siehe auch Hirschmann 1920b und Reznicek 1961, S. 28–31.
42 In seiner Monographie über Goltzius behauptet Lawrence Nichols, dass Rubens den älteren Meister nicht nur nachahmte, wie es üblich war, sondern dass Goltzius auch von seinem jüngeren Kollegen inspiriert wurde, insbesondere von Rubens' klassizistischen Gemälden jener Zeit. In einem anregenden Beitrag über künstlerische Rivalität unterstreicht auch Anna Tummers den guten Ruf der Haarlemer Künstler zu Beginn des 17. Jahrhunderts als Anziehungsfaktor für Rubens, aber sie nuanciert den gegenseitigen Austausch zwischen Rubens und Goltzius, indem sie davon ausgeht, dass die beiden Künstler bei sechs verschiedenen Gelegenheiten ähnliche Themen malten, sich aber nie gegenseitig zitierten. Ihrer Meinung nach reagierten sie beide auf Tizian, ihren älteren und berühmten Vorgänger. Nichols 2013, S. 58–61; Tummers 2015.
43 Es wurde oft behauptet, Goltzius habe sich hauptsächlich für Rubens' klassizistische Szenen interessiert, aber das ist nicht ganz richtig. Rubens' klassizistische Periode begann erst 1612, und Goltzius' Œuvre zeigt auch Einflüsse aus Werken vor dieser Periode: Rubens' *Venus und Adonis* in Düsseldorf und *Lot und seine Töchter* stammen aus den Jahren 1609/10 bzw. 1610.
44 McGrath et al. 2022, Bd. 1, S. 256–262.
45 Sluijter 1991, S. 396, Nr. 24.
46 Eck 2008, bes. S. 81–109.
47 Hemmer 2015.
48 Dies findet sich in der Korrespondenz von Rubens, insbesondere in seinen Briefen vom 28. April, 7., 12., 20. und 29. Mai 1618. Siehe Rooses/Ruelens 1887–1909, Bd. 2 (1898), S. 136, 146, 150, 161, 177.
49 Peter Sutton behauptet, der Künstler habe Altarbilder „für Kirchen in Flandern gemalt (die *Auferstehung des Lazarus* von 1623, Liebfrauenkirche, Brügge; die *Mariä Himmelfahrt* von 1648, St.-Peter-Kirche, Gent, heute im Museum voor Schone Kunsten, Gent)". Übers. n. Sutton 1999, S. 116. Nachforschungen von Marloes Hemmer und Karolien De Clippel haben ergeben, dass die ältesten Provenienzen beider Gemälde nicht bekannt sind und die frühesten Hinweise nur bis ins 18. Jahrhundert zurückreichen. Selbst wenn die Gemälde im Kontext von Brügge bzw. Gent angesiedelt sind, fehlen Belege für einen Auftrag. Gent 2007, Bd. 1, S. 97; Stadsarchief Gent 1797, Nr. 269.
50 Siehe u. a. Walsh 1974a; Walsh 1974b; Duverger 1976.
51 De Clippel 2003; De Clippel 2006, Nr. 16.
52 Haarlem/Zürich/Washington 2004.
53 Oder, um die Formulierung Michael Baxandalls aufzugreifen, sie trafen Entscheidungen, die ihr Bewusstsein für Trends, Sitten und Moden anderer niederländischer Städte veranschaulichen. Baxandall 1985.

This is a slightly reworked and updated version of an article published in *De Zeventiende Eeuw* in December 2012. We are grateful to Anna Tummers for her encouragement and feedback.

1 For instance, during his noteworthy inaugural lecture at the Centre for the Study of the Golden Age in Amsterdam in 2002, the renowned art historian Christopher Brown singled out Haarlem as the archetype of a Dutch city school in terms of painting. Brown 2002.
2 Biesboer 2008. At the level of national schools, the divergence between the Dutch school and its Flemish counterpart was the topic of an essay by Theodore Rabb, see Rabb 2011, pp. 78 and 83.
3 De Marchi/Miegroet 2006; Vermeylen 2004.
4 For a more general essay on cultural transmission in the Low Countries, see De Clippel/Vermeylen 2012.
5 On the causes of the large-scale emigration of Flemish artists during the Dutch Revolt, see Vermeylen 2014.
6 Marnef 1996; Biesboer 2002, pp. 1–2.
7 Biesboer 2002, pp. 2–3; Biesboer et al. 1996, p. 10.
8 On this, as well as the rest of this paragraph, see Biesboer 2002, pp. 2–3; Biesboer et al. 1996, p. 10.
9 This database is in essence an online version of Groenendijk 2008.
10 "[…] hier sulcken schilders te vinden," quoted in Briels 1976, p. 150.
11 Bok 2001.
12 Boers-Goossens 2001.
13 Boers-Goossens 1999.
14 Vermeylen 2003, pp. 127–139; Biesboer 2002, p. 18.
15 De Vries 1981; Verhoeven 2009b; Verhoeven 2009a.
16 Certainly by the 1620s, people traveling from Antwerp to Haarlem boarded a coach in the direction of Dordrecht (via Breda), from where they took a barge to Leiden and then traveled onward to Haarlem by either coach or boat. We would like to thank Gerrit Verhoeven for supplying us with this information; Biesboer 2002, p. 5.
17 See note 15.
18 De Clippel 2006, p. 22.
19 Houbraken 1718–1721, vol. 1, pp. 90–91.
20 Barrett 2012, pp. 24–51.
21 Thiel-Stroman 1989b, p. 19; Thiel-Stroman 1989a, p. 377, doc. 17; p. 378, doc. 22.
22 Thiel-Stroman 2006, pp. 163–164, 168.
23 Lohse Belkin 2009, vol. 1, p. 36; pp. 164–165, cat. 72; pp. 218–219, cat. 108.
24 Lohse Belkin 2009, vol. 1, pp. 218–219, cat. 108.
25 Lohse Belkin 2009, vol. 1, pp. 36, 219.
26 Amsterdam/New York/Toledo 2003, p. 266.
27 Amsterdam/New York/Toledo 2003, pp. 203–204.
28 Amsterdam/New York/Toledo 2003, pp. 205–206.
29 On this travel, see Gelder 1950/51, pp. 119–120; Smet 1977.
30 Amsterdam/New York/Toledo 2003, pp. 33–39, 203–209.
31 Balis 1993; Balis 2007.
32 Renger 1974a; Renger 1975; see also Huvenne 2004.
33 See for example Huvenne 2004, p. 13.
34 Barrett 2012, pp. 18–23. Rubens received his first privilege in 1619. See Van Hout 2004.
35 See Greenwich/Berkeley/Cincinnati 2004, p. 92.
36 Suggested dates vary from 1611 to 1614. See Held 1980, p. 432, and McGrath 1997, vol. 1, p. 50 (1614); Peter Sutton in Greenwich/Berkeley/Cincinnati 2004, p. 92 (ca. 1613); David Jaffé in London 2005, p. 161 (1611).
37 Gelder 1931, p. 52; D'Hulst/Vandenven 1989, cat. 4 (copy 2); London 2005, p. 171.
38 Barrett 2012, cat. 20.
39 Sluijter 2005.
40 Mander (1604) 1994, vol. 1, fols. 285v23, 286r21, and vol. 5, pp. 214, 218; see also Taylor 1998.
41 The part of Gerbier's poem where Rubens comes onto the scene is published with commentary by David Freedberg. See Freedberg 1983; see also Hirschmann 1920b; Reznicek 1961, pp. 28–31.
42 In his monograph on Goltzius, Lawrence Nichols asserts that Rubens not only emulated the older master, as was common practice, but that Goltzius was also inspired by his younger peer, especially by Rubens's classicizing paintings of that period. In an inspiring paper on artistic rivalry, Anna Tummers also underlines the solid reputation of the Haarlem artists at the beginning of the seventeenth century as a pull factor for Rubens, but she nuances the mutual exchange between Rubens and Goltzius, assuming that the two artists painted similar themes on six different occasions, but never cited one another. In her opinion, they both responded to Titian, their senior and famous predecessor. Nichols 2013, pp. 58–61; Tummers 2015.
43 It has often been pretended that Goltzius was mostly interested in Rubens's classicistic scenes, but this is not entirely correct. Rubens's classicist period only started in 1612, and Goltzius's oeuvre shows influences from works before that period too: Rubens's *Venus and Adonis* in Düsseldorf and *Lot and His Daughters* date from 1609–1610 and 1610 respectively.
44 McGrath et al. 2022, vol. 1, pp. 256–262.
45 Sluijter 1991, p. 396, n. 24.
46 Eck 2008, esp. pp. 81–109.
47 Hemmer 2015.
48 This appears in Rubens's correspondence, specifically his letters of April 28, May 7, May 12, May 20, and May 29, 1618. See Rooses/Ruelens 1887–1909, vol. 2 (1898), pp. 136, 146, 150, 161, 177.
49 Peter Sutton asserts that the artist painted altarpieces "for churches in Flanders (the *Resurrection of Lazarus* of 1623, Church of Our Lady, Bruges; *Assumption of the Virgin* of 1648, Saint Peter's church, Ghent, now in the Museum of Fine Arts, Ghent)." Sutton 1999, p. 116. Research by Marloes Hemmer and Karolien De Clippel has revealed that the earliest provenances of both paintings are missing and that the earliest references go back to the eighteenth century only. Even if the paintings are situated in the Brugge and Ghent context respectively, evidence of a commission is missing. Gent 2007, vol. 1, p. 97; Stadsarchief Gent 1797, no. 269.
50 See among others Walsh 1974a; Walsh 1974b; Duverger 1976.
51 De Clippel 2003; De Clippel 2006, n. 16.
52 Haarlem/Zürich/Washington 2004.
53 Or to use Baxandall's terminology, they made choices which illustrate their awareness of trends, manners, and fashions in other Netherlandish towns. Baxandall 1985.

NADINE M. ORENSTEIN

Hendrick Goltzius

Virtuoser Druckgraphiker
und bahnbrechender Verleger

Hendrick Goltzius

Virtuoso Printmaker
and Groundbreaking Publisher

Hendrick Goltzius' *Hochzeit von Amor und Psyche* (1587) ist eine extravagante Druckgraphik, die in einem der fruchtbarsten Momente in der Karriere des Künstlers entstand (Abb. 1). Die Darstellung, die zu Recht als Manifest des manieristischen Stils bezeichnet wird, besteht aus über achtzig sich elegant drehenden Figuren, die von kurvig-runden bis zu sehr muskulösen Gestalten reichen und sich in einer himmlischen Umgebung befinden, welche von langen, gewundenen Wolkenbändern begrenzt wird.[1] Die Protagonisten der Szene – Amor, der Gott der Liebe, erkennbar an seinen großen Flügeln, und Psyche, seine sterbliche Braut – sitzen in typisch manieristischer Weise weit entfernt im Mittelgrund des Bildes und könnten dem Betrachter so leicht entgehen. Goltzius stach das Werk von beeindruckender Größe in drei Kupferplatten, die auf drei Papierbögen gedruckt wurden. So etwas hatte man in der Kupferstichkunst noch nicht gesehen. Sein Freund und Biograph Karel van Mander (1548–1606) schrieb, der Druck zeige ein „herrliches

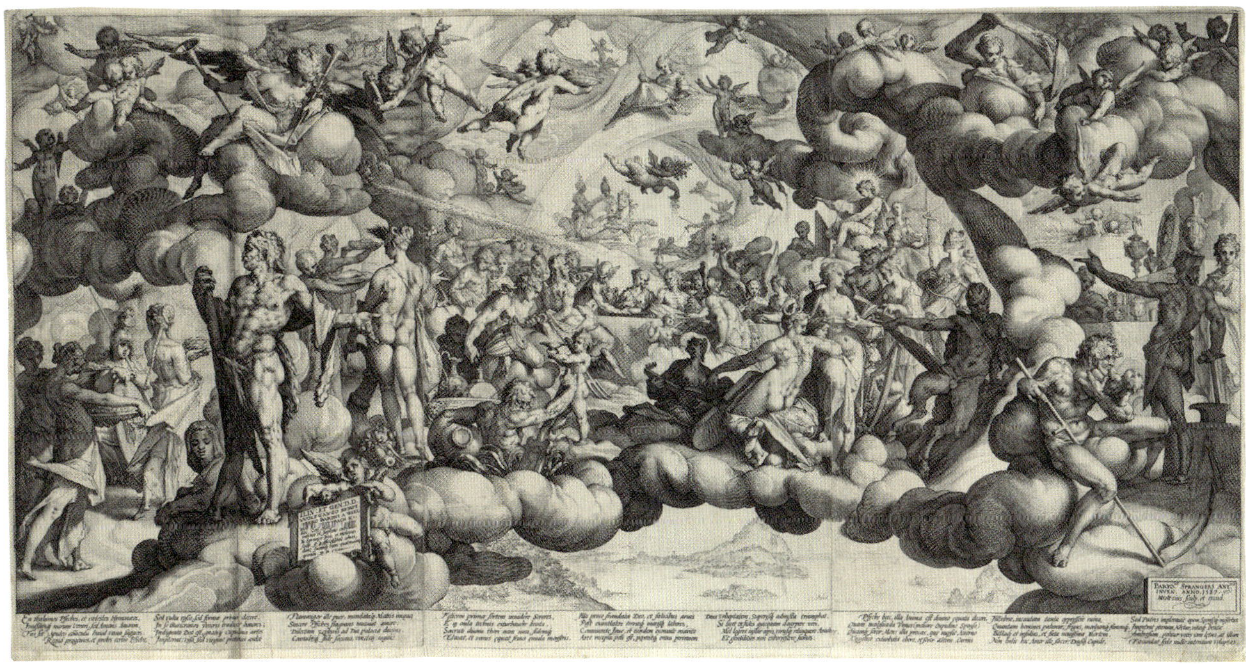

1 Bartholomeus Spranger (Inventor / designer), Goltzius (Stecher, Verleger / engraver, publisher)
Hochzeit von Amor und Psyche / The Wedding of Cupid and Psyche, 1587
Kupferstich / engraving SGSM, Inv. 1987:31 D

Hendrick Goltzius's *The Wedding of Cupid and Psyche* (1587) is an extravaganza of a print created at one of the most fertile moments in the artist's career (fig. 1). Aptly termed the manifesto of the Mannerist style, the depiction consists of over eighty elegantly torquing figures, ranging from the sinuous to the highly muscled, inhabiting a heavenly setting defined by long, twisting bands of clouds.[1] The protagonists of the scene—Cupid, the god of love, recognizable by his large wings, and Psyche, his mortal bride—are seated far off in the middle plane in typical Mannerist fashion and might easily escape the viewer's notice. Goltzius engraved the impressively sized piece on three copper plates that were printed on three sheets of paper. Nothing quite like this had been seen before in engraving. His friend and biographer Karel van Mander (1548–1606) wrote that the print was "a grand piece . . . which overflows with sweet and appealing Nectar and which offers equal immortality to the designer and engraver."[2] This astounding work, a high

Götterbankett, das von dem süßem Nektar der Anmut überfließt und dem Zeichner wie dem Stecher gleichermaßen Unsterblichkeit sichert".[2] Dieses erstaunliche Werk, ein Höhepunkt in Goltzius' Œuvre, ist das Ergebnis einer der großen Long-Distance-Kooperationen zwischen Entwerfer und Stecher: Bartholomeus Spranger (1546–1611), der am kaiserlichen Hof in Prag tätig war, und Goltzius in seiner Werkstatt im nordniederländischen Haarlem. Sprangers gezeichneter Entwurf für den Druck wurde mit all seiner Kühnheit und Komplexität zum Katalysator für den Kupferstecher, der sich der Herausforderung stellte und seine Kupferstichtechnik mit gewagten, anschwellenden Linien neu erfand.

Die *Hochzeit von Amor und Psyche* ist zwar nur eines der zahlreichen außergewöhnlichen von Goltzius geschaffenen Werke, doch es verkörpert in vielerlei Hinsicht jene Herangehensweise an die Druckgraphik und das Verlagswesen, die sein Werk einzigartig machte: die markante Linienführung, die große, extravagante Komposition, das kühne und erotisch aufgeladene mythologische Sujet und der internationale Kontext, in dem es geschaffen und veröffentlicht wurde. Dieser Aufsatz wird einige dieser Aspekte im Werk des Künstlers beleuchten.[3]

Goltzius, von Anfang an ehrgeizig und mit den Werken berühmter Vorgänger wie Albrecht Dürer (1471–1528), Lucas van Leyden (1494–1533) und Cornelis Cort (1533–1578) vertraut, machte sich die Kompositionen dieser Künstler und ihre Art, den Stichel zu führen, so sehr zu eigen, dass van Mander ihn einen „Proteus oder Vertumnus der Kunst" nannte, „fähig, sich in jeden Stil hineinzufinden".[4] Diesen Weg verfolgte er während seiner gesamten Laufbahn bis hin zu späteren Werken wie der zarten *Pietà* (1596), welche von zweien seiner großen Vorgänger aus Nord- und Südeuropa inspiriert ist: Er ahmte die

point of Goltzius's oeuvre, is the result of one of the great long-distance collaborations between designer and engraver: Bartholomeus Spranger (1546–1611), active at the imperial court in Prague, and Goltzius in his workshop in Haarlem, in the Northern Netherlands. Spranger's drawn design for the print, with all of its daring and complexity, became a catalyst for the engraver, who rose to the challenge and reinvented his engraving technique with bold, swelling flows of lines.

While *The Wedding of Cupid and Psyche* is just one of numerous extraordinary works created by Goltzius, it captures in many ways the approach to printmaking and publishing that made his work unique—the prominent linework, large extravagant composition, bold and sexy mythological subject matter, and an international context for its creation and publication. This essay will look at some of these aspects of the artist's work.[3]

Ambitious from the start and well-versed in the work of illustrious predecessors, most notable among them Albrecht Dürer (1471–1528), Lucas van Leyden (1494–1533), and Cornelis Cort (1533–1578), Goltzius soaked in these artists' compositions and manner of handling the burin so deftly that Van Mander called him "a Proteus or Vertumnus in art. Because he can transform himself to all forms of working methods."[4] He continued on this path throughout his career with such later works as the delicate *Pietà* (1596), which merged inspiration from two of his great predecessors of northern and southern Europe: he imitated the refinement of line and seeming tactility of Dürer's engravings with a Michelangelesque treatment of the subject that relates to the Italian's famous sculpture in the Vatican (fig. p. 235).[5] In the series

verfeinerte Linienführung und die scheinbare Taktilität von Dürers Stichen nach und verschmolz sie mit einer michelangelesken Behandlung des Themas, die sich auf die berühmte Skulptur des Italieners im Vatikan bezieht (Abb. S. 235).[5] In der Serie *Christi Geburt und Jugend* (1594/95) griff Goltzius bekanntlich auf eine Reihe von Künstlern nördlich und südlich der Alpen zurück, darunter Federico Barocci und Tizian, die er aufgrund von Druckgraphiken nach ihren Werken kannte. Van Mander berichtet, dass seine Übernahme der Stile von Dürer in der *Beschneidung Christi* (1594; Abb. S. 199) und Lucas van Leyden in der *Anbetung der Könige* (1594) so erfolgreich war, dass Käufer Abzüge der Drucke als tatsächliche Werke der frühen Meister kauften – ein Selbstporträt im Hintergrund der *Beschneidung* hatte Goltzius vorab unkenntlich gemacht.[6] In seinen Werken zeigt sich immer wieder eine tiefe Vertrautheit mit der Kunst seiner Vorgänger und die Fähigkeit, die spezifische Eigenart dieser aufzugreifen – eine Gabe, die Druckgraphik-Kenner jener Zeit zu schätzen wussten und mit anderen in ihrem Kreis diskutierten.

Eine von Goltzius' Haupttätigkeiten zu Beginn seiner Produktion bestand darin, Stiche nach Entwürfen zeitgenössischer Maler anzufertigen. So sah er angesichts von Werken von Künstlern wie Spranger und Cornelis Cornelisz. van Haarlem (1562–1638) die Herausforderung, auf ihrer Grundlage neue gewagte Drucke zu schaffen, in denen die Ausführung des Stichs ebenso wie die Bildsprache selbst manieristische Ideale zum Ausdruck brachten. *Die vier Himmelsstürmer* (1588), nach Gemälden von Cornelisz. van Haarlem, ist eine Tour de force unter den Druckgraphiken dieser Zeit: Die verblüffende Serie von vier runden Kupferstichen zeigt jeweils eine Figur in ähnlicher Pose aus verschiedenen Blickwinkeln, die fast filmisch in der Luft taumelt (Abb. S. 190 f.). In der Platte des *Ikarus* ist die markante,

The Birth and Early Life of Christ (1594–95), Goltzius famously drew on a range of artists both north and south of the Alps, including Federico Barocci and Titian, which he would have known from prints after their work. Van Mander recounts that his assimilation of the styles of Dürer in *The Circumcision* (1594; fig. p. 199) and Lucas van Leyden in *The Adoration of the Magi* (1594) were so successful that people bought impressions of the prints as actual works by the early masters—the artist had obscured a portrait of himself in the background of *The Circumcision*.[6] We repeatedly find in his works a deep familiarity with the art that preceded him and an ability to take these artists on in their own idioms, a gift that connoisseurs of prints at the time would have appreciated and discussed with others in their circle.

One of the main activities of his production early on was to engrave prints after the designs of contemporary painters. He saw in such artists as Spranger and Cornelis Cornelisz. van Haarlem (1562–1638), for instance, a challenge to create bold new prints in which the execution of the engraving expressed Mannerist ideals just as much as the imagery itself. *The Four Disgracers* (1588), after paintings by Cornelisz. van Haarlem, is a tour de force among prints of the time: Each of the four roundels in this astounding series renders a figure in a similar pose from a different angle, tumbling almost cinematically in midair (figs. pp. 190–191). In the plate of *Icarus*, the pronounced curving cross-hatching that delineates the shadows of the figure's back is so prominent that it suggests a woven net that catches the falling figure.

Goltzius acquired the skills for printmaking and the connections necessary for establishing himself in Haarlem early in life. We know a good deal about his life thanks to Van Mander, who devoted

geschwungene Kreuzschraffur, welche die Schatten des Rückens der Figur abgrenzt, so ausgeprägt, dass sie ein gewebtes Netz suggeriert, das die fallende Figur auffängt.

Schon früh erwarb Goltzius die für die Druckgraphik erforderlichen Fähigkeiten und knüpfte die nötigen Verbindungen, um sich in Haarlem zu etablieren. Dank van Mander, der dem Künstler eines der längsten Kapitel in seinem *Schilder-boeck* (1604) widmete, wissen wir viel über sein Leben.[7] Als Sohn eines Glasmalers wuchs er in Duisburg auf, unweit der heutigen deutsch-niederländischen Grenze. Im Alter von 16 Jahren begann er, mit Dirck Volckertsz. Coornhert (1522–1590) zu arbeiten, einem Künstler, Theologen und Diplomaten, der in den 1540er- und 1550er-Jahren mit dem Maler Maarten van Heemskerck (1498–1574) eine große Anzahl von Drucken hergestellt hatte. Goltzius lernte nicht nur das Stechen, sondern auch das Entwerfen von Druckgraphiken auf der Grundlage von Coornherts allegorischen Konzepten, und diese Erfahrung verschaffte dem angehenden und sichtlich talentierten jungen Graveur eine Grundlage, die ihm beim Aufbau seiner Karriere gute Dienste leistete. Im März 1577 kehrte Coornhert nach Haarlem zurück, und Goltzius, inzwischen 19 Jahre alt, folgte ihm einige Monate später. In Haarlem angekommen, scheint Coornhert einen wesentlichen Anteil daran gehabt zu haben, dass Goltzius mit einem Netzwerk von Druckern und Verlegern in Verbindung kam, darunter mit Coornherts ehemaligem Schüler Philips Galle (1537–1612), der in Antwerpen ansässig war. Zwischen 1577 und 1582 stach Goltzius zahlreiche Drucke für Galle sowie für Aux Quatre Vents, den Verlag von Volcxken Diericx (1514–1600), der Witwe des bedeutenden Antwerpener Verlegers Hieronymus Cock, für den Coornhert gearbeitet hatte (*Die Verkündigung* nach Maerten de Vos, um 1579; Abb. S. 129). Goltzius' Heirat mit

one of the longest chapters in his *Schilder-boeck* (1604) to the life of the artist.[7] The son of a glass painter, he grew up in Duisburg, not far from the present border of Germany and the Netherlands. Around the age of sixteen, he began to work with Dirck Volckertsz. Coornhert (1522–1590), an artist, theologian, and diplomat who had produced a large number of prints with the painter Maarten van Heemskerck (1498–1574) in the 1540s and 1550s. Goltzius learned not only to engrave prints but also to design them based on Coornhert's allegorical concepts, and this experience provided the budding and already visibly talented young engraver with a grounding that served him well as he built his career. Coornhert returned to Haarlem in March 1577 and Goltzius, now nineteen years old, followed a few months later. Once in Haarlem, Coornhert seems to have been instrumental in connecting Goltzius with a network of printmakers and publishers, among them his former student Philips Galle (1537–1612), who were established in Antwerp. Between 1577 and 1582, Goltzius engraved numerous prints for Galle as well as for Aux Quatre Vents, the publishing house of Volcxken Diericx (1514–1600), widow of the great Antwerp print publisher Hieronymus Cock, for whom Coornhert had worked (*The Annunciation* after Maerten de Vos, ca. 1579; fig. p. 129). Goltzius's marriage to Margaretha (Grietgen) Jansdochter (1549/50–1631) in 1579 provided Goltzius with some stability and eventually with his most devoted pupil and assistant: his stepson Jacob Matham (1571–1631), who ultimately took over the business.

Goltzius's early engravings suggest an artist in the process of evolving, yet they also demonstrate a bold self-confidence. Two inscriptions on prints belonging to the series *The Rewards of Labor, Industry,*

Margaretha (Grietgen) Jansdochter (1549/50–1631) im Jahr 1579 bescherte diesem eine gewisse Stabilität und bald dann seinen treuesten Schüler und Assistenten, seinen Stiefsohn Jacob Matham (1571–1631), der schließlich das Geschäft übernahm.

Goltzius' frühe Stiche lassen auf einen Künstler schließen, der sich noch in der Entwicklung befindet, zeugen aber auch von einem ausgeprägten Selbstvertrauen. Zwei Inschriften auf Drucken, die zu der Serie *Der Lohn der Arbeit, des Fleißes, der Übung und der Kunstfertigkeit* (1582) gehören, scheinen Goltzius' Ambitionen zu verdeutlichen: „Immer wenn Arbeit und Fleiß sich zum Bund die Hände reichen, dann bedenkt auch die Kunst im Herzen Themen, die der Göttin Pallas Themen würdig sind"; und „Wer nur mit Liebe und fleißig die edlen Künste betreibt, der wird pures Gold und reichlich Lob einstreichen" (Abb. 2).[8] Zu seinen frühesten Veröffentlichungen gehören Werke nach Anthonie Blocklandt (1533/34–1583) und Dirck Barendsz. (1534–1592), den führenden niederländischen Malern seiner Zeit. Dies sind keine zaghaften Werke. *Lots Flucht aus Sodom* (1582) nach Blocklandt ist kühn und zeichnet sich durch einen klaren Bildaufbau aus. Die Figuren sind groß und

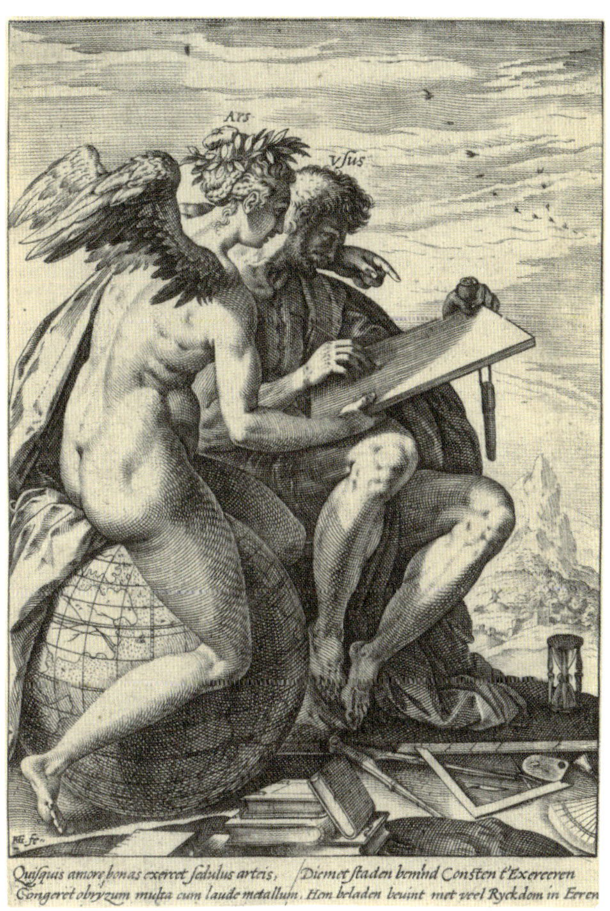

2 Hendrick Goltzius (Inventor, Stecher, Verleger / designer, engraver, publisher)
Ars et usus / Kunst und Ausübung / Practice and Art, 1582
Aus der Serie *Der Lohn der Arbeit …* / from the series *The Rewards of Labor …*, 1582
Kupferstich / engraving SGSM, Inv. 30945 D

Practice, and Art (1582) seem to spell out Goltzius's aspirations: "When Labor is paired with Industry, Art also brings forth ingenious finds" and "He who practices the arts lovingly and with care, will gain much praise and pure gold" (fig. 2).[8] His earliest publications include pieces after the leading Dutch painters of his day, Anthonie Blocklandt (1533/34–1583) and Dirck Barendsz. (1534–1592). These are not timid works. *Lot's Flight from Sodom* (1582) after Blocklandt is bold and compositionally clear. The figures are large and despite prominent swaths of drapery, the female bodies are revealed. The artist's pronounced engraving lines have become more conspicuous, integral parts of the image rather than mere conduits for describing the scene. *The Venetian Wedding* after Barendsz. (1584; fig. 4) is another large and ambitious early print by the engraver. Printed from two copperplates, this expansive scene populated with thirty figures is based on a work by Barendsz. known to us now via Goltzius's drawing for the engraving (fig. 3).[9] Shimmering fabrics draw the eye of the viewer through the arc of the figures in the foreground. In the drawn design for the print, the shine of the

bringen trotz der auffälligen Faltenwürfe die weiblichen Körper deutlich zur Geltung. Die ausgeprägten Gravurlinien des Künstlers sind auffälliger geworden und sind nun ein integraler Bestandteil des Bildes und nicht mehr nur Mittel zur Beschreibung der Szene. *Die venezianische Hochzeit* nach Barendsz. (1584; Abb. 4) ist ein weiteres großes und anspruchsvolles Frühwerk Goltzius'. Diese mittels zweier Kupferplatten gedruckte weitläufige Szene mit dreißig Figuren basiert auf einem Werk von Barendsz., das wir heute dank Goltzius' Vorzeichnung für den Stich kennen (Abb. 3).[9] Schimmernde Stoffe ziehen den Blick des Betrachters durch den Bogen der Figuren im Vordergrund. In der Vorzeichnung für den Druck wird der Glanz des Stoffes durch breite, blau lavierte Flächen angedeutet, während im Stich Goltzius' lineare Interpretation der Lavierungen den Schimmer, der nun die Szene beherrscht, noch verstärkt.

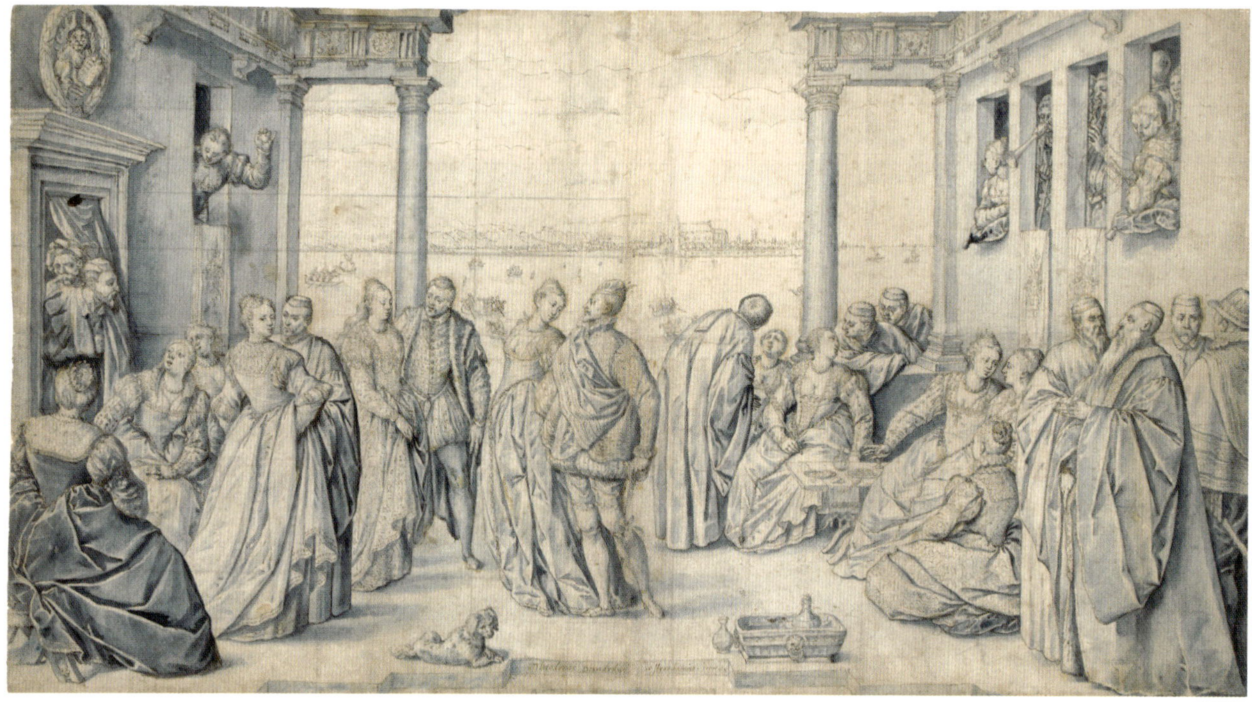

3 Goltzius, nach / after Dirck Barendsz.
Die venezianische Hochzeit / The Venetian Wedding, ca. 1584
Vorzeichnung / preparatory drawing, Feder, laviert / ink, wash Amsterdam, Rijksmuseum, Inv. RP-T-1937-14

fabric is indicated by broad areas of blue wash, while in the engraving Goltzius's linear interpretation of the washes accentuates the shimmer which now dominates the scene.

A similar fascination with glistening fabric appeared in the artist's images of standard-bearers from 1585 and 1587, in which large shimmering flags cut through the images and occupy as much space as the figures themselves, who are fancily dressed in elaborately decorated textiles. Sporting a fancy feathered cap and dangling earring, the *Standard-Bearer* of 1587, who elegantly strides to the left as he turns his head behind him, may have been intended as a portrait (fig. 5); inscriptions identify him at least twice as Gerrit Velsterman, a standard-bearer of the city of Haarlem.[10] Goltzius created many finely drawn and engraved portraits during his early years, which no doubt provided a good source of income as he was getting a start. He was a gifted portraitist and this interest continued throughout his career. *Portrait*

Eine ähnliche Faszination für glitzernde Stoffe zeigt sich auch in den Bildern der Fahnenträger von 1585 und 1587, in denen große schimmernde Fahnen die Bilder durchschneiden und ebenso viel Raum einnehmen wie die Figuren selbst, die in aufwendig verzierte Textilien gekleidet sind. Der *Fahnenträger* von 1587, der mit einer eleganten Federmütze und einem baumelnden Ohrring ausgestattet ist und elegant nach links schreitet, während er den Kopf nach hinten dreht, könnte als Porträt gedacht gewesen sein (Abb. 5); Inschriften weisen ihn mindestens zweimal als Gerrit Velsterman, einen Fahnenträger der Stadt Haarlem, aus.[10] Goltzius schuf in seinen frühen Jahren viele fein gezeichnete und gestochene Porträts, die ihm zweifellos eine gute Einnahmequelle boten, als er seine ersten Schritte als Künstler machte. Er war ein begabter Porträtist, und dieses Interesse hielt während seiner gesamten Laufbahn an. Das *Bildnis eines*

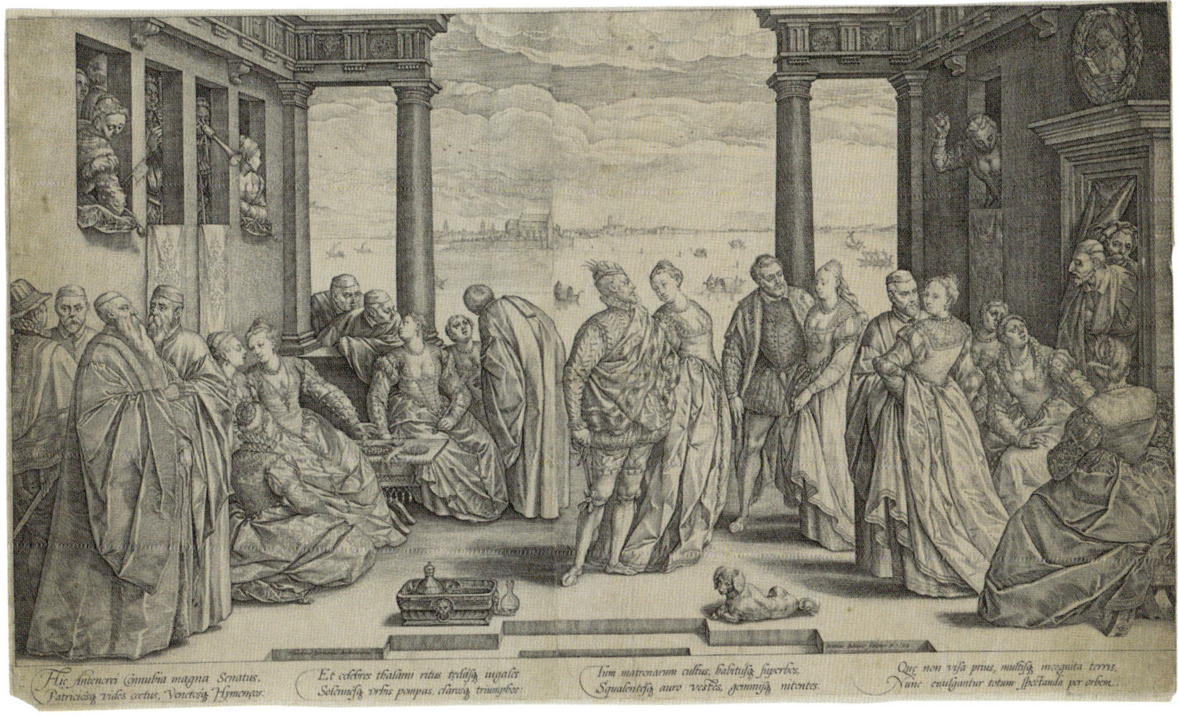

4 Goltzius (Zeichner, Stecher / draftsman, engraver), nach / after Dirck Barendsz.
Die venezianische Hochzeit / The Venetian Wedding, 1584
Kupferstich / engraving SGSM, Inv. 2021:493 D

of an Unknown Man (1580; fig. p. 262, D), like many of his early prints, was produced as a medallion. Here the inscriptions are reversed in the impression on the paper, an indication that they appeared in the correct direction on the original plate. Goltzius rendered portraits not only of local residents of Haarlem, friends, and family but also of significant political figures, which attests to his reputation as a portraitist early on. He engraved the *Portraits of Willem van Oranje* (1533–1584) and his third wife, *Charlotte* of Bourbon (1546/47–1582), in 1581 (figs. pp. 258 and 259), and the *Portrait of Robert Dudley* (1532–1588), governor-general of the United Provinces, in 1586 (fig. p. 263, G). The portrait of Dudley was produced as a gold medallion from which prints were made.[11] While his early portrait drawings were mainly created in metalpoint, in the late 1580s he turned to colored chalks, a medium with which he created some of his most remarkable large drawn pieces, such as the arresting *Portrait of Gillis van Breen* (1588; fig. p. 261). With

Unbekannten (1580; Abb. S. 262, D) geht, wie viele seiner frühen Drucke, auf ein Medaillon zurück. Hier sind die Inschriften im Abdruck auf dem Papier spiegelverkehrt, ein Hinweis darauf, dass sie auf dem Originalmedaillon in der richtigen Richtung erschienen. Goltzius porträtierte nicht nur Einwohner Haarlems, Freunde und Familienangehörige, sondern auch bedeutende politische Persönlichkeiten, was von seinem frühen Ruf als Porträtist zeugt. 1581 stach er etwa die *Bildnisse des Willem van Oranje* (1533–1584) und seiner dritten Frau *Charlotte* von Bourbon (1546/47–1582) (Abb. S. 258 f.) sowie 1586 das *Bildnis des Robert Dudley* (1532–1588), dem Generalgouverneur der Vereinigten Provinzen (Abb. S. 263, G). Das Porträt von Dudley wurde als Goldmedaillon hergestellt, von dem Abdrucke genommen wurden.[11] Während seine frühen Bildniszeichnungen hauptsächlich mit dem Silberstift ausgeführt sind, wandte sich Goltzius in den späten 1580er-Jahren der farbigen Kreide zu, einem Medium, mit dem er einige seiner bemerkenswertesten großformatigen Zeichnungen schuf, so etwa das fesselnde *Bildnis des Gillis van Breen* (1588; Abb. S. 261). Mit mehreren farbigen Kreiden hielt Goltzius den Drucker in einem ungeschützten Moment fest, mit fliegendem Haar und einer großen, fein gezeichneten Krause um den Hals schaut er gedankenverloren in die Ferne.

multiple colored chalks, Goltzius captured the printer in an unguarded moment, his hair flying as he gazes off in thought, wearing a large, delicately rendered ruff collar. One of the artist's most charming portraits is the engraving of the *Portrait of Frederick de Vries* of 1597 (fig. p. 257). Frederick (ca. 1590–1614) was the son of Goltzius's friend Dirck de Vries (1554–1612), a painter who lived in Venice at the time. The boy and his brother had been entrusted to the care of Goltzius, who symbolized himself as the guardian dog who looks knowingly out of the image. In the guise of a knight, the boy mounts his "steed" and holds a dove as though it were a falcon.[12]

The period between 1586 and 1590 represents one of the high points of the artist's career and his Spranger-influenced

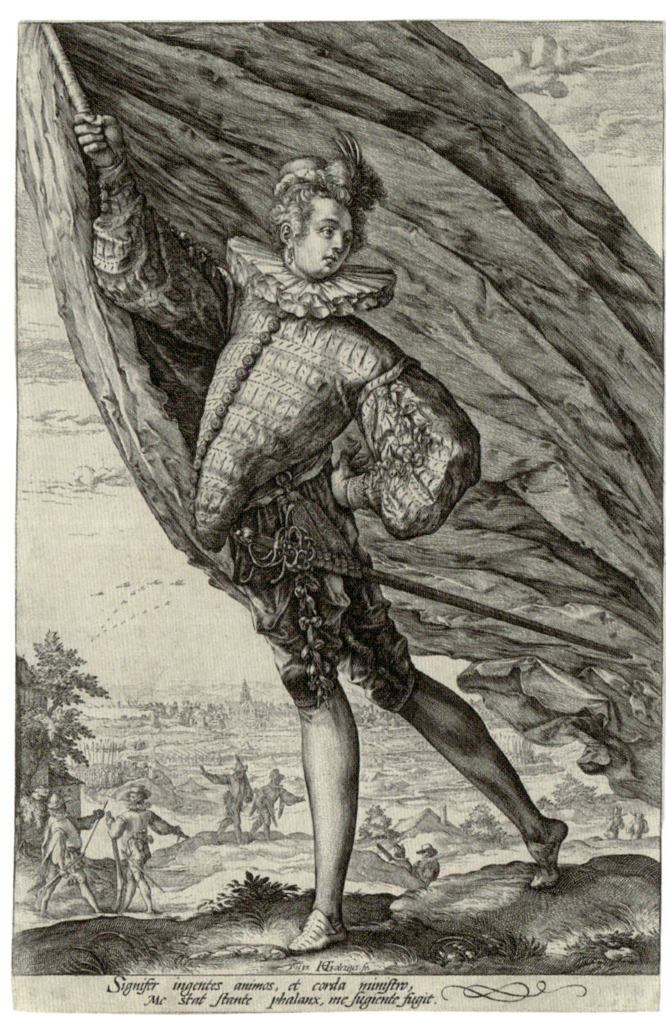

5 Hendrick Goltzius (Inventor, Stecher / designer, engraver)
Der Fahnenträger, nach links gewandt /
The Standard-Bearer, Turned to Left, 1587
Kupferstich / engraving SGSM, Inv. 30955 D

Eines der reizvollsten Porträts des Künstlers ist der Kupferstich mit dem *Bildnis des Frederick de Vries* von 1597 (Abb. S. 257). Frederick (um 1590–1614) war der Sohn von Goltzius' Freund Dirck de Vries (1554–1612), einem Maler, der zu dieser Zeit in Venedig lebte. Der Junge und sein Bruder waren der Obhut von Goltzius anvertraut worden, der sich selbst als Wachhund symbolisierte, der wissend aus dem Bild herausschaut. In der Gestalt eines Edelmanns besteigt der Junge sein „Ross" und hält eine Taube so in der Hand, als wäre sie ein Falke.[12]

Die Zeit zwischen 1586 und 1590 stellt einen der Höhepunkte in Goltzius' Karriere und seines von Spranger beeinflussten manieristischen Stils dar. Seine erste Begegnung mit dem Werk Sprangers fand statt, als van Mander, 1583 frisch in Haarlem eingetroffen, Goltzius Zeichnungen des international bekannten Künstlers zeigte, welcher Hofmaler Kaiser Rudolfs II. (1552–1612) in Prag war. Goltzius war von dem Werk so angetan, dass er 1585 den Vorsatz fasste, der Hauptstecher von Sprangers Entwürfen zu werden, ein Ziel, das er schnell erreichen sollte. Während seine ersten Drucke nach Spranger noch relativ harmlos anmuten, scheint die *Hochzeit von Amor und Psyche* für den Künstler ein Erweckungserlebnis gewesen zu sein: Er erkannte, dass er einen Stich anfertigen musste, der es mit der verblüffenden figürlichen Extravaganz der Vorlage aufnehmen konnte. Zwar ist der Stich auf 1587 datiert, doch wahrscheinlich hatte Goltzius schon ein oder zwei Jahre früher mit der Arbeit daran begonnen, da die Zeichnung und die Probedrucke zur Genehmigung und weiteren Bearbeitung zwischen Prag und Haarlem hin- und hergeschickt wurden.[13] Die neu entdeckte Virtuosität des Künstlers begann sich nun auch in seinen Drucken und Entwürfen zu zeigen. Jedes weitere Hauptwerk aus dieser Zeit – *Römische Helden* (1586; Abb. S. 111),

Mannerist style. His first encounter with Spranger's work came when Van Mander, newly arrived in Haarlem in 1583, showed Goltzius drawings by the internationally known painter, court artist to Emperor Rudolf II (1552–1612) in Prague. Goltzius was so taken with the work that by 1585 he had set out to become the main engraver of Spranger's designs, a goal that he quickly achieved. While his first prints after Spranger are relatively tame, *The Wedding of Cupid and Psyche* seems to have been the moment of epiphany for the artist, as he realized that he needed to make an engraving that would rival the astounding figural extravaganza. While the print is dated 1587, it is likely that Goltzius had begun working on it one or two years earlier, as the drawing and proof impressions would have been sent back and forth between Prague and Haarlem for approval and further work.[13] The artist's newfound virtuosity began to extend throughout his prints and designs. Each additional major piece from this period—*The Roman Heroes* (1586; figs. p. 111), *The Four Disgracers* (1588; figs. pp. 190–191), *Hercules Killing Cacus* (1588; figs. pp. 180–181), *Mars and Venus* (1585; fig. p. 137), *Apollo* (1588; fig. 6), and *The Creation of the World* (1589; figs. pp. 201–203)—features ever more startling displays of engraving brilliance, multiplying bulging muscles, and twisting, lissome bodies.

In this period, Goltzius also experimented with woodcut. He created about eighteen woodcuts, mainly in the chiaroscuro technique. Works like *Hercules Killing Cacus* (figs. pp. 180–181) combine a line-block printed in black with one or more tone-blocks printed in color to form a complete image. The ensemble was printed in different color variations. The technique had rarely been employed since the early sixteenth century in Italy and Germany, but once again the artist's protean mind took on earlier masters.

Die vier Himmelsstürmer (1588; Abb. S. 190 f.), *Herkules erschlägt Cacus* (1588; Abb. S. 180 f.), *Mars und Venus* (1585; Abb. S. 137), *Apoll* (1588; Abb. 6) und *Die Erschaffung der Welt* (1589; Abb. S. 201–203) – zeichnet sich durch eine immer verblüffendere Brillanz der Gravur, durch eine Vervielfältigung der prallen Muskeln und durch gewundene, geschmeidige Körper aus.

In dieser Zeit experimentierte Goltzius auch mit dem Holzschnitt. Er schuf etwa 18 Holzschnitte, hauptsächlich in Chiaroscuro-Technik. Werke wie *Herkules erschlägt Cacus* kombinieren einen schwarz gedruckten Linienblock mit einem oder mehreren farbig gedruckten Tonblöcken zu einem vollständigen Bild. Das Ensemble wurde in unterschiedlichen Farbvarianten gedruckt. Diese Technik kam seit dem frühen 16. Jahrhundert in Italien und Deutschland nur noch selten zum Einsatz, doch auch hier griff der Künstler mit seinem proteischen, wandlungsfähigen Geist auf frühere Meister zurück. Die Tonblöcke in *Herkules erschlägt Cacus* (1588) verleihen dem Bild Tiefe und Klarheit, doch der Linienblock scheint unnötig mit Details überfrachtet zu sein. In *Proserpina* aus der Serie *Demogorgon und die Gottheiten* (um 1588–1590; Abb. 7) ist Goltzius' Verständnis für die Möglichkeiten des Mediums gewachsen; hier vermitteln die Tonblöcke sowohl kompositorische Details als auch Schatten.

Die Zeit zwischen 1585 und 1590 markiert auch den Höhepunkt der Produktivität des Verlags des Künstlers. In dieser Zeit gab er etwa 208 Drucke heraus, von denen 151 von einem Team von Assistenten angefertigt

The tone-blocks in *Hercules Killing Cacus* (1588) provide depth and clarity to the image, but the line-block seems unnecessarily filled with detail. In *Proserpine*, from the series *Demogorgon and the Deities* (ca. 1588–1590; fig. 7), Goltzius's understanding of the possibilities of the medium has grown; here the tone-blocks communicate compositional detail as well as shadows.

The period between 1585 and 1590 also marks the height of productivity of the artist's publishing house. During this time, he issued some 208 prints with a team of assistants who created 151 of them. Goltzius had established a print publishing business in Haarlem in 1582 and quickly found success. Only five years later, in 1587, he created *The Wedding of Cupid and Psyche.* He signaled his new enterprise on prints from 1582 such as *Lot and His Daughters Leaving Sodom*, specifying in Dutch, French, or Latin that the works were printed in Haarlem.[14] By declaring his established base in Haarlem, a town that in the previous ten years had suffered under a siege by the Spanish and then from a great fire that destroyed about a third of the city, he was bringing attention not only to his own new publishing business but also to the return of the city. In addition, Goltzius was making plain that these works were not issued in Antwerp, the city in the Southern Netherlands that had dominated the northern European print market since the mid-sixteenth century.

6 Hendrick Goltzius (Inventor, Stecher / designer, engraver)
Apoll / Apollo, 1588
Kupferstich / engraving SGSM, Inv. 30961 D

wurden. Goltzius hatte 1582 in Haarlem einen Druckereibetrieb gegründet und feierte schnell Erfolge. Nur fünf Jahre später, im Jahr 1587, schuf er die *Hochzeit von Amor und Psyche*. Auf Drucken aus dem Jahr 1582 wie *Lot und seine Töchter verlassen Sodom* bewarb er sein neues Unternehmen, indem er auf Niederländisch, Französisch oder Latein kundtat, dass die Werke in Haarlem gedruckt wurden.[14] Indem er erklärte, dass er sich in Haarlem niedergelassen hatte, einer Stadt, die in den vorangegangenen zehn Jahren unter der Belagerung durch die Spanier und dann unter einem großen Brand gelitten hatte, der etwa ein Drittel Haarlems zerstörte, machte er nicht nur auf sein eigenes neues Verlagsgeschäft aufmerksam, sondern auch auf das Comeback dieser Stadt. Außerdem stellte Goltzius damit heraus, dass diese Werke nicht im südniederländischen Antwerpen erschienen, der Stadt, die seit Mitte des 16. Jahrhunderts den nordeuropäischen Druckmarkt beherrschte.

Im 16. Jahrhundert hätte ein Kunstverleger den Entwerfer, den Kupferstecher, den Drucker, den Dichter und den Kalligraphen bei der Herstellung eines Drucks zusammengebracht und außerdem über die notwendigen Geräte, Mitarbeiter und Materialien verfügt. In Goltzius' Fall kennen wir zwar die Namen einiger der Stecher, Dichter, Lehrlinge und Drucker, die seine Werkstatt durchliefen, aber viele andere bleiben anonym.[15] Wie schon erwähnt, ging es ihm eindeutig darum, sich von der vorangegangenen Verlegergeneration in Antwerpen zu unterscheiden, der Stadt, die bis zu seiner Niederlassung in Haarlem das Zentrum des nordeuropäischen Druckgewerbes gewesen war. Im Gegensatz zu früheren Verlegern wie Hieronymus Cock und Philips Galle schuf er einen Verlag, der sich auf seinen eigenen Stil konzentrierte, sich auf Stiche mit überwiegend mythologischen und allegorischen Themen spezialisierte und sich an ein

In the sixteenth century, a print publisher would have brought together the designer, engraver, printer, poet, and calligrapher in the production of a print, as well as the necessary equipment, staff, and materials. In Goltzius's case, although we know the names of some of the engravers, poets, apprentices, and printers who passed through his workshop, many more remain anonymous.[15] As mentioned above, he clearly set out to distinguish himself from the preceding generation of publishers based in Antwerp, the city that had been the center of the northern European print trade until he set up shop in Haarlem. In contrast to earlier publishers like Hieronymus Cock and Philips Galle, he created a publishing business focused on his own house style, specializing in engraving largely mythological and allegorical themes and directed toward an international humanist, art-appreciating audience. He employed a number of engravers trained to reproduce his designs in his style; we know the ones who were permitted to sign their work: Jacob Matham, his stepson; Jacques de Gheyn II (1565–1629) and Jan Harmensz. Muller (1571–1628), who each worked for Goltzius for about two years before moving out on their own; and Jan Saenredam (1565/66–1607), who started working for him just before the trip to Italy in 1590 to 1591 and who, after a falling out with Goltzius, continued to engrave prints for the workshop from his home in Assendelft.[16] Goltzius produced countless finished drawings like *The Seven Virtues* (1585–1588; fig. p. 158) that served as templates for the engravers. They would have been expert at transferring the outlines onto the copper plate and then translating the areas of wash on the drawings into Goltzius-style engraved hatching. To achieve a certain uniformity, Goltzius necessarily would have had to exercise a good deal of supervision over what

internationales, humanistisches, kunstinteressiertes Publikum richtete. Er beschäftigte eine Reihe von Stechern, die darin geschult waren, seine Entwürfe in seinem Stil zu reproduzieren; wir kennen diejenigen, die ihre Arbeiten signieren durften: seinen Stiefsohn Jacob Matham sowie Jacques de Gheyn II (1565–1629) und Jan Harmensz. Muller (1571–1628), die jeweils etwa zwei Jahre lang für Goltzius arbeiteten, bevor sie sich selbstständig machten, und Jan Saenredam (1565/66–1607), der kurz vor Goltzius' Italienreise 1590/91 für ihn zu arbeiten begann und nach einem Zerwürfnis von seinem Haus in Assendelft aus weiterhin Drucke für die Werkstatt stach.[16] Goltzius schuf unzählige detailliert ausgeführte Zeichnungen wie *Die sieben Tugenden* (1585–1588; Abb. S. 158), die den Stechern als Vorlagen dienten. Diese waren Experten darin, die Umrisse auf die Kupferplatte zu übertragen und die lavierten Flächen auf den Zeichnungen in Schraffuren im Stil von Goltzius umzusetzen. Um eine gewisse Einheitlichkeit zu erreichen, musste dieser zwangsläufig ein hohes Maß an Kontrolle ausüben über das, was sie produzierten. Das HG-Monogramm des Künstlers, das auf so vielen seiner Werke eingraviert ist, scheint sowohl ein Symbol für Vortrefflichkeit als auch für seine Urheberschaft zu sein.

In seiner Rolle als Verleger musste sich Goltzius auch um den Druck und den Vertrieb der Blätter sowie um deren Finanzierung und Schutz kümmern. Die Verleger verkauften ihre Drucke in Geschäften und über Händlernetze im In- und Ausland. Die Informationen über Goltzius' verlegerische Praxis sind begrenzt, doch durch van Mander und aus anderen Quellen

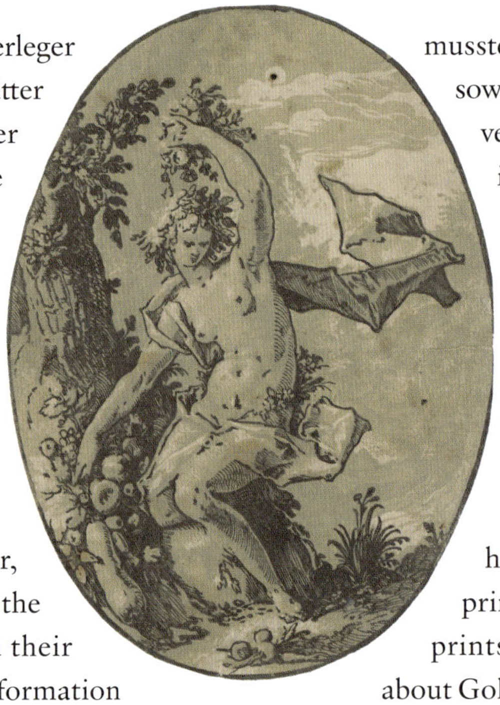

they produced. The artist's HG monogram, inscribed on so much of his work, seems as much a symbol of excellence as a conveyor of his authorship.

In his role as publisher, he would also have seen to the printing and distribution of the prints, as well as their financing and protection. Publishers sold their prints in shops and via networks of dealers at home and abroad. Information about Goltzius's practice is limited, but we do know from Van Mander and other sources that he brought work to the Frankfurt Book Fair, one of the main venues at the time for selling prints internationally.[17] For example, Dominicus Lampsonius (1532–1599) in Liège wrote to Abraham Ortelius (1527–1598) in Antwerp, asking whether he could buy one of the impressions of *The Wedding of Cupid and Psyche* that Ortelius had purchased there.[18] Dedications and privileges were reliable sources of financing, protection, and prestige for some publishers. The inscription on the plaque at the bottom left of *The Wedding of Cupid and Psyche* indicates that Goltzius and Spranger together dedicated the print to Wolfgang Rumpf (1535/36–1605), chamberlain to the Holy Roman Emperor Rudolf II. Rumpf had often mediated on behalf of artists with the emperor at the court in Prague where Spranger was court artist. In 1586, a year earlier, Goltzius had already dedicated the remarkable series of *Roman Heroes* to the emperor himself. Honor and some financial reward would have resulted from such dedications. According to Van Mander, Goltzius received for his dedication of

7 Goltzius (Inventor, Holzschneider / designer, woodcutter), Willem Jansz. Blaeu (Verleger / publisher)
Proserpina / Proserpine, ca. 1588–1590
Aus der Serie *Demogorgon und die Gottheiten* / from the series *Demogorgon and the Deities*, ca. 1588–1590
Chiaroscuro-Holzschnitt / chiaroscuro woodcut SGSM, Inv. 151648 D

wissen wir, dass er Arbeiten zur Frankfurter Buchmesse brachte, einem der wichtigsten Orte für den internationalen Verkauf von Druckgraphiken in jener Zeit.[17] So schrieb Dominicus Lampsonius (1532–1599) in Lüttich an Abraham Ortelius (1527–1598) in Antwerpen und fragte, ob er einen der Abzüge der *Hochzeit von Amor und Psyche* kaufen könne, die Ortelius dort erworben hatte.[18] Widmungen und Privilegien waren für einige Verleger zuverlässige Quellen der Finanzierung, des Schutzes und des Prestiges. Die Inschrift auf der Kartusche unten links auf der *Hochzeit von Amor und Psyche* weist darauf hin, dass Goltzius und Spranger den Druck gemeinsam Wolfgang Rumpf (1535/36–1605), dem Kammerherrn des habsburgischen Kaisers Rudolf II., widmeten. Rumpf hatte am Prager Hof, wo Spranger Hofkünstler war, oft im Namen von Künstlern beim Kaiser vermittelt. Bereits 1586, ein Jahr zuvor, hatte Goltzius dem Kaiser die bemerkenswerte Serie der *Römischen Helden* gewidmet. Solche Widmungen waren ehrenvoll und gingen mit einer gewissen finanziellen Belohnung einher. Laut van Mander erhielt Goltzius für seine Widmung der Serie *Christi Geburt und Jugend* an den Herzog von Bayern „eine goldene Kette mit einer schönen Goldmedaille, die das Porträt des Gesichts des Herzogs trägt".[19]

Privilegien erfüllten eine ähnliche Funktion wie das heutige Urheberrecht, um Werke vor Nachahmung zu schützen. Wie Widmungen muss auch ein Privileg des Kaisers des Heiligen Römischen Reichs mit einem gewissen Prestige verbunden gewesen sein. Am 12. April des Jahres 1595 erhielt Goltzius von Rudolf II. ein allgemeines Privileg, das die unberechtigte Vervielfältigung aller seiner Drucke für einen Zeitraum von sechs Jahren untersagte, unter der Bedingung, dass er dem Hof von jedem Druck drei Abzüge überließ. Auf dieses Privileg berief sich Goltzius auf späteren Stichen wie *Der hl. Hieronymus* nach

the *Birth and Early Life of Christ* series to the Duke of Bavaria "a golden chain with a beautiful gold medal, which has the portrait of the face of the Duke on it."[19]

Privileges functioned something like present-day copyrights to protect work from being copied. Like dedications, a privilege from the Holy Roman emperor must have also brought with it a certain amount of prestige. On April 12, 1595, Goltzius received a general privilege from Rudolf II barring the unauthorized copying of all his prints for a period of six years on the condition that he present the court with three impressions of every print. Goltzius referred to the privilege on subsequent engravings such as *St. Jerome* after Jacopo Palma II (ca. 1548–1628), created the following year and inscribed in the lower right corner with "Cum privil. Sa. C. M." (1596; fig. p. 117). This privilege expired in 1601, by which time direction of the business had been assumed by Matham, who then acquired a privilege of his own from the court in Prague. While the Rudolphine privileges would have been of use in the territory belonging to the Holy Roman Empire, they would not have been of assistance in his own country and this provides some indication of the international audience and approval that he sought.

Goltzius's work took a new direction around 1589, about the time that he was planning a long-desired trip to Italy. According to Van Mander, Goltzius had suffered from consumption for some time and, believing that he did not have long to live, decided to finally make the trip. The work produced before his departure reflects his eagerness to see Italy. In the large *Judgment of Midas* (1590; fig. pp. 194–195) a sense of golden light pervades the scene and the figures now are large and weighty. They no longer

Jacopo Palma II (um 1548–1628), der im folgenden Jahr 1596 entstand und in der rechten unteren Ecke mit der Inschrift „Cum privil. Sa. C. M." (Abb. S. 117) versehen war. Dieses Privileg erlosch 1601. Zu diesem Zeitpunkt hatte Matham die Leitung der Geschäfte übernommen und ein eigenes Privileg vom Prager Hof erworben. Während die rudolfinischen Privilegien in den zum Heiligen Römischen Reich gehörenden Gebieten sicherlich von Nutzen waren, hätten sie ihm in seinem eigenen Land nichts genützt – ein Hinweis auf das internationale Publikum und die Zustimmung, die er suchte.

Goltzius' Arbeit schlug um 1589, etwa zu der Zeit, als er eine lang ersehnte Reise nach Italien plante, eine neue Richtung ein. Van Mander zufolge litt Goltzius schon seit einiger Zeit an Schwindsucht. In dem Glauben, dass er nicht mehr lange zu leben hatte, beschloss er, die Reise endlich anzutreten. Die vor seiner Abreise entstandenen Werke spiegeln seinen Eifer wider, Italien zu sehen. Im großen *Midasurteil* (1590; Abb. S. 194 f.) scheint die Szene von goldenem Licht erfüllt zu sein und die Figuren sind nun groß und gewichtig. Sie schreiten und gestikulieren nicht mehr dynamisch, sondern unterhalten sich gesittet in kleinen Gruppen, und die Protagonisten befinden sich eindeutig in der Mitte des Kreises. Goltzius zitiert hier sowohl die Musenfiguren aus Raffaels *Parnass*, die er von einer Druckgraphik Marcantonio Raimondis (1470/82–1527/34) kannte, als auch die schimmernden Stoffe seiner eigenen *Venezianischen Hochzeit*. Man nimmt an, dass dieser italienische Einfluss auf van Mander zurückzuführen ist, aber man kann sich auch vorstellen, dass der Künstler in Erwartung seiner Reise alle seine italienischen Drucke und andere verwandte Quellen vor sich ausgebreitet hat.[20] Während seiner Reise überließ er das Geschäft Matham und Saenredam, die beide nach Goltzius' Entwürfen Stiche für die Serie der Ovid'schen *Metamorphosen* anfertigten.

stride and gesticulate dynamically, but rather gently converse in small groups, and the protagonists are unmistakably at the circle's center. He quoted both the figures of the Muses from Raphael's *Parnassus*, known to him from a print by Marcantonio Raimondi (1470/82–1527/34), and the shimmering fabrics of his own *Venetian Wedding*. It has been suggested that this Italian influence in the print is due to the influence of Van Mander, but we can also envision the artist laying out before him all of his Italian prints and other related sources in anticipation of his journey.[20] During his travels he left the business in the hands of Matham along with Saenredam, both of whom produced engravings for the series of Ovid's *Metamorphoses* from Goltzius's designs.

Goltzius returned from Italy refreshed and with numerous drawings of the art he saw there, including Classical sculptures and frescoes by Raphael (1483–1520), Polidoro da Caravaggio (ca. 1499–ca. 1543), and others. These fueled his workshop's production (*The Farnese Hercules*, 1592; *The Triumph of Galatea*, 1592; and *The Punishment of Niobe*, 1594; figs. pp. 223, 243, 244–245). He made fewer prints himself, but some of his most exceptional pieces were created at this time: the *Pietà*, the *Birth and Early Life of Christ* series, the abovementioned *Portrait of Frederick de Vries*, and the *Passion of Christ* series in the style of Lucas van Leyden (figs. pp. 235; 110, 198, 199; 257; 35, 104, 156, 196–197).

Goltzius gave up printmaking in 1600 in favor of painting. His friend Van Mander, among others, considered painting the highest form of art and Goltzius had been moving in small ways in this direction over the previous years, working with color and brushwork in his drawings, his "pen works," and

Goltzius kehrte erfrischt und mit zahlreichen Zeichnungen der Kunst, die er dort gesehen hatte, aus Italien zurück, darunter antike Skulpturen sowie Fresken von Raffael (1483–1520), Polidoro da Caravaggio (um 1499 – um 1543) und anderen. Diese regten die Produktion in seiner Werkstatt an (*Herkules Farnese*, 1592; *Triumph der Galatea*, 1592; und *Die Bestrafung der Niobe*, 1594; Abb. S. 223, 243, 244 f.). Auch wenn er nun selbst weniger Drucke anfertigte, entstanden doch einige seiner außergewöhnlichsten Werke in dieser Zeit: die *Pietà*, die Serie *Christi Geburt und Jugend*, das bereits erwähnte *Bildnis des Frederick de Vries* und die Serie *Die Passion Christi* im Stil von Lucas van Leyden (Abb. S. 235; 110, 198, 199; 257; 35, 104, 156, 196 f.).

1600 gab Goltzius die Druckgraphik zugunsten der Malerei auf. Sein Freund van Mander und andere hielten die Malerei für die höchste Form der Kunst, und Goltzius hatte sich in den Jahren zuvor in kleinen Schritten in diese Richtung bewegt, indem er in seinen Zeichnungen, seinen Federkunststücken und sogar in seinen Druckgraphiken mit Farbe und Pinsel arbeitete.[21] In nur 18 Jahren seit der Gründung seines Verlags und 13 Jahren seit der *Hochzeit von Amor und Psyche* war Goltzius zu einem weithin bewunderten, international erfolgreichen Graphiker und Verleger geworden. Nun suchte er nach neuen künstlerischen Wegen. Als Peter Paul Rubens Goltzius 1612 besuchte, traf er sich mit dem erfolgreichsten Künstler der nördlichen Niederlande, einem international bekannten Maler, der eine äußerst lukrative Druckwerkstatt betrieb und es schaffte, ausländische Höfe für seine Graphiken zu gewinnen. Es bleibt unserer Phantasie überlassen, sich vorzustellen, wie das Gespräch zwischen diesen beiden Gleichgesinnten verlief.

even his prints.[21] In a mere eighteen years since establishing his publishing business and thirteen years since *The Wedding of Cupid and Psyche*, Goltzius had become a widely admired, internationally successful printmaker and publisher, and he was now looking for new artistic avenues to explore. When Peter Paul Rubens visited Goltzius in 1612, he was meeting with the most successful artist in the Northern Netherlands, an internationally famous painter who ran a highly successful printmaking business and succeeded in engaging foreign courts in support of his prints. One can only imagine the discussion that took place between these kindred spirits.

1 Oberhuber 1958, S. 127.
2 Mander (1604) 2000, S. 337, fol. 284r.
3 Zu Goltzius' Druckgraphiken siehe NHD Goltzius 2012; Amsterdam/New York/Toledo 2003 und Filedt Kok 1991/92.
4 Mander (1604) 2000, S. 339, fol. 285r.
5 Huigen Leeflang, in: Amsterdam/New York/Toledo 2003, S. 226f.
6 Mander (1604) 2000, S. 339, fol. 284v, und Huigen Leeflang, in: Amsterdam/New York/Toledo 2003, S. 207f. und Kat. 75.
7 Mander (1604) 2000, S. 328–345, fol. 281v–287r.
8 Übers. zit. nach: Dessau 2017, Kat. IV.1 und 2 (Übers. Lara Elisabeth Vogel).
9 Amsterdam, Rijksmuseum, Inv. RP-T-1937-14. Traditionell galt die Zeichnung als Werk von Barendsz., bis Martin Royalton-Kisch die heute allgemein anerkannte Neuzuschreibung an Goltzius vornahm. Royalton-Kisch 1989, S. 14–26.
10 Amsterdam/New York/Toledo 2003, S. 78f.
11 Das Goldmedaillon wird im Birmingham Museum and Art Gallery aufbewahrt (Inv. 1532-1885).
12 Marijn Schapelhouman, in: Amsterdam/New York/Toledo 2003, S. 165.
13 Huigen Leeflang erörtert einen solchen Austausch zwischen Jan Harmensz. Muller und Spranger; siehe Leeflang 2008.
14 Folgende Publikationen dieses Jahres weisen die Inschrift auf: *Die büßende hl. Maria Magdalena* (NHD Goltzius 2012, 49), die aus vier Tafeln bestehende *Der Lohn der Arbeit, des Fleißes, der Übung und der Kunstfertigkeit* (NHD Goltzius 2012, 199–202), *Lot und seine Töchter verlassen Sodom* (NHD Goltzius 2012, 312) und *Der tote Erlöser und die vier Evangelisten* (NHD Goltzius 2012, 314). *Moses und die Gesetzestafeln*, das im folgenden Jahr gedruckt wurde, trägt ebenfalls diese Inschrift (NHD Goltzius 2012, 1).
15 Marjolein Leesberg gibt eine gute Einschätzung zu den Druckgraphikern, welche die Werkstatt durchliefen; siehe NHD Goltzius 2012, S. lii–lviii; ebenfalls zu diesem Thema Filedt Kok 1991/92.
16 Amsterdam/New York/Toledo 2003, S. 204f.
17 Mander (1604) 2000, S. 337, fol. 284v.
18 Hessels 1887, S. 353–355.
19 Mander (1604) 2000, S. 339, fol. 285r.
20 Leesberg 1991/92, S. 416–420.
21 Seine Hinwendung zur Malerei wird von Lawrence W. Nichols ausführlich diskutiert; siehe Nichols 2013, S. 19–29.

1 Oberhuber 1958, p. 127.
2 Mander (1604) 1994, fol. 284r.
3 On Goltzius's prints, see NHD Goltzius 2012; Amsterdam/New York/Toledo 2003; and Filedt Kok 1991/92.
4 Mander (1604) 1994, fol. 285r.
5 Huigen Leeflang in Amsterdam/New York/Toledo 2003, pp. 226–227.
6 Mander (1604) 1994, fol. 284v, and Huigen Leeflang in Amsterdam/New York/Toledo 2003, pp. 207–208 and cat. 75.
7 Mander (1604) 1994, fols. 281v–287r.
8 Amsterdam/New York/Toledo 2003, cats. 10.1 and 10.2.
9 Amsterdam, Rijksmuseum, inv. RP-T-1937-14. The drawing had been traditionally given to Barendsz. until Martin Royalton-Kisch proposed the attribution of the drawing to Goltzius that is now generally accepted; Royalton-Kisch 1989, pp. 14–26.
10 Amsterdam/New York/Toledo 2003, pp. 78–79.
11 The gold medallion is preserved in the Birmingham Museum and Art Gallery (inv. 1532-1885).
12 Marijn Schapelhouman in Amsterdam/New York/Toledo 2003, p. 165.
13 Such an exchange between Jan Harmensz. Muller and Spranger is discussed by Huigen Leeflang, see Leeflang 2008.
14 The following publications of that year display the inscription: *St. Mary Magdalene Penitent* (NHD Goltzius 2012, 49), the four-plate *The Rewards of Labor, Industry, Practice, and Art* (NHD Goltzius 2012, 199–202), *Lot and His Daughters Leaving Sodom* (NHD Goltzius 2012, 312), and *The Dead Savior and the Four Evangelists* (NHD Goltzius 2012, 314). *Moses and the Tablets of the Law*, published the following year, also bears the inscription (NHD Goltzius 2012, no. 1).
15 Marjolein Leesberg provides a good assessment of the printmakers who passed through the workshop in NHD Goltzius 2012, pp. lii–lviii; also on this topic, see Filedt Kok 1991/92.
16 Amsterdam/New York/Toledo 2003, pp. 204–205.
17 Mander (1604) 1994, fol. 284v.
18 Hessels 1887, pp. 353–355.
19 Mander (1604) 1994, fol. 285r.
20 Leesberg 1991/92, pp. 416–420.
21 His conversion to painting is discussed at length by Lawrence W. Nichols, see Nichols 2013, pp. 19–29.

NILS BÜTTNER

Rubens-Graphik

Von der kontrollierten Wiederholung zur globalen Verbreitung

Rubens in Print

From Controlled Reproduction to Global Dissemination

ANFÄNGE

Peter Paul Rubens war von gedruckten Bildern fasziniert. Davon zeugt die Genauigkeit, mit der er in seiner Jugend die Bibel-Illustrationen des Tobias Stimmer (1539–1584) studierte. Jeden der im Schnitt nur sechs Zentimeter hohen Holzschnitte hat er akribisch analysiert und einzelne Figuren herauskopiert, die ihm als besonders ausdrucksstark erschienen. Viele Jahre später, auf einer Reise durch Holland, hat er diese Praxis auch seinem späteren Biographen empfohlen, dem Maler Joachim von Sandrart (1606–1688).[1] Der weist gleich mehrfach auf die ihm unvergessliche Begegnung hin, wobei er sich besonders an eine Fahrt auf dem Fährboot erinnerte. Dort habe ihm Rubens berichtet, dass er in seiner Jugend die Holzschnitte von Stimmer und Hans Holbein II (1497/98–1543) nachgezeichnet habe.[2]

Auch andere druckgraphische Werke haben Rubens' Stil geprägt und wurden ihm dauerhaft zum Vorbild.[3] Das gilt zum Beispiel für die Werke von Otto van Veen (1556–1629), bei dem Rubens in die Lehre ging. Zum Fundus von van Veens Werkstatt gehörten auch Arbeiten von dessen Lehrer Dominicus Lampsonius (1532–1599), deren Fermente sich immer wieder in Rubens' Arbeiten nachweisen lassen.[4] Lampsonius wiederum griff Bilderfindungen seines Lehrmeisters Lambert Lombard (1505/06–1566) auf, wies aber auch Cornelis Cort (1533–1578) auf italienische Werke hin, die dieser dann reproduzierte.[5] Cort nutzte dafür eine damals neue Technik, bei der durch das Anschwellenlassens der Strichstärke in den Schattenpartien zusätzliche Schraffurlagen unnötig wurden (Abb. S. 100).[6] Diese sogenannte Taillentechnik, die Rubens' Vorstellung einer technisch perfekten Reproduktion prägte, wurde zur Grundlage für die Stichtechnik des Hendrick Goltzius. Auch dessen revolutionäre Graphiken fanden Eingang in Rubens'

BEGINNINGS

Peter Paul Rubens was fascinated by printed images. This is evident from the rigor with which he studied the Bible illustrations of Tobias Stimmer (1539–1584) in his youth. He meticulously analyzed each of the woodcuts, which were only six centimeters high on average, and copied out individual figures that he found particularly expressive. Many years later, on a trip through Holland, he also recommended this practice to his later biographer, the painter Joachim von Sandrart (1606–1688).[1] The latter referred to this unforgettable encounter several times, especially recalling a ferry boat trip. On this occasion, Rubens told him that in his youth he had copied the woodcuts by Stimmer and Hans Holbein II (1497/98–1543).[2]

Among the other printed works that influenced Rubens's style and became enduring models for him are those of Otto van Veen (1556–1629), to whom Rubens was apprenticed.[3] Van Veen's workshop also included the works of his teacher Dominicus Lampsonius (1532–1599), traces of whose influence can be repeatedly discerned in Rubens's works.[4] Lampsonius, in turn, drew on the pictorial inventions of his teacher, Lambert Lombard (1505/06–1566), while also identifying Italian works for Cornelis Cort (1533–1578) to reproduce.[5] Cort used a technique—novel at the time—that involved swelling the line width in the shaded areas, making additional hatched layers unneccessary (fig. p. 100).[6] This so-called taille technique, which shaped Rubens's idea of a technically perfect reproduction, became the basis of Hendrick Goltzius's engraving technique. Goltzius's revolutionary prints also found their way into Rubens's pictorial repertoire, which was committed to the ideals of the Renaissance and its ancient

Bildrepertoire, das den Idealen der Renaissance und ihrer antiken Vorbilder verpflichtet war. Von Rubens' Bilddenken zeugt auch ein theoretisches Studienbuch, dessen Original verloren ist, von dem aber einzelne lose Blätter und vier umfangreiche Kopien überliefert sind.[7] Dieses Konvolut von Skizzen und Ideen referiert, abgesehen von Monumenten der antiken Skulptur, vor allem auf Bilder aus der Zeit vor 1550.[8] Überhaupt zeigt sich, dass Rubens' ästhetisches Ideal zutiefst in den Werken der oben genannten Künstler und ihrer Bildwelten wurzelte. Dabei ist es bezeichnend, dass er – anders als die meisten anderen Zeichner – zumeist nicht ganze Drucke kopierte, sondern nur einzelne Haltungen und Handlungen, in denen Emotionen in besonders sprechender Weise zum Ausdruck gebracht waren.[9] Rubens' Anspruch war es, im Sinne eines künstlerischen Wettstreits Bilderfindungen aufzugreifen, sie seiner eigenen Bildsprache anzuverwandeln und sie auf diese Weise zu überbieten. Diesen Anspruch teilte er mit dem 19 Jahre älteren Hendrick Goltzius.[10]

BILDSPRACHE

Goltzius wurde von seinen Zeitgenossen Cornelis Schonaeus (1541–1611) und Karel van Mander (1548–1606) für seine Fertigkeit gelobt, Stile berühmter Künstler meisterhaft zu imitieren.[11] Sich berühmter Vorbilder zu bedienen und sie nachzuahmen, galt keineswegs als verwerflich; im Gegenteil. Wenn man ein Vorbild in der Absicht aufgriff, es zu verbessern oder gar zu übertreffen, galt dies sogar als besonders löblich. In der Kunsttheorie der Zeit, die ihre Begriffe und Ideale der Rhetorik entlehnte, bezeichnete man das als *aemulatio*.[12] Diesem für die Ästhetik der Zeit zentralen Begriff lag die Idee zugrunde, dass jedes neue Kunstwerk nicht allein in der Nachfolge älterer Werke stehe, sondern mit ihnen in einen Wettstreit trete. Das hat Goltzius

models. Rubens's pictorial conception is evidenced by a theoretical notebook as well; although the original is lost, loose individual sheets and four extensive copies have survived.[7] Apart from monuments of ancient sculpture, this collection of sketches and ideas refers primarily to paintings from the period before 1550.[8] Rubens's aesthetic ideal was altogether deeply rooted in the works of the abovementioned artists and their pictorial worlds. A particularly distinctive aspect of his copying practice is that, unlike most other draftsmen, Rubens did not usually copy entire prints, but only individual postures and actions in which emotions were expressed in an especially eloquent manner.[9] Rubens took up pictorial inventions in the spirit of an artistic competition and adapted them to his own visual language, aspiring to surpass the originals. He shared this ambition with Hendrick Goltzius, who was nineteen years his senior.[10]

VISUAL LANGUAGE

Goltzius was praised by his contemporaries Cornelis Schonaeus (1541–1611) and Karel van Mander (1548–1606) for his skill at masterfully imitating the styles of famous artists.[11] Drawing on and even imitating the work of famous models was by no means considered objectionable. On the contrary, imitating an exemplary work with the intention of improving or even surpassing it was considered particularly praiseworthy. In the art theory of the time, which borrowed its concepts and ideals from rhetoric, this was referred to as *aemulatio*.[12] This concept, central to the aesthetics of the time, was based on the idea that new works of art did not merely come after older works, but entered into competition with them. This was

getan, der sich in seinen sogenannten *Meisterstichen* mit den allseits bewunderten Kupferstichen von Albrecht Dürer und Lucas van Leyden auseinandergesetzt hat.[13] Auch Rubens hat diese älteren Stiche als vorbildlich verstanden und kopiert. Es ist deshalb sicher kein Zufall, dass Rubens' intensive Auseinandersetzung mit Goltzius genau in jene Zeit fällt, in der er auch selbst Werke der deutschen Renaissance kopierte.[14] Dabei ist Rubens' *Pilatus* (1596–1600; Abb. S. 157) eine *aemulatio*, die zwar das Vorbild erkennbar kopiert, dabei jedoch zugleich auf dessen Überbietung abzielt.[15] Rubens kombinierte den thronenden Pilatus aus Goltzius' Kupferstich mit zwei in verschiedene Richtungen schauenden Köpfen nach dem vierten Blatt der Stichfolge, das Christus vor Caiaphas zum Gegenstand hat (Abb. S. 104). Er veränderte den Bildausschnitt, rückte die Szene näher heran und verlieh ihr durch diese Neuordnung und eine stärkere Ausarbeitung der Physiognomien eine psychologische Wirksamkeit, die der Vorlage fehlt.[16]

Rubens hat selbst schon früh bekundet, dass er immer bestrebt gewesen sei, „mit keinem noch so großen Mann verwechselt zu werden".[17] Der selbstbewussten Behauptung steht die schon früh bezeugte Tatsache entgegen, dass Rubens' Historienbilder, die vor seinem Umzug nach Italien entstanden, den Werken von Otto van Veen zum Verwechseln ähnlich sehen.[18] Es gelang Rubens aber schon in den ersten Jahren seines Italienaufenthaltes zwischen 1600 und 1608, einen eigenen Stil zu entwickeln. Seine zunehmend charakteristische Bildsprache zeigt sich nicht nur in Gemälden mit selten oder nie dargestellten Themen, sondern gerade in solchen Bildern, in denen er traditionelle Bildgegenstände und Motive der christlichen Ikonographie besonders wirkmächtig umsetzte. Er schuf Bilder, die dem Publikum im Gedächtnis bleiben. Es ist seine unverwechselbare malerische Handschrift, die diese Wirkmacht entfaltet

Goltzius's approach in his so-called *Masterpieces*, which emulated the universally admired engravings by Albrecht Dürer and Lucas van Leyden.[13] Rubens also saw these older engravings as exemplary and copied them. Surely, therefore, it is not a coincidence that Rubens's intense engagement with Goltzius took place precisely at the time when he was also copying works from the German Renaissance.[14] Rubens's *Pilate* (1596–1600; fig. p. 157) is an *aemulatio* which, while recognizably copying its model, also aims to surpass it.[15] Rubens combined the enthroned Pilate from Goltzius's engraving with two figures looking in different directions from the fourth print in the *Passion* series, which depicts Christ before Caiaphas (fig. p. 104). He also changed the crop of the image and drew the scene closer. Through this rearrangement and a stronger elaboration of the physiognomies, he gave his drawing a psychological impact the original lacks.[16]

Rubens himself professed early on that he had always endeavored "not to be confused with any man, no matter how great."[17] This self-confident assertion is countered by the fact, attested to early on, that the history paintings Rubens created before his move to Italy look remarkably similar to the works of Otto van Veen.[18] Rubens succeeded in developing his own style, however, in the first years of his stay in Italy from 1600 to 1608. His increasingly characteristic pictorial language can be seen not only in his portrayal of subjects that were rarely or never depicted by other artists, but also in his use of traditional pictorial subjects and motifs from Christian iconography to particularly powerful effect. He created works that lingered in the memory of their audience. It is his distinctive

und Wiedererkennbarkeit garantiert. Keines seiner überwältigenden Altarwerke hat er mit einer Signatur versehen. Sein Stil ist sein Markenzeichen.[19]

KÜNSTLERISCHER WETTSTREIT UND FRÜHER RUHM

Rubens war es ein Anliegen, sich einen Namen zu machen. Sein Ehrbestreben ist nicht nur durch die erfolgreiche Teilnahme an Künstlerkonkurrenzen belegt, sondern hat auch in seinen Briefen Niederschlag gefunden. Als Hofmaler des Herzogs von Mantua bat Rubens am 2. Dezember 1606 seinen Dienstherrn um die Genehmigung, in Rom bleiben zu dürfen, weil sein Ehrbestreben ihn getrieben habe, sich um die Gestaltung des Hochaltars der Oratorianer-Kirche Santa Maria in Vallicella zu bewerben.[20] Er habe diesen Wettbewerb gegen die tüchtigsten Maler Italiens gewonnen und schließlich gereiche es doch auch dem Herzog zur Ehre, wenn dessen Diener in Rom zu Ruhm gelange. Rubens durfte bleiben und machte sich ans Werk, wobei die vollendete Erstfassung des Gemäldes von den Auftraggebern abgelehnt wurde. Die zweite Version sicherte Rubens seinen Platz unter den erfolgreichen Malern des barocken Rom. Unmittelbar nach der Einweihung kehrte er im Dezember 1608 nach Antwerpen zurück.[21] Wenige Wochen zuvor war dort seine Mutter gestorben, für deren Seelenheil sein Bruder und er einen Altar und regelmäßige Messen stifteten.[22] Dabei mag es dem Maler nicht ungelegen gekommen sein, dass er die vergeblich gemalte Erstfassung des Altarwerkes für die Oratorianer-Kirche aus Italien mit in die Heimat gebracht hatte.[23] Sie fand als Epitaph der verstorbenen Mutter in Antwerpen ihren Platz, wo sie zugleich für den Maler Werbung machte. Schon bald gab es in der Schelde-Stadt kein bedeutendes öffentliches

painterly signature that unfolds this power and guarantees recognizability. He did not sign any of his stunning altarpieces—his style is his trademark.[19]

ARTISTIC COMPETITION AND EARLY FAME

Rubens was keen to make a name for himself. His quest for honor is not only evidenced by successful participation in art competitions, but also reflected in his letters. As court painter to the Duke of Mantua, Rubens asked his patron on December 2, 1606, for permission to stay in Rome because his ambition had compelled him to apply to design the high altar of the Oratorian church of Santa Maria in Vallicella.[20] Boasting that he had won this competition against the most talented painters in Italy, he suggested that it would be to the duke's honor if his servant achieved fame in Rome. Rubens was allowed to stay and set to work, although the first completed version of the painting was rejected by its patrons. The second version secured Rubens's place among the successful painters of Baroque Rome. Immediately after the altar's consecration in December 1608, he returned to Antwerp,[21] where his mother had died a few weeks earlier. Rubens and his brother donated an altar and regular masses for her salvation.[22] Rather conveniently, the painter had brought the first, rejected, version of the altarpiece for the Oratorian church back home from Italy.[23] It found its place in Antwerp as an epitaph to his deceased mother—and it also promoted the painter. Soon a work by Rubens could be admired in virtually every significant public building in the city on the Scheldt. The ubiquity of his paintings is also evidenced by a letter from the merchant Jan le Grand,

Gebäude mehr, in dem man nicht ein Werk von Rubens bewundern konnte. Die Allgegenwart seiner Bilder bezeugt auch ein Brief des Kaufmanns Jan le Grand, der im März des Jahres 1611 einem Bekannten eine beeindruckende Liste ihm bekannter Gemälde aufzählt und mitteilt, dass man Rubens den „Gott der Maler" nenne.[24] Die in Italien errungenen Erfolge blieben in den Niederlanden unsichtbar. Man kann es sich im Jahrhundert der allgegenwärtigen Bilder kaum mehr vorstellen, wie schwierig es einst war, sich vom Werk eines Malers ein Bild zu machen. Und dabei wurde noch vor drei Dezennien auch in kunsthistorischen Kontexten regelmäßig mit kläglichen Schwarz-Weiß-Photos und -Diapositiven gearbeitet, weil farbige Abbildungen von Gemälden nicht verfügbar waren. Selbst die heute aus dem Museumskontext kaum mehr wegzudenkenden monographischen Ausstellungen sind eine gemessen an den Gegenständen ihrer Beschäftigung junge Erfindung. So fand zum Beispiel die erste Rubens-Werkschau erst 1927 in Antwerpen statt.[25] Zu Rubens' Zeit, lange vor der Erfindung des Museums und des öffentlichen Ausstellungswesens, bedeutete ein erfolgreich verkauftes Bild zugleich, dass es am Ort seiner Entstehung den Blicken entzogen war und weitgehend unsichtbar blieb. Die in Rom errungenen Erfolge blieben auch in Mantua unsichtbar, wo man ohne zu reisen auch nicht wissen konnte, was Rubens in Genua geleistet hatte. Wohl auch aus diesem Grund hat Rubens in Verona seinem Freund Jan van den Wouwer (1576–1636) versprochen, eines der seinerzeit entstandenen Gemälde reproduzieren zu lassen (Abb. S. 113).[26] Die von Cornelis Galle I (1576–1650) gestochene Reproduktion einer Judith mit dem Haupt des Holofernes war ausweislich der darunter angebrachten Widmung der erste Kupferstich nach einem Gemälde von Rubens, das heute verschollen ist.[27]

who in March 1611 sent an acquaintance an impressive list of paintings he knew and wrote that Rubens was called the "god of painters."[24] The successes achieved in Italy remained invisible in the Netherlands, however. In our present century of omnipresent images, it is hard to imagine how difficult it once was to obtain an overview of a painter's oeuvre. And yet just three decades ago, even in art-historical contexts, people regularly worked with paltry black-and-white photographs and slides because color images of paintings were not available. Even the monographic exhibitions that have become an integral part of the museum context today are a recent invention when compared to the objects they display. The first Rubens exhibition, for example, only took place in Antwerp in 1927.[25] In Rubens's time, long before the invention of the museum and public exhibitions, successfully selling a painting resulted in it being hidden from view in the place of its creation and remaining largely invisible. Rubens's successes in Rome remained unseen in Mantua, where it was in turn impossible to know what he had achieved in Genoa without going on a journey. It was probably also for this reason that Rubens promised his friend Jan van den Wouwer (1576–1636) in Verona that he would have one of the paintings created during his Italian sojourn reproduced (fig. p. 113).[26] The reproduction, depicting Judith with the head of Holofernes, was engraved by Cornelis Galle I (1576–1650). According to the dedication below it, this was the first engraving after a painting by Rubens, which is now lost.[27]

REPRODUKTIONEN

Die Wiederholung von Bildern und Motiven war eine Möglichkeit der Selbstvermarktung, die Rubens intensiv genutzt hat. Gemalte Wiederholungen waren die Regel, wobei davon auszugehen ist, dass Rubens keine der einmal von ihm gemalten Kompositionen je selbst wiederholt hat. Das war Aufgabe der Werkstattmitarbeiter, die den Stil ihres Meisters, der sich selbst Unverwechselbarkeit zum Ziel gesetzt hatte, möglichst exakt zu imitieren hatten. Die Ergebnisse wurden dann von Rubens ganz selbstverständlich als seine Werke ausgegeben. Ein Beispiel für diese Praxis ist ein Porträt, um das Nicolas-Claude Fabri de Peiresc (1580–1637) den Maler lange gebeten hatte.[28] Am 19. Mai 1628 bedankte sich Peiresc bei Rubens dafür, dass der bereit sei, sich von seinem Selbstporträt zu trennen.[29] Die Erstfassung dieses Gemäldes befand sich allerdings zu diesem Zeitpunkt schon gar nicht mehr im Besitz des Malers, der dieses Bild bereits Jahre zuvor an Charles I. (1600–1649) nach London gesandt hatte (Abb. 1).[30] In einem Brief vom 2. Dezember 1628 brachte Rubens dann seine Hoffnung zum Ausdruck, dass sein Bildnis („il mio ritratto") gut an seinem Bestimmungsort angekommen sei (Abb. 2).[31] Der Beschenkte dürfte kaum einen Zweifel gehegt haben, dass das ihm übersandte Gemälde, das den Maler zeigte, auch von diesem selbst gemalt war. Die malerische Ausführung erweist jedoch, dass auch diese Wiederholung ein Produkt der Werkstatt ist.

Die oft leicht modifizierte Wiederholung von beliebten Bilderfindungen wurde zu einer Spezialität der Rubens-Werkstatt und manch stolzer Besitzer vermeintlich eigenhändiger Originale besaß nur Kopien, die teils sogar außerhalb der Werkstatt dieses Meisters entstanden waren. Schon einer seiner ersten Biographen, Roger de Piles (1635–1709), hatte das daraus resultierende Problem erkannt, dass ein

REPRODUCTIONS

The replication of images and motifs was a means of self-promotion that Rubens used extensively. Painted copies were the rule, although it can be assumed that Rubens never repeated any of his compositions himself. This was the task of the workshop assistants, who were entrusted with imitating, as exactly as possible, the unmistakable style of their master. The results were then quite naturally passed off by Rubens as his own work. One example of this practice is a portrait that Nicolas-Claude Fabri de Peiresc (1580–1637) had long asked the painter for.[28] On May 19, 1628, Peiresc thanked Rubens for his willingness to part with this self-portrait.[29] However, at this time the first version of the painting was no longer in the painter's possession, as he had sent it to King Charles I (1600–1649) in London years earlier (fig. 1).[30] In a letter to Peiresc dated December 2, 1628, Rubens expressed his hope that his portrait ("il mio ritratto") had arrived safely at its destination (fig. 2).[31] The recipient would have had little reason to doubt that the painting sent to him, which depicted the painter, was indeed painted by him. However, the painterly execution proves that this replica is a product of the workshop.

The repetition of popular pictorial inventions, often slightly modified, became a specialty of Rubens's workshop, with many a proud owner of supposed originals actually possessing copies, some of which had even been created outside the master's workshop. One of his first biographers, Roger de Piles (1635–1709), recognized the resulting problem: the dubious quality of some of these productions

Teil dieser Hervorbringungen durch die zweifelhafte Qualität dem guten Ruf des Malers eher schadete.[32] Joachim von Sandrart hingegen sah den Vorteil, dass Antwerpen durch Rubens „eine ungemeine Kunst-Schule wurde“.[33]

Das internationale Publikum wünschte Gemälde, die jenes spezifische Erscheinungsbild repräsentierten, das man unmittelbar als „Rubens“ erkennen konnte. Deshalb erbat sich der Tischler Jaspar Billeau im Rahmen der Honorarvereinbarung im Gegenzug für die Anfertigung der Treppen für Rubens' Wohnhaus explizit eine „Kopie“. Als er sich vertraglich eine „copye naer eenich stuck van synder hant“ – eine Kopie nach einem Stück von seiner Hand – zusichern ließ, wollte er vermutlich nicht etwa ein Bild, bei dem sichergestellt war, dass es vom Meister selbst gemalt war, sondern vielmehr eines, das jeder sofort als einen Rubens erkannte.[34] Die Vorstellungen von dem, was als „Original“ oder „Kopie“ galt, waren

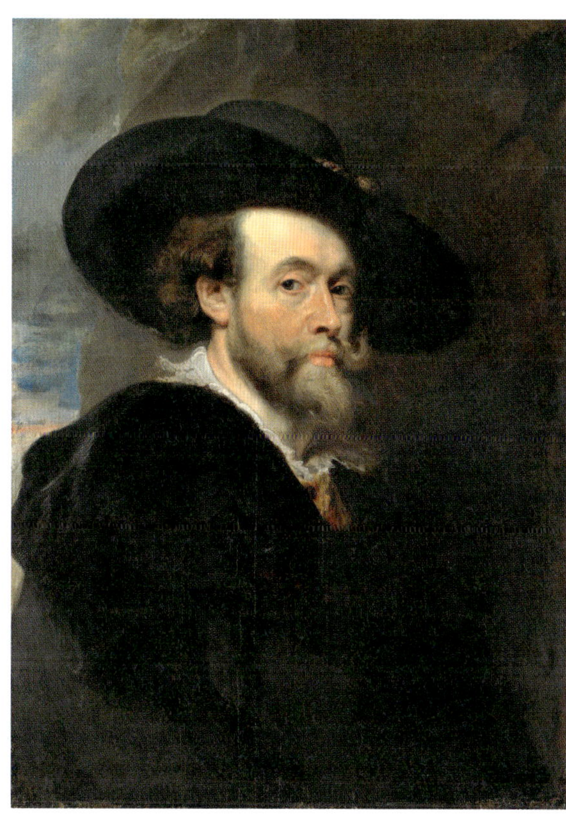

1 Peter Paul Rubens
Selbstbildnis / Self-Portrait, 1623
Öl auf Holz / oil on panel
London, Royal Collection Trust, Inv. RCIN 400156

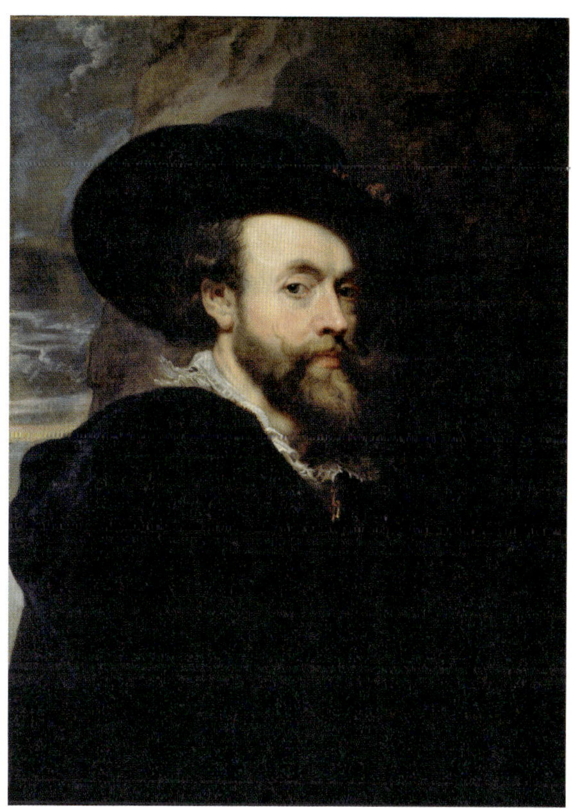

2 Peter Paul Rubens (Werkstatt / workshop)
Selbstbildnis / Self-Portrait, 1623
Öl auf Holz / oil on panel
Canberra, National Gallery of Australia, Inv. NGA 83.53

tended to damage the painter's reputation.[32] Joachim von Sandrart, on the other hand, saw the benefit that, through Rubens, Antwerp "became an exceptional art school."[33]

International audiences wanted paintings with the specific look that made them instantly recognizable as "a Rubens." For this reason, the carpenter Jaspar Billeau explicitly requested a "copy" as part of the fee agreement in return for building the stairs for Rubens's house. When he contractually agreed to a "copye naer eenich stuck van synder hant"—a copy after a piece by his own hand—he presumably

gänzlich andere als heute.[35] Es gibt deshalb kaum eines der etwa 1800 Rubens-Gemälde nur einmal. Es lässt sich sogar zeigen, dass die Zweitfassung parallel zur ersten Version ausgeführt wurde, wobei der mit der Ausführung beauftragte Maler Seite an Seite mit Rubens an der möglichst exakten Kopie arbeitete. Oft übertrug Rubens auch die Ausführung von Landschaften und Stillleben-Elementen an spezialisierte Maler, die dann neben der Erstfassung auch gleich die Kopie staffierten.[36] Mit Blick auf diese Werkstatt und eine stetig wachsende Flut von Aufträgen lag es nahe, sich auch für die Anfertigung druckgraphischer Reproduktionen Hilfe zu suchen, für die es ebenfalls einen expandierenden Markt gab, zumal Rubens' Bilder zunehmend als vorbildhaft galten.

RUBENS-GRAPHIK

Im Verlauf des 17. Jahrhunderts erschienen mehr als 800 druckgraphische Reproduktionen von Rubens-Werken, die nach seinen Gemälden, aber nur zum Teil auch unter seiner Aufsicht ausgeführt wurden.[37] Selbst nach den von ihm verantworteten Drucken entstanden gedruckte Kopien, deren Zahl in den folgenden Jahrhunderten weiter anstieg.[38] Es waren diese druckgraphischen Reproduktionen, die über Jahrhunderte die Vorstellung von Rubens' Œuvre prägen sollten, wobei der französische Begriff „Œuvre" im Verständnis der Zeit unmittelbar auf die graphischen Reproduktionen der Werke eines Künstlers bezogen war.[39] Schon im Verlauf des 17. Jahrhunderts wurden deshalb erste Versuche unternommen, das Gesamtwerk des Künstlers in druckgraphischen Reproduktionen zusammenzustellen, wobei die 1644 von Michel de Marolles (1600–1681), Abt von Baugerais und Villeloin, begonnene Sammlung, die später in

was not expecting a picture that was certain to have been painted by the master himself, but rather one that would immediately be recognized as a Rubens.[34] The notion of what was considered an "original" as opposed to a "copy" was completely different from that of today.[35] As a result, hardly any of the approximately 1,800 Rubens paintings exist only once. It can even be shown that in some cases, the second version was executed in parallel to the first, with the commissioned painter working side by side with Rubens to create the most exact copy possible. Rubens also often entrusted the rendering of landscapes and still-life elements to specialized painters who contributed to the first version as well as the copy.[36] In view of these workshop practices and a steadily growing flood of commissions, it seemed obvious to also seek help for making printed reproductions, for which there was likewise an expanding market, especially since Rubens's pictures were increasingly regarded as exemplary.

RUBENS PRINTS

In the course of the seventeenth century, more than eight hundred printed reproductions of Rubens's paintings appeared, only some of which were executed under his supervision.[37] Even the prints he had authorized were in turn used as models for more printed copies, the number of which continued to increase in the following centuries.[38] It was these printed reproductions that were to shape the perception of Rubens's oeuvre for centuries, whereby the French term *œuvre* was at the time understood to refer directly to the graphic reproductions of an artist's works.[39] Because of this, first attempts to compile

den Besitz des französischen Königs gelangte, auf diesem Gebiet Maßstäbe setzte.[40] Er stellte alle nur irgend verfügbaren Drucke in Klebealben zusammen, lange vor der Publikation des ersten gedruckten Verzeichnisses von Rubens' Drucken, dem 1751 publizierten *Catalogue des estampes gravées d'après Rubens* von Robert Hecquet (1693–1775).[41] Dieses Buch wurde von Pierre-François Basan (1723–1797) grundlegend überarbeitet und 1767 als dritter Band des *Dictionnaire des graveurs anciens et modernes* publiziert, das zur Grundlage der neueren Rubens-Forschung wurde.[42]

Die unter Rubens' Aufsicht ausgeführten Stiche sind durch ein vergleichbares graphisches Erscheinungsbild ausgezeichnet, das auf eine malerische Wirkung abzielte, die auch Goltzius anstrebte. Es kann deshalb nicht verwundern, dass Rubens sich in seinem Bestreben, die bestmöglichen Reproduktionen zu erreichen, 1612 nach Holland wandte, wo er Goltzius besuchte, der, längst nicht mehr als Stecher aktiv, mit Rubens auf dessen Feld der Malerei wetteiferte.[43] Rubens kooperierte dafür mit dessen Stiefsohn und Schüler Jacob Matham (1571–1631), um das bald nach der Rückkehr aus Italien für das Haus eines Freundes entstandene Gemälde *Samson und Delilah* reproduzieren zu lassen (Abb. S. 103).[44] Wie bei der späteren Zusammenarbeit mit dem Haarlemer Kupferstecher Jan Harmensz. Muller (1571–1628) erweisen schon diese Blätter, dass Rubens ganz dezidiert nach einer zwar präzisen, aber doch zugleich malerischen Umsetzung seiner Bilder suchte. Der heute gern verwandte Begriff der „Rubens-Graphik" ist deshalb zumal auf die unmittelbar unter seiner Aufsicht entstandenen Werke durchaus anwendbar.[45] Seine Rechtfertigung erfährt er durch die strenge Kontrolle, unter der die gestochenen Reproduktionen entstanden. Sie klingt schon in einem Brief an, in dem Rubens am 23. Januar 1619 Pieter van Veen

printed reproductions of Rubens's complete works were made as early as the seventeenth century. The collection begun in 1644 by Michel de Marolles (1600–1681), Abbé of Baugerais and Villeloin, set the standard in this field and later came into the possession of the French king.[40] De Marolles compiled all available prints in albums long before the first register of Rubens's prints, the *Catalogue des estampes gravées d'après Rubens* by Robert Hecquet (1693–1775), was published in 1751.[41] This book was thoroughly revised by Pierre-François Basan (1723–1797) and published in 1767 as the third volume of the *Dictionnaire des graveurs anciens et modernes*, which became the basis for more recent research on Rubens.[42]

The engravings executed under Rubens's supervision are characterized by a graphic appearance that aimed for a painterly effect, one that Goltzius also strove for. It is therefore not surprising that Rubens, in his efforts to achieve the best possible reproductions, in 1612 turned to Holland, where he visited Goltzius, who, no longer active as an engraver, was now a competitor with Rubens in the field of painting.[43] Rubens collaborated with Goltzius's stepson and pupil Jacob Matham (1571–1631) to have the painting *Samson and Delilah*, which had been created for a friend's house soon after the artist's return from Italy, reproduced (fig. p. 103).[44] These prints show that—as with his later collaboration with the Haarlem-based engraver Jan Harmensz. Muller (1571–1628)—Rubens was already resolutely seeking a precise yet painterly realization of his pictures. The term "Rubens prints," which is often used today, is therefore indeed applicable to the works created directly under his supervision.[45] It is justified by the strict control under which the engraved reproductions were created. This can be discerned in a letter to Pieter van Veen

gegenüber äußert, wie streng er darauf geachtet habe, „dass sich der Stecher sorgsam bemüht, der Vorlage zu folgen, wie ich es auch für angezeigt halte, die Arbeit unter meiner Aufsicht ausführen zu lassen".[46]

Die Ausführung seines ersten Reproduktionsstiches hatte Rubens an Cornelis Galle I übertragen, der es meisterhaft verstand, alle Details der gemalten Vorlage in klar umrissene Hell-Dunkel-Kontraste zu übersetzen. Dabei blieb aber die auf Präzision zielende individuelle graphische Handschrift Galles sehr deutlich spürbar. Rubens wünschte aber sanftere Modellierungen und mehr Stofflichkeit und Tiefenwirkung, wie er sie in seiner Malerei pflegte. Er sah sich deshalb nach einem anderen Stecher um. Seine Wahl fiel auf den Kupferstecher Lucas Vorsterman I (1595/96–1674/75), der Rubens als die richtige Wahl erschien, da er sich nach eigenem Bekunden entschlossen hatte, die Arbeit lieber unter seinen Augen von einem jungen Menschen ausführen zu lassen, „der von dem Wunsch beseelt ist, Gutes zu schaffen, als von angesehenen Meistern gemäß deren Launen".[47] Dieser Stecher pflegte die von Cort entwickelte und von Goltzius weiterentwickelte Technik mit an- und abschwellenden Linien, die es ermöglichte, im schwarzweißen Medium malerische Wirkungen zu erzielen. Allerdings kam es zwischen dem Maler und seinem Stecher zu Misshelligkeiten, nachdem Vorsterman bereits zahlreiche bekannte Kompositionen in Kupferstiche umgesetzt hatte, die Rubens mit Widmungen an Freunde und berühmte Gönner versehen ließ. Eines der Blätter, das *Bildnis des Charles de Longueval*, versah Vorsterman jedoch mit einer eigenen Widmung (Abb. S. 269).[48] Ob das der Anlass oder die Folge der Auseinandersetzung zwischen beiden war, lässt sich nicht mehr mit Bestimmtheit sagen. Rubens hatte das Bildnis in einer eigens angefertigten Ölskizze vorbereitet (Abb. 3), die Vorsterman virtuos in den gleich großen Kupferstich übersetzte.[49] Bei dem sich

on January 23, 1619, in which Rubens wrote of how strictly he had endeavored "to have an engraver who was more expert in imitating his model, but it seemed the lesser evil to have the work done in my presence."[46]

Rubens had entrusted the execution of his first reproductive engraving to Cornelis Galle I, who was a master at translating all the details of the original painting into clearly defined contrasts of light and dark. At the same time, Galle's individual graphic style, which aimed for precision, remained very clearly perceptible. Rubens, however, desired the softer modeling and greater sense of materiality and depth that characterized his paintings. He therefore looked for another engraver and selected Lucas Vorsterman I (1595/96–1674/75), who Rubens felt was the right choice as he had decided, by his own account, that he would rather have the work done under his own eye by a "well-intentioned young man than by great artists according to their fancy."[47] Vorsterman used the technique of swelling and diminishing lines developed by Cort and further evolved by Goltzius, which made it possible to achieve painterly effects in the black-and-white medium. Disagreements arose between painter and engraver after Vorsterman had converted numerous well-known compositions into engravings, which Rubens had inscribed with dedications to friends and famous patrons. Vorsterman, however, added his own dedication to one of the prints, the *Portrait of Charles de Longueval* (fig. p. 269).[48] Whether this was the cause or the consequence of the dispute between the two can no longer be said with certainty. Rubens had prepared the portrait in a specially made oil sketch (fig. 3) which Vorsterman masterfully translated into a copper engraving of the same size.[49] The dispute, which dragged on for years, seems to have been about the assessment of the engraver's performance.[50]

von nun an über Jahre hinziehenden Streit scheint es um die Bewertung der Leistung des Stechers gegangen zu sein.[50] Offensichtlich fühlte Vorsterman sich nicht der Qualität seiner Arbeit entsprechend bezahlt, denn er betonte, wie Rubens in einem Brief an van Veen referiert, „dass seine [Vorstermans] Stechkunst und sein berühmter Name diesen Stichen den einzigen Wert verleihen".[51] Rubens scheint das anders gesehen zu haben, wobei Vorsterman sich auf die damals etablierte Honorarpraxis berufen konnte, die den Zeitaufwand monetisierte. Deshalb wurde, wie die Kassenbücher des Verlages Plantin-Moretus verraten, die rein handwerkliche Leistung des Stechers mit einem vielfach höheren Betrag abgegolten als die zeichnerische Invention. So erhielt Rubens für den Entwurf eines Titelblattes 20 Gulden gutgeschrieben, während dem ausführenden Stecher knapp das Vierfache bezahlt wurde.[52] Was Rubens an Vorsterman zahlte, ist nicht dokumentiert, es dürfte sich aber an den ortsüblichen Löhnen orientiert haben. Einen Nachfolger für den rebellischen Vorsterman fand Rubens in dessen Schüler und Mitarbeiter Paulus Pontius (1603–1658), mit dem er in den folgenden Jahren eng zusammenarbeitete, wobei er verschiedentlich auch Boëtius à Bolswert (1570/90–1633) und dessen jüngeren Bruder Schelte (1586–1659) sowie Hans Witdoeck (1615–1639/42) mit Aufträgen bedachte.

Vorsterman evidently did not feel that he was remunerated in accordance with the quality of his work, emphasizing, as Rubens relayed in a letter to Van Veen, "that it is his [Vorsterman's] engraving alone and his illustrious name that give these prints any value."[51] Rubens seems to have disagreed, while Vorsterman was able to appeal to the established fee practice of the period, which monetized the time spent on the work. It is for this reason, as the cashbooks of the Plantin-Moretus publishing house reveal, that an engraver's purely manual work was rewarded with a much higher sum than the actual graphical invention. For example, Rubens received twenty guilders for the design of a title page,

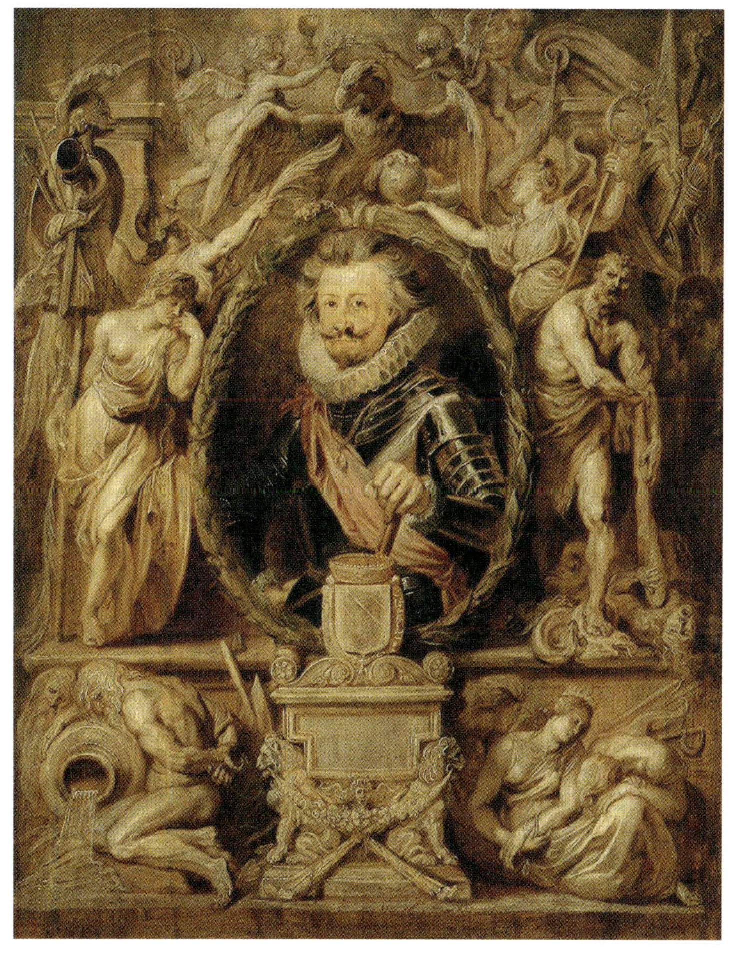

3 Peter Paul Rubens
Bildnis des / Portrait of Charles de Longueval, 1621
Vorzeichnung / preparatory drawing
Öl auf Holz / oil on panel St. Petersburg, The State Hermitage Museum, Inv. GE-508

PRODUKTION UND HERSTELLUNGSPROZESS

In der Regel überließ Rubens selbst das Anfertigen der für die Reproduktion benötigten gezeichneten Vorlage einem Mitarbeiter.[53] Die notwendige Vorlage zur Reproduktion der zwischen 1616 und 1618 für das Kapuzinerkloster in Aachen entstandenen *Anbetung der Hirten* (Abb. 4) wird beispielsweise Anthonis van Dyck (1599–1641) zugeschrieben, der damals in Rubens' Werkstatt arbeitete.[54] Die von Rubens überarbeitete Zeichnung (Abb. 5) wurde dann von Lucas Vorsterman in einen Kupferstich übersetzt (Abb. S. 124).[55] Einzig die für seinen Freund Balthasar Moretus I (1574–1641) entworfenen Buchtitelblätter scheint Rubens selbst gezeichnet zu haben (Abb. S. 143).[56] Dass er sich trotz seiner hohen Qualitätsansprüche zumeist nicht selbst als Vorlagenzeichner engagierte, eröffnete ein Übungsfeld für die Mitarbeiter.[57] Deshalb ließ er auch die Vorzeichnung zu dem nach seinem Ritterschlag zur Reproduktion vorgesehenen Selbstbildnis durch den Stecher Paulus Pontius anfertigen (Abb. 6).[58] Dafür hat er jeden Schritt der Herstellung kritisch begleitet und die gezeichnete Vorlage und auch Probedrucke korrigiert, bis der von ihm gewünschte Ausdruck erreicht war.[59]

Von etlichen durch Rubens beauftragte Graphiken sind Probedrucke mit eingezeichneten Korrekturen erhalten, die traditionell ihm zugeschrieben werden. Besonders viele derartige Blätter, die zugleich das frühe sammlerische Interesse an Rubens' Graphik dokumentieren, haben sich im Louvre in Paris erhalten. Dorthin, so berichtet schon Pierre Jean Mariette (1694–1774), seien sie aus der Sammlung von Everhard Jabach (1618–1695) gelangt, der sie wiederum aus Rubens' Nachlass erworben habe.[60] Zumeist mit Pinsel und Tusche sind in diesen Blättern Überarbeitungen angebracht, deren Ziel es augenscheinlich

while the engraver was paid almost four times that amount.[52] What Rubens paid Vorsterman has not been documented, but it is likely to have been in line with local wages. Rubens found a successor to the rebellious Vorsterman in the latter's student and collaborator Paulus Pontius (1603–1658), with whom he worked closely in the following years, occasionally also commissioning Boëtius à Bolswert (1570/90–1633) and his younger brother Schelte (1586–1659), as well as Hans Witdoeck (1615–1639/42).

PRODUCTION AND MANUFACTURING PROCESS

As a rule, Rubens left even the creation of the preparatory drawings required for reproduction to an assistant.[53] For example, the preparatory drawing necessary for the reproduction of *The Adoration of the Shepherds* (fig. 4), created between 1616 and 1618 for the Capuchin monastery in Aachen, is attributed to Anthony van Dyck (1599–1641), who was working in Rubens's workshop at the time.[54] After being revised by Rubens, the drawing (fig. 5) was then translated into an engraving by Lucas Vorsterman (fig. p. 124).[55] Only the book title pages designed for his friend Balthasar Moretus I (1574–1641) appear to have been drawn by Rubens himself (fig. p. 143).[56] The fact that, despite his high quality standards, he did not usually craft the preparatory drawings himself provided his assistants with good practice.[57] When the engraver Paulus Pontius made the preparatory drawing for the self-portrait slated for reproduction after his knighthood (fig. 6),[58] Rubens critically supervised every step of the production process, correcting the preparatory drawing and proof impressions until the desired expression was achieved.[59]

war, die Figuren zu präzisieren und die Verteilung von Licht und Schatten malerisch zu modellieren.[61] Dass die Reproduktion die gleiche Seitenrichtung wie das gemalte Vorbild aufwies, scheint dabei von nachrangigem Interesse gewesen zu sein. Von den als Kern des Rubens-Œuvres geltenden 56 Stichen sind tatsächlich nur fünf in der gleichen Seitenrichtung wie das Gemälde ausgeführt, das sie interpretieren.[62]

Dafür blieb in der Regel das Format des Gemäldes bei der graphischen Reproduktion erhalten. Wo es ein Altarwerk zu reproduzieren galt, dessen Bilderzählungen sich über die Flügel eines aufgeschlagenen Triptychons ausbreitete, musste – wie etwa im Falle der *Kreuzaufrichtung* (1638; Abb. S. 204 f.) – die Bildvorlage so stark überarbeitet werden, dass Rubens selbst einen neuen Entwurf ausführte. Doch blieb auch im Falle dieser Neufassung das Querformat erhalten. Die einzige Ausnahme

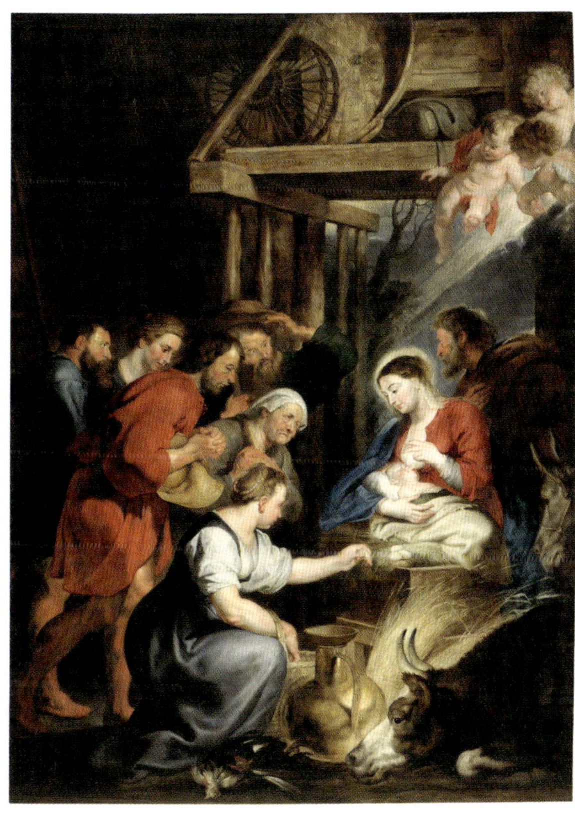

4 Peter Paul Rubens
Die Anbetung der Hirten / The Adoration of the Shepherds, 1616–1618
Öl auf Leinwand / oil on canvas
Rouen, Musée des Beaux-Arts, Inv. 1803.6

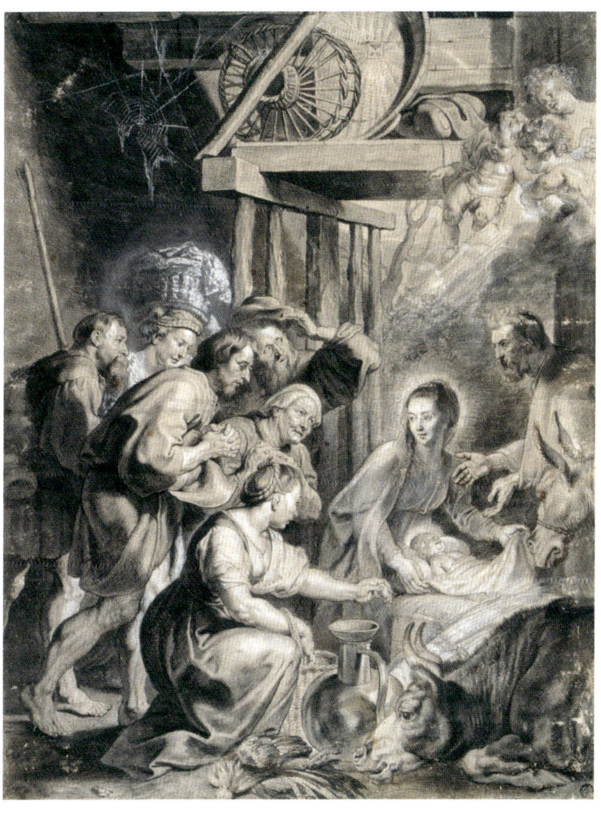

5 Anthonis / Anthony van Dyck, nach / after Rubens
Die Anbetung der Hirten / The Adoration of the Shepherds, ca. 1618
Vorzeichnung / preparatory drawing
Schwarze Kreide, von Rubens überarbeitet, Feder, laviert, weiß gehöht / black chalk, retouched by Rubens, ink, wash, white highlights Paris, Louvre, Inv. 20309, recto

Proof impressions of several prints commissioned by Rubens have survived with drawn-in corrections, which are traditionally attributed to him. A particularly large number of such sheets, which also serve to document early collectors' interest in Rubens's prints, have been preserved in the Louvre in Paris. According to Pierre Jean Mariette (1694–1774), they came from the collection of Everhard Jabach (1618–1695), who had acquired them from Rubens's estate.[60] These prints were mostly reworked with brush and ink, apparently with the intention of making the figures more precise and modeling the distribution

von dieser Regel ist der auf dem schlanken, hochformatigen Seitenflügel eines Altarwerks in Mecheln basierende *Der wunderbare Fischzug* (1633–1638; Abb. 7), den Rubens als Querformat neu entwarf.[63]

Rubens' in seinen Korrekturen bezeigter Anspruch an die graphische Umsetzung hat ihn davon abgehalten, sich selbst auf dem Gebiet der Druckgraphik zu erproben. Er mag sich zwar einmal in der Technik der Radierung geübt haben, über das Stadium eines ersten Experimentierens mit der Radiernadel ist er jedoch nie hinausgelangt. Die an einem der Deckenbilder für die Antwerpener Jesuitenkirche orientierte Darstellung *Die hl. Katharina* (1621–1630) blieb zu Lebzeiten des Malers unpubliziert (Abb. S. 178 f.).[64] Erst nach seinem Tod wurde das unvollendete Blatt vermutlich durch Lucas Vorsterman mit dem Grabstichel vollendet, wobei die Ergänzungen auch Schelte à Bolswert oder Pieter Soutman (1593/1601–1657) zugeschrieben wurden.[65] Rubens und seinen Zeitgenossen waren präzise und durch ihr Format und ihre malerische Wirkung imponierende Reproduktionen wichtiger als die erst von der französischen Kunsttheorie des 18. Jahrhunderts als Qualitätskriterium etablierte Eigenhändigkeit in der graphischen Umsetzung, die in eine bis heute

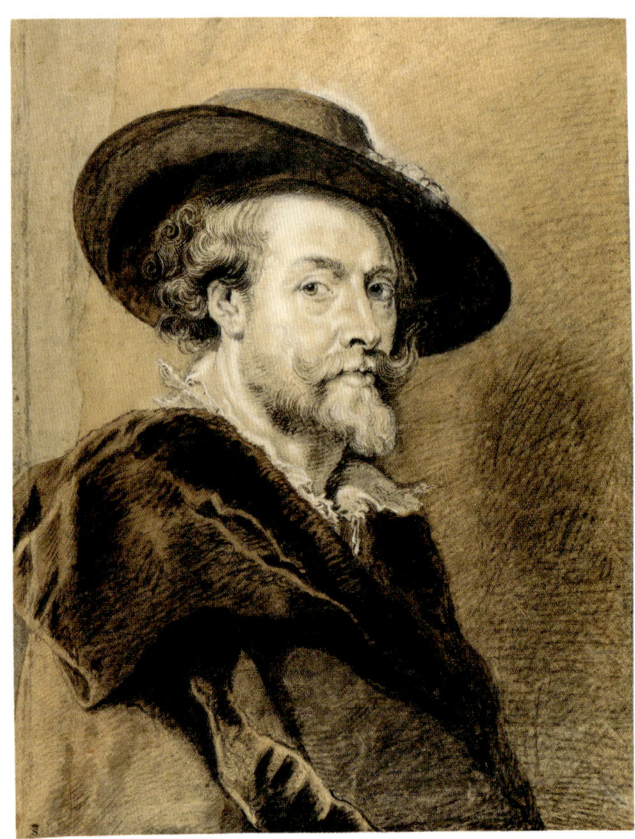

6 Paulus Pontius, nach / after Rubens
Selbstbildnis / Self-Portrait, 1623–1630
Vorzeichnung / preparatory drawing
Kreide, Feder, mit weißer Kreide gehöht und korrigiert / chalk, ink, highlights and corrections in white chalk
Köln, Wallraf-Richartz-Museum & Fondation Corboud, Inv. Dep. 2022 / 90

of light and shadow in a painterly manner.[61] It does not seem to have been important for the reproduction to be in the same direction as the original painting. Of the fifty-six engravings considered to be the core of Rubens's oeuvre, only five are actually executed in the same direction as the respective painting they interpret.[62]

By contrast, the format of a painting was generally retained in the graphic reproduction. Where an altarpiece was to be reproduced whose pictorial narratives extended across the wings of an open triptych, the preparatory drawing had to be so heavily reworked—as in the case of *The Raising of the Cross* (1638; fig. pp. 204–205)—that Rubens himself executed a new design. However, even in the case of this new version, the horizontal format was retained. The only exception to this rule is *The Miraculous Draught* (1633–38; fig. 7), based on the slender portrait-format side wing of an altarpiece in Mechelen, which Rubens redesigned in a horizontal format.[63]

The high standards Rubens applied to the graphical realization, evident in his corrections, prevented him from trying his hand at the field of printmaking himself. Although he may have practiced

wirksame Geringschätzung der „Reproduktionsgraphik“ gegenüber der „Originalgraphik“ mündete, in der ein Künstler seinen eigenen Entwurf selbst umgesetzt hatte.[66]

Für Rubens war die eigenhändige Ausführung kein Kriterium. Sein Ziel war allein eine virtuose graphische Umsetzung, die geeignet war, dem Medium neue Qualitäten abzuringen. Auf dem Gebiet des reproduzierenden Holzschnittes gelang ihm das im letzten Jahrzehnt seines Lebens mit Hilfe des Formschneiders Christoffel Jegher (1596–1652/53), der dem Holzschnitt als traditioneller Technik in den Jahren der Zusammenarbeit mit Rubens zwischen 1632 und 1634 völlig neue Facetten abgewann. Auch

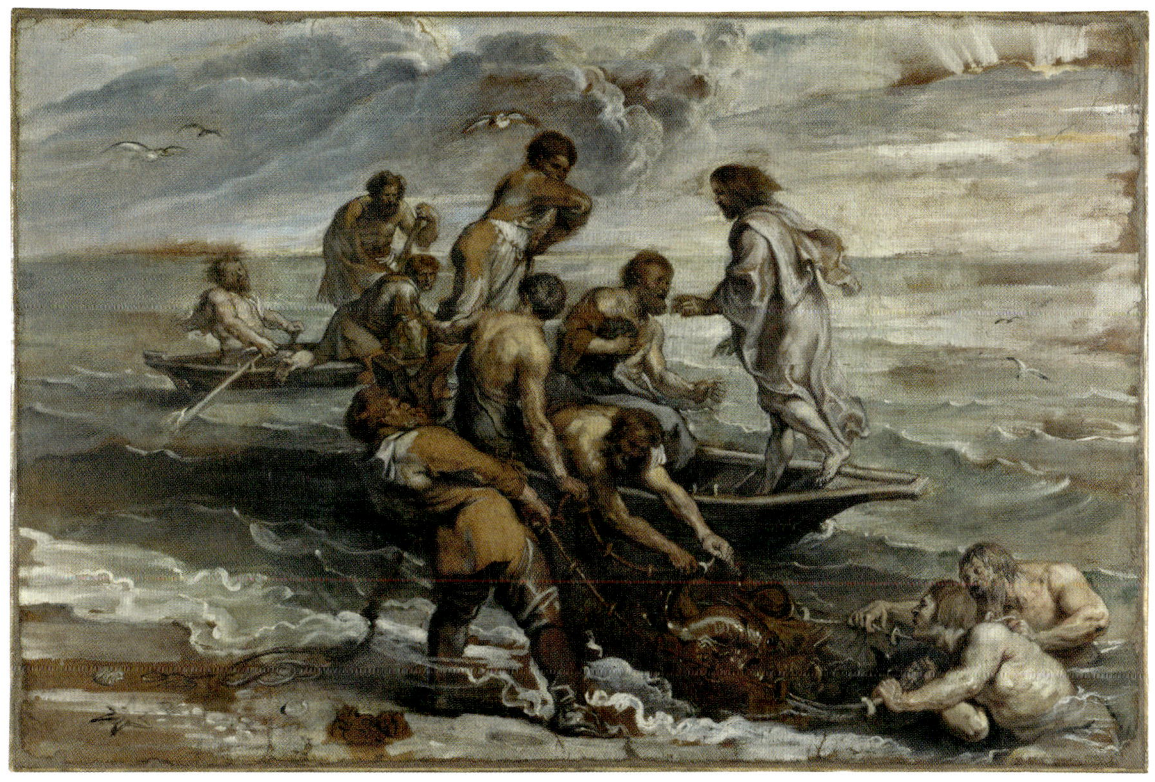

7 Peter Paul Rubens
Der wunderbare Fischzug / The Miraculous Draught, ca. 1618/19, vollendet / finished 1633–1638
Vorzeichnung / preparatory drawing
Schwarze Kreide und Öl auf Papier auf Leinwand / black chalk and oil on paper on canvas London, National Gallery, Inv. 680

the technique of etching once, he never progressed beyond the stage of initial experimentation with the etching needle. The print *St. Catherine* (1621–1630; figs. pp. 178–179), based on one of the ceiling paintings for the Jesuit church in Antwerp, remained unpublished during the painter's lifetime.[64] It was only after his death that the unfinished plate was completed with the burin, probably by Lucas Vorsterman, although the additions have also been attributed to Schelte à Bolswert or Pieter Soutman (1593/1601–1657).[65] Rubens and his contemporaries attached more importance to precise reproductions that were impressive in terms of their format and painterly effect than to the individuality of the graphical rendering. The latter was only established as a criterion of quality by French art theory in the eighteenth century and led to a disdain for “reproductive prints” as opposed to “original prints” (where an artist had realized his own design himself) which continues to this day.[66]

von Jeghers Holzschnitten haben sich Umdrucke (Abb. S. 183) und Abzüge mit von Rubens angebrachten Korrekturen erhalten, die zeigen, dass Rubens auf ein das Publikum überwältigendes visuelles Gesamtbild abzielte. Dieser Anspruch wird schon in der Auswahl der Motive deutlich, wie dem in starker Untersicht gezeigten *Herkules erschlägt die Missgunst* (1633–1635; Abb. S. 182).[67] Jegher reproduzierte eines der Bildfelder aus der Decke des Banqueting House in London, die Rubens kurz zuvor entworfen hatte.[68] Diese Technik hatte einen plakativen Effekt, der auch auf größere Distanz zu wirken vermochte und doch dazu einlud, die Details zu studieren. Zumal mit den in einigen Fällen zusätzlich aufgedruckten farbigen Partien boten diese Drucke dem interessierten Publikum ein staunenswertes druckgraphisches Experiment (Abb. S. 184 f., 266). Anders als die Kupferstiche wurden die Holzschnitte Jeghers nicht nachgeahmt und kopiert, wobei die von anderen Formschneidern nicht wieder erreichte Technik sicher ein besserer Schutz vor Nachahmung war als der auf einigen der Holzschnitte mitgedruckte Vermerk „CUM PRIVILEGIIS".

PRIVILEGIEN

Seit dem Jahr 1618 bemühte sich Rubens, ein Privileg für die nach seinen Inventionen gestochenen Werke zu erlangen. Er nutzte seine weitgespannten persönlichen und politischen Kontakte, um für die von ihm beauftragten Druckgraphiken Privilegien zu erhalten. 1619 wurde ihm dieses Recht durch den „allerchristlichsten" französischen König zuerkannt, außerdem von Erzherzog Albrecht VII. von Österreich (1559–1621) und seiner Frau, der spanischen Infantin Isabella Clara Eugenia (1566–1633), die seit 1598 souverän über die südlichen Niederlande herrschten.[69] Spätestens seit dem Waffenstillstand von 1609 war es aber eine

Executing the work himself was not important to Rubens. His sole aim was a masterly graphical realization that was capable of wresting new qualities from the employed medium. In the field of reproductive woodcuts, he achieved this in the last decade of his life with the help of the woodcutter Christoffel Jegher (1596–1652/53), who took the traditional technique of woodcutting to completely new heights in the years he worked with Rubens, from 1632 to 1634. Surviving prints and counterproofs of Jegher's woodcuts (fig. p. 183) with corrections made by Rubens show that he intended to create a dazzling visual effect that would overwhelm the viewer. This ambition is evident in the choice of motifs as well, such as *Hercules Slaying Envy* (1633–35; fig. p. 182), depicted in pronounced low-angle perspective.[67] For this work, Jegher reproduced one of the panels from the ceiling of the Banqueting House in London, which Rubens had designed shortly before.[68] The technique Jegher employed had a striking impact that was effective at a greater distance while simultaneously inviting the viewer to study the details. With the addition of printed colored sections in particular, as was done in some cases (figs. pp. 184–185, 266), these prints presented an astonishing sense of experimentation in printmaking to an interested audience. Unlike the copper engravings, Jegher's woodcuts were not imitated or copied, with protection against imitation lying more in other woodcutters' inability to achieve the applied technique rather than in the note "CUM PRIVILEGIIS" that was printed on some of the woodcuts.

politisch anerkannte Realität, dass die sieben nördlichen Provinzen ein eigenes Staatswesen waren. Rubens bemühte sich auch für die vereinigten niederländischen Provinzen ein Privileg zu erhalten und sandte 1619 eine Liste von begonnenen und geplanten Stichen an den als Vermittler in dieser Sache tätigen Bruder seines einstigen Lehrers, den Advokaten Pieter van Veen (1563–1629), der in Den Haag lebte und arbeitete.[70] Die Liste ist ein interessantes Dokument, da sie von Rubens' Ambitionen auf dem Gebiet der graphischen Reproduktion seiner Werke zeugt (Abb. 8). Dem Ansinnen war allerdings erst Erfolg beschieden, nachdem sich der kunstsinnige englische Gesandte am Hof in Den Haag für Rubens verwandt hatte. Zum Dank für seinen Einsatz widmete Rubens Sir Dudley Carleton (1573–1632) im Jahr 1620 den Kupferstich nach seiner *Kreuzabnahme* (Abb. S. 207), der bereits mit dem dreifachen Privileg erschien: „Mit den Privilegien des allerchristlichen Königs, der [süd-]niederländischen Fürsten und der [nord-]niederländischen Generalstände."[71]

Die meisten Verleger hofften mit dem Erwerb eines Privilegs die Investitionen zu schützen, die in Herstellung und Vertrieb geflossen waren, da sie um den Verkaufserlös fürchten mussten, wenn ihre Produkte nachgeahmt wurden.[72] Für Rubens dürften die mit Blick auf seine sonstigen Einkünfte geringen

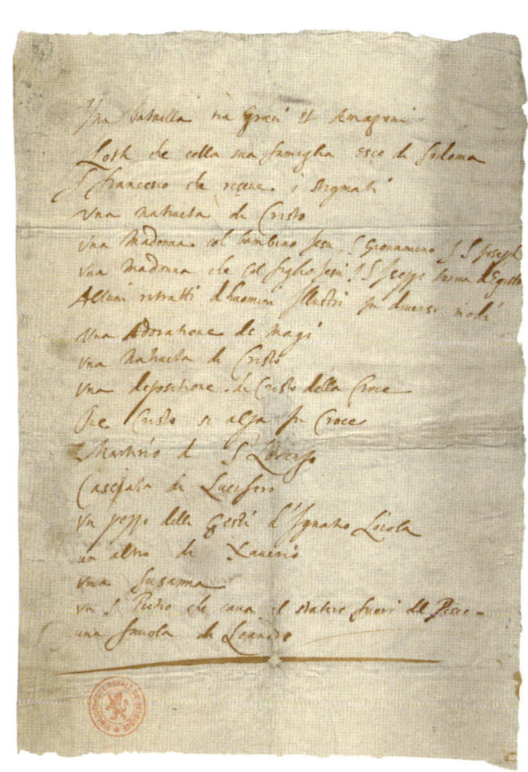

8 Seite aus einem Brief von Rubens an Pieter van Veen mit einer Liste geplanter Stiche, 23. Januar 1619 / page from a letter from Rubens to Pieter van Veen with a list of planned prints, January 23, 1619
Brussel, Koninklijke Bibliotheek van België, Sig. Ms. II 1559.3r

PRIVILEGES

Beginning in 1618, Rubens endeavored to obtain a privilege for the works engraved after his inventions, using his extensive personal and political contacts for this purpose. In 1619, this right was granted to him by the "most Christian" French king, as well as by Archduke Albert VII of Austria (1559–1621) and his wife, the Spanish Infanta Isabella Clara Eugenia (1566–1633), who had been the governors of the Southern Netherlands since 1598.[69] Since the truce of 1609 at the latest, however, it was a politically recognized reality that the seven Northern provinces were a separate state. Rubens thus also endeavored to obtain a privilege for the United Provinces of the Netherlands and in 1619 sent a list of engravings he had begun and planned to his former teacher's brother, the advocate Pieter van Veen (1563–1629), who lived and worked in The Hague.[70] This list is an interesting document, as it testifies to Rubens's ambitions in the field of reproductive prints of his works (fig. 8). However, his request was only successful after the art-loving English envoy to the court in The Hague interceded on Rubens's behalf. In 1620, Rubens thanked Sir Dudley Carleton (1573–1632) for his efforts by dedicating to him the engraving after his *The Descent from the Cross* (fig. p. 207), which was released with a triple privilege: "With the Privileges of the most Christian King, the Belgian governors, and the Dutch Estates-General."[71]

Herstellungskosten nicht der zentrale Beweggrund gewesen sein. Auch ging es ihm sicher nicht um den Schutz geistigen Eigentums. Die Privilegien schützten nicht die Rechte der Bilderfinder, sondern wurden stets dem für Vertrieb und Verkauf zuständigen Verleger zuerkannt, der eher selten mit dem entwerfenden Künstler identisch war, wie das bei vielen Rubens-Graphiken der Fall ist.[73] Dabei beantragte Rubens auch Privilegien für in seinem Auftrag hergestellte Reproduktionen, die nicht auf seine Bilderfindungen zurückgingen. Rubens und seinen Zeitgenossen galt das Kopieren von Werken anderer sogar als eine Form der Ehrbezeugung. So zum Beispiel, wenn Rubens nach seinen gezeichneten oder gemalten Kopien von Werken Bruegels, Tizians oder Leonardos graphische Reproduktionen anfertigen ließ. Das von zwei Platten gedruckte Blatt zeigt, so die Stichunterschrift, „das staunenerregende Abendmahl des Leonardo da Vinci, der in den Armen des Königs von Frankreich starb" (1632; Abb. S. 246 f.).[74] Ausweislich der Unterschrift hatte Pieter Soutman es nach einer Zeichnung umgesetzt, die Rubens nach dem Gemälde Leonardos angefertigt hatte. Dabei ist augenfällig, dass es bei der Reproduktion nicht zwingend um die möglichst exakte Abbildung von Leonardos Fresko ging. Abgesehen von der Seitenverkehrung, die einem auf beinahe allen Stichen nach Rubens begegnet, wenn nicht gerade die segnende oder zum Kampf erhobene Hand einer im Bild gezeigten Figur zwingend die Seitenrichtigkeit vorgab, hat Rubens auch tiefgreifende kompositionelle und inhaltliche Änderungen vorgenommen. Statt der von Leonardo gezeigten Architektur ist zur Betonung der Figur Christi ein Vorhang eingesetzt und der bei Leonardo dezent gedeckte Tisch ist fast vollständig geleert. Auch das Thema hat sich verschoben, worauf auch die Stichunterschrift verweist: von der Ankündigung des Verrates, der in Leonardos Gemälde in den Physiognomien so deutlich ablesbar ist,

By acquiring a privilege, most publishers hoped to protect the investments they had made in production and distribution, as they feared that they would lose sales revenue if their products were imitated.[72] This was probably not the main motivation for Rubens, as the production costs were low in view of his other income. Nor was he, in all likelihood, concerned with protecting intellectual property. The privileges did not protect the rights of the inventors of images, after all, but were granted to the publisher responsible for distribution and sales, who—unlike in Rubens's case—was rarely the same person as the designing artist.[73] Rubens also applied for privileges for reproductions he commissioned that were not based on his own pictorial inventions. He and his contemporaries even regarded copying the works of others as a form of tribute. For example, Rubens had reproductive prints made after his drawn or painted copies of works by Bruegel, Titian, and Leonardo. According to the engraved caption, one sheet, printed from two plates, shows "The Astonishing [Last] Supper by Leonardo da Vinci, Who Died in the Arms of the King of France" (1632; fig. pp. 246–247).[74] According to the signature, Pieter Soutman realized the engraving after a drawing that Rubens had made after Leonardo's painting. What is striking is that the reproduction was not necessarily intended to depict Leonardo's fresco as accurately as possible. Apart from the print showing the motif in reverse—as was the case in almost all engravings after Rubens, except for when the hand of a depicted figure, either blessing or raised in battle, prescribed the same direction as the original—he also made far-reaching changes to the composition and content. Instead of the architecture shown by Leonardo, a curtain has been inserted to emphasize the figure of Christ, and the table set discreetly

auf den Beginn des Abendmahls. Sowohl die Verbreitung einer fremden Bilderfindung wie auch eine derartige Veränderung des Bildsinns würden heute als Verletzung des Copyrights juristisch geahndet. Doch das heute so selbstverständliche Urheberrecht an einer Bilderfindung gab es zu Rubens' Zeit noch nicht. Insgesamt wurden 56 Stiche mit dem dreifachen Privileg des Künstlers publiziert, das aber nicht das Bildmotiv, sondern die für die Herstellung der Graphik unternommene Investition schützte.

Wenn Rubens sich in einem Prozess gegen einen französischen Kopisten bemühte, sein Privileg durchzusetzen, dann ging es ihm vor allem darum, auf dem internationalen Markt seine hohen Qualitätsmaßstäbe zu realisieren. Wie gezeigt, legte er bei der Herstellung der Reproduktionen seiner Werke höchste Qualitätsstandards an, die er mit seinem Namen verbunden sehen wollte. Um sie bei allen Werken sicherzustellen, die mit seinem Namen verknüpft waren, bedurfte er eines Privilegs, das ihn vor schlechten Nachahmungen und entstellenden Kopien schützte. Zugleich wird es noch um etwas anderes gegangen sein, das mit der modernen Vorstellung von einem Privileg als „Copyright" auf eine künstlerische Idee ebenfalls wenig zu tun hat. Die Vergabe von Privilegien wurde nämlich von Seiten der Regierungen auch als Medium politischer Kontrolle eingesetzt. So durften weder in den südlichen Niederlanden noch in Frankreich Graphiken vertrieben werden, die nicht einem Zensor vorgelegen hatten und mit einem Vertriebsprivileg versehen waren.[75] Als es darum ging, ein Privileg für die nördlichen Provinzen zu erwerben, war es deshalb das zentrale Argument, dass Rubens' Graphiken kein geheimer oder politischer Sinn innewohne.[76] Die Notwendigkeit, ein Privileg zu erhalten, um seine Blätter vertreiben zu dürfen, illustriert ein Brief, den Rubens 1635 an Peiresc sandte und in dem er die Befürchtung ausspricht, seine

by Leonardo is almost completely empty. The subject has also shifted, as the caption points out, from the announcement of the betrayal, so clearly visible in the facial expressions in Leonardo's painting, to the start of the Last Supper. Both the dissemination of someone else's pictorial invention and such an alteration of its pictorial meaning would today be punishable by law as an infringement of copyright. But the copyright for a pictorial invention, which is taken for granted today, did not exist in Rubens's time. A total of fifty-six engravings were published with the artist's triple privilege, whose purpose was not, however, to protect the motif but rather the investment made in producing the print.

When Rubens sought to assert his privilege in a lawsuit against a French copyist, he was primarily concerned with enforcing his high quality standards on the international market. As shown above, he applied the highest quality standards to the reproductions of his works and wanted this excellence to be associated with his name. In order to ensure this for all works linked to his name, he needed a privilege that protected him from poor imitations and distorted copies. At the same time, there must have been something else at stake, which again has little to do with the modern notion of a privilege as a "copyright" on an artistic idea. The granting of privileges was, for example, also used by governments as a means of political control. Thus, neither in the Southern Netherlands nor in France were prints allowed to be distributed unless they had been submitted to a censor and granted a distribution privilege.[75] When it came to acquiring a privilege for the Northern provinces, the key argument was therefore that Rubens's prints had no secret or political meaning.[76] The necessity of obtaining a privilege to distribute his prints is illustrated by a letter that Rubens

Stiche nicht in Frankreich vertreiben zu dürfen.[77] Eine solche Einschränkung wäre wohl der Mehrung seines künstlerischen Ruhmes gar zu abträglich gewesen.

WIDMUNGEN

Die in allen europäischen Staaten strenge Zensur musste Rubens nicht fürchten, da seine Stiche mehrheitlich religiöse Themen und Motive zeigten, die katholischen und protestantischen Kunden gleichermaßen vertraut waren. Von dem Kundenkreis, den Rubens für die gedruckten Reproduktionen im Sinn hatte, zeugen auch die auf vielen Blättern angebrachten Widmungen. Die bei Weitem meisten Stiche nach Rubens' Gemälden tragen Widmungen der Stecher und sind nicht vom Maler dediziert. Die Verpflichtung, die den bedachten Personen aus solcher Dedikation erwuchs, wird in der kulturellen Praxis ablesbar, derartige Zueignungen in barer Münze zu vergelten.[78] Die dafür gezahlten Beträge dürften dabei vor allem für die Stecher interessant gewesen sein, die die gedruckten Blätter als Leistung ihrer Handwerkskunst gerne hochstehenden Persönlichkeiten zueigneten. Es scheint, als habe Rubens nach seiner Auseinandersetzung mit Vorsterman keine Versuche mehr unternommen, daran zu rühren und auf einer Dedikation in seinem Namen zu bestehen. Mit Ausnahme der Widmung unter dem ersten Reproduktionsstich, *Judith enthauptet Holofernes* (1616; Abb. S. 113), sind fast alle persönlichen Dedikationen von Rubens unter den wenigen Blättern zu finden, die von Vorsterman gestochen wurden. Jene fünfzehn von den mehr als hundert in seinem Auftrag entstandenen Kupferstiche, die mit einer persönlichen Widmung von Rubens versehen sind, wurden dabei in der Hauptsache dem Bekannten- und Freundeskreis des ersten Jahrzehnts seiner Antwerpener Zeit

sent to Peiresc in 1635, in which he expressed his fear that he would not be allowed to distribute his engravings in France.[77] Such a restriction would have been too detrimental for the growth of his artistic fame.

DEDICATIONS

Rubens did not have to fear the strict censorship prevalent in all European countries, as the majority of his engravings depicted religious themes and motifs that were equally acceptable to Catholic and Protestant customers. The dedications on many prints also bear witness to the clientele Rubens had in mind for the printed reproductions. The vast majority of engravings after Rubens's paintings bear dedications by the engravers rather than the painter. Such dedications obliged the recipients to take part in the cultural practice of rewarding these in cash.[78] These sums were probably of particular interest to the engravers, who aspired to dedicate the prints to high-ranking personalities as a mark of their outstanding craftsmanship. It seems that after his dispute with Vorsterman, Rubens made no further attempts to address this matter or insist on a dedication in his name. With the exception of the dedication beneath the first engraved reproduction, *Judith Beheading Holofernes* (1616; fig. p. 113), almost all of Rubens's personal dedications can be found among the few prints engraved by Vorsterman. The fifteen engravings bearing a personal dedication by Rubens—out of more than one hundred engravings commissioned in total—were mainly dedicated to his circle of friends and acquaintances during his first decade in Antwerp.[79] Unlike his engravers, Rubens was probably interested not in pecuniary gain but in other forms of obligation that were effective in social relationships.

dediziert.[79] Anders als seinen Stechern dürfte es Rubens auch hier nicht um den pekuniären Vorteil gegangen sein, sondern vielmehr um andere Formen von Verbindlichkeiten, die in seinem sozialen Beziehungsgefüge wirksam waren. So dankte er beispielsweise mit der Widmung der *Kreuzaufrichtung* seinem Freund Cornelis van der Geest (1577–1638) für die Vermittlung des Auftrages für das Altarwerk gleichen Themas (Abb. S. 204 f.). In anderen Dedikationen dankte Rubens Männern, die ihn bei der Beschaffung von Vertriebsprivilegien unterstützt hatten, wie Pieter van Veen, oder Persönlichkeiten, von deren intellektuellem, militärischem oder fürstlichem Ruhm er durch die gemeinsame Nennung ihrer Namen profitieren konnte.[80] Die illustre Gesellschaft verlieh seinem Namen Glanz und wird zu seinem Ruhm beigetragen haben. Gerade die von ihm entworfenen 58 Buch-Titelblätter dürften hierzu einen nicht unwesentlichen Beitrag geleistet haben, die von frühen Sammlern als bedeutender Teil seines druckgraphischen Werkes zusammengetragen wurden.[81]

Rubens' Engagement auf dem Gebiet der graphischen Reproduktion seiner Bilderfindungen zielte fraglos auf die Mehrung seines künstlerischen Ruhmes. Das verdeutlicht auch ein Brief, den der Maler im Zusammenhang mit seinen Auseinandersetzungen um ein französisches Privileg 1635 an Peiresc sandte. Er würde, so heißt es darin, gegebenenfalls darauf verzichten, seine Stiche in Frankreich zu verbreiten: „Wenn also die ganze Schwierigkeit nur darin besteht, so gebe ich gern zu, dass man meine Stiche aus dem Königreiche Frankreich verbanne; ich begnüge mich mit dem übrigen Europa, um Ehren zu erlangen, was ich weit höher schätze als alle anderen Vorteile."[82] Durch die graphische Vervielfältigung erfuhren Rubens' Bilder eine ungeheure Verbreitung. Die in höchster technischer Perfektion ausgeführten Reproduktionen machten seine Kompositionen in ganz Europa bekannt und trugen zur Hebung seiner

For example, he thanked his friend Cornelis van der Geest (1577–1638) for procuring the commission for the altarpiece with the same subject by dedicating *The Raising of the Cross* to him (fig. pp. 204–205). In other dedications, Rubens thanked men who had supported him in obtaining distribution privileges, such as Pieter van Veen (1562–1629), or personalities from whose intellectual, military, or princely renown he could benefit by the joint mention of their names.[80] The illustrious company added glamour to his name and would have contributed to his fame. In particular, the fifty-eight book title pages he designed—considered an important part of his printed work by early collectors—are likely to have made a significant contribution to this effect.[81]

Rubens's commitment to the printed reproduction of his pictorial inventions was undoubtedly aimed at increasing his artistic fame. This is illustrated by a letter that the painter sent to Peiresc in 1635 in connection with his disputes over a French privilege. According to the letter, he would refrain from distributing his engravings in France if necessary: "If this, therefore, constitutes the difficulty, I am willing to have my prints banished from all the kingdom of France; there is enough opportunity in the rest of Europe for me to gain some honor, which I esteem more than any other profit."[82] Thanks to printed reproductions, Rubens's pictures became immensely popular. These reproductions, executed to the highest technical perfection, made his compositions known throughout Europe and helped to enhance his artistic reputation and prestige. At the same time, however, they also disseminated their own unique graphical repertoire and the specific style of the Rubens print, which was adapted by numerous artists and used both for reproductions and their own graphical inventions.

künstlerischen Reputation und seines Ansehens bei. Zugleich aber verbreiteten sie auch das ihnen eigene graphische Repertoire und den spezifischen Stil der Rubens-Graphik, der von zahlreichen Künstlern adaptiert und für Reproduktionen, aber auch für eigene graphische Inventionen aufgegriffen wurde.

RUHM UND NACHRUHM

Rubens hat sehr systematisch darauf hingewirkt, seine Werke und damit auch sich selbst international bekannt zu machen. Dabei wurden nur die wenigsten Reproduktionen seiner Werke unter seiner Aufsicht hergestellt. Insgesamt sind es knapp hundert Blätter, die tatsächlich in seinem Auftrag und unter seiner Kontrolle produziert und vertrieben wurden. Diese Rubens-Graphiken wurden, kaum publiziert, vielfach kopiert und nachgeahmt. Man kann davon ausgehen, dass die Verbreitung seiner Bilder schon im Wissen darum geschah, dass die Drucke von anderen Künstlern als Vorlagen genutzt werden würden. Bis weit ins 18. Jahrhundert entstanden, um den nicht nachlassenden Bedarf an Rubens-Gemälden zu stillen, gemalte Kopien der Kupferstiche, die teils im gleichen Format ausgeführt waren. Ein typisches Beispiel dafür ist die von Johann Christian Sperling (1689–1746) ausgeführte Kopie (Abb. 9) nach einem Reproduktionsstich Vorstermans, den Rubens 1620 Erzherzog Albrecht gewidmet hatte (Abb. S. 115).[83] Sperlings um das Jahr 1730 entstandene *Anbetung der Könige* hing dabei in der Gemäldegalerie des Schlosses Ludwigsburg beinahe unmittelbar neben einer weiteren gemalten Kopie von unbekannter Hand, die die gleiche zugrunde liegende Komposition seitenrichtig zeigte.[84] Zur Allgegenwart von Rubens' Kompositionen in fürstlichen Gemäldegalerien und bürgerlichen Sammlungen kamen unzählige von Rubens inspirierte Bildwerke, mit denen zumal in den Jahrhunderten nach seinem Tod auch zahlreiche protestantische Kirchen geschmückt wurden.[85] Die Ausstrahlung reichte über den protestantischen Norden Deutschlands bis weit nach Skandinavien.[86] Mit Missionaren und auf Handelsschiffen erreichten Rubens' Bilderfindungen den amerikanischen Kontinent, genauer die kanadische Provinz Québec, Mexiko und Argentinien, aber auch Afrika, Asien und Australien.[87] Vor allem dank der druckgraphischen Reproduktionen wurde Rubens zum ersten globalen Künstler. Die enorme Wirkung seiner Bilderfindungen ist bis heute nicht erloschen und auch die technisch virtuosen graphischen Reproduktionen vermögen bis heute zu faszinieren.

1 Zu Rubens' Reise durch Holland vgl. Büttner 2023a. Zur Rubens-Vita des Joachim von Sandrart vgl. Büttner 2015b.

2 Sandrart 1675, Bd. 2, S. 252, 254. Zu diesen Zeichnungen ausführlich Lohse Belkin 2009, Bd. 1, S. 110–143, Nr. 14–58 und S. 155–166, Nr. 65–73; Bd. 2, Abb. 52–143 und S. 163–196.

3 Vgl. Jaffé 2021.

4 Denhaene 1990, S. 283, Abb. 345, für die Rezeption der *Kauernden Venus* des Doidalsas, die auch Rubens studierte und zitierte. Zu Lambert Lombards Auseinandersetzung mit *Herkules und Anteaus* ebd., S. 285, Abb. 346, S. 301, Abb. 371, S. 146, Abb. 164; diese ist gut mit Rubens' Zeichnung mit Herkulestaten im British Museum vergleichbar (um 1630–1635). Vgl. Held 1986, S. 10, 28, 107, 154, Nr. 217, Taf. 216; vgl. auch Wouk 2018.

5 Vgl. Baroni Vannucci 1997, Bd. 1, S. 141, Abb. 8, zu Federico Zuccaros *Moses und Aaron*-Fresko in den Belvedere-Apartments; zu Corts 1567 entstandenem Stich ebd., S. 145, Abb. 25; vgl. auch Jaffé 1966, Bd. 2, fol. 35r, S. 230.

6 Vgl. Pollack 2020; Münster 1976, S. 48.

7 Grundlegend dazu Balis (2001) 2023 sowie den in Vorbereitung befindlichen Band des Corpus Rubenianum Ludwig Burchard.

8 Mit den formierenden Vorbildern des jungen Rubens und der Frage, wie es ihm gelang, aus dieser etwas biederen akademischen Tradition auszubrechen, hat sich David Jaffé ausführlich auseinandergesetzt. Vgl. London 2005, bes. S. 11–20; siehe auch Anm. 3.

9 Schon Giovanni Pietro Bellori (1613–1696) hat diesen Anspruch des theoretischen Studienbuchs erkannt und treffend beschrieben: „Non era egli semplice pratico ma erudito, essendosi veduto un libro di sua mano, in cui si contengono osservazioni di ottica, simmetria, proporzioni, anatomia, architettura, ed una ricerca de' principali affetti ed azzioni cavati da descrizzioni di poeti, con le dimostrazioni de pittori. Vi sono battaglie, naufragi, giuochi, amori ed altre passioni ed avvenimenti, trascritti alcuni versi di Virgilio e d'altri, con rincontri principalmente di Rafaelle e dell'antico." Vgl. Bellori (1672) 2020, S. 112 f.

10 Vgl. hierzu Müller/Pfisterer 2011, hier bes. die Beiträge Silver 2011 und Büttner 2011b.

11 Mander 1604, Bd. 1, S. 395, fol. 284, sowie den Kommentar in Bd. 5, S. 201; Leesberg 2017a.

12 Siehe Anm. 10.

13 Siehe Abb. S. 110, 198 f. im vorliegenden Katalog.

14 Vgl. Lohse Belkin 2009, S. 36.

15 Vgl. ebd., S. 219 f., Nr. 110, Abb. 310; Reznicek 1992.

16 Für diese und weitere Beobachtungen vgl. Sonnabend 2018.

17 Rooses/Ruelens 1887–1909, Bd. 1 (1887), S. 145: „che mai patirò avendo avuto sempre per raccommandato il confondermi con nessuno qual si voglia grand huomo."

18 Der Neffe des Malers hatte dem Maler und Kunstschriftsteller Roger de Piles 1676 seinen Eindruck mitgeteilt, dass Rubens' vor der Reise nach Italien entstandene Werke „eine gewisse Ähnlichkeit mit denen von Otto Van Veen hatten, seinem Meister" („ils avoient quelque ressemblance avec ceux d'Octave Van Veen, son maistre"). Vgl. Ruelens 1883, S. 166. Die Aussage wird durch zahlreiche in ihrer Zuschreibung umstrittene Gemälde

FAME AND POSTHUMOUS REPUTATION

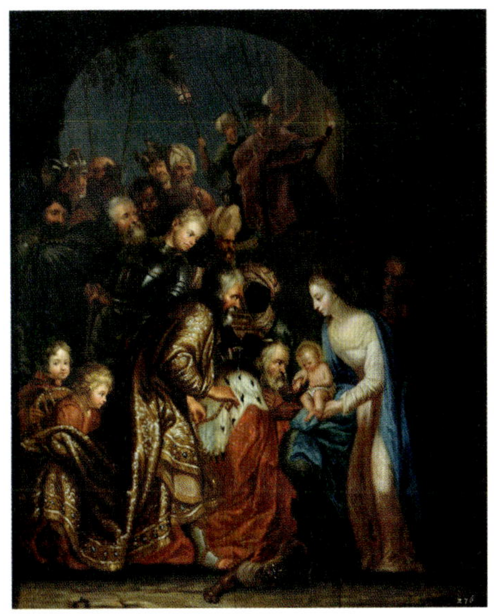

9 Johann Christian Sperling, nach / after Rubens
Die Anbetung der Könige /
The Adoration of the Magi, ca. 1730
Öl auf Holz / oil on panel
Schloss Ludwigsburg, Staatliche Schlösser und Gärten Baden-Württemberg, Inv. Sch.L. 4256

Rubens worked highly systematically to make his works—and thus also himself—internationally known. However, very few reproductions of his works were created under his supervision. In total, just under a hundred prints were actually produced and distributed on his behalf and under his control. These Rubens prints were copied and imitated many times as soon as they were published. It can be assumed that his pictures were distributed in the knowledge that the prints would be used as templates by other artists. To satisfy the ever-increasing demand for Rubens paintings, painted copies of the engravings were created well into the eighteenth century, some of them executed in the same size and format as the prints. A typical example of this is the copy created by Johann Christian Sperling (1689–1746) (fig. 9) after a reproduced engraving by Vorsterman that Rubens had dedicated to Archduke Albert (1620; fig. p. 115).[83] Sperling's *The Adoration of the Magi*, painted around 1730, hung in the picture gallery of Ludwigsburg Palace almost directly next to another painted copy by an unknown hand, which showed the composition in the same direction.[84] In addition to the omnipresence of Rubens's compositions in princely picture galleries and bourgeois collections, countless works inspired by Rubens were also used to decorate numerous Protestant churches, especially in the centuries following his death.[85] His influence reached far beyond the Protestant north of Germany to Scandinavia.[86] Through missionaries and on merchant ships, Rubens's pictorial inventions reached the American continent—more precisely the Canadian province of Quebec, Mexico, and Argentina—as well as Africa, Asia, and Australia.[87] Rubens became the first global artist, primarily thanks to his printed reproductions. The enormous impact of his pictorial inventions has not waned to this day, and the technical mastery of the reproductive prints, too, is as fascinating as ever.

1 On Rubens's journey through Holland, see Büttner 2023a. On Joachim von Sandrart's life of Rubens, see Büttner 2015b.

2 Sandrart 1675, vol. 2, pp. 252, 254. For detailed information on these drawings, see Lohse Belkin 2009, vol. 1, pp. 110–143, nos. 14–58, and pp. 155–166, nos. 65–73; vol. 2, figs. 52–143 and pp. 163–196.

3 See Jaffé 2021.

4 See Denhaene 1990, p. 283, fig. 345, on the reception of the *Crouching Venus* by Daedalsas, which Rubens also studied and invoked. On Lambert Lombard's discussion of *Hercules and Antaeus*, see Denhaene 1990, p. 285, fig. 346, p. 301, fig. 371, p. 146, fig. 164; this is readily comparable with Rubens's drawing of the deeds of Hercules in the British Museum (ca. 1630–1635). See Held 1986, pp. 10, 28, 107, 154, no. 217, pl. 216; see also Wouk 2018.

5 See Baroni Vannucci 1997, vol. 1, p. 141, fig. 8, on Federico Zuccaro's *Moses and Aaron* fresco in the Belvedere Apartments; on Cort's 1567 engraving see Baroni Vannucci 1997, p. 145, fig. 25; see also Jaffé 1966, vol. 2, fol. 35r, p. 230.

6 See Pollack 2020; Münster 1976, p. 48.

7 For foundational information on this, see Balis (2001) 2023 and the forthcoming volume of the *Corpus Rubenianum Ludwig Burchard*.

8 David Jaffé has dealt extensively with the formative role models of the young Rubens and the question of how he succeeded in breaking out of this somewhat tame academic tradition. See London 2005, esp. pp. 11–20; see also note 3 above.

9 Giovanni Pietro Bellori (1613–1696) already recognized and aptly described this aspiration of the theoretical notebook: "Non era egli semplice pratico ma erudito, essendosi veduto un libro di sua mano, in cui si contengono osservazioni di ottica, simmetria, proporzioni, anatomia, architettura, ed una ricerca de' principali affetti ed azzioni cavati da descrizzioni di poeti, con le dimostrazioni de pittori. Vi sono battaglie, naufragi, giuochi, amori ed altre passioni ed avvenimenti, trascritti alcuni versi di Virgilio e d'altri, con rincontri principalmente di Rafaelle e dell'antico." See Bellori (1672) 2020, pp. 112–113.

10 See Müller/Pfisterer 2011, esp. the contributions Silver 2011 and Büttner 2011b.

11 Mander (1604) 1916, vol. 1, p. 395, fol. 284, as well as the commentary in vol. 5, p. 201; Leesberg 2017a.

12 See note 10.

13 See figs. pp. 110, 198–199 in this catalog.

14 See Lohse Belkin 2009, p. 36.

15 See Lohse Belkin 2009, pp. 219–220, no. 110, fig. 310; Reznicek 1992.

16 For these and other observations, see Sonnabend 2018.

17 Rooses/Ruelens 1887–1909, vol. 1 (1887), p. 145: "che mai patirò avendo avuto sempre per raccommandato il confondermi con nessuno qual si voglia grand huomo."

18 The painter's nephew had told the painter and art writer Roger de Piles in 1676 of his impression that Rubens's works created before his journey to Italy "bore a certain resemblance to those of Otto van Veen, his master" ("ils avoient quelque ressemblance avec ceux d'Octave Van Veen, son maistre"). See Ruelens 1883, p. 166. This statement is confirmed by numerous paintings whose attribution is disputed and which are alternately attributed to Rubens and Van Veen. See on this Jaffé 2021.

19 See Atkins 2012.

bestätigt, die wechselnd mal Rubens, mal van Veen zugeschrieben werden. Vgl. dazu Jaffé 2021.

19 Vgl. Atkins 2012.

20 Vgl. Rooses/Ruelens 1887–1909, Bd. 1 (1887), S. 354; Zoff 1918. Zu dem Auftrag siehe Mühlen 1998 und zuletzt Paolini 2022.

21 Vgl. Büttner 2006, S. 42.

22 Vgl. Sweertius 1613, S. 143; Génard 1877, S. 17, 390.

23 Rubens, *Papst Gregor der Große und andere Heilige*, 1607/08, Öl auf Leinwand, 477 × 288 cm, Grenoble, Musée de Grenoble, Inv. MG 97; siehe Vlieghe 1972, Bd. 2, S. 43–50, Nr. 109.

24 Monballieu 1965, S. 196.

25 Vgl. Büttner 2006, S. 144; Büttner 2011a.

26 Vgl. Nils Büttner, in: Braunschweig 2004, S. 230–232, Nr. 47; Meier 2020a, S. 13–15, 141–144, Nr. 8.

27 Zum verschollenen Gemälde vgl. D'Hulst/Vandenven 1989, S. 158, Nr. 50. Erhalten geblieben ist aber die Vorzeichnung, ebd., S. 163, Nr. 50b.

28 Bereits am 8. März 1627 hatte Peiresc in einem Brief an den französischen Maler Jean Chalette (1581–1644) seine Freude darüber zum Ausdruck gebracht, dass Rubens sich bereiterklärt habe, ihm ein Selbstbildnis zuzusenden. Vgl. dazu Jaffé 1988; Biffis 2021, bes. S. 6 f.

29 Rooses/Ruelens 1887–1909, Bd. 4 (1904), S. 414: „Con che finisco, rendendole infinite gratie della final concessione del suo ritratto."

30 Bezeichnet: „Petrus Paullus Rubens | Se ipsum expressit | A. D. MDCXXIII." Vgl. Vlieghe 1987, S. 153 f., Nr. 135, Abb. 171, 176; Büttner 2015a, S. 39–53.

31 Vgl. Vlieghe 1987, S. 153 f., Nr. 135, Copy 1. Rooses/Ruelens 1887–1909, Bd. 5 (1907), S. 11: „Spero che V. S. haveva gia ricevuto il mio ritratto che consignai molti giorni, inanzi la mia partenza d'Anversa, al cogniato del Sr Pycqueri come egli mi haveva ordinato." Da Rubens direkt nach Versand des Gemäldes nach Spanien aufgebrochen war, blieb er lange Zeit unsicher, ob das Bild seinen Adressaten erreicht habe. Ein Brief an Pierre Dupuy erweist, dass Rubens noch am 22. April 1629 keine Eingangsbestätigung erhalten hatte, da er noch immer hoffte, „dass er es erhalten hat, da ich es einige Zeit nach meiner Abreise aus Flandern mit sicherer Post geschickt habe." Übers. n. Rooses/Ruelens 1887–1909, Bd. 5 (1907), S. 29: „mio ritratto che spero avera ricevuto poiche il mandai per via sicura qualq. tempo inanci la mia partenza di Fiandra."

32 Piles 1699, S. 396 f.: „La réputation de Rubens s'étenduë par toute l'Europe, il n'y eût pas un Peintre qui ne voulût avoir un morceau de sa main; & comme il étoit éxtrémement sollicité de toutes parts, il fit faire sur ses Desseins coloriéz, & par d'habiles Disciples un grand nombre de Tableaux, qu'il retouchoit ensuite avec des yeux frais, avec un intelligence vive, & avec une promptitude de main qui y répandoit entiérement son Esprit, ce qui luy aquit beaucoup de biens en peu de tems: mais la différence de ces fortes de Tableaux, qui passoient pour être de luy, d'avec ceux qui étoient véritablement de sa main, fit du tort à sa réputation; car ils étoient la plûpart mal dessinez, & légérement peints."

33 Sandrart 1675, Bd. 2, S. 292.

34 Dokument vom 2. November 1616, Antwerpen, FelixArchief, N#3838 (Notariaatsarchief: Kaspar Van der Herstraeten Sr.: Protocollen en staten 1615–1616), fol. 167r: „Ende tvoers. werk alsoo loffelyck ende behoirlyck gestelt ende volmaeckt synde soo sal den voers. Sgr Rubbens aen Jasper bovens die voers. beloeffde somme alnoch schenken een stuck schilderye tsy op doeck oft paneel wesende copye naer eenich stuck van synder hant gemaeckt, tselve stellende tsyner Sgr Rubbens discretie."

35 Vgl. dazu ausführlich Büttner 2008; Tieze 2012.

36 Vgl. Büttner 2017a. Grundlegend zur Werkstattpraxis sind bis heute die Beiträge von Arnout Balis; siehe Balis 1993 und Balis 2007.

37 Einen umfassenden Überblick werden die in Vorbereitung befindlichen Rubens-Bände des New Hollstein geben, die Jaco Rutgers und Simon Turner verantworten. Zur Einführung vgl. Meier 2020a und Antwerpen/Québec 2004; eine gute Zusammenfassung bieten Rutgers 2019; Kaulbach 2021.

38 Das bis heute grundlegende Verzeichnis von George Voorhelm Schneevoogt (Voorhelm Schneevoogt 1873) führte fast 2200 auf.

39 Furetière 1690, Bd. 2, o. S.: „À l'égard des Peintres & Graveurs, on appelle l'oeuvre d'un Maître, le recueil de toutes fes pièces gravées qu'on en trouve." Vgl. auch Bonne 2022.

40 Vgl. Brakensiek 2003, S. 17–39, 549–553; Büttner 2023b.

41 Hecquet 1751.

42 Basan 1767.

43 Vgl. dazu den Beitrag von Karolien De Clippel und Filip Vermeylen auf S. 24–49 in diesem Katalog. Dieser Beitrag zuvor in: De Clippel/Vermeylen 2012, S. 138–160. Zu Rubens in Holland zuletzt Büttner 2023a, S. 89–102.

44 Rubens, *Samson und Delilah*, um 1609/10, Öl auf Holz, 185 × 205 cm, London, National Gallery, Inv. NG6461. Vgl. D'Hulst/Vandenven 1989, S. 107–113, Nr. 31; Antwerpen/Wien 2007, S. 11–34; De Clippel/Vermeylen 2012, S. 149–155; Rutgers 2019, S. 107.

45 Vgl. Renger 1974a, bes. S. 147–161. Vgl. auch Nico Van Hout, in: Antwerpen/Québec 2004, S. 56–69; Büttner 2011a.

46 „Havrei ben voluto chel intagliator fosse riuscito piu esperto ad imitar ben il prototypo pur mi pare minor male di vederli fare in mia presenza", schrieb Rubens am 23. Januar 1619 an Pieter van Veen. Rooses/Ruelens 1887–1909, Bd. 2 (1898), S. 199.

47 „Vederli fare in mia presenza per mano di un giovane ben intentionato che di gran valenthuomini secondo il lor capriccio", schrieb Rubens am 23. Januar 1619 an Pieter van Veen. Rooses/Ruelens 1887–1909, Bd. 2 (1898), S. 199.

48 Vgl. Nico Van Hout, in: Antwerpen/Québec 2004, S. 55, Anm. 44; Meier 2020a, S. 31, 64–67, 187–191, Nr. 27; Bertram 2021.

49 Vgl. Held 1980, S. 395–398, Nr. 294; Vlieghe 1987, S. 67–71, Nr. 82; Gritsay/Babina 2008, S. 251–253, Nr. 309.

50 Brief vom 30. April 1622. Rooses/Ruelens 1887–1909, Bd. 2 (1898), S. 399–401.

51 „Presumendo che l'intaglio suo solo facçia valer queste stampe qualque cosa et il suo nome tanto illustre", schrieb Rubens am 30. April 1622 an van Veen. Rooses/Ruelens 1887–1909, Bd. 2 (1898), S. 399 f.

52 Vgl. Bouchery/Wijngaert 1941, S. 113 f.; Renger 1974a, S. 127, Anm. 30.

53 Vgl. dazu Carl Depauw, in: Antwerpen 1999, S. 42–71 und S. 60 f., Nr. 2.

54 Vgl. Devisscher/Vlieghe 2014, Bd. 1, S. 76–81, Nr. 15.

55 Vgl. ebd., S. 82–87, Nr. 15b; Meier 2020a, S. 52 f.

56 Vgl. Renger 1974a, S. 144; Judson/Van de Velde 1978; Bertram/Büttner 2018; Bertram 2018; Meier 2020a, bes. S. 53–55.

57 Das Entwerfen derartiger Blätter war auch ökonomisch nicht interessant, wie auch der Verkauf der gedruckten Blätter, deren Ertrag trotz großer Auflagen doch eher gering war. Vgl. Renger 1974a, S. 126 f.; Renger 1975, S. 212.

58 Vgl. Büttner 2015a, S. 148–150, Nr. 9; Meier 2020a, S. 213–215, Nr. 32.

59 Vgl. Büttner 2006, S. 106 f., 204, Anm. 148, 249. Demnächst dazu auch Thomas Klinke, Köln, der das Blatt 2023 erstmals ausführlich kunsttechnologisch untersucht hat.

60 „J'ai vu nombre de morceaux préparés par Rubens pour les gravures, et j'en possède plusieurs que M. Crozat avoit rassemblés et que Jabach avoit fait achetter autrefois à la vente du cabinet de Rubens qui se fit après la mort de ce grand peintre." Chennevières/Montaiglon (Mariette) 1851–1860, Bd. 5 (1858/59), S. 70.

61 Vgl. Renger 1974a, S. 137.

62 Vgl. Meier 2020a, S. 23.

63 Vgl. Bulckens 2017, S. 116–121, Nr. 26; Meier 2020a, S. 21, 105–107, 246–248, Nr. 46.

64 Vgl. Vlieghe 1972, S. 116 f., Nr. 75; Nils Büttner, in: Braunschweig 2004, S. 207–209, Nr. 38; Nico Van Hout, in: Antwerpen/Québec 2004, S. 70–75.

65 Vgl. Meier 2020a, S. 244–246, Nr. 45.

66 Vgl. Brakensiek 2011; Luckschewitz 2020.

67 Vgl. Nils Büttner, in: Braunschweig 2004, S. 178, Nr. 25; Martin 2005, Bd. 1, S. 255 f., Nr. 6d; Meier 2020a, S. 283–285, Nr. 59.

68 Rubens, *Herkules erschlägt die Missgunst*, um 1634–1636, Öl auf Leinwand, 549 × 239 cm (oval), London, Whitehall Palace, Banqueting House; Rubens-Werkstatt, *Herkules erschlägt die Missgunst*, um 1632, Öl auf Holz, 638 × 486 mm, Boston, MA, Museum of Fine Arts, Inv. 47.1543. Vgl. Martin 2005, S. 249–254, Nr. 6.

69 Vgl. Brussel 1998.

70 Vgl. Meier 2020a, S. 15, Abb. 10, S. 57–63, 383 f., Quellen Nr. 3–4.

71 Vgl. Stuttgart 2021, S. 324, Nr. 68.

72 Vgl. Jan van der Stock, in: Schallaburg 1991, S. 187.

73 Vgl. Jeroom Machiels, in: Machiels 1997, S. 15–60; Miedema 1985, bes. S. 482 f.; Orenstein 2006.

74 Vgl. dazu Münster 1976, S. 160 f.; Büttner 2011a, S. 66 f.; Meier 2020a, S. 333–337, Nr. 74.

75 „Et à la charge que led. Rubens mettra deux exemplaires en blanc dud. recueil en nostre bibliotheque, aussy tost qu'il sera achevé d'imprimer à peine de deschéange du fruict de ce présent privilège", heißt es zum Beispiel im französischen Privileg. Rooses/Ruelens 1887–1909, Bd. 2 (1898), S. 209. Auch während des 1633 in Paris geführten Prozesses ist vom „dépôt légal" die Rede. Vgl. ebd., Bd. 6 (1909), S. 126–129.

76 „Per conto delli suggetti non potrà nascervi difficolta alcuna non toccando al stato in modo alcuno ma schietti senza ambiguità ò senso mistico, come V. S. vedra nella lista qui annessa", schrieb Rubens am 23. Januar 1619 an van Veen. Rooses/Ruelens 1887–1909, Bd. 2 (1898), S. 199.

77 Rooses/Ruelens 1887–1909, Bd. 6 (1909), S. 126 f.

78 Vgl. Büttner 2006, S. 224, Anm. 159.

79 Vgl. Renger 1975, S. 204; Münster 1976, S. 186.

80 Vgl. Büttner 2006, S. 146–148.

81 Siehe Anm. 40.

82 Zit. nach Zoff 1918, S. 450. „Se in questo consiste la difficoltà io mi contento che le mie stampe siano bandité di tutto ìl regno di Francia, bastondomi il rimamente d'Europa per cavarne qualche honore, che stimo assai più ch' alcun altro interesso", schrieb Rubens am 16. August 1635 in einem Brief an Peiresc. Rooses/Ruelens 1887–1909, Bd. 6 (1907), S. 126 f.

83 Vgl. Stuttgart 2021, S. 325, Nr. 71.

84 Anonym, *Die Anbetung der Könige*, Ende 17. Jh., Öl auf Kastanie (?), 100,8 × 72 cm, Staatliche Schlösser und Gärten Baden-Württemberg, Schloss Ludwigsburg, Inv. Sch.L. 4124.Vgl. Stuttgart 2021, S. 325, Nr. 72.

85 Vgl. Büttner 2020.

86 Charlotta Krispinsson, Copies and Replicas in 17th Century Northern Europe: Image, Medium, and Practice (in Vorbereitung).

87 Vgl. Jaffé 1984; Porter/Béland 2004; Hyman 2021; Biffis 2021.

20 See Rooses/Ruelens 1887–1909, vol. 1 (1887), p. 354; English translation in Magurn 1955, pp. 39–40. On the commission, see Mühlen 1998 and, most recently, Paolini 2022.
21 See Büttner 2006, p. 42.
22 See Sweertius 1613, p. 143; Génard 1877, pp. 17, 390.
23 Rubens, *St. Gregory Surrounded by Saints*, 1607/08, oil on canvas, 477 × 288 cm, Grenoble, Musée de Grenoble, inv. MG 97; see Vlieghe 1972, vol. 2, pp. 43–50, no. 109.
24 Monballieu 1965, p. 196.
25 See Büttner 2006, p. 144; Büttner 2011a.
26 See Nils Büttner, in: Braunschweig 2004, pp. 230–232, no. 47; Meier 2020a, pp. 13–15, 141–144, no. 8.
27 On the lost painting, see D'Hulst/Vandenven 1989, p. 158, no. 50. The preparatory drawing has survived, D'Hulst/Vandenven 1989, p. 163, no. 50b.
28 As early as March 8, 1627, Peiresc had expressed his delight in a letter to the French painter Jean Chalette (1581–1644) that Rubens had agreed to send him a self-portrait. See Jaffé 1988; Biffis 2021, esp. pp. 6–7.
29 Rooses/Ruelens 1887–1909, vol. 4 (1904), p. 414: "Con che finisco, rendendole infinite gratie della final concessione del suo ritratto."
30 Inscribed: "Petrus Paullus Rubens | Se ipsum expressit | A. D. MDCXXIII." See Vlieghe 1987, pp. 153–154, no. 135, figs. 171, 176; Büttner 2015a, pp. 39–53.
31 See Vlieghe 1987, pp. 153 154, no. 135, copy 1. Rooses/Ruelens 1887–1909, vol. 5 (1907), p. 11: "Spero che V. S. haveva gia ricevuto il mio ritratto che consignai molti giorni, inanzi la mia partenza d'Anversa, al cogniato del Sr Pycqueri come egli mi haveva ordinato." As Rubens had left for Spain immediately after sending the painting, he remained unsure for a long time whether it had reached its addressee. A letter to Pierre Dupuy shows that Rubens had not yet received confirmation of receipt as of April 22, 1629, as he still hoped "he has received it, for I sent it by a safe route shortly before my departure from Flanders." English translation from Magurn 1955, p. 297. Original wording in: Rooses/Ruelens 1887–1909, vol. 5 (1907), p. 29: "mio ritratto che spero avera ricevuto poiche il mandai per via sicura qualq. tempo inanci la mia partenza di Fiandra."
32 Piles 1699, pp. 396–397: "La réputation de Rubens s'étenduë par toute l'Europe, il n'y eût pas un Peintre qui ne voulût avoir un morceau de sa main; & comme il étoit éxtrémement sollicité de toutes parts, il fit faire sur ses Desseins coloriéz, & par d'habiles Disciples un grand nombre de Tableaux, qu'il retouchoit ensuite avec des yeux frais, avec un intelligence vive, & avec une promptitude de main qui y répandoit entiérement son Esprit, ce qui luy aquit beaucoup de biens en peu de tems: mais la différence de ces fortes de Tableaux, qui passoient pour être de luy, d'avec ceux qui étoient véritablement de sa main, fit du tort à sa réputation; car ils étoient la plûpart mal dessinez, & légérement peints."
33 Sandrart 1675, vol. 2, p. 292. English translation from Sandrart (1675) 2019, p. 47.
34 Document dated November 2, 1616, Antwerp, FelixArchief, N#3838 (Notariaatsarchief: Kaspar Van der Herstraeten Sr.: Protocollen en staten 1615–1616), fol. 167r: "Ende tvoers. werk alsoo loffelyck ende behoirlyck gestelt ende volmaeckt synde soo sal den voers. Sgr Rubbens aen Jasper bovens die voers. beloeffde somme alnoch schenken een stuck schilderye tsy op doeck oft paneel wesende copye naer eenich stuck van synder hant gemaeckt, tselve stellende tsyner Sgr Rubbens discretie."
35 For more details on this, see Büttner 2008; Tieze 2012.
36 See Büttner 2017a. Arnout Balis's contributions on the workshop practice are still seminal today, see Balis 1993 and Balis 2007.
37 A comprehensive overview will be provided by the *New Hollstein* volumes on Rubens currently in preparation, for which Jaco Rutgers and Simon Turner are responsible. For an introduction, see Meier 2020a and Antwerpen/Québec 2004; Rutgers 2019 and Kaulbach 2021 offer good summaries.
38 George Voorhelm Schneevoogt's seminal catalogue raisonné (Voorhelm Schneevoogt 1873) lists almost 2,200.
39 Furetière 1690, vol. 2, unpaginated: "À l'égard des Peintres & Graveurs, on appelle l'oeuvre d'un Maître, le recueil de toutes fes pièces gravées qu'on en trouve." See also Bonne 2022.
40 See Brakensiek 2003, pp. 17–39, 549–553; Büttner 2023b.
41 Hecquet 1751.
42 Basan 1767.
43 See the contribution by Karolien De Clippel and Filip Vermeylen on pp. 24–49 in this catalog (first published in De Clippel/Vermeylen 2012). On Rubens in Holland, see, most recently, Büttner 2023a.
44 Rubens, *Samson and Delilah*, ca. 1609/10, oil on panel, 185 × 205 cm, London, National Gallery, inv. NG6461. See D'Hulst/Vandenven 1989, pp. 107–113, no. 31; Antwerp/Vienna 2007, pp. 11–34; De Clippel/Vermeylen 2012, pp. 149–155; Rutgers 2019, p. 107.
45 See Renger 1974a, esp. pp. 147–161; see also Nico Van Hout, in: Antwerp/Québec 2004, pp. 56–69; Büttner 2011a.
46 "Havrei ben voluto chel intagliator fosse riuscito piu esperto ad imitar ben il prototypo pur mi pare minor male di vederli fare in mia presenza," Rubens wrote to Pieter van Veen on January 23, 1619. Rooses/Ruelens 1887–1909, vol. 2 (1898), p. 199. English translation from Magurn 1955, p. 69.
47 "Vederli fare in mia presenza per mano di un giovane ben intentionato che di gran valenthuomini secondo il lor capriccio," Rubens wrote to Pieter van Veen on January 23, 1619. Rooses/Ruelens 1887–1909, vol. 2 (1898), p. 199. English translation from Magurn 1955, p. 69.
48 See Nico Van Hout, in: Antwerp/Québec 2004, p. 55, n. 44, Meier 2020a, pp. 31, 64–67, 187–191, no. 27; Bertram 2021.
49 See Held 1980, pp. 395–398, no. 294; Vlieghe 1987, pp. 67–71, no. 82; Gritsay/Babina 2008, pp. 251–253, no. 309.
50 Letter of April 30, 1622. Rooses/Ruelens 1887–1909, vol. 2 (1898), pp. 399–401.
51 "Presumendo che l'intaglio suo solo facçia valer queste stampe qualque cosa et il suo nome tanto illustre," Rubens wrote to Van Veen on April 30, 1622. Rooses/Ruelens 1887–1909, vol. 2 (1898), pp. 399–400. English translation from Magurn 1955, p. 87.
52 See Bouchery/Wijngaert 1941, pp. 113–114; Renger 1974a, p. 127, n. 30.
53 See Carl Depauw, in: Antwerpen 1999, pp. 42–71 and 60–61, no. 2.
54 See Devisscher/Vlieghe 2014, vol. 1, pp. 76–81, no. 15.
55 See Devisscher/Vlieghe 2014, vol. 1, pp. 82–87, no. 15b; Meier 2020a, pp. 52–53.
56 See Renger 1974a, p. 144; Judson/Van de Velde 1978; Bertram/Büttner 2018; Bertram 2018; Meier 2020a, esp. pp. 53–55.
57 The design of prints was not economically interesting, nor was their sale, as revenue was rather low despite large print runs. See Renger 1974a, pp. 126–127; Renger 1975, p. 212.
58 See Büttner 2015a, pp. 148–150, no. 9; Meier 2020a, pp. 213–215, no. 32.
59 See Büttner 2006, pp. 106–107, 204, n. 148, 249. Soon see also Thomas Klinke, Cologne, who examined the sheet in detail in 2023 for the first time in terms of conservation science.
60 "J'ai vu nombre de morceaux préparés par Rubens pour les gravures, et j'en possède plusieurs que M. Crozat avoit rassemblés et que Jabach avoit fait achetter autrefois à la vente du cabinet de Rubens qui se fit après la mort de ce grand peintre." Chennevières/Montaiglon 1851–1860, vol. 5 (1858/59), p. 70.
61 See Renger 1974a, p. 137.
62 See Meier 2020a, p. 23.
63 See Bulckens 2017, pp. 116–121, no. 26; Meier 2020a, pp. 21, 105–107, 246–248, no. 46.
64 See Vlieghe 1972, pp. 116–117, no. 75; Nils Büttner, in: Braunschweig 2004, pp. 207–209, no. 38; Nico Van Hout, in: Antwerp/Québec 2004, pp. 70–75.
65 See Meier 2020a, pp. 244–246, no. 45.
66 See Brakensiek 2011; Luckschewitz 2020.
67 See Nils Büttner, in: Braunschweig 2004, p. 178, no. 25; Martin 2005, vol. 1, pp. 255–256, no. 6d; Meier 2020a, pp. 283–285, no. 59.
68 Rubens, *Hercules Slaying Envy*, ca. 1634–1636, oil on canvas, 549 × 239 cm (oval), London, Whitehall Palace, Banqueting House; Rubens workshop, *Hercules Slaying Envy*, ca. 1632, oil on wood, 638 × 486 mm, Boston, MA, Museum of Fine Arts, inv. 47.1543. See Martin 2005, pp. 249–254, no. 6.
69 See Brussel 1998.
70 See Meier 2020a, p. 15, fig. 10, pp. 57–63, 383–384, source nos. 3–4.
71 See Stuttgart 2021, p. 324, no. 68.
72 See Jan van der Stock, in: Schallaburg 1991, p. 187.
73 See Jeroom Machiels, in: Machiels 1997, pp. 15–60; Miedema 1985, esp. pp. 482 483; Orenstein 2006
74 See Münster 1976, pp. 160–161; Büttner 2011a, pp. 66–67; Meier 2020a, pp. 333–337, no. 74.
75 "Et à la charge que led. Rubens mettra deux exemplaires en blanc dud. recueil en nostre bibliotheque, aussy tost qu'il sera achevé d'imprimer à peine de deschéange du fruict de ce présent privilège," reads, for example, the French privilege. Rooses/Ruelens 1887–1909, vol. 2 (1898), p. 209. The "dépôt légal" was mentioned during the trial in Paris in 1633 as well. See Rooses/Ruelens 1887–1909, vol. 6 (1909), pp. 126–129.
76 "Per conto delli suggetti non potrà nascervi difficolta alcuna non toccando al stato in modo alcuno ma schietti senza ambiguità ò senso mistico, come V. S. vedra nella lista qui annessa," Rubens wrote to Van Veen on January 23, 1619. Rooses/Ruelens 1887–1909, vol. 2 (1898), p. 199.
77 Rooses/Ruelens 1887–1909, vol. 6 (1909), pp. 126–127. For the English translation, see Magurn 1955, pp. 397–398.
78 See Büttner 2006, p. 224, n. 159.
79 See Renger 1975, p. 204; Münster 1976, p. 186.
80 See Büttner 2006, pp. 146–148.
81 See note 40.
82 "Se in questo consiste la difficoltà io mi contento che le mie stampe siano banditè di tutto il regno di Francia, bastondomi il rimamente d'Europa per cavarne qualche honore, che stimo assai più ch' alcun altro interesso," Rubens wrote in a letter to Peiresc on August 16, 1635. Rooses/Ruelens 1887–1909, vol. 6 (1907), pp. 126–127. English translation from Magurn 1955, p. 400.
83 See Stuttgart 2021, p. 325, no. 71.
84 Anonymous, *The Adoration of the Magi*, late seventeenth century, oil on chestnut (?), 100.8 × 72 cm, Staatliche Schlösser und Gärten Baden-Württemberg, Ludwigsburg Palace, inv. Sch.L. 4124. See Stuttgart 2021, p. 325, no. 72.
85 See Büttner 2020.
86 Charlotta Krispinsson, Copies and Replicas in 17th Century Northern Europe: Image, Medium, and Practice (in preparation).
87 See Jaffé 1984; Porter/Béland 2004; Hyman 2021; Biffis 2021.

Der Katalog folgt bei der Schreibweise und den Lebensdaten der niederländischen Künstler in der Regel der Künstlerdatenbank des RKD – Nederlands Instituut voor Kunstgeschiedenis, die online verfügbar ist. Alle übrigen Künstlernamen und Lebensdaten entsprechen der Nennung der Union List of Artist Names® Online des Getty Research Institute. Komplexe Datierungen (z. B. unterschiedliche Daten für den Entwurf und den Druck) werden oft verkürzt wiedergegeben, können im Detail jedoch neben weiteren Angaben online nachgelesen werden: https://www.sgsm.eu/sgsm-online/. Die Abkürzung SGSM steht für Staatliche Graphische Sammlung München.

For the spelling and dates of birth/death of Netherlandish artists, this catalog generally follows the database of the RKD – Netherlands Institute for Art History. The spelling and dates of birth/death of all other artists correspond with the Union List of Artist Names® Online of the Getty Research Institute. Complex dates (e.g. divergent dates for design and printing) are often given in abbreviated form. More details about these dates, along with further information on individual works, are provided online at https://www.sgsm.eu/sgsm-online/. SGSM stands for Staatliche Graphische Sammlung München.

Katalog — Catalog

NINA SCHLEIF

I. Werkstattbetrieb und Stecher

Wie organisierten Hendrick Goltzius und Peter Paul Rubens die Produktion ihrer Druckgraphiken? Ein Kupferstich nach Jan van der Straet (1523–1605), auch Stradanus genannt, zeigt eine vereinfachte (und wohl idealisierte) Ansicht, wie wir uns einen Werkstattbetrieb um 1600 vorzustellen haben (Abb. S. 97). Hier saß nicht ein genialischer Künstler „im stillen Kämmerlein" und stach und druckte alleine Kupferplatten ab. Im Stradanus-Stich wird anschaulich, dass die handwerkliche Produktion von Druckgraphik eine arbeitsteilige, sehr aufwendige und platzfordernde Angelegenheit war. Die Darstellung zeigt einige Akteure und nötige Arbeitsschritte. Deutlich wird auch, dass die Ausbildung für die beteiligten Berufe im Kindesalter begann.

Wo Goltzius seine Werkstatt hatte und wie groß sie war, wissen wir nicht.[1] Im Fall von Rubens gibt es nur den Hinweis, dass seine Stecher Korrekturen in seiner Gegenwart vornehmen mussten.[2] Doch wo diese Spezialisten ihrer Arbeit nachgingen und die übrigen Mitarbeiter anleiteten, während sie für Rubens arbeiteten, liegt im Dunkeln.[3] Dokumentiert ist einzig, dass Rubens' von Christoffel Jegher (1596–1652/53) angefertigte Holzschnitte im Verlagshaus Plantin-Moretus (Officina Plantiniana) in hohen Auflagen auf den Buchdruckpressen abgezogen wurden.[4]

Bei Stradanus' Blick in die Werkstatt bleiben die geistigen Urheber von Kupferstichen unsichtbar, aber sie werden in den Stichen selbst genannt, was der gängigen Praxis entsprach: Erwähnt werden hier nicht nur die Erfinder der Motive („inventor", „invenit", lat. für Erfinder, erfinden), sondern auch die (meist gelehrten) Autoren der Texte (ohne eigene Bez.), ferner die Stecher („sculptor", „sculpsit", lat. für Bildhauer, Stecher, stechen) sowie die Verleger („excudit", „excudebat", lat. für formen, gestalten).

Eine zentrale Rolle innerhalb der Werkstätten spielten die jeweiligen Stecher, denn ihnen vertrauten die Meister die Aufgabe an, den „Goltzius-Stil" bzw. den „Rubens-Stil" auf so hohem Niveau umzusetzen, dass er trotz stilistischer Veränderungen als Marke über Jahrzehnte erkennbar blieb. Beide Künstler machten es sich daher zur Aufgabe, die begabtesten Talente ihrer Generation aufzuspüren und auszubilden und diese wiederum eine Nachfolgergeneration ausbilden zu lassen, die dann ebenfalls nach den beiden Meistern tätig wurde.

Diese Stecher, aber auch Radierer und Holzschneider waren von herausragender Bedeutung für die Qualität der Druckgraphiken von Goltzius und Rubens. Beide Künstler verfolgten das Ziel, möglichst die Besten ihres Faches an sich zu binden, um eine verlässliche Zusammenarbeit und effiziente Produktion zu gewährleisten. Zu Goltzius' wertvollsten Stechern zählten Jacob Matham, Jan Saenredam, Jacques de Gheyn II und Jan Harmensz. Muller. Rubens beschäftigte über die Jahre hinweg Lucas Vorsterman I, Paulus Pontius, Boëtius und Schelte à Bolswert, Marinus van der Goes, Nicolaes Lauwers, Hans Witdoeck, Pieter Soutman und den bereits erwähnten Christoffel Jegher.

I. Workshop Operation and Engravers

How did Hendrick Goltzius and Peter Paul Rubens organize the production of their prints? An engraving after Jan van der Straet (1523–1605), also known as Stradanus, depicts a simplified (and likely idealized) view of a workshop around 1600 (fig. p. 97). What we see in this print is far from the stereotype of a brilliant artist sitting in his private closet, engraving and printing copperplates in solitude. The Stradanus engraving clearly reveals that the manual production of prints was a highly complex and space-consuming affair involving an intricate division of labor. The illustration shows some of the protagonists and required work steps. It also becomes apparent that the training for the relevant professions began in childhood.

We do not know the location or size of Goltzius's workshop.[1] When it comes to Rubens, the only indication is that his engravers had to make corrections in his presence.[2] Where, however, these specialists went about their work, which included instructing the other workshop staff, is unknown.[3] All that is documented is that Rubens's woodcuts, executed by Christoffel Jegher (1596–1652/53), were printed in large quantities on the letterpresses in the Plantin-Moretus publishing house (Officina Plantiniana).[4]

In Stradanus's view of the workshop, the intellectual authors of the engravings remain invisible. In line with common practice, however, they are named in the engravings themselves, which mention not only the designers of the motifs (identified by *inventor*, *invenit*, Lat. for "designer," "to invent") but also the engravers (*sculptor*, *sculpsit*, Lat. for "sculptor," "engraver," "to engrave") and publishers (*excudit*, *excudebat*, Lat. for "to form," "to shape"), as well as the (mostly scholarly) authors of the epigrams (without any special appellation).

The engravers played a central role in the workshops, as the masters entrusted them with the task of implementing the "Goltzius style" or the "Rubens style" to such a high standard that it remained recognizable as a brand for decades, despite stylistic changes. Both artists therefore made it their mission to seek out and train the most gifted talents of their generation and to have them in turn train a successor generation, who then also worked after the two masters.

These engravers, as well as etchers and woodcutters, were of outstanding importance for the quality of the prints by Goltzius and Rubens. Both artists aimed to attract the best in their field in order to ensure reliable collaboration and efficient production. Goltzius's most prized engravers included Jacob Matham, Jan Saenredam, Jacques de Gheyn II, and Jan Harmensz. Muller. Over the years, Rubens employed Lucas Vorsterman I, Paulus Pontius, Boëtius and Schelte à Bolswert, Marinus van der Goes, Nicolaes Lauwers, Hans Witdoeck, Pieter Soutman, and the aforementioned Christoffel Jegher.

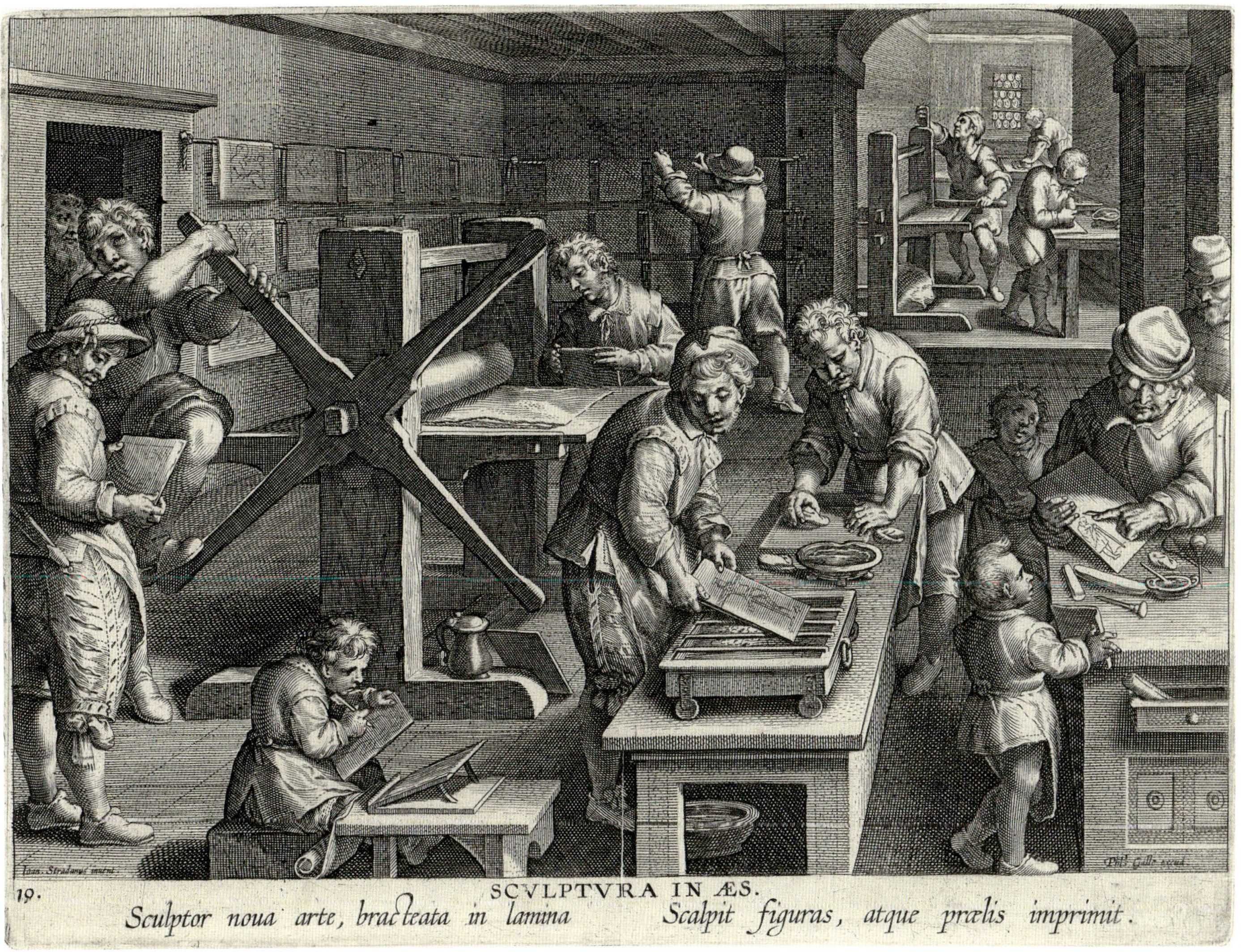

Theodoor Galle (Stecher / engraver), nach / after J. van der Straet
SCULPTURA IN AES / Kupferstecherwerkstatt / A Printer's Workshop, ca. 1580–1601
Aus / from J. van der Straet, *Nova Reperta*, Antwerpen, nach / after 1612
Kupferstich / engraving SGSM, Inv. 1966:13-19 D

Obwohl Goltzius und Rubens durch eine Generation sowie eine Landesgrenze getrennt waren, gab es einen kleinen Kreis Stecher, der Werke für beide Künstler schuf. Hierzu zählte auch Jan Harmensz. Muller (1571–1628). Zwei weitere seien hier beispielhaft anhand ihrer Nachtszenen nach Goltzius und Rubens vorgestellt: Jacob Matham und Lucas Vorsterman I. Nachtszenen waren traditionell herausfordernd für Stecher, galt es doch, genug Licht ins Dunkel zu bringen, damit Details sichtbar werden, und zugleich die Übergänge zwischen Hell und Dunkel überzeugend zu gestalten.

Jacob Matham (1571–1631) war der Stiefsohn von Goltzius, den seine Frau Margaretha Jansdochter mit in die Ehe gebracht hatte (Abb. S. 98). Bereits als Kind band der Stiefvater ihn in die Arbeit in der Kupferstichwerkstatt ein und brachte ihm das Handwerk bei. Während seiner

Although Goltzius and Rubens were separated by a generation and a national border, there was a small circle of engravers who created works for both of them. One of these engravers was Jan Harmensz. Muller (1571–1628). Below, I will present two others, Jacob Matham and Lucas Vorsterman I, and discuss their work on the basis of night scenes engraved after both Goltzius and Rubens. Night scenes were traditionally challenging for engravers, as it was necessary to bring enough light into the darkness to make details visible, while simultaneously creating convincing transitions between light and dark.

Jacob Matham (1571–1631; fig. p. 98) was Goltzius's stepson, brought into his marriage to Margaretha Jansdochter. Goltzius involved Matham from childhood on in the work of the engraving

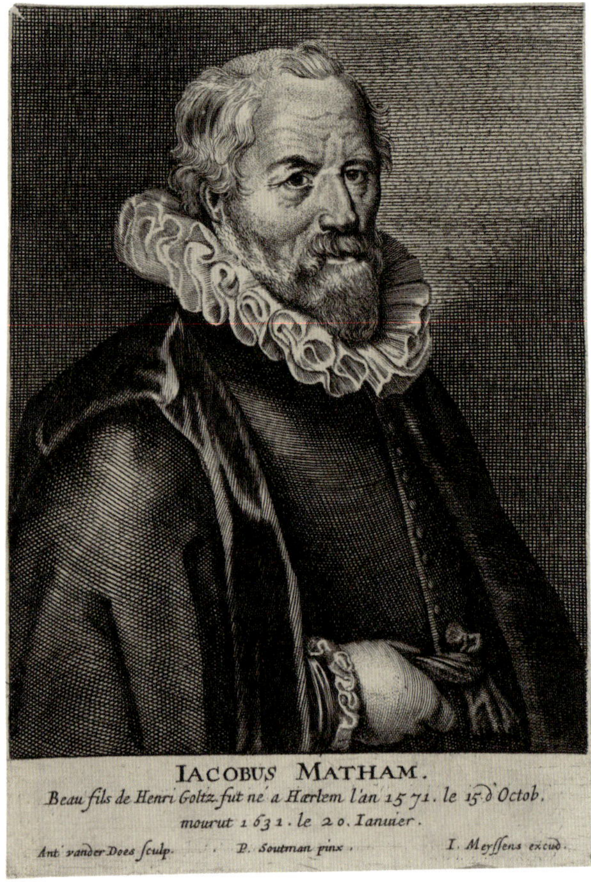

Antony van der Does (Stecher, Radierer / engraver, etcher),
nach / after Pieter Soutman
Bildnis des / Portrait of Jacob Matham, nach / after 1631
Kupferstich, Radierung / engraving, etching SGSM, Inv. 101398 D

etwa einjährigen Italienreise 1590/91 übertrug Goltzius Matham die Verantwortung für seinen Betrieb. Auch als Goltzius sich ab 1598 vom Kupferstich ab- und der Malerei zuwandte, war es Matham, in dessen Hände er seine florierende Werkstatt übergab. 1601 wurde das kaiserliche Privileg, das Goltzius 1595 erhalten hatte, an den Stiefsohn übertragen.[5] Obwohl Matham alle Handgriffe von Goltzius lernte, schuf er seine besten Stiche nach den Erfindungen anderer, vor allem nach Goltzius und in einem Fall nach Rubens. Anhand von zwei Nachtszenen lässt sich zeigen, wie Matham bemüht war, ihren Wünschen und Vorstellungen bei der Umsetzung ihrer Kompositionen gerecht zu werden.

Um das Jahr 1600 hatte Goltzius eine Nachtszene entworfen, die später von Matham gestochen und 1615 verlegt wurde: *Die Mondgöttin Diana begleitet einen jungen Mann, der Laute spielt* (Abb. S. 102). Formen und Figuren sind ein spätmanieristischer Nachklang früherer von Goltzius erdachter Götterlieben. Dieser Stil scheint Matham mehr zugesagt zu haben als das Drama mit viel irdischeren Körpern und spannungsgeladener Handlung, das er für und nach Rubens stach: Um die Zeit des Besuchs von Rubens in Haarlem 1612 fertigte Matham seinen einzigen Stich nach einem Gemälde des

workshop, teaching him the craft. During his approximately one-year stay in Italy from 1590 to 1591, Goltzius entrusted Matham with running his business, and when Goltzius ceased engraving and turned instead to painting in 1598, it was Matham in whose hands he placed his flourishing workshop. In 1601, the imperial privilege that Goltzius had received in 1595 was transferred to his stepson.[5] Although Matham learned all the tricks of the trade from Goltzius, he created his best engravings based on the inventions of others, especially Goltzius and, in one case, Rubens. Two night scenes show how Matham strove to live up to their wishes and ideas in the realization of their compositions.

Around 1600 Goltzius designed a night scene which Matham later engraved: *Diana as Luna Accompanying a Young Man Serenading in a Garden of Love* (fig. p. 102) was published in 1615. The forms and figures are a late Mannerist echo of earlier loves of the gods conceived by Goltzius. This style seems to have had a greater appeal for Matham than the night scene he engraved for and after Rubens that contained much more earthly bodies and suspenseful action. *Samson and Delilah* was Matham's only engraving following a painting by the Fleming and was crafted around the time of Rubens's visit to Haarlem in 1612 (fig. p. 103). He probably saw the preparatory oil sketch of the painting in Antwerp, or perhaps Rubens brought it with him on his journey to Haarlem.[6] It is quite conceivable that the Fleming hoped that this work sample would help him decide if Matham might be a suitable engraver for his own planned workshop in Antwerp. Rubens appears to have been only partially satisfied with the result.[7] The print was dedicated to Rubens's close friend Nicolaas Rockox, the influential burgomaster of Antwerp, and the artist had a text by his brother Philip placed beneath the motif. In the end, though, this was the only print that Matham produced after Rubens's paintings.

The first engraver with whom Rubens realized an entire series of motifs was Lucas Vorsterman I (1595/96–1674/75; fig. p. 99). We do not know how and when Rubens became aware of this young man. Vorsterman's earliest dated engraving was made in 1607, and his ambition was probably to become one of the best in his field: by making copies after the *Passion of Christ* series by Goltzius, he revealed who he was emulating (fig. p. 104).[8] Nico Van Hout believes Rubens may have become aware of Vorsterman's talent as a result of these copies: "Possibly, it was these exercises in virtuosity and patience that came to Rubens's attention and that led him to hire Vorsterman."[9] Comparing one of Vorsterman's copies with its model, Goltzius's *Christ before Caiaphas* (1597), makes clear how confidently and vividly the young artist executed this print. Although Vorsterman intensified the chiaroscuro effects of the night scene, he succeeded so convincingly that it appears as if the night light and the torches could not possibly illuminate the scene in any other manner. He also knew how to bring the figures to life, thereby emphasizing the contrast between his own style and Goltzius's, which was deliberately old-fashioned, harking back as it did to that of Lucas van Leyden. Deviating from

Flamen: *Samson und Delilah* (Abb. S. 103). Vermutlich sah er die vorbereitende Ölskizze des Gemäldes in Antwerpen oder Rubens führte sie auf seiner Reise nach Haarlem mit sich.[6] Es ist durchaus denkbar, dass der Flame sich von dieser Arbeitsprobe versprach, Klarheit über die Eignung Mathams für seine Pläne einer eigenen Druckproduktion zu erlangen. Rubens scheint mit dem Ergebnis nur bedingt zufrieden gewesen zu sein.[7] Die Widmung des Blatts galt Rubens' engem Freund Nicolaas Rockox, dem einflussreichen Bürgermeister Antwerpens. Unter das Motiv ließ er einen Text seines Bruders Philip setzen. Dieses blieb jedoch das einzige Blatt, das Matham nach Rubens' Malerei anfertigte.

Der für Rubens erste wichtige Stecher, mit dem er eine ganze Reihe von Motiven realisierte, war Lucas Vorsterman I (1595/96–1674/75; Abb. S. 99). Wann und wie Rubens auf den jungen Mann aufmerksam wurde, wissen wir nicht. Vorstermans frühester datierter Stich entstand 1607 und sein Ehrgeiz war wohl, einer der Besten zu werden, denn indem er Kopien nach der Serie *Die Passion Christi* von Goltzius anfertigte, legte er offen, wem er nacheiferte (Abb. S. 104).[8] Nico Van Hout hält es für möglich, dass Rubens aufgrund dieser Kopien auf das Talent von Vorsterman aufmerksam wurde: „Es waren wohl diese Übungen in Virtuosität und Geduld, die Rubens zu Augen kamen und den Künstler schließlich zu der Entscheidung führten, Vorsterman in Dienst zu nehmen."[9] Vergleicht man eine von Vorstermans Kopien mit seinem Vorbild, Goltzius' Szene mit *Christus vor Caiaphas* (1597), stellt man fest, wie souverän und lebendig er diesen Nachstich ausführte. Zwar verstärkte der Stecher die Hell-Dunkel-Effekte der Nachtszene, aber dies gelang ihm so überzeugend, dass es wirkt, als könnte das nächtliche Licht und die Fackeln die Szene nur so erleuchten, wie Vorsterman sie zeigt. Auch wusste er den Figuren trotz des von Goltzius bewusst gewählten altertümlichen (weil auf Lucas van Leyden zurückgehenden) Stils Lebendigkeit zu verleihen. Abweichend von der Vorlage setzte Vorsterman unten links in das Motiv selbstbewusst das Monogramm des Haarlemer Meisters, das ligierte „HG":[10] einerseits, um seiner Bewunderung für Goltzius Ausdruck zu verleihen, andererseits, um zu unterstreichen, dass seine Kopie dem Meister würdig war.

Jahre später schuf Vorsterman auch eine Nachtszene für Rubens, die zu dessen Bravourstücken im Kupferstich gezählt wird (Abb. S. 105): das *Martyrium des hl. Laurentius* (1621) nach dem Rubens-Gemälde in der Alten Pinakothek in München. Hier bestand die Herausforderung für Vorsterman darin, die dramatischen Lichteffekte in unterschiedlichen Stofflichkeiten, auf der nackten Haut, der Kleidung und in den Rauchschwaden, plausibel zu machen. Auch diesmal hängte der Stecher die Messlatte für sich hoch, war doch allen Kennern bewusst, dass Rubens den Vergleich mit Cornelis Corts Stich nach Tizians Komposition (1571) desselben Themas anstrebte (Abb. S. 100).[11] Kein geringeres Werk musste übertroffen werden in Komposition und Ausführung! Ein Vergleich der Darstellung von nackter Haut des Märtyrers zeigt, dass Vorsterman der Triumph gelungen war: Wo Cort die Körperoberfläche in Schraffuren und Kreuzschraffuren aufbaute und damit zwar Volumen, nicht aber Textur erreichte, erzielte Vorsterman mit kurzen, weichen Schraffuren und eingestreuten Punkten den Eindruck von Verwundbarkeit der Haut.

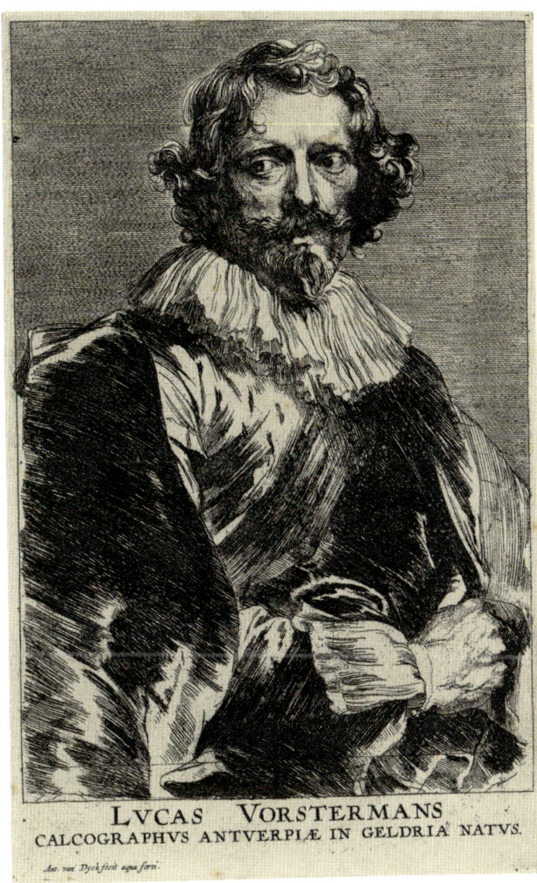

Anthonis / Anthony van Dyck (Radierer / etcher)
Bildnis des / Portrait of Lucas Vorsterman I, 1630/41
Radierung / etching SGSM, Inv. 69696 D

the original, Vorsterman self-assuredly placed the Haarlem master's initials, the interlaced "HG,"[10] at the bottom left of the motif, partly to express his admiration for Goltzius and partly to emphasize that his copy was worthy of the master.

Years later, Vorsterman created a night scene for Rubens which came to be considered one of his engraved masterpieces: the *The Martyrdom of St. Lawrence* (1621; fig. p. 105), after the painting by Rubens in the Alte Pinakothek in Munich. Here, the challenge for Vorsterman lay in making the dramatic light effects palpable on different surfaces and substances: the bare skin, the clothing, and the clouds of smoke. Once again, the bar was high, as all connoisseurs were aware that Rubens was aiming for a comparison with Cornelis Cort's engraving after Titian's painting of the same subject (1571; fig. p. 100), a work whose exceptional composition and execution were second to none.[11] A comparison of the depictions of the martyr's naked skin shows that Vorsterman succeeded in surpassing Cort's engraving: whereas Cort composed the surface of the body using hatching and cross-hatching, and thus achieved a sense of volume but not texture, Vorsterman's short, soft hatching and interspersed stipples express the vulnerability of the skin.

1 „The location of his studio and publishing house is unknown. It is possible that he worked at home but, given the size of his output and the number of apprentices and assistants he had, it seems more likely that he had a separate workplace." Huigen Leeflang, in: Amsterdam/New York/Toledo 2003, S. 17.

2 Rooses/Ruelens 1887–1909, Bd. 2 (1898), S. 199. Brief von Rubens an Pieter van Veen, 23. Januar 1619: „[...] vederli fare in mia presenza per mano [...]." In dtsch. Übers. siehe Zoff 1918, S. 95: [...] die Arbeit unter meinen Augen [...] ausführen zu lassen [...]."

3 In ihren kürzlich veröffentlichen Bänden zur Baugeschichte des Rubenshuis in Antwerpen gibt Nora De Poorter keinen Hinweis darauf, dass in Rubens' Antwerpener Wohnsitz eine Druckwerkstatt eingerichtet gewesen wäre oder auch nur Platz gehabt hätte; siehe De Poorter/Bauduoin 2022.

4 In den Kassenbüchern ist dokumentiert, dass die Auflagen auf Kosten von Rubens gedruckt wurden, dem man zum Beispiel für das Drucken von 2000 Holzschnitten und das dazugehörige Papier 72 Gulden und 30 Stuiver in Rechnung stellte; siehe Bouchery/Wijngaert 1941, S. 100f. Dank an Nils Büttner für den Hinweis auf diese Angaben.

5 Vgl. das Kapitel „Privilegien" im vorliegenden Katalog, S. 116–127.

6 Letzteres vermuten Meier 2020a, S. 130, und Büttner 2023a, S. 90.

7 NHD Matham 2007, 10, führt einen von Rubens überarbeiteten Probedruck und insgesamt fünf Zustände für das Blatt an.

8 Die Datierung seiner Kopien nach Goltzius ist in Quellen leider nicht belegt, wird aber zwischen 1607 und dem Beginn seiner Tätigkeit für Rubens 1619 anzusetzen sein. Christiaan Schuckman schreibt lediglich: „The series probably dates from Vorsterman's youth." NHD Vorsterman I 1993, 14–25.

9 „Het zijn well deze oefeningen in virtuositeit en geduld die Rubens onder ogen kreeg en de kunstenaar uiteindelijk deden besluiten om Vorsterman in dienst te nemen." Nico Van Hout, in: Antwerpen/Québec 2004, S. 41 (Übers. der Autorin).

10 Dieses Monogramm fehlt in der Abbildung im NHD Vorsterman I 1993, 17.

11 Vgl. NHD Cort 2000, 127.

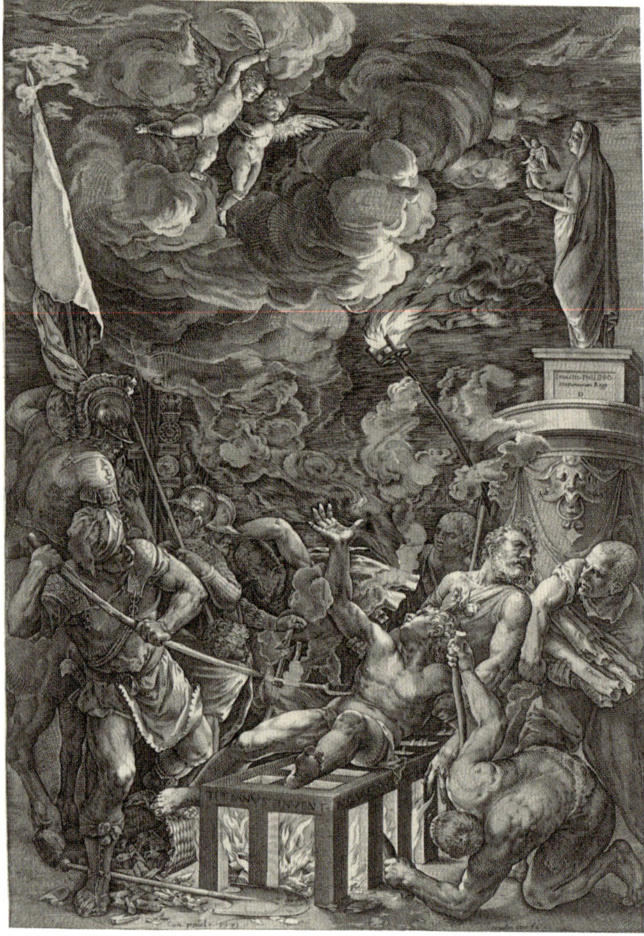

Cornelis Cort (Stecher / engraver), nach Tizian / after Titian
Das Martyrium des hl. Laurentius / The Martyrdom of St. Lawrence, 1571
Kupferstich / engraving SGSM, Inv. 7904 D

1 "The location of his studio and publishing house is unknown. It is possible that he worked at home but, given the size of his output and the number of apprentices and assistants he had, it seems more likely that he had a separate workplace." Huigen Leeflang, in: Amsterdam/New York/Toledo 2003, p. 17.

2 Rooses/Ruelens 1887–1909, vol. 2 (1898), p. 199. Letter from Rubens to Pieter van Veen, January 23, 1619: "[. . .] vederli fare in mia presenza per mano [. . .]." For an English translation, see Magurn 1955, p. 69: "[. . .] to have the work done in my presence [. . .]"

3 In her recently published volumes on the architectural history of the Rubenshuis in Antwerp, Nora De Poorter gives no indication that Rubens's Antwerp residence would have had a printing workshop or even room for one; see De Poorter/Bauduoin 2022.

4 It is documented in the account books that the editions were printed at Rubens's expense: he was charged seventy-two guilders and thirty stuivers for the printing of two thousand woodcuts and the required paper, for example; see Bouchery/Wijngaert 1941, pp. 100–101. Thanks to Nils Büttner for pointing out this information.

5 See the chapter "Privileges," pp. 116–127.

6 The latter is assumed by Meier 2020a, p. 130, and Büttner 2023a, p. 90.

7 NHD Matham 2007, 10, cites a proof impression, revised by Rubens, and a total of five states for the print.

8 The dating of his copies after Goltzius is unfortunately not documented, but can be placed between 1607 and the beginning of his work for Rubens in 1619. Christiaan Schuckman merely writes: "The series probably dates from Vorsterman's youth." NHD Vorsterman I 1993, 14–25.

9 "Het zijn well deze oefeningen in virtuositeit en geduld die Rubens onder ogen kreeg en de kunstenaar uiteindelijk deden besluiten om Vorsterman in dienst te nemen." Nico Van Hout, in: Antwerpen/Québec 2004, p. 41 (author's translation).

10 These initials are missing in the print illustrated in NHD Vorsterman I 1993, 17.

11 See NHD Cort 2000, 127.

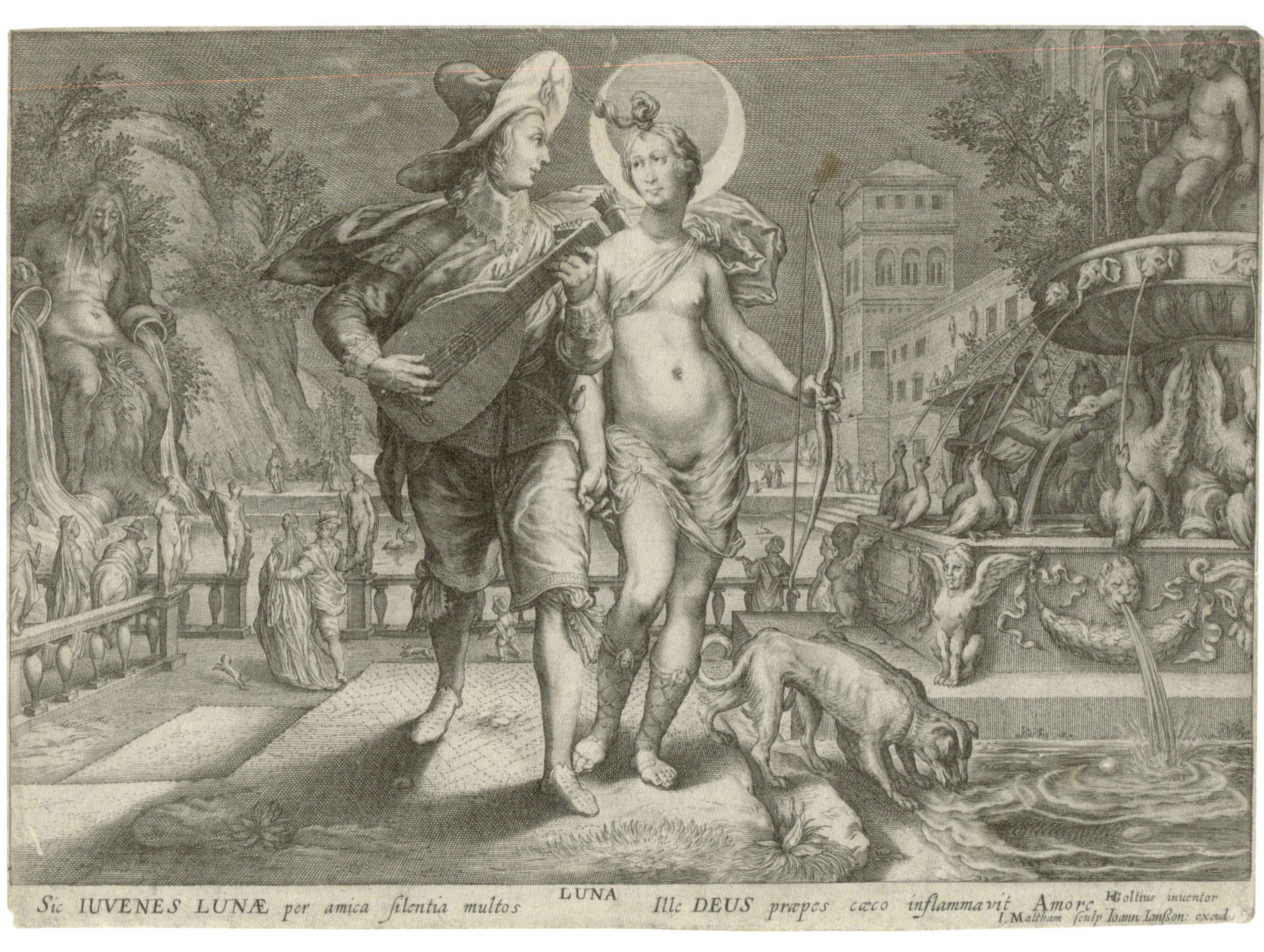

Goltzius (Inventor / designer), Jacob Matham (Stecher / engraver), Jan Janszoon I (Verleger / publisher)
Die Mondgöttin Diana begleitet einen jungen Mann, der Laute spielt / Diana as Luna Accompanying a Young Man Serenading in a Garden of Love, ca. 1600/15
Kupferstich / engraving SGSM, Inv. 31127 D

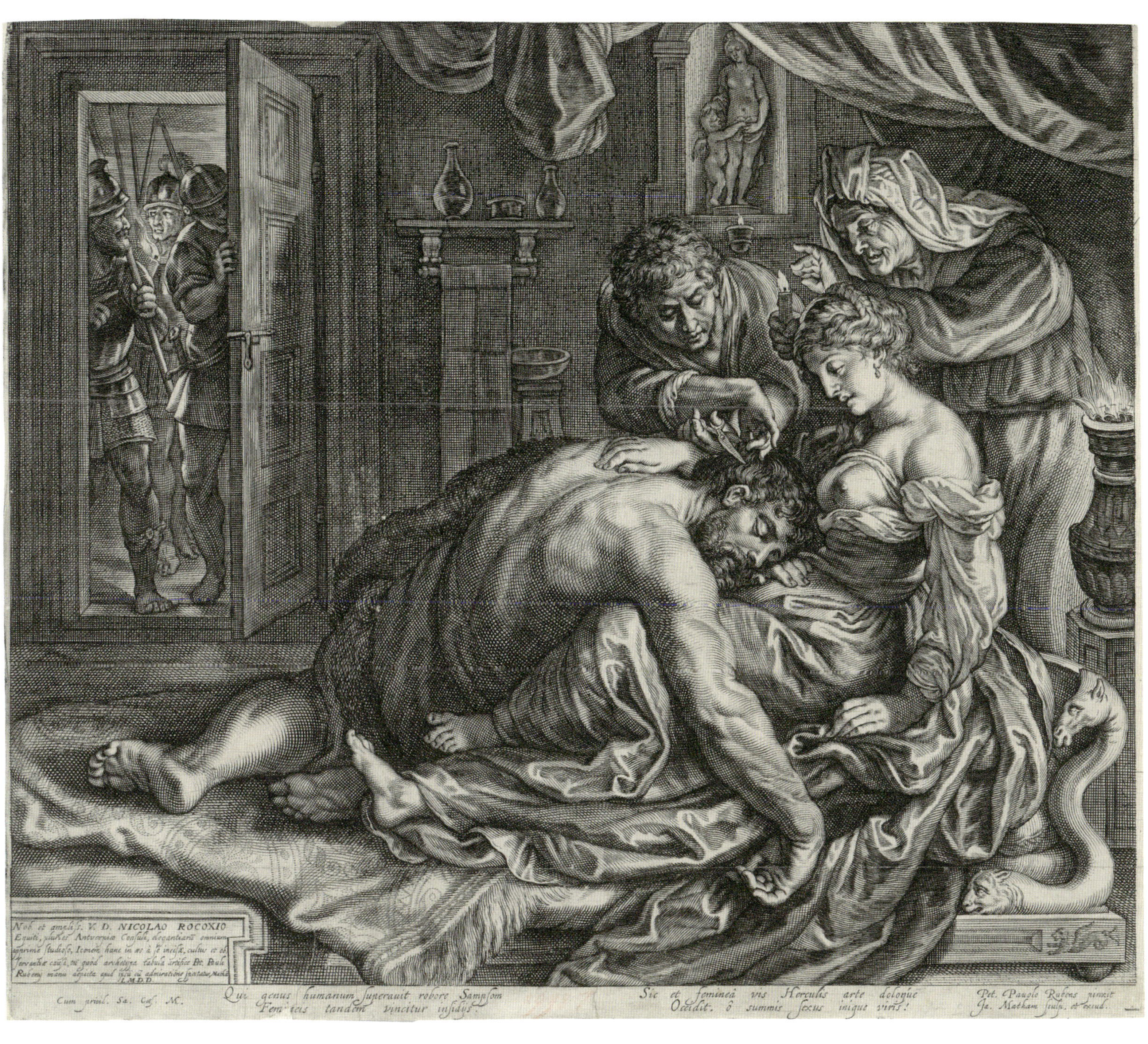

Jacob Matham (Stecher / engraver), nach / after Rubens
Samson und / and Delilah, ca. 1613
Kupferstich / engraving SGSM, Inv. 29987 D

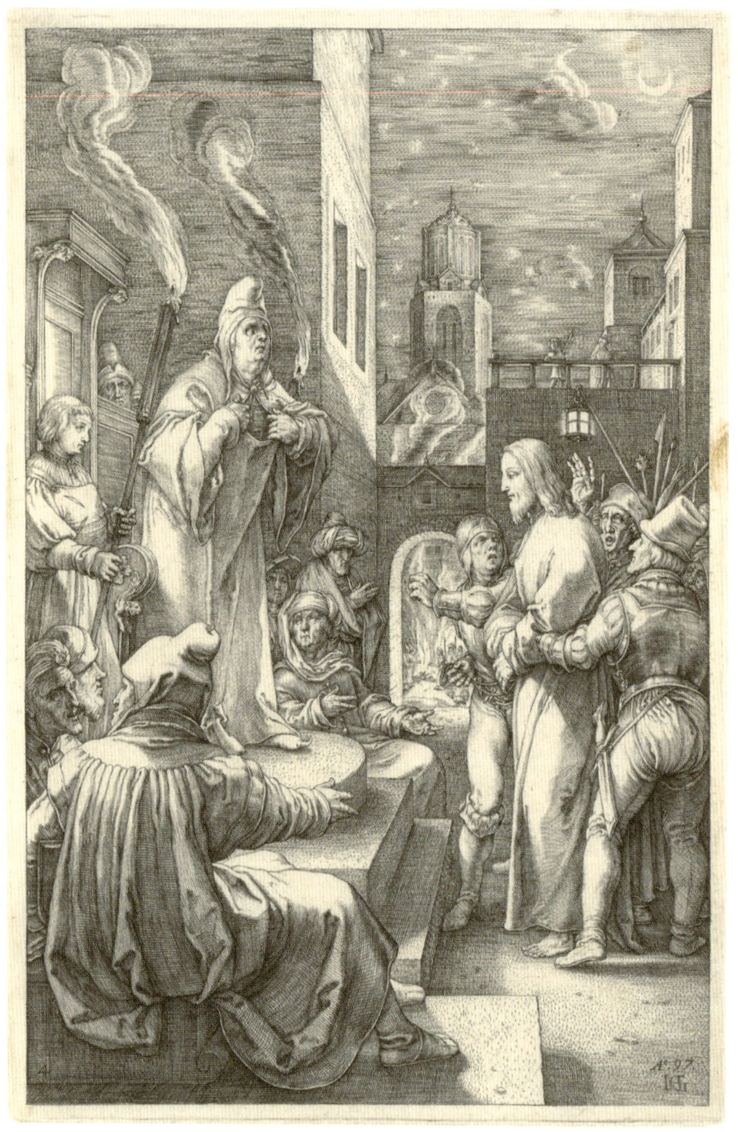

Hendrick Goltzius (Inventor, Stecher / designer, engraver)
Christus vor / Christ before Caiaphas, 1597
Aus der Serie *Die Passion Christi* / from the series *The Passion of Christ*, 1596–1598
Kupferstich / engraving SGSM, Inv. 30909 D

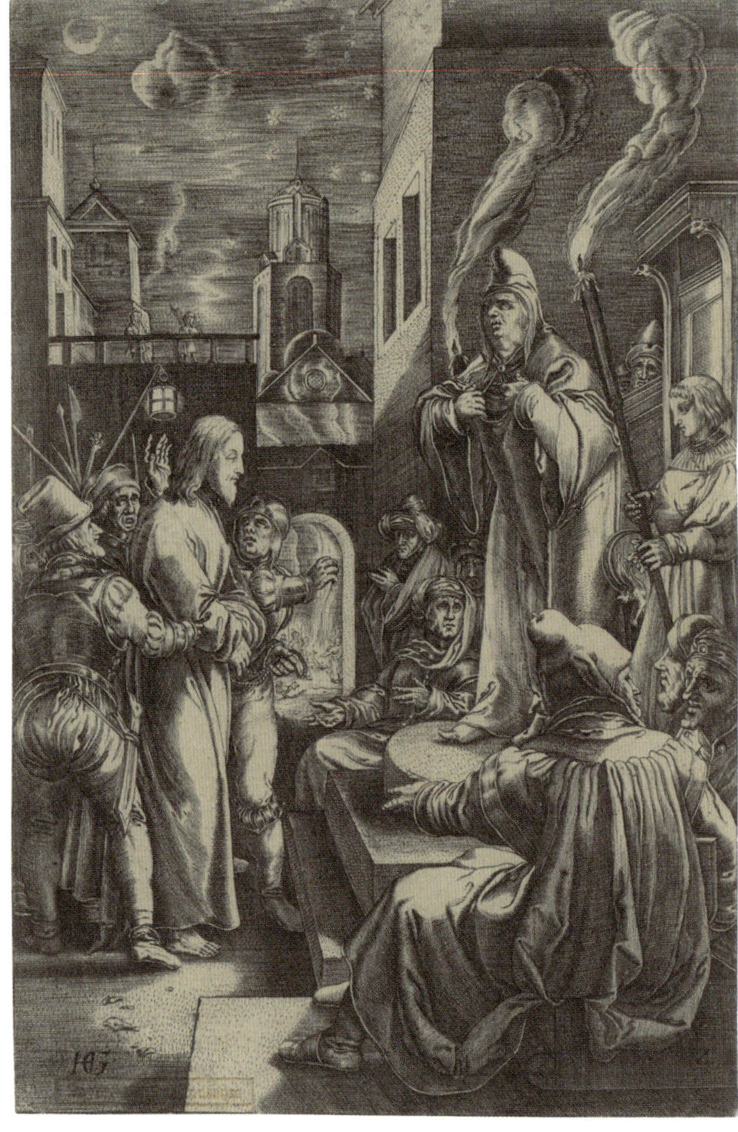

Lucas Vorsterman I (Stecher / engraver), Kopie nach / copy after Goltzius
Christus vor / Christ before Caiaphas, nach / after 1607
Kupferstich / engraving SGSM, Inv. 210219 D

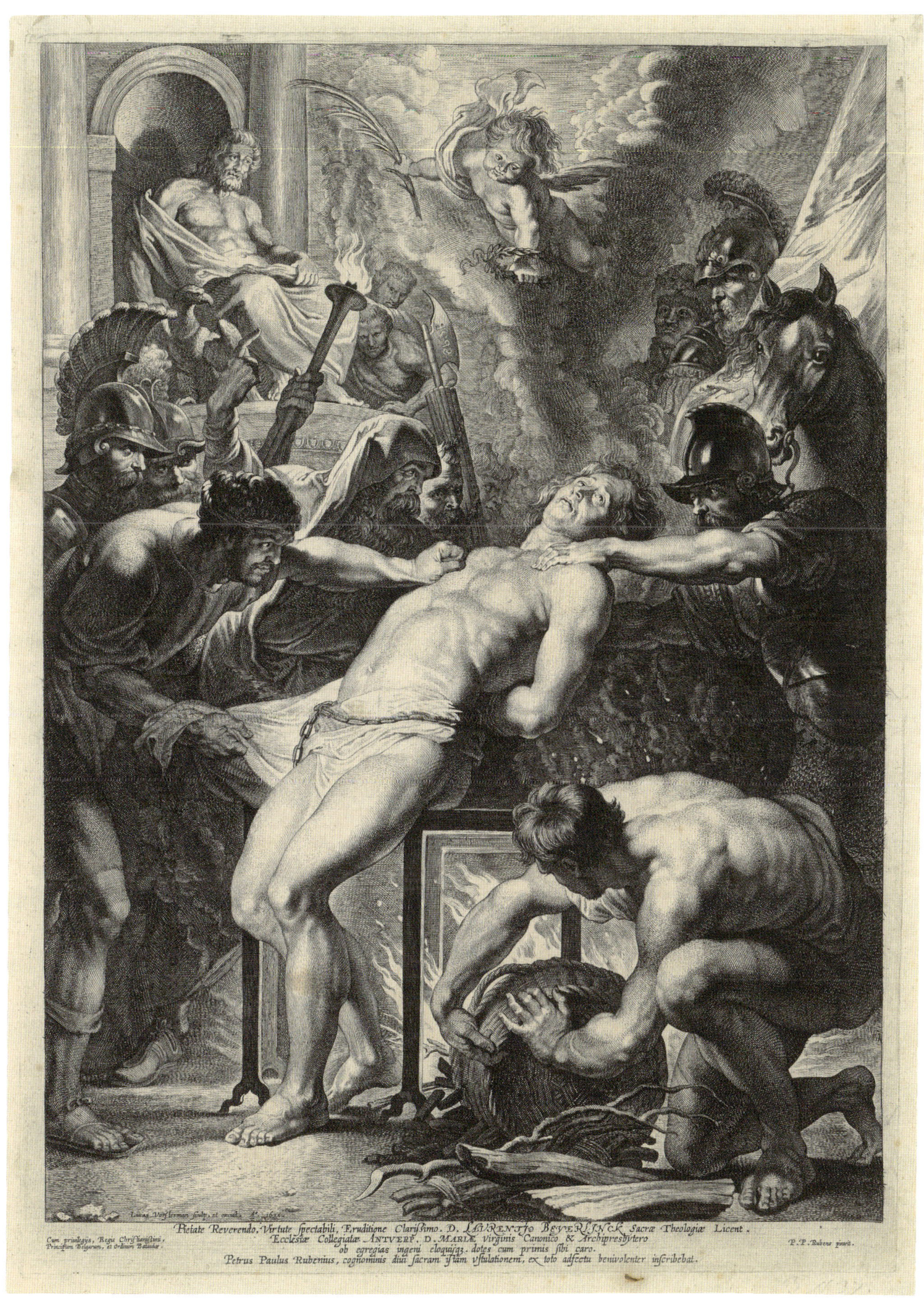

Rubens (Inventor / designer), Lucas Vorsterman I (Stecher, Verleger / engraver, publisher)
Martyrium des hl. Laurentius / The Martyrdom of St. Lawrence, 1621
Kupferstich / engraving SGSM, Inv. 30254 D

II. Widmungen

Die in den Stichen selbst gut sichtbar angebrachten Widmungen liefern wertvolle Informationen zur Entstehung der Werke und Motivation der Künstler. Jede sichtbare Widmung implizierte eine persönliche Beziehung zwischen dem Widmenden und dem Empfänger. Auf diese Weise konnten Künstler zeigen, bei welchen Fürsten sie in der Gunst stehen wollten und standen. Auch gibt es sehr persönliche Widmungstexte, die einen spezifischen Dank an einen Freund richten und damit öffentlich eine Freundschaft zelebrieren. Bei Goltzius wie Rubens finden sich zudem Widmungen an einflussreiche Persönlichkeiten oder etwa Künstlerkollegen. Auch Stecher und Verleger konnten Stiche aus der Autorschaft von Goltzius oder Rubens mit eigenen Widmungen versehen. Widmungen legten Netzwerke offen, die das eigene Ansehen mehrten.

Hendrick Goltzius richtete Widmungen seiner Stiche eher selten an persönliche Freunde wie etwa seinen Künstlerkollegen Dirck de Vries.[1] Seine Hauptwerke sind vielmehr einzelnen Fürsten oder einflussreichen Persönlichkeiten an deren Höfen gewidmet. Die nach seiner Italienreise entstandenen *Meisterstiche* (1594/95) veröffentlichte er als Gabe für den bayrischen Herzog Wilhelm V. (1548–1626), auf den er womöglich während seines Zwischenstopps in München persönlich getroffen war. Thea Vignau-Wilberg hat darauf hingewiesen, dass sich Goltzius mit der Darstellung *Die Verkündigung* (Abb. S. 106, 110), dem ersten Blatt dieser Serie, das auch den Widmungstext trägt, mit seinem Münchner Künstlerkollegen Hans Sadeler (1550–1600) messen wollte. Dessen Stich der *Verkündigung* bezog sich auf ein Altarbild des Peter Candid (1546/50–1628) in einer Kapelle der Münchner Michaelskirche.[2] Diese Kapelle war Renata, der Gemahlin Wilhelm V., gewidmet. So traten die beiden Stiche nicht nur künstlerisch, sondern auch hinsichtlich ihrer Widmungen in Konkurrenz.[3] Diese feinen lokalen Anspielungen wird der Widmungsempfänger verstanden und geschätzt haben, denn er erwiderte die Ehrbezeugung, indem er Goltzius mit einer Goldkette und einer goldenen Medaille dankte.[4]

II. Dedications

Dedications, which were prominently included in the engravings themselves, provide valuable information about the creation of the works and the motivation of the artists. Each highly visible dedication announced a personal relationship between the dedicator and the recipient. In this way, artists were able to indicate whose princely patronage they sought and had found. There are also very personal dedication texts that express specific gratitude to a friend and thereby publicly celebrate a friendship. In the case of Goltzius and Rubens, we also find dedications to powerful figures and fellow artists. Engravers and publishers were able to add their own dedications to engravings after Goltzius or Rubens as well. Dedications revealed networks that served to enhance one's own reputation.

It was the exception rather than the rule for Hendrick Goltzius to dedicate an engraving to personal friends, such as his fellow artist Dirck de Vries.[1] Generally, his main works were dedicated to individual princes or influential figures at their courts. He published the *Masterpieces* (1594/95), created after his trip to Italy, as a gift for the Bavarian Duke Wilhelm V (1548–1626), whom he may have met personally during his stop in Munich. Thea Vignau-Wilberg has pointed out that with *The Annunciation* (figs. pp. 106, 110)—the first print of the series, and the one bearing the dedication text—Goltzius wanted to compete with his friend Hans Sadeler (1550–1600), who was Wilhelm V's court engraver. Sadeler's engraving of *The Annunciation* was based on an altarpiece by Peter Candid (1546/50–1628) in a chapel in St. Michael's Church in Munich.[2] This chapel was dedicated to Renata, the wife of Wilhelm V. The two engravings thus competed not only artistically but in terms of their dedications.[3] The duke must have understood and appreciated these subtle local allusions, as he returned the tribute by thanking Goltzius with a gold chain and a gold medal.[4]

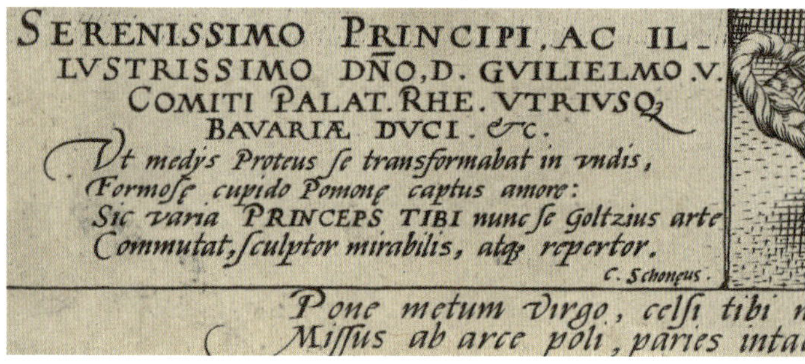

Widmungstext aus / dedicatory text from
Die Verkündigung / *The Annunciation*
von / by Hendrick Goltzius, 1594
SGSM, Inv. 1962:219 D, Detail

„Dem großartigen Prinzen und sehr berühmten Herrn, Wilhelm V., Pfalzgraf und Herzog beider Bayern etc. So wie Proteus sich mitten im Wasser verwandelte [und wie Vertumnus, der] ergriffen war von leidenschaftlicher Liebe zur wohlgestalteten Pomona, so verwandelt sich jetzt Goltzius für dich, Fürst, durch seine vielfältige Kunst. Er ist ein wundervoller Stecher und Bilderfinder."[5]

"To the exalted Prince and August Lord, the lord William V. Count Palatine and Duke of the two Bavarias, etc. As Proteus changed amidst the waves out of burning love for the beautiful Pomona, so does Goltzius, the admirable engraver and inventor, with his varied art, for you, Oh Prince."[5]

Auch die beeindruckende Serie *Römische Helden* (1586) schuf Goltzius als Huldigung an einen Potentaten, in diesem Fall den Habsburger Kaiser Rudolf II. (1552–1612), der ihm 1595 ein Privileg für seine Bildfindungen verleihen sollte. In den sich stolz präsentierenden Kriegern und ihrer überbetonten körperlichen und – damit impliziert – charakterlichen Stärke sollte sich der Kaiser selbst wiedererkennen, sie waren als Fürstenlob gemeint (Abb. S. 107, 111).[6] Die Titelseite mit einer *Allegorie der Stadt Rom* bekräftigte den Herrschaftsanspruch Rudolfs II. als Kaiser des Heiligen Römischen Reichs. Goltzius selbst bezeichnete sich in der Widmung demütig als „chalcographus“, als Kupferstecher. Rudolf II. war durchaus bewusst, dass Goltzius mehr als ein einfacher Handwerker war. In der Sammlung des Kaisers befanden sich einige der schönsten Werke des Niederländers, unter anderem auch vier oder fünf seiner hochgeschätzten, aber seltenen „Federkunststücke“, bei denen Goltzius mit der Feder die Stichtechnik nachahmte.[7]

Goltzius also created the impressive *Roman Heroes* series (1586) as an homage to a potentate, in this case the Habsburg Emperor Rudolf II (1552–1612), who was to grant him a privilege for his paintings in 1595. The emperor was intended to recognize himself in the proudly presented warriors and their overemphasized physical prowess—and, by implication, their strength of character—all of which Goltzius intended as praise for the ruler (figs. pp. 107, 111).[6] The title page with an *Allegory of Rome* affirmed Rudolf II's claim to rule as Holy Roman emperor. In the dedication, Goltzius humbly described himself as a "chalcographus," a copper engraver. Rudolf II was well aware that Goltzius was more than a simple craftsman, however. The emperor's collection contained some of the Dutchman's finest works, including four or five of his highly prized but rare "pen works," in which Goltzius imitated the look of engraving using a pen.[7]

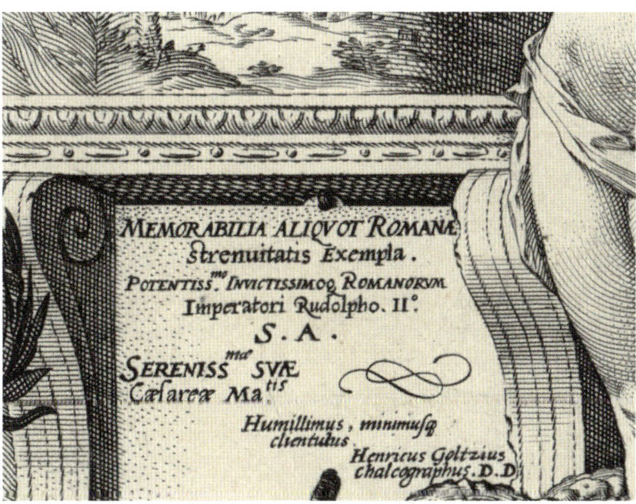

Widmungstext aus / dedicatory text from
Allegorie der Stadt Rom / Allegory of Rome
von / by Hendrick Goltzius, 1586
SGSM, Inv. 30936 D, Detail

„Einige denkwürdige Beispiele römischer Heldentaten für den höchst mächtigen und unbesiegbaren römischen Kaiser Rudolf II. vom ganz niedrigen und winzigsten Diener Ihrer erhabenen Majestät, dem Kupferstecher Hendrick Goltzius, als Geschenk.“[8]

"Some memorable examples of Roman deeds, commended and dedicated to the high and mighty and invincible Emperor of the Roman Empire, Rudolf II, by the humble and insignificant servant, the engraver Hendrick Goltzius."[8]

Mit der Inschrift auf dem Stich, der heute als *Die große Judith* (um 1616) betitelt wird, widmete Peter Paul Rubens die Darstellung der alttestamentlichen Heldin, die den Holofernes enthauptet, seinem Freund Jan van den Wouwer (1576–1636), einen humanistisch gebildeten Antwerpener Juristen (Abb. S. 108, 113). Er löse damit ein Versprechen ein, das er während eines gemeinsamen Aufenthalts in Verona (1602) gegeben habe, so der Widmungstext. Dieses Motiv ließ Rubens den Antwerpener Stecher Cornelis Galle I (1576–1650) ausführen. Hans Jakob Meier hat darauf hingewiesen, dass diese Widmung „in der Geschichte der Druckgraphik [...] ohne Beispiel bleibt“, denn Rubens habe damit offiziell sein Debüt im Kupferstich benannt ebenso wie die Entscheidung, seine Gemälde mittels Stichen zu verbreiten.[9] Bereits mit diesem ersten Stich verfolgte Rubens die stark kollaborative Arbeitsweise, die er später für alle unter seiner Aufsicht ausgeführten Stiche beibehielt: Er machte Korrekturen sowohl in der Vorzeichnung wie auch in einem Probedruck. Seine Anweisungen für den Stecher zielten darauf, starke

With the inscription on the engraving now titled *The Great Judith* (ca. 1616; figs. pp. 108, 113), Peter Paul Rubens dedicated his depiction of the Old Testament heroine beheading Holofernes to his friend Jan van den Wouwer (1576–1636), a humanist and Antwerp lawyer. According to the dedicatory text, he was thereby fulfilling a promise he had made during a joint stay in Verona (1602). Rubens had this motif executed by the engraver Cornelis Galle I (1576–1650) from Antwerp. Hans Jakob Meier has pointed out that this dedication "remains without precedent in the history of printmaking [. . .]," as Rubens had thus officially announced both his debut in engraving and his decision to disseminate his paintings by means of engravings.[9] Already with this first engraving, Rubens followed the highly collaborative working method that he later employed for all prints executed under his supervision: he made corrections to both the preparatory drawing and the proof impression. His instructions for the engraver were

Hell-Dunkel-Kontraste zu verstärken, die laut Konrad Renger „das Kennzeichen der Rubens-Stiche überhaupt" wurden.[10] Vermutlich geht auch die eng an Goltzius' Linienführung orientierte Ausführung, die für Galle ungewöhnlich war, auf einen expliziten Wunsch von Rubens zurück.[11] Mit seinen Widmungen an Freunde erreichte Rubens zweierlei: Er nutzte diese Geste als Freundschaftsbeweis gegenüber Vertrauten, aber zugleich als Mittel der Offenlegung seiner Netzwerke innerhalb humanistischer Zirkel.

aimed at enhancing the strong contrasts between light and dark, which according to Konrad Renger became "the absolute hallmark of Rubens engravings."[10] It is likely that Rubens explicitly requested the style, which was closely modeled on Goltzius's line design—a technique that was unusual for Galle.[11] Rubens achieved two objectives with his personal dedications, using this gesture as a sign of cameraderie toward his friends and as a means of making known his networks in humanist circles.

Clariss.o et amicissimo viro D. IOANNI *WOVERIO paginam hanc auspicalem primumque suorum operum typis æneis expressum* PETRVS PAVLLVS RVBENIVS *promissi iam olim Veronæ à se facti memor* DAT DICAT.

Widmungstext aus / dedicatory text from
Judith enthauptet Holofernes (*Die große Judith*) / *Judith Beheading Holofernes* (*The Great Judith*), ca. 1616
SGSM, Inv. 29994 D, Detail

„Dem höchst berühmten und befreundeten Mann, Herrn Jan Wover, ist diese erste und vorausweisende Seite seiner von Kupfer zu druckenden Werke in Gedenken des einst in Verona von Peter Paul Rubens gemachten Versprechens übergeben und zugeeignet."[12]

"Peter Paul Rubens, recalling the promise he made a long time ago at Verona, presents and dedicates this preliminary page and the first of his works to be printed from copper plates to that most illustrious and well-disposed gentleman, Mr. Jan van den Wouver."[12]

Wie Goltzius wusste auch Rubens, gezielte Stichwidmungen an Fürsten zu richten, die viel sachlicher formuliert waren als Widmungen an Freunde. Dem Statthalter der südlichen Niederlande Erzherzog Albrecht VII. (1559–1621) zeigte sich Rubens 1620 mit einer seiner schönsten Variationen der *Anbetung der Könige* besonders erkenntlich (Abb. S. 108, 115). 1609, kurz nach seiner Rückkehr aus Italien, war Rubens von Albrecht zum Hofmaler in Brüssel berufen worden. Den Ausschlag für die Widmung auf diesem Stich gab aber wohl die Gewährung eines Privilegs für Rubens' Stiche, das Albrecht 1619 bewilligt hatte und das hier unter der Widmung zu sehen ist. Mit dem allegorisch gelesenen Motiv der Huldigung des Christuskindes durch die Könige war auch ein Herrscherlob verbunden: an Albrecht als gläubigen Katholiken und Unterstützer von Spaniens Kampf gegen den aufständischen Norden, dem die Niederlande eine Waffenruhe zwischen 1609 und 1621 verdankten.

Like Goltzius, Rubens was also well-versed in addressing specific dedications to princes and rulers. These were more straightforward and contained fewer details than his dedications to friends. In 1620, Rubens showed his special appreciation for the governor of the Southern Netherlands, Archduke Albert VII (1559–1621), with one of his most beautiful variations of *The Adoration of the Magi* (figs. pp. 108, 115). Shortly after his return from Italy in 1609, Rubens had been appointed court painter in Brussels by Albert. The decisive factor for the dedication on this engraving, however, was probably the granting of a privilege for Rubens's engravings. This privilege, which Albert had approved in 1619, can be seen here below the dedication. The allegorical motif of the magi paying homage to the Christ Child was also intended to praise the ruler: Albert was a devout Catholic and supporter of Spain's fight against the religious revolt, to whom the Netherlands owed a truce between 1609 and 1621.

SERENISSIMO ET POTENTISSIMO ALBERTO AVSTR. ARCHID. BVRG. ET BELGARVM CLEMENTISSIMO D.no AR
P. P. Rubens pinxit. *Cum privilegiis, Regis Christianissimi,*

Widmungstext aus / dedicatory text from
Die Anbetung der Könige / *The Adoration of the Magi*, 1620
SGSM, Inv. 30058 D, Detail

„Dem durchlauchtigsten und mächtigen Albrecht, Erzherzog von Österreich und gnädigstem Herzog von Burgund und Belgien, widmet Peter Paul Rubens demütig und in ehrerbietiger Treue diese Probe seiner Kunst und frommen Gefühle."[13]

"To the most high and mighty Albert, Archduke of Austria, and the most serene Duke of Burgundy and Belgium, Peter Paul Rubens humbly and faithfully dedicates and consecrates this sample of his work and devotion."[13]

1 An diesen richtete er laut Bildinschrift das ungewöhnliche Bildnis, das er von dessen Sohn Frederick de Vries (Abb. S. 257) angefertigt hatte und bei dem der Künstler aufgrund der unkonventionellen Ikonographie mit großem Aufsehen rechnen konnte. Vgl. das Kapitel „Meisterdrucke" im vorliegenden Katalog, S. 186–217.
2 Vgl. München 2005, Kat. A15. Der Stich von Sadeler in der SGSM, Inv. 17027 D.
3 Näheres zum Schicksal des bzw. der Widmungsexemplare siehe Nina Schleif auf S. 290 im vorliegenden Katalog.
4 Mander (1604) 2000, S. 339. Es handelte sich wohl um einen sogenannten Gnadenpfennig; vgl. Staatliche Münzsammlung München, Inv. 6-03942 oder 6-02639.
5 Übers. zit. nach Hamburg 2002, Kat. 44 (A. Wolkenhauer).
6 Die Alt-Philologin Uta Schmidt-Clausen zeigt, dass neben dem Herrscherlob auch die „Prognose seines grenzenlosen Ruhms" im Fokus der Serie steht; siehe Schmidt-Clausen 2016, S. 318.
7 Huigen Leeflang, in: Amsterdam/New York/Toledo 2003, S. 235.
8 Übers. zit. nach Hamburg 2002, Kat. 13.1 (A. Wolkenhauer).
9 Meier 2020a, S. 13, 15.
10 Konrad Renger, in: Göttingen/Hannover/Nürnberg 1977, Kat. 21, S. 46. Zur Vorzeichnung und dem Probedruck vgl. Renger 1974a, S. 134.
11 Das vermutet Konrad Renger, in: Göttingen/Hannover/Nürnberg 1977, Kat. 21, S. 46. Dem folgt Büttner 2011a, S. 120.
12 Übers. der Autorin. Davon abweichend und freier die Übersetzung bei Meier 2020a, Kat. 8.
13 Übers. zit. nach Meier 2020a, S. 165.

1 According to the inscription, Goltzius addressed the unusual portrait of De Vries's son Frederick de Vries (fig. p. 257) to him, for which the artist could expect a great deal of attention thanks to its unconventional iconography. See the chapter "Masterprints" in this catalog, pp. 186–217.
2 See München 2005, cat. A15. The engraving by Sadeler is in the SGSM, inv. 17027 D.
3 For more on the fate of the dedication copy or copies, see Nina Schleif, p. 290, in the present catalog.
4 Mander (1604) 1994, fol. 285r03. This was probably a so-called *Gnadenpfennig* medallion; for specimens of this type, see Staatliche Münzsammlung Munich, inv. 6-03942 or 6-02639.
5 Translation from Amsterdam/New York/Toledo 2003, cat. 75.
6 The Classical philologist Uta Schmidt-Clausen shows that alongside praise for the ruler, the series also focuses on the "forecast of his boundless fame" (trans. Julian Jain); see Schmidt-Clausen 2016, p. 318.
7 Huigen Leeflang, in: Amsterdam/New York/Toledo 2003, p. 235.
8 Translation from Amsterdam/New York/Toledo 2003, cat. 29.
9 Meier 2020a, pp. 13, 15. Translation by Julian Jain.
10 Konrad Renger, in: Göttingen/Hannover/Nürnberg 1977, cat. 21, p. 46. Translation by Julian Jain. On the preparatory drawing and proof impression, see Renger 1974a, p. 134.
11 This is assumed by Konrad Renger, in: Göttingen/Hannover/Nürnberg 1977, cat. 21, p. 46, and accepted by Büttner 2011a, p. 120.
12 Translation from Hottle 2004, pp. 57 and 59.
13 Translated from the Latin by the author.

VOTIONIS SVAE SPECIMEN, PETRVS PAVLVS RVBENS, EX FIDO CVLTV HVMILITER DEDICAT CONSECRATQVE.
garum, & Ordinum Batauiæ. Lucas Vorsterman sculp. et excud. An. 1620.

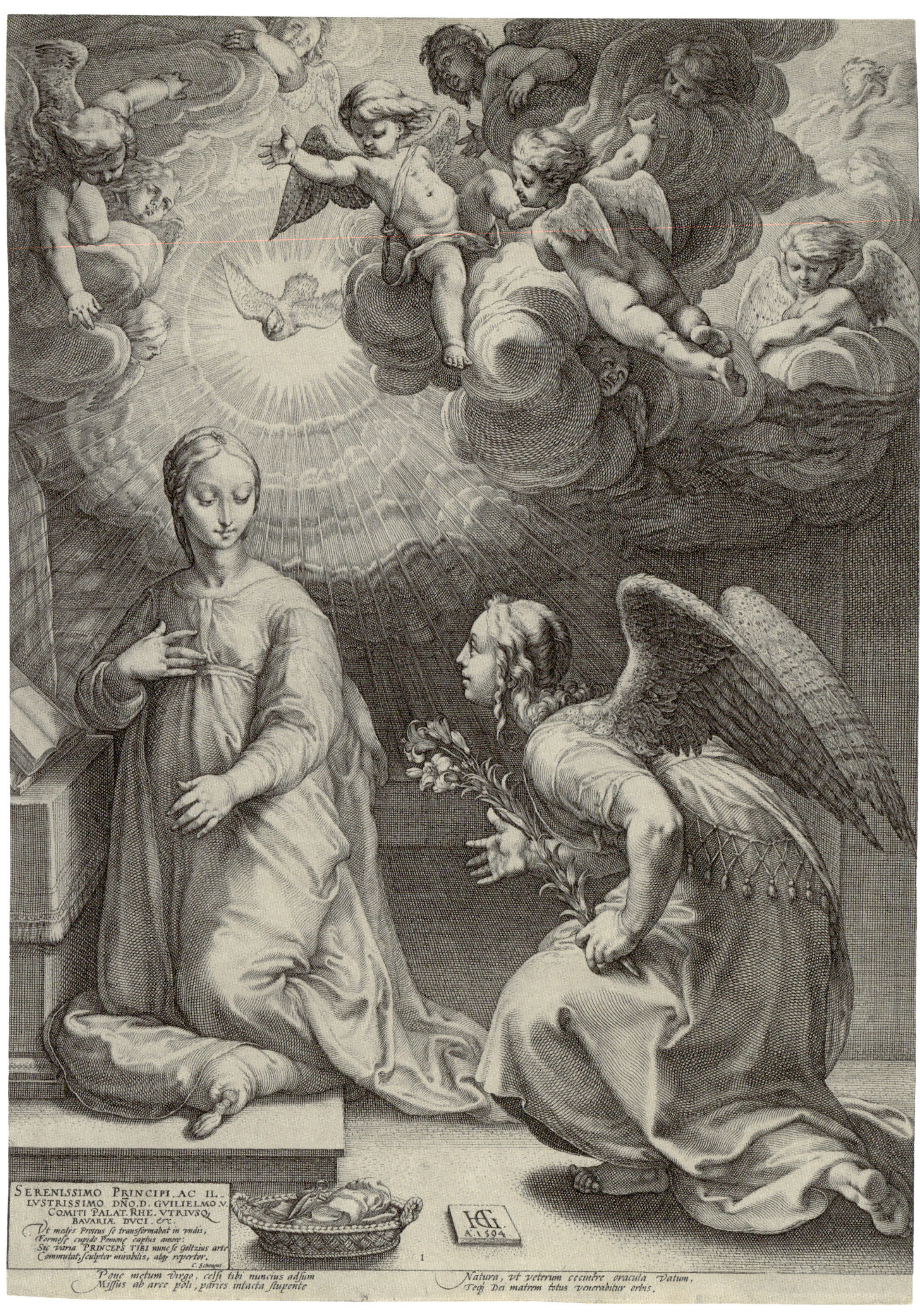

Hendrick Goltzius (Inventor, Stecher, Verleger / designer, engraver, publisher)

Die Verkündigung / The Annunciation, 1594

Aus der Serie *Christi Geburt und Jugend (Meisterstiche)* / from the series *The Birth and Early Life of Christ (Masterpieces)*, 1594/95

Widmung an Wilhelm V., Herzog von Bayern / dedicated to Wilhelm V, Duke of Bavaria von / by Goltzius

Kupferstich / engraving SGSM, Inv. 1962:219 D

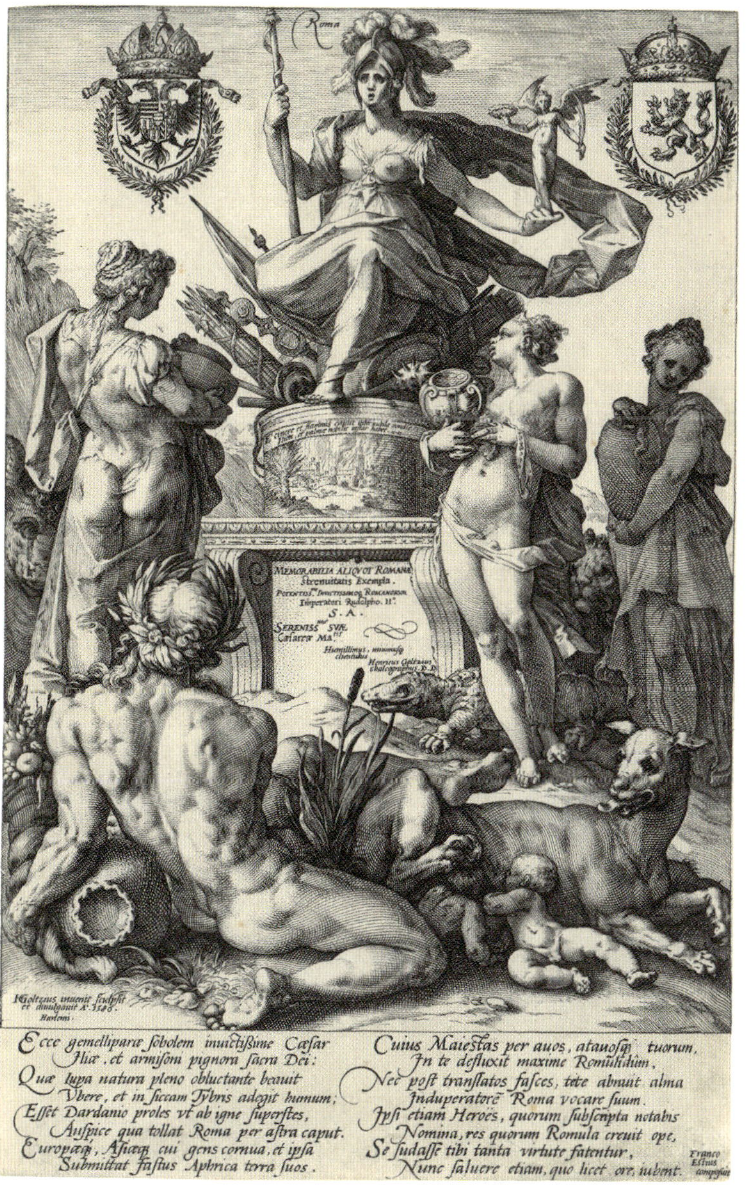

Goltzius (Inventor, Stecher, Verleger / designer, engraver, publisher)
Allegorie der Stadt Rom / Allegory of Rome, 1586
Aus der Serie *Römische Helden* / from the series *Roman Heroes*, 1586
Widmung an Rudolf II. / dedicated to Rudolf II von / by Goltzius
Kupferstich / engraving SGSM, Inv. 30936 D

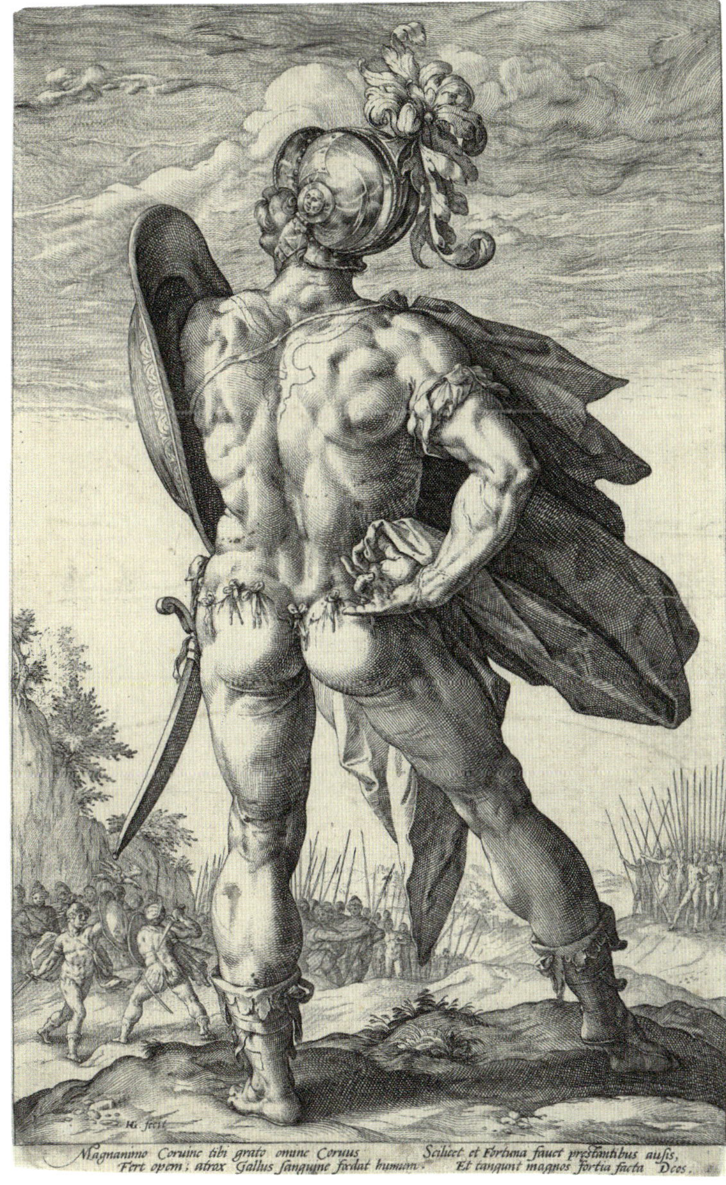

Goltzius (Inventor, Stecher, Verleger / designer, engraver, publisher)
Marcus Valerius Corvus, 1586
Aus der Serie *Römische Helden* / from the series *Roman Heroes*, 1586
Widmung an Rudolf II. / dedicated to Rudolf II von / by Goltzius
Kupferstich / engraving SGSM, Inv. 30937 D

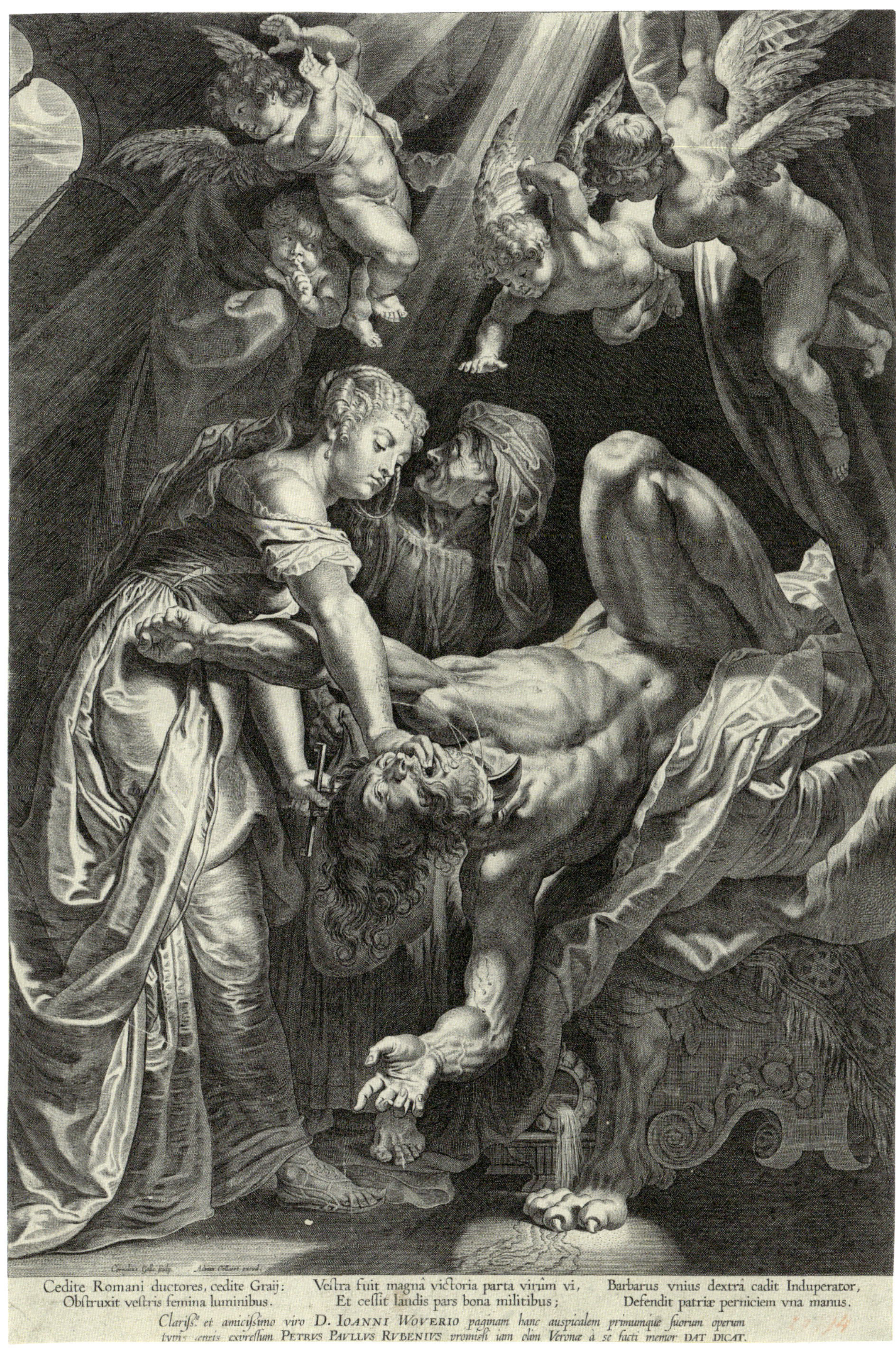

Cornelis Galle I (Stecher / engraver), nach / after Rubens, Adriaen Collaert (Verleger / publisher)
Judith enthauptet Holofernes (Die große Judith) / Judith Beheading Holofernes (The Great Judith), ca. 1616
Widmung an / dedicated to J. van den Wouwer von / by Rubens
Kupferstich / engraving SGSM, Inv. 29994 D

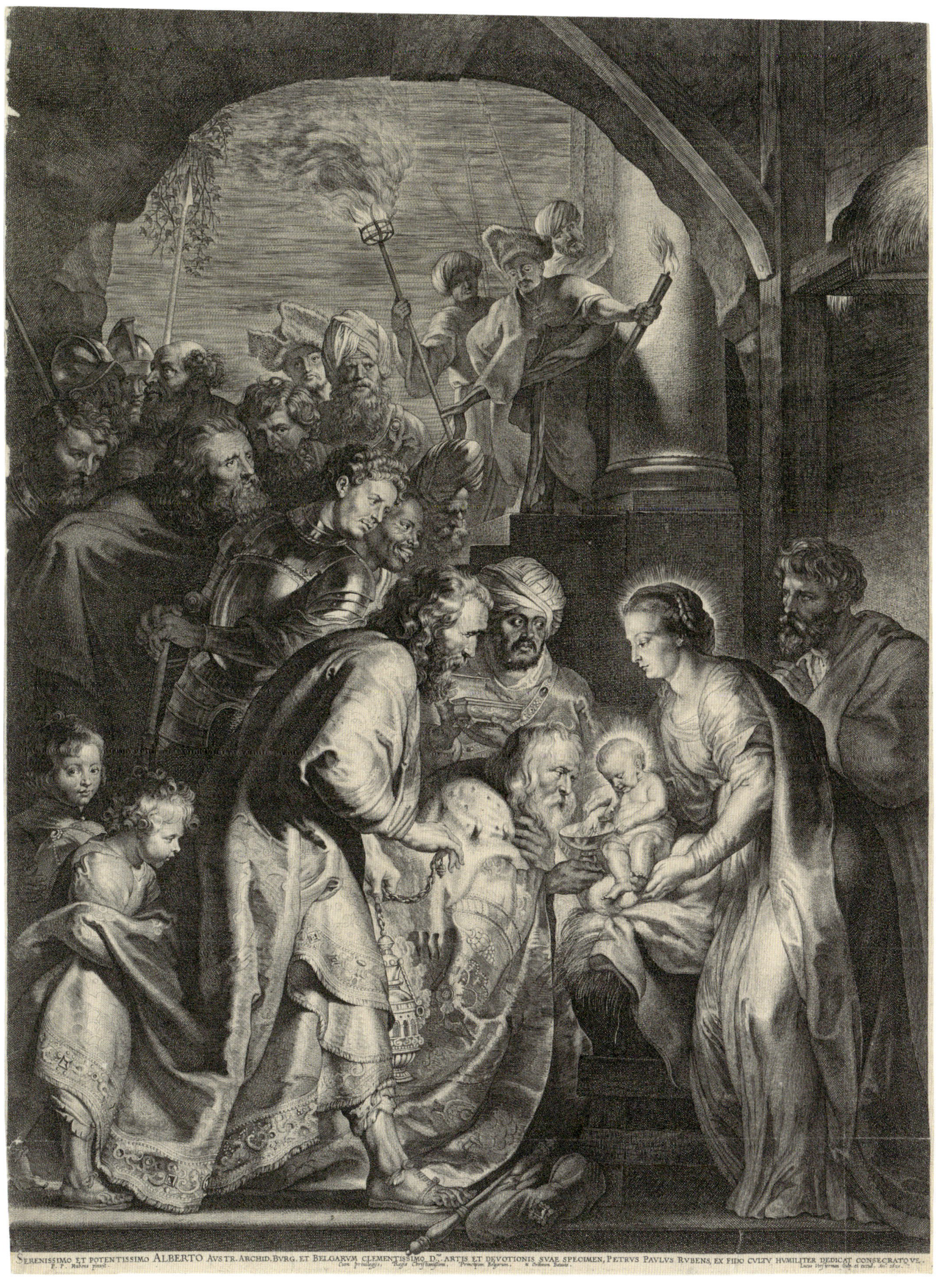

Rubens (Inventor / designer), Lucas Vorsterman I (Stecher, Verleger / engraver, publisher)
Die Anbetung der Könige / The Adoration of the Magi, 1620
Widmung an Albrecht VII. / dedicated to Albert VII von / by Rubens
Kupferstich / engraving SGSM, Inv. 30058 D

III. Privilegien

Mit einem Privileg, einer Art frühmodernem Copyright, suchten Künstler im späten 16. und frühen 17. Jahrhundert einzelne Stiche oder Werke ganzer Jahrgänge zu schützen. Kernphrase der in den Kupferstichen vermerkten Formulierungen war das lateinische „cum privilegium", das an gut sichtbarer Stelle und mit Hinweis auf den jeweils Erteilenden platziert war. Wie Nadine M. Orenstein ausgeführt hat, dienten Privilegien „nicht als Schutz geistigen Eigentums, sondern als Schutz für eine bestimmte Platte und deren Verkauf".[1] Die Motive selbst waren also den Kopisten preisgegeben, aber Künstler erhofften sich, zumindest „vor schlechten Nachahmungen und schlechten Kopien" geschützt zu sein, wie Nils Büttner für Rubens annimmt.[2]

Das Einwerben von Privilegien für Druckgraphik war durchaus nicht für alle Künstler interessant, doch Hendrick Goltzius und Peter Paul Rubens bildeten um 1600 diesbezüglich namhafte Ausnahmen. Während Goltzius am 12. April 1595 ein generelles Privileg für sechs Jahre von Kaiser Rudolf II. in Prag erhielt,[3] bemühte sich Rubens um Privilegien für drei Länder: die Vereinigten Provinzen (erteilt am 8. Juni 1619 für sieben Jahre),[4] Frankreich (erteilt am 3. Juli 1619 für zehn Jahre) und die Spanischen Niederlande (erteilt am 16. Januar 1620 zunächst für Brabant, von 1630 bis 1642 für das gesamte Herrschaftsgebiet Spaniens).[5] Alle diese Privilegien wurden wohl nach ihrem Ablauf verlängert. In seinem Fall sind die drei Privilegien für die Kunstwissenschaft ein Indiz, dass Rubens selbst an der Produktion eines Stichs beteiligt war, und in manchen Fällen lässt sich die jeweilige Privilegsformel, die mit wechselnden Herrschern anders lautete, für eine Datierung von Stichen heranziehen, auf denen selbst kein Datum vermerkt ist (mehr hierzu unten).

Obwohl kein unmittelbarer finanzieller Gewinn aus Privilegien bekannt ist, scheinen sie sich in den Augen einiger Künstler auch der Nachfolgegeneration ausgezahlt zu haben, denn diese beantragten und erhielten Privilegien für den Vertrieb von Werken ihrer Meister: Jacob Matham erhielt nach Ablauf des Privilegs seines Stiefvaters 1601 von Rudolf II. ein unbefristetes Privileg; ebenso Jan Harmensz. Muller (1606) und Jacques de Gheyn II (1610); Pieter Soutman erlangte 1636 ein generelles Privileg in Holland.

Beide Künstler, Goltzius und Rubens, mussten früh Kopien oder nicht autorisierte Stiche nach ihren Blättern erdulden, insofern war ihr Bemühen um Privilegien der Versuch, diese ausufernde Produktion einzudämmen. Die unerlaubten Kopien wie auch gegen sie gerichtete Privilegien bestätigten jedoch gleichermaßen, dass es sich hier um bedeutsame oder doch verkaufsträchtige Werke handelte. So paradox es scheinen mag, vermehrten diese unerwünschten Kopien den Ruhm der Künstler. Auf diese Weise wurde das echte Privileg eines Künstlers zu einem Gütesiegel: In solchen Blättern war die Qualität des Stichs und des Motivs vom Künstler selbst geprüft und gebilligt worden. Dass es aber auch „unechte" Privilegien gab, zeigt die Werkauswahl in diesem Kapitel.

Nachdem Goltzius 1595 ein Privileg für das Heilige Römische Reich von Kaiser Rudolf II. erhalten hatte, begann er, dies in seinen Stichen

III. Privileges

In the late sixteenth and early seventeenth centuries, artists tried to protect individual prints or the works created within a certain time period with a privilege, a kind of early modern copyright. The core phrase used in engravings, the Latin "cum privilegium," was joined with a mention of the privilege grantor and placed in a conspicuous part of the print motif. As Nadine M. Orenstein explained with respect to privileges, "They did not serve as a protection of intellectual property but rather as a protection of the specified plate and selling of that plate."[1] The images themselves, in this sense, were still exposed to the risk of being copied, but artists nevertheless hoped to be protected "from bad imitations and bad copies," as Nils Büttner has assumed was the case for Rubens.[2]

Requesting privileges by no means made sense for every artist, but around 1600 Hendrick Goltzius and Peter Paul Rubens were notable exceptions to the rule. While Goltzius obtained a general privilege for six years from Emperor Rudolf II in Prague on April 12, 1595,[3] Rubens requested privileges for three countries: the United Provinces (granted on June 8, 1619, for seven years),[4] France (granted on July 3, 1619, for ten years), and the Spanish Netherlands (granted on January 16, 1620, initially for Brabant, but expanded to the entire territory under Spanish control from 1630 to 1642).[5] All these privileges were extended when their expiration dates neared. In Rubens's case, the three privileges are an indication for art historians that Rubens himself was involved in the production of a certain print. In some cases, the specific wording of a privilege allows us to determine when a print bearing no date was made, because the wording changed with different rulers (see below).

Even though we know of no immediate financial reward stemming from privileges, some artists of the following generation seem to have found them worth obtaining. These artists requested and were granted privileges for selling works by their masters: Jacob Matham obtained an unlimited privilege from Rudolf II once that of his stepfather expired in 1601, and Jan Harmensz. Muller and Jacques de Gheyn II also received privileges under which they issued prints after Goltzius (in 1606 and 1610 respectively). Pieter Soutman was granted a general privilege for the Northern Netherlands in 1636.

Both artists, Goltzius and Rubens, had to tolerate copies and unauthorized prints after their works early on, and their efforts to obtain privileges may have been an attempt at containing this sprawling production. Both the unauthorized copies and the privileges directed against them, however, confirm that the works in question were notable or at least valuable. As paradoxical as it may sound, these undesired copies increased the artists' fame. In this manner, an authentic privilege became a hallmark of excellence: the quality of the print and the motif had been assessed and approved by the artist himself. There were also works bearing falsified privileges, though, as will become evident in the prints illustrated in the present chapter.

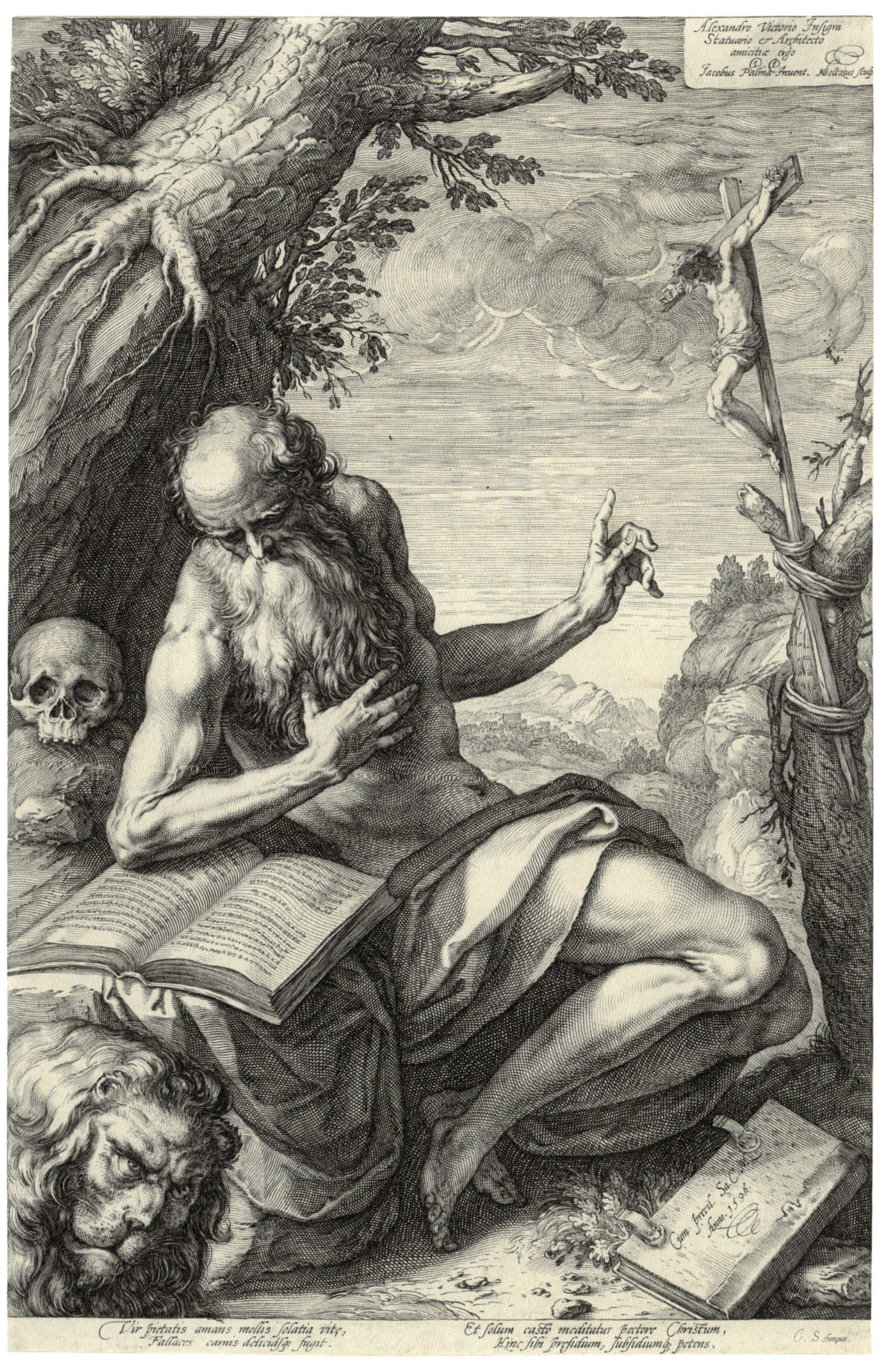

Goltzius (Stecher / engraver), nach / after Jacopo Palma II
Der hl. Hieronymus / St. Jerome, 1596
Kupferstich / engraving SGSM, Inv. 31003 D

sichtbar zu machen. In seinem viel beachteten Stich *Der hl. Hieronymus* (1596) ist die Formel „Cum privil. Sa. C. M." gut sichtbar auf dem Buch am Boden vor dem Heiligen angebracht (Abb. S. 117). Im Vergleich zu dieser zentralen Stelle ist die Widmung an den Bildhauer Alessandro Vittoria oben rechts im Bildfeld leicht zu übersehen. Das Goltzius-Werkverzeichnis listet für dieses Motiv allein vier Zustände und sechs Kopien auf, eine weitere fand sich in den Beständen der Staatlichen Graphischen Sammlung München.[6]

Jacob Matham (1571–1631) verfügte seit 1601 über das kaiserliche Privileg für die von ihm herausgegebenen Stiche, und so findet es sich etwa in dem Stich nach Goltzius' *Die büßende hl. Maria Magdalena* (um 1607–1612), einem in der Zeit der sogenannten Gegenreformation besonders häufig gewählten Motiv: „Cum privil. Sa. Cæ M." (Abb. S. 119). Der Katholik Matham hielt sich mit diesem Stich an die Auflage aus Prag: Seine auf diese Weise geschützten Werke durften nicht gegen den katholischen Glauben verstoßen.[7]

In der Staatlichen Graphischen Sammlung München werden eine Reihe von Kopien nach Goltzius-Stichen aufbewahrt, die zeigen, wie prekär der Schutz war, den ein Privileg bot. Da ist zum Beispiel eine seitengleiche Kopie nach dem *Bildnis des Frederick de Vries* (1597), die kurz nach dem Original entstanden sein muss (Abb. S. 123, 257). Der anonyme Stecher schuf nicht nur eine Nachahmung des Motivs (die sichtbar macht, wie meisterhaft im Vergleich Goltzius' Werk war), er kopierte auch gleich das Monogramm von Goltzius, die Datierung sowie die Privilegsformel an gleicher Stelle unten links.

Dasselbe Phänomen findet sich in der zeitgenössischen Kopie nach *Das letzte Abendmahl* (1598) aus der Serie *Die Passion Christi* von Goltzius, einem seiner Hauptwerke (Abb. 122). Wie im Original findet sich die Privilegsformel unten rechts auf dem Absatz, ebenso wie das Künstlermonogramm, alles in der Absicht, Käufer über die Autorschaft zu täuschen. Die Tatsache aber, dass solche Kopien von den kapitalen Werken Goltzius' angefertigt wurden, trug wie ausgeführt letztlich zu ihrem Ruhm bei. Und ambitionierte, gelehrte Sammler von Goltzius' Kunst machten es sich vielleicht auch zur Aufgabe, beim Kauf Kopie und Original unterscheiden zu können.

An dieser Stelle soll ein weiteres Werk angeführt werden, obwohl es das Goltzius-Privileg nicht trägt: eine von drei in der Staatlichen Graphischen Sammlung vorhandenen Kopien nach seinem Stich *Pietà* (1596), die stattdessen eine andere ungewöhnliche Inschrift aufweist (Abb. S. 121, 235). In diesem Fall war die Abwesenheit der Privilegsformel sogar besonders wichtig für den Fälscher: Denn er wünschte dieses Werk nicht als eines des Haarlemer Meisters auszugeben, sondern als eines von Albrecht Dürer! Deshalb fügte er unten rechts dessen Monogramm AD ins Bild ein. Die angestrebte Verwechslung bezog womöglich Schützenhilfe aus einer Anekdote, die seit 1604 in Karel van Manders Lebensbeschreibung von Hendrick Goltzius zu lesen war. Dort wurde berichtet, der Künstler habe auf der Frankfurter Messe nicht nur Sammler, sondern auch Stecher darin täuschen können, dass das Motiv der *Beschneidung* von Dürer sei, indem er das Blatt künstlich alterte und das berühmte Monogramm hinzufügte, vor allem aber, weil sein Stechstil das Vorbild so perfekt imitierte.[8]

After Goltzius obtained a privilege for the Holy Roman Empire from Emperor Rudolf II in 1595, he started placing it ostentatiously in his prints. In his much noted engraving *St. Jerome* (1596), the wording "Cum privil. Sa. C. M." is highly visible on the book in front of the saint (fig. p. 117). In contrast to this central position, the print's dedication to the sculptor Alessandro Vittoria in the upper right part of the image might easily be overlooked. The Goltzius catalogue raisonné lists four states and six copies by other artists for this print alone, to which an additional copy recently found in the holdings of the Staatliche Graphische Sammlung München can be added.[6]

In 1601 Jacob Matham (1571–1631) obtained an imperial privilege that covered every print he published. Among the works carrying this privilege is an engraving after Goltzius's *St. Mary Magdalene Repentant* (ca. 1607–1612), a motif that was highly popular with Catholic collectors: "Cum privil. Sa. Cæ M." (fig. p. 119). With this print, the Catholic Matham adhered to the requirement from Prague: No works issued with this privilege could go against the Catholic faith.[7]

The Staatliche Graphische Sammlung München keeps a number of copies after Goltzius prints that show just how precarious the protection granted by a privilege was. One example is the copy (after 1597) in the same direction after the *Portrait of Frederick de Vries* that must have been made shortly after the original (figs. pp. 123, 257). Not only did the anonymous engraver imitate the motif (thus providing evidence of just how masterful Goltzius's work is in comparison), but he also copied the artist's monogram, "HG," and the date, as well as the wording of the privilege, which he positioned in the lower left corner, just as Goltzius had.

The same phenomenon appears in a copy (after 1598) of *The Last Supper* from the series *The Passion of Christ* by Goltzius, one of his capital works (fig. p. 122). As in the original, the privilege and the artist's monogram are positioned in the lower right on the step, all in an attempt to trick customers into believing that Goltzius was the creator of the print. The fact that such copies were made of Goltzius's major works only added to their fame. Ambitious and learned collectors might pride themselves on being able to tell such copies from the originals.

An additional work is worth mentioning in this context, even though it does not bear the Goltzius privilege. One of the three copies (after 1596) kept in the SGSM after Goltzius's famous print *Pietà* offers a different, rather unusual inscription (figs. pp. 121, 235). In this case the absence of Goltzius's privilege was especially important to the forger, for he wished to present this work as being not by the Haarlem master but by Albrecht Dürer! For that reason he added the monogram "AD" in the lower right corner. This attempted deception may be connected to an anecdote that Karel van Mander related in his 1604 biography of Hendrick Goltzius. The story was that the artist had been able to mislead collectors and engravers alike at the Frankfurt Fair into believing that his print *The Circumcision* was actually done by Dürer. To accomplish this he had artificially aged the paper, added the famous monogram, and, above all, masterfully imitated the style of Dürer's engravings.[8]

Rubens konnte ab 1620 seine Stiche mit den drei oben genannten Privilegien versehen. Zu dieser Zeit arbeitete er produktiv mit Lucas Vorsterman I (1595/96–1674/75) zusammen. So entstand etwa eine *Anbetung der Hirten* (1620), die mit folgender Privilegsformel versehen war (Abb. S. 124): „Cum priuilegijs, Regis Christianißimi, Principum Belgarum, & Ordinum Batauiæ." („Mit den Privilegien des höchst christlichen Königs, des Fürsten der Belgier & der Generalstaaten"). Anstelle von „Batauiæ" konnte auch das Wort „Confœderatorum" (Bund) stehen.

Mit dem Tod des Erzherzogs Albrecht VII. (1559–1621), der gemeinsam mit der spanischen Infantin Isabella Clara Eugenia (1566–1633) souverän über die südlichen Niederlande regiert hatte, fiel die Herrschaft nach seinem Tod an den spanischen König.[9] Die Erzherzogin blieb aber bis zu ihrem Tod seine Statthalterin, weshalb die Formulierung mit „Ihrer Durchlaucht, der Infantin" auf sie zugeschnitten werden musste. Sie lautete zwischen 1621 und 1633: „Cum priuilegijs Regis Cristianissimi Serenissimæ Infantis et Ordinum Confœderatorum." Der Stich *Die Flucht nach Ägypten* (1632), angefertigt von Marinus van der Goes (1606/07–1639), fällt in diese Zeit und war entsprechend mit dieser Formulierung versehen (Abb. S. 126).

Die Statthalterin verstarb 1633 und ihr folgte der Kardinalinfant Ferdinand nach, unter dem Rubens wieder zur ersten Formulierung zurückkehrte. Aufgrund dieser Veränderungen in der Privilegsformel kann die Entstehungszeit mancher nicht datierter Stiche genauer eingekreist werden.

Eine Besonderheit findet sich in den Holzschnitten, die Rubens als Verleger ausweisen und von Christoffel Jegher (1596–1652/53) Anfang der 1630er-Jahre geschnitten wurden. Auf ihnen ist nur die Kurzform „Cum priuilegijs" vermerkt, eine Variante, die womöglich der schwierigeren Anbringung von Inschriften in Langholz geschuldet war (siehe Abb. S. 145, 182f., 184 f., 208 f.).

Auch nach Rubens' Tod lohnte es sich für Verleger, Stiche nach seinen Gemälden mit einem Privileg zu versehen. Das Blatt *Christus in Emmaus* (1643/um 1700) ist solch ein Fall (Abb. S. 127). 1643 legte Pieter Soutman seine eigene Zeichnung nach dem gleichnamigen Rubens-Bild seinem Schüler Pieter van Sompel für die Umsetzung in

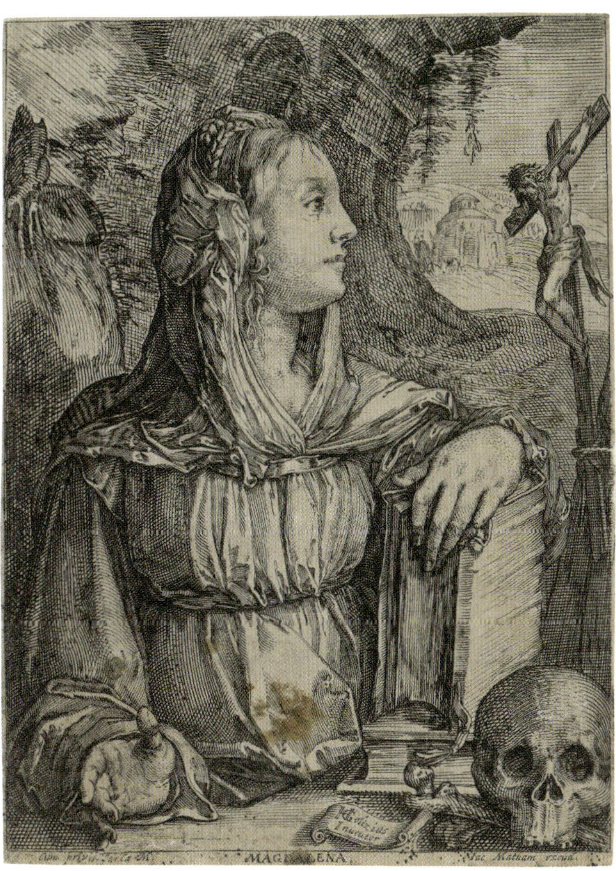

Goltzius (Inventor / designer),
Jacob Matham (zugeschr. Stecher / attr. engraver, Verleger / publisher)
Die büßende hl. Maria Magdalena / St. Mary Magdalene Repentant, ca. 1607–1612
Kupferstich / engraving SGSM, Inv. 31163 D

From 1620 on, Rubens used the three privileges mentioned above in his prints. At this time he was working productively with Lucas Vorsterman I (1595/96–1674/75). Together, they crafted *The Adoration of the Shepherds* (1620), which bears the wording of the three privileges (fig. p. 124): "Cum priuilegijs, Regis Christianißimi, Principum Belgarum, & Ordinum Batauiæ." (With the privileges of the highest Christian king, the leader of the Belgians & the States General.) Instead of "Batauiæ," the word "Confœderatorum" (confederation) was sometimes used.

Upon the death of Archduke Albert VII (1559–1621), who together with the Infanta Isabella Clara Eugenia (1566–1633) had served as sovereign ruler of the Southern Netherlands, rule fell to the Spanish king.[9] However, the Infanta remained governor until her death, and for that reason the wording was changed to "Her Majesty, the Infanta." Accordingly, between 1621 and 1633 the privilege read: "Cum priuilegijs Regis Cristianissimi Serenissimæ Infantis et Ordinum Confœderatorum." The print *The Flight into Egypt* (1632) was engraved by Marinus van der Goes (1606/07–1639) during this time and therefore displays this wording (fig. p. 126).

The Infanta Isabella died in 1633 and was followed by the Cardinal-Infante Ferdinand, under whose rule Rubens returned to the initial wording of his privilege for the Southern Netherlands. Because of these changes in the wording of the privileges, the dates for some prints from that era can be more precisely determined.

The woodcuts that Rubens published in the early 1630s, engraved by Christoffel Jegher (1596–1652/53), stand out in regard to his privilege. They bear only the abbreviated wording "Cum priuilegijs," perhaps because of the difficulty of cutting inscriptions in side grain (see figs. pp. 145, 182–183, 184–185, 208–209).

Even after Rubens's death, it seems to have paid off for publishers to add privileges to prints after his paintings. The print *The Supper at Emmaus* (1643/ca. 1700) is a case in point (fig. p. 127). In 1643 Pieter Soutman gave his own drawing after Rubens'

einen Kupferstich vor und fügte sein Privileg in die Platte ein.[10] Die Platte wurde einige Jahrzehnte später von dem Amsterdamer Verleger Gerard Valck erworben und mit dessen Adresse versehen, ohne dass Soutmans Privileg getilgt worden wäre.

Das folgende Beispiel, eine Kopie im Gegensinn der oben besprochenen *Anbetung der Hirten* (1620) von Rubens / Vorsterman (Abb. S. 124), belegt dagegen, dass das Privilegsystem auch nach Rubens' Tod 1640 seine Berechtigung behielt (Abb. S. 125). Der Pariser Verleger und Stecher François Ragot (tätig in den 1630er-Jahren, gest. 1670) hatte anscheinend ein gutes Auskommen mit seinen Kopien nach Rubens-Graphik, denn von ihm kennen wir kaum Blätter nach anderen Künstlern. Er versah das vorliegende Blatt mit einem Privileg des französischen Königs, welches er 1641 für Stiche nach Rubens erhalten hatte.[11] Ragot fertigte besonders viele Kopien nach Vorsterman- und Pontius-Blättern an, alle jedoch gespiegelt zu den Vorlagen (siehe das Kapitel „Nachbilder", S. 270–289).

painting *The Supper at Emmaus* to his student Pieter van Sompel to be transferred into an engraving, to which Soutman added his own privilege.[10] The printing plate was bought decades later by the Amsterdam publisher Gerard Valck, who added his address but left Soutman's privilege untouched.

Such infringements notwithstanding, our final example, a copy in reverse (ca. 1641) of the abovementioned *The Adoration of the Shepherds* by Rubens / Vorsterman, confirms that the system of privileges remained in use even after Rubens's death in 1640 (figs. pp. 124, 125). The Parisian publisher and engraver François Ragot (active from around the 1630s, died 1670) seems to have prospered from his copies after Rubens prints, because we know of his issuing hardly any prints after other artists. He protected the print shown here with a privilege from the French king which he had obtained in 1641 for prints after Rubens.[11] Ragot produced many prints after Vorsterman and Pontius in particular, all of them reverse copies of the originals (see the chapter "Afterimages," pp. 270–289).

1 Orenstein 2006, S. 314 (Übers. der Autorin). Dieser Aufsatz bietet eine sehr genaue Analyse der Situation um 1600 sowie eine tabellarische Übersicht über die in Holland beantragten und bewilligten Privilegien.
2 Büttner 2011a, S. 127.
3 Der Wortlaut zit. bei Nichols 1991/92, S. 91, unter 12. April 1595.
4 Siehe Rutgers 2021, S. 104.
5 Die präzisen Daten und Quellen zitiert Renger 1974a, S. 125, sowie ders., in: Göttingen/Hannover/Nürnberg 1977, S. 15. Die Texte der Privilegien für Frankreich und die Spanischen Niederlande samt informativen Kommentaren sind leicht erreichbar in Meier 2020a, Quellen 7–9; für Holland vgl. Orenstein 2006. – Gelder 1950/51, S. 128, sowie Orenstein 2006, S. 317, berichten, dass der Maler Balthasar Flessiers bereits 1614 das erste Privileg für einen Stich von Andries Jacobsz. Stock, einem Schüler von Jacques de Gheyn II, nach einem Rubens-Gemälde erhielt (SGSM, Inv. 29980 D). – Für Bücher war es durchaus üblich, Privilegien in mehreren Ländern zu beantragen, vor Rubens jedoch nicht für Druckgraphik. Rubens' Lehrer Otto van Veen beantragte 1608 Privilegien für zwei Emblembücher in Holland, Frankreich und Spanien (Orenstein et al. 1993, S. 171). Der Gelehrte Justus Lipsius erhielt für seine Bücher Privilegien vom deutschen Kaiser, dem französischen König sowie den südlichen Niederlanden (Hottle 2004, S. 82, Anm. 39).
6 Vgl. NHD Goltzius 2012, 330. Die dort nicht aufgeführte Kopie SGSM, Inv. 93746 D, im Gegensinn mit einem Text von Laurentius Beyerlinck, dem Antwerpener Theologen und Zensor. Ihm widmete Rubens seinen Stich *Martyrium des hl. Laurentius*; siehe S. 99 sowie Abb. S. 105.
7 Der Wortlaut in: Nichols 1991/92, S. 91, unter 12. April 1595. An das Prager Privileg war die Auflage geknüpft, dass die Stiche nichts enthalten dürften, das gegen den katholischen Glauben oder die Gesetze des Heiligen Römischen Reichs verstieße, was aus heutiger Sicht einer religiösen und politischen Zensur entspricht.
8 Mander (1604) 2000, S. 338. Für diesen Zweck tilgte er ebenso das Selbstporträt aus den Abzügen, die er mit zur Frankfurter Messe nahm.
9 Vgl. Brussel 1998 zur Regentschaft von und insbesondere zur künstlerischen Blüte unter Albrecht und Isabella.
10 1611 hatte Willem van Swanenburg einen ersten Stich nach Rubens' Gemälde angefertigt; siehe SGSM, Inv. 30120 D. Vgl. Renger 1974a, S. 133 f., sowie Meier 2020a, Kat. 1.
11 Vgl. Antwerpen/Québec 2004, S. 38.

1 Orenstein 2006, p. 314. This essay provides a precise analysis of the situation around 1600, as well as a table with an overview of the privileges requested and granted in the Northern Netherlands.
2 Büttner 2011a, p. 127.
3 For the exact wording, see Nichols 1991/92, p. 91, under April 12, 1595.
4 See Rutgers 2021, p. 104.
5 For the precise dates and sources, see Renger 1974a, p. 125, and Renger, in: Göttingen/Hannover/Nürnberg 1977, p. 15. The wording of the privileges for France and the Spanish Netherlands with informative commentary are easily accessible in Meier 2020a, Quellen 7–9; for the Northern Netherlands, see Orenstein 2006. – Gelder 1950/51, p. 128, and Orenstein 2006, p. 317, recount that the painter Balthasar Flessiers obtained a privilege for a print engraved by Andries Jacobsz. Stock, a student of Jacques de Gheyn II, after a painting by Rubens as early as 1614 (SGSM, inv. 29980 D). – For books it was common practice to request privileges in several countries, but Rubens was the first to do this for prints. His teacher Otto van Veen in 1608 requested privileges for two emblem books in the Northern Netherlands, France, and Spain (Orenstein et al. 1993, p. 171). The scholar Justus Lipsius obtained privileges for his books from the German emperor and the French king, as well as in the Southern Netherlands (Hottle 2004, p. 82, n. 39).
6 See NHD Goltzius 2012, 330. The copy not listed there, SGSM, inv. 93746 D, is in reverse and has an inscription authored by Laurentius Beyerlinck, the Antwerp theologian and censor. Rubens dedicated his print *The Martyrdom of St. Lawrence* to him; see p. 99 and fig. p. 105.
7 For the wording, see Nichols 1991/92, p. 91, under April 12, 1595. Attached to the privilege from Prague was the condition that prints not contain anything directed against the Catholic faith or the laws of the Holy Roman Empire. Today this would be seen as religious and political censorship.
8 Mander (1604) 1994, p. 397, fol. 284v. For this purpose he also removed his self-portrait from the copies he took to the Frankfurt Fair.
9 See Brussel 1998 on the regency and especially the artistic blossoming under Albert and Isabella.
10 In 1611 Willem van Swanenburg had crafted the first print after this Rubens painting (see SGSM, inv. 30120 D). See Renger 1974a, pp. 133–134, and Meier 2020a, cat. 1.
11 See Antwerpen/Québec 2004, p. 38.

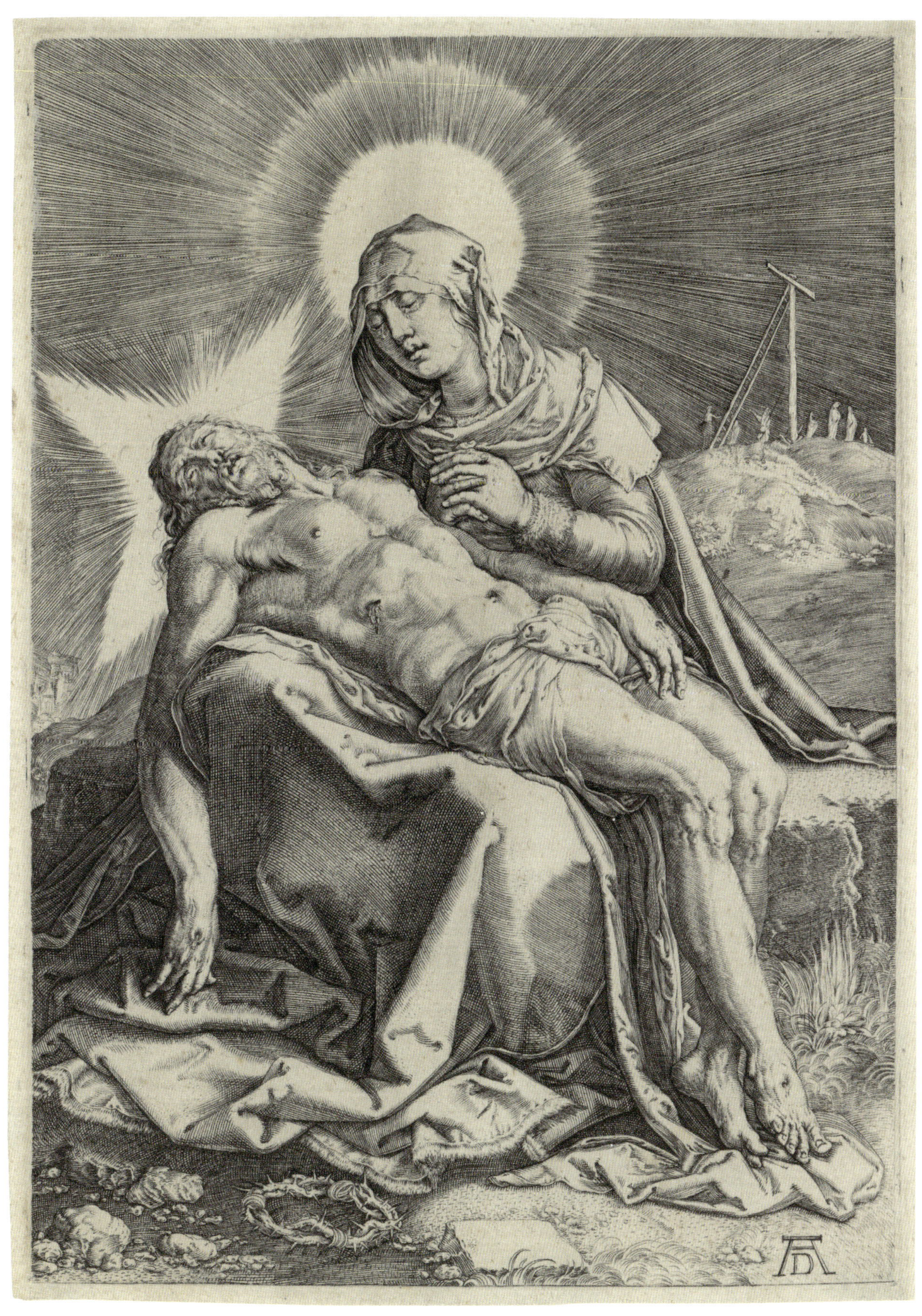

Anonymer Stecher / anonymous engraver, Kopie nach / copy after Goltzius
Pietà, nach / after 1596
Kupferstich / engraving SGSM, Inv. 63754 D

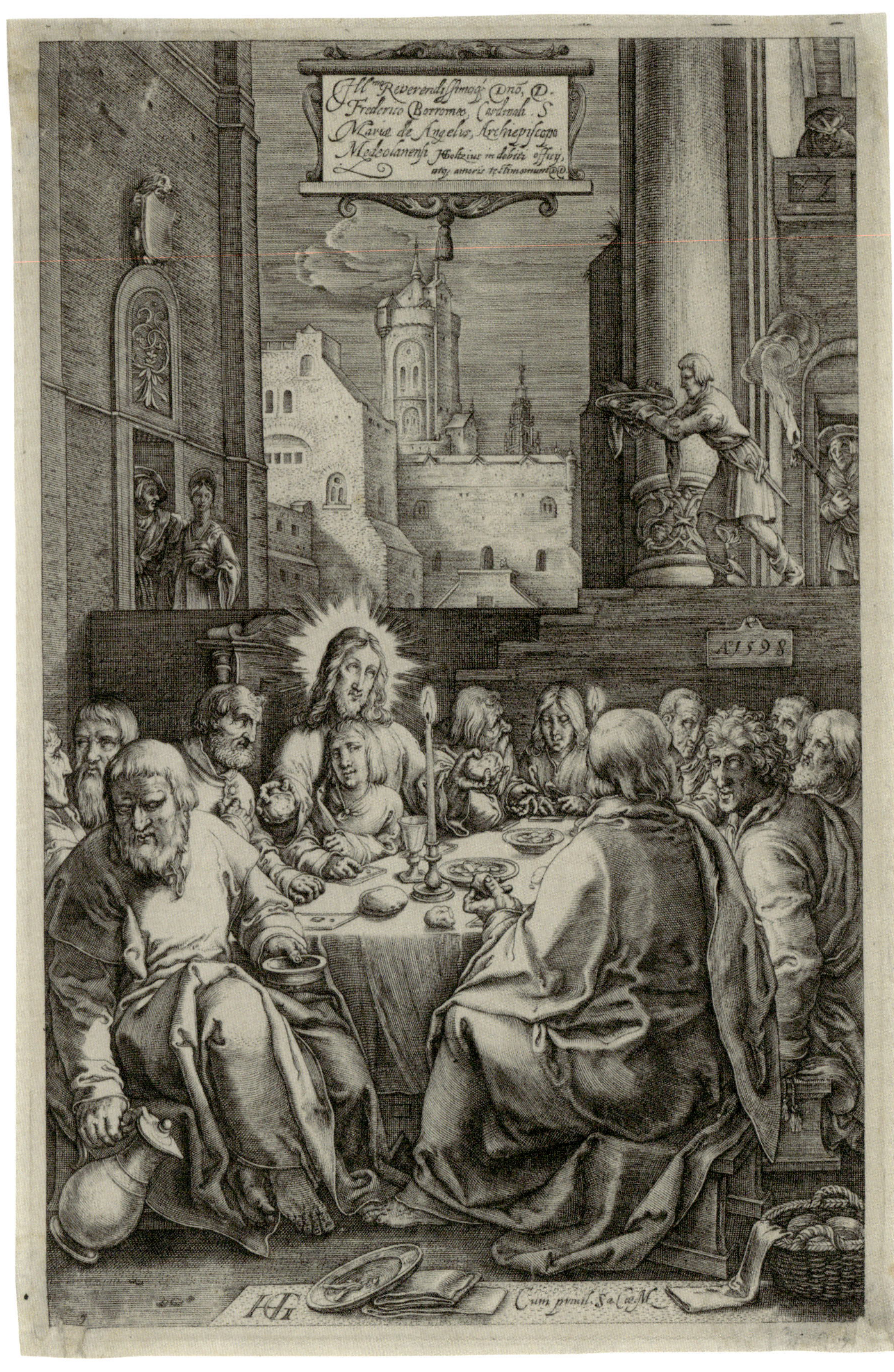

Anonymer Stecher / anonymous engraver, Kopie nach / copy after Goltzius
Das letzte Abendmahl / The Last Supper, nach / after 1598
Kupferstich / engraving SGSM, Inv. 66249 D

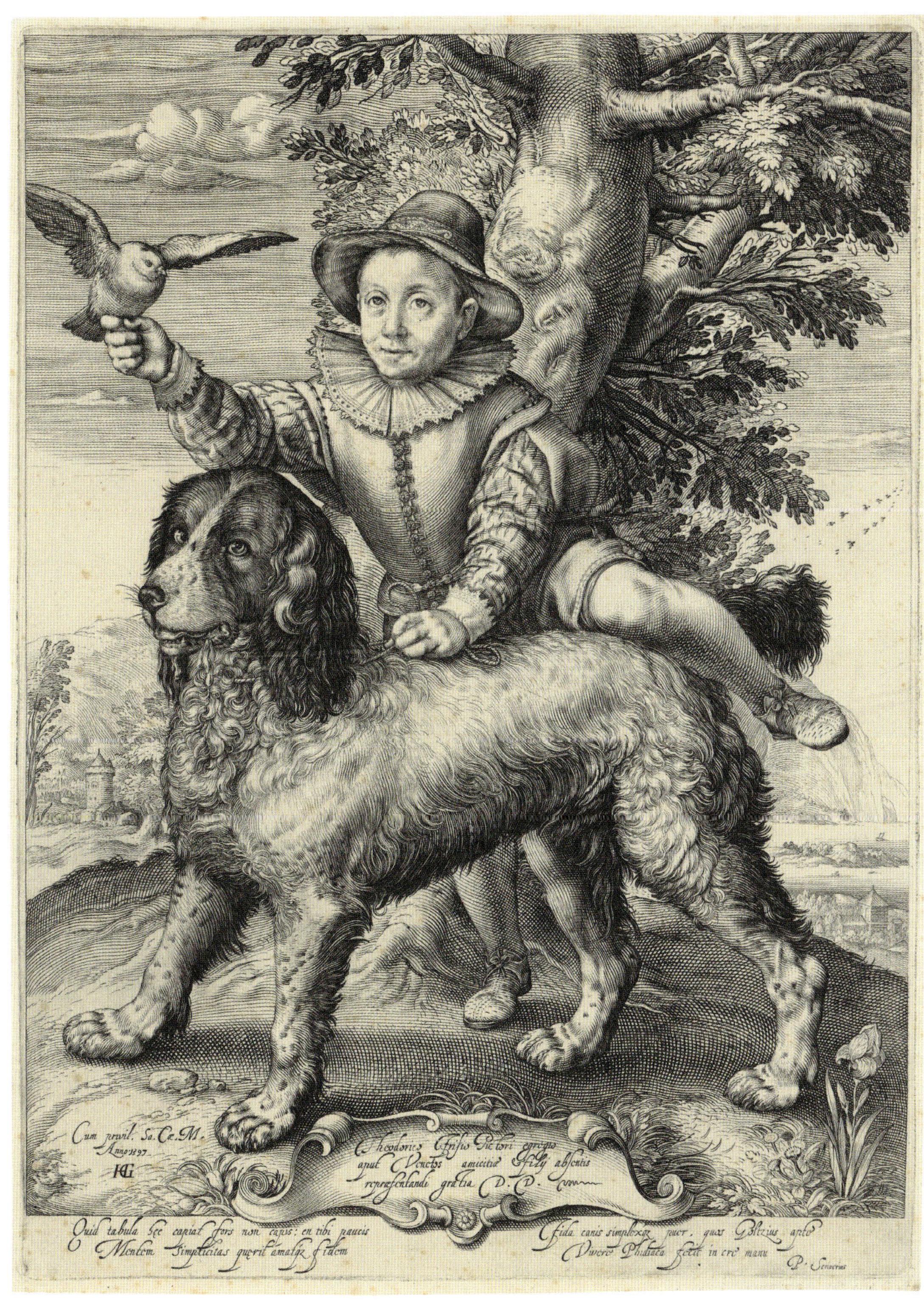

Anonymer Stecher / anonymous engraver, Kopie nach / copy after Goltzius
Bildnis des Frederick de Vries (Der Hund des Goltzius) / Portrait of Frederick de Vries (Goltzius's Dog), nach / after 1597
Kupferstich / engraving SGSM, Inv. 31020 D

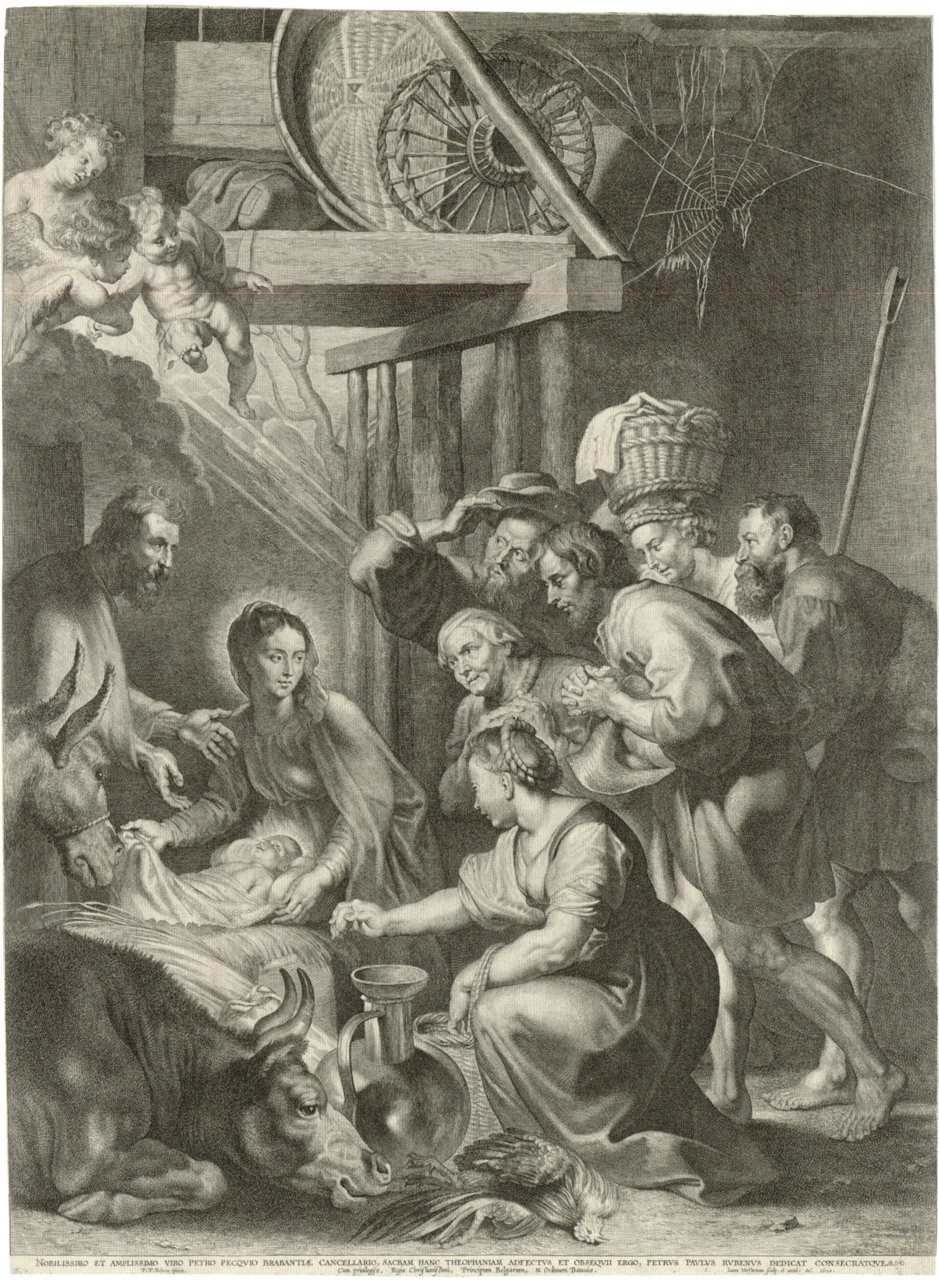

Rubens (Inventor / designer), Lucas Vorsterman I (Stecher, Verleger / engraver, publisher)
Die Anbetung der Hirten / The Adoration of the Shepherds, 1620
Kupferstich / engraving SGSM, Inv. 30040 D

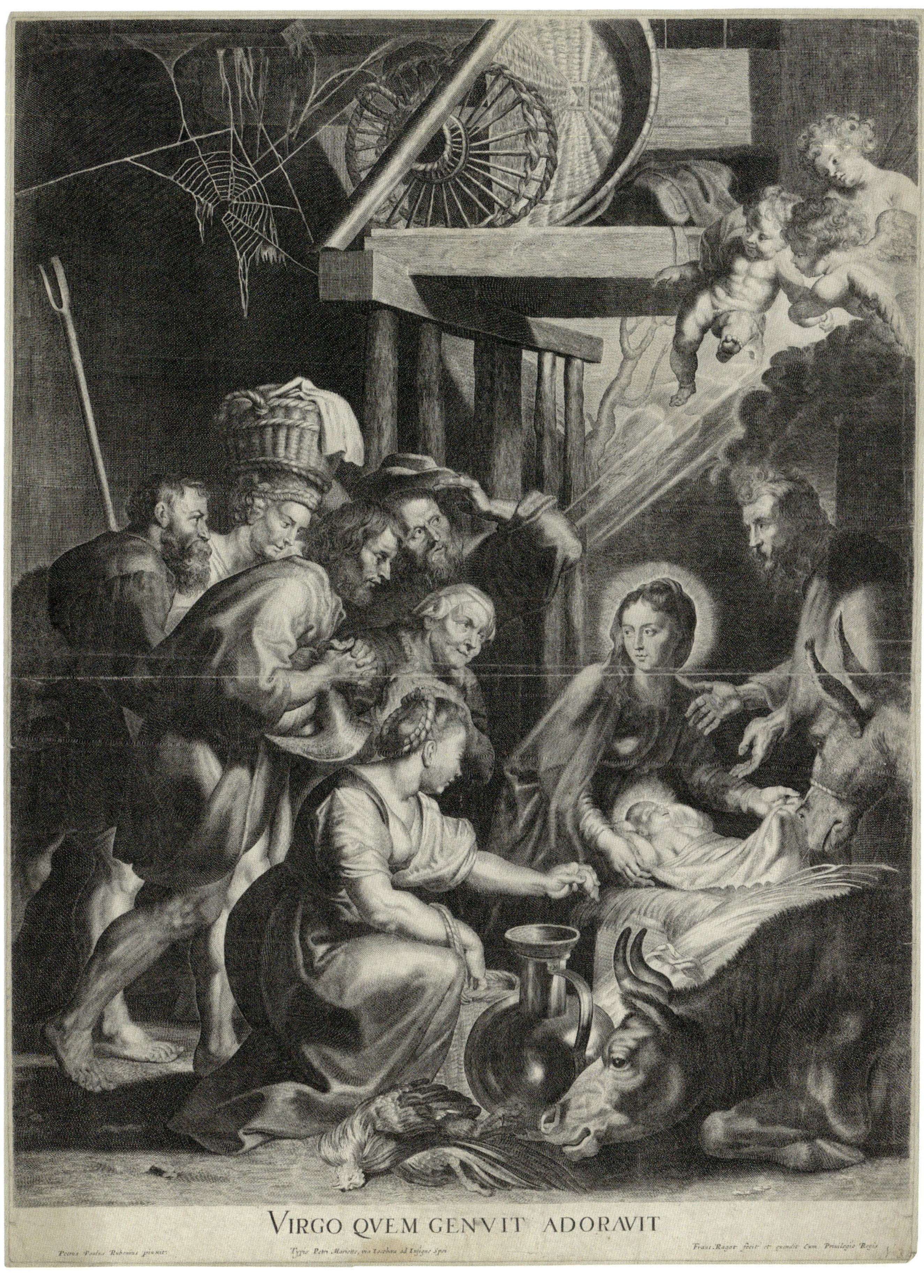

François Ragot (Stecher, Verleger / engraver, publisher), Kopie nach / copy after Lucas Vorsterman I, nach / after Rubens
Die Anbetung der Hirten / The Adoration of the Shepherds, ca. 1641
Kupferstich / engraving SGSM, Inv. 2022:47 D

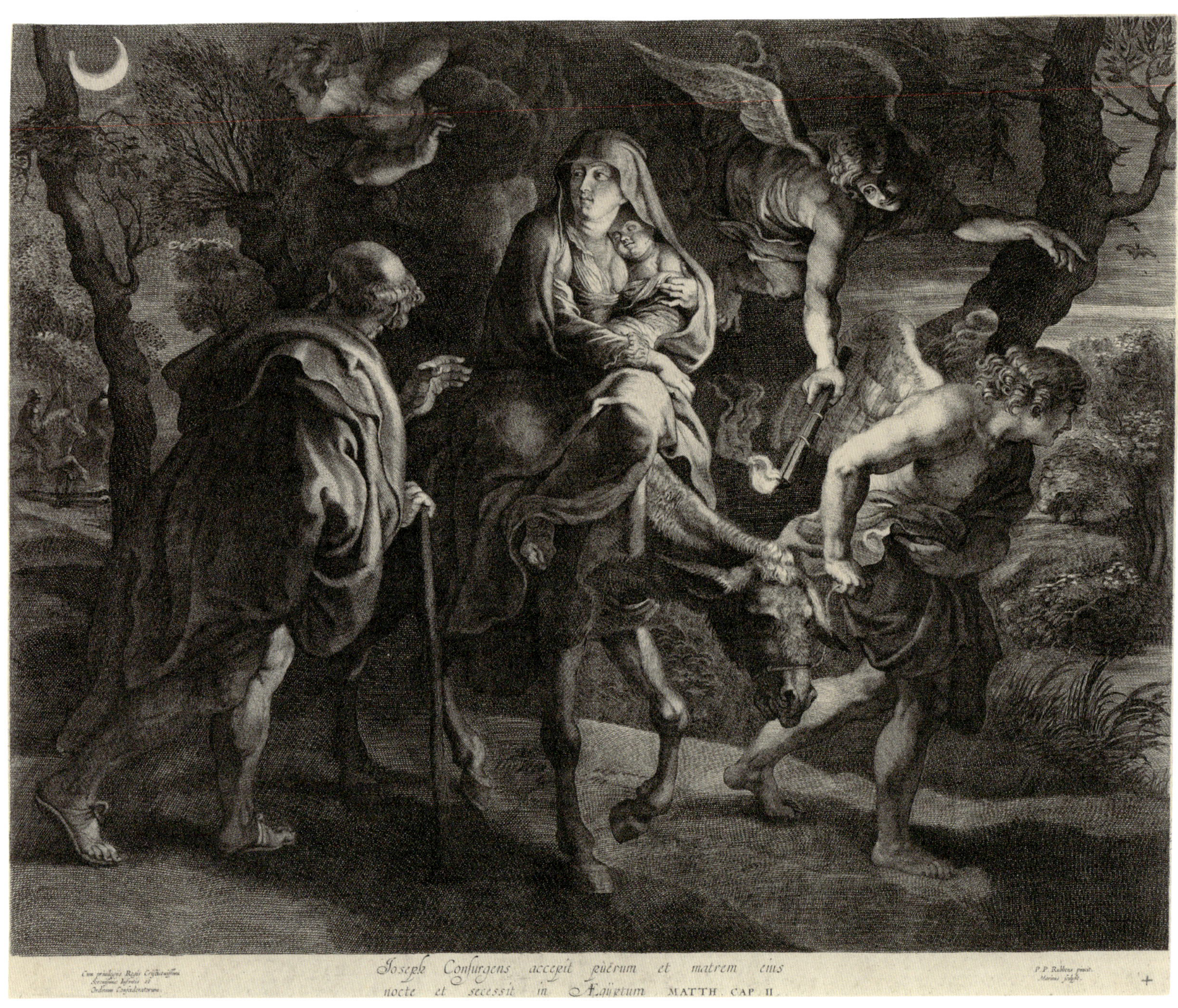

Rubens (Inventor / designer), Marinus van der Goes (Stecher / engraver)
Die Flucht nach Ägypten / The Flight into Egypt, 1632
Kupferstich / engraving SGSM, Inv. 30061 D

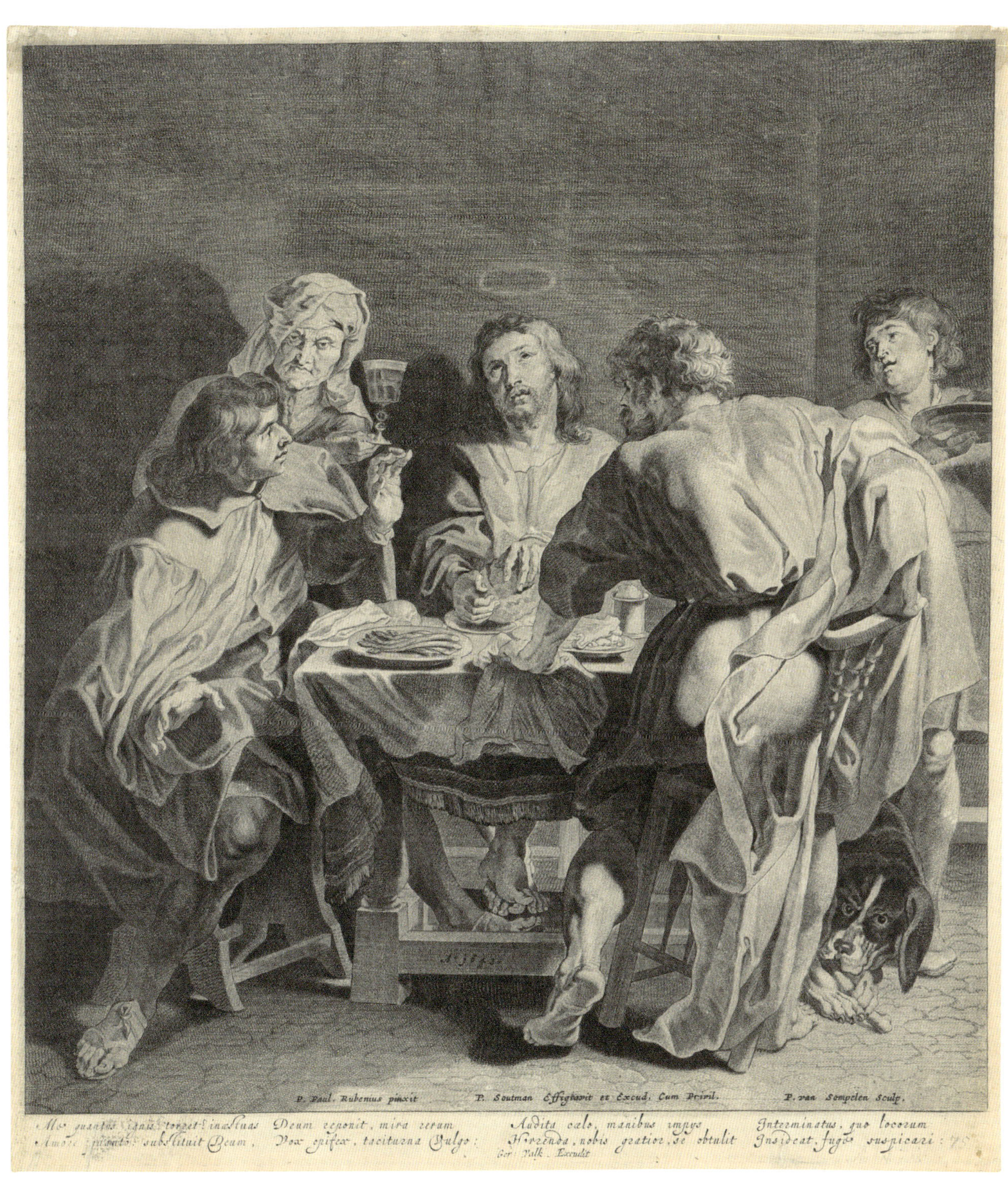

Pieter Soutman (Zeichner, Verleger / draftsman, publisher),
Pieter van Sompel (Stecher / engraver), nach / after Rubens, Gerard Valck (Verleger / publisher)
Christus in Emmaus / The Supper at Emmaus, 1643/ca. 1700
Kupferstich / engraving SGSM, Inv. 30119 D

IV. Verleger

Wer über die Verbreitung von Goltzius- und Rubens-Stichen in Europa und der weiteren Welt spricht, muss die Unterscheidung vornehmen zwischen der Tätigkeit der Verleger und dem Handel. Seit dem 16. Jahrhundert fiel in der Regel dem Verleger die Rolle zu, ein Programm für sein Sortiment zu entwerfen und für dessen Umsetzung zu sorgen. Der Verleger war der Projektmanager, der sich um Vorlagen renommierter Künstler, um passende Stecher, um talentierte Schriftsetzer oder Kalligraphen sowie um gelehrte Autoren für Bildunterschriften kümmerte. Auch oblag ihm, dafür zu sorgen, dass entsprechende Werkstätten und die dort tätigen Handwerker vorhanden waren. Er musste in Honorare und Material investieren, bevor überhaupt ein Gewinn zu erzielen war. Den eigentlichen Handel mit Druckgraphik besorgten, wo kein eigenes Ladengeschäft an das Verlagshaus angeschlossen war, andere, etwa reisende oder emigrierte Händler, Geschäftsbesitzer und Vertreter auf Messen.[1] Das Transportwesen war bereits im 16. Jahrhundert in Europa gut ausgebaut. Goltzius-Graphik konnte jedoch nicht nur in Europa erworben werden, sondern wurde anscheinend auch in fernere Ecken der Erde geschickt.[2] Dasselbe gilt für Rubens-Graphik, die sich, wie Nils Büttner in seinem Beitrag anführt (S. 90), in allen Herren Ländern verbreitete.

Anhand ihrer Druckgraphiken kann man die Vernetzung beider Künstler mit Verlegern sichtbar machen, welche in der Lage waren, die Reichweite der geschaffenen Blätter zu vergrößern. Solche Verleger waren bereits zu Lebzeiten von Goltzius und Rubens tätig, sie profitierten aber noch Jahrzehnte und darüber hinaus vom Handel mit den immer weiter verkauften Druckplatten der innovativen Stiche dieser Künstler sowie mit Kopien.

Am Anfang seiner Tätigkeit als Kupferstecher schuf Hendrick Goltzius Werke im Auftrag von bereits etablierten Verlegern wie Philips Galle oder Hieronymus Cock in Antwerpen, dessen internationales Verlagshaus In de Vier Winden (Aux Quatre Vents) ganz Europa belieferte. Diese Arbeiten entsprachen im Stil konventionellen Stichen, für die eine bestimmte Kundschaft bereits ins Auge gefasst worden war, oder dem Verlagsprogramm. Ein solches Blatt und entsprechendes Sujet ist *Die Verkündigung* (Abb. S. 129), die Goltzius nach einer Vorlage von Maerten de Vos um 1579 für Hieronymus Cock schuf. Damit empfahl sich der Haarlemer Künstler einem der damals größten Kundenkreise wie auch anderen potenziellen Auftraggebern und Kollegen. Ab 1582 mischte Goltzius den Markt für Druckgraphik in den Niederlanden mit seiner eigenen verlegerischen Tätigkeit in Haarlem komplett auf und schuf in den folgenden 19 Jahren ein Sortiment mit mehr als 400 verkäuflichen Stichen, das mit anderen europäischen Verlegern quantitativ mithalten konnte, diese qualitativ jedoch oft übertraf.[3] Beispiele für Blätter, die er selbst verlegte, sind die 1585 entstandene *Kreuzigung* (Abb. S. 135) sowie aus demselben Jahr *Mars und Venus, von Vulkan überrascht* (Abb. S. 137), eine Arbeit, die sich an Entwürfen des Prager Hofkünstlers Bartholomeus Spranger orientiert.

Nachdem sich Goltzius ab 1598 aus der Druckgraphik zurückgezogen und seinem Stiefsohn Jacob Matham seine Werkstatt

IV. Publishers

When we consider the distribution of Goltzius and Rubens prints throughout Europe and other parts of the world, it is important to distinguish between the tasks of publishers and of print merchants. Beginning in the sixteenth century, it was, as a rule, the publishers who determined the specialization of their publishing house and decided how to put it into practice. Publishers were project managers whose task it was to commission designs from renowned artists; find the right engravers, typesetters, or calligraphers; and hire learned authors for inscriptions and epigrams. They also provided the print workshops, as well as the assistants who worked there, and had to invest in salaries and materials before seeing any revenue. Unless there was a shop connected to the publishing house, the actual trade in prints was delegated to others, such as traveling or emigrant merchants, shopkeepers, and salesmen at fairs.[1] The transport business was well developed in sixteenth-century Europe. Goltzius prints could be had not only in Europe but also in farther reaches of the globe.[2] The same is true for Rubens prints, which were to be found, as Nils Büttner relates in his essay (p. 91), in many countries.

By evaluating the information provided in their prints, we can uncover the artists' networks with publishers, which considerably expanded the distribution of their prints. Such publishers were active during Goltzius's and Rubens's lifetimes, but continued to benefit for decades to come from selling the artists' printing plates and copies after their prints.

When Hendrick Goltzius first started out as an engraver he worked on behalf of established publishers like Philips Galle or Hieronymus Cock in Antwerp, whose international publishing house In de Vier Winden (Aux Quatre Vents) sold to all of Europe. In terms of style, these early works were conventional engravings intended for an already existent clientele or for the publishers' specialized product line. One such print and motif was *The Annunciation* (fig. p. 129), which Goltzius engraved for Hieronymus Cock around 1579 after a design by Maerten de Vos (1532–1603). With this work the Haarlem artist commended himself to one of the largest clienteles as well as to potential customers and colleagues. From 1582 on Goltzius completely revolutionized the print market in the Netherlands with his own publishing enterprise in Haarlem. In the following nineteen years, his production amounted to more than four hundred prints, an output that was comparable with other European publishers in terms of quantity but surpassed them in terms of quality.[3] Examples of prints he himself published are the 1585 *Crucifixion* (fig. p. 135) and *Mars and Venus Surprised by Vulcan* of the same year (fig. p. 137), a piece that emulated designs by the Prague court artist Bartholomeus Spranger.

After Goltzius stopped engraving around 1598 and entrusted his print workshop to his stepson Jacob Matham, he also passed on his stock, which continued to be profitable. The Goltzius

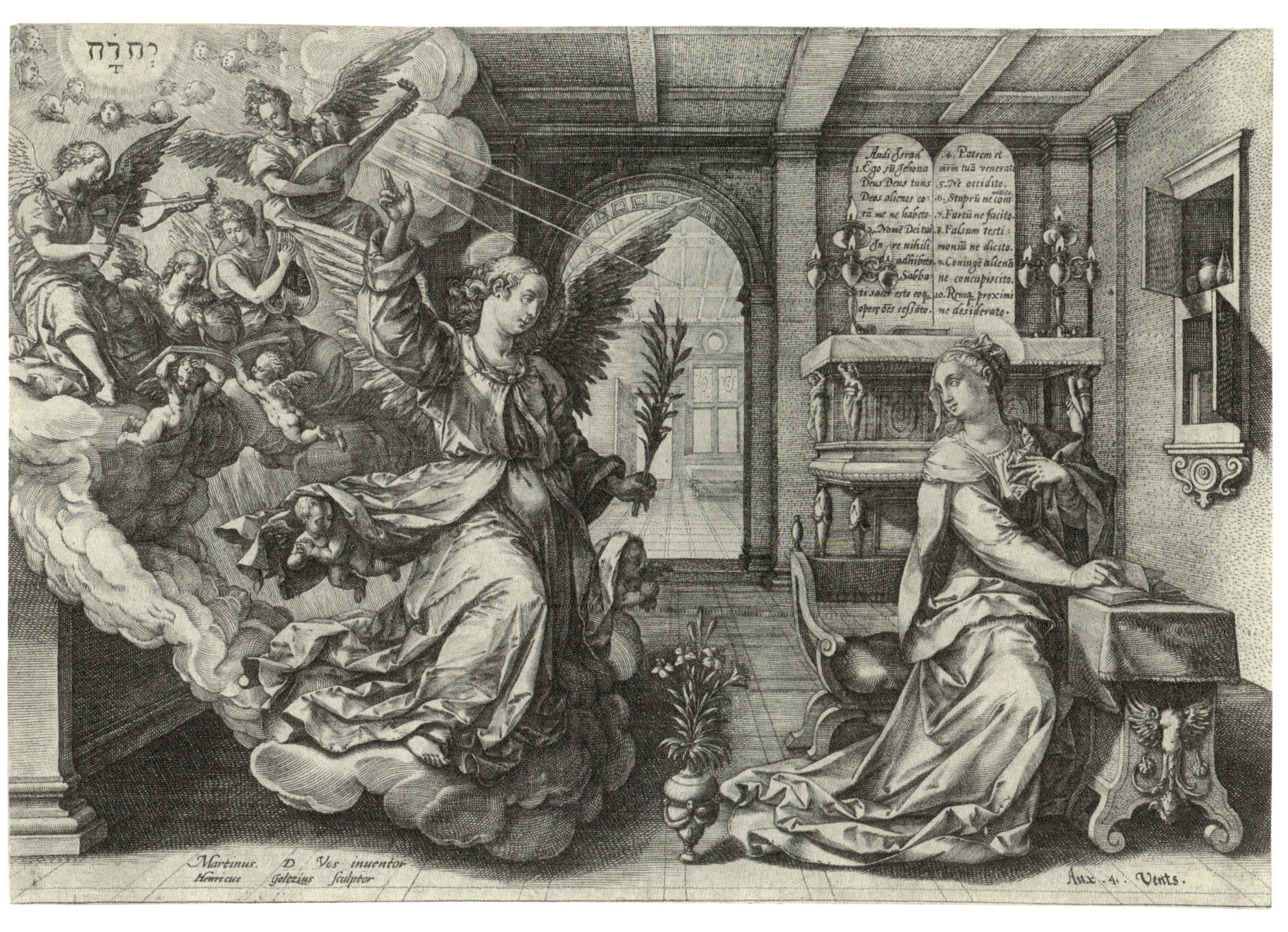

Goltzius (Stecher / engraver), nach / after Maerten de Vos, Aux Quatre Vents (Verlag / publisher)
Die Verkündigung / The Annunciation, ca. 1579
Kupferstich / engraving SGSM, Inv. 28684 D

übergeben hatte, ging auch das Sortiment an diesen über und das lukrative Geschäft wurde fortgeführt. Das Goltzius-Warenlager war langfristig so ertragreich, dass ein großer Teil später an den Jacques-de-Gheyn-Schüler Robert de Baudous (1574/75–1659) überging und von ihm an den Buchhändler Jan Janszoon I (gest. 1630) in Arnhem.[4] Einige Blätter im Münchner Bestand, wie der Abzug *Allegorie der Liebe, des Gesichtssinns und der Kunst* (Abb. S. 138), stammen aus dessen Verlag.

Der große Erfolg der Goltzius-Graphik ließ sich auch an den vielen Kopien messen, die in ganz Europa auftauchten. Eines der meist kopierten Motive war die *Fünf-Sinne*-Serie, die Jan Saenredam 1595/96 nach Goltzius-Blättern gestochen hatte. In Augsburg hatte sich der (aus Antwerpen stammende) Stecher und Verleger Dominicus Custos (1559/60–1615) seit Ende der 1570er-Jahre mit seinem Verlagsprogramm auf solche unautorisierten Kopien spezialisiert.[5] Dies entbehrte nicht einiger Brisanz, war doch sein Vater, der Maler Peeter Baltens, ein enger Freund von Goltzius. Zudem stand Custos ab 1607 im Dienst Rudolfs II. in Prag, der bis 1601 Goltzius, im Anschluss dann Matham ein kaiserliches Privileg für die Stichproduktion erteilt hatte. Auch die *Trilogie der Hochzeiten* (1595–1615/16), darunter das Motiv *Hochzeit, basierend auf weltlicher Liebe*, nahm Custos als Raubkopie in sein Sortiment auf (Abb. S. 139), trug aber so zu dessen Verbreitung auch in Deutschland bei.[6] Die Tatsache, dass Goltzius- und Rubens-Stiche nachgestochen wurden, zeugte folglich ebenfalls vom Erfolg ihrer Kompositionen und vergrößerte diesen.

Sowohl Goltzius als auch Rubens schätzten das Buchwesen als ein Medium mit europaweiter Reichweite für ihre Stiche. Eine kleine, aber feine Gruppe von Goltzius' Bildnissen fand sich als Illustrationen in Büchern wieder.[7] Für die Erstausgabe des kunsttheoretischen Buches *Het schilder-boeck* (Das Buch über die Malerei), das von dem befreundeten Autor und Künstler Karel van Mander 1604 verfasst wurde und für Goltzius' Rezeption überhaupt wichtig werden sollte, stach Jan Saenredam das Bildnis des Autors nach einem Gemälde von Goltzius (Abb. S. 141). Während der Porträtkopf selbst den Konventionen der Zeit entsprach, fällt die Ornamentik des Rahmens ins Auge. Diese dekorativen Elemente, die sich durch den Buchdruck weit verbreiteten, sind laut Huigen Leeflang der Ursprung des sogenannten Ohrmuschelstils (niederl. *kwab*), der um 1610 eine kurze, aber intensive Mode in der bildenden Kunst und in der Goldschmiedekunst auslöste.[8] Solche Röllchenformen erfreuten sich besonders im Umkreis des Prager Hofs großer Beliebtheit und lassen erahnen, dass der Schritt vom Manierismus hin zu barocken Gestaltungsformen kein so großer war.

Entwürfe für Buchtitelseiten und -illustrationen waren die frühesten Werke im Bereich der Druckgraphik, die Peter Paul Rubens schuf.[9] Seit 1608, also noch bevor er mit *Die große Judith* sein erstes signiertes Einzelblatt veröffentlichte (Abb. S. 113), entwarf er regelmäßig für das Verlagshaus Plantin-Moretus in seiner Heimatstadt Antwerpen Buchillustrationen, später auch allegorische Titelblätter, die den Wert von Büchern humanistischer Autoren steigerten und Rubens' eigenes Ansehen mehrten. Um den monetären Lohn für diese Arbeiten ging es ihm nicht, wie aus einem Brief seines Verlegers hervorgeht.[10] Denn die Stecher wurden viel besser bezahlt als Rubens selbst.[11] So überrascht es nicht, dass er sich seine Entlohnung vom Verleger nicht in bar, sondern

brand was so lucrative that later even his printing plates changed hands. Some of them went to Robert de Baudous (1574/75–1659), a student of Jacques de Gheyn II, and then to the bookseller Jan Janszoon I (died 1630) in Arnhem.[4] Some of the prints in the collection of the Staatliche Graphische Sammlung München, like the copy of *Allegory of Love, Sight and Art* (fig. p. 138), were issued by Janszoon.

The great success of Goltzius prints can also be measured by the many unauthorized copies that started to appear in all of Europe. One of the most frequently copied motifs was the series *The Five Senses* Jan Saenredam had engraved in 1595/96 after Goltzius. In Augsburg, the engraver and publisher (and Antwerp native) Dominicus Custos (1559/60–1615) specialized in such unauthorized copies.[5] This was a delicate arrangement, because his father was the painter Peeter Baltens, a close friend of Goltzius's. In addition, from 1607 on Custos was a court painter of Rudolf II in Prague, who had awarded Goltzius an imperial print privilege that after 1601 was transferred to Jacob Matham and his print production. This notwithstanding, Custos offered, among other pirated copies, the motif *Marriage for Worldly Love* (1595–1615/16) from Goltzius's series *Three Kinds of Marriages* (fig. p. 139). Then again, such copies increased the visibility of Goltzius's prints, in this case in Germany.[6] The fact that the Goltzius and Rubens prints were copied in various ways and places testified to their success and increased it.

Both Goltzius and Rubens valued books as a medium that gave their prints a wider reach throughout Europe. A small but fine group of Goltzius portraits was created specifically as book illustrations.[7] For the first edition of the painter Karel van Mander's art-theory book *Het schilder-boeck* (The book on painting), which was published in 1604 and was to have a great impact on Goltzius's general reception, Jan Saenredam engraved the author's likeness after a painting Goltzius had made of his friend (fig. p. 141). While the portrait head complied with the conventions of the day, the ornamental frame is noteworthy. Its decorative elements, which had a wide reach because they were part of this book, must according to Huigen Leeflang be considered the origin of the auricular style (*kwab* in Dutch), which came into fashion briefly but forcefully in the fine arts and in the goldsmiths' art.[8] The little rolled ornaments enjoyed great popularity in the circles of the Prague court and indicate that the step from Mannerist to Baroque aesthetics was not a big one.

Book title pages and illustrations were the earliest prints for which Peter Paul Rubens created designs.[9] Beginning in 1608—even before he published *The Great Judith*, his first single-leaf print (see fig. p. 113)—Rubens regularly designed allegorical title pages on behalf of the publishing house Plantin-Moretus in Antwerp. These were meant to increase the value of books by humanist authors, and also to boost his own standing. It was not the monetary rewards he was interested in, as we learn from a letter written by his publisher.[10] After all, engravers received higher salaries than he did.[11] Not surprisingly, he had the publisher remunerate him in

in Büchern aus dessen Sortiment erbat. Der Künstler profitierte von dem Marketing-Effekt dieser Buchillustrationen, die ihm zunehmende Bekanntheit und damit Ruhm einbrachten. Bis kurz vor seinem Tod schuf er Vorlagen für solche in Büchern verbreiteten Stiche, insgesamt eine Anzahl von fast sechzig.[12] Bemerkenswerterweise – und dieser Punkt spricht dafür, dass er selbst an dieser Tätigkeit Freude hatte – sind diese Stichvorlagen die einzigen in seinem Œuvre, die er komplett eigenhändig ausführte und nicht von einem Assistenten anlegen ließ und im Anschluss überarbeitete.[13] Auch behielt er sich die Arbeit an diesen Entwürfen für Sonn- und Feiertage vor, denn an den übrigen Tagen hätte sein viel höheres übliches Salär für Gemälde das ganze Buchprojekt für den Verleger unrentabel gemacht.[14] Bei Rubens' 1638 entworfenem Titelblatt für die dritte Auflage des populären, 1618 erstmals erschienenen Buchs *Legatus* (Der Gesandte) des Politikers Frederik van Marselaer (Abb. S. 143) ist anzunehmen, dass der Künstler sich auch mit dem Inhalt auseinandersetzte, denn als Gesandter in unterschiedlichen fürstlichen Diensten betätigte sich Rubens viele Jahre lang.[15] Folglich gehörte er selbst zum anvisierten humanistisch gebildeten Rezipientenkreis der Bücher, für den er Illustrationen schuf.[16]

Der Haarlemer Künstler Pieter Soutman (1593/1601–1657) hatte seine Graphikausbildung wohl bei Jacob Matham erhalten und war 1615/16 von Rubens als Assistent angeworben worden. Bis 1624 arbeitete er in Antwerpen an Gemälden des Meisters mit.[17] Während dieser Zeit machte er vermutlich für seine eigenen Zwecke Nachzeichnungen von einigen Rubens-Kompositionen. Nachdem er wieder in seine Heimatstadt zurückgekehrt war, fertigte er Graphiken nach diesen Zeichnungen an und trat auch selbst als Verleger der Blätter auf. In der Bildunterschrift zu *Die Niederlage des Sanherib* (Abb. S. 148 f.), das ein Gemälde (München, Alte Pinakothek) umsetzt, hielt sich Soutman Folgendes zugute: „Effigiauit et excud" – nachgezeichnet und verlegt. Mit seinen Stichen nach Rubens war er in den nordlichen Niederlanden ab 1636 sehr erfolgreich und leitete darin auch Schüler wie Jacob Louys, Pieter van Sompel oder Willem van der Leeuw an.

Letztgenannter Soutman-Schüler radierte Rubens' Darstellung *Lot und seine Töchter* (Abb. S. 147) nach einer Stichvorlage, die Soutman wohl vor 1624 in Rubens' Atelier in einer Zeichnung nach dem Gemälde festgehalten hatte. Das etwas pikante Motiv scheint auch für den nordniederländischen Markt interessant gewesen zu sein, denn der vornehmlich in Amsterdam tätige Verleger Cornelis Danckerts nahm es in sein Sortiment auf. Dieser hatte sein Handwerk zwischen 1625 und 1627 im Pariser Kunsthandel gelernt und unterhielt seither geschäftliche Kontakte dorthin. Danckerts hatte sich nach seiner Rückkehr nach Amsterdam und der Gründung seines Verlags ab 1630 um Originaldruckplatten von Goltzius bemüht – erfolgreich: Ihm gehörten einige wichtige Motive, allen voran die Platten für die Serie *Die Passion Christi*. Zugleich führte er aber auch Graphik der viel aktuelleren Künstler Rubens und Rembrandt.

Eine Dependance in Paris hatte der Antwerpener Verleger Anton Goetkint (ab 1621 Anton Bonenfant), der auch Motive nach Rubens anbot, darunter das vielleicht von Michel Lasne gestochene und von Schelte à Bolswert überarbeitete Blatt *Die Hl. Familie mit dem Papagei* (Abb. S. 146). Goetkint hatte zudem Kontakte nach Italien und offerierte auch Motive italienischer Künstler wie Tizian, Parmigianino,

books from the existing stock rather than cash. The artist nonetheless benefited from the marketing effect of his book illustrations, which added to his profile and fame. He continued crafting designs for book illustrations and title pages until shortly before his death, amounting to almost sixty in total.[12] It is noteworthy—and speaks for the fact that he enjoyed this task—that these designs are the only ones in his print oeuvre that are entirely by his own hand instead of being prepared by an assistant to be reworked afterward by him.[13] He reserved this kind of work for Sundays and holidays, because his salary on other days would have had to be as high as for paintings and this would have made any book project unprofitable for the publisher.[14] In 1638 Rubens designed the title page for the third edition of the popular book *Legatus* (The legate) by the politician Frederik van Marselaer (fig. p. 143). The artist was likely familiar with the content of this book, which was first published in 1618, for he himself had been a legate at various courts for many years.[15] We may conclude, then, that Rubens was part of the intended humanist audience of the books for which he designed these illustrations.[16]

The Haarlem artist Pieter Soutman (1593/1601–1657), who had probably received his training from Jacob Matham, became Rubens's assistant in 1615/16. He worked in the master's painting studio in Antwerp until 1624.[17] During this time he probably made drawings of several Rubens compositions for his own purposes. After returning to Haarlem in 1628, he started producing prints after these drawings, some of which he published himself. In the inscription of *The Defeat of Sennacherib* (fig. pp. 148–149), which reproduces a painting (now in the Alte Pinakothek, Munich), Soutman credited himself as follows: "Effigiauit et excud," drawn and published by. From 1636 onward he was very successful in the Northern Netherlands with his prints after Rubens, and he set his apprentices, among them Jacob Louys, Pieter van Sompel, and Willem van der Leeuw, on this path as well.

The latter Soutman apprentice engraved Rubens's depiction of *Lot and His Daughters* (fig. p. 147), working from a drawing Soutman had probably made before 1624 in Rubens's studio after the painting. This somewhat suggestive motif seems to have been of interest to the Northern Netherlandish art market as well, because the Amsterdam publisher Cornelis Danckerts carried it in his stock. Having learned his trade between 1625 and 1627 on the Paris art market, Danckerts continued to cultivate contacts there. After returning to Amsterdam and founding his publishing house, he had tried since 1630 to get his hands on Goltzius printing plates—with success: some important plates, such as those for *The Passion of Christ*, came into his possession. But he also carried prints by the more current artists Rubens and Rembrandt.

The Antwerp publisher Anton Goetkint (from 1621 Anton Bonenfant) ran a second shop in Paris where he also offered prints after Rubens paintings, among them *The Holy Family with the Parrot* (fig. p. 146), possibly engraved by Michel Lasne and reworked by Schelte à Bolswert. Goetkint also had contacts in Italy and was able to offer motifs by Italian artists like Titian, Parmigianino, Ludovico Carracci, and Guido Reni.[18] Flemish

Ludovico Carracci und Guido Reni.[18] Den flämischen Barock vertraten bei ihm neben Werken von Rubens auch solche von Anthonis van Dyck. Das hier gezeigte Motiv stand (laut Bildunterschrift) unter dem Schutz eines Privilegs, das Goetkint 1635 beim französischen König eingeholt hatte, um mit Kupferstichen handeln zu dürfen. Hieraus können wir schließen, dass diese Kopie zwischen 1635 und Goetkints Tod 1644 entstanden ist.

Nicht annähernd in dem Maße wie Goltzius, aber doch in wohlüberlegten Fällen fungierte Rubens selbst als Verleger einiger seiner Blätter. Weil das nicht automatisch bedeutete, dass er auch den Vertrieb übernahm, darf man vermuten, dass es ihm auch in diesem Punkt um das mit seinem Namen verknüpfte Prestige ging.[19] So behielt er sich das Verlegerrecht für die Stiche nach den Tizian-Bildnissen *Kaiser Karl V.* (Abb. S. 133) und *Isabella d'Este* (Abb. S. 241) vor. Ebenso blieben alle mit Christoffel Jegher geschaffenen Holzschnitte bei seiner Verlegeradresse, hier etwa *Die Marienkrönung* (Abb. S. 145).

Baroque art was represented by Rubens as well as Anthony van Dyck. The print shown here of the Holy Family was covered (according to the inscription) by the privilege that Goetkint had acquired in 1635 in order to obtain permission to sell engravings. It follows, then, that this print dates from sometime between 1635 and Goetkint's death in 1644.

In a few well-considered cases—but not nearly as often as Goltzius—Rubens functioned as publisher of his own prints. Because he left the distribution to others, we may assume that here, too, he was interested less in profit than the prestige these prints conferred on his name.[19] For example, he reserved the publisher's address for himself on the prints after Titian's *Portraits of Emperor Charles V* and *Isabella d'Este* (figs. pp. 133, 241). In addition, he assumed the publisher's role for all woodcuts created in collaboration with Christoffel Jegher, such as *The Coronation of the Virgin* (fig. p. 145).

1 Für Rubens ist besonders ein Händler, Jacques Moermans, verbürgt, doch mehr als der Name ist bislang nicht bekannt. Vgl. Nico Van Hout, in: Antwerpen/Québec 2004, S. 38.
2 Karel van Mander erwähnt, dass Goltzius' Stiche in Rom zum Verkauf angeboten wurden, als er 1590 dort eintraf. Mander (1604) 2000, S. 334. – Huigen Leeflang spricht von einem „international network", das Goltzius' Werke in Europa verteilte. Leeflang 2012, S. 33, siehe auch S. 24. – Zu einem Fund von Goltzius-Graphiken 1871 in Nova Zembla, dem heute russischen Nowaja Semlja im Nordpolarmeer, vgl. Marjolein Leesberg, in: NHD Goltzius 2012, S. lxviii.
3 Der Experte zu Goltzius' verlegerischer Tätigkeit, Jan Piet Filedt Kok, formuliert: „Goltzius became the first in the Northern Netherlands to publish prints for an international audience, which subsequently put an end to the quasi-monopoly of Antwerp, moving the centre of the printmaking business to Holland." Filedt Kok 2014, S. 676.
4 So Marjolein Leesberg, in: NHD Goltzius 2012, S. lxi und lxii.
5 Zur Biographie von Custos siehe F[riederike] Thomas und C[laudia] D[äubler]-H[auschke], sv. Custos, Dominicus, in: AKL, Bd. 23, S. 209 f., sowie Jörg Diefenbacher, Introduction, in: NHD Custos I, S. xxiii– cxxvii.
6 Vgl. NHD Goltzius 2012, S. lxix. In der SGSM befindet sich zudem eine Kopie aus der *Fünf-Sinne*-Serie (*Der Geschmack*, Inv. 253946 D) von Custos. Eine Kopie des 19. Jahrhunderts, *Der Sehsinn*, ist im Kapitel „Nachbilder" auf S. 278 im vorliegenden Katalog abgebildet.
7 Auflagen von Kupferstichen bewegten sich zwischen 1000 und 4000 Exemplaren (vgl. Büttner 2011a, S. 125, und Diels 2009, S. 202); Buchauflagen erreichten um 1600, je nach Popularität des Titels, Auflagen zwischen 300 und 5000 Exemplaren (vgl. Judson/Van de Velde 1978 und Bertram/Büttner 2018, hier die Aufl. bei der jeweiligen Kat.-Nr.).
8 Vgl. Leeflang 2019, bes. S. 251 f.
9 Zu Rubens als Buchillustrator vgl. Judson/Van de Velde 1978; Bertram/Büttner 2018.
10 Brief von Balthasar Moretus an Balthasar Cordier, 15. September 1630; siehe Judson/Van de Velde 1978, Bd. 2, S. 385, Nr. 53.
11 Während Rubens je nach Größe bis zu 20 Gulden pro Entwurf erhielt, wurde der Stecher für seine Arbeit und das Material mit 75 Gulden entlohnt. Vgl. Evers 1944, S. 168, sowie Judson/Van de Velde 1978, Appendix III.
12 Auf diese Anzahl kommt Nils Büttner auf S. 89 im vorliegenden Katalog. Die Autoren des Werkverzeichnisses der Buchillustrationen geben 84 Vorlagen an; siehe Judson/Van de Velde 1978.
13 Vgl. Renger 1974a, S. 247. Zuletzt auch besonders beachtet von Wood 2020, bes. S. 49 und S. 53–55.
14 Wie Anm. 10 (Brief an Balthasar Cordier).
15 Zu Rubens' inhaltlicher Auseinandersetzung mit diesem Buch vgl. Büttner 2006, S. 64–68.
16 Rubens besaß ein Exemplar der zweiten Auflage von 1626; vgl. Arents 2001, S. 117. Vgl. auch Judson/Van de Velde 1978, Kat. 84, und Bertram/Büttner 2018, Kat. 54 (NB).
17 Zu Soutmans Biographie siehe U[lrike] B. Wegener, sv. Soutman, Pieter, in: AKL, Bd. 105, S. 159. Zu seinem Werk siehe Barrett 2012.
18 Zu Goetkints Biographie siehe U[lrich] R[üter], sv. Goetkint, Anton, in: AKL, Bd. 57, S. 80.
19 Konrad Renger betont: „Die eigene Herausgabe bedeutet nicht, daß er alle Blätter auch selbst vertrieben haben muß. Agenten und andere Verleger können durchaus auf seine Rechnung daran beteiligt gewesen sein." Renger 1975, S. 171, Anm. 15a.

1 For Peter Paul Rubens, there is a report of one merchant, Jacques Moermans, but his name is all we know of him. See Nico Van Hout, in: Antwerpen/Québec 2004, p. 38.
2 Karel van Mander mentions that Goltzius's prints were offered on the art market when Goltzius arrived in Rome in 1590. Mander (1604) 1994, pp. 390–391, fol. 283r–283v. – Huigen Leeflang refers to an "international network" that disseminated Goltzius's works throughout Europe. Leeflang 2012, p. 33, see also p. 24. – On the 1871 discovery of Goltzius prints in Nova Zembla, today's Novaya Zemlya in the Russian Arctic Ocean, see Marjolein Leesberg, in: NHD Goltzius 2012, p. lxviii.
3 The expert on Goltzius's publishing activities, Jan Piet Filedt Kok, states: "Goltzius became the first in the Northern Netherlands to publish prints for an international audience, which subsequently put an end to the quasi-monopoly of Antwerp, moving the centre of the printmaking business to Holland." Filedt Kok 2014, p. 676.
4 Marjolein Leesberg, in: NHD Goltzius 2012, pp. lxi and lxii.
5 For biographical information on Custos, see F[riederike] Thomas and C[laudia] D[äubler]-H[auschke], s.v. Custos, Dominicus, in: AKL, vol. 23, pp. 209–210, and Jörg Diefenbacher, introduction, in: NHD Custos I, pp. xxiii–cxxvii.
6 See NHD Goltzius 2012, p. lxix. In the SGSM there is another copy from the series *The Five Senses* (*Taste*, inv. 253946 D) by Custos. For a nineteenth-century copy of *Sight*, see the chapter "Afterimages" on p. 278 of the present catalog.
7 Print runs of engravings ranged between one thousand and four thousand copies (see Büttner 2011a, p. 125, and Diels 2009, p. 202); around 1600, print runs of books ranged from three hundred to five thousand copies, depending on the popularity of the title (see Judson/Van de Velde 1978 and Bertram/Büttner 2018, who list each print run in the respective catalog entry).
8 See Leeflang 2019, esp. pp. 251–252.
9 On Rubens as book illustrator, see Judson/Van de Velde 1978; Bertram/Büttner 2018.
10 Letter from Balthasar Moretus to Balthasar Cordier, September 15, 1630; see Judson/Van de Velde 1978, vol. 2, p. 385, cat. 53.
11 While Rubens charged, depending on size, up to twenty guilders per design, the engraver was paid seventy-five guilders for his work and materials. See Evers 1944, p. 168, and Judson/Van de Velde 1978, appendix III.
12 This is the number Büttner cites, see p. 89 in the present catalog. The authors of the catalogue raisonné of books counted eighty-four titles; see Judson/Van de Velde 1978.
13 See Renger 1974a, p. 247. This was also recently discussed by Wood 2020, esp. pp. 49 and 53–55.
14 See note 10 (letter to Balthasar Cordier).
15 On Rubens's intellectual interest in this book, see Büttner 2006, pp. 64–68.
16 Rubens owned a copy of the second edition of 1626; see Arents 2001, p. 118. See also Judson/Van de Velde 1978, cat. 84, and Bertram/Büttner 2018, cat. 54 (NB).
17 For Soutman's biography, see U[lrike] B. Wegener, s.v. Soutman, Pieter, in: AKL, vol. 105, p. 159. On his oeuvre, see Barrett 2012.
18 On Goetkint's biography, see U[lrich] R[üter], s.v. Goetkint, Anton, in: AKL, vol. 57, p. 80.
19 Konrad Renger points out: "Publishing the prints himself did not mean he also had to take care of selling them. He may have paid agents and other publishers to get involved." Renger 1975, p. 171, n. 15a. Translation by the author.

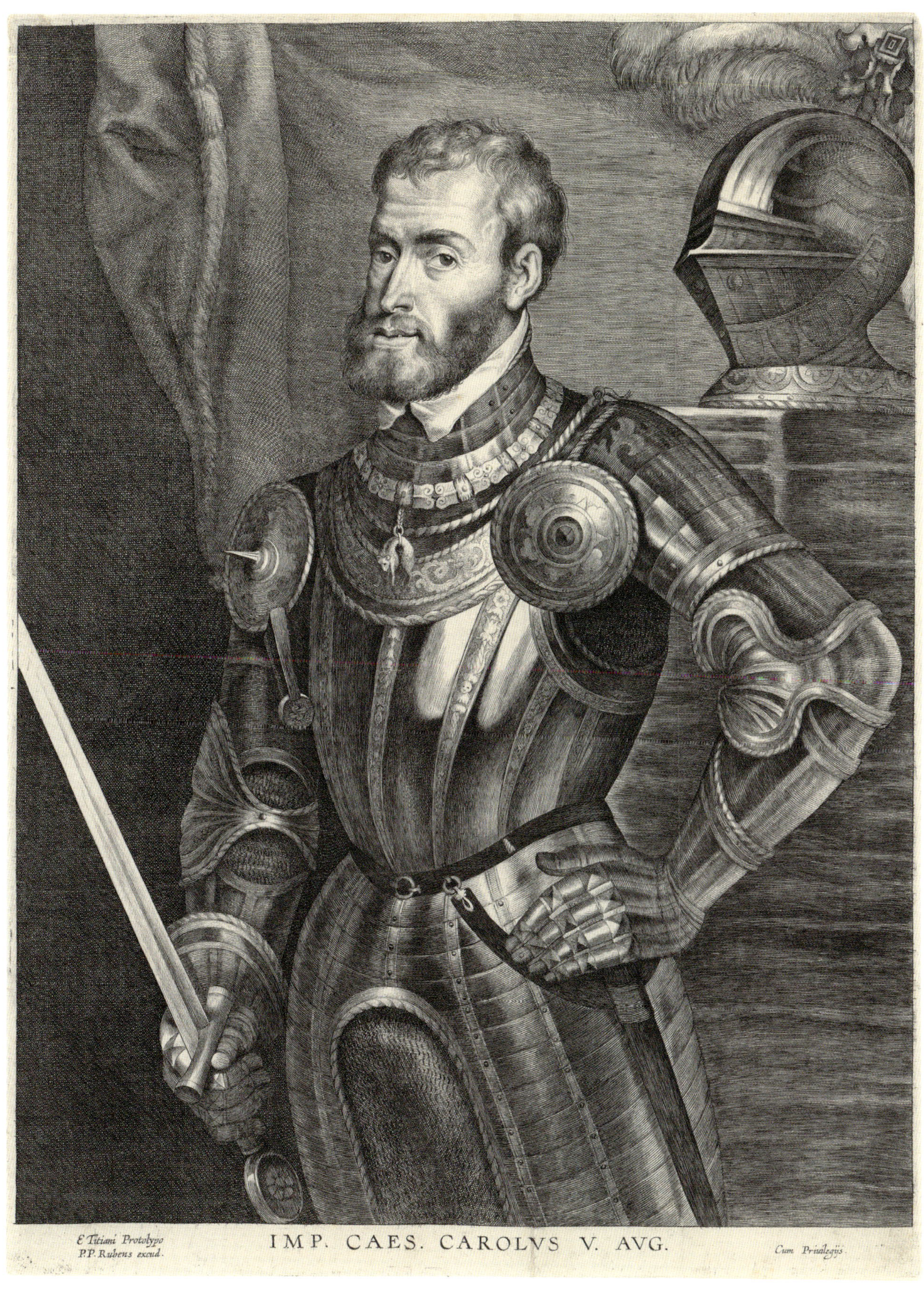

Rubens (Inventor, Verleger / designer, publisher), Lucas Vorsterman I? (Stecher / engraver), nach Tizian / after Titian
Bildnis von Kaiser Karl V. / Portrait of Emperor Charles V, ca. 1620
Kupferstich / engraving SGSM, Inv. 127611 D

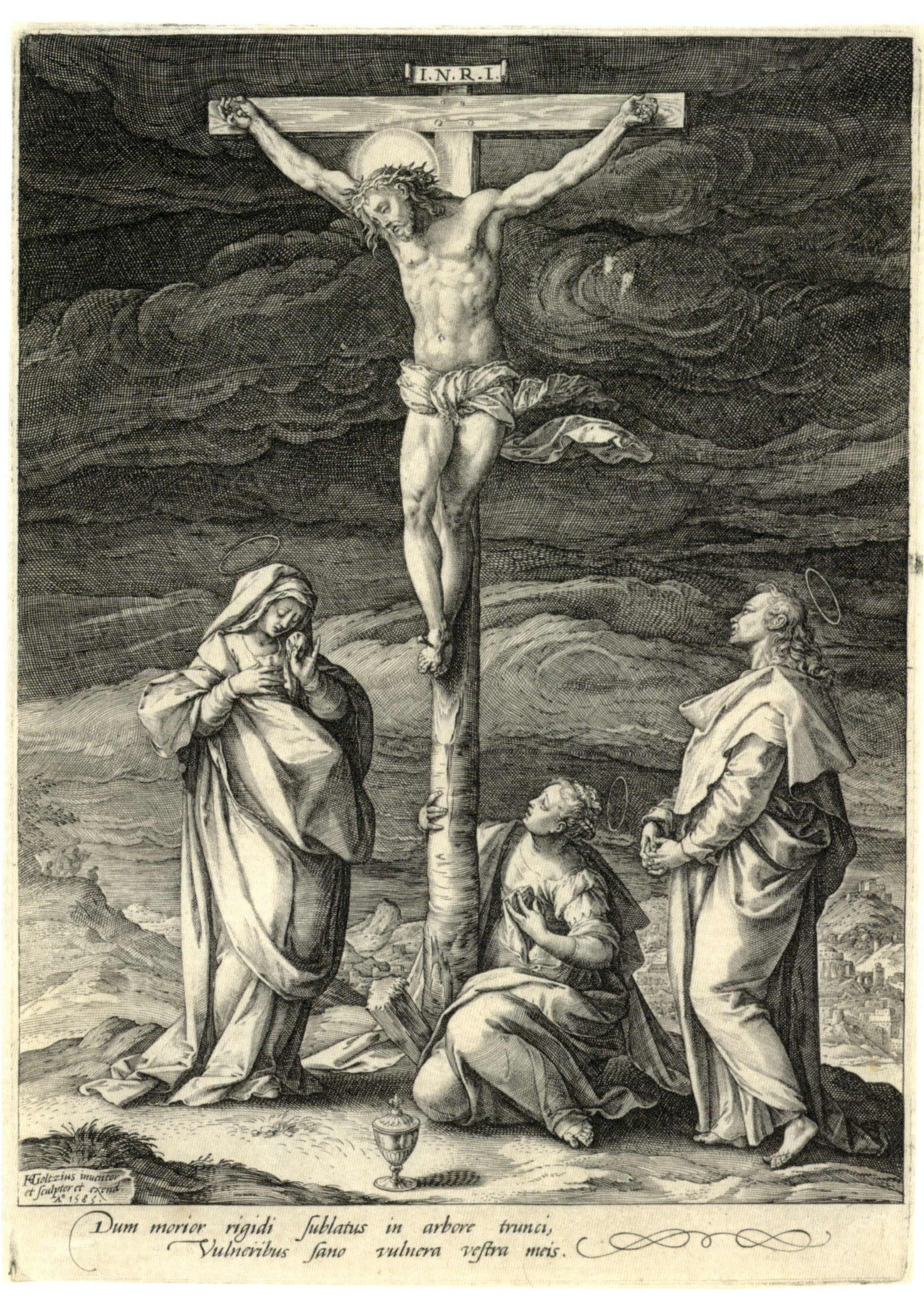

Hendrick Goltzius (Inventor, Stecher, Verleger / designer, engraver, publisher)
Die Kreuzigung / The Crucifixion, 1585
Kupferstich / engraving SGSM, Inv. 101283 D

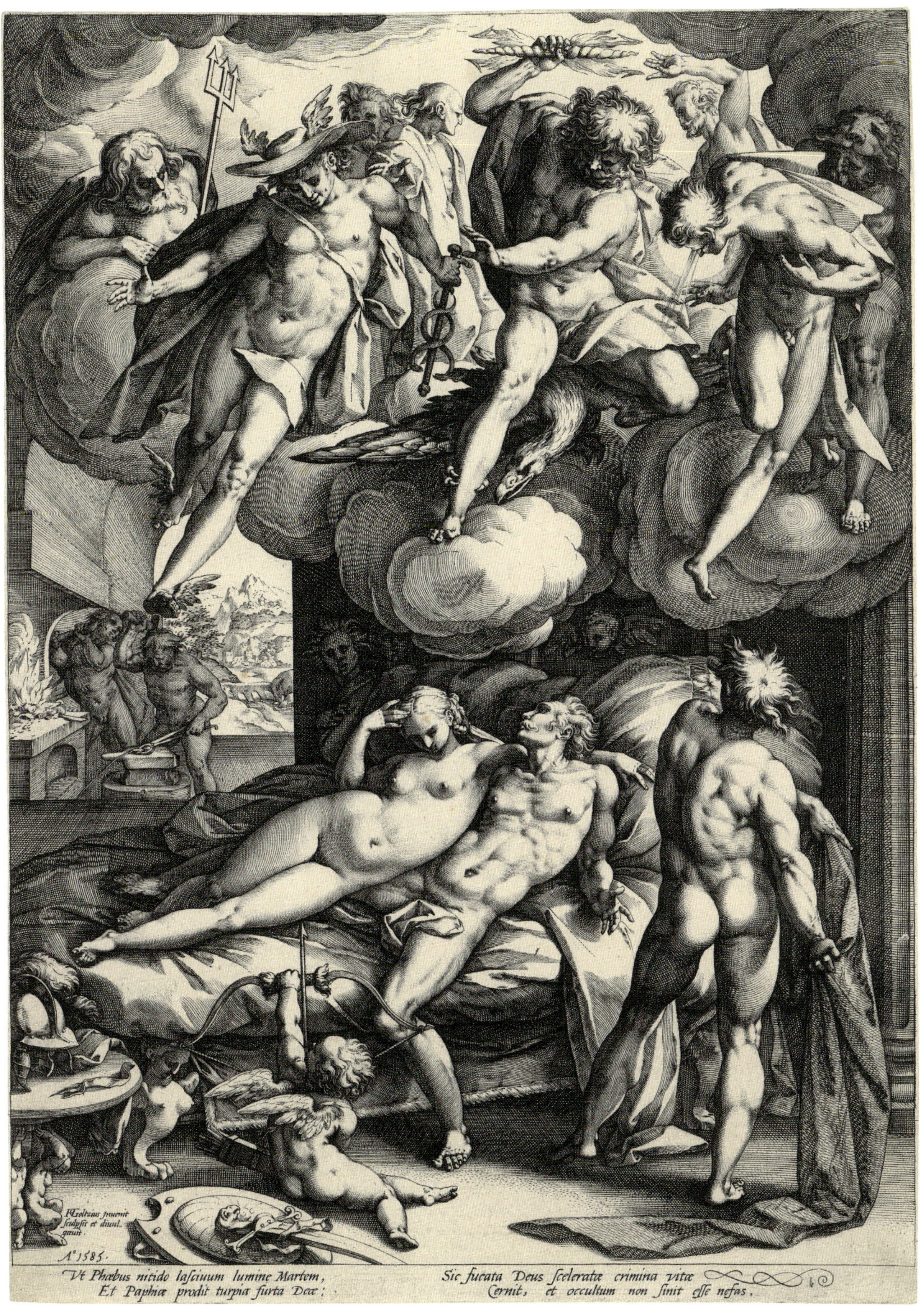

Hendrick Goltzius (Inventor, Stecher, Verleger / designer, engraver, publisher)
Mars und Venus, von Vulkan überrascht / Mars and Venus Surprised by Vulcan, 1585
Kupferstich / engraving SGSM, Inv. 30959 D

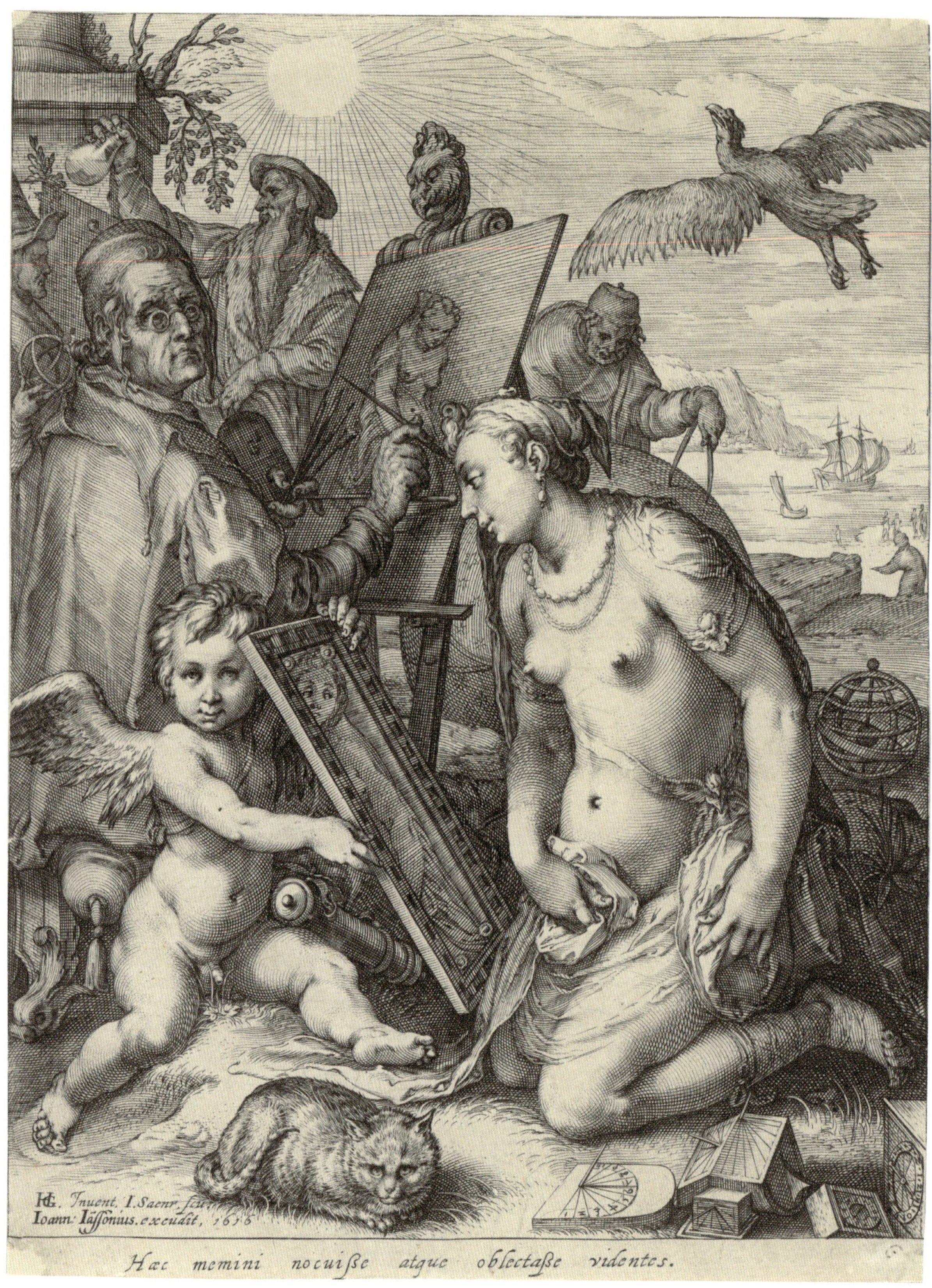

Goltzius (Inventor / designer), Jan Saenredam (Stecher / engraver), Jan Janszoon I (Verleger / publisher)
Allegorie der Liebe, des Gesichtssinns und der Kunst / Allegory of Love, Sight and Art, 1598/1616
Kupferstich / engraving SGSM, Inv. 191 D

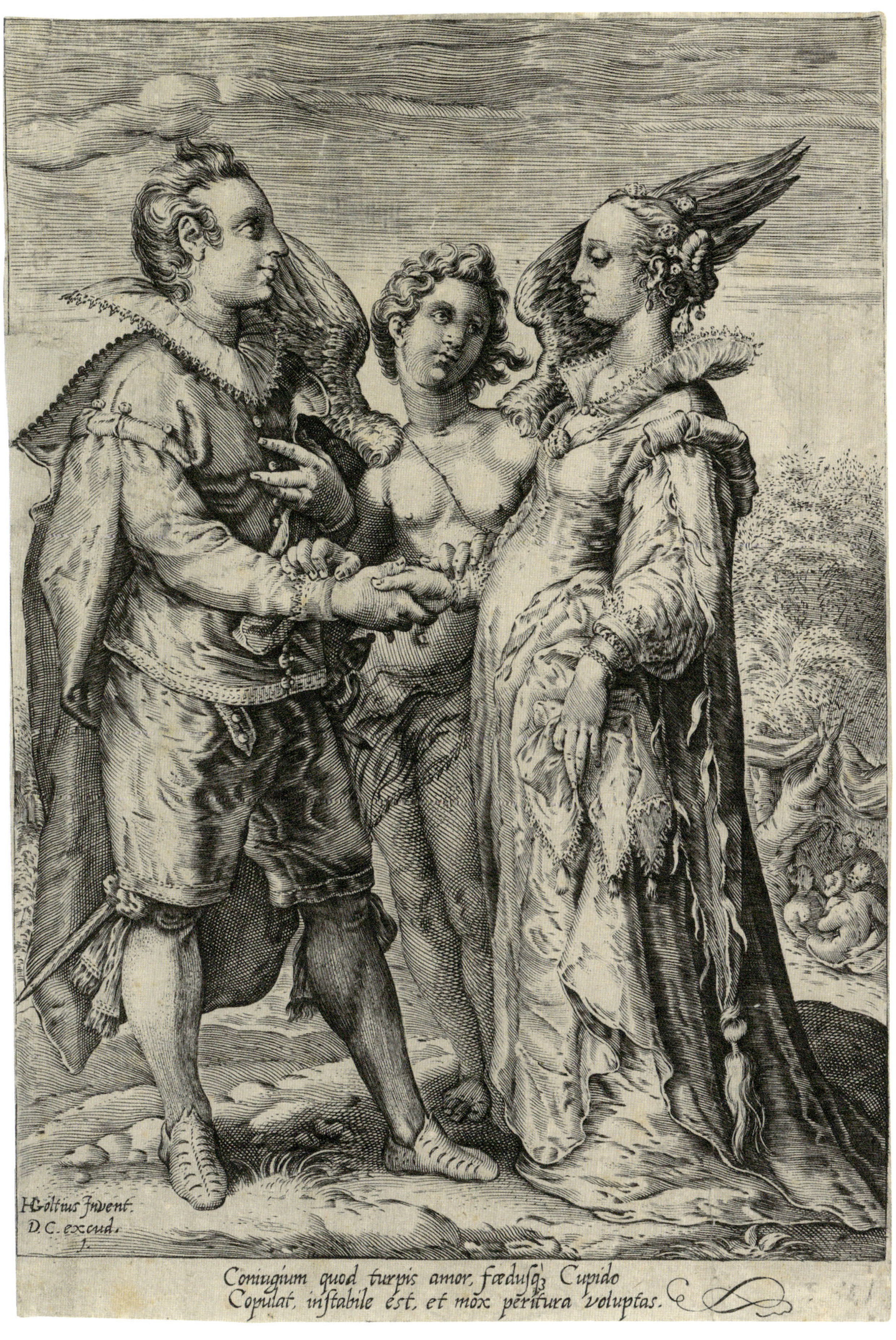

Anonymer Stecher / anonymous engraver, Kopie nach / copy after Goltzius, Dominicus Custos (Verleger / publisher)
Hochzeit, basierend auf weltlicher Liebe / Marriage for Worldly Love, 1615/16
Aus der Serie *Trilogie der Hochzeiten* / from the series *Three Kinds of Marriages*, 1615/16
Kupferstich / engraving SGSM, Inv. 31045 D

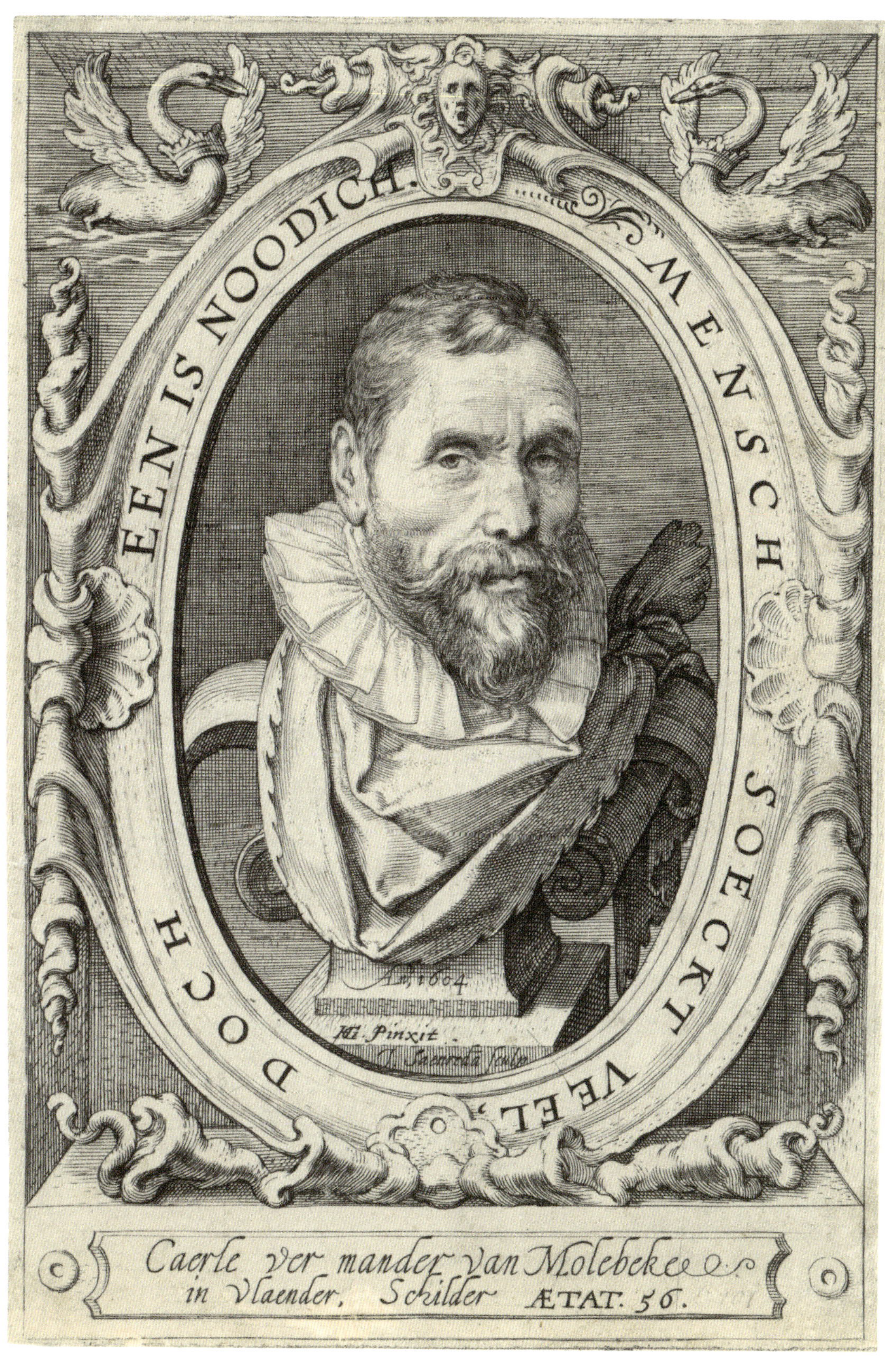

Goltzius (Inventor / designer), Jan Saenredam (Stecher / engraver), Paschier van Wesbusch (Verleger / publisher)
Bildnis des / Portrait of Karel van Mander, 1604
Illustration aus / from K. van Mander, *Het schilder-boeck …*, 1604
Kupferstich / engraving SGSM, Inv. 31051 D

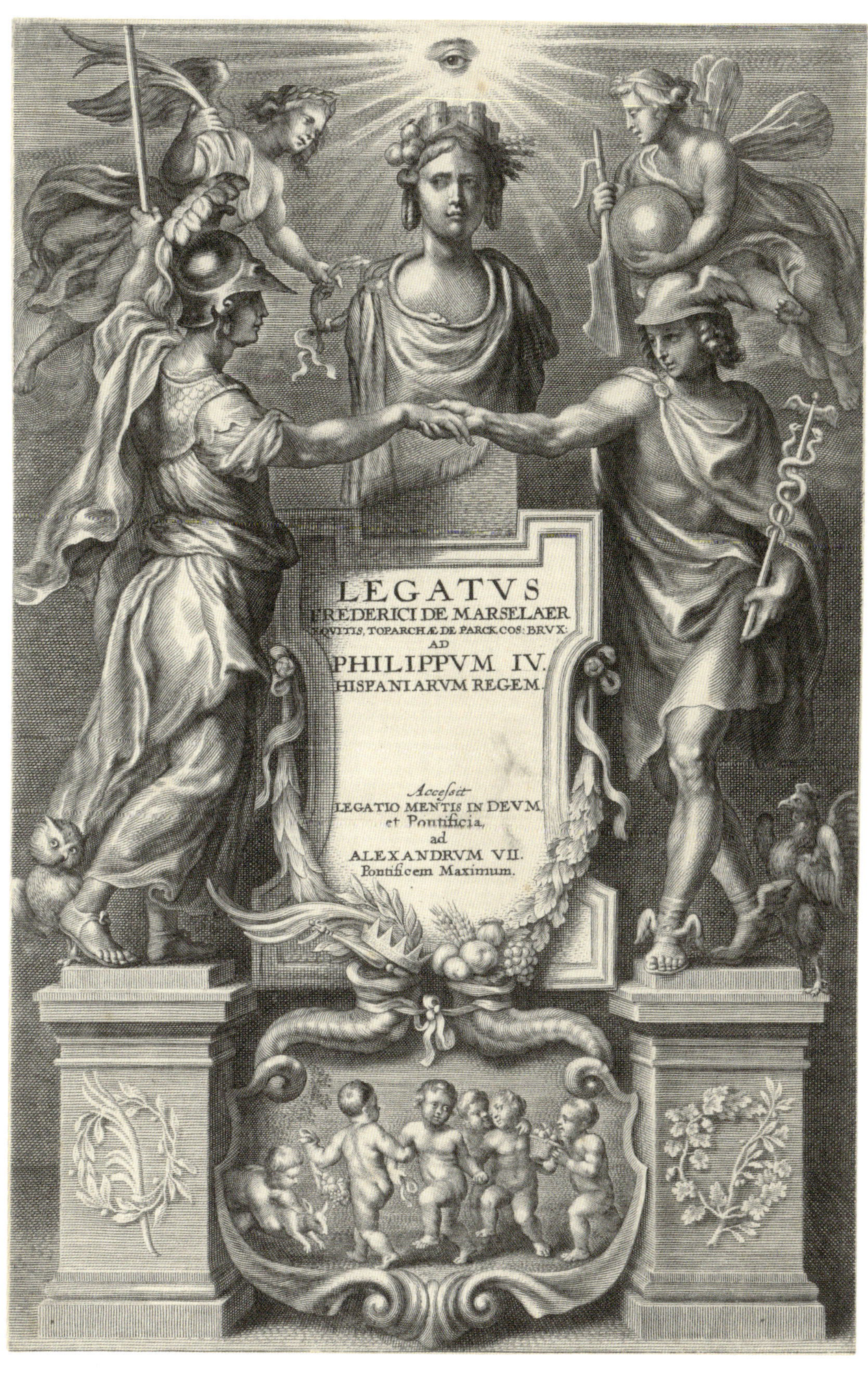

Cornelis Galle II (Stecher / engraver), nach / after Rubens, Plantiniana (Verlag / publisher)
Buchtitel / book title, 1638/66
Aus / from F. de Marselaer, *Legatus*, Antwerpen 1666
Kupferstich / engraving SGSM, Inv. 30553 D

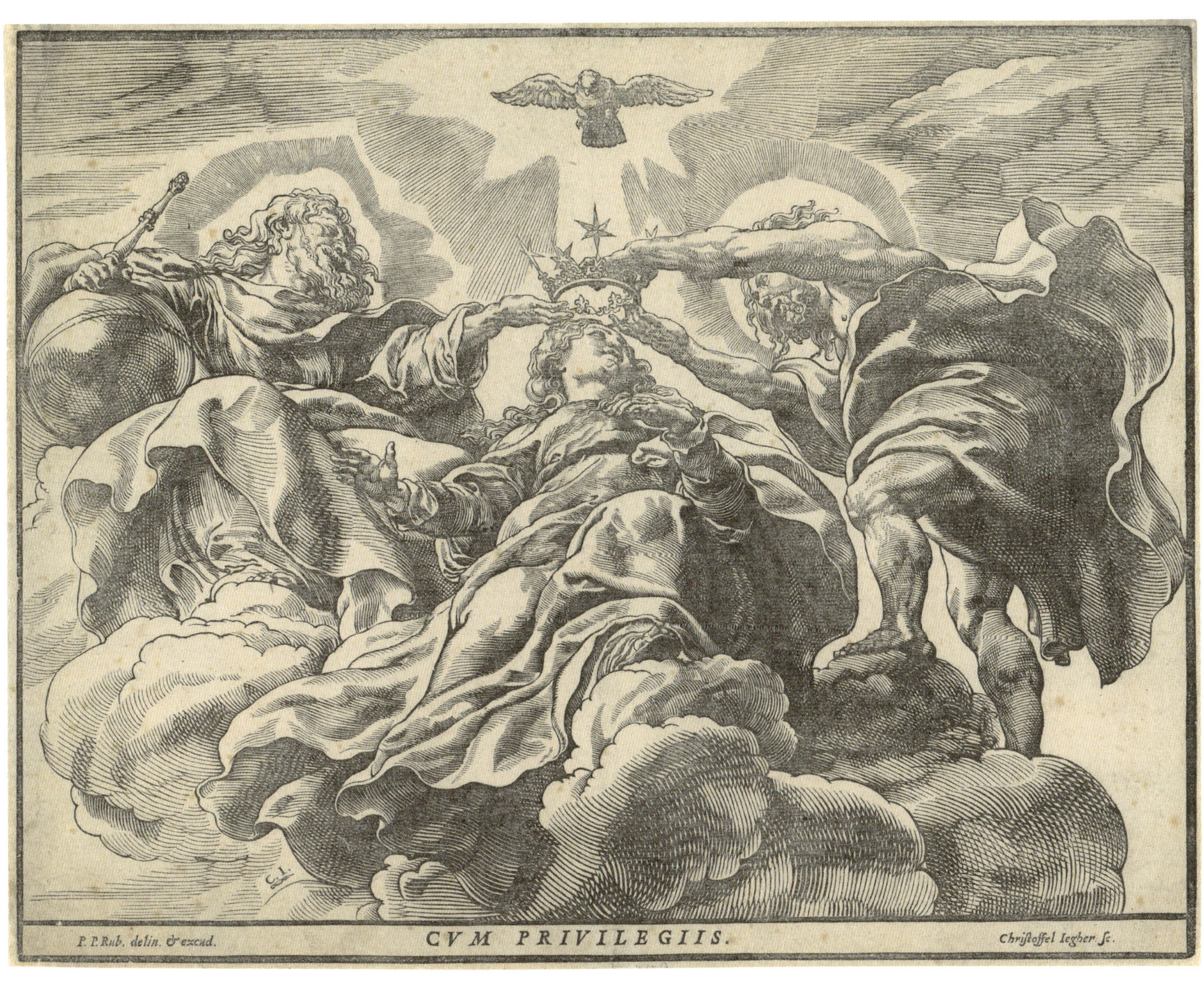

Rubens (Inventor, Verleger / designer, publisher), Christoffel Jegher (Holzschneider / woodcutter)
Die Marienkrönung / The Coronation of the Virgin, 1633–1635
Holzschnitt / woodcut SGSM, Inv. 150811 D

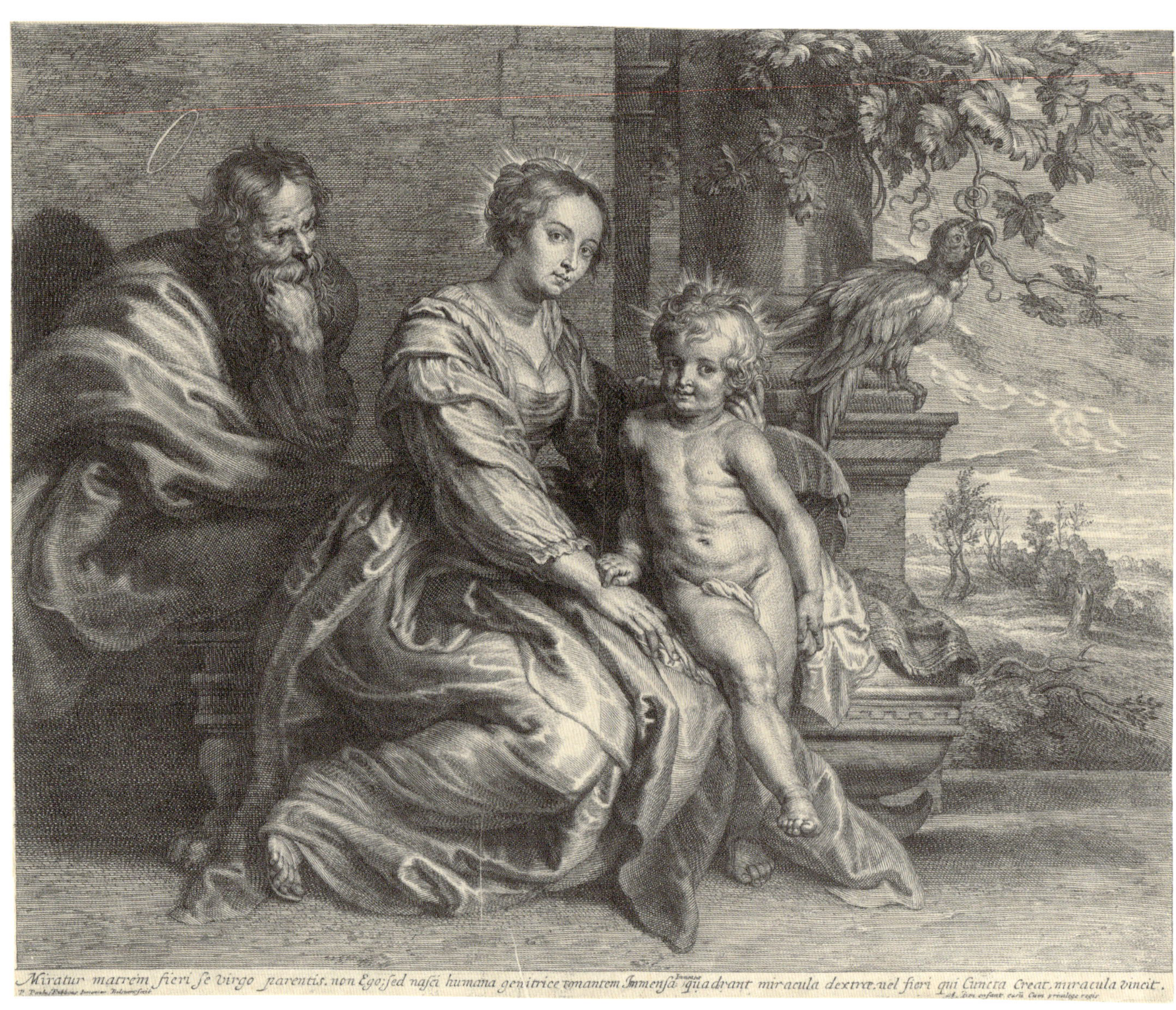

Michel Lasne? (Stecher / engraver), Schelte à Bolswert (Stecher / engraver), nach / after Rubens, Anton Goetkint (Verleger / publisher)
Die Hl. Familie mit dem Papagei / The Holy Family with the Parrot, 1635–1644
Kupferstich / engraving SGSM, Inv. 30173 D

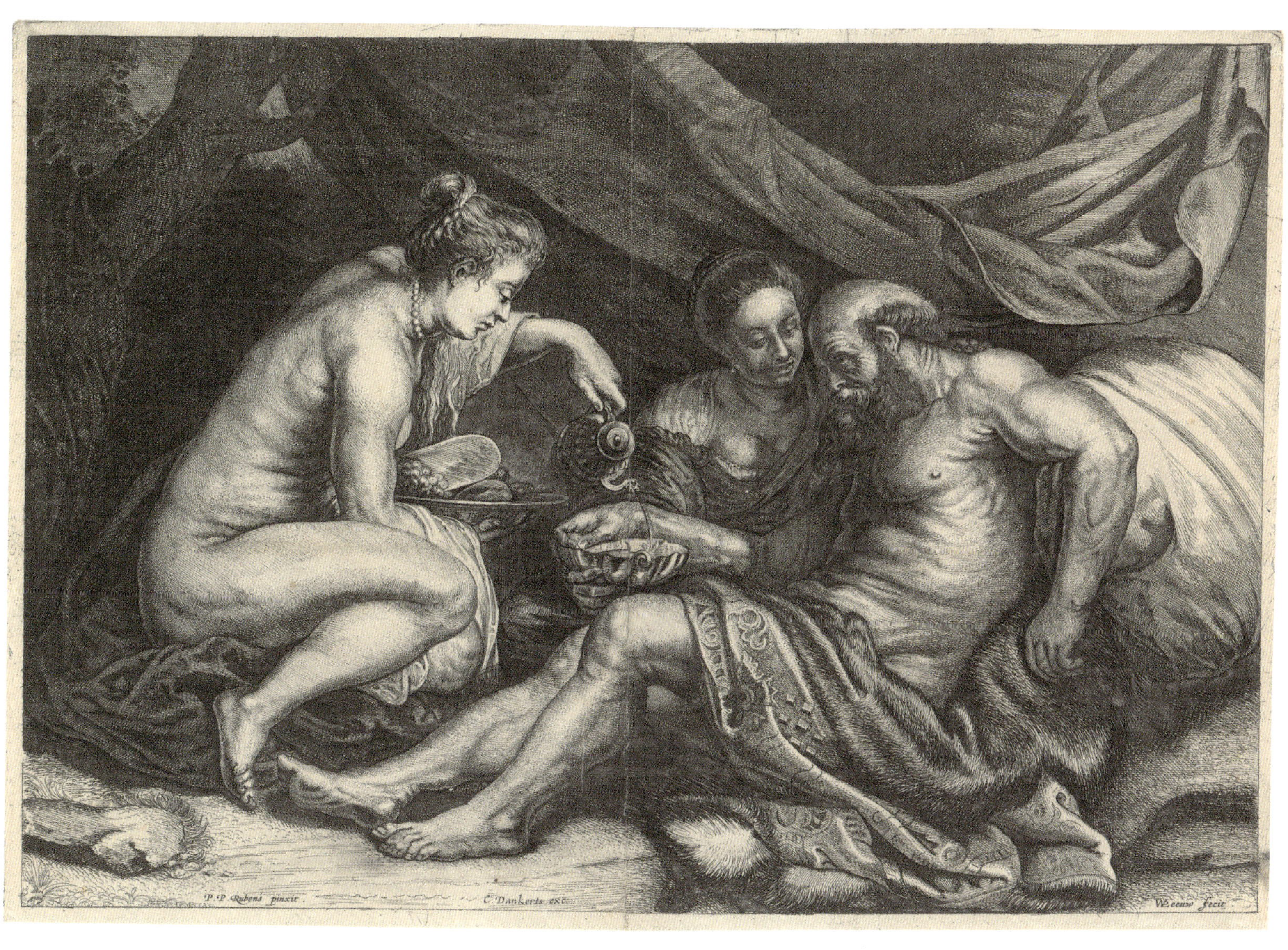

Willem van der Leeuw (Stecher / engraver), nach / after Rubens, Cornelis Danckerts (Verleger / publisher)
Lot und seine Töchter / and His Daughters, 1630–1634
Kupferstich / engraving SGSM, Inv. 111408 D

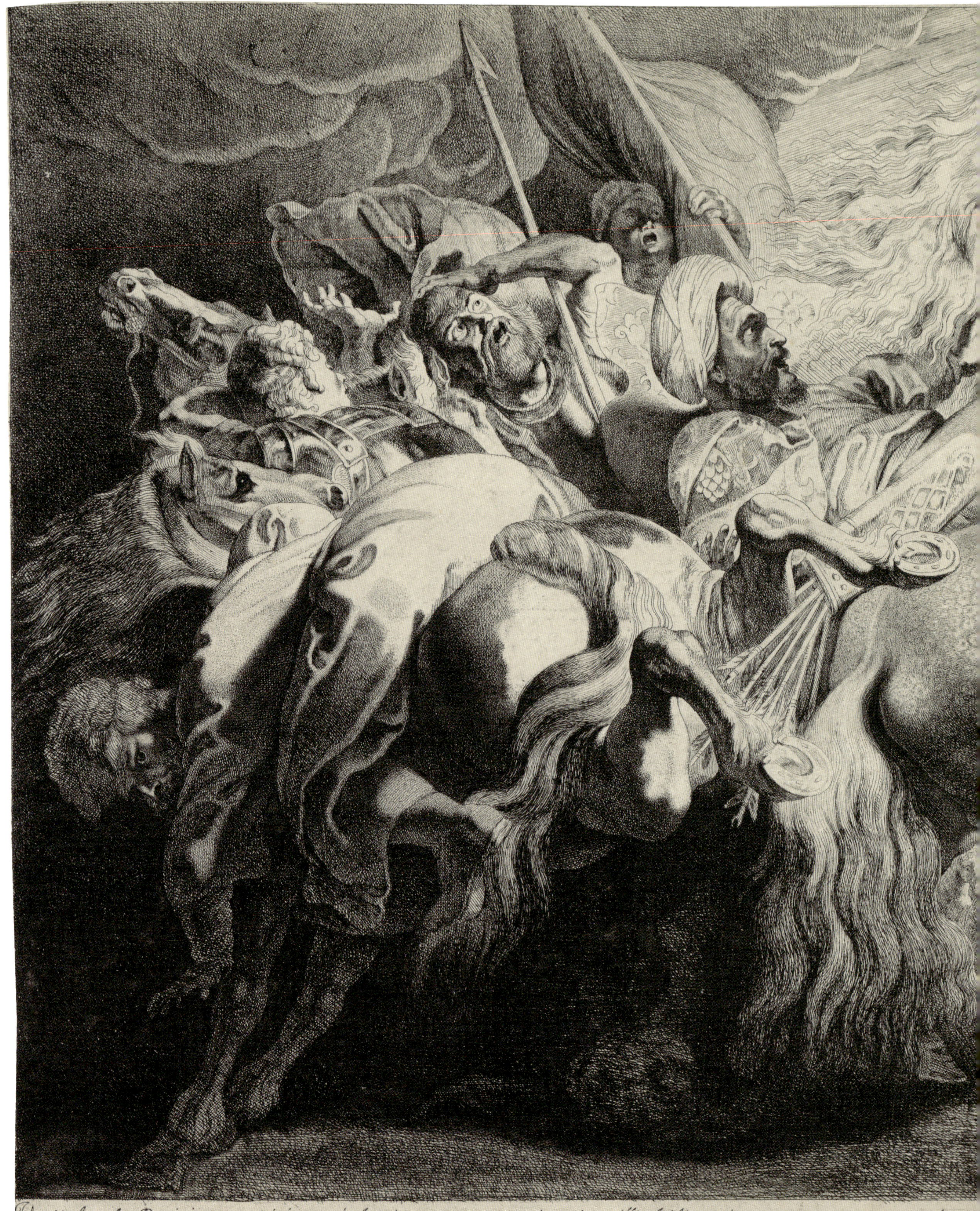

Venit Angelus Domini, et percussit in castris Assyriorum centum octuaginta quinq. millia. Vidit omnia corpora mortuorum, et recedens

P. P. Rubens Pinxit

Cum Privil.

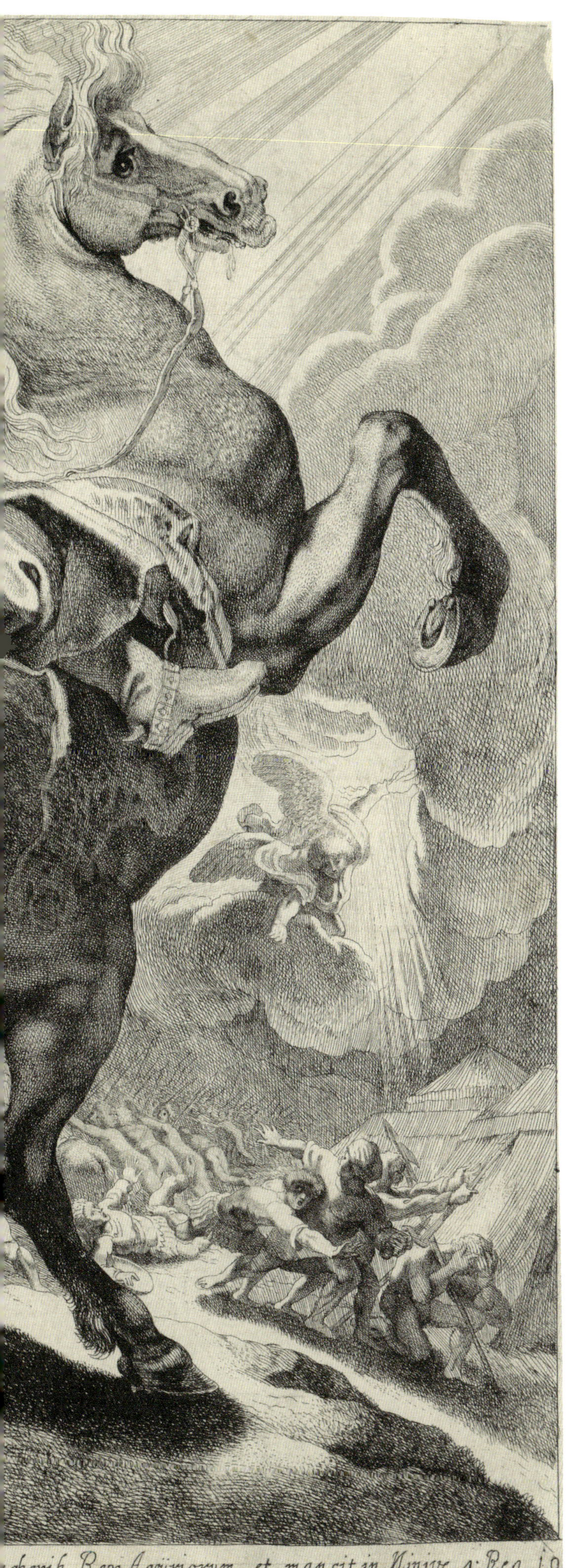

Pieter Soutman (Stecher, Radierer, Verleger / engraver, etcher, publisher), nach / after Rubens
Die Niederlage des Sanherib / The Defeat of Sennacherib, nach / after 1638
Kupferstich / engraving SGSM, Inv. 29992 D

V. Druckgraphik und Zeichnungen

Unerlässlich im Produktionsprozess von Druckgraphik waren Zeichnungen. Bei Hendrick Goltzius dienten sie ihm selbst und seinen Stechern als Vorlagen für die Stiche. Weil Goltzius-Zeichnungen bereits zu seinen Lebzeiten geschätzt wurden, sind sehr viele seiner Stichvorlagen erhalten. Bei Peter Paul Rubens hatten diese, meist angefertigt von seinen Atelierassistenten, zunächst die Funktion als ricordi, als Erinnerungen an Bildkompositionen. Manche Gemälde wurden erst Jahre oder Jahrzehnte, nachdem sie das Atelier verlassen hatten, in Druckgraphik umgesetzt, was Anlass war, die Zeichnungen für diesen Zweck zu überarbeiten. Viele herausragende Stichvorlagen von Rubens befinden sich heute als Teil eines Konvoluts im Louvre, sie wurden von Anthonis van Dyck (1599–1641) in Rubens' Atelier angefertigt. Bis über Rubens' Tod hinaus blieben sie ein gut gehüteter Schatz[1] und wurden, auch nachdem diese Zeichnungen 1657 auf den Markt gekommen waren, von Sammlern für ihre Qualität geschätzt und im Konvolut belassen.[2] Stichvorlagen konnten folglich ungeachtet ihrer Funktion von großer Qualität sein und verraten zudem vieles über den Entstehungsprozess von Stichen. Quantitativ jedoch überwiegen Nachzeichnungen nach Drucken. Meist waren dies Übungen von Werkstattassistenten oder Schülern, aber vereinzelt kopierte auch ein angehender Meister (wie Rubens) ein großes Vorbild (wie Goltzius).

In diesem Katalog steht nicht die Zeichnung im Mittelpunkt, die traditionell höher geschätzt wird als die Druckgraphik, sondern Letztere. Eine solche konservative Wertung – Zeichnung vor Druckgraphik – verstellt oft den Blick und lässt außer Acht, dass sich beide Medien gegenseitig befruchten und ihr jeweiliger Gewinn sowie ihr Zusammenspiel überaus vielfältig sein können. Dass diese Abhängigkeit ganz unterschiedliche, teils überraschende Facetten haben kann und dass sie zudem informativ ist, zeigen die Gegenüberstellungen von zusammengehörigen Paaren in diesem Kapitel.

Erstmals überhaupt treffen am Beispiel des Motivs *Christus vor Pilatus* in unserer Ausstellung eine Goltzius-Stichvorzeichnung, der ausgeführte Goltzius-Stich und die sich darauf beziehende Rubens-Nachzeichnung aufeinander (Abb. S. 156 f.). Für die gesamte Serie *Die Passion Christi* (1596–1598) sind die Vorzeichnungen von Goltzius im Museum der bildenden Künste Leipzig erhalten. Am *Pilatus*-Blatt sehen wir, dass es dem Haarlemer Künstler im Vorfeld darum ging, die Anlage der Architektur sowie der Figuren festzulegen. Die Gebäude und perspektivischen Fluchten konstruierte Goltzius mit dem Lineal, während er sich im Vordergrund über die Positionen, Körperhaltungen und Kleidung der um Pilatus versammelten Personen klar wurde. Die Figur neben dem Kopf des Pilatus entfernte er wieder, sie taucht dann im Stich auch nicht mehr auf. Auffällig sind die starken Konturlinien, die vom Nachzeichnen beim Übertragen (dem sogenannten Griffeln) auf die Druckplatte herrühren. Durch den Druck zeichneten sie sich auf dem Kupfer ab und dienten dort als Vorzeichnung für Goltzius, während er stach.

Der Stich unterscheidet sich von der Vorzeichnung vor allem durch die filigranen Details, die der Künstler in der Zeichnung

V. Prints and Drawings

Drawings were indispensable in the production of prints. For Hendrick Goltzius and his engravers, they served as templates for preparing the copperplates. Because Goltzius drawings were highly esteemed even during his lifetime, many of these preparatory drawings have survived. For Peter Paul Rubens, the drawings produced by his assistants functioned as *ricordi*, as records of his paintings' compositions. Some paintings were not turned into prints until years or even decades after they had left his studio. At that point and in a second step, he reworked the drawings by his assistants. Some exceptional preparatory drawings made by Anthony van Dyck (1599–1641) in Rubens's studio have stayed together as a group and are today kept in the Louvre. Rubens guarded these like a treasure until his death,[1] and even after they entered the art market in 1657 they were highly valued by collectors and remained together as a set.[2] Preparatory drawings, therefore, could be of excellent quality despite their functional purpose. In addition, they tell us much about the production of prints. In terms of quantity, however, there are more drawings after prints. Most of these were exercises by workshop assistants or apprentices, but every now and then an aspiring master (like Rubens) copied a great paragon (like Goltzius).

In this catalog the focus is not on drawings but on prints, even though the former traditionally have been regarded more highly. Such a conservative valuation (of drawings over prints) tends to obscure our gaze and disregard the fact that each medium fertilizes the other, leading to a multiplicity of interactions. This interdependence generates various and sometimes surprising facets and can be informative as well, as is demonstrated by the juxtapositions chosen for this chapter.

For the first time, our exhibition unites Goltzius's preparatory drawing *Christ before Pilate* with his print after it and with the Rubens drawing after this print (figs. pp. 156–157). The preparatory drawings for the entire series *The Passion of Christ* (1596–1598) are kept at the Museum der bildenden Künste Leipzig. In the drawing for the *Pilate* scene we can see that the Haarlem artist's intention was to ascertain the positions of the architecture and figures. Goltzius constructed the buildings and building lines with a ruler while he clarified for himself the specific positions, postures, and dresses of the figures surrounding Pilate. He erased a figure next to Pilate's head. As a consequence, it does not appear in the print. The dark contour lines that catch our eye result from the composition being traced with a stylus onto the copperplate. Due to the pressure applied, they left marks in the copper and served as a preliminary design for Goltzius once he started engraving.

The print differs from the preparatory drawing mostly in the delicate details that were only hinted at in the drawing, or not shown at all. In the print Goltzius rendered the details with the utmost care, emulating his idol Lucas van Leyden and thereby turning those details into a distinct narrative element.

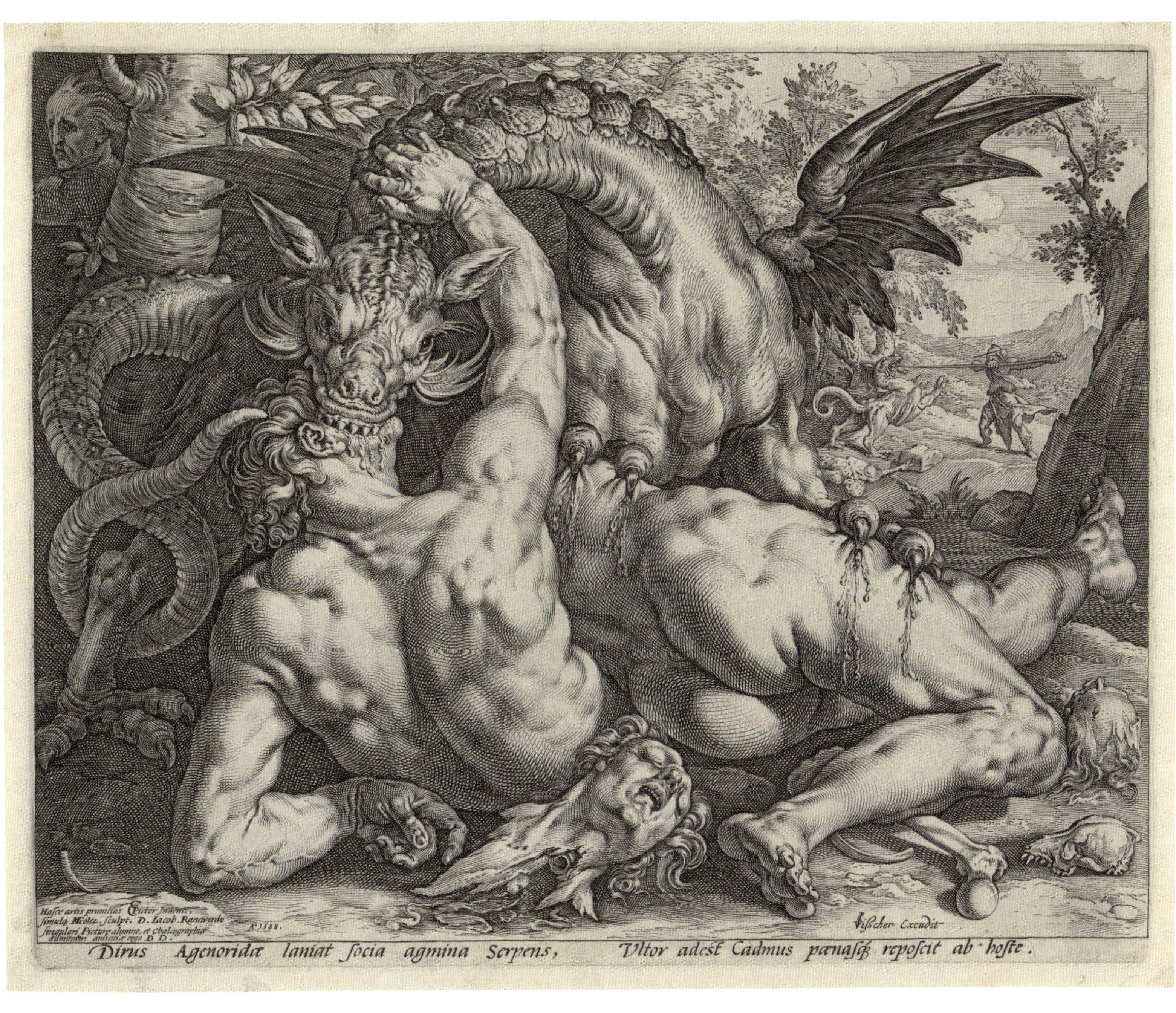

Goltzius (Stecher / engraver), nach / after Cornelis Cornelisz. van Haarlem, Claes Jansz. Visscher (Verleger / publisher)
Der Drache verschlingt die Gefährten des Cadmus / The Dragon Devouring the Companions of Cadmus, 1588
Kupferstich / engraving SGSM, Inv. 31004 D

manchmal nur andeutete, manchmal gar nicht vorgefasst hatte, die er jetzt aber in feinster Manier und dem ziselierenden Vorbild Lucas van Leydens folgend ausführte, sodass sie zu einem wichtigen eigenen Erzählelement wurden.

Kurz vor 1600, als diese Stichfolge entstand, war Rubens selbst noch angehender Künstler. Als er den Goltzius-Stich bald nach dessen Veröffentlichung zu sehen bekam, faszinierte ihn offensichtlich, dass nicht Christus die Hauptfigur war, sondern Pilatus und dass dieser als imposanter, nicht unsympathischer Mann dargestellt war. Was ihm augenfällig auch gefiel, war die Rückenfigur rechts, die uns zwar die Schulter zukehrt, aber ein überzeugender Blickfang ist. Zumindest kopierte Rubens nicht den ganzen Stich, sondern legte sein Augenmerk auf diese beiden Figuren und zeichnete sie nach, um sie sich einzuprägen.[3] Die beiden Figuren ganz links in der Zeichnung entnahm er einem anderen Blatt der *Passion*, *Christus vor Caiaphas* (Abb. S. 104). Goltzius' Linienführung im Stich spielt in Rubens' Nachzeichnung keine Rolle. Wie jeder angehende Künstler in dieser Zeit übte sich Rubens im Kopieren bedeutender Vorbilder, in diesem Fall Goltzius.

Als zweites Beispiel zeigen wir, wie eine Stichvorlage von Goltzius selbst aussah. Die in der Münchner Sammlung befindliche Darstellung *Die sieben Tugenden* (1585–1588) wurde 1588 von Jacob Matham (1571–1631) in einen Stich umgesetzt (Abb. S. 158 f.).[4] Hier kann man von einer Ökonomie der Angaben sprechen. Goltzius gab mit schnellen, wenigen Konturlinien die Figuren vor. Mittels Lavierungen und Höhungen deutete er die Verteilung von Licht und Schatten an. Über Details wie die Burg auf einem Berg in der Landschaft hinten muss es einen mündlichen Austausch gegeben haben, in der Zeichnung selbst ist nur ganz matt ein Berg angedeutet. Aus dieser Gegenüberstellung von Stichvorlage und Stich ist abzulesen, wie effizient die Werkstatt von Goltzius organisiert gewesen sein muss. Nur so ist schließlich auch die große Menge an Stichen zu erklären, die aus ihr hervorging.

Die meisten der Schüler- oder Lehrlingsnachzeichnungen sind anonym. Auch übertreffen sie, wie erwähnt, zahlenmäßig die noch erhaltenen Stichvorzeichnungen namentlich bekannter Künstler. In den Beständen der Staatlichen Graphischen Sammlung München finden sich gleich zwei Nachzeichnungen von namenlosen Epigonen zu Goltzius' Stich *Der Drache verschlingt die Gefährten des Cadmus*. Bei diesem 1588 datierten Blatt nach einem Gemälde von Cornelis Cornelisz. van Haarlem handelt es sich um eine der blutrünstigsten Darstellungen, die Goltzius in seiner Graphik verarbeitet hat (Abb. S. 151). Obwohl er ganz ohne Farbe auskommen musste, gelang es ihm, die besonders brutalen Bildelemente – den das menschliche Gesicht wegbeißenden Drachenkopf sowie dessen sich in das Fleisch des anderen Körpers bohrende Krallen – noch anschaulicher als im Gemälde herauszustellen. Auch die muskulösen Körper der beiden Opfer wirken realistischer, trotz einer gewissen Überspitzung.[5]

Einen der beiden Kopisten haben vor allem die Schaueraspekte gereizt (Abb. S. 153 unten). Er sparte die erzählerischen Momente drumherum aus und konzentrierte sich auf das Kerngeschehen, das er zunächst mit einem Graphitstift vorzeichnete, dann in drastischen Kontrasten lavierte und schließlich mit dünner Feder und Höhungen mehr schlecht als recht zu imitieren suchte.

Rubens was still an aspiring artist when this print series was created, just before 1600. When he saw Goltzius's print shortly after it was published, he was apparently fascinated by the fact that the elder artist had made the central figure not Christ but Pilate, and that he rendered him as an imposing, not disagreeable man. He also seems to have liked the figure on the right, which is a convincing eye-catcher despite turning his back and shoulder to us. Not surprisingly then, Rubens copied only these two figures rather than the entire motif, to have them at his disposal and commit them to memory.[3] The two figures at the left edge of the sheet are copied from another print in the *Passion of Christ* series, *Christ before Caiaphas* (fig. p. 104). The style Goltzius had chosen for his lines in this print was of no interest to Rubens in his drawing. Like all aspiring artists of the time, Rubens copied important paragons for practice, in this case Goltzius.

Our second example demonstrates what a preparatory drawing by Goltzius looked like. The drawing *The Seven Virtues* (1585–88), now in the collection of the Staatliche Graphische Sammlung München, was turned into an engraving by Jacob Matham (1571–1631) in 1588 (figs. pp. 158–159).[4] The drawing displays an economy of means. Goltzius rendered the figures quickly and with only a few contour lines, indicating the distribution of light and shadow with a brush and highlights. Details like the castle on top of a mountain in the background must have been requested orally, for in the drawing the mountain is barely indicated. This juxtaposition of preparatory drawing and print makes clear how efficiently Goltzius must have organized his workshop and explains the large number of prints that issued from it.

Most of the drawings by apprentices and assistants are anonymous. In terms of numbers, they surpass, as mentioned above, the extant preparatory drawings by artists we know by name. In the collection of the Staatliche Graphische Sammlung München are two drawings by nameless epigones of Goltzius's print *The Dragon Devouring the Companions of Cadmus*. This work, dated 1588 and based on a painting by Cornelis Cornelisz. van Haarlem, is one of the most gruesome depictions in all of Goltzius's prints (fig. p. 151). Even though he had to do entirely without color, he succeeded in making the ghastly details (the human face being bitten off by the dragon, claws piercing flesh) stand out even more luridly than they did in Cornelisz.'s painting. The muscular bodies of both victims appear more realistic even though they are, in fact, exaggerated.[5]

One of our two copyists was especially intrigued by the shocking parts (fig. p. 153, bottom). He neglected the narrative elements around them and zoomed in on the action in the center, which he tried to imitate rough-and-ready first with outlines in graphite before adding dramatic contrasts in brush and finally working over it in a fine pen and with highlights.

The anonymous epigone of the second drawn copy wanted to capture the entire composition (fig. p. 153, top). He used a grid in pencil to facilitate the copying of all elements from the print. Over a rough underdrawing in red chalk he placed a

Anonym / anonymous, Kopie nach / copy after Goltzius
Der Drache verschlingt die Gefährten des Cadmus / The Dragon Devouring the Companions of Cadmus, nach / after 1588
Graphit, Feder, Rötel, Kreide, laviert / graphite, ink, red chalk, chalk, wash SGSM, Inv. 8970 Z

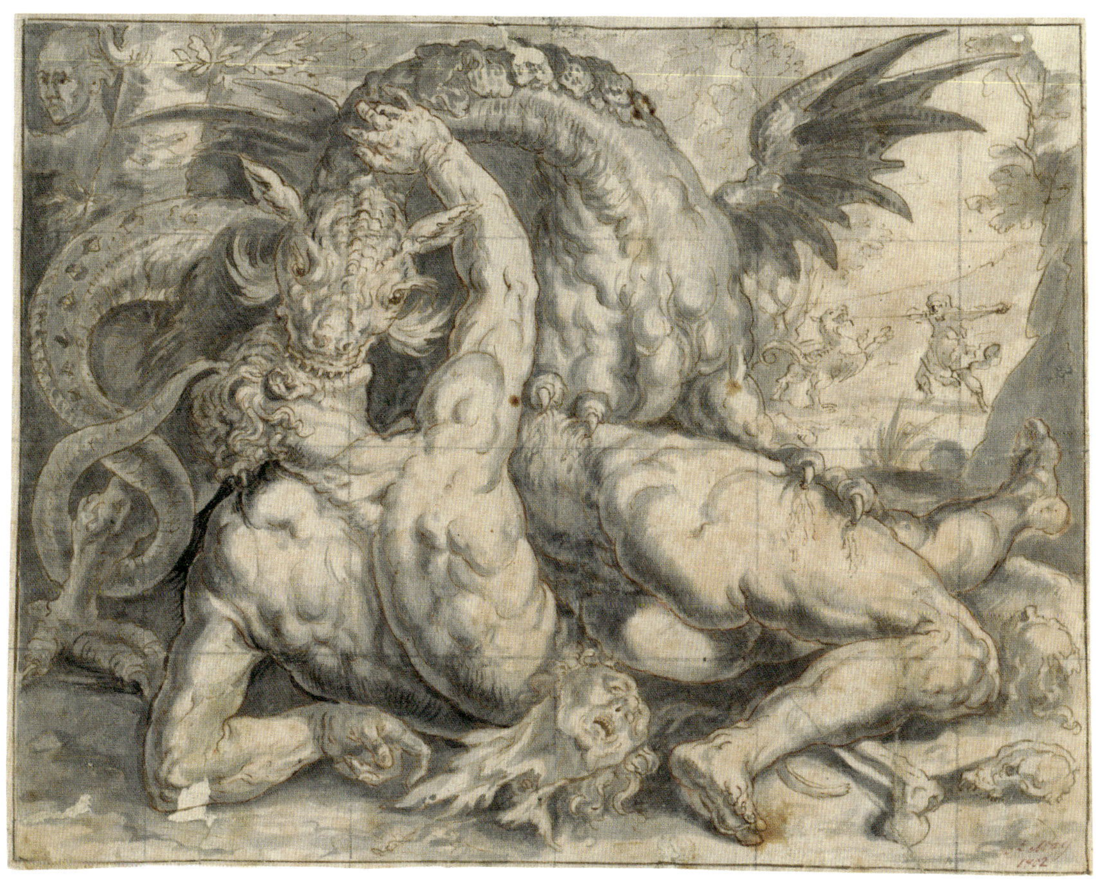

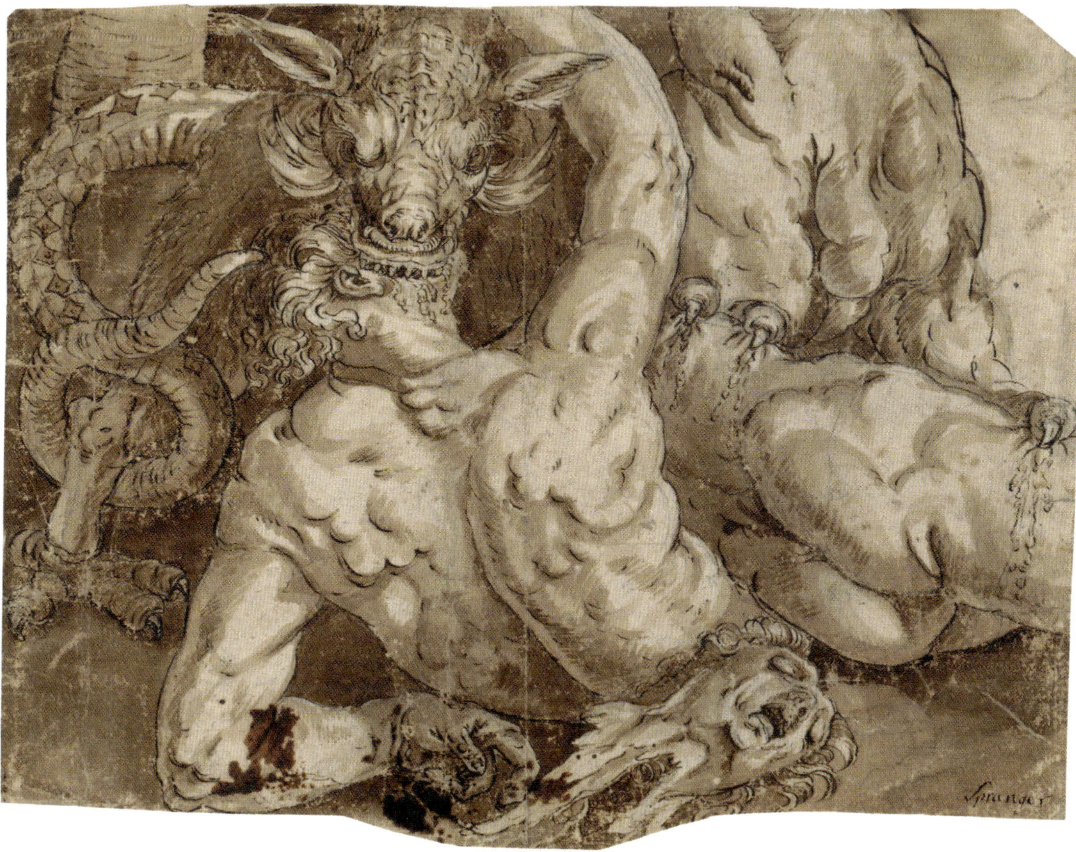

Anonym / anonymous, Kopie nach / copy after Goltzius
Der Drache verschlingt die Gefährten des Cadmus / The Dragon Devouring the Companions of Cadmus, nach / after 1588
Graphit, Feder, laviert / graphite, ink, wash SGSM, Inv. 41057 Z

Der anonyme Schüler der zweiten Zeichnung wollte die gesamte Komposition wiedergeben (Abb. S. 153 oben). Dabei behalf er sich mit einer Quadrierung in Bleistift, um die einzelnen Bildelemente leichter übertragen zu können. Über eine grobe Unterzeichnung in Rötel ging er sehr viel gekonnter und bedachter mit Feder und Lavierungen hinweg. Der Gesamteindruck kommt dem Stich sehr nahe, auch in Hinblick auf die Lichtverteilung.

Der Rubens-Stich *Tomyris mit dem Haupt des Cyrus* (Abb. S. 163) war ungemein beliebt, wie zahllose Kopien (auch aus dem 18. Jahrhundert) belegen.[6] Paulus Pontius (1603–1658) setzte ihn 1630 meisterlich für Rubens nach der Stichvorlage um, die als Leihgabe in unserer Ausstellung zu sehen ist (Abb. S. 162). Diese war wohl bereits Mitte der 1620er-Jahre nach einem Gemälde desselben Themas von Rubens' Assistenten als Kohlezeichnung angelegt worden und dann mit Tinte und farbigen Gouachen in den Details präzisiert worden. Vor der Umsetzung in den Stich durch Pontius Jahre später überarbeitete Rubens das Blatt selbst mit Pinsel und Gouache in Grau und Weiß.[7] Diese Ausarbeitung war für Pontius wichtig, nachdem er die Zeichnung auf die Kupferplatte durchgegriffelt hatte, denn Rubens' Überarbeitungen gaben ihm die Lichtverteilung und auch die Oberflächenbehandlungen von Stoffen oder Metallen vor. Das Blatt wurde mit Rubens' dreifachem Privileg versehen, Ausdruck davon, dass der Meister es für ein gelungenes Vorzeigewerk hielt, das als Botschafter für seine Kunst werben konnte.

Einen anderen ungewöhnlichen Typus Zeichnung in Zusammenhang mit einer Stichproduktion stellt die anonyme Kreidezeichnung nach einem Zwischenzustand von Rubens' Gemälde *Das Kleine Jüngste Gericht* (um 1621/22)[8] vor (Abb. S. 164). Das Besondere in diesem Fall ist, dass Rubens sein Gemälde im Rahmen einer Planänderung während der Ausführung oben um eine Lünette erweiterte, durch deren Figuren das Motiv von einem *Engelsturz* zu einem *Jüngsten Gericht* erweitert wurde, denn über dem Erzengel Michael thront jetzt der Weltenrichter. Auch die trompetenden Engel fügte der Künstler im Rahmen dieser Änderung im Gemälde hinzu, und diese fehlen in Zeichnung und Stich. Der Stich von Jonas Suyderhoef (1614–1686), der denselben Bildausschnitt wie die Zeichnung zeigt, ist 1642 datiert, also nach Rubens' Tod und etwa zwanzig Jahre nach Fertigstellung des Gemäldes (Abb. S. 165). Konrad Renger hat daher vermutet, dass Stich und Zeichnung auf dieselbe gezeichnete Vorlage zurückgehen, eine uns heute unbekannte oder verlorene Zeichnung[9] – vielleicht eine jener Zeichnungen, die Pieter Soutman während seiner Zeit in Rubens' Atelier von damals dort zu sehenden Gemälden gemacht hatte.

Eine ganz außergewöhnliche Art der Zeichnung, die auf das Engste mit dem Kupferstich verbunden ist, ist das von Hendrick Goltzius zwar nicht erfundene, aber von ihm zur unübertroffenen Blüte gebrachte „Federkunststück".[10] Eine Handvoll solcher Werke schuf er, meist bereits mit dem Rezipienten im Kopf.[11] Diese gemäldegroßen Zeichnungen, die mit der Feder die Ästhetik des Kupferstichs nachahmen, gingen bereits zu Lebzeiten vor allem in Kunstkammern ein. Kaiser Rudolf II. etwa besaß vier oder fünf solcher Kostbarkeiten von Goltzius.[12] Goltzius' Stiefsohn und Assistent Jacob Matham wusste um den Erfolg,

more skilled and considered drawing in pen and brush. The appearance of the whole comes close to the print, including in the distribution of light.

The Rubens print *Queen Tomyris with the Head of Cyrus* (fig. p. 163) was very popular, as numerous copies (even from the eighteenth century) attest.[6] In 1630, Paulus Pontius (1603–1658) made a masterful engraving for Rubens after the preparatory drawing that is on loan to our exhibition (fig. p. 162). In its initial design this drawing had been sketched in charcoal, probably in the mid-1620s by one of Rubens's assistants after the painting of the same subject. The details were then refined with ink and color gouaches. Years later—and before Pontius proceeded to engrave the design—Rubens reworked the sheet with brush and gouache in gray and white.[7] This further specification in the drawing was important for Pontius: after he had transferred the composition with a burin to the copperplate, Rubens's marks indicated to him the distribution of light as well as the surface treatment of fabrics and metals. Rubens had his three privileges added to the print, an expression of the fact that he considered it a successful showpiece that could serve as an ambassador of his art.

An anonymous chalk drawing (fig. p. 164) after an intermediary state of Rubens's painting *The Small Last Judgment* (ca. 1621/22) represents a different, highly unusual kind of drawing.[8] Remarkably, Rubens changed his plan for this painting while he was already at work on it, deciding to add a round arch to the top of the composition. The figures thus added to the composition thematically transformed the planned *Fall of the Damned* into a *Last Judgment*, because God now appeared above the Archangel Michael, judging all souls and nations. As part of the changes, the artist also added trumpeting angels to the top portion of the painting. An engraving by Jonas Suyderhoef (1614–1686) shows the same portion of the painting as the chalk drawing and is dated 1642, after Rubens's death and a full twenty years after he finished the painting (fig. p. 165). All of Rubens's additions to the painting are missing in both the drawing and the print. Hence, Konrad Renger speculates that the print and drawing both copied the same template, a drawing that is unknown to us today or has been lost,[9] possibly one of the drawings that Pieter Soutman made of the paintings in Rubens's studio during his time there.

Yet another kind of exceptional drawing, one that is closely related to engravings, is the "pen work," which, although not invented by Hendrick Goltzius, reached unprecedented heights in his hands.[10] He created a handful of these works with specific recipients in mind.[11] These drawings—the size of paintings—emulate in pen the aesthetics of engraving. Even during his lifetime, Goltzius's "pen works" entered *Kunstkammer* collections. Emperor Rudolf II owned four or five such treasures.[12] Goltzius's stepson and assistant Jacob Matham was aware that these exceptional works bestowed much honor on their maker, and he also created a few.[13] One of them, signed by Matham and dated 1604, *Pen Work with Three Heads Symbolizing the Three Ages of Man and Utensils for Drawing*

der mit solch außergewöhnlichen Werken zu erzielen war, und fertigte auch eine kleine Anzahl hiervon an.[13] Eines dieser Werke, das von Matham signierte und auf 1604 datierte *Federkunststück mit drei Köpfen verschiedener Lebensalter und Utensilien des Zeichnens und Stechens*, befindet sich in den Beständen der Staatlichen Graphischen Sammlung München (Abb. S. 160 f.). Nicht nur technisch ist dieses Werk darauf angelegt, auf mehreren Ebenen gelesen zu werden, sondern auch ikonographisch. Von Weitem erweckt es den Anschein eines Stiches, von Nahem entpuppt es sich als akribisch detailliert ausgeführte Federzeichnung. Augenscheinlich sehen wir ein Stillleben mit fragmentarischen Skulpturenköpfen, doch tatsächlich handelt es sich um ein allegorisches Selbstbildnis des Zeichners. Seine Arbeitsutensilien – die Feder oben links, das schärfende Messer unten links, Tintenfass und Stiftetui im Vordergrund, der Grabstichel im Kästchen rechts – und seine Bildvorlagen – die beiden antiken Köpfe, das Buch auf dem Kasten hinten links –, aber schließlich auch sein eigener Porträtkopf rechts ergeben im Ganzen ein ungewöhnliches Selbstbildnis. Ob Matham dieses Werk selbst behielt oder verschenkte, wissen wir nicht. Aber wie auch die „Federkunststücke" von Goltzius gelangte es schließlich in königlichen Besitz, namentlich den von Ludwig I. von Bayern (1786–1868), welcher es den königlichen Sammlungen vermachte.

and Engraving, is now in the collection of the Staatliche Graphische Sammlung München (fig. pp. 160–161). This work was meant to impress on several levels, in terms of both technique and iconography. Although it looks like a print from afar, in close-up it turns out to be a meticulously executed pen drawing. We are ostensibly looking at a still life with the heads from three sculptures, but this is actually an allegorical self-portrait of the draftsman. His utensils—the quill in the upper left, the sharpening knife in the lower left, inkwell and pen case in the foreground, the burin in the small box on the right—and his objects of study—the two Classical heads, the book on top of the box on the left—together with his own face on the sculpted head on the right all combine to form a wholly unusual self-portrait. We do not know if Matham kept this work for himself or gave it away as a gift. But just like Goltzius's "pen works," it eventually belonged to a king—namely, Ludwig I of Bavaria (1786–1868), who bequeathed it to the royal collections.

1 Zur Geschichte vom Verbleib von Rubens' Zeichnungen unmittelbar nach dessen Tod vgl. Büttner 2006, S. 214, Anm. 23, sowie Büttner 2015c, S. 114.
2 Vgl. zuletzt Anne-Marie Logan, in: Logan/Lohse Belkin 2021, S. 13. Ausführlicher Wood 2020, S. 57–63.
3 Zu Rubens' Nachzeichnungen nach Goltzius siehe Lohse Belkin 2009, Nr. 110; Logan/Lohse Belkin 2021, Nr. 15–18; Sonnabend 2018.
4 Vgl. Reznicek 1961, K81.
5 Vgl. die interessante Besprechung bei Meier 2020b, S. 56 f., der auch Parallelen zu Rubens zieht.
6 Vgl. hierzu New York 2005, Kat. 55, bes. S. 184. Die SGSM bewahrt zwei Stiche von Gaspard Duchange (Inv. 30397 D und 2023:64 D) sowie eine anonyme aus der zweiten Hälfte des 17. Jahrhunderts auf (Inv. 2023:85 D; nicht bei McGrath 1997, Nr. 2 oder 3).
7 Das Gemälde befindet sich heute im Museum of Fine Arts Boston, Inv. 41.40.
8 München, Alte Pinakothek, Inv. 611.
9 Konrad Renger, in: Renger/Denk 2002, S. 324.
10 Vor ihm hatte Bartolomeo Passerotti (1529–1592) in Italien diese besondere Art der Zeichnung gepflegt. Vgl. Reznicek 1961, S. 11, und Nichols 1991/92, S. 10.
11 Vgl. Nichols 1992 sowie Larionov 2021.
12 Vgl. Huigen Leeflang, in: Amsterdam/New York/Toledo 2003, S. 235.
13 Yvonne Bleyerveld hat 15 erhaltene „Federkunststücke" Mathams gezählt; siehe Bleyerveld 2022, S. 31 und Anm. 6 samt Liste.

1 For the history of Rubens's drawings immediately after his death, see Büttner 2006, p. 214, n. 23, and Büttner 2015c, p. 114.
2 See, most recently, Anne-Marie Logan, in: Logan/Lohse Belkin 2021, p. 13. For more details, see Wood 2020, pp. 57–63.
3 On Rubens's drawings after Goltzius, see Lohse Belkin 2009, no. 110; Logan/Lohse Belkin 2021, nos. 15–18; Sonnabend 2018.
4 See Reznicek 1961, K81.
5 See the interesting discussion in Meier 2020b, pp. 56–57, who also draws parallels to Rubens.
6 On this point, see New York 2005, cat. 55, esp. p. 184. The SGSM holds two prints by Gaspard Duchange (inv. 30397 D and 2023:64 D), as well as an anonymous print from the second half of the seventeenth century (inv. 2023:85 D; not in McGrath 1997, no. 2 or 3).
7 The painting is now in the Museum of Fine Arts Boston, inv. 41.40.
8 The painting is in Munich, Alte Pinakothek, inv. 611.
9 Konrad Renger, in: Renger/Denk 2002, p. 324.
10 Before him, Bartolomeo Passerotti (1529–1592) had practiced this special kind of drawing in Italy. See Reznicek 1961, p. 11, and Nichols 1991/92, p. 10.
11 See Nichols 1992 and Larionov 2021.
12 See Huigen Leeflang, in: Amsterdam/New York/Toledo 2003, p. 235.
13 Yvonne Bleyerveld counts fifteen "pen works" by Matham; see Bleyerveld 2022, p. 31 and n. 6 with a list.

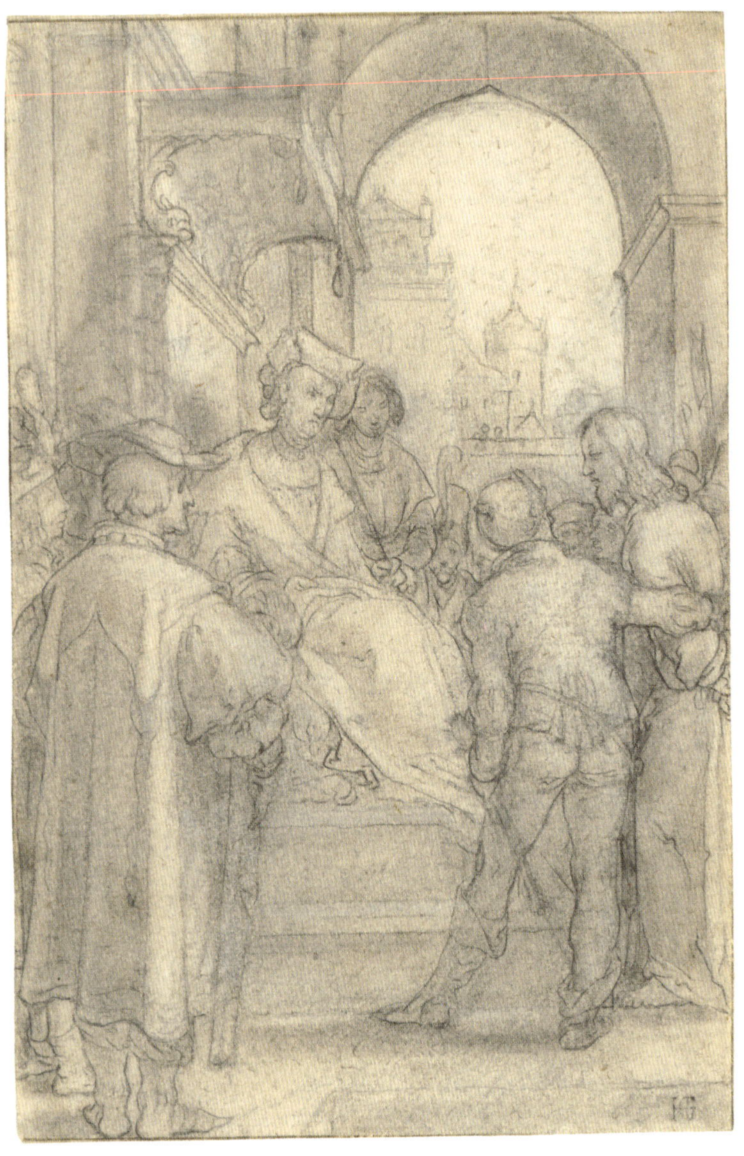

Hendrick Goltzius
Christus vor Pilatus / Christ before Pilate, ca. 1596
Vorzeichnung / preparatory drawing
Kreide, weiß gehöht / chalk, white highlights
Leipzig, Museum der bildenden Künste, Inv. Nl. 442

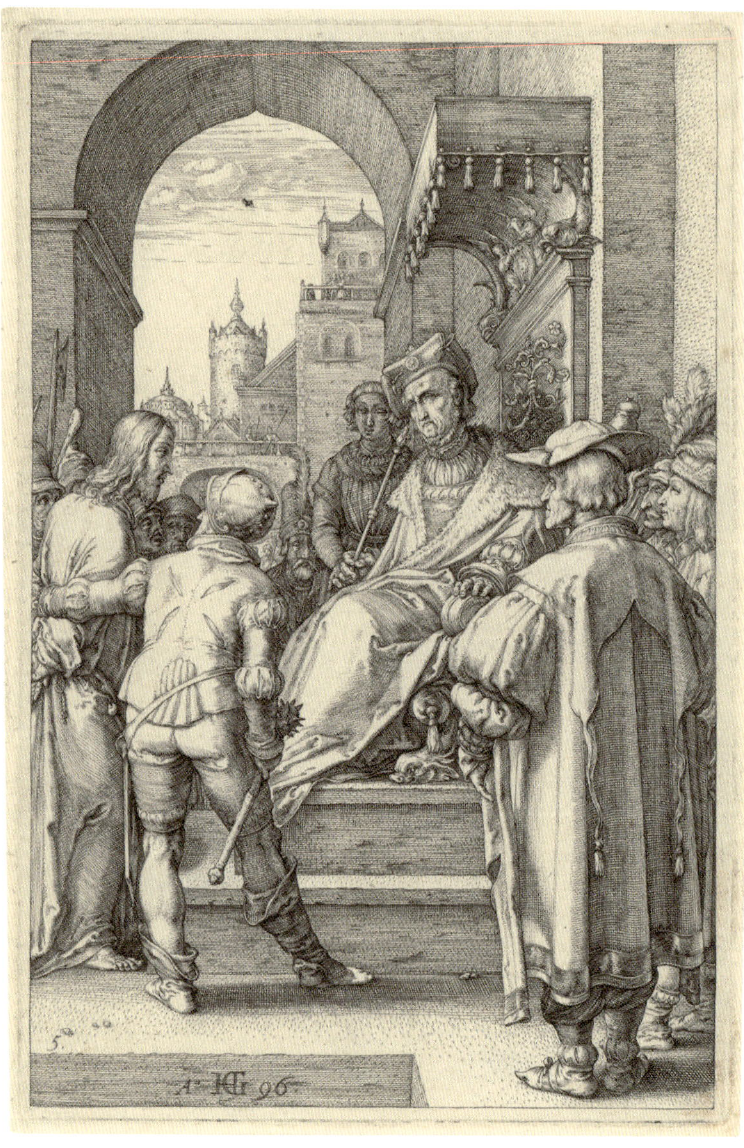

Hendrick Goltzius (Inventor, Stecher / designer, engraver)
Christus vor Pilatus / Christ before Pilate, 1596
Aus der Serie *Die Passion Christi* / from the series *The Passion of Christ*, 1596–1598
Kupferstich / engraving SGSM, Inv. 30910 D

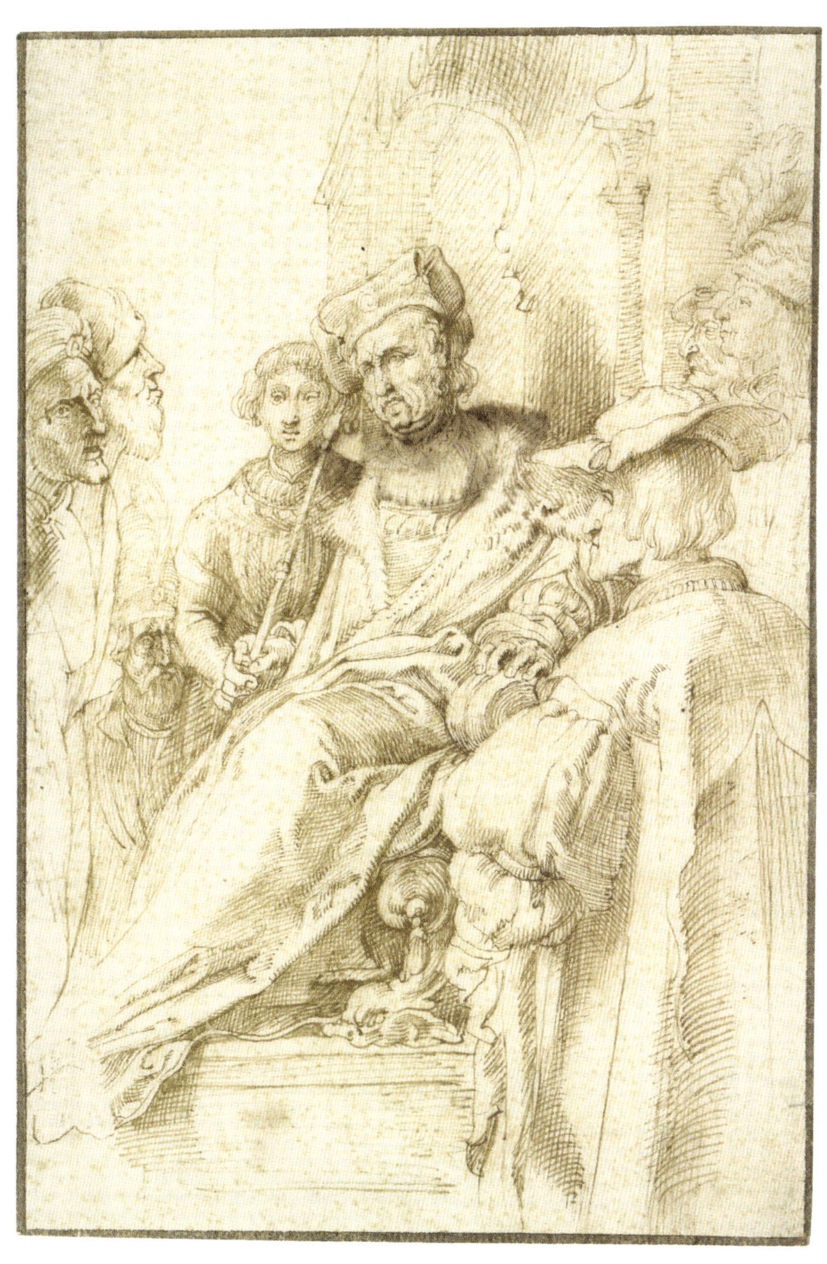

Rubens, Kopie nach / copy after Goltzius
Pilatus / Pilate, 1596–1600
Feder / ink Frankfurt am Main, Städel Museum, Inv. 806

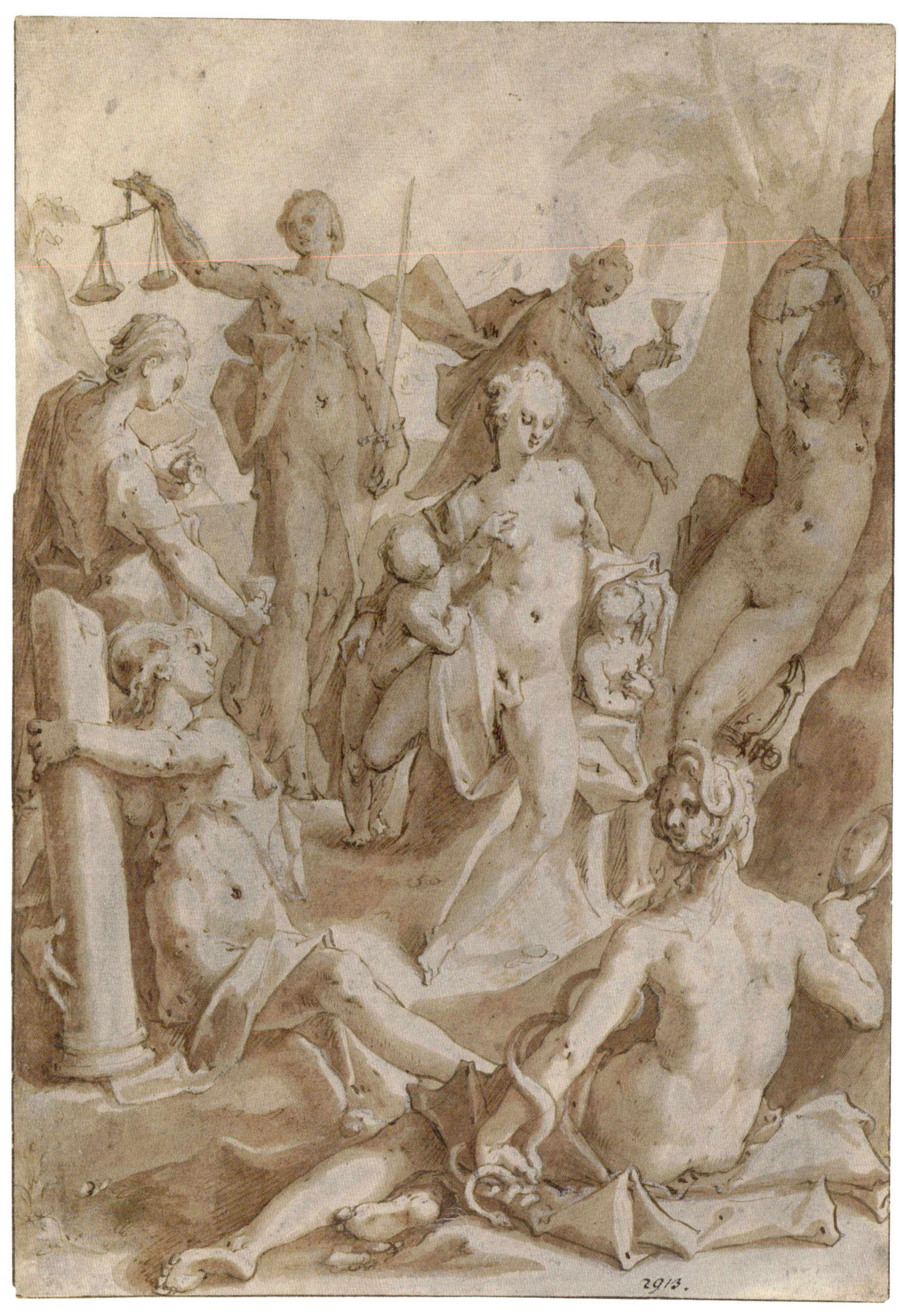

Hendrick Goltzius
Die sieben Tugenden / The Seven Virtues, 1585–1588
Vorzeichnung / preparatory drawing
Feder, laviert, weiß gehöht / ink, wash, white highlights SGSM, Inv. 1043 Z

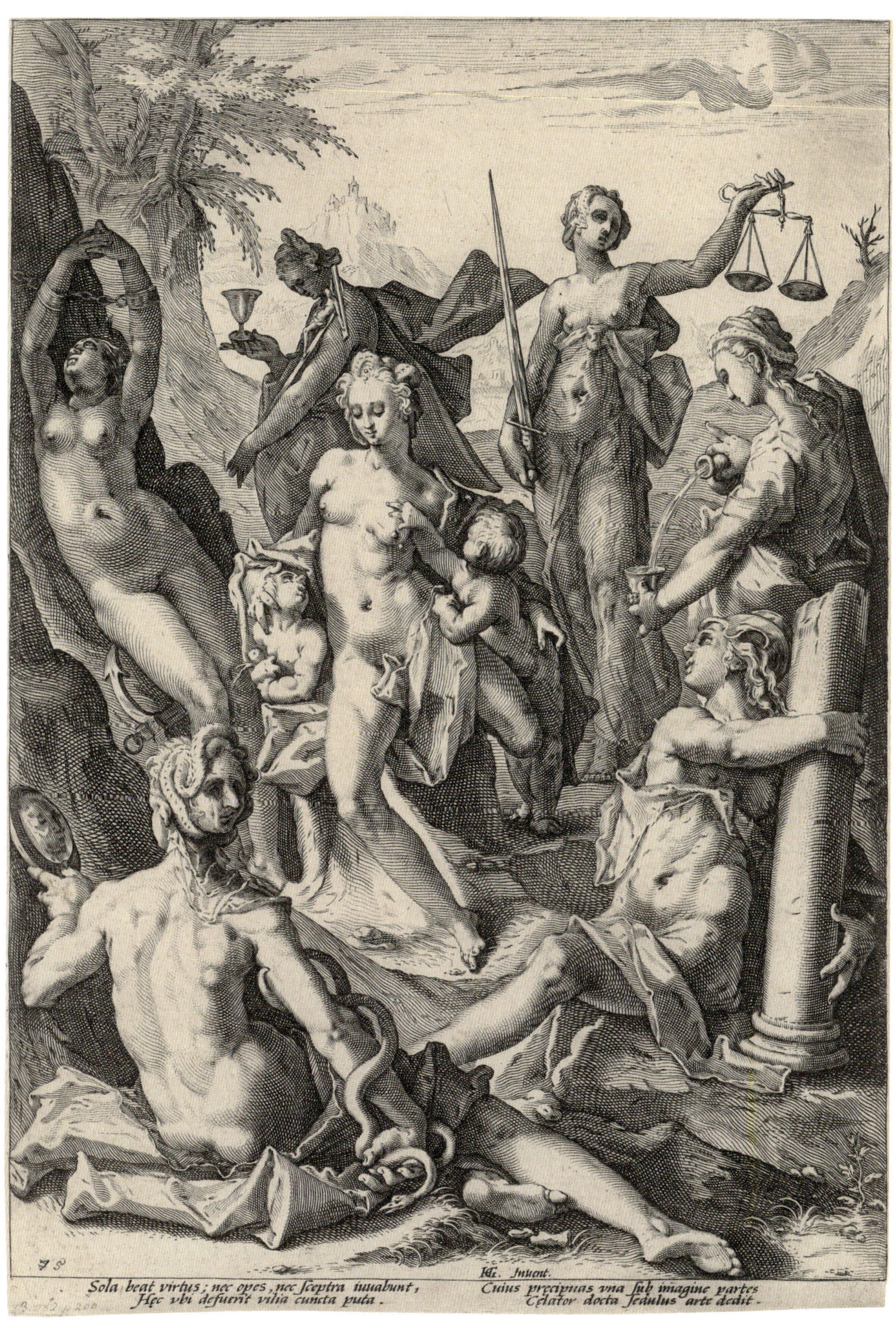

Goltzius (Inventor, Verleger / designer, publisher), Jacob Matham (zugeschr. Stecher / attr. engraver)
Die sieben Tugenden / The Seven Virtues, 1588
Kupferstich / engraving SGSM, Inv. 31183 D

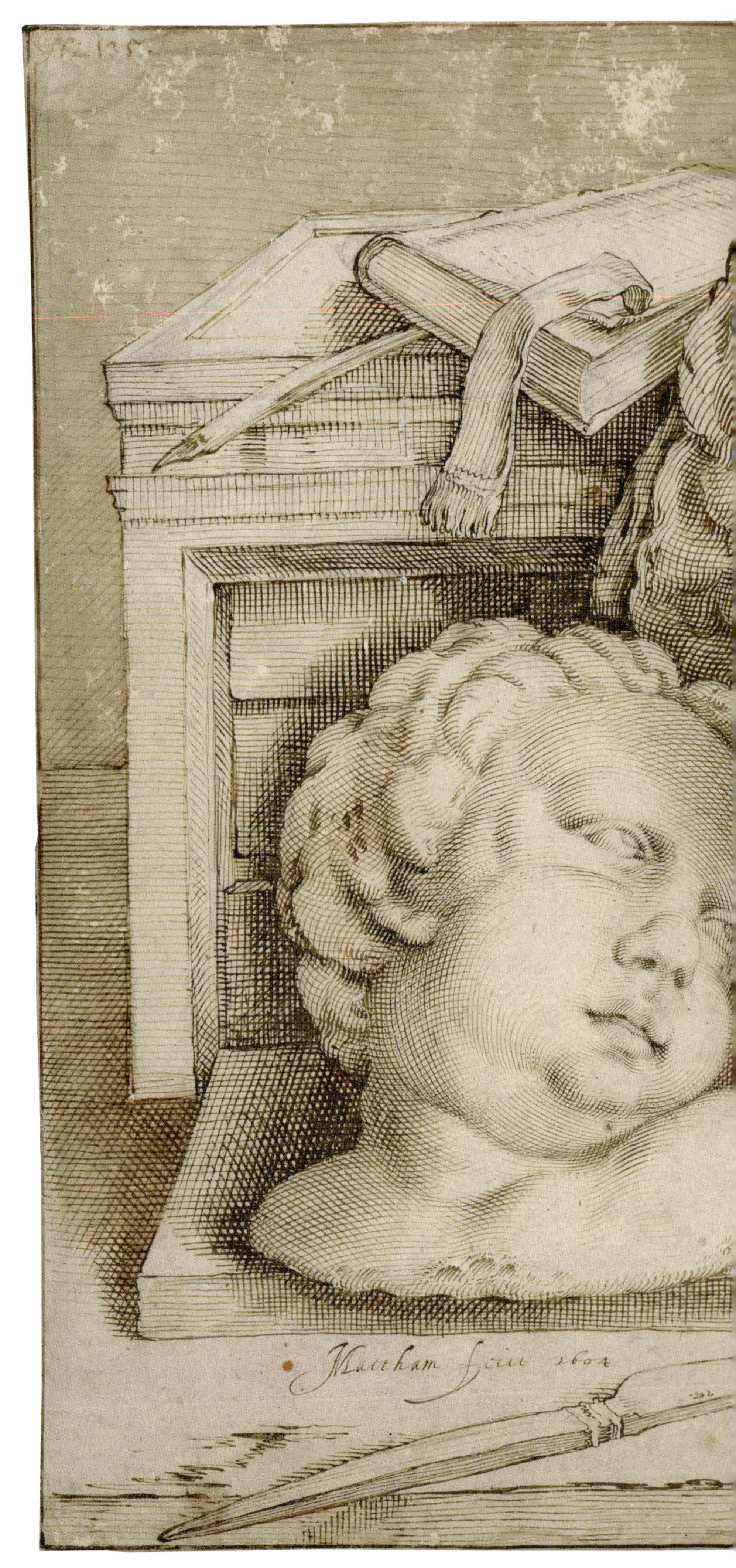

Jacob Matham
Federkunststück mit drei Köpfen verschiedener Lebensalter und Utensilien des Zeichnens und Stechens / Pen Work with Three Heads Symbolizing the Three Ages of Man and Utensils for Drawing and Engraving, 1604
Feder, Graphit, laviert / ink, graphite, wash
SGSM, Inv. 21128 Z

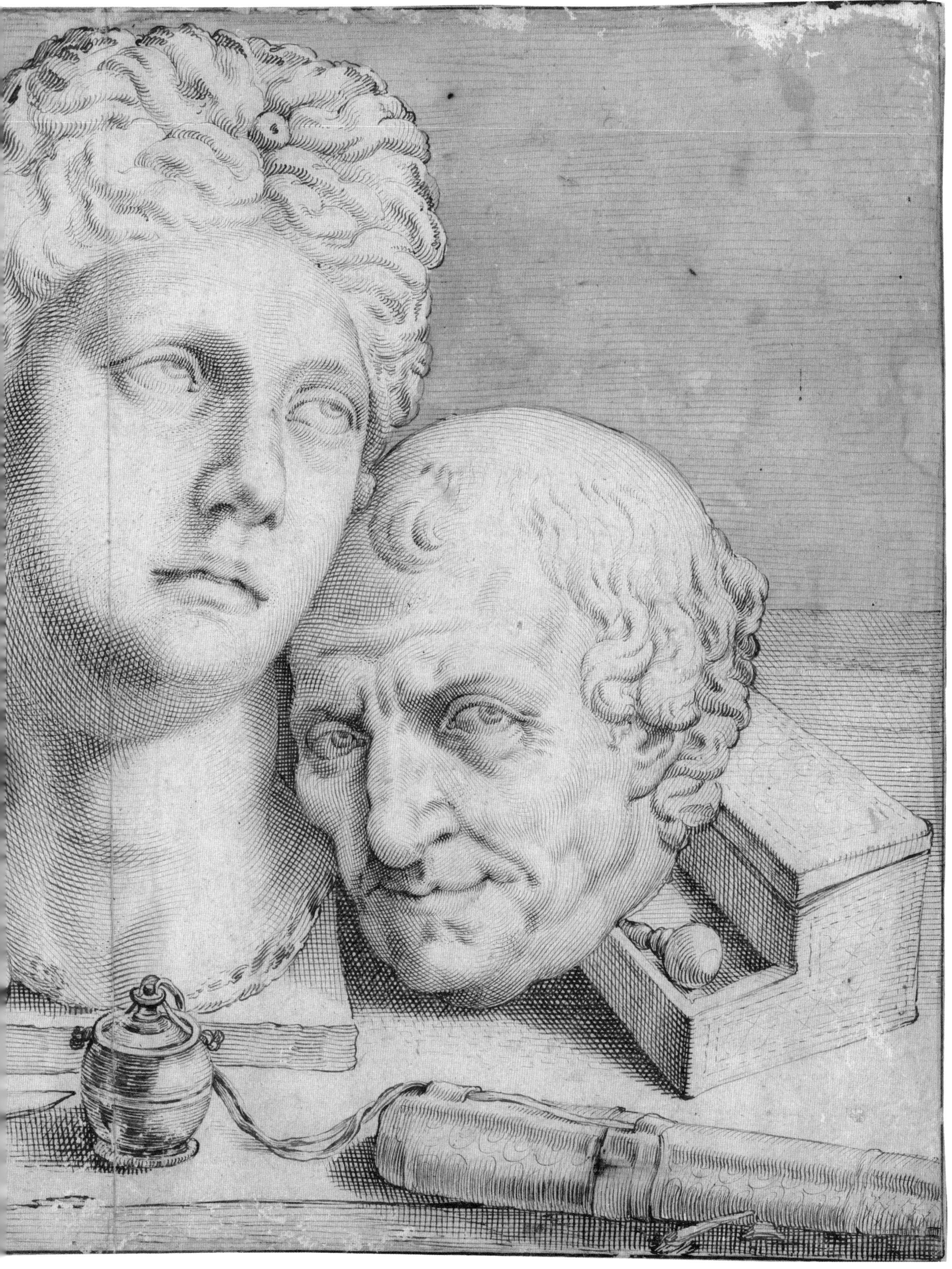

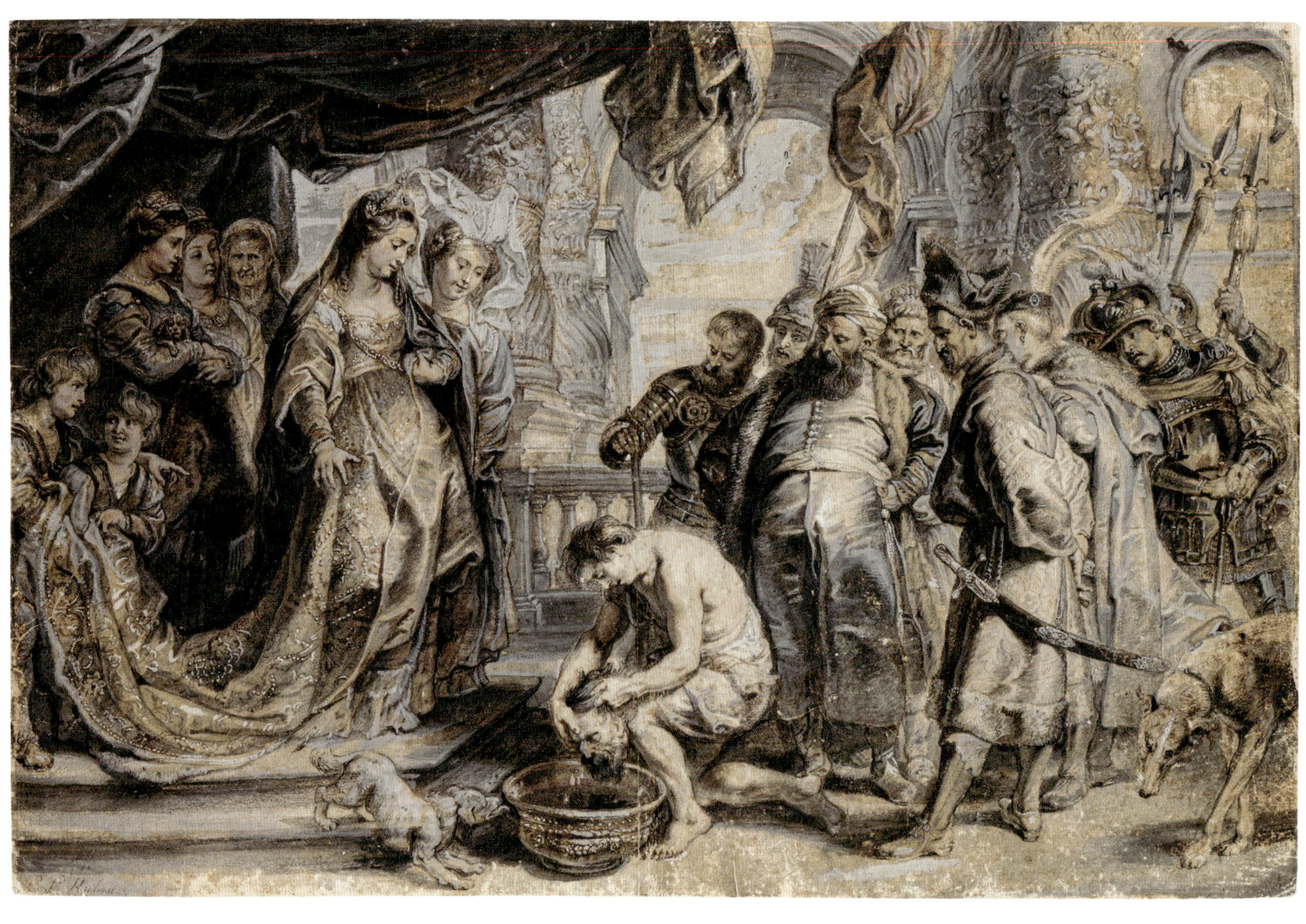

Rubens und Werkstatt / and workshop
Tomyris mit dem Haupt des Cyrus / Queen Tomyris with the Head of Cyrus, ca. 1630
Vorzeichnung / preparatory drawing
Kreide, Feder, laviert, Aquarell, weiß gehöht / chalk, ink, wash, watercolor, white highlights München, Privatsammlung / private collection

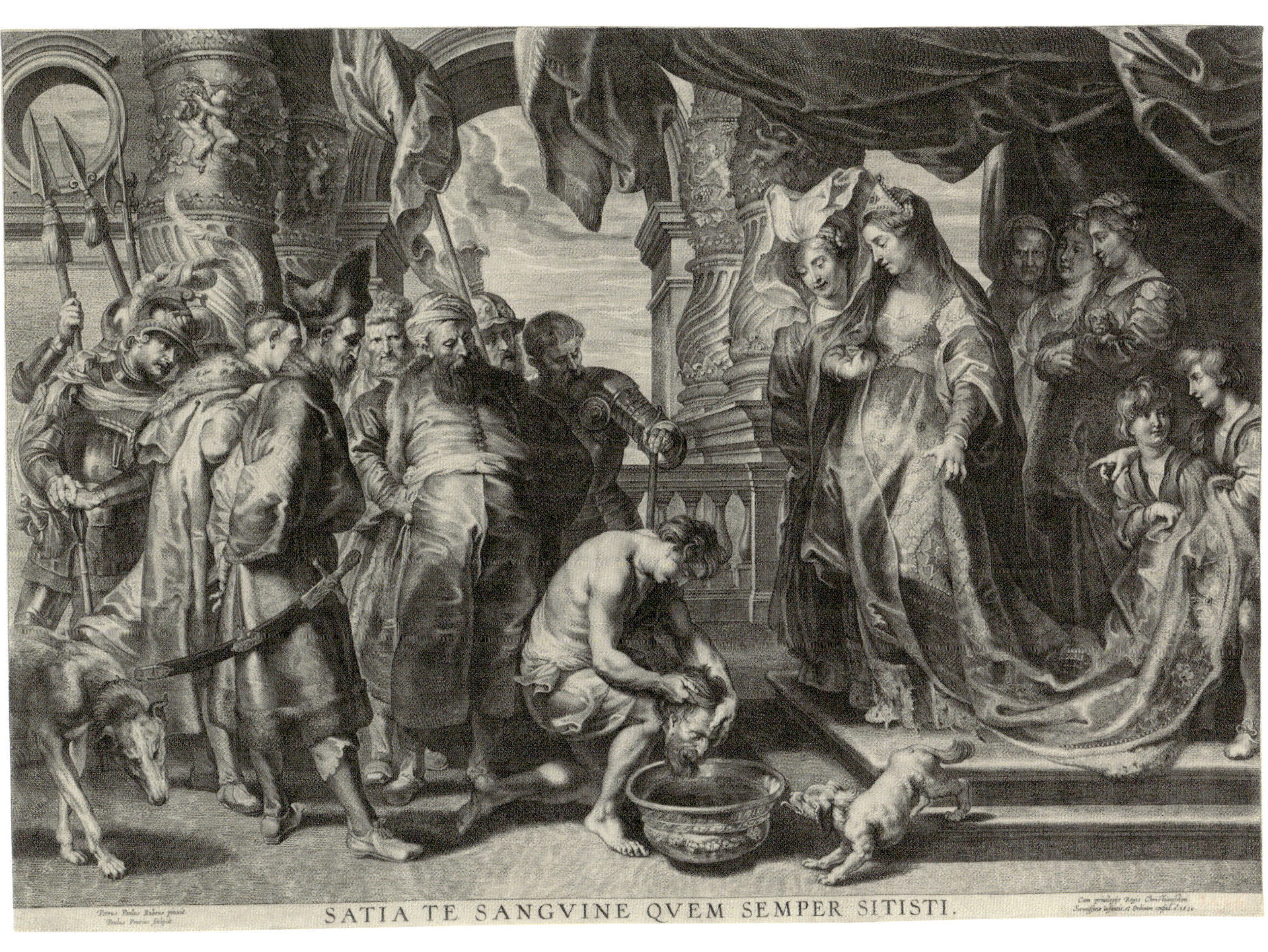

Rubens (Inventor / designer), Paulus Pontius (Stecher / engraver)
Tomyris mit dem Haupt des Cyrus / Queen Tomyris with the Head of Cyrus, 1630
Kupferstich / engraving SGSM, Inv. 30396 D

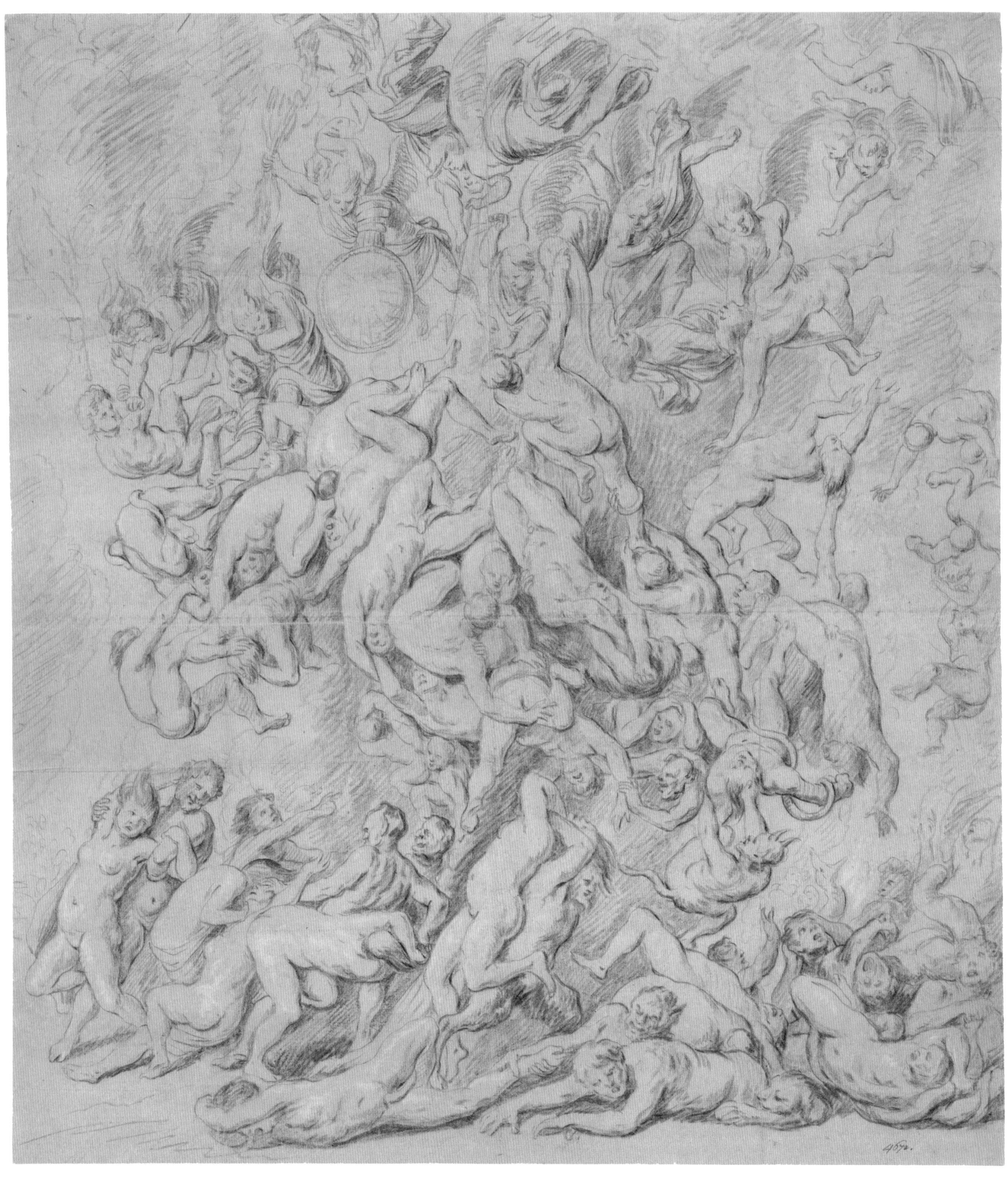

Anonym / anonymous, nach / after Rubens
Das Kleine Jüngste Gericht / The Small Last Judgment, ca. 1621/22
Kreide, weiß gehöht / chalk, white highlights SGSM, Inv. 14081 Z

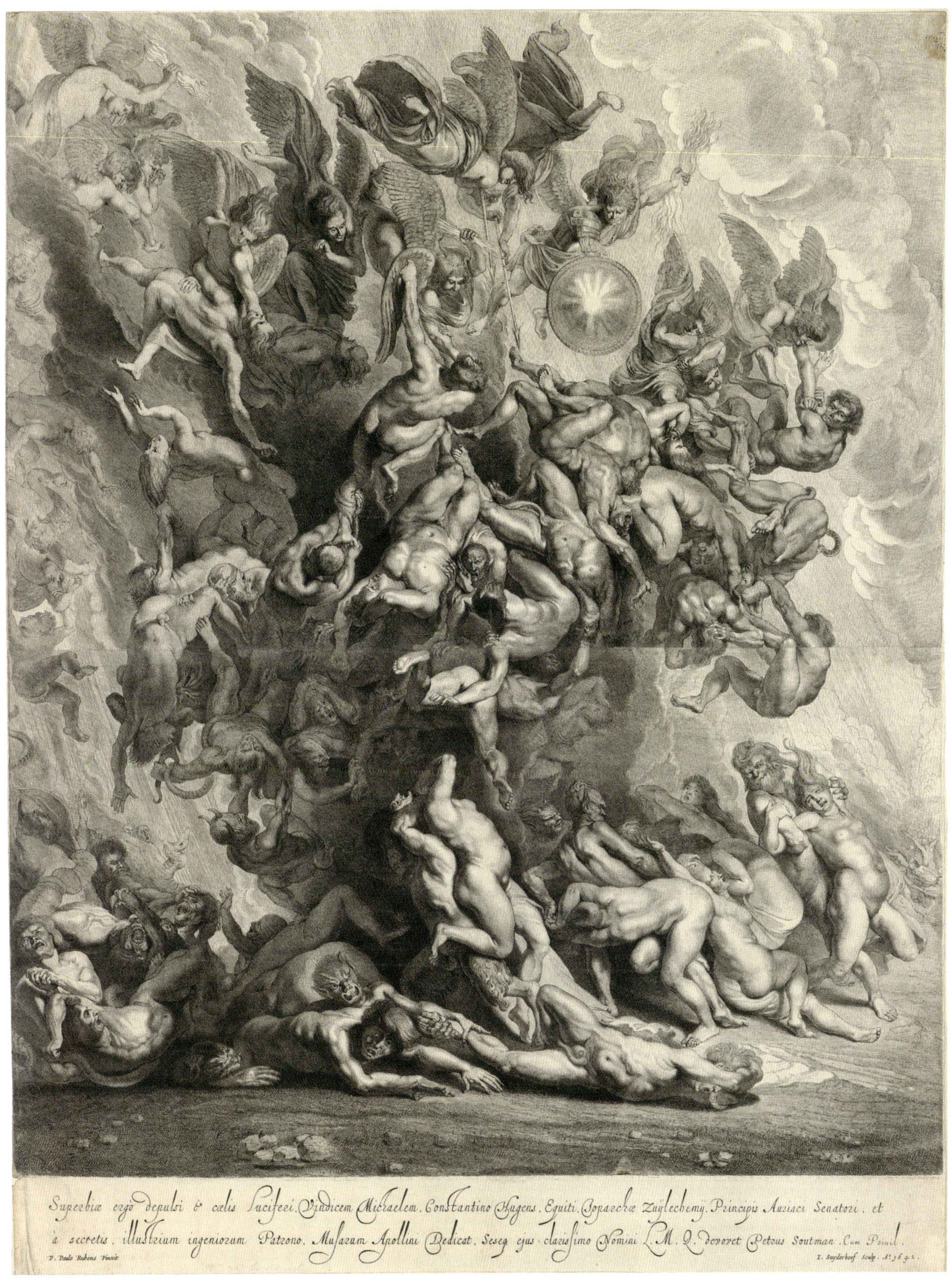

Jonas Suyderhoef (Stecher / engraver), nach / after Rubens
Das Kleine Jüngste Gericht / The Small Last Judgment, 1642
Kupferstich / engraving SGSM, Inv. 2023:32 D

VI. Technische Experimente

Zu den Möglichkeiten, sich mit Druckgraphiken zu profilieren, zählte auch das technische Experiment, also besonders gewagte, ungewöhnliche oder innovative Materialbearbeitungen. Auf diesem Gebiet verfolgten Hendrick Goltzius, der selbst ein hervorragender Stecher war, und Peter Paul Rubens, der die Umsetzung Spezialisten übertrug, ähnliche Taktiken, um ihre Kundschaft zu beeindrucken und auch die eigene Freude an Neuem wachzuhalten.

Unser Fokus liegt auf drei technischen Herausforderungen, die sowohl Goltzius als auch Rubens annahmen und meisterten: zum einen übergroße Bildformate, also Werke, die von mehreren Platten gedruckt werden mussten, weil sie das Standardmaß einer Druckplatte überstiegen; zum anderen die Radiertechnik, die erst mit Rembrandt (1606/07–1669) den Status eines anerkannten, selbstständigen Ausdrucksmittels erlangen sollte;[1] und schließlich der Holzschnitt, dieses älteste der europäischen Druckmedien, dem beide Künstler mit raffinierten Neuschöpfungen bis dahin ungesehene und nachhaltige Impulse verliehen.[2]

GROSSFORMATE

Unter Großformate fallen jene Stiche, für deren Umsetzung mehr als eine Kupferplatte nötig war. Mit solchen oft gemäldegroßen Kompositionen ließen sich Sammler beeindrucken. So wurde etwa Rubens' Gemälde *Amazonenschlacht* (um 1618) in der Übertragung von Lucas Vorsterman I immerhin von sechs Platten gedruckt.[3] In den Werkstätten setzten diese Werke jedoch sehr erfahrene Stecher und Drucker voraus, denn die Bildnähte auf den Platten wie auf dem Papier passgenau zusammenzuführen, war eine Kunst für sich.

Mit seinem Stichwerk *Hochzeit von Amor und Psyche* (1587) nach einer eigens für diesen Zweck von dem Prager Hofkünstler Bartholomeus Spranger angefertigten Zeichnung schuf Goltzius ein Blatt, das in die Geschichte der Druckkunst einging (siehe hierzu auch Nadine M. Orenstein, S. 50–66, sowie Abb. S. 172 f.). Seine unerhörte Größe – 430 mm in der Höhe und 845 mm in der Breite – war ein Grund hierfür, aber zudem hatte man eine solch elegante Choreographie so vieler Figuren (über achtzig), solche extravaganten Wolkendarstellungen und eine solche Vielfalt an unterschiedlichen Strichführungen in einem Stich noch nicht gesehen. Karel van Mander, Biograph von Spranger und Goltzius, lobte bereits 1604 „Sprangers' herrliches Götterbankett, das von dem süßen Nektar der Anmut überströmt und dem Zeichner wie dem Stecher gleichermaßen Unsterblichkeit sichert".[4]

Auf einen ähnlichen Überwältigungseffekt setzte wohl auch Pieter Soutman, als er 1642 Rubens' *Der Höllensturz der Verdammten* (um 1621) in einem Stich von zwei Platten mit dem Gesamtmaß 569 × 418 mm herausbrachte (Abb. S. 167). Auch hier galt es, eine große Figurengruppe überzeugend zu arrangieren, die freilich nur einen Ausschnitt aus Rubens' noch viel umfangreicherem Gemälde[5] zeigt. Dem Thema des Sturzes gerecht werdend, legte Soutman das Motiv als Hochformat an und fügte die beiden Blätter, die von zwei Platten gedruckt werden mussten, übereinander zusammen. So gelang es ihm, den siebenköpfigen Drachen, Sinnbild für die sieben Kardinalsünden, aus

VI. Technical Experiments

One way for print artists to win acclaim was by technical experimentation, pursuing especially daring, unusual, or innovative means of handling materials and instruments. In this respect, Hendrick Goltzius, himself a brilliant engraver, and Peter Paul Rubens, who entrusted the execution of his engravings to specialists, pursued similar strategies. Their intention was to impress their customers and to keep alive their own joy in experimenting.

The present exhibition focuses on three technical challenges that both Goltzius and Rubens accepted and mastered: large-format works that were printed from several plates because they exceeded the standard formats of printing plates; the technique of etching, which was to attain the status of an accepted and autonomous means of expression only with Rembrandt (1606/07–1669);[1] and, finally, the woodcut, the oldest of the European printing techniques, to which both artists lent unseen and lasting impulses with ingenious new works.[2]

LARGE FORMATS

The category of large formats comprises prints that needed more than one copperplate to be realized, enabling artists to impress collectors with compositions the size of paintings. Lucas Vorsterman I engraved Rubens's painting *The Battle of the Amazons* (ca. 1618), for example, from a total of six plates.[3] Such works demanded highly experienced engravers and printers in the workshops, because the borders had to match on the plates as well as the paper, and achieving this was an art unto itself.

With *The Wedding of Cupid and Psyche* (1587), after a drawing crafted especially for this purpose by the court artist Bartholomeus Spranger, Goltzius created an engraving that entered print history (for a discussion of this print, see Nadine M. Orenstein, pp. 50–66, and fig. pp. 172–173). One of the reasons for this work's exceptional status is its unprecedented size of 430 mm in height and 845 mm in width. But it also boasts an extremely elegant choreography of a great number of figures (more than eighty), an extravagant formation of clouds, and a great richness in the style of lines and their arrangements. As early as 1604, Karel van Mander, biographer of both artists, praised ". . . Sprangher's Heavenly Banquet, which overflows with sweet and appealing Nectar, and which offers equal immortality to the designer and engraver."[4]

Pieter Soutman aimed for a similarly stunning effect in his print *The Fall of the Damned*, after Rubens's painting (ca. 1621). He published this work, which was printed from two plates to arrive at a total size of 569 × 418 mm (fig. p. 167), in 1642. In this case, too, the task was to successfully arrange quite a number of figures, even though the print showed only a detail from Rubens's much larger painting.[5] Suitably, Soutman decided on portrait format for the theme of the fall and mounted the sheets from the two plates vertically. In so doing, he moved the seven-headed dragon, a symbol of the seven deadly sins, from the position it had

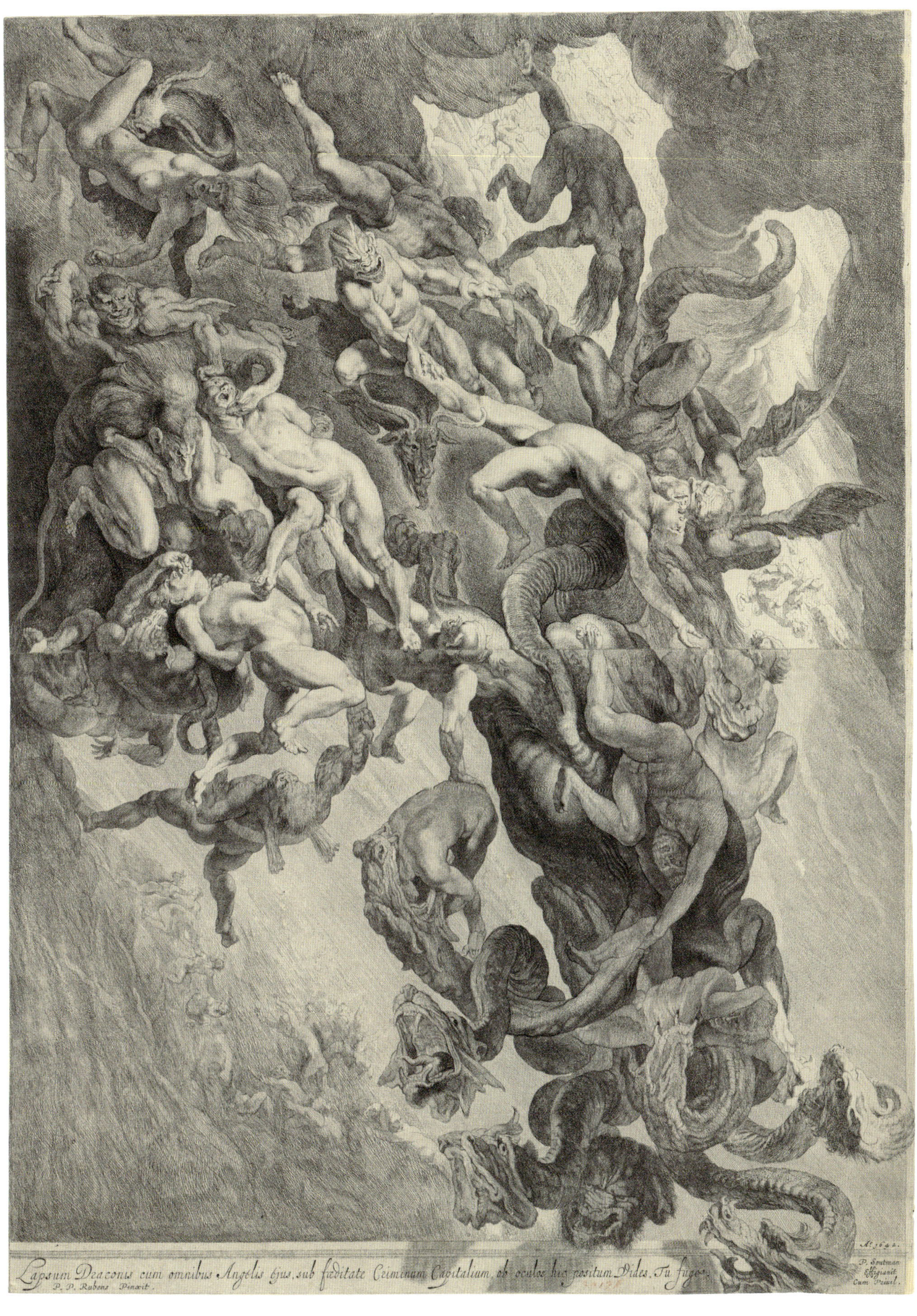

Pieter Soutman (Stecher / engraver), nach / after Rubens
Der Höllensturz der Verdammten / The Fall of the Damned, 1642
Kupferstich / engraving SGSM, Inv. 30128 D

seiner seitlichen Position im Gemälde in den Mittelpunkt des Stiches zu rücken und dadurch einer breiteren Öffentlichkeit die „Highlights" des Gemäldes bekannt zu machen, das damals in einer Privatsammlung aufbewahrt wurde.[6]

Auf einen eher meditativen Eindruck zielte Rubens wohl, als er um 1635 Schelte à Bolswert beauftragte, die Mitteltafel seines Altargemäldes *Der wunderbare Fischzug* von 1617/18 in einen Kupferstich umzusetzen (Abb. S. 174 f.). Dem Stecher lag eine Kreide- und Ölzeichnung vor (Abb. S. 83). Als Bolswert bereits mit der Umsetzung begonnen hatte, beschloss Rubens wohl, für den Stich die Komposition von einem Hochformat in ein ausladendes Querformat zu erweitern.[7] Die beiden Anstückungen rechts und links erklären sich also aus dieser Planänderung während des Herstellungsprozesses. Für die Darstellung ergab sich auf diese Weise mehr Luft um die Figurengruppe sowie die Möglichkeit, „weit geöffnete Flächen von Wasser und Himmel darzustellen", worin dieses Großformat nach Einschätzung von Hans Jakob Meier im 17. Jahrhundert singulär blieb.[8]

RADIERUNG

Das Thema Radierung hat sowohl Goltzius als auch Rubens beschäftigt. Diese Ätztechnik wurde zwar bereits seit dem frühen 16. Jahrhundert praktiziert, hatte sich aber gegen den Kupferstich noch nicht als eigenständiges Medium durchsetzen können. Im Werk beider Künstler finden sich jedoch immer wieder Blätter, in denen manche Partien als Radierung ausgeführt wurden. Sowohl Goltzius als auch Rubens hatten erkannt, dass mit dieser Technik eine leichtere Handhabe wie auch ein der Zeichnung ähnlicherer Ausdruck entstand, der einen ganz eigenen Reiz hatte. Ein Grund, warum beide sich letztlich nicht zu dieser Technik durchringen konnten, waren vielleicht die deutlich geringeren Auflagen, die mit radierten Platten gegenüber gestochenen erzielt werden konnten.[9]

Bei Goltzius waren das einige Landschaften, die kurz nach 1603 wohl dem Radierer Gerrit Adriaensz. Gauw (gest. 1638) ins Auge fielen und als verbreitungswürdig erschienen. Sowohl bei der *Berglandschaft mit sitzendem Reisenden* als auch bei der *Landschaft mit Daedalus und Ikarus* ist man aufgrund stilistischer Ähnlichkeiten geneigt, an die innovativen Schöpfungen Pieter Bruegels I (1526/30–1569) in der zweiten Hälfte des 16. Jahrhunderts zu denken (Abb. S. 176 f.). Eben diese hatte Karel van Mander, der Kunsttheoretiker, Maler und langjährige Freund von Goltzius, angehenden Malern zur Nachahmung anempfohlen, denn Bruegels Vorbild lehre, „da er in den felsigen Alpen war, ohne viel Mühe das Hinabblicken in die schwindeligen Täler, steile Klippen, wolkenküssende Fichten, weite Fernsichten und rauschende Ströme zu machen".[10] Doch während es bei Bruegel um eine Synthese von real Gesehenem und Imaginiertem ging, beließ es Goltzius bei der Naturbeobachtung. Als einer der Ersten zeichnete er oft *en plein air*, also im Freien. Die beiden (leicht mit dem Grabstichel nachgearbeiteten) Radierungen von Gauw sollten Goltzius' Stil in seinen Landschaftszeichnungen nachahmen und als Reproduktionen einem größeren Publikum nahebringen. Sie hinkten in der Ausführung qualitativ jedoch ihren Vorlagen hinterher.

in the painting (slightly to the side) to the center of the print. Soutman's print thus brought the "highlights" of the painting, which was at the time kept in a private collection, to a wider audience.[6]

Rubens seems to have had a more meditative effect in mind when in 1635 he had Schelte à Bolswert engrave the middle panel of an altarpiece (1617/18) depicting the *The Miraculous Draught* (fig. pp. 174–175). Bolswert worked after a chalk and oil drawing (fig. p. 83). After he had already begun work on the drawing, Rubens apparently decided to switch from portrait to landscape format and to extend the composition on both sides.[7] This change of plans during the production of the print explains the additions on the left and right, which opened up more space in the composition for the figures. The new format also made it possible to depict "wide open expanses of water and sky," making this large print unique, according to Hans Jakob Meier, in the seventeenth century.[8]

ETCHING

The technique of etching was intellectually interesting to both Goltzius and Rubens. This acid-based intaglio process had been practiced since the early sixteenth century but had not yet caught up to engraving as an autonomous and valid technique. Still, prints in which some parts were etched can be found in the oeuvres of both artists. Goltzius and Rubens alike recognized that the etching needle was easier to handle than the burin and had an effect comparable to that of the pen, but with an appeal all its own. One reason why both in the end refrained from using etching more widely may have been that in comparison with engraving it yielded lower print runs.[9]

A few landscapes from Goltzius's drawing oeuvre must have caught the eye of the etcher Gerrit Adriaensz. Gauw (died 1638) shortly after 1603, for he turned them into prints. Both the *Mountainous Landscape with a Seated Traveller* and the *Landscape with Daedalus and Icarus* are reminiscent in terms of style of the innovative creations of Pieter Bruegel I (1526/30–1569) in the second half of the sixteenth century (figs. pp. 176–177). Karel van Mander, an art theoretician, painter, and close friend of Goltzius's, had recommended to aspiring painters the imitation of Bruegel's landscapes, arguing that his example taught "because he was in the rocky Alps, how to depict without much effort the view into a deep valley, steep cliffs, spruces kissing the clouds, faraway clear views and hissing ravines."[10] Yet while Bruegel showed a synthesis of imagined sights and his own observations, Goltzius stuck to the latter. He was one of the first artists to make drawings en plein air, in nature. Gauw's two etchings (which he reworked slightly with a burin) were meant to imitate the drawing style of Goltzius's landscapes and, as they were reproductions, make them better known to a wider audience. In terms of quality, however, they fell short of Goltzius's drawings.

Pieter Soutman verdanken wir die besten Radierungen nach Rubens-Kompositionen, aber diese entstanden, nachdem die beiden getrennte Wege gegangen waren, also nicht auf die Initiative des Meisters hin.[11] Da aber die Radiernadel eine große Affinität zum Zeichenstift hat, was die leichtere Führbarkeit und den Ausdruck angeht, hat die Kunstwissenschaft lange annehmen wollen, dass auch große Künstler, die sonst nicht selbst Druckgraphik angefertigt haben, bei einigen Blättern selbst zur Radiernadel gegriffen hätten. Neben zwei weiteren Motiven wurde Rubens das Radieren der *Hl. Katharina* vielfach zugeschrieben (Abb. S. 178 f.).[12] Über die hohe Qualität der radierten Partien ist sich die Forschung einig. Ein noch existierender, von Rubens selbst überarbeiteter Probedruck der *Hl. Katharina* belegt, dass er in die Arbeit an diesem Stich involviert war. Inzwischen hat sich unter Forschern die Auffassung durchgesetzt, dass zumindest die radierten Partien von Rubens selbst stammen, dass aber fraglich ist, ob die mit dem Grabstichel nachgearbeiteten Stellen mit Rubens' Wissen oder Zustimmung erfolgten und dass dieser Stich erst posthum verlegt wurde.[13] Ein Grund für Rubens' Experiment mit der Radierung könnte gewesen sein, dass sie einen „schnelleren Arbeitsablauf" ermöglichte.[14] Denn, das belegen Konrad Renger zufolge alle drei ihm zugeschriebenen Radierungen: um den Ausdruck zeichnerischer Leichtigkeit, die diese Technik erzeugt, ging es ihm nicht.[15]

HOLZSCHNITT

Hendrick Goltzius und Peter Paul Rubens sind in dieser Ausstellung mit Holzschnitten vertreten, die die Wirkung auf die Spitze treiben, welche ihre druckgraphischen Œuvres entfalten. Diese Wirkung beziehen Goltzius' *Herkules erschlägt Cacus* (1588) und Rubens' *Herkules erschlägt die Missgunst* (1633–1635) eben nicht ausschließlich aus ihren gewalttätigen Sujets und ihren imposanten Formaten. In beiden Fällen ist es auch das gewählte Medium, der Holzschnitt, der diese Werke so kraftvoll macht. Natürlich kannten beide Künstler die bahnbrechenden Holzschnitte von Albrecht Dürer (1471–1528). Mehr noch aber als dieses Vorbild erahnt man in ihren Blättern Arbeiten nach italienischen Künstlern wie Tizian (um 1488–1576) und Parmigianino (1503–1540)[16] oder die des Holzstechers Ugo da Carpi (1480–1532), die beiden vor Augen standen und die zu übertreffen vielleicht ein Ziel war. Innerhalb beider Werke beschränkte sich die Produktion von Holzschnitten auf wenige Jahre: auf die Zeit von 1588 bis 1590 für etwa achtzehn Motive bei dem Haarlemer Künstler und von 1632 bis um 1635 für neun bei seinem Antwerpener Kollegen. Aus dieser Befristung lässt sich schließen, dass beide diese Technik als Experiment ansahen, das nach gewisser Zeit seinen Reiz verlor. Während Goltzius sich wohl selbst im Holzschneiden versuchte, aber einen externen Drucker betraute, führte Rubens den für das Verlagshaus Plantin-Moretus bereits tätigen Holzschneider Christoffel Jegher (1596–1652/53) zu einer bis dahin ungeahnten Größe und ließ seine Abzüge dort anfertigen.[17]

Der 1588 datierte *Herkules*-Holzschnitt von Goltzius entfaltet seine Kraft durch die dynamische Gestaltung des brutalen Themas und die Größe des Blattes, was beides dazu beiträgt, das Drama zu steigern (Abb. S. 180). Für den Künstler war es wohl faszinierend, dass der Druck mithilfe der beiden Tonplatten, mit denen die Farbe aufgebracht

The most extensive use of the etching needle in Rubens prints was made by Pieter Soutman, but only after the two had gone their separate ways, and not at Rubens's initiative.[11] Because the etching needle is similar in its use and expression to the draftsman's pen, art historians have long speculated that a number of famous artists who were not trained as engravers may have tried their hand at etching now and then. Rubens has frequently been credited with having etched three motifs, including *St. Catherine* (figs. pp. 178, 179).[12] Scholars agree on the excellent quality of the etched parts of this print. An extant proof impression of *St. Catherine* shows reworkings by Rubens and is therefore an indication that he was involved in its production. Scholars currently believe that the etched parts are to be attributed to Rubens, but they doubt that he knew of or consented to the print being reworked with a burin, and there is also a consensus that this print was pulled only after his death.[13] One reason for Rubens's experiment with etching could have been that it facilitated a "faster workflow."[14] All three etchings attributed to Rubens, according to Konrad Renger, refute a common assumption about etching: that the artist used it to emulate the immediacy of drawing.[15]

WOODCUT

Our exhibition presents woodcuts by both Hendrick Goltzius and Peter Paul Rubens that can be seen as the culmination of their graphic oeuvres. Prints like Goltzius's *Hercules Killing Cacus* (1588) and Rubens's *Hercules Slaying Envy* (1633–1635) do not only derive their force from the brutal stories they tell. Rather, in both cases it is also the chosen medium, the woodcut, that makes these works so powerful. Naturally, both artists were familiar with the woodcuts of Albrecht Dürer (1471–1528). Yet in the woodcuts of both Goltzius and Rubens there are reminiscences of the woodcuts of Titian (ca. 1488–1576) and Parmigianino (1503–1540),[16] as well as the woodcutter Ugo da Carpi (1480–1532), which they may have sought to surpass. Both artists created woodcuts for only a very limited period of time: from 1588 to 1590 for eighteen motifs in the case of Goltzius, and from 1632 to 1635 for nine in the case of Rubens. This limitation indicates that for both artists, the woodcut technique was an experiment which eventually lost its charm. While Goltzius seems to have been personally active as a woodcutter, engaging only an external printer, Rubens hired the woodcutter Christoffel Jegher (1596–1652/53), whom he knew from his prior work for the publisher Plantin-Moretus, where he also had the woodcuts printed. Their collaboration yielded some especially fine specimens in this technique.[17]

The Goltzius woodcut *Hercules Killing Cacus* is dated 1588 and unfolds its force through the dynamic composition of this brutal story as well as the sheer size of the print: both of these heighten the drama (fig. p. 180). One area of fascination for us—as, surely, for the artist—is that this print exists in a variety of different shades produced by varying the colors used in the tone-blocks (which supply the color in the motif). This flexibility allowed for varied effects. In the process of preparing for this exhibition, we

wurde, ganz unterschiedliche Wirkungen entfaltete. Während der Aufarbeitung unseres Bestands fand sich neben dem bekannten ein weiterer Abzug des Werkes (Abb. S. 181), sodass in der Ausstellung die Wirkung verschiedener Tonalitäten im Verbund mit dem Linienblock, der die Zeichnung des Motivs vorgibt, geprüft werden kann. Während die hellere Fassung die Aufmerksamkeit auf die Handlung lenkt, entfaltet der dunklere Druck eine bedrohliche Stimmung, die von den starken Lichtkontrasten herrührt. Nach Ansicht der Expertin Marjolein Leesberg spiegelt der blassere Abzug die Absichten des Künstlers eher wider als der kräftigere.[18]

In unserer Ausstellung hängt der Anfang der 1630er-Jahre entstandene Holzschnitt *Herkules erschlägt die Missgunst* (Abb. S. 182) nicht ohne Hintergedanken in der Nähe von Goltzius' *Herkules*. Wenn es an irgendeiner Stelle ein motivisches Erbe zu benennen gibt, dann hier. Wie sein berühmter ältere Künstlerkollege, so entschied sich auch Rubens für eine Frontal-, keine Seitenansicht des Kampfes, und auch er stellte die schiere körperliche Kraft heraus, mit der Herkules seinen Gegner tötet. Aber während der Ältere die Körpervolumen durch Muskelmasse und den Chiaroscuro-Effekt der Tonplatten anschaulich machte, schälte der Jüngere seine Figuren aus dem kaum bearbeiteten Hintergrund heraus und ließ sie aus der Untersicht hervortreten wie eine kunstvoll austarierte, sich auftürmende Skulptur. Diesem phänomenalen Rubens-Blatt meint man ablesen zu können, dass es zum Ziel hatte, sich mit einem bestimmten Vorbild zu messen. Gut möglich, dass dieses Vorbild der *Herkules* von Goltzius war.

Auch für den Rubens-*Herkules* fand sich während unserer Bestandserschließung ein weiterer, bislang unbekannter Abzug, in diesem Fall ein sogenannter Umdruck (Abb. S. 183).[19] Ein solcher wird angefertigt, indem auf einen frischen Abzug ein weiteres Blatt Papier gelegt und mit diesem nochmal in die Presse gelegt wird. Für den *Herkules* war bislang kein solcher Umdruck bekannt, den Rubens in anderen Fällen gern auch für Korrekturen verwendete. Das Münchner Exemplar weist jedoch keine solchen Korrekturen auf. Ungewöhnlich im Vergleich mit anderen erhaltenen Umdrucken ist der schwache Farbauftrag, was wohl Hinweis darauf ist, dass man den Abzug von einem bereits getrockneten Blatt genommen hat, dessen Farbe mit Lauge druckbar gemacht wurde.[20]

Einer von zwei Holzschnitten, bei denen Rubens sich neben dem Linienblock für einen Tonblock entschied, ist *Die Ruhe auf der Flucht nach Ägypten* (1633–1635; Abb. S. 184 f.). Motivisch verband Rubens hier eine Waldlandschaft mit einer neutestamentlichen Szene. Josef ruht an einem Baum am Fluss, während Maria den schlafenden Jesus in den Armen hält. Der Künstler wollte die Szene in der Dämmerung zeigen. Um diesen Ausdruck überzeugender zu vermitteln, entschied er sich noch während der Arbeit am Linienblock, auch einen Tonblock anfertigen zu lassen. Das alles geht aus den erhaltenen Probedrucken hervor, auf denen Rubens seine Korrekturen vermerkte. Konrad Renger hat spekuliert, ob Rubens' Begegnung mit Goltzius' Chiaroscuro-Holzschnitten ihn zu diesem Experiment inspiriert haben könnte, aber auch farbige italienische Vorbilder sind denkbar.[21]

discovered a second print of this work (fig. p. 181) besides the one already known in our holdings. Now visitors can see how the two different colorations, in combination with the line-block (which outlines the motif), change its overall effect. While the lighter print directs our attention to the scene, the darker print's stark contrasts in color convey an ominous mood. According to expert Marjolein Leesberg, the paler print better resembles the artist's intention than the one in darker colors.[18]

In our exhibition we present Rubens's woodcut *Hercules Slaying Envy* (fig. p. 182) in close proximity to Goltzius's *Hercules Killing Cacus*—for good reason. If there is ever a debt to be named with respect to motif, it is here. Like his famous older colleague, Rubens decided to depict the fight from the front, and also like him, he emphasized the sheer physical force Hercules uses to kill his enemy. But while Goltzius suggested physical mass by exaggerating the muscles and using the tone-block for a chiaroscuro effect, Rubens modeled his figures before an almost empty background and showed them from below, like a skillfully balanced towering sculpture. This phenomenal Rubens woodcut looks as if it were meant to be measured against a certain paragon. Possibly, this paragon was the *Hercules* by Goltzius.

The preparation for our exhibition also brought to light a second hitherto unknown print of the Rubens *Hercules*, or, more precisely, a counterproof of it (fig. p. 183).[19] To obtain a counterproof, a sheet of paper is positioned on top of a fresh print and both are placed in the press once more. Rubens liked to use counterproofs for corrections. No such counterproof was known for the *Hercules* motif until now. This one, however, shows no correction marks. Its very light color is also unusual and may be an indication that it was taken from a dry print whose paint was reactivated with the help of a mild lye.[20]

One of two woodcuts where Rubens decided to use a tone-block in addition to the line-block was *The Rest on the Flight to Egypt* (1633–35; fig. pp. 184–185). In terms of motif, Rubens here fused a landscape with a New Testament story. Joseph is leaning on a tree next to the river while Mary holds the sleeping infant Jesus in her arms. The artist intended to have this scene set at dusk. To achieve this impression more convincingly he decided, even while work on the line-block was well on its way, to add a tone-block. We know all this from the extant proof impressions on which Rubens made his corrections. Konrad Renger speculated that it might be his knowledge of Goltzius's chiaroscuro woodcuts that inspired Rubens to experiment with color, but Italian precursors are also conceivable.[21]

1 Zu Radierungen allgemein im späten 16. Jahrhundert vgl. Grieken 2023, S. 47; zu Rubens und seinen Radierungen vgl. Wijngaert 1940, S. 19–21, 23; Renger 1975, S. 166–172; Diels 2009, S. 10, 243.
2 Zu Goltzius’ Holzschnitten vgl. Nancy Bialler, in: Amsterdam/Cleveland 1992; Mazur-Contamine 1994; Nico Van Hout, in: Antwerpen/Québec 2004, S. 92–107; Marjolein Leesberg, in: NHD Goltzius 2012, 293–310 sowie S. lf.; Leesberg 2015; zu denen von Rubens vgl. Myers 1966; Renger 1975, S. 172–200; Parshall 2005.
3 Der Stich (Gesamtmaß ca. 850 × 1200 mm) nach dem Gemälde in München, Alte Pinakothek, Inv. 324. Vgl. Meier 2020a, Kat. 25.
4 Mander (1604) 2000, S. 337.
5 München, Alte Pinakothek, Inv. 320.
6 Zur Sammlungsgeschichte des Gemäldes siehe Renger/Denk 2002, S. 330–333, bes. S. 333.
7 Diese Produktionsgeschichte hat Konrad Renger als Erster rekonstruiert (Renger 1974b, S. 7 f., sowie Renger 1974a, S. 151 f.), und sie wird aktuell noch akzeptiert (siehe Wood 2020, S. 59). – Nico Van Hout hat angeführt, dass Rubens nach 1630 für seine Graphiken das Querformat bevorzugte und dass dies auch eine Motivation für diese Änderung gewesen sein könnte (Antwerpen/Québec 2004, S. 85).
8 Meier 2020a, Kat. 46, S. 248.
9 Vgl. Diels 2009, S. 202.
10 Mander (1604) 1916, S. 207.
11 Um die 30 Radierungen „nach Rubens“ schuf auch Willem Panneels, der eine Zeitlang Rubens’ Vertrauen genoss, diese Arbeiten aber wahrscheinlich ohne des Meisters Zustimmung schuf. Hollstein, Bd. XV, führt 36 Nummern unter seinem Namen an, die SGSM hat 29 Blätter (sowie einen Verlust), darunter manche Motive in unterschiedlichen Druckzuständen. Zu Panneels siehe auch das Kapitel „Nachbilder“, S. 272.
12 Bei den beiden anderen Motiven handelt es sich um die *Alte Frau mit Knabe und Kerzen* (SGSM, Inv. 30407 D) und um eine *Büste des Seneca* (Abb. S. 219).
13 Siehe Renger 1975, S. 168, 170. Mit anderer Argumentation, aber gleichem Schluss Meier 2020a, Kat. 45. Vgl. auch den Beitrag von Nils Büttner im vorliegenden Katalog, S. 82.
14 Vgl. Renger 1975, S. 171.
15 Vgl. ebd.
16 Karel van Mander empfahl angehenden Künstlern das Studium von Parmigianinos Holzschnitten explizit an. Vgl. Mander (1604) 1916, S. 58 f., Kap. II, Abs. 12.
17 Für das Drucken von Holzschnitten ist eine andere Druckpresse, nämlich eine Schraubpresse, als jene für Kupferplatten nötig. – Leesberg 2015, S. 164, führt Argumente an, die dafür sprechen, dass Goltzius die Druckstöcke selbst anfertigte. Auf S. 165 nennt sie den Haarlemer Gillis Rooman als wahrscheinlichen Drucker. – Vor den Holzschnitt-Einzelblättern hatte Jegher bereits Holzschnitte nach Entwürfen von Rubens als Buchillustrationen bei Plantin-Moretus ausgeführt, daher boten sich die Werkstätten der Officina Plantiniana an. Diese entsprachen jedoch ganz konventionellen Arbeiten für den Buchdruck. Vgl. Nico Van Hout, in: Antwerpen/Québec 2004, S. 93.
18 NHD Goltzius 2012, S. li; Leesberg 2015, S. 167 f.
19 Zu Funktionen und Beispielen von Umdrucken vgl. Seigneur 2004 sowie Stijnman 2012, S. 321.
20 Dies vermutet Ad Stijnman in einer E-Mail an die Autorin vom 5. Januar 2024. Vgl. Stijnman 2012, S. 159, für das Verfahren, Umdrucke von älteren Drucken zu nehmen, woraus mattere Abdrücke hervorgehen als die von druckfrischen Abzügen genommenen. Die Autorin dankt folgenden weiteren Kollegen für den Gedankenaustausch zu diesem Blatt: Konrad Renger, Jaco Rutgers, Joanna Seidenstein und Vanessa Selbach.
21 Renger 1975, S. 195.

1 On late sixteenth-century etchings, see Grieken 2023, p. 47; on Rubens and etchings, see Wijngaert 1940, pp. 19–21; Renger 1975, pp. 166–172; Diels 2009, pp. 10, 243.
2 On Goltzius’s woodcuts, see Nancy Bialler, in: Amsterdam/Cleveland 1992; Mazur-Contamine 1994; Nico Van Hout, in: Antwerpen/Québec 2004, pp. 92–107; Marjolein Leesberg, in: NHD Goltzius 2012, 293–310 and pp. l–li; Leesberg 2015; on those by Rubens, see Myers 1966; Renger 1975, pp. 172–200; Parshall 2005.
3 The print (ca. 850 × 1200 mm) is after the painting in Munich, Alte Pinakothek, inv. 324. See Meier 2020a, cat. 25.
4 Mander (1604) 1994, p. 394, fol. 284r.
5 The painting is in Munich, Alte Pinakothek, inv. 320.
6 For the collection history of the painting, see Renger/Denk 2002, pp. 330–333, esp. p. 333.
7 Konrad Renger was the first to reconstruct the production process (Renger 1974b, pp. 7–8, and Renger 1974a, pp. 151–152), and his account is still accepted (see Wood 2020, p. 59). – Nico Van Hout points out that Rubens preferred landscape format for his prints after 1630 and that this preference may have been a cause for the change in format (Antwerpen/Québec 2004, p. 85).
8 Meier 2020a, cat. 46, p. 248.
9 See Diels 2009, p. 202.
10 “. . . Daer hy, als in de hoornigh’ *Alpes* rootsich, / Ons leert te maken, sonder groote quellingh, / Het diep afsien in een swijmende dellingh, / Steyle clippen, wolck-cussende Pijnboomen, / Verre verschietens, en ruysschende stroomen.” Mander 1604, ch. 8, §25. Translation by the author.
11 Willem Panneels, who enjoyed Rubens’s trust for some time, crafted approximately thirty etchings “after Rubens,” but he probably did so without the master’s approval. Hollstein, vol. XV, lists thirty-six numbers under Panneels’s name. The SGSM holds twenty-nine prints (and records one lost print), some of them in different states. For more on Panneels, see the chapter “Afterimages,” p. 272.
12 The other two motifs are: *Old Woman and a Boy with Candles* (SGSM, inv. 30407 D) and *Bust of Seneca* (fig. p. 219).
13 See Renger 1975, pp. 168, 170. For different arguments but the same conclusion, see Meier 2020a, cat. 45. See also Nils Büttner in the present catalog, pp. 82–83.
14 See Renger 1975, p. 171.
15 See Renger 1975, p. 171.
16 Karel van Mander explicitly recommended that aspiring artists study Parmigianino’s woodcuts. See Mander 1604, ch. 2, §12.
17 A different printing press—namely, a screw press—is used for woodcuts than for engravings. – Leesberg 2015, p. 164, lists arguments that support the theory that Goltzius engraved the printing blocks himself. On p. 165 she names Gillis Rooman as the likely printer. – Before crafting individual woodcut prints for Rubens, Jegher had engraved woodcuts after designs by Rubens as book illustrations for Plantin-Moretus, which is why this print workshop seems to have been the obvious choice. However, these early woodcuts fully conformed with conventional book illustrations. See Nico Van Hout, in: Antwerpen/Québec 2004, p. 93.
18 NHD Goltzius 2012, p. li; Leesberg 2015, pp. 167–168.
19 On the functions of counterproofs, and for examples, see Seigneur 2004 and Stijnman 2012, p. 321.
20 This is a theory kindly shared by Ad Stijnman in an email to the author of January 5, 2024. See Stijnman 2012, p. 159, for the procedure of taking counterproofs from dried prints, which may result in duller counterproofs than those taken from fresh prints. The author also wishes to thank the following colleagues for sharing their thoughts on this print: Konrad Renger, Jaco Rutgers, Joanna Seidenstein, and Vanessa Selbach.
21 Renger 1975, p. 195.

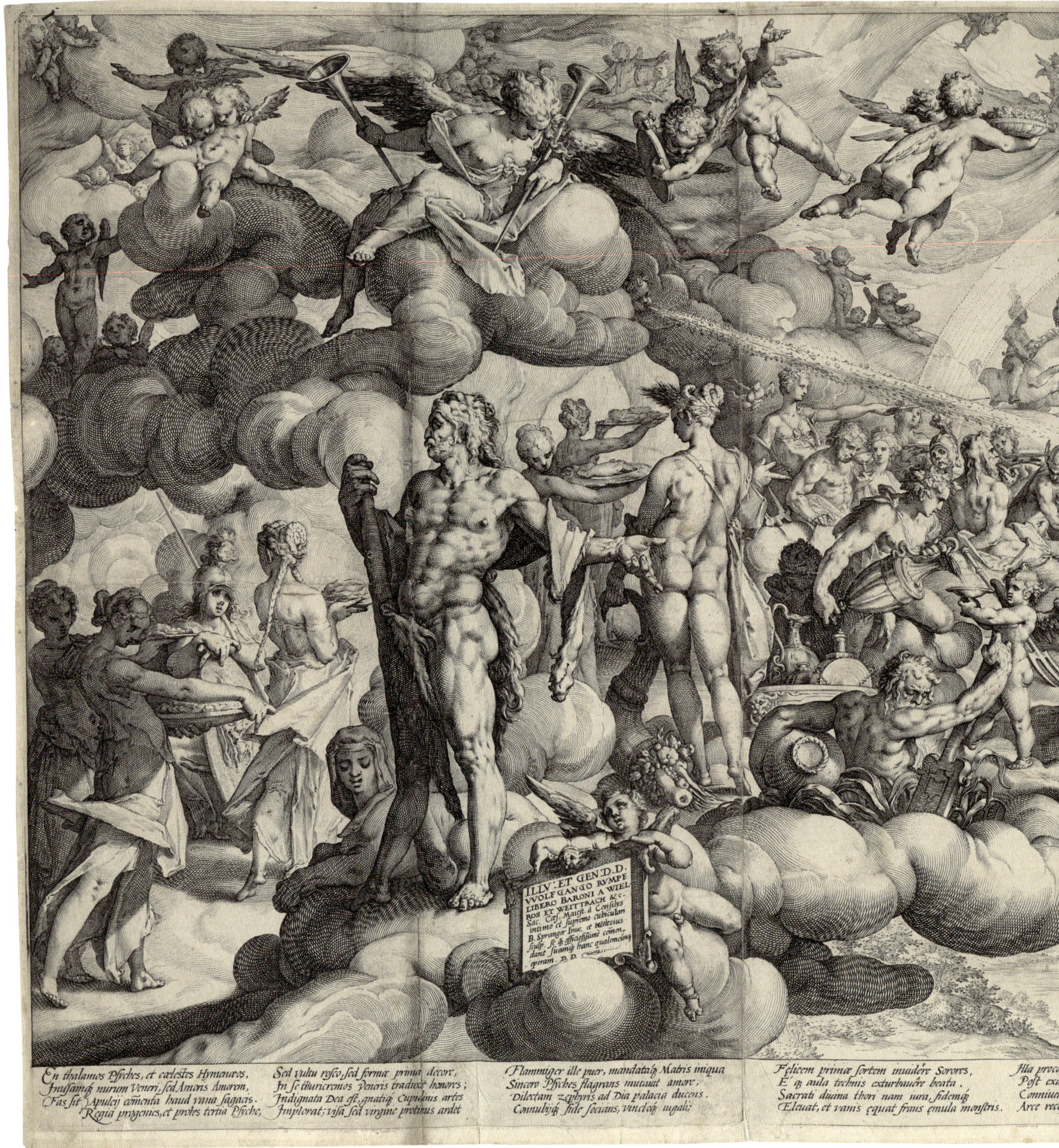

Bartholomeus Spranger (Inventor / designer), Goltzius (Stecher, Verleger / engraver, publisher)
Hochzeit von Amor und Psyche / The Wedding of Cupid and Psyche, 1587
Kupferstich / engraving SGSM, Inv. 1987:31 D

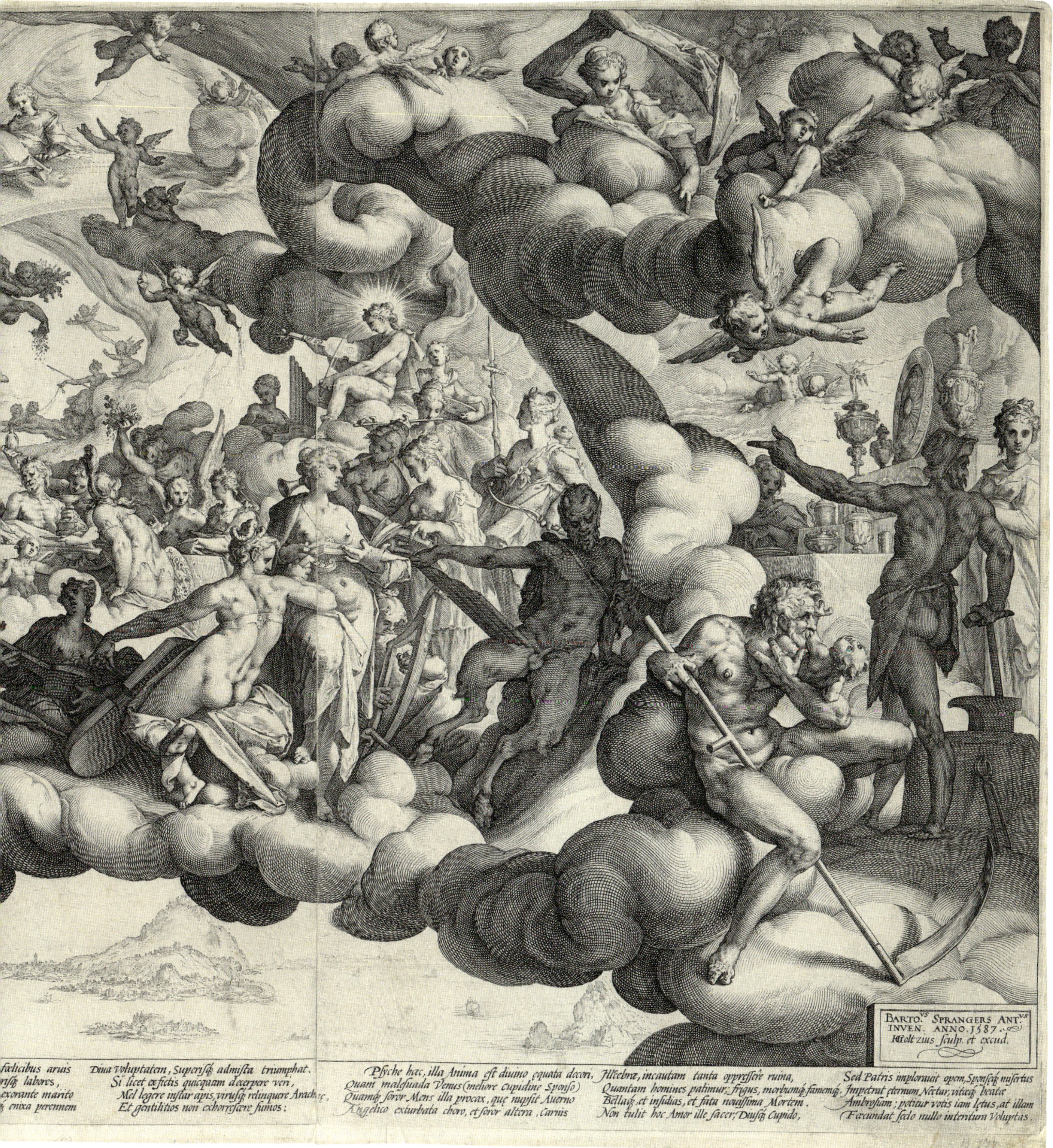
BARTO.VS SPRANGERS ANT.VS
INVEN. ANNO. 1587.
HGoltzius sculp. et excud.
fœlicibus aruis
risq; labores,
exorante marito
; enixa perennem
Diua Voluptatem, Superisq; admista triumphat.
Si licet ex fictis quicquam decerpere veri,
Mel legere instar apis, virusq; relinquere Arachnę,
Et gentilitios non exhorrescere fumos:
Psyche hæc, illa Anima est diuino ęquata decori,
Quam malesuada Venus (meliore Cupidine Sponso)
Quamq; soror Mens illa procax, quę nupsit Auerno
Angelico exturbata choro, et soror altera, Carnis
Illecebræ, incautam tanta oppressere ruina,
Quantam homines patimur; frigus, morbumq; famemq;
Bellaq; et insidias, et fata nouissima Mortem.
Non tulit hoc Amor ille sacer; Diuisq; Cupido,
Sed Patris implorauit opem, Sponsęq; misertus
Impetrat ęternum Nectar; vitaq; beatæ
Ambrosiam; potitur votis iam lętus, at illam
Fœcundat seclo nullo interitura Voluptas.

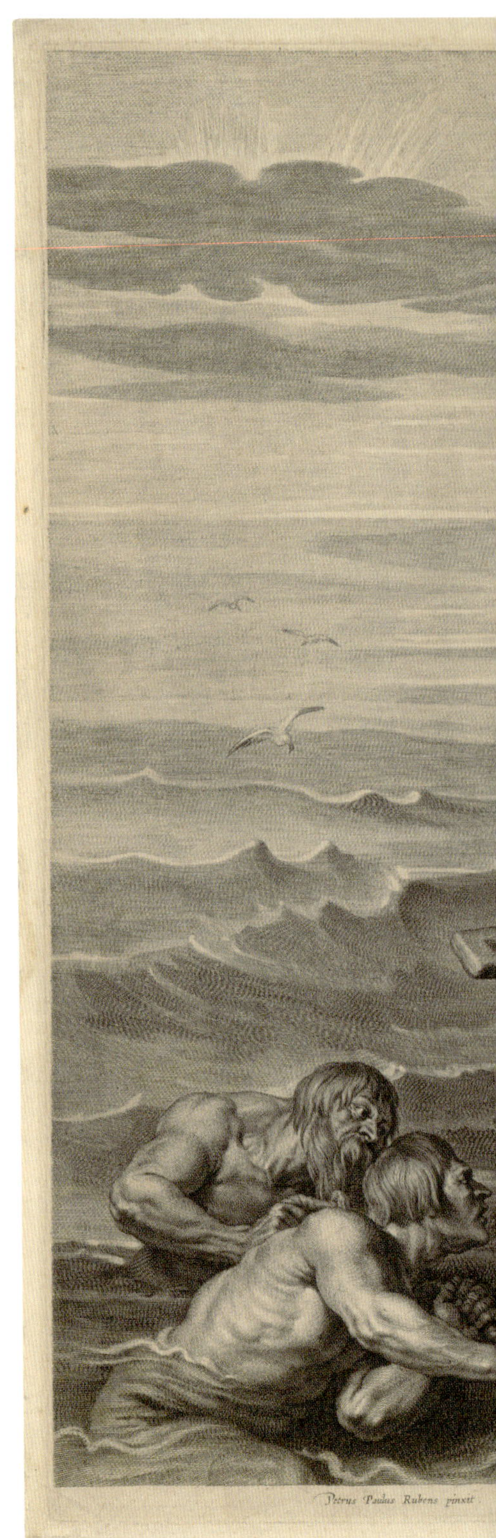
Petrus Paulus Rubens pinxit

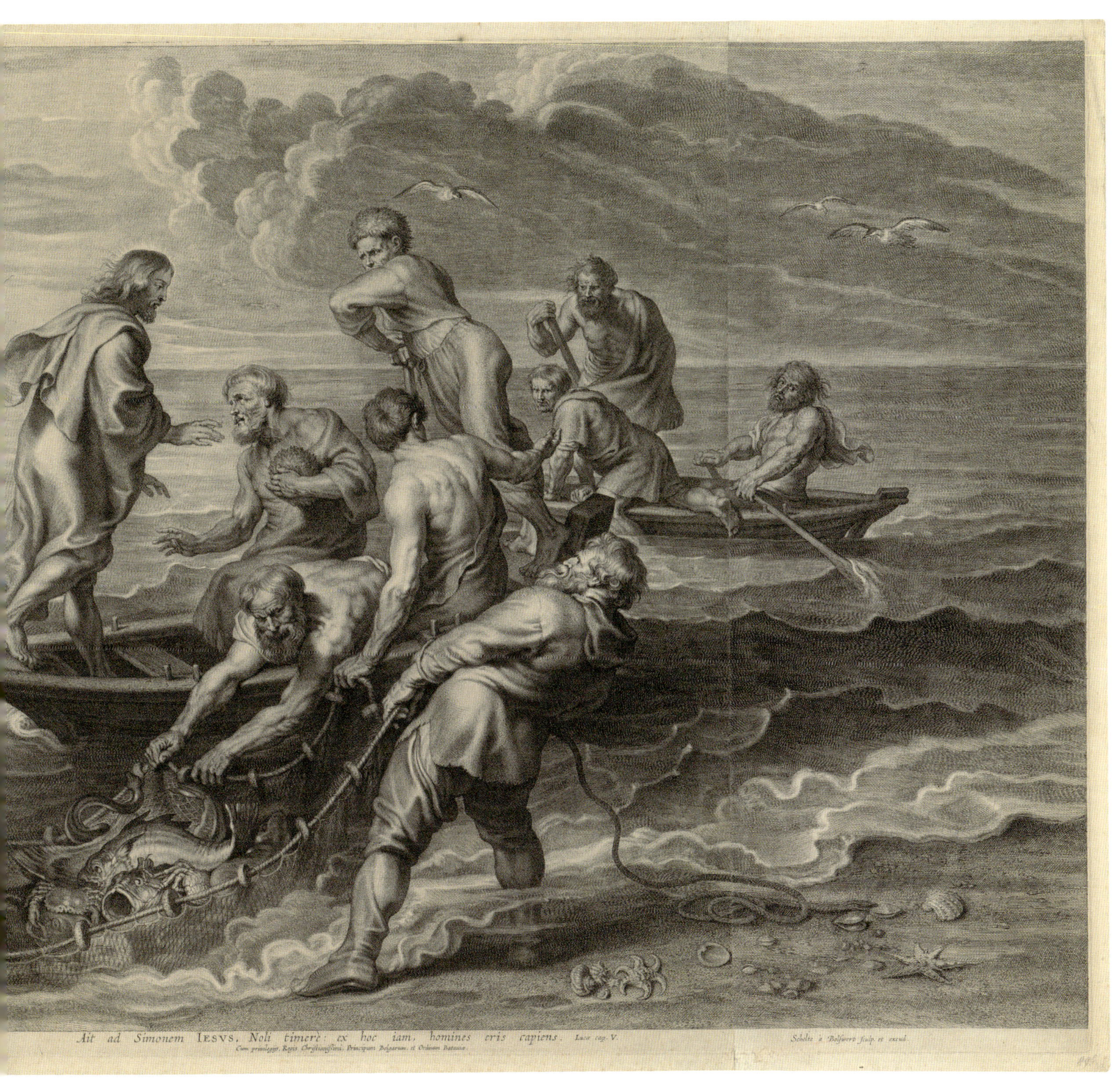

Rubens (Inventor / designer), Schelte à Bolswert (Stecher, Verleger / engraver, publisher)
Der wunderbare Fischzug / The Miraculous Draught, ca. 1635
Kupferstich / engraving SGSM, Inv. 2010:71 D

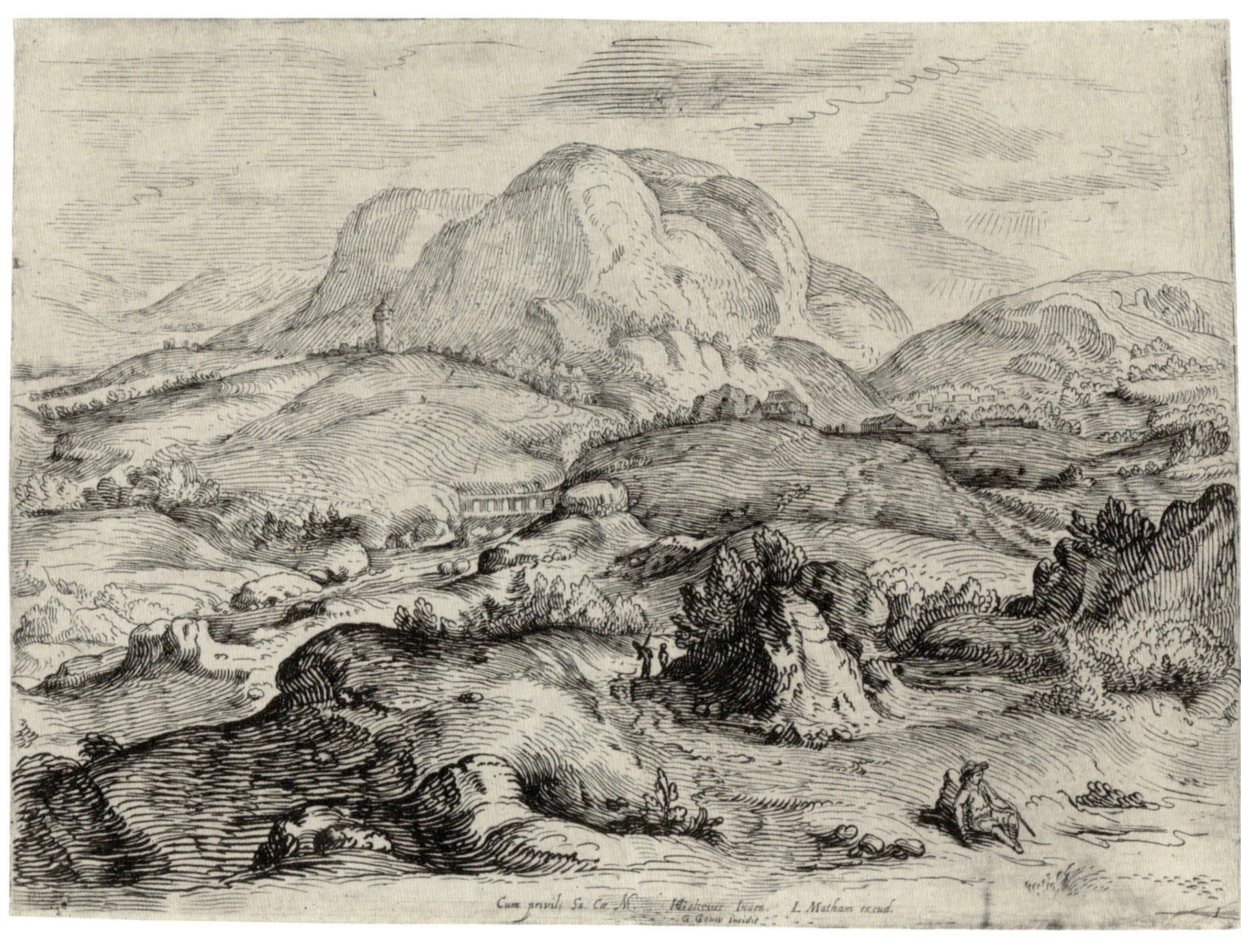

Gerrit Adriaensz. Gauw (zugeschr. Stecher, Radierer / attr. engraver, etcher), nach / after Goltzius, Jacob Matham (Verleger / publisher)
Berglandschaft mit sitzendem Reisenden / Mountainous Landscape with a Seated Traveller (OBEN / ABOVE)
Landschaft mit Daedalus und Ikarus / Landscape with Daedalus and Icarus (RECHTS / RIGHT), nach / after 1603
Radierung, Kupferstich / etching, engraving SGSM, Inv. 31235 D; 31190 D

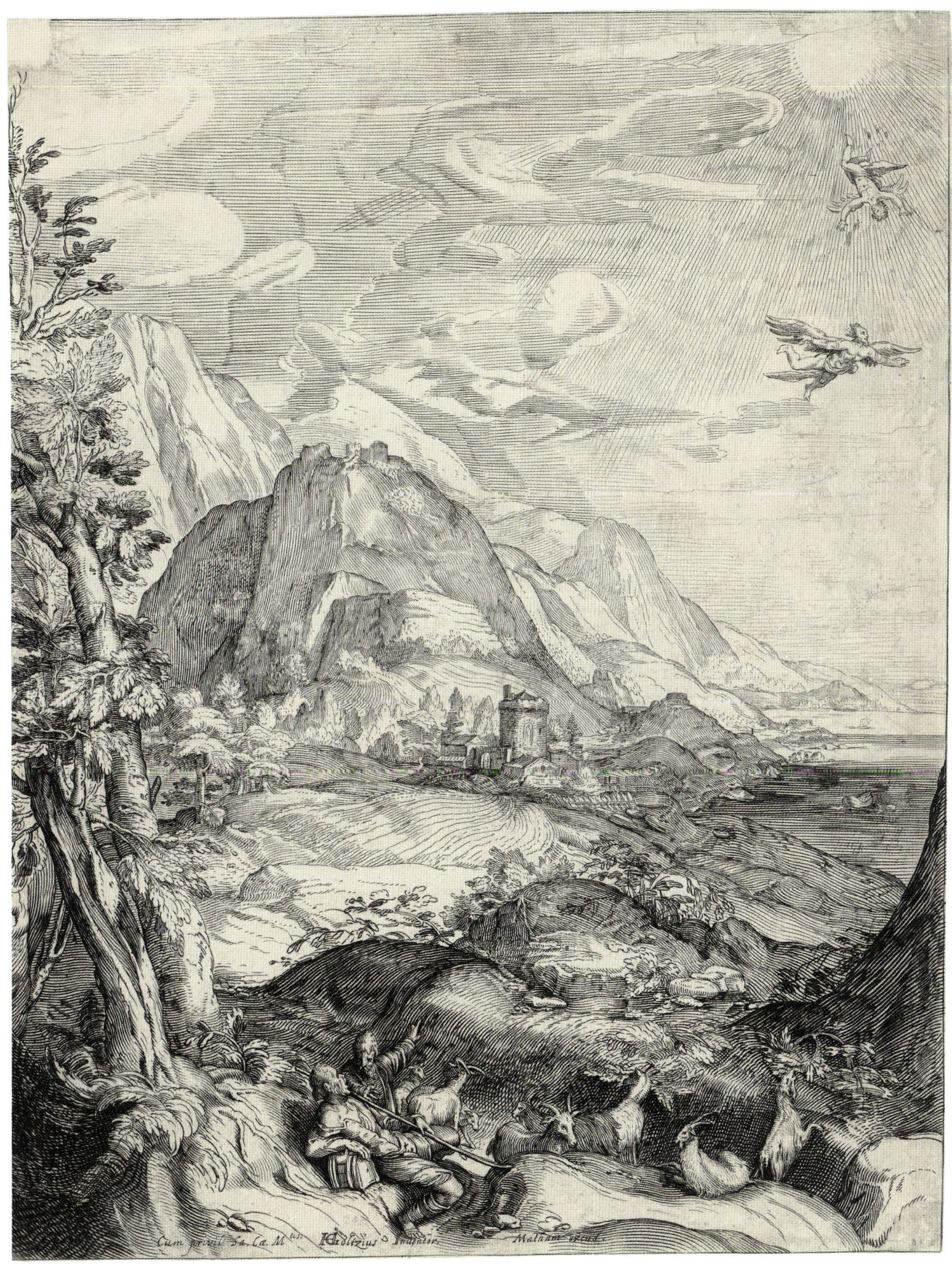
Cum privil. Sa. Ca. M^tis
HGoltzius Inventor.
Malham excud.

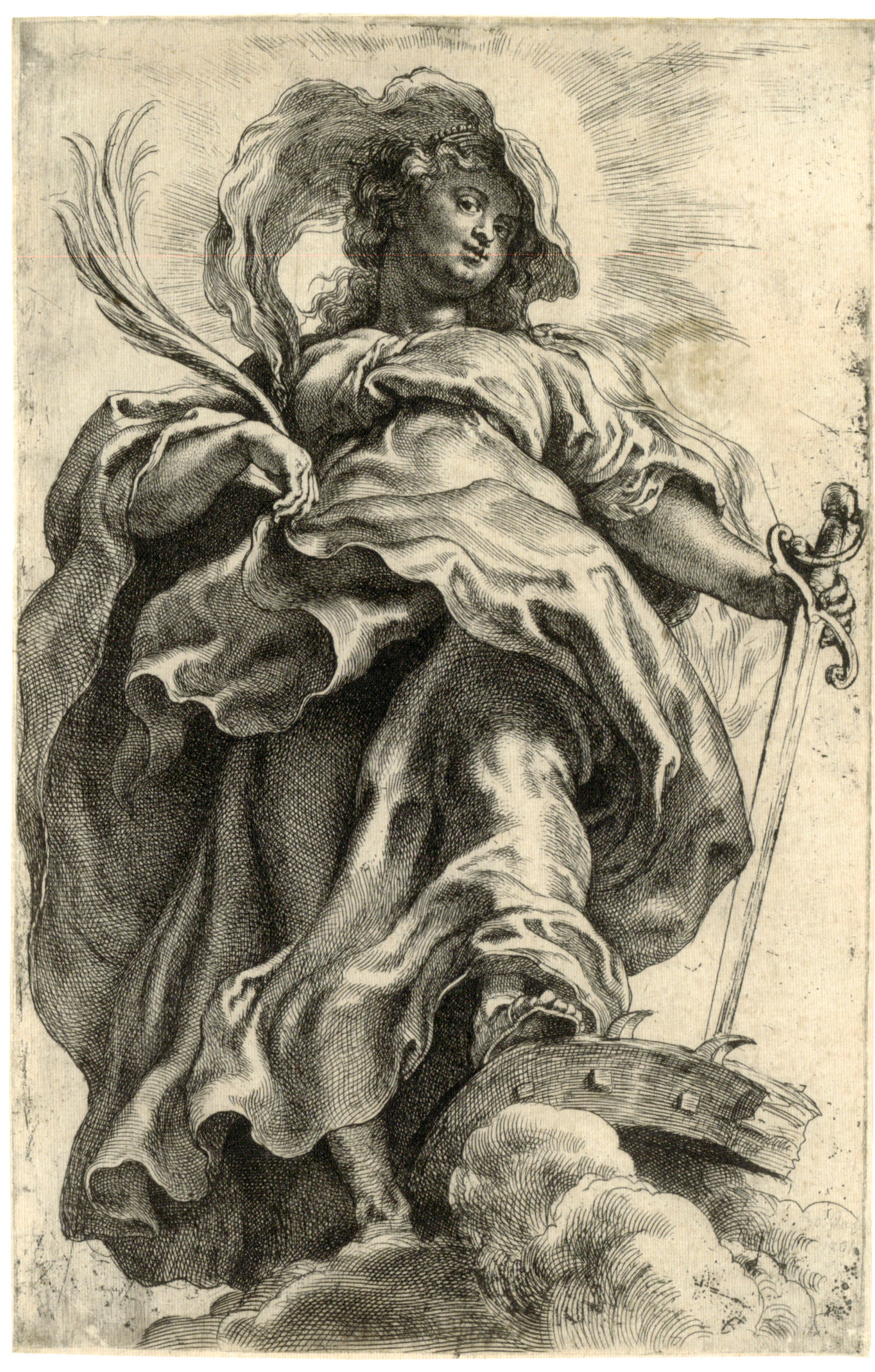

Rubens (Inventor, Radierer / designer, etcher), anonymer Stecher / anonymous engraver
Die hl. Katharina / St. Catherine, 1621–1630
Radierung, Kupferstich / etching, engraving, Zustand / state II? SGSM, Inv. 30269 D

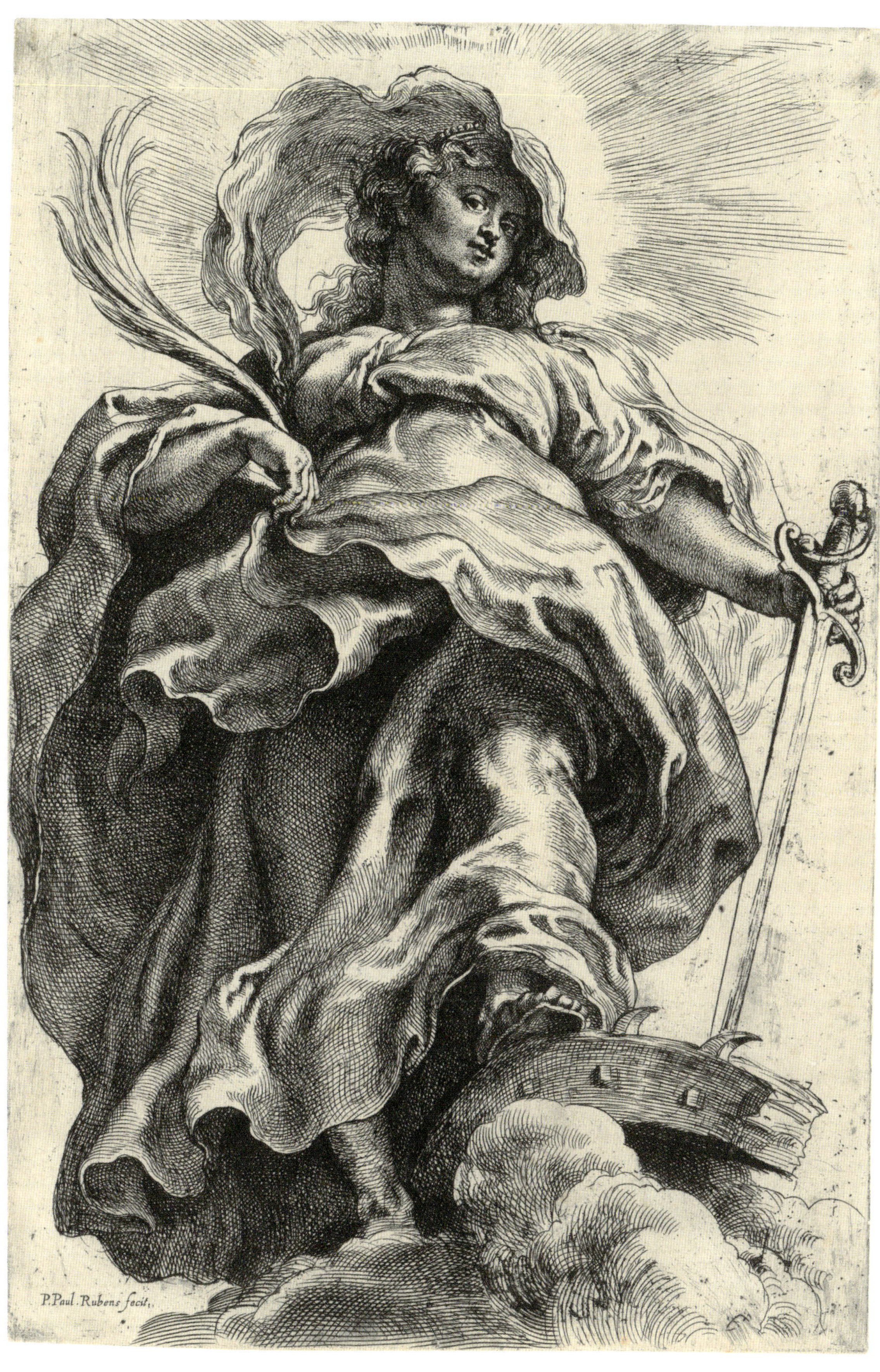

Rubens (Inventor, Radierer / designer, etcher), anonymer Stecher / anonymous engraver
Die hl. Katharina / St. Catherine, 1621–1630
Radierung, Kupferstich / etching, engraving, Zustand / state III SGSM, Inv. 30270 D

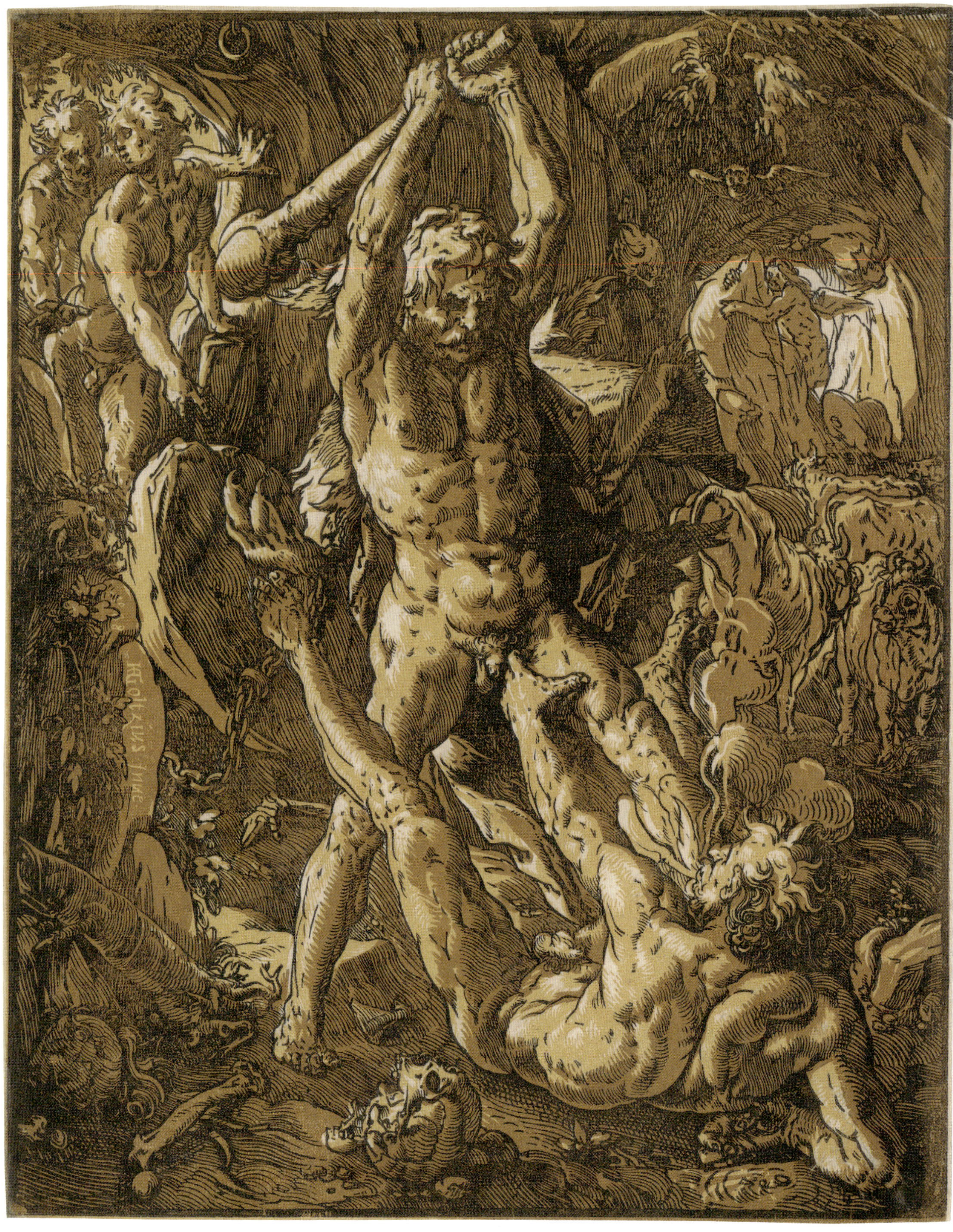

Hendrick Goltzius (Inventor, Holzschneider, Verleger / designer, woodcutter, publisher)
Herkules erschlägt Cacus / Hercules Killing Cacus, 1588
Chiaroscuro-Holzschnitt / chiaroscuro woodcut SGSM, Inv. 30975 D

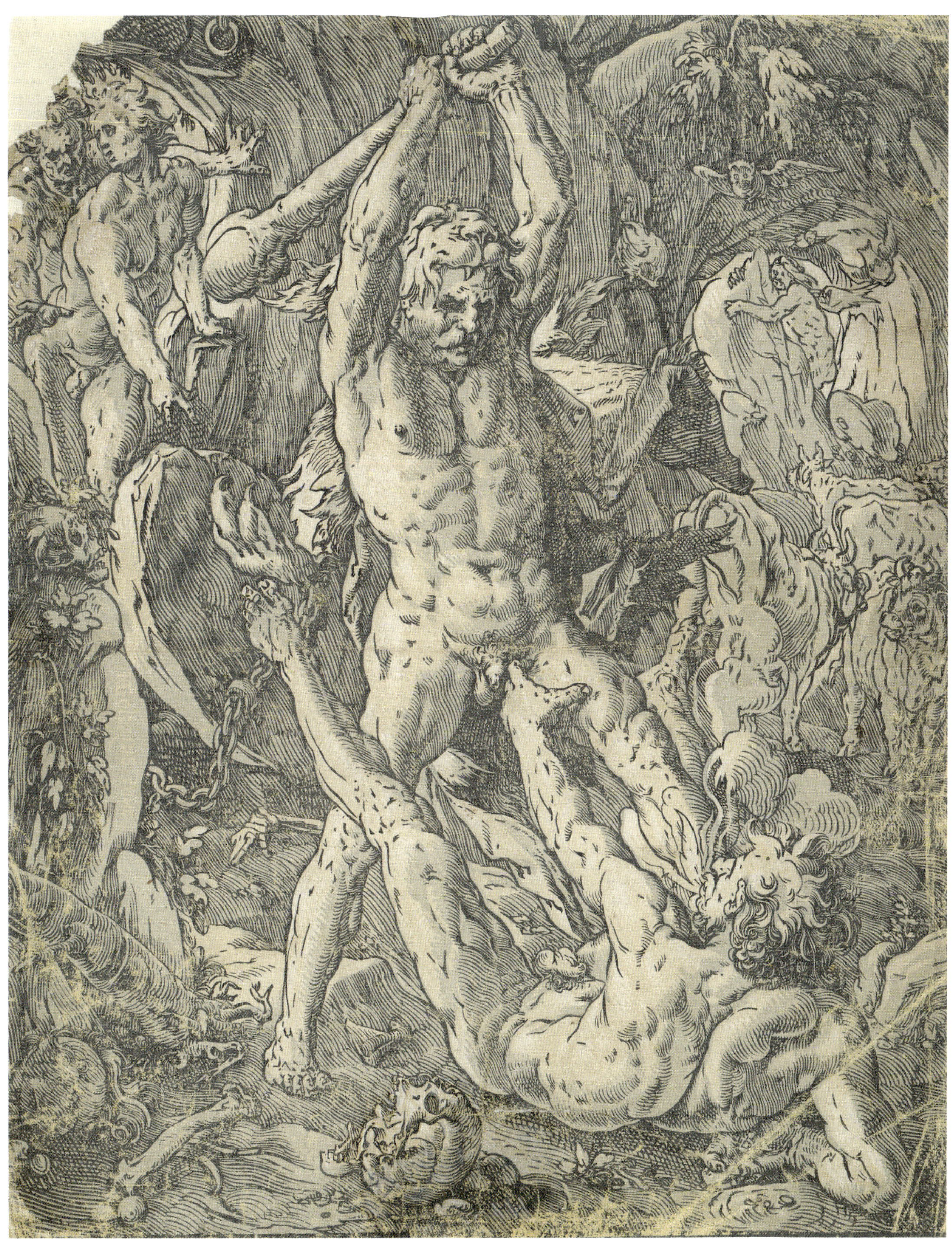

Hendrick Goltzius (Inventor, Holzschneider, Verleger / designer, woodcutter, publisher)
Herkules erschlägt Cacus / Hercules Killing Cacus, 1588
Chiaroscuro-Holzschnitt / chiaroscuro woodcut SGSM, Inv. 2021:1 D

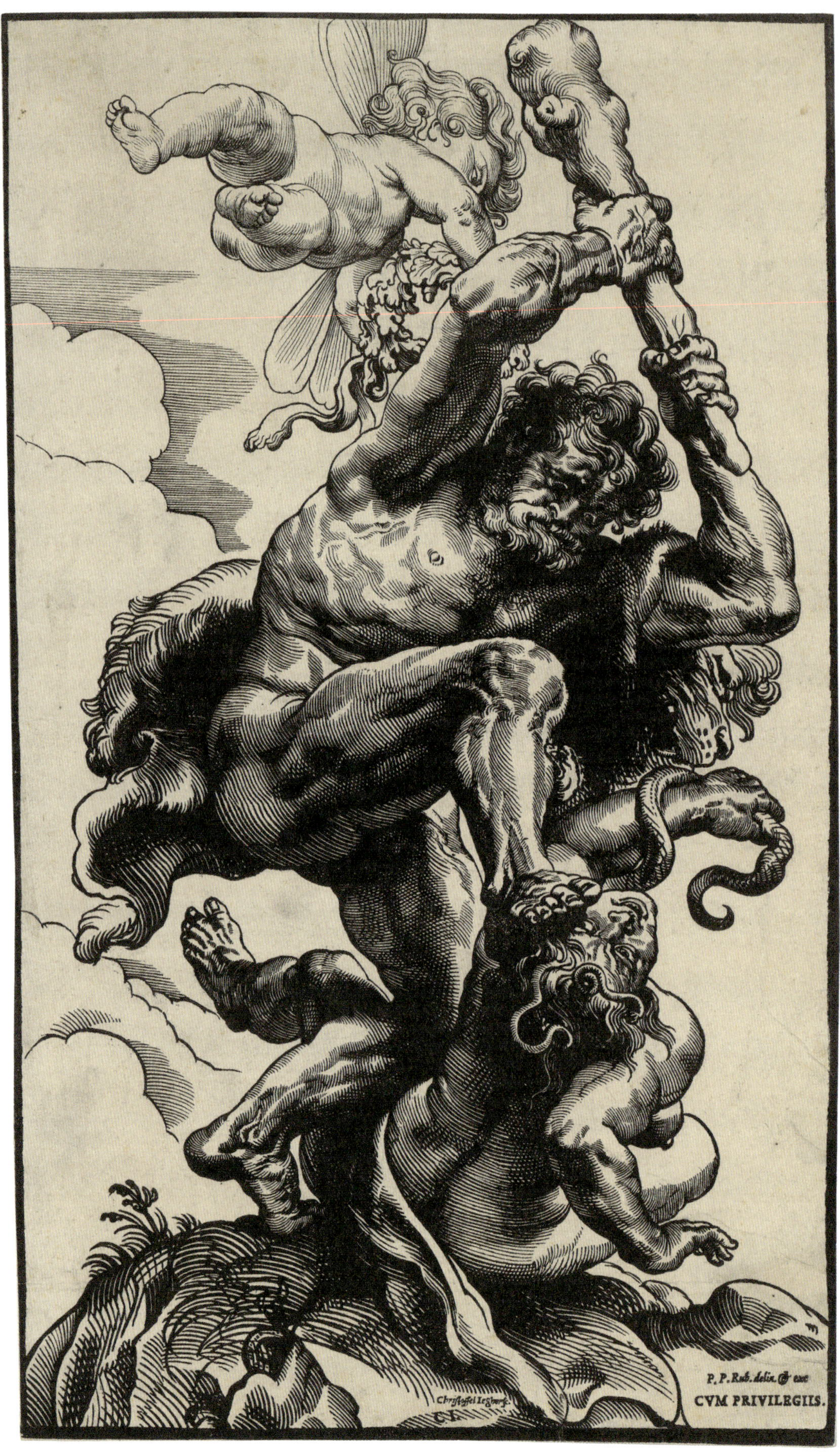

Rubens (Inventor, Verleger / designer, publisher), Christoffel Jegher (Holzschneider / woodcutter)
Herkules erschlägt die Missgunst / Hercules Slaying Envy, 1633–1635
Holzschnitt / woodcut SGSM, Inv. 148971 D

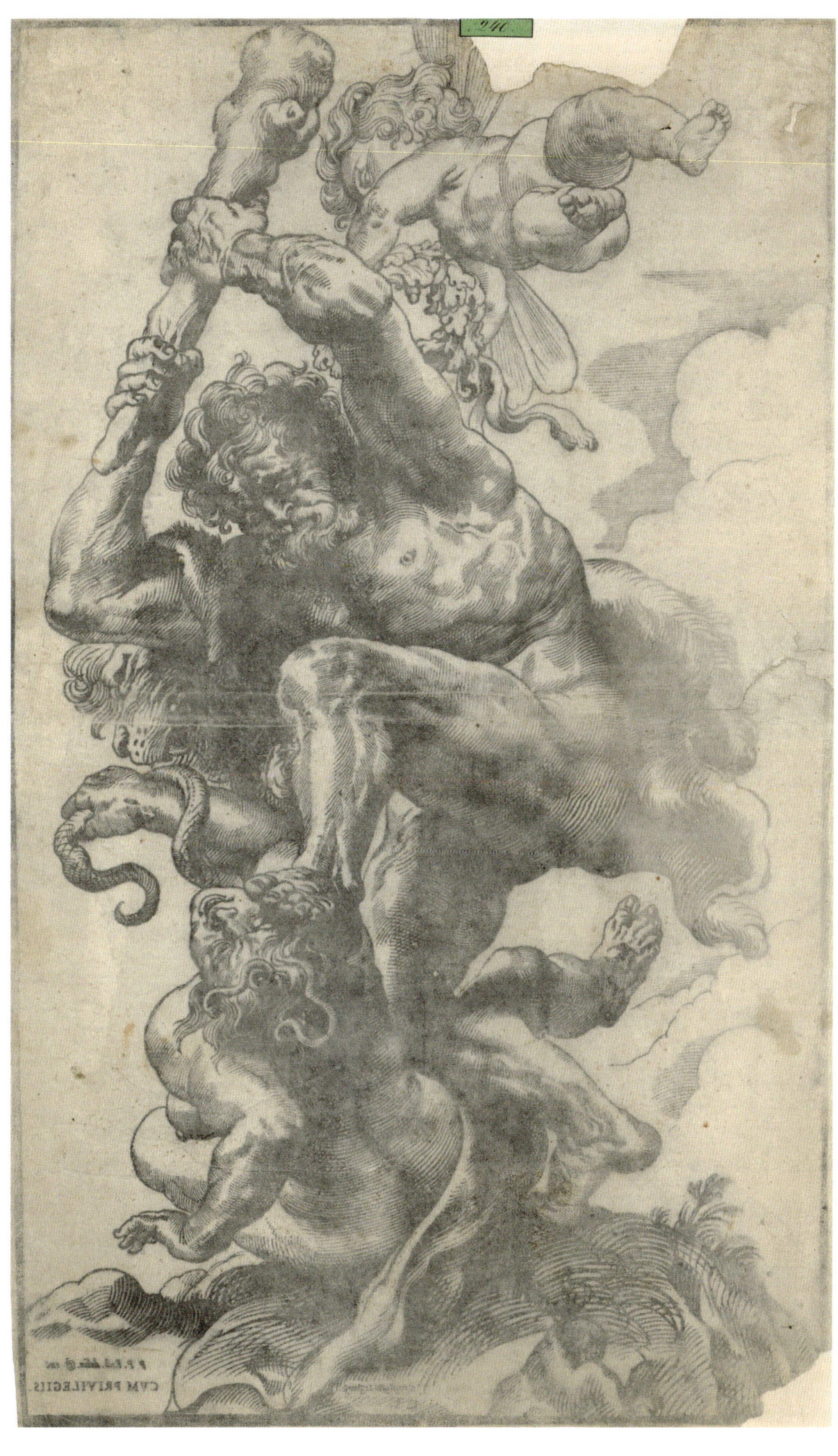

Rubens (Inventor, Verleger / designer, publisher), Christoffel Jegher (Holzschneider / woodcutter)
Herkules erschlägt die Missgunst / Hercules Slaying Envy, 1633–1635
Umdruck / counterproof, Holzschnitt / woodcut SGSM, Inv. 2021:494 D

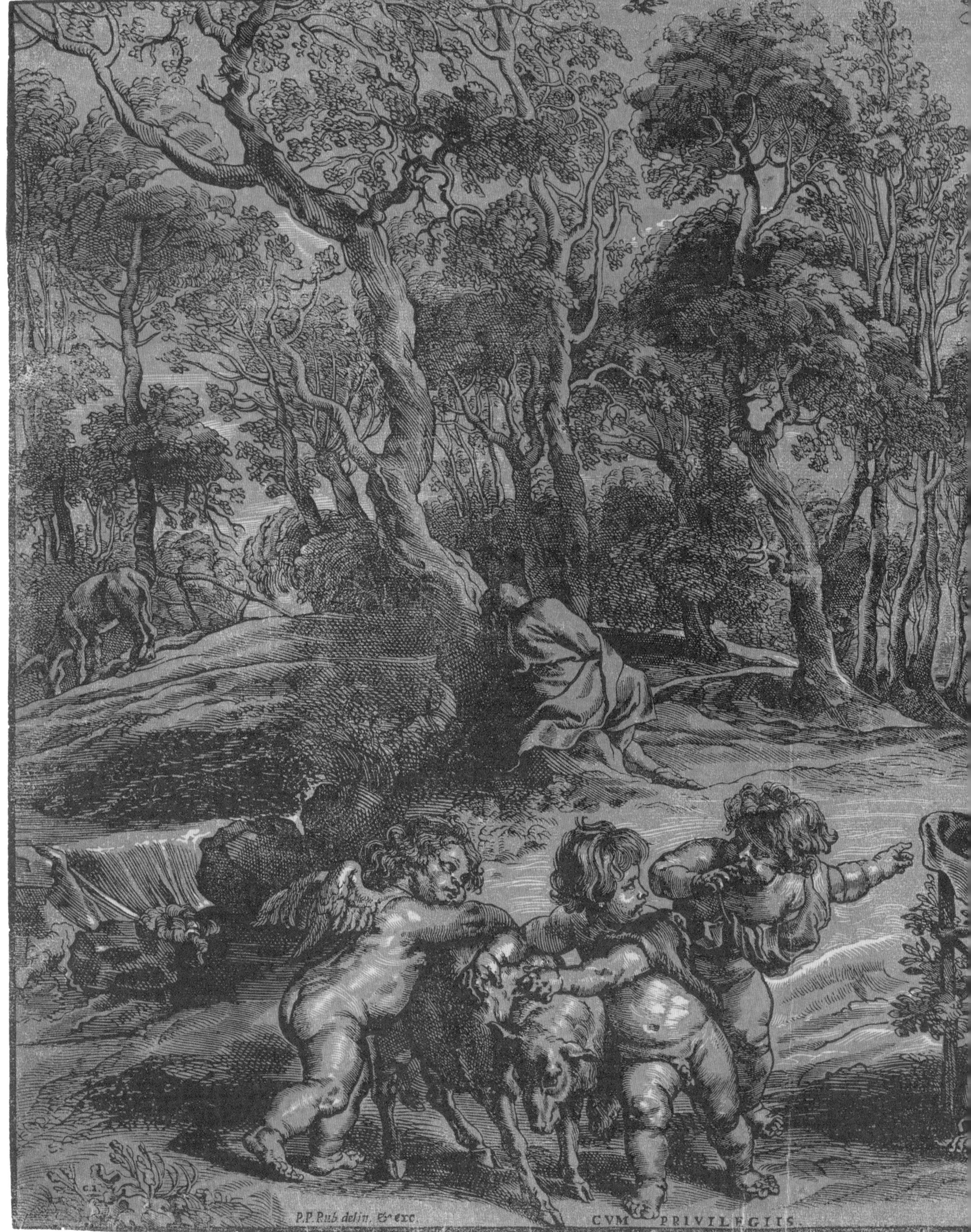

P.P. Rub. delin. & exc.
CVM PRIVILEGIIS.

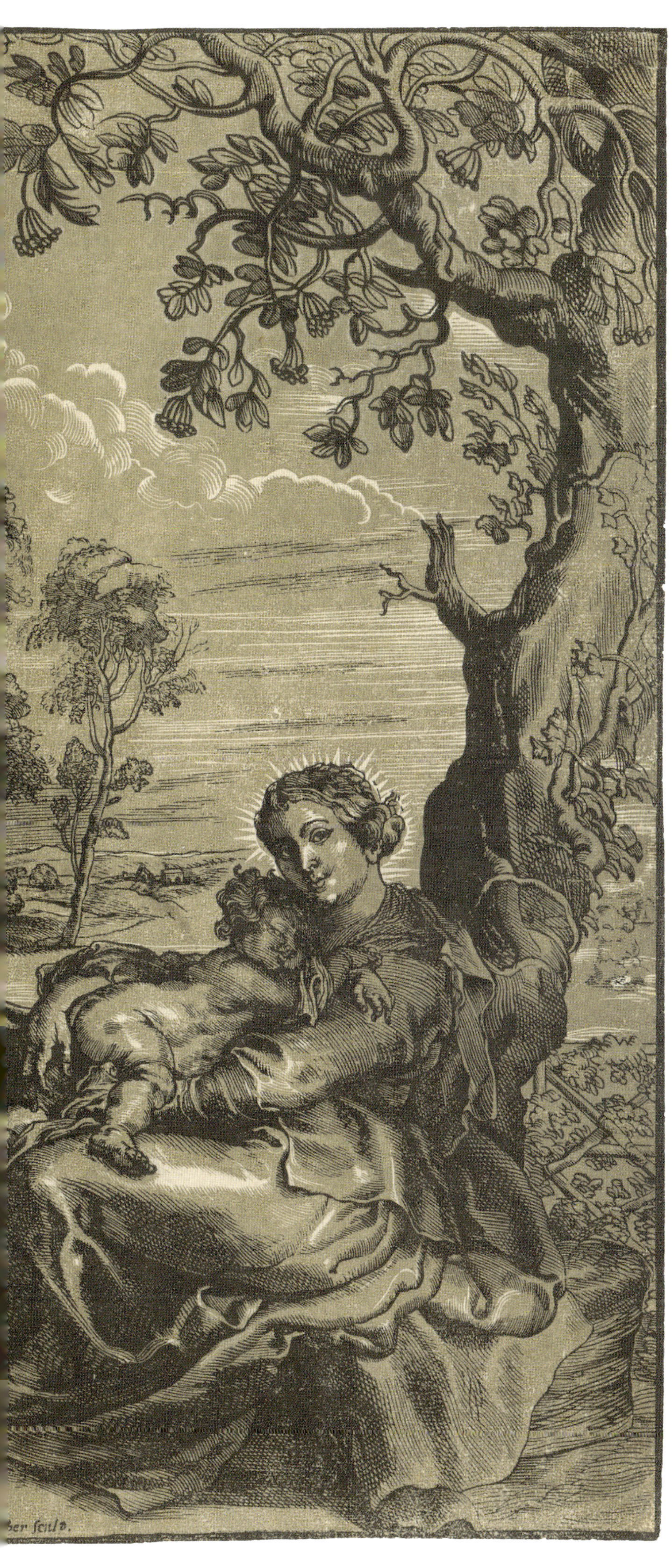

Rubens (Inventor, Verleger / designer, publisher),
Christoffel Jegher (Holzschneider / woodcutter)
Die Ruhe auf der Flucht nach Ägypten /
The Rest on the Flight to Egypt, 1633–1635
Chiaroscuro-Holzschnitt / chiaroscuro woodcut
SGSM, Inv. 30152 D

VII. Meisterdrucke

Der Blick aus der Gegenwart in die Vergangenheit macht es leicht, jene Werke zu benennen, die im Œuvre eines Künstlers eine besonders breite Rezeption erfahren haben. Aber sowohl Hendrick Goltzius als auch Peter Paul Rubens dürften es bereits bei der Produktion bestimmter Kunstwerke darauf angelegt haben, herausragende Druckgraphiken zu schaffen. Sie wählten hierzu die besten Stecher und Vorlagen und entsprechende Themen aus. So entstanden Werke wie *Die vier Himmelsstürmer* von Goltzius oder *Die Kreuzabnahme* von Rubens, die bis heute einen großen Wiedererkennungseffekt und eine erwiesene Nachwirkung haben. Dieses Kapitel stellt einige der Blätter vor, die sich ihre Kraft und Geltung durch viele Moden hinweg bewahrt haben und als Marken für die beiden Künstler stehen.

Die vier Himmelsstürmer (1588) von Goltzius erkennen heute noch Menschen wieder, denen der Name des Künstlers nichts mehr sagt (Abb. S. 190 f.). Doch während die Stiche von Goltzius stammen, gehen die Bildideen auf Gemälde eines Haarlemer Freundes, des Malers Cornelis Cornelisz. van Haarlem (1562–1638) zurück, die zum Teil verloren sind. Die Stiche jedoch schmücken viele Buchdeckel und wirken auch in Zeiten von Photographie und Film enorm modern. Die vier Sünder *Ixion*, *Phaeton*, *Ikarus* und *Tantalus*, die sich der Hybris (Überheblichkeit gegenüber den Göttern) schuldig gemacht haben, werden im tödlichen freien Fall gezeigt. Die Faszination, die Stürzenden beobachten zu können, während man selbst in Sicherheit ist, fesselt uns auch heute noch. Vor den abwechselnd hellen und dunklen Hintergründen und mit den starken Verkürzungen ziehen die Körper der Männer unsere Blicke auf sich. Wäre man ein Sammler im 16. Jahrhundert und hätte diese Stiche zu Hause, würde man die Rundbilder zudem drehen, um die moralisierenden Bildumschriften zu lesen. Die fallenden Körper würden dadurch noch mehr in Bewegung versetzt werden.[1]

Der große Herkules (1589) oder, wie er aus ersichtlichen Gründen auch genannt wurde, der *Knollenmann*, kommt uns dagegen heute etwas lächerlich vor mit seinen unzähligen Muskelpaketen (Abb. S. 187). Es fällt schwer, bei seinem Anblick nicht zu schmunzeln. Was aber, wenn wir Martin Kirves darin folgen, dass der Körper dieses Helden nur der visuelle Ausdruck eines „ebenso machtvollen Geistes" wäre?[2] Dem gelehrten Betrachter in der Zeit von Goltzius und Rubens ist diese Metapher deutlich gewesen, er erkannte in diesem Herkules einen Tugendhelden. Dasselbe lässt sich auch für die Serie der ähnlich muskelbepackten *Römischen Helden* (1586) sagen (Abb. S. 111), die alle Vorbilder für ein tugendhaftes Leben sind. Laut dem mit Goltzius befreundeten Biographen Karel van Mander (1548–1606) ließ sich in diesen Blättern auch die „Heldenkraft [der] Zeichenkunst" ablesen, womit der Autor eine weitere metaphorische Lesart für den *Großen Herkules* und die *Römischen Helden* aufzeigte.[3]

Das Midasurteil (1590), eines der letzten Werke, die Goltzius vor seiner Abreise nach Italien fertigstellte, war sicher als Aushängeschild für des Künstlers technische und intellektuelle Meisterschaft gedacht und vielleicht führte Goltzius einige Exemplare dieses Stichs im Reisegepäck mit, um in Italien für Aufsehen zu sorgen (Abb. S. 194 f.). In

VII. Masterprints

It is easy to name in retrospect those works in an artist's oeuvre that enjoyed an especially wide reception. Both Hendrick Goltzius and Peter Paul Rubens probably created some of their prints with the intention of having them recognized as extraordinary within the history of the medium. To achieve this they chose exceptional engravers, designs, and subjects. Thanks to this approach, images like Goltzius's *The Four Disgracers* and Rubens's *The Descent from the Cross* have made a great impact and enjoyed lasting recognition. This chapter presents some of the prints whose potency and status has been preserved throughout changing times and that function, so to speak, as signets for these artists.

Today *The Four Disgracers* (1588; figs. pp. 190–191) by Goltzius are recognized even by people who are not familiar with the artist's name. Goltzius engraved these prints after paintings by his Haarlem friend Cornelis Cornelisz. van Haarlem (1562–1638), some of which are lost today. The prints now adorn many book covers and appear very modern to us, even in our time of photography and film. The four sinners, *Ixion*, *Phaeton*, *Icarus*, and *Tantalus*, who all committed the sin of hubris, presuming to take on a godlike status, are shown in their deadly falls. Our fascination with watching the men falling while we as viewers remain safe is as strong now as it was when the engravings were first created. In front of alternately white and black backgrounds, the bodies of these men, with their stark foreshortening, still catch our eye. As sixteenth-century collectors in possession of these works, we would rotate the paper while reading the moralizing inscriptions around the prints and thereby make the figures spin even more.[1]

The Great Hercules (1589; fig. p. 187), in contrast, appears a bit ridiculous to our modern eyes because of his exaggerated muscles. It is hard not to smile at his appearance. But what if we followed Martin Kirves in his argument that this hero's physique is simply the visual expression of his "equally powerful spirit"?[2] Learned viewers in Goltzius's and Rubens's times would have been familiar with this metaphor and recognized in this Hercules a hero of virtue. The same holds true for the equally muscle-packed *Roman Heroes* (1586; figs. p. 111), who are all role models for a virtuous life. Goltzius's friend and biographer Karel van Mander (1548–1606) wrote that these prints also expressed the "heroic power of . . . draftsmanship," thereby offering yet another metaphorical interpretation for *The Great Hercules* and the *Roman Heroes*.[3]

The Judgment of Midas (1590; fig. pp. 194–195), one of the last works Goltzius finished before his departure for Italy, was most certainly intended as a figurehead for the artist's technical and intellectual mastery. Perhaps Goltzius carried a few copies of this print in his luggage with hopes of causing a stir in Italy. In the center of his composition is not, as the title suggests, King Midas, but Apollo, the loser of the musical contest that Midas decided between Apollo and Pan. With its large format (427 × 680 mm), a

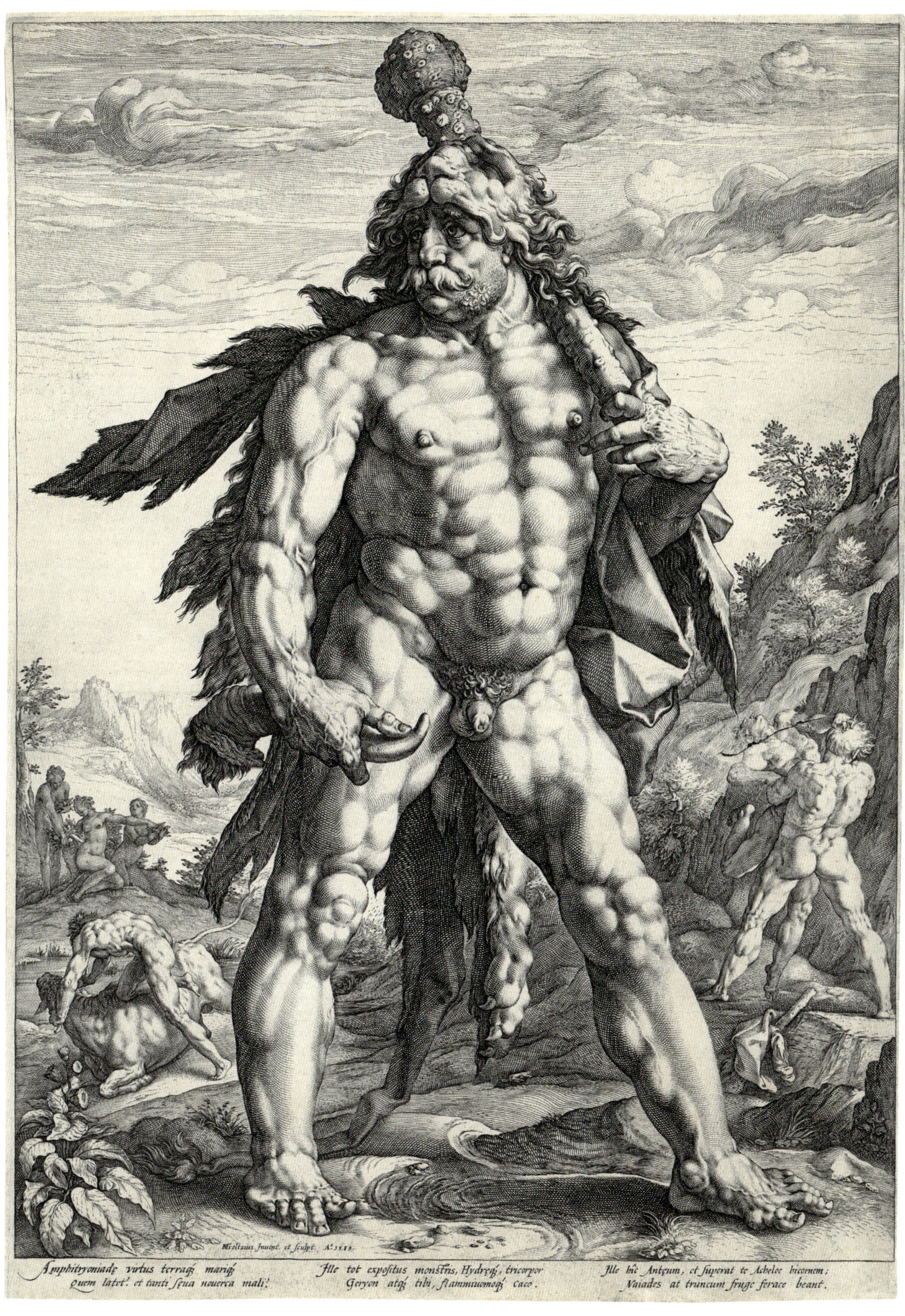

Hendrick Goltzius (Inventor, Stecher, Verleger / designer, engraver, publisher)
Der große Herkules (Knollenmann) / The Great Hercules, 1589
Kupferstich / engraving SGSM, Inv. 1987:26 D

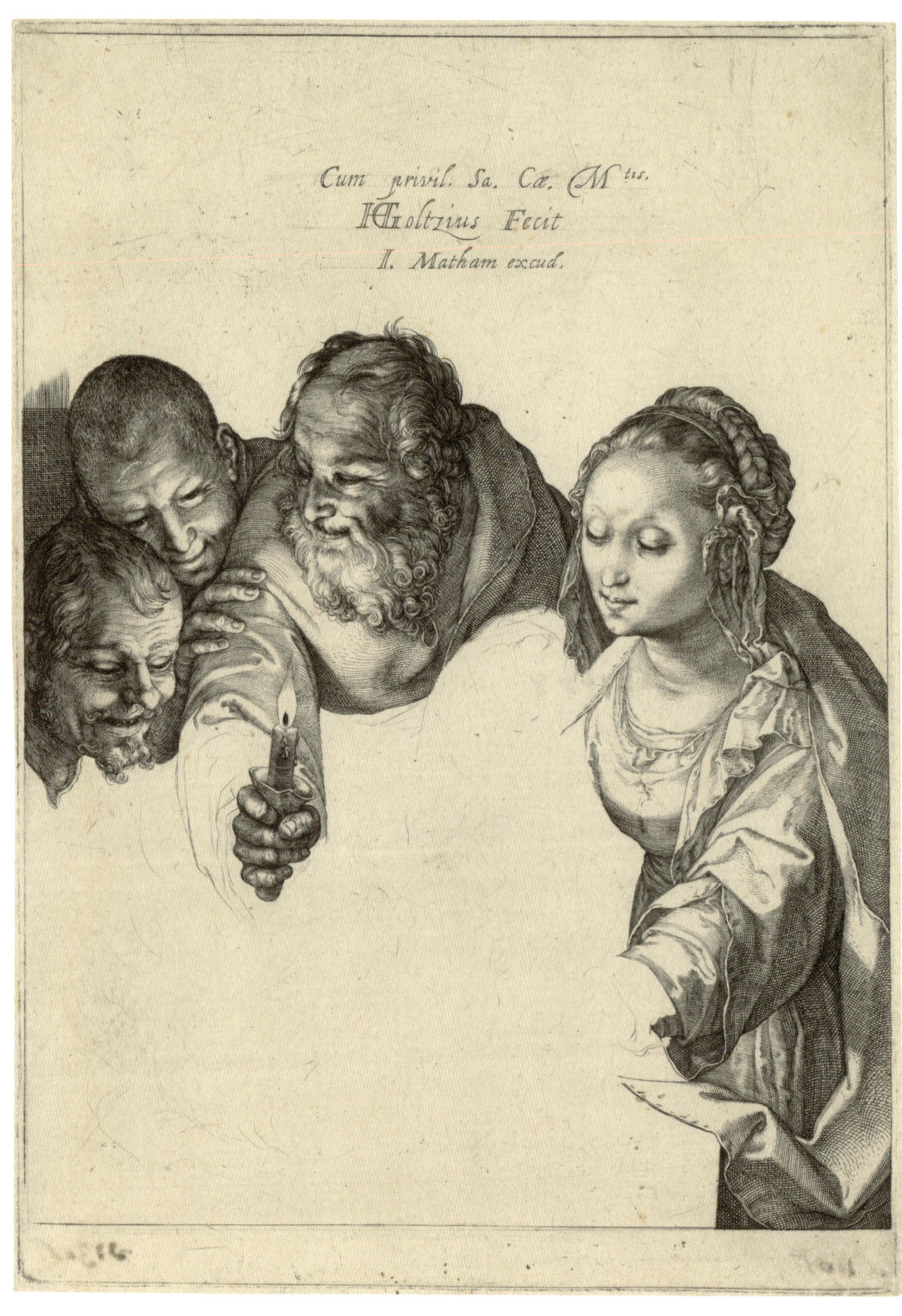

Goltzius (Stecher, Radierer / engraver, etcher), nach Tizian / after Titian, Jacob Matham (Verleger / publisher)
Die Anbetung der Hirten / The Adoration of the Shepherds, 1599/1615
Radierung, Kupferstich / etching, engraving, Zustand / state I SGSM, Inv. 30899 D

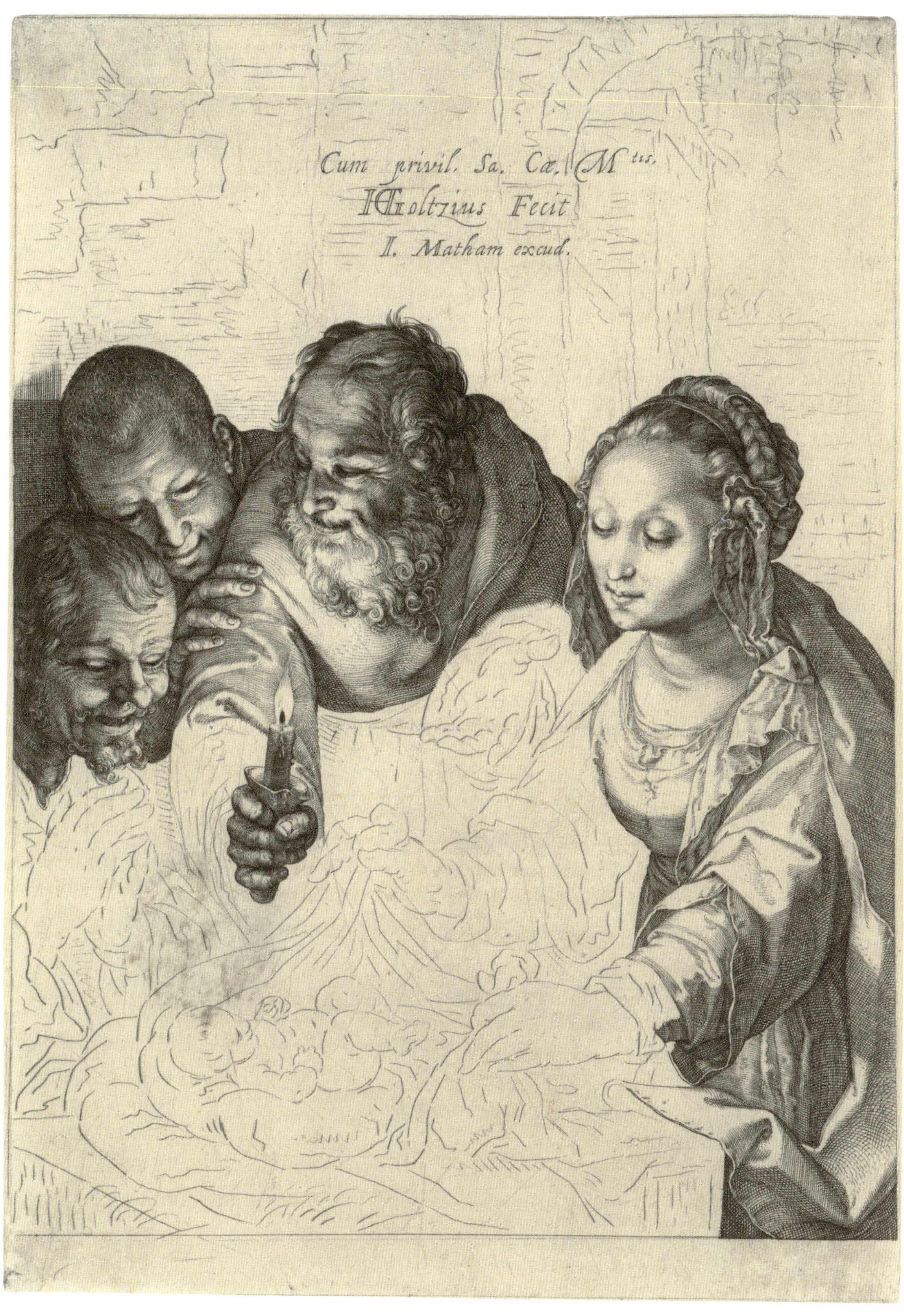

Goltzius (Stecher, Radierer / engraver, etcher), nach Tizian / after Titian, Jacob Matham (Verleger / publisher)
Die Anbetung der Hirten / The Adoration of the Shepherds, 1599/1615
Radierung, Kupferstich / etching, engraving, Zustand / state III SGSM, Inv. 30900 D

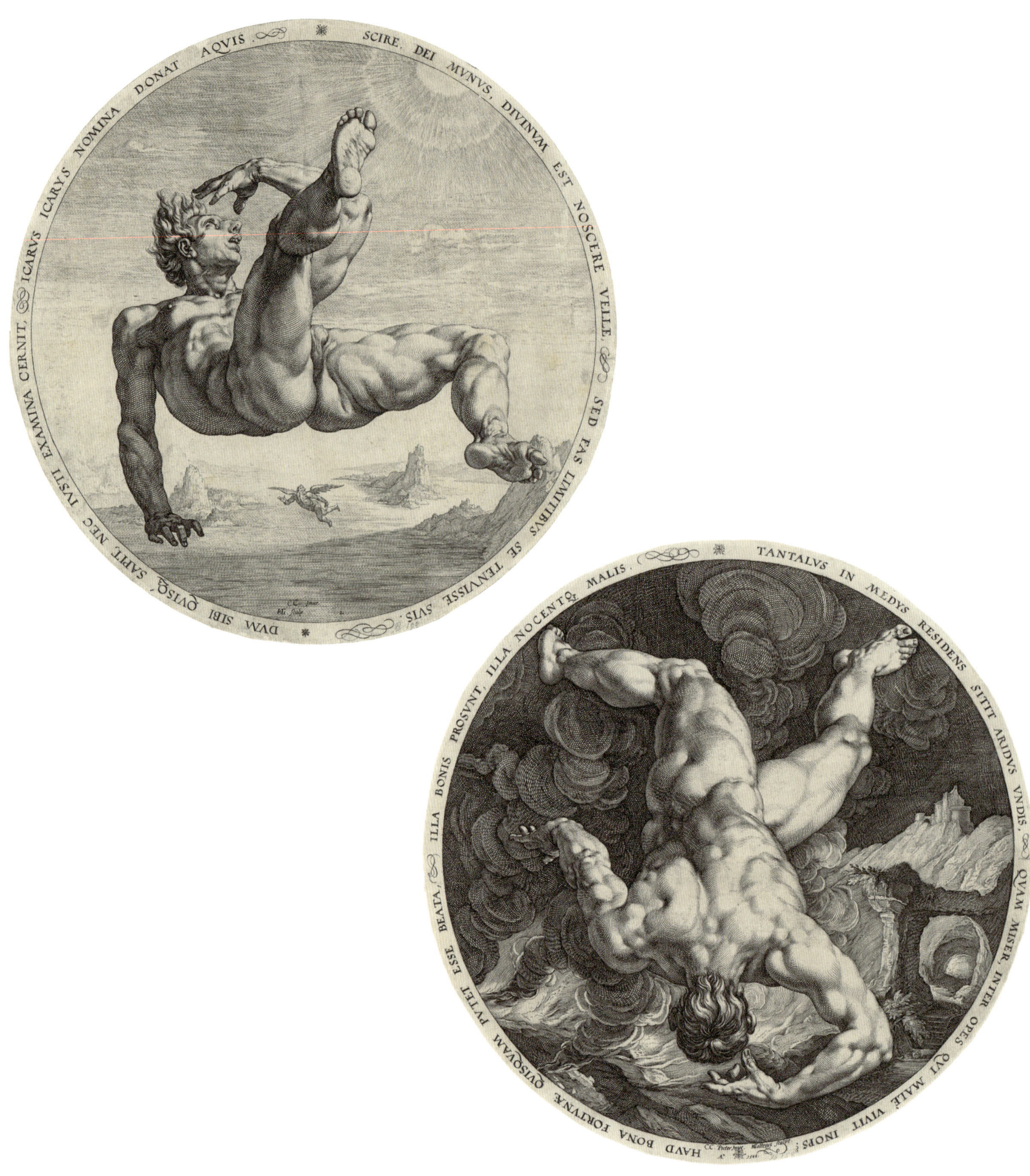

Goltzius (Inventor, Stecher, Verleger / designer, engraver, publisher), nach / after Cornelis Cornelisz. van Haarlem
Ikarus / Icarus, *Tantalus*, *Ixion*, *Phaeton* (VON LINKS / FROM LEFT), 1588
Aus der Serie *Die vier Himmelsstürmer* / from the series *The Four Disgracers*, 1588
Kupferstich / engraving SGSM, Inv. 31006 D; 31005 D; 31008 D; 31007 D

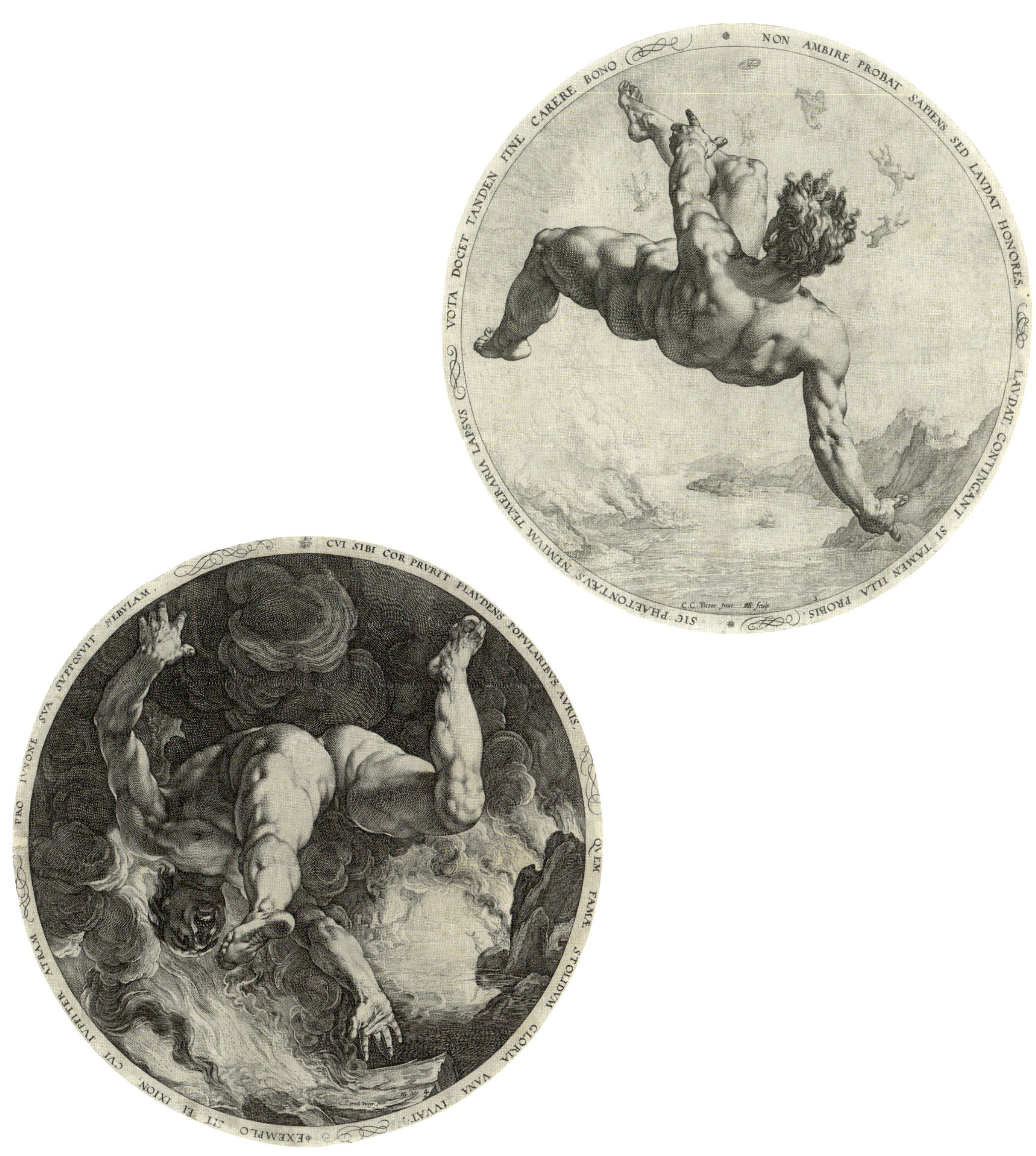
NON AMBIRE PROBAT SAPIENS SED LAVDAT HONORES, LAVDAT, CONTINGANT SI TAMEN ILLA PROBIS.
SIC PHAETONTÆVS NIMIVM TEMERARIA LAPSVS VOTA DOCET TANDEN FINE CARERE BONO
CVI SIBI COR PRVRIT PLAVDENS POPVLARIBVS AVRIS, QVEM FAMÆ STOLIDVM GLORIA VANA IVVAT,
EXEMPLO SIT EI IXION, CVI IVPITER AVRAM PRO IVNONE SVA SVPPOSVIT NEBVLAM.

seiner Komposition steht nicht der titelgebende König im Mittelpunkt, sondern Apoll, der Verlierer des Musikwettstreits, den Midas zwischen Apoll und Pan entscheiden musste. Mit seinem großen Format (427 × 680 mm), der wohlüberlegten und austarierten Komposition der Figuren, mit seinen Anspielungen auf italienische Vorbilder (Raffael) wie auf den Stil von Bartholomeus Spranger und schließlich mit dem gelehrten lateinischen Text konnte dieses Werk auf ganz unterschiedlichen Ebenen beeindrucken. Eine Moral der dargestellten Geschichte war entsprechend der Bildunterschrift von Willem Hessels van Est (lat. Estius), dass nur Kenner wirkliche Kunst von Blendwerk unterscheiden können.[4] Damit war impliziert, dass der Empfänger der Widmung und, in Erweiterung, auch die Betrachter dieses Stichs sich als Kenner erweisen, wenn sie Goltzius' Blatt als große Kunst würdigten.

Die wie die *Himmelsstürmer* im Rundformat ausgeführte Serie *Die Erschaffung der Welt* (1589) umfasst zwei Szenen, die in der Geschichte der Kunst bis dahin ohne Beispiel waren (Abb. S. 201–203). Für die Scheidung von Licht und Dunkel am ersten Schöpfungstag und die Scheidung von Tag und Nacht am vierten fand der Künstler originelle Neuschöpfungen. Die übrigen Schöpfungstage folgen konventionelleren Bildtypen. Eine weitere Besonderheit dieser Serie ist, dass Goltzius mit dem Stechen der Blätter den Amsterdamer Künstler Jan Harmensz. Muller (1571–1628) beauftragte und er selbst nur als „Inventor", als Erfinder, sowie als Verleger auftrat. Über die Hintergründe, wie es zu dieser Konstellation kam, wissen wir nichts. Aber Muller verstand es, den Goltzius-Stil umzusetzen, und stellte mit dieser Folge die vorzügliche Qualität seiner Arbeit unter Beweis. Jahre später sollte er zwei Porträts nach Rubens stechen (Abb. S. 264 f.).

Nach Goltzius' Rückkehr aus Italien entstanden zwei religiöse Serien, auf die der Künstler besonders stolz war und die seinen Ruhm unter seinen Zeitgenossen wie bei vielen nachfolgenden Künstlergenerationen sicherten. Mit der sechsteiligen Folge *Christi Geburt und Jugend*, seinen sogenannten *Meisterstichen* (1594/95), brachte er zur Blüte, was zuvor bereits in anderen Werken angeklungen war: Er machte sich die Stile von namhaften Künstlern zu eigen und setzte sie in eigenen Bildentwürfen um.[5] Bei der Szene *Die Anbetung der Hirten* folgte er Stichen italienischer Vorbilder wie Tizian und Jacopo Bassano (Abb. S. 198), bei *Die Beschneidung Christi* solchen des großen Vorbilds Albrecht Dürer (Abb. S. 199).[6] Dieses Vorgehen bedeutete ein Sich-Messen mit den Meistern der Vergangenheit und brachte Goltzius die Betitelung „Proteus" ein, womit gemeint war, dass er in virtuoser Weise stilistisch wandel- und anpassungsfähig war.[7] Diesen Titel des alten, weisen und wandlungsfähigen Meeresgottes formulierte Cornelis Schonaeus im Widmungstext des ersten Blatts der *Meisterstiche*, der *Verkündigung* (Abb. S. 110). Van Mander zufolge freute es Goltzius über alle Maßen, wenn Betrachter seine Werke für solche der Künstler hielten, denen er mit seinem wechselnden Stil huldigte.[8]

Die zwölf Blätter der *Passion Christi* (1596–1598) waren stilistisch eine Hommage an Lucas van Leyden, den großen niederländischen Meister des frühen 16. Jahrhunderts, aber die erfindungsreichen Kompositionen verdanken wir Goltzius. Weil er die Serie dem Mailänder Erzbischof Federico Borromeo widmete, einem bedeutenden Sammler nordischer wie italienischer Kunst, liegt es nahe, auch bei dieser Serie anzunehmen, dass es Goltzius um eine idealtypische

carefully planned and balanced composition of figures, allusions to Italian models (Raphael) and Bartholomeus Spranger's style, and a learned Latin text, this work was destined to impress on many different levels. One of its morals, according to the epigram by Willem Hessels van Est (Estius in Latin), was that only connoisseurs can distinguish between true and false art.[4] This implied that the recipient of the print's dedication and, by extension, the viewers of the print would prove to be connoisseurs if and when they praised Goltzius's work as great art.

Like *The Four Disgracers*, the prints in the series *The Creation of the World* (1589) were composed as roundels. The iconography of two of the scenes was unprecedented in art history (figs. pp. 201–203). For the division of light and darkness on the first day and the division of Day and Night on the fourth, the artist invented original new images. The other motifs follow conventional iconography. It is noteworthy that Goltzius commissioned the Amsterdam artist Jan Harmensz. Muller (1571–1628) as engraver for these prints and relinquished his own roles to those of "inventor" (or designer) and publisher. We know nothing further about this collaboration. But Muller succeeded in realizing the Goltzius style and proved his own excellence as an engraver with this series. Years later he was to engrave two portraits after Rubens (figs. pp. 264–265).

After Goltzius returned from Italy, he created two religious series of which he was very proud and which secured him lasting fame among both his contemporaries and subsequent generations of artists. In his six-part series *The Birth and Early Life of Christ*, his so-called *Masterpieces* (1594/95), he brought to fruition what he had been practicing in earlier works: He appropriated the engraving styles of famous artists in compositions that were fully his own.[5] For *The Adoration of the Shepherds* he looked to the prints of Italian precursors like Titian and Jacopo Bassano (fig. p. 198), while he modeled *The Circumcision* on his great idol Albrecht Dürer (fig. p. 199).[6] This method not only signaled that he wanted to be compared with the masters of the past but also earned him the title "Proteus," which meant that he was a virtuoso of stylistic changeability and adaptability.[7] Cornelis Schonaeus used this epithet of the old, wise, and changeable ocean god in the dedication of the first print of the *Masterpieces*, *The Annunciation* (fig. p. 110). According to Van Mander, it made Goltzius extremely happy whenever viewers believed his works to be by those artists to whom he had paid tribute with his flexible style.[8]

The twelve prints of *The Passion of Christ* (1596–1598) were a stylistic tribute to Lucas van Leyden, the great Netherlandish master of the early sixteenth century. However, the imaginative compositions were entirely Goltzius's own. Because he dedicated the series to the archbishop of Milan, Federico Borromeo, an important collector of northern and Italian art, it makes sense to conclude that Goltzius aimed in his series for a synthesis of the artistic characteristics of these two regions.[9] *Christ on the Cross* (no. 10; fig. p. 196) and *The Resurrection* (no. 12, fig. p. 197), like all the other scenes in the series, testify to Goltzius's ambition to secure himself a place in art history by means of comparison with and

Zusammenführung der Eigenheiten dieser Kunstlandschaften ging.[9] *Die Kreuzigung* (Blatt 10; Abb. S. 196) und *Die Auferstehung* (Blatt 12; Abb. S. 197) zeigen hier stellvertretend für die Serie, dass Goltzius sich mit ihr selbstbewusst einen Platz in der Kunstgeschichte sichern wollte, indem er den Vergleich mit und das Übertreffen von anerkannten Vorläufern suchte. Die große Anzahl von Kopien, die nach Erscheinen der Serie angefertigt wurde (auch jene Nachzeichnung von Rubens in unserer Ausstellung; Abb. S. 157), ist der beste Beweis, dass er dieses Ziel erreichte.[10]

Erst 1615 gab Goltzius' Stiefsohn Jacob Matham (1571–1631) das heute sehr populäre Motiv der unfertig gebliebenen Hirtenanbetung heraus, von dem die Staatliche Graphische Sammlung München zwei Zustände besitzt und zeigt (Abb. S. 188 f.). Die Platte war wohl 1599 in Goltzius' Werkstatt liegengeblieben. Da er es laut Karel van Mander nicht schätzte, unfertige Werke zu zeigen geschweige denn zu publizieren, darf man sich fragen, warum Goltzius sein Einverständnis zur Veröffentlichung gab. Van Mander berichtet aber von einer Aussage Goltzius', die er gehört habe, „wonach Tizian, es ist wert zu hören, in einer Christnacht einen Hirten den Kopf voraus herankommen lässt, auf dessen Stirn erscheint nur ein einziges Licht, um sich gut herauszuheben, während der ganze Rest abflauend ins Dunkel versinkt".[11] Karel van Mander zufolge waren die fertiggestellten Bildteile die einzig Nötigen, um zu zeigen, dass Goltzius Tizian das Wasser reichen konnte.[12]

Die „Meisterdrucke" von Rubens zeichnen sich durch eine noch größere thematische Vielfalt als bei Goltzius aus. Daher gibt es nicht das eine Blatt, das stellvertretend für sein Gesamtwerk herausgestellt werden könnte. Mit der *Kreuzaufrichtung* (1638), einem Stich von Hans Witdoeck (1615–1639/42) von drei Platten, und der *Kreuzabnahme* (1620), gestochen von Lucas Vorsterman I (1595/96–1674/75), brachte Rubens Motive in die Graphik, die zu seinen großen Bildschöpfungen der Frühzeit gehörten und die nun auch außerhalb Antwerpens bestaunt werden konnten (Abb. S. 204 f., 207).[13] Mit den beiden zugrunde liegenden Gemälden hatte er die Ikonographie dieser Themen revolutioniert und die Stiche stellten sicher, dass Künstler wie Rembrandt (1606/07–1669) oder Thomas Gainsborough (1727–1788) Rubens' Inventionen präsent hatten, als sie selbst Neues zu dieser Thematik schaffen wollten.[14] Die besonders persönlich formulierten Widmungen dieser Stiche an bedeutende Persönlichkeiten, in deren Schuld Rubens stand, den Antwerpener Sammler Cornelis van der Geest (1577–1638) und den englischen Gesandten in Den Haag Sir Dudley Carleton (1573–1632), verliehen beiden Blättern – und damit ihrem geistigen Schöpfer – zusätzliche Prominenz. Van der Geest hatte Rubens für den bedeutenden Auftrag vorgeschlagen, aus dem *Die Kreuzaufrichtung* hervorging, daher war Rubens' Widmung des Stichs an ihn ein später Dank für seine Unterstützung sowie eine Ehrerweisung an den kurz zuvor Verstorbenen. Mit der Widmung des Stichs *Die Kreuzabnahme* an Sir Dudley Carleton bedankte sich Rubens dafür, dass dieser ihm bei der Erlangung des Privilegs für die nördlichen Niederlande behilflich gewesen war. Diese Widmungen legten darüber hinaus sein Netzwerk einflussreicher Männer offen.

Das alttestamentliche Thema *Susanna und die beiden Alten* hat Rubens vielfach behandelt, darunter in dem viel gerühmten Stich, den Lucas Vorsterman I 1620 fertigte (siehe das Kapitel „Antike", S. 222).

outshining of famous precursors. The large number of copies that appeared after publication of the series (including Rubens's drawing that incorporates elements from two of the scenes and that is on view in our exhibition; fig. p. 157), is the best proof that he achieved this goal.[10]

It was not until 1615 that Goltzius's stepson Jacob Matham (1571–1631) published the unfinished engraving *Adoration of the Shepherds*, a work that is popular to this day and of which the Staatliche Graphische Sammlung München holds and shows two states (figs. pp. 188, 189). The plate probably remained untouched in Goltzius's studio after 1599. Because the artist allegedly did not like to show unfinished work, and much less to publish it, we may well wonder why he gave Matham permission to print it. However, Karel van Mander relates having heard Goltzius speak of "... how Titian, it is worth hearing, had a shepherd approach, head first, and on that head a single light was seen so as to make him stand out while everything else was dipped in darkness."[11] Thus, according to Van Mander, the finished parts of Goltzius's print were all that was necessary to prove him to be Titian's equal.[12]

Rubens's "Masterprints" are remarkable for their great variety of subject matter. Accordingly, no one single work is representative of the oeuvre. With *The Raising of the Cross* (1638), an engraving from three plates by Hans Witdoeck (1615–1639/42), and *The Descent from the Cross* (1620), an engraving by Lucas Vorsterman I (1595/96–1674/75), Rubens had two major early altar paintings translated into prints so that they might be known outside Antwerp (figs. pp. 204–205, 207).[13] With his inventions for these altarpieces Rubens had revolutionized the way these scenes were depicted, and thanks to the wide distribution of his prints, artists like Rembrandt (1606/07–1669) and Thomas Gainsborough (1727–1788) were sure to become aware of Rubens's compositions when they themselves looked for new ideas for representing the scenes.[14] The dedications on these two prints were phrased in an especially personal manner and addressed to important public figures to whom Rubens was indebted: the Antwerp collector Cornelis van der Geest (1577–1638) and the English envoy to The Hague, Sir Dudley Carleton (1573–1632). These dedications secured additional prominence for the prints—and for their creator. Van der Geest had suggested entrusting Rubens with the important commission from which *The Raising of the Cross* derived. Therefore, Rubens's dedication of the print to him was both a belated show of gratitude and a tribute to his benefactor, who had died shortly before. With his dedication of the print of *The Descent from the Cross*, Rubens expressed his indebtedness to Sir Dudley Carleton for having helped him gain the printing privilege for the Northern Netherlands. Both dedications thus served to make visible Rubens's network of influential figures.

Rubens treated the Old Testament story of *Susanna and the Elders* several times, among them the famous 1620 engraving by Lucas Vorsterman I (see the chapter "Antiquity," p. 222). Christoffel Jegher's (1596–1652/53) woodcut of 1633 to 1635 places the scene in a garden setting, for which a landscape format was more

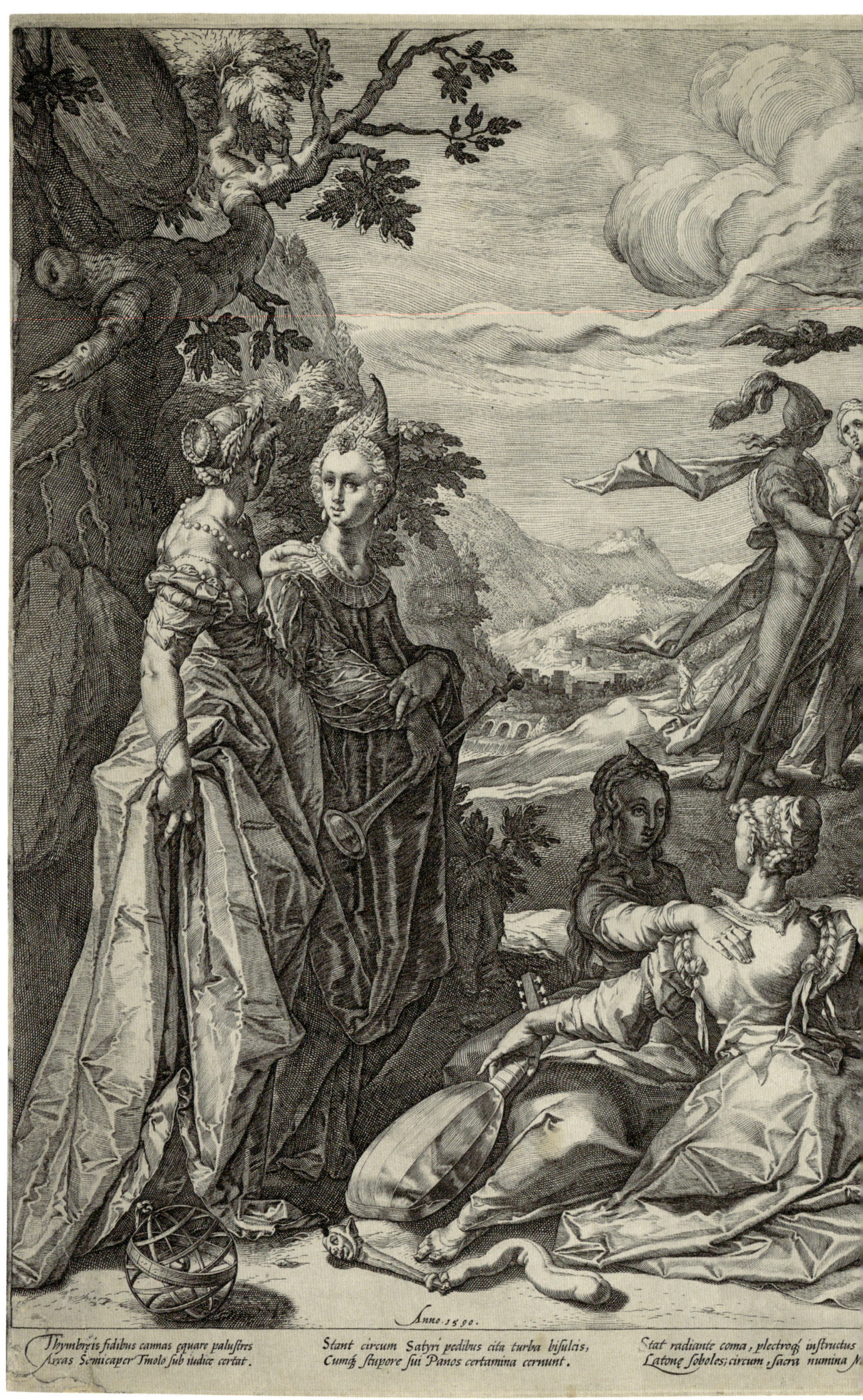

Hendrick Goltzius (Inventor, Stecher, Verleger / designer, engraver, publisher)
Das Midasurteil / The Judgment of Midas, 1590
Kupferstich / engraving SGSM, Inv. 1961:1237 D

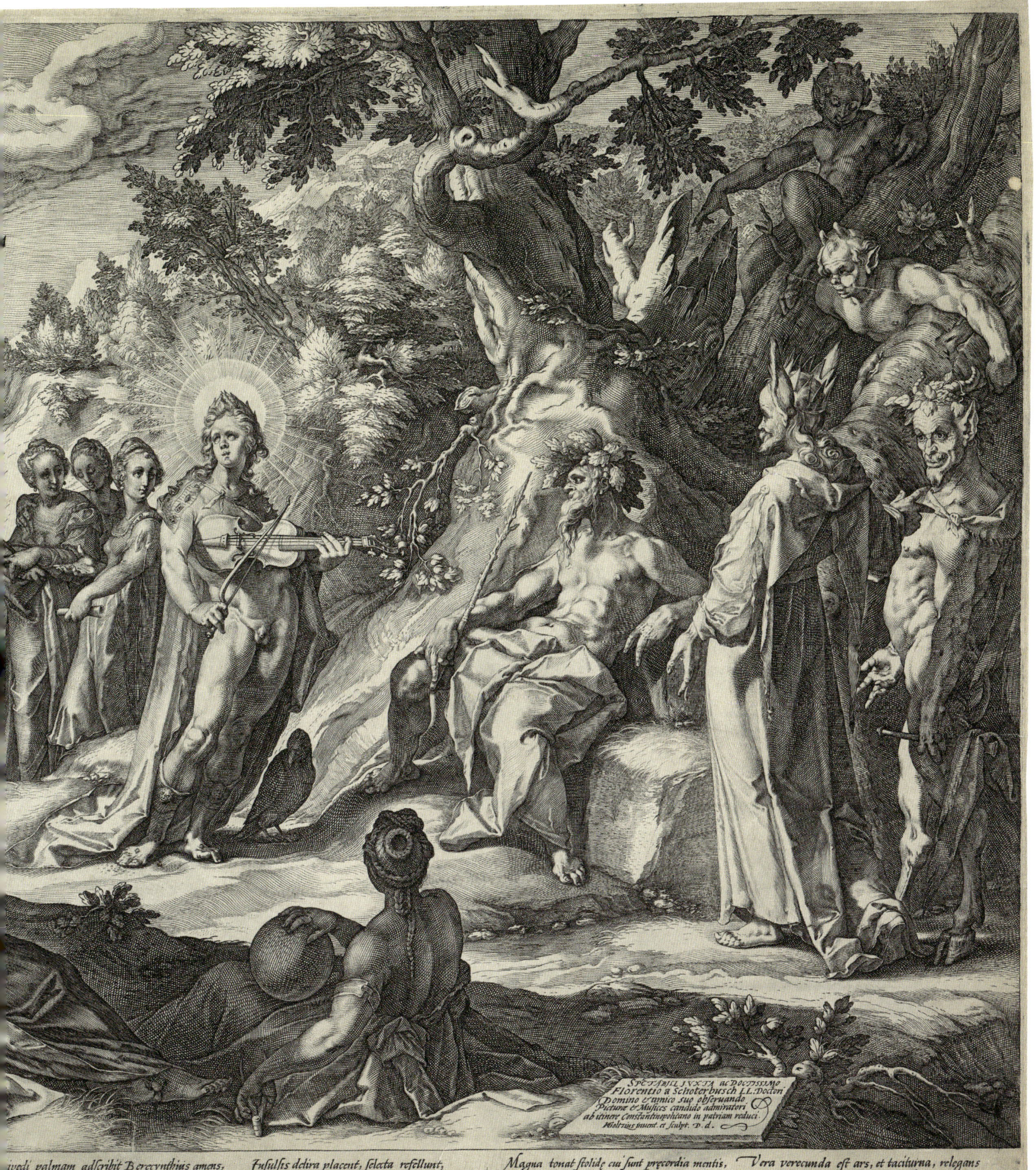
SPCTABILI IUXTA ac DOCTISSIMO
Florentio a Schoterbusch I.L. Doctori
Domino & amico suo obseruando
Picturæ & Musices candido admiratori
ab itinere Constantinopolitano in patriam reduci.
Holtzius inuent. et sculpt. D.d.
…ipedi palmam adscribit Berecynthius amens,
…us Phœbe tibi, cui Pindi cura, cui Hæmi.
Insulsis delira placent, selecta refellunt,
Atq; vltra crepidam sutor male taxat Apellem.
Magna tonat stolidę cui sunt pręcordia mentis,
Inscitiaq; Bavi strepitas, et ineptule Mevi.
Vera verecunda est ars, et taciturna, relegans
Clangentes lituos tumidi blateronibus oris.
Franco Estius,

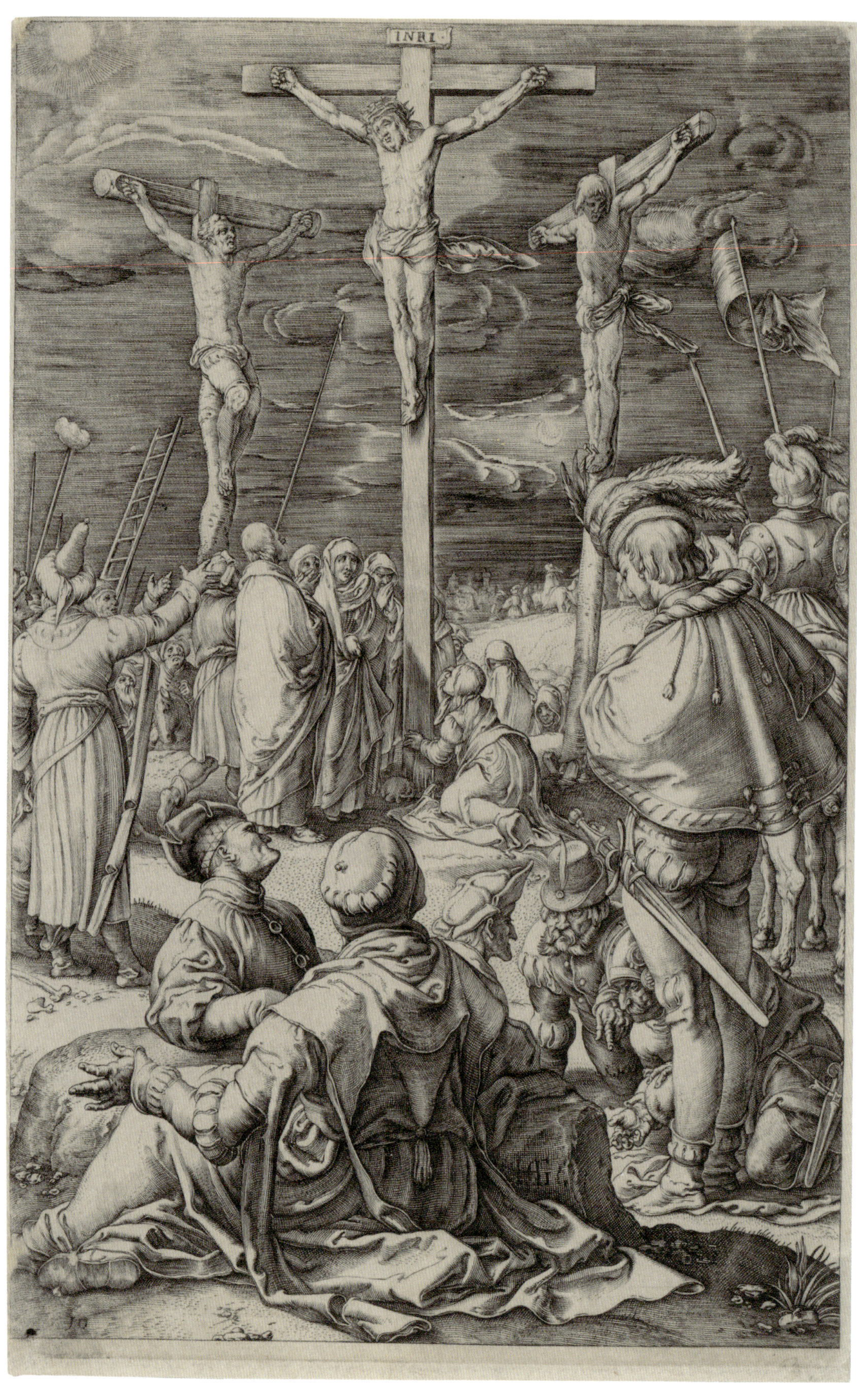

Hendrick Goltzius (Inventor, Stecher / designer, engraver)
Die Kreuzigung / Christ on the Cross, 1596–1598
Aus der Serie *Die Passion Christi* / from the series *The Passion of Christ*, 1596–1598
Kupferstich / engraving SGSM, Inv. 30915 D

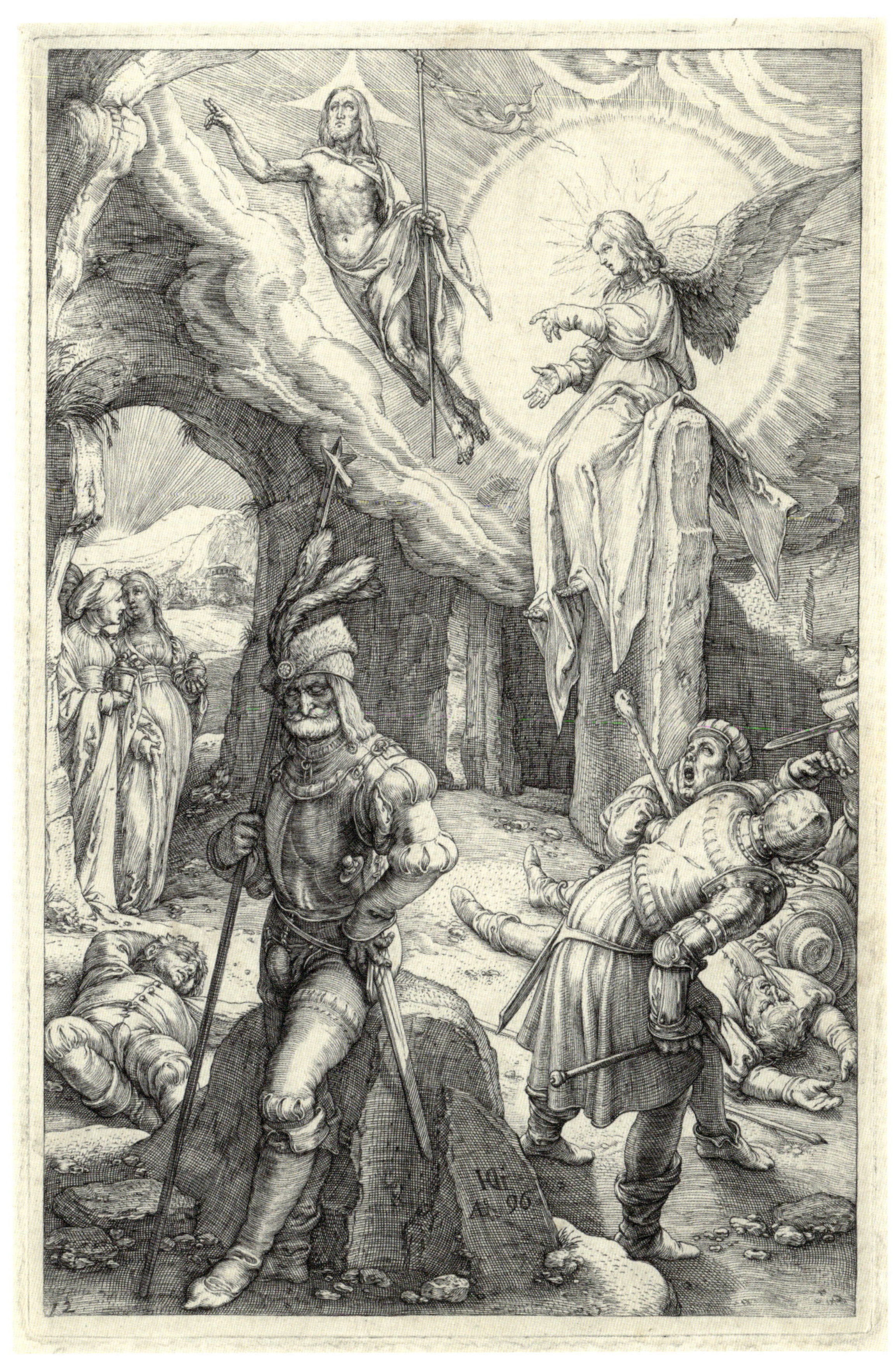

Hendrick Goltzius (Inventor, Stecher / designer, engraver)
Die Auferstehung / The Resurrection, 1596
Aus der Serie *Die Passion Christi* / from the series *The Passion of Christ*, 1596–1598
Kupferstich / engraving SGSM, Inv. 30917 D

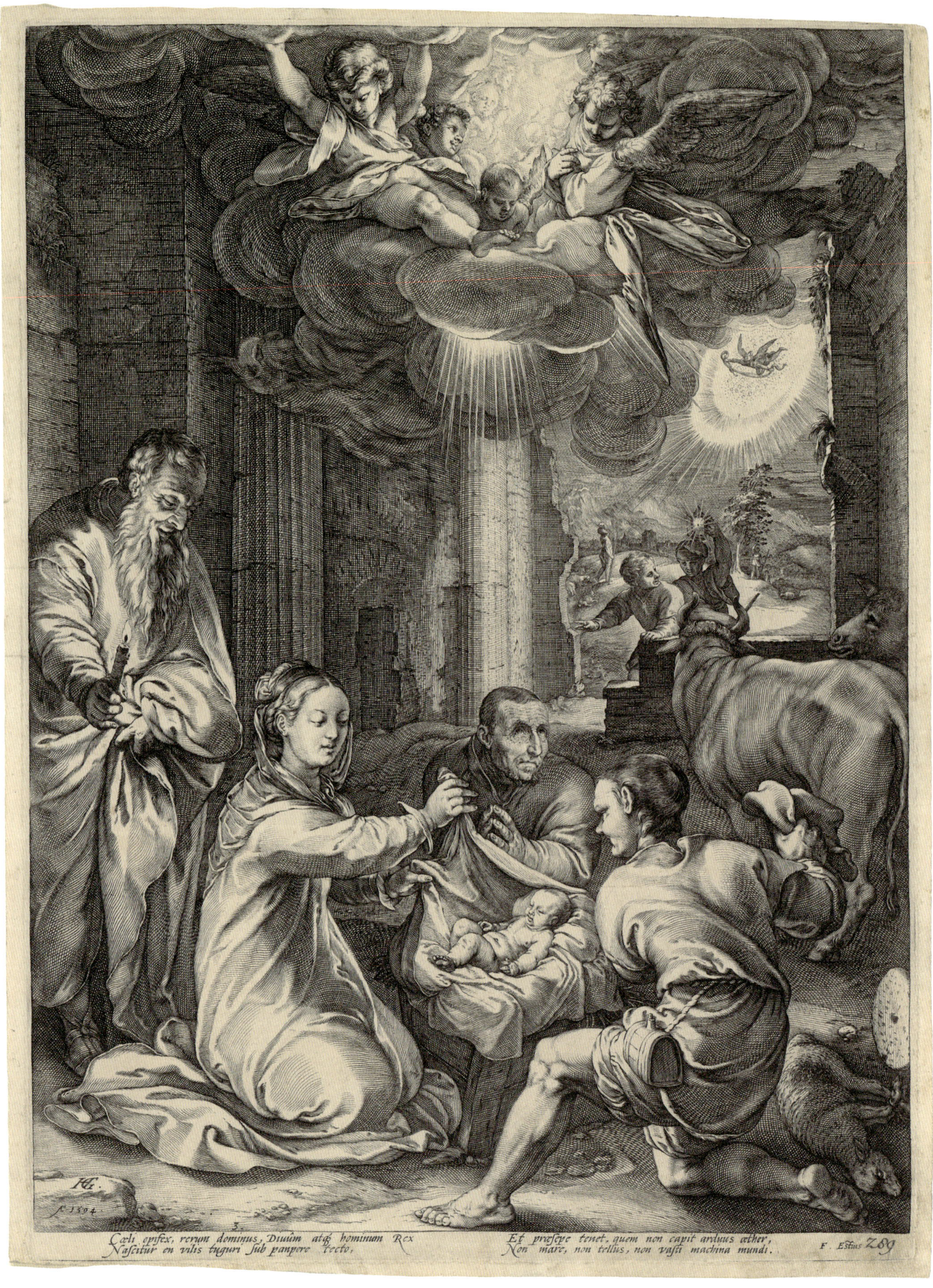

Hendrick Goltzius (Inventor, Stecher, Verleger / designer, engraver, publisher)
Die Anbetung der Hirten / The Adoration of the Shepherds, 1594
Aus der Serie *Christi Geburt und Jugend (Meisterstiche)* / from the series *The Birth and Early Life of Christ (Masterpieces)*, 1594/95
Kupferstich / engraving SGSM, Inv. 1988:88 D

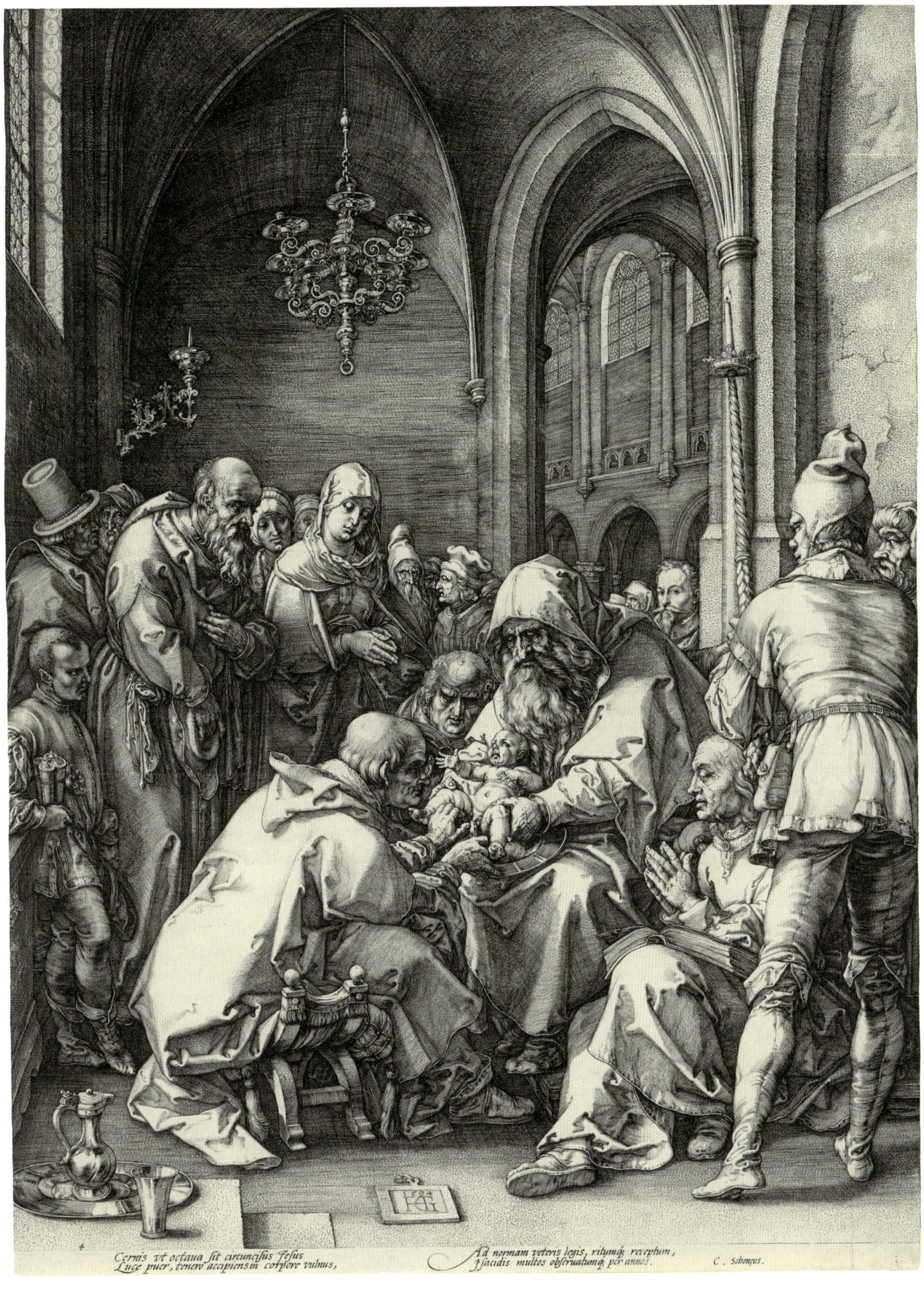

Hendrick Goltzius (Inventor, Stecher, Verleger / designer, engraver, publisher)
Die Beschneidung Christi / The Circumcision, 1594
Aus der Serie *Christi Geburt und Jugend (Meisterstiche)* / from the series *The Birth and Early Life of Christ (Masterpieces)*, 1594/95
Kupferstich / engraving SGSM, Inv. 1988:84 D

Der Holzschnitt von Christoffel Jegher (1596–1652/53), der zwischen 1633 und 1635 entstand, zeigt das Geschehen in einer Gartenlandschaft, wofür sich das Querformat besser eignete (Abb. S. 208). Dieses Motiv stand am Beginn der Zusammenarbeit zwischen Rubens und Jegher.

Unter den Werken in dieser Abteilung sind auch solche, die die nordniederländischen Brüder Boëtius (1570/90–1633) und Schelte (1586–1659) à Bolswert unabhängig von Rubens, aber nach seinen Erfindungen anfertigten (Abb. S. 210–212). Obwohl die Blätter nicht die dem Meister verliehenen Privilegien tragen und wohl nicht unter seiner Aufsicht entstanden, scheint es gerechtfertigt, sie hier anzuführen. Denn die von ihnen gestochenen Rubens-Motive, wie *Das Urteil des Salomon* (vor 1633), *Die Bekehrung des Paulus* (1633) oder *Diana kehrt von der Jagd zurück* (um 1638), fanden ihr Publikum bereits in der ersten Hälfte des 17. Jahrhunderts und prägten das Bild, das man sich in den folgenden Jahrhunderten von Rubens machte.

Fehlen dürfen in der Gruppe der Arbeiten, die im engen Umkreis, jedoch ohne explizite Autorisierung von Rubens entstanden, auch nicht die Werke von Pieter Soutman (1593/1601–1657), der zeitweise als Rubens' Assistent arbeitete. Er erkannte das Potenzial, das die großen Jagdszenen auf dem internationalen Graphikmarkt entfalten würden. Fünf Rubens-Gemälde, die als solche nur fürstlichen Sammlungen vorbehalten blieben, übersetzte er in Stiche, darunter *Die Nilpferdjagd* (um 1640/41), die die rasante Dramatik des Gemäldes (um 1616) zu vermitteln weiß (Abb. S. 213). Damit machte Soutman die Jagden auch einem bürgerlichen Publikum zugänglich. Vermutlich basierend auf Zeichnungen, die er 1628 aus dem Atelier des Meisters zurück in seine Heimat Haarlem gebracht hatte, stach Soutman sie kurz nach Rubens' Tod. Soutmans *Nilpferdjagd* wurde bereits kurz nach Erscheinen des Blatts ein erstes Mal von Willem van der Leeuw (1603–1665) kopiert.[15] Von Pietro Antonio Martini (1738–1797) besitzt die Staatliche Graphische Sammlung München eine der vielen weiteren Kopien, diese datiert 1772.[16]

Obwohl mit dem Stich *Eine Flusslandschaft im Mondschein* (um 1638) zu Rubens' Lebzeiten nur eine einzige Landschaft mit Rubens' Privilegien entstand, entwickelten sich die Graphiken in diesem Genre zu einer eigenen Sparte in der Stichproduktion nach Rubens (Abb. S. 216 f.).[17] 26 unterschiedliche Motive nach Rubens' gemalten Landschaften erschienen in den Folgejahren im Druck, verantwortet von den Antwerpener Verlegern Gilles Hendricx (tätig 1637/38) und Martinus van den Enden I (1605–1654/74), die das Marktinteresse an solchen Rubens-Kompositionen erkannten und deren Nachstiche initiierten.[18] Die hier ausgewählten, alle um 1638 entstandenen Stiche deuten die Bandbreite der Rubens'schen Landschaften an, die in seinem gemalten Spätwerk zu seinem bevorzugten Genre wurden (Abb. S. 214–217). *Eine Flusslandschaft im Mondschein* gilt in der Kunstgeschichte als erste Nachtszene ohne Staffage, also ohne Verknüpfung mit einer Geschichte.[19] In der *Gewitterlandschaft mit Philemon und Baucis* steht das Naturphänomen, nicht die antike Erzählung im Mittelpunkt von Rubens' Interesse.[20] Und die *Landschaft mit dem verlorenen Sohn* verbindet Landschafts- mit Genredarstellung und trotz der dramatischen Bibelgeschichte wird hier ein arkadisches Idyll geschildert.[21] Der Einfluss, den Rubens' Landschaften, vermittelt durch seine Stiche, etwa auf die englischen Landschaftsmaler des 18. Jahrhunderts hatten, kann nicht überschätzt werden.[22]

suitable (fig. p. 208). This work marks the beginning of the collaboration between Rubens and Jegher.

Among the works in this chapter are some that the Northern Netherlandish brothers Boëtius (1570/90–1633) and Schelte (1586–1659) à Bolswert engraved independently from Rubens but after his inventions (figs. pp. 210–212). Even though these sheets neither carry the master's privileges nor were made under his supervision, it seems justified to include them in this selection. Rubens motifs such as *The Judgment of Solomon* (before 1633), *The Conversion of St. Paul* (1633), and *Diana Returning from the Hunt* (ca. 1638) found their audience in the first half of the seventeenth century and shaped the way subsequent centuries would perceive his art.

Among the group of prints that were created in close proximity to Rubens but without his explicit authorization are the works by Pieter Soutman (1593/1601–1657), who had worked for a time as his assistant. Understanding the potential the large hunting scenes might have on the international print market, Soutman transferred five Rubens paintings, which were typically reserved for princely collections, into prints. Among these was the *Hippopotamus Hunt* (ca. 1640/41; fig. p. 213), which compellingly conveys the fast-paced drama of the painting (ca. 1616). Soutman made these hunts available to a non-aristocratic audience. Probably working from drawings he had executed in Rubens's studio and brought back with him to Haarlem in 1628, Soutman etched and engraved them shortly after Rubens's death in 1640. Soutman's *Hippopotamus Hunt* was copied soon after its release by Willem van der Leeuw (1603–1665).[15] The Staatliche Graphische Sammlung München also holds a copy by Pietro Antonio Martini (1738–1797) dated 1772, one of many copies to follow.[16]

Although *Landscape with the Moon and Stars* (ca. 1638) was the only landscape to carry Rubens's privileges, this genre would go on to occupy its very own space within his print oeuvre (fig. pp. 216–217).[17] In the following years, twenty-six different landscape motifs after Rubens's painted landscapes were issued by the Antwerp publishers Gilles Hendricx (active 1637–1638) and Martinus van den Enden I (1605–1654/74). These two had recognized that there was a market for such Rubens compositions and initiated their print production.[18] The prints shown in this exhibition were all created around 1638 and give a good impression of the spectrum of Rubens landscapes, which developed into a favorite genre in his late work (figs. pp. 214–217). *Landscape with the Moon and Stars* is considered the first night scene without staffage—that is, without a narrative pretext.[19] In *Landscape with a Thunderstorm and Philemon and Baucis*, it is the natural phenomenon of the thunderstorm rather than the Classical story that is of interest to Rubens.[20] The *Landscape with the Prodigal Son* combines the landscape with a genre motif and, disregarding the Bible story, depicts an Arcadian idyll.[21] The influence Rubens's landscapes had, by way of the prints after them—for example, on the eighteenth-century British landscapists—cannot be overestimated.[22]

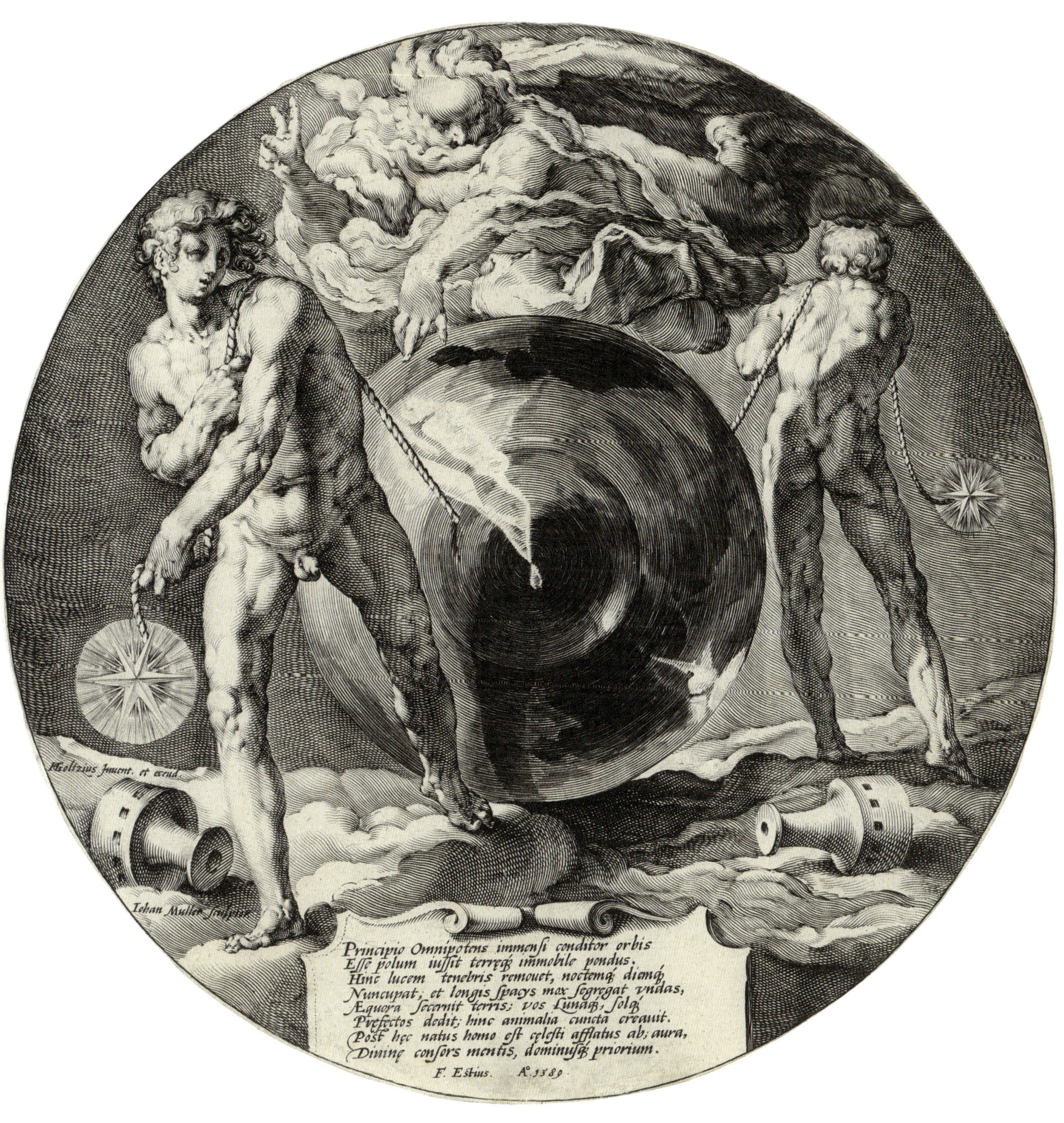

Goltzius (Inventor, Verleger / designer, publisher), Jan Harmensz. Muller (Stecher / engraver)
Gott erschafft Himmel und Erde aus dem Chaos / God Creating Heaven and Earth from a Sphere Representing Unformed Chaos, 1589
Titelblatt der Serie *Die Erschaffung der Welt* / title page of the series *The Creation of the World*, 1589
Kupferstich / engraving SGSM, Inv. 31238 D

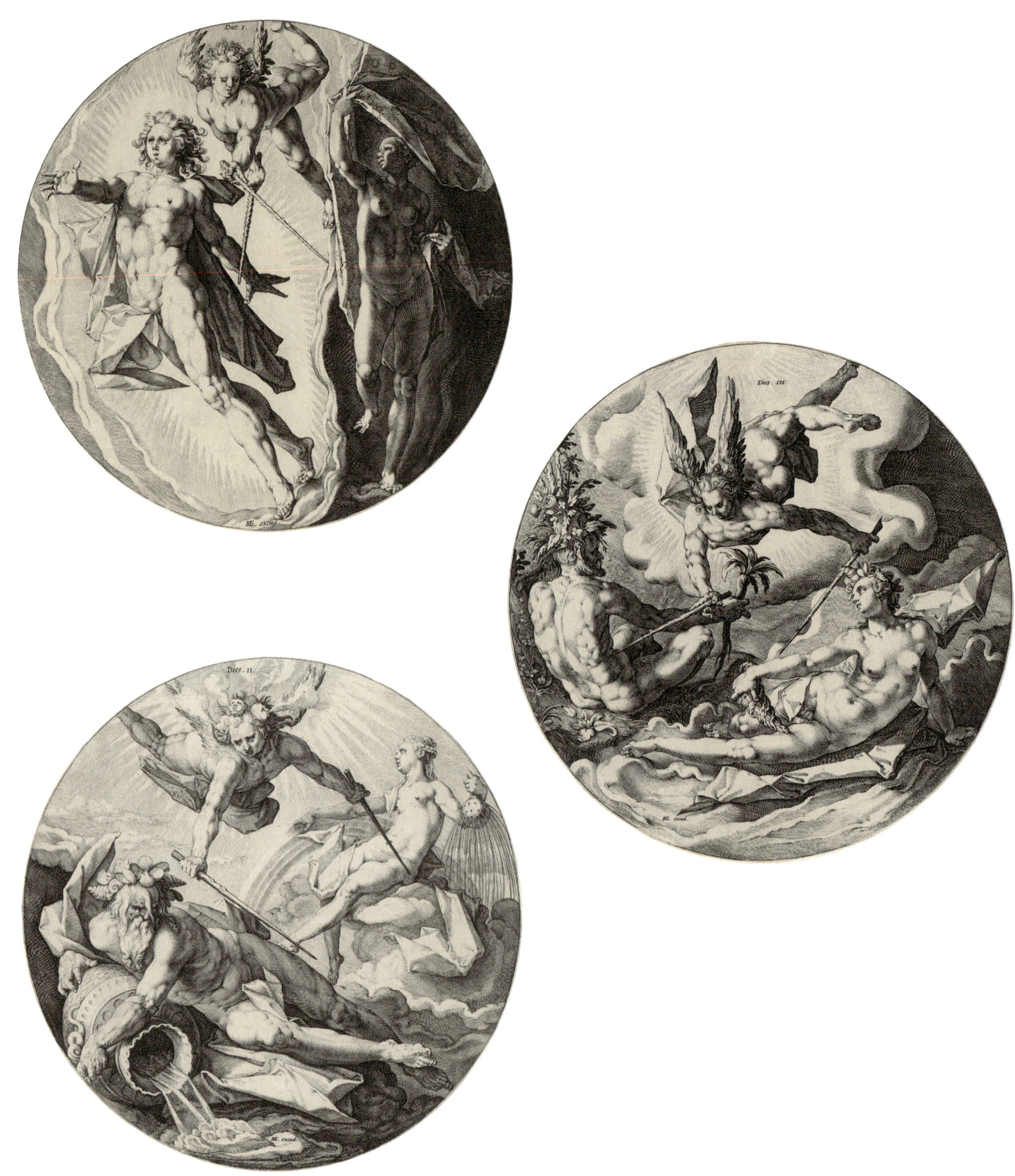

Goltzius (Inventor, Verleger / designer, publisher), Jan Harmensz. Muller (Stecher / engraver)
Die Schöpfungstage 1 bis 6 / Days 1 through 6, 1589
Aus der Serie *Die Erschaffung der Welt* / from the series *The Creation of the World*, 1589
Kupferstich / engraving SGSM, Inv. 31239–31244 D

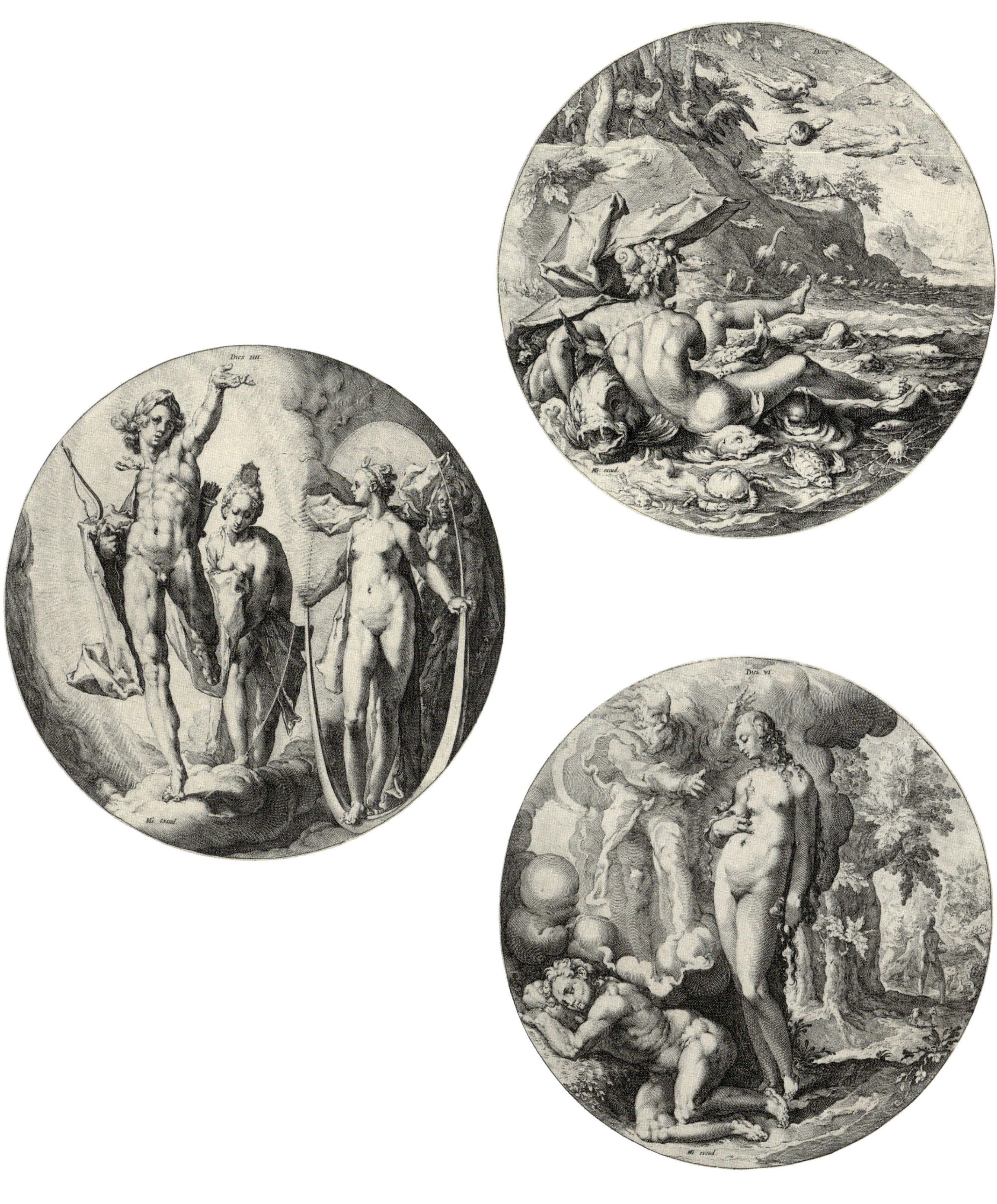
Dies V
Dies IIII
Dies VI

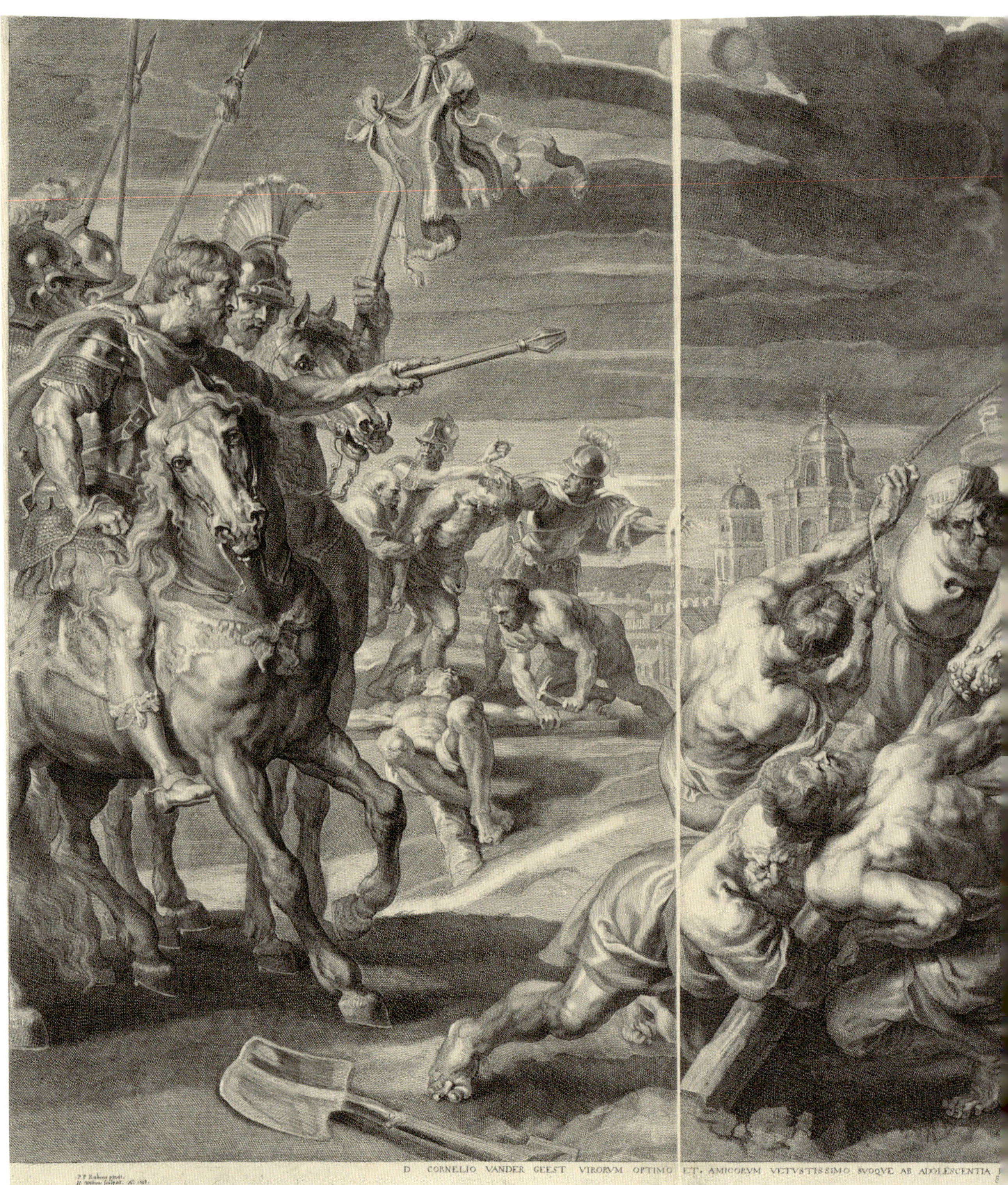
D CORNELIO VANDER GEEST VIRORVM OPTIMO ET. AMICORVM VETVSTISSIMO SVOQVE AB ADOLESCENTIA

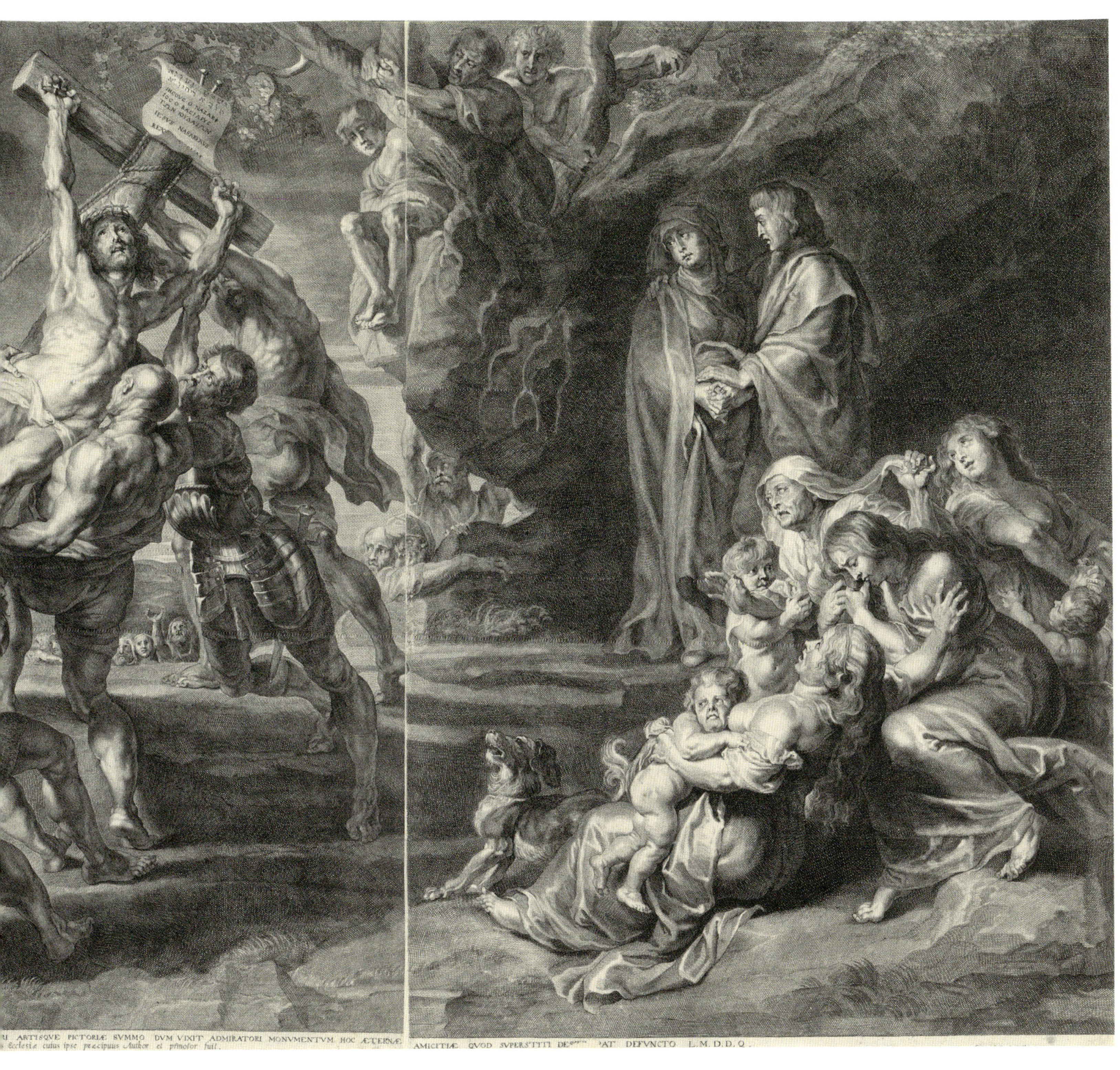

Rubens (Inventor / designer), Hans Witdoeck (Stecher / engraver)
Die Kreuzaufrichtung / The Raising of the Cross, 1638
Kupferstich / engraving SGSM, Inv. 30094-a–c D

1 Vgl. Arbeitsgruppe Estius 2017, S. 110.
2 Kirves 2017, S. 74 f.
3 „de heldighe cracht der Teycken-const". Mander (1604) 2000, S. 337, 284v07–08.
4 Vgl. Amsterdam/New York/Toledo 2003, Kat. 39, bes. S. 114.
5 Besonders ausführlich zu dieser Serie als Ausdruck künstlerischer *aemulatio* äußert sich Wandrey 2018 sowie viele Aufsätze von Walter S. Melion.
6 Huigen Leeflang weist darauf hin, dass Goltzius sich an den in Stichen überlieferten Werken orientierte, nicht an den Gemälden, die den italienischen Graphiken zugrunde lagen. Er kommt daher auch zu dem Schluss, dass die Serie als „commentary on the history and status of printmaking" gemeint war. Leeflang 2012, S. 36 f.
7 1604 wurde diese Betitelung von Karel van Mander in seiner Biographie von Goltzius wiederholt, Mander verlieh dem Künstler zudem den Beinamen „Vertumnus" (der Gott der Jahreszeiten, der sich jederzeit verwandeln kann). Mander (1604) 2000, S. 339.
8 Mander (1604) 2000, S. 338. Vgl. auch meinen Beitrag auf S. 234–247 im vorliegenden Katalog.
9 Goltzius könnte Borromeo in Rom getroffen haben, bevor dieser 1595 zum Erzbischof von Mailand ernannt wurde und dorthin zurückkehrte. Der Erzbischof dankte dem Künstler für die Widmung mit einer Goldkette und einer Goldmedaille. Vgl. Nichols 1991/92, S. 118, sub „1650 or earlier". Borromeo plante damals, seine Kunstschätze als Lehrsammlung angehenden Künstlern zu öffnen. Ab 1618 war diese Sammlung zugänglich. Vertreten waren Künstler wie Caravaggio und Raffael, aber auch Bernard van Orley, Lucas van Leyden und Jan Brueghel I.
10 NHD Goltzius 2012, 17–28, führt 11 Kopien zuzüglich etlicher Auflagen auf.
11 „[…] Hoe Titianus (t'is weerdich om hooren) / In eenen Kerstnacht met den hoofde vooren / Maeckt' eenen Herder / comende ghestreken / Al waer op ,t voorhooft / om wel doen uysteken / Een eenich hoogsel maer en is verschenen / Daer al de reste vliet bedommelt henen." Mander (1604) 1916, S. 279.
12 Zu einer Kopie, in der die Leerstellen ergänzt sind, siehe Abb. S. 277 im Kapitel „Nachbilder" im vorliegenden Katalog.
13 *Die Kreuzaufrichtung* malte Rubens 1611 bis 1614 für die Antwerpener Kirche der hl. Walburga (später versetzt in die Kathedrale). Zunächst war vorgesehen, dass Lucas Vorsterman das Motiv stechen sollte, aber dazu kam es nie. – Das Altarmittelbild der *Kreuzabnahme* (1611) wurde für eine Kapelle in der Antwerpener Kathedrale geschaffen. Später entstanden auch Stiche nach dem *Hl. Christophorus* und der *Heimsuchung*, Motiven der Altarflügel.
14 Rubens' *Kreuzabnahme* fand Nachhall in Rembrandts Darstellung desselben Themas, dem Gemälde in der Alten Pinakothek in München, Inv. 395. Der Hinweis auf Gainsboroughs Faszination für Rubens' *Kreuzabnahme* bei Meier 2020a, Kat. 17, S. 169.
15 Vgl. SGSM, Inv. 30489 D.
16 Vgl. SGSM, Inv. 30490 D.
17 Vgl. Kleinert 2014, Kap. 3, bes. S. 134. Kleinert widerspricht der bisher vorherrschenden Meinung der Rubens-Forschung und glaubt für einige Motive der sogenannten *Kleinen Landschaften*, dass Rubens sie vor seinem Tod wahrscheinlich gesehen habe.
18 Vgl. Nico Van Hout, in: Antwerpen/Québec 2004, S. 116 f. Auch die Tatsache, dass für diese Motivgruppe keine Stichvorlagen erhalten sind, führt Van Hout überzeugend als weiteres Argument für die Projektinitiative durch die Verleger an.
19 Vgl. Kleinert 2014, S. 76 f. – Auf ihre Nähe zu Adam Elsheimers *Flucht nach Ägypten*, 1609, München, Alte Pinakothek, Inv. 216, gestochen 1613 von Hendrick Goudt, ist vielfach hingewiesen worden.
20 Vgl. Kleinert 2014, S. 96–99.
21 Vgl. ebd., S. 107–109.
22 Vgl. hierzu Nico Van Hout, in: Antwerpen/Québec 2004, S. 118–120. Van Hout nennt John Constable, William Turner und Joshua Reynolds als Bewunderer der Rubens-Landschaften. Zur europäischen Rezeption vgl. Kleinert 2014, Kap. 4.

1 Cf. Arbeitsgruppe Estius 2017, p. 110.
2 Kirves 2017, pp. 74–75.
3 Mander (1604) 1994, p. 397, fol. 284v07–08.
4 See Amsterdam/New York/Toledo 2003, cat. 39, esp. p. 114.
5 For an extensive discussion of this series as an expression of artistic *aemulatio*, see Wandrey 2018, as well as the writings of Walter S. Melion.
6 Huigen Leeflang points out that for inspiration Goltzius looked to the prints rather than the Italian paintings they were modeled on. He therefore concludes that the series was meant as a "commentary on the history and status of printmaking." Leeflang 2012, pp. 36–37.
7 In 1604 Karel van Mander repeated this epithet in his biography of Goltzius. In addition, he called him "Vertumnus" (the God of the seasons who can change at will). Cf. Mander (1604) 1994, p. 398, fol. 285r11.
8 Mander (1604) 1994, p. 387, fol. 284v09ff. See also the chapter by Schleif on pp. 234–247 in the present catalog.
9 Goltzius may have met Borromeo in Rome before the latter was named archbishop of Milan and returned there. The archbishop thanked the artist for the dedication with a gold chain and medal. See Nichols 1991/92, p. 118, under "1650 or earlier." Borromeo was planning at the time to make his art collection available to artists for study. From 1618 on, the collection was accessible. It held works by artists like Caravaggio, Raphael, Bernard van Orley, Lucas van Leyden, and Jan Brueghel I.
10 NHD Goltzius 2012, 17–28, lists eleven copies and several editions.
11 Mander 1604, fol. 49r v34. Translation by the author.
12 For a copy with the unfinished parts filled in, see fig. p. 277 in the chapter "Afterimages" in the present catalog.
13 Rubens painted *The Raising of the Cross* between 1611 and 1614 for Antwerp's St. Walburga Church (the work was later transferred to the cathedral). Initially, Rubens had planned for Lucas Vorsterman to engrave this motif, but nothing came of that. – The painting *The Descent from the Cross* (1611) was commissioned for the center part of the altar in a chapel of the Antwerp cathedral. Later, Rubens had prints made after the side panels showing *St. Christophorus* and *The Visitation*.
14 Rubens's *Descent from the Cross* was echoed in Rembrandt's painting of the same title, held at the Alte Pinakothek, Munich, inv. 395. The connection to Gainsborough's fascination with Rubens's *Descent from the Cross* is discussed by Meier 2020a, cat. 17, p. 169.
15 See SGSM, inv. 30489 D.
16 See SGSM, inv. 30490 D.
17 See Kleinert 2014, ch. 3, esp. p. 134. Kleinert rejects the position formerly held by Rubens scholars and is convinced that Rubens saw some of the motifs from the series of the so-called *Small Landscapes* before his death: "Rubens probably saw some of these engravings."
18 See Nico Van Hout, in: Antwerpen/Québec 2004, pp. 116–117. The fact that no preparatory drawings are extant for this group of motifs, Van Hout argues, is a further argument that the initiative for this project came from the publishers.
19 See Kleinert 2014, pp. 76–77. – Its debt to Hendrick Goudt's print after Adam Elsheimer's *Flight into Egypt* (1609), Alte Pinakothek, Munich, inv. 216, has been acknowledged in the literature.
20 See Kleinert 2014, pp. 96–99.
21 See Kleinert 2014, pp. 107–109.
22 On this, see Nico Van Hout, in: Antwerpen/Québec 2004, pp. 118–120. Van Hout names John Constable, William Turner, and Joshua Reynolds as admirers of Rubens's landscapes. On the European reception of these works, see Kleinert 2014, ch. 4.

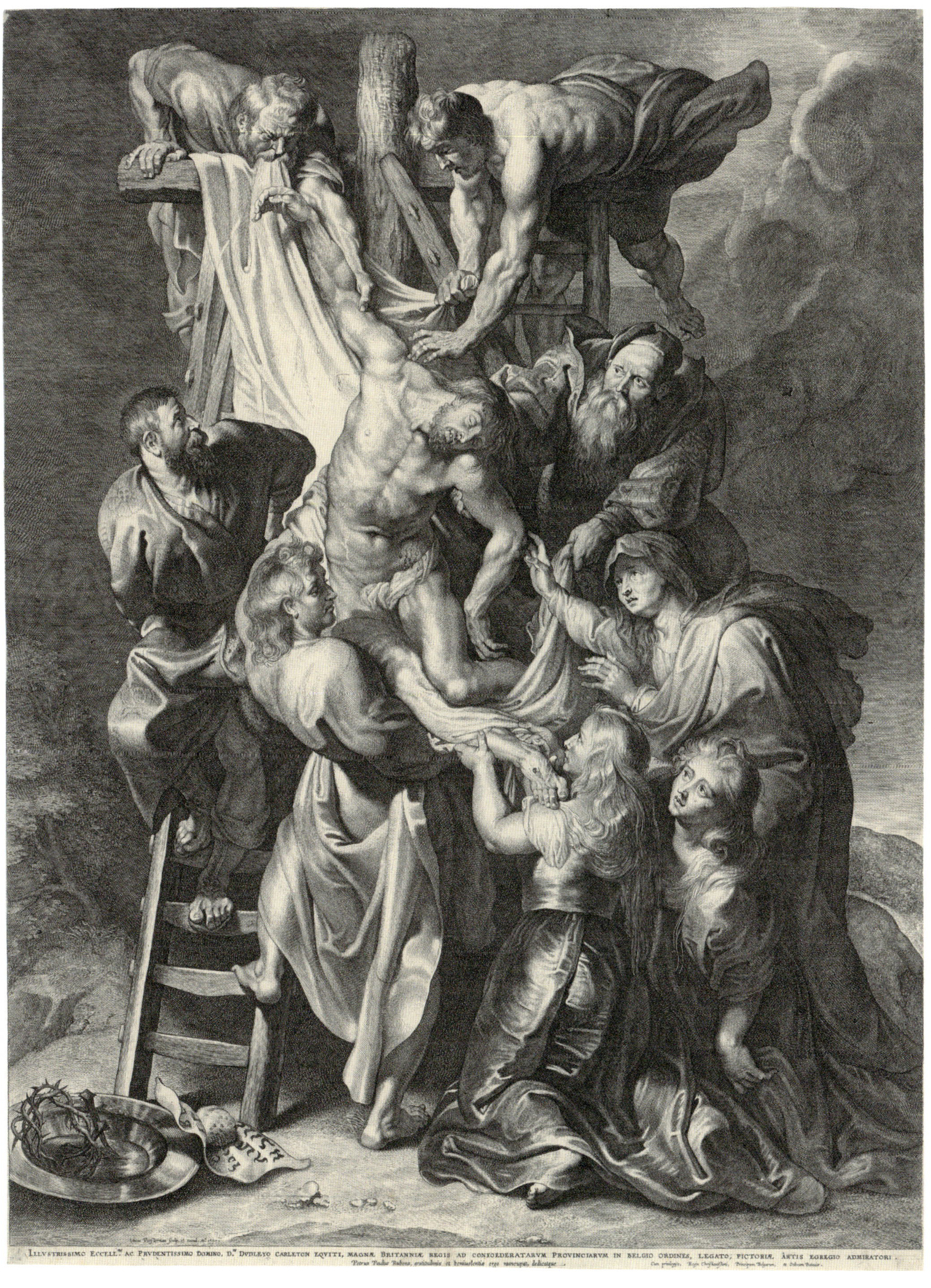

Rubens (Inventor / designer), Lucas Vorsterman I (Stecher, Verleger / engraver, publisher)
Die Kreuzabnahme / The Descent from the Cross, 1620
Kupferstich / engraving SGSM, Inv. 30107 D

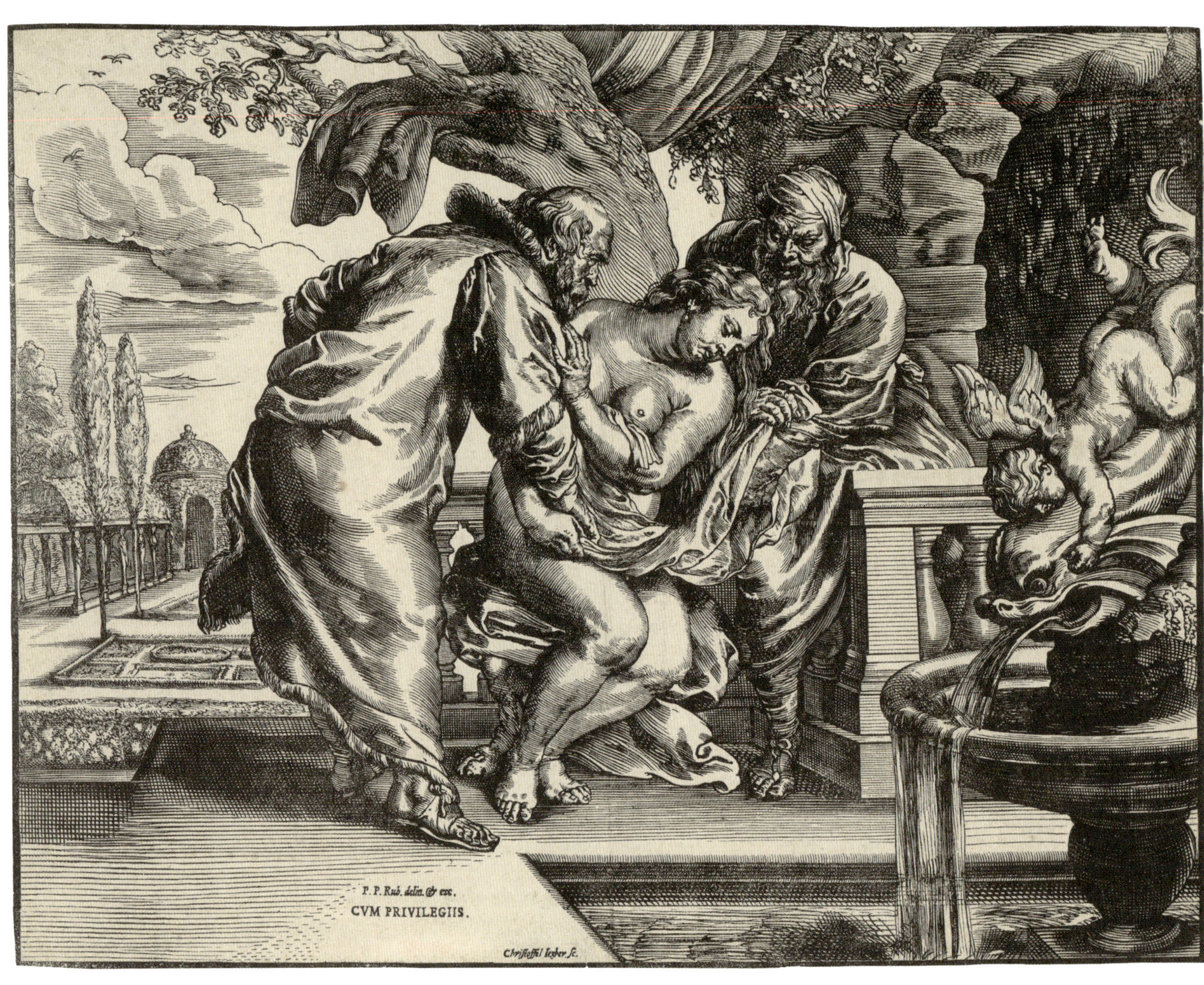

Rubens (Inventor, Verleger / designer, publisher), Christoffel Jegher (Holzschneider / woodcutter)
Susanna und die beiden Alten / Susanna and the Elders, 1633–1635
Holzschnitt / woodcut SGSM, Inv. 30004 D

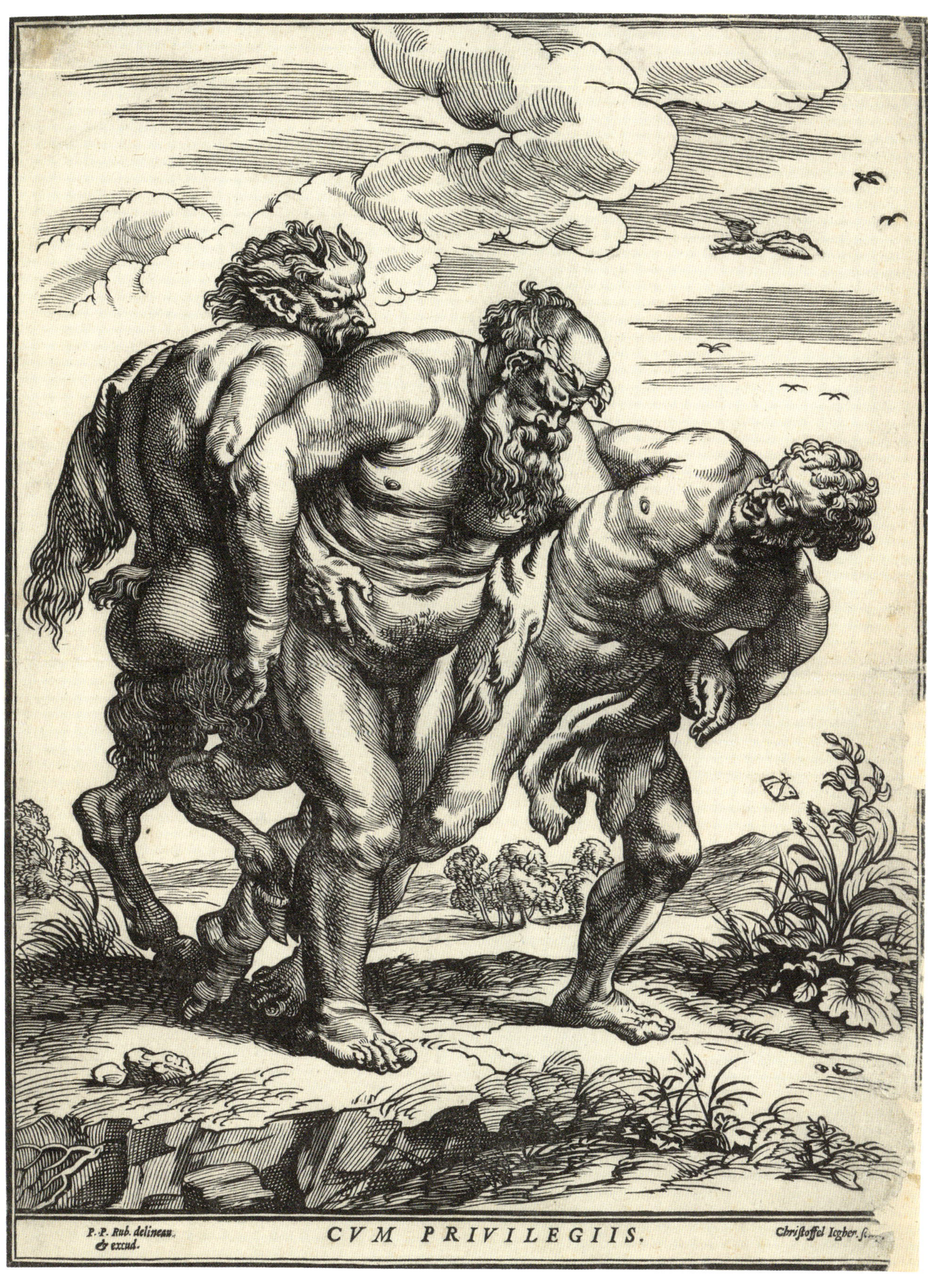

Rubens (Inventor, Verleger / designer, publisher), Christoffel Jegher (Holzschneider / woodcutter)
Der trunkene Silen / Drunken Silenus, 1633–1635
Holzschnitt / woodcut SGSM, Inv. 111422 D

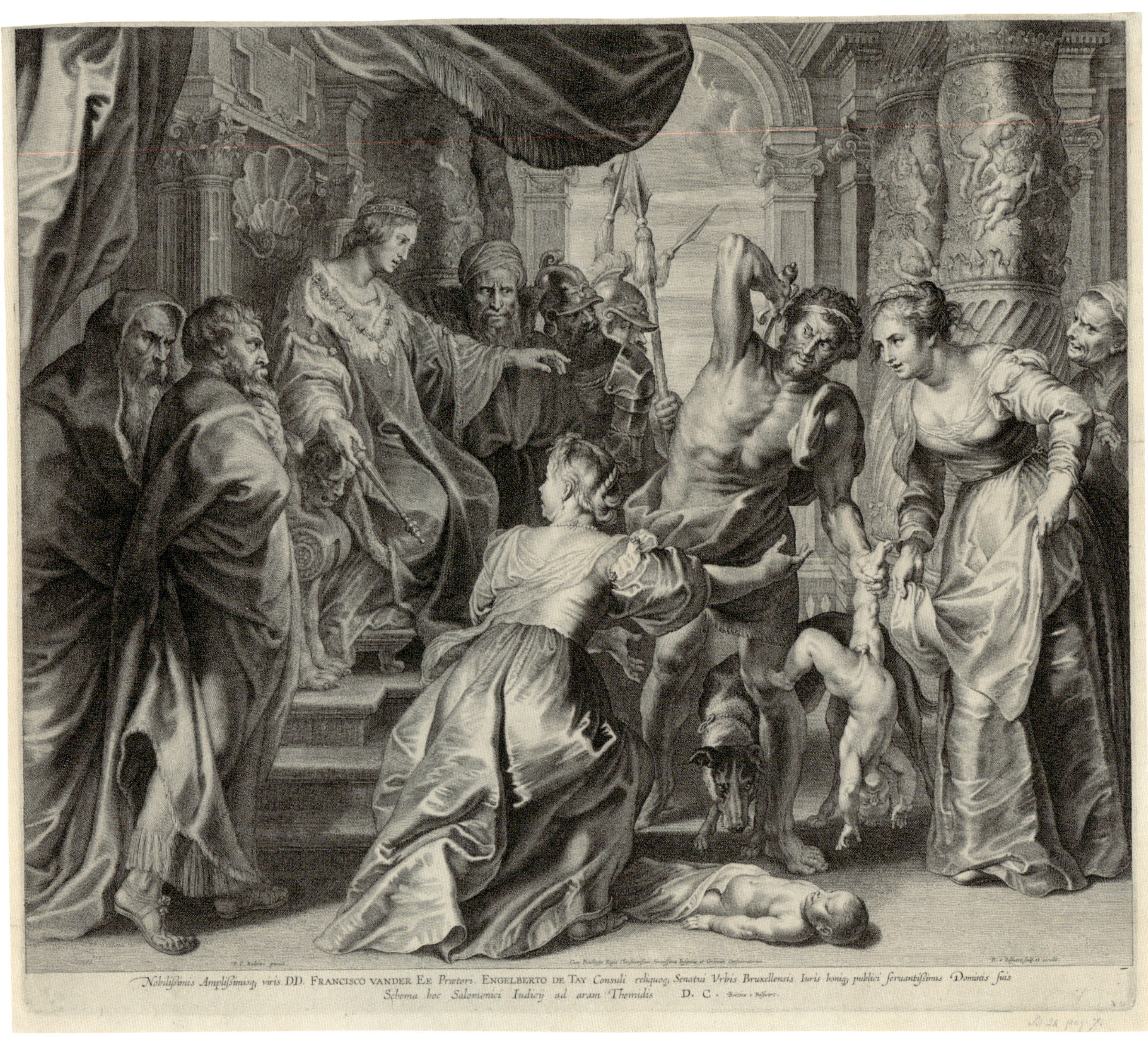

Boëtius à Bolswert (Stecher, Verleger / engraver, publisher), nach Rubens
Das Urteil des Salomon / The Judgment of Solomon, vor / before 1633
Kupferstich / engraving SGSM, Inv. 29990 D

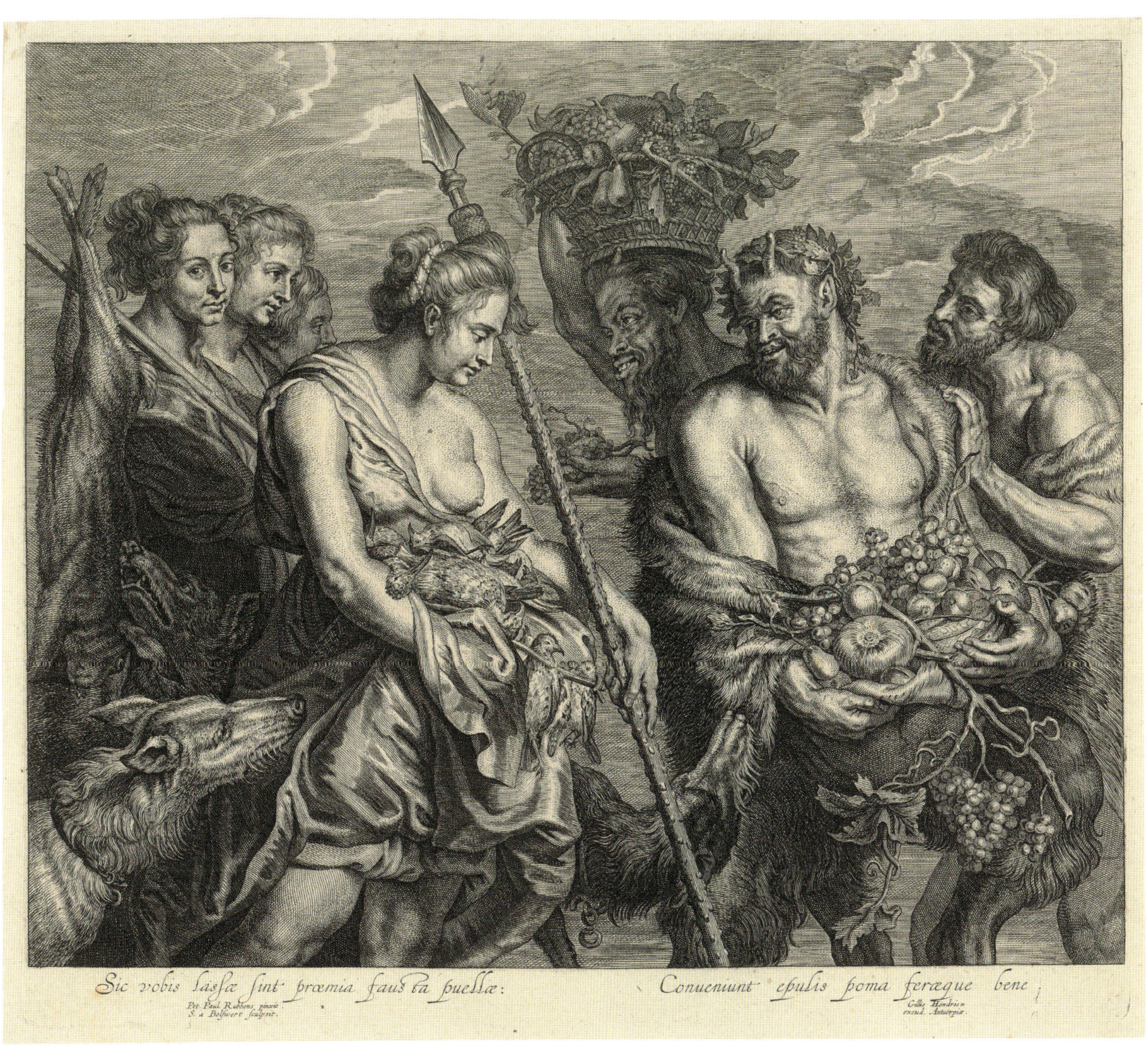

Schelte à Bolswert (Stecher / engraver), nach / after Rubens, Gilles Hendricx (Verleger / publisher)
Diana kehrt von der Jagd zurück / Diana Returning from the Hunt, ca. 1638
Kupferstich / engraving SGSM, Inv. 30453 D

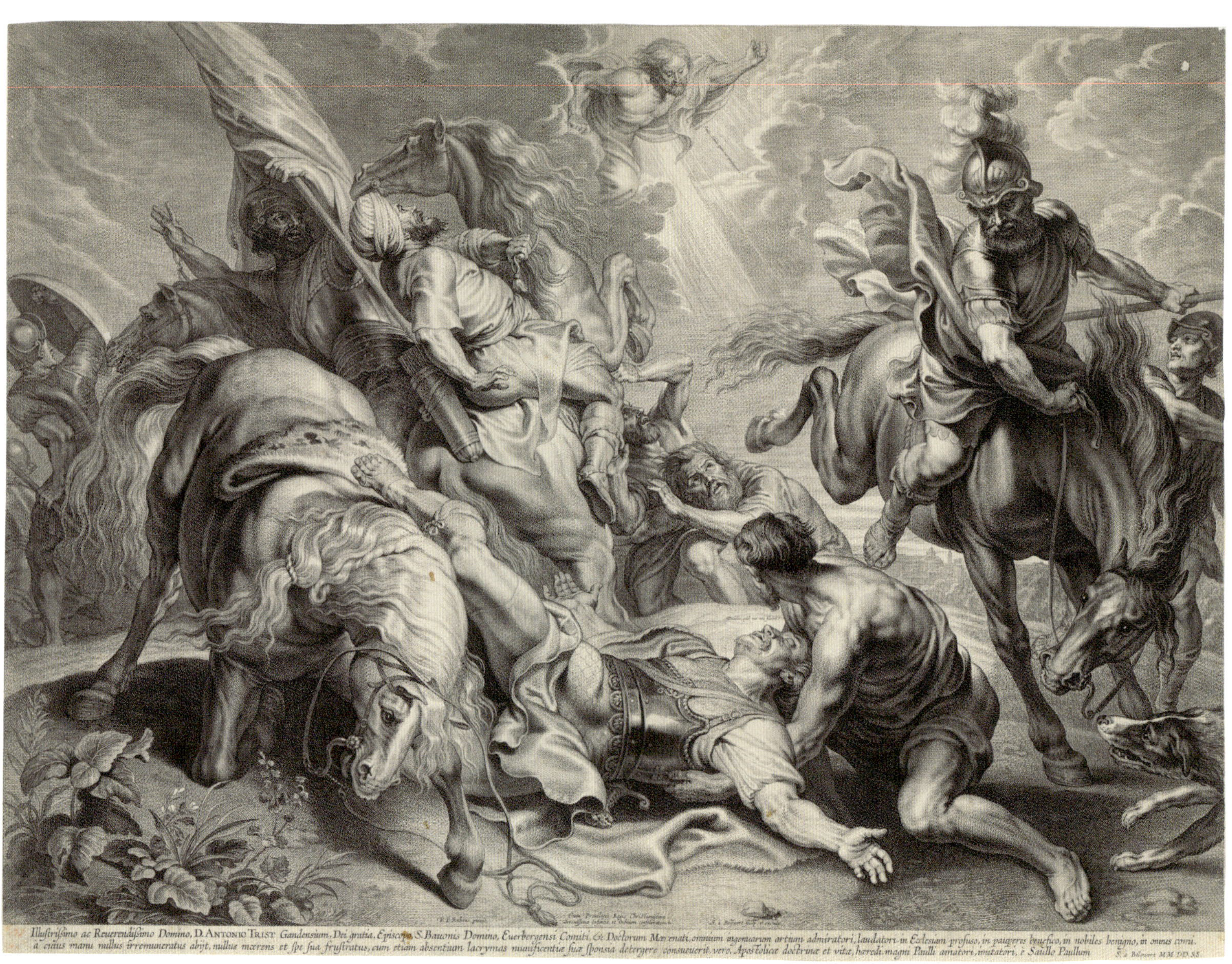

Schelte à Bolswert (Stecher, Verleger / engraver, publisher), nach / after Rubens
Die Bekehrung des Paulus / The Conversion of St. Paul, 1633
Kupferstich / engraving SGSM, Inv. 215618 D

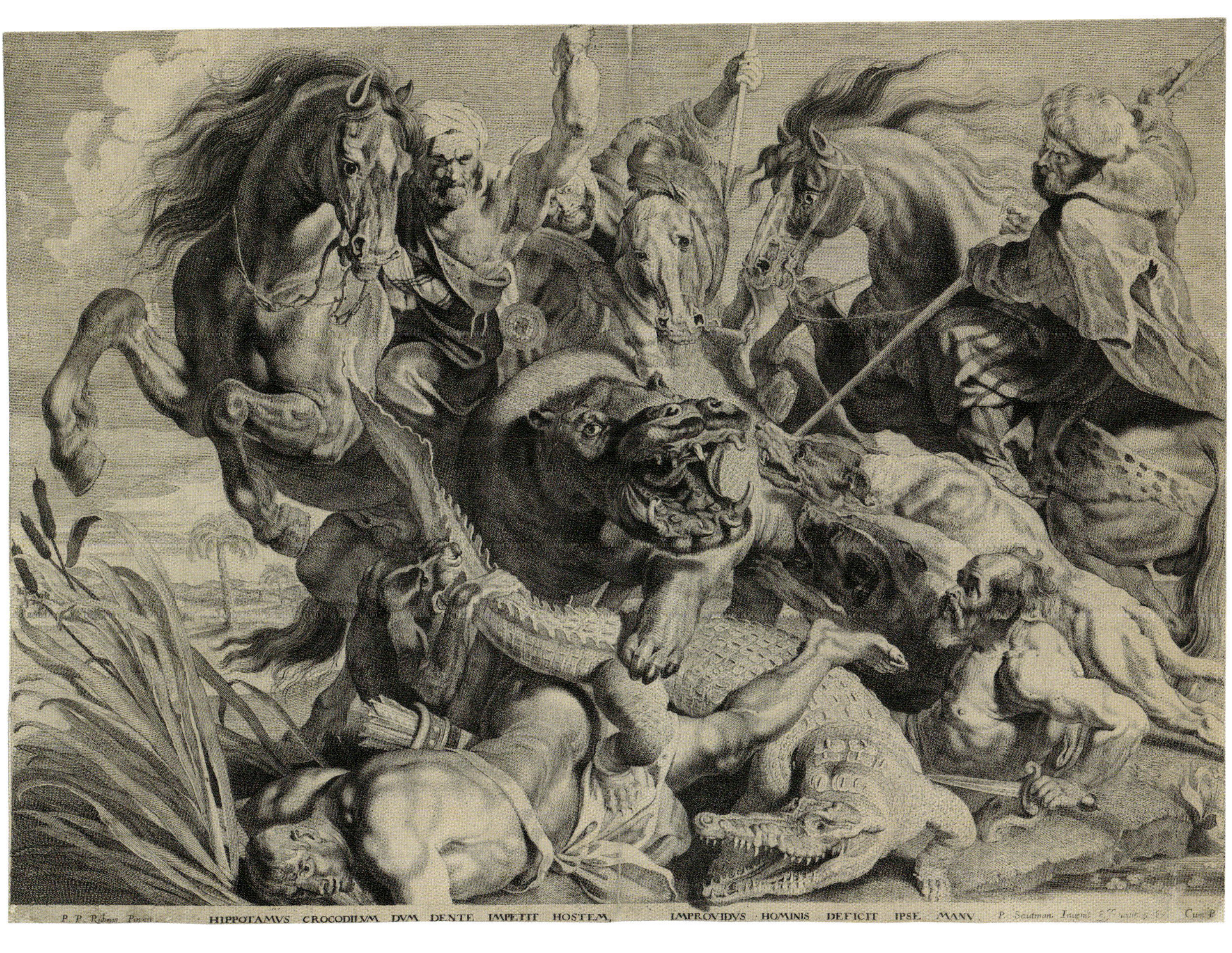

Pieter Soutman (Stecher, Radierer, Verleger / engraver, etcher, publisher), nach / after Rubens
Die Nilpferdjagd / Hippopotamus Hunt, ca. 1640/41
Kupferstich, Radierung / engraving, etching SGSM, Inv. 2021:506 D

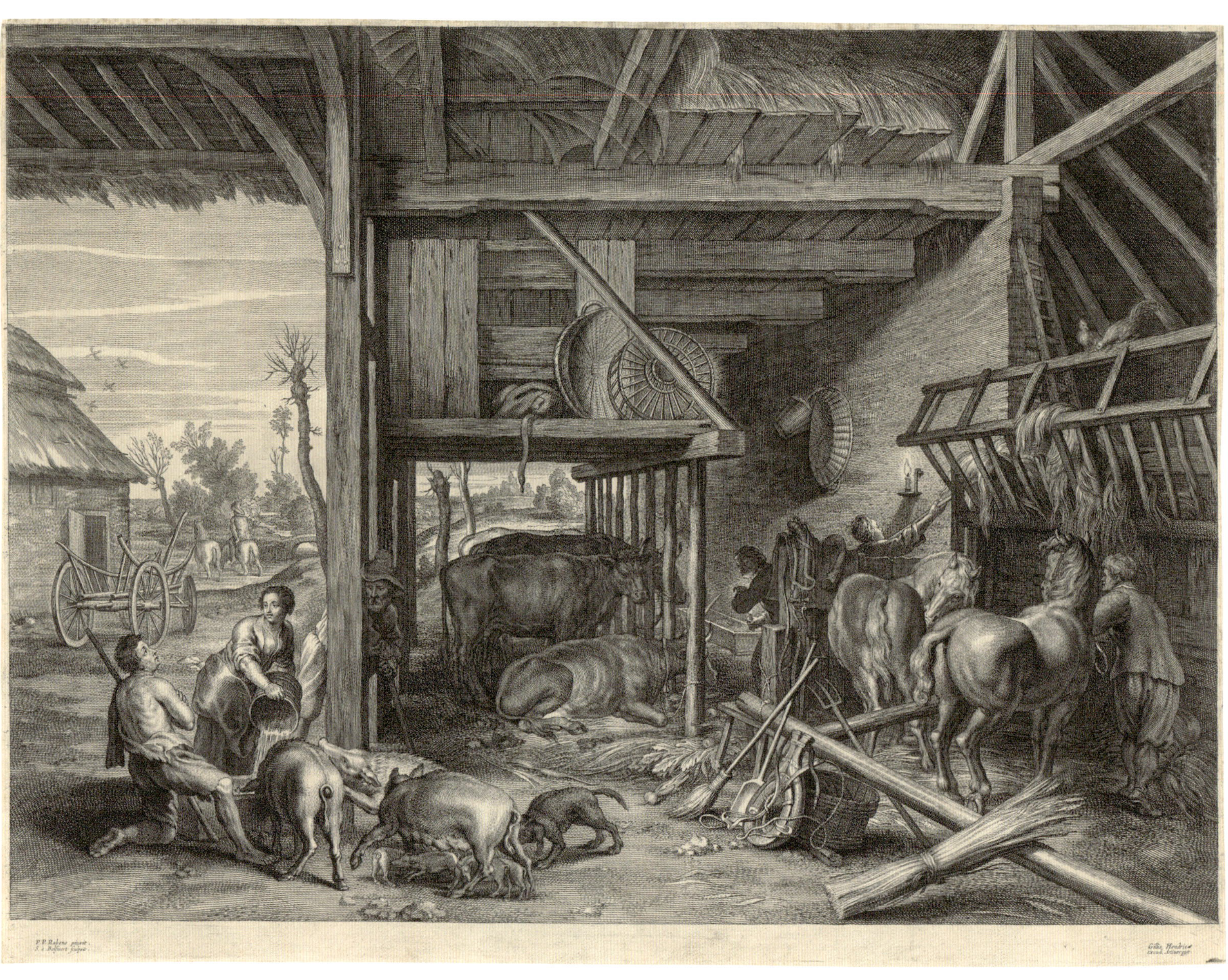

Schelte à Bolswert (Stecher / engraver), nach / after Rubens, Gilles Hendricx (Verleger / publisher)
Landschaft mit dem verlorenen Sohn / Landscape with the Prodigal Son, ca. 1638
Kupferstich / engraving SGSM, Inv. 30529 D

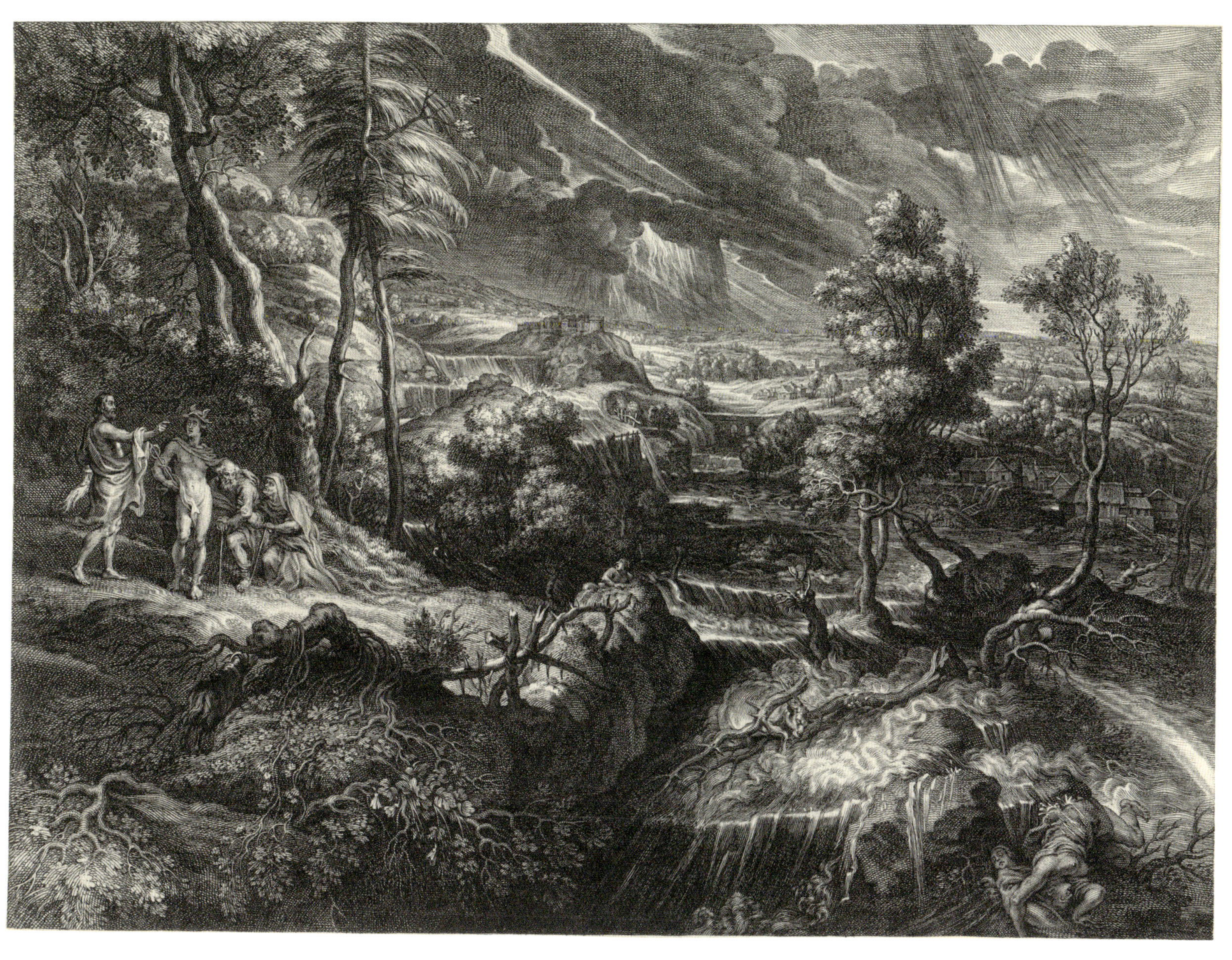

Schelte à Bolswert (Stecher / engraver), nach / after Rubens, Gilles Hendricx (Verleger / publisher)
Gewitterlandschaft mit Philemon und Baucis / Landscape with a Thunderstorm and Philemon and Baucis, ca. 1638
Kupferstich / engraving SGSM, Inv. 30528 D

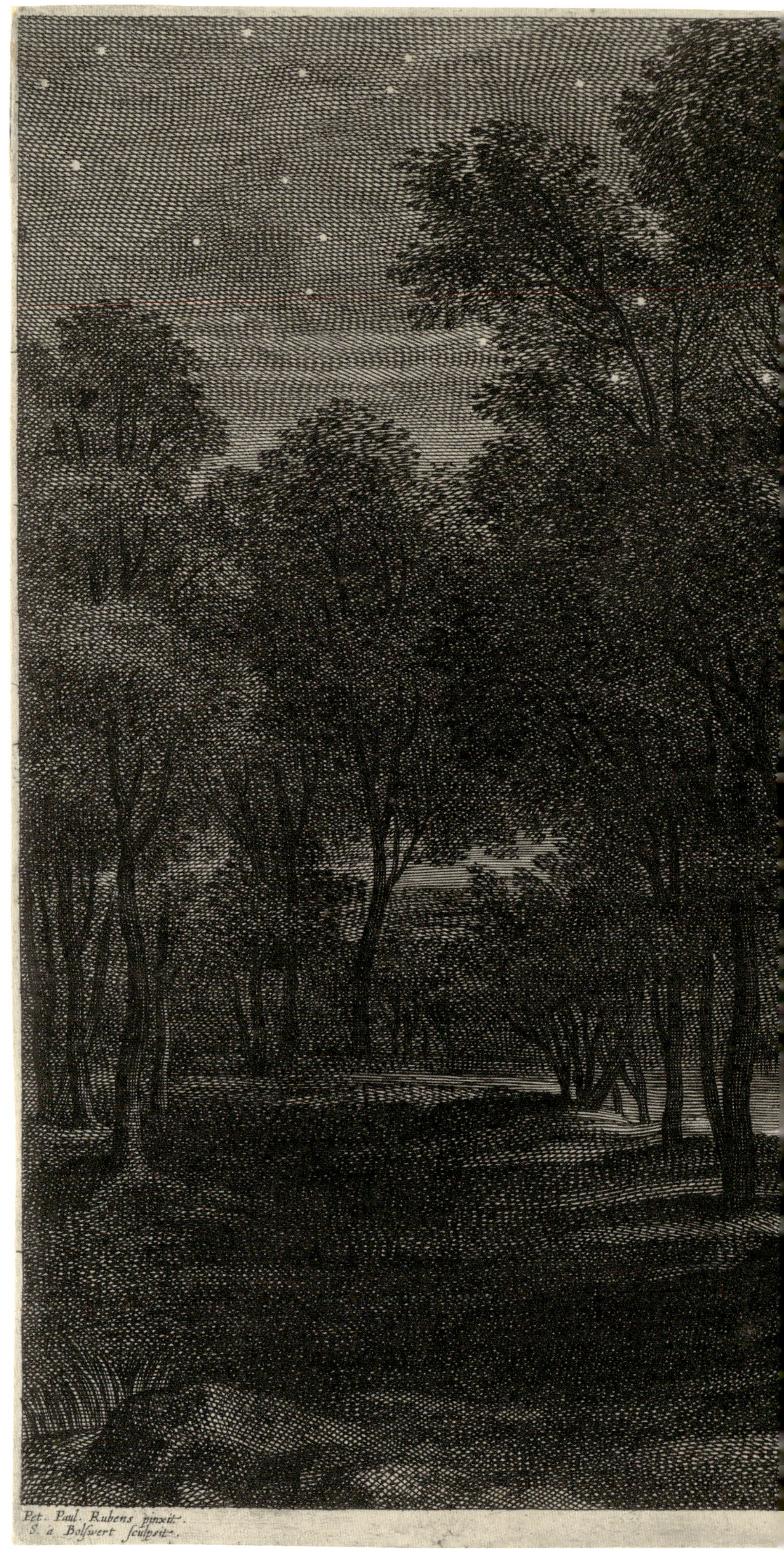

Schelte à Bolswert (Stecher, Radierer / engraver, etcher),
nach / after Rubens,
Gilles Hendricx (Verleger / publisher)
Eine Flusslandschaft im Mondschein /
Landscape with the Moon and Stars, ca. 1638
Kupferstich, Radierung / engraving, etching
SGSM, Inv. 30521 D

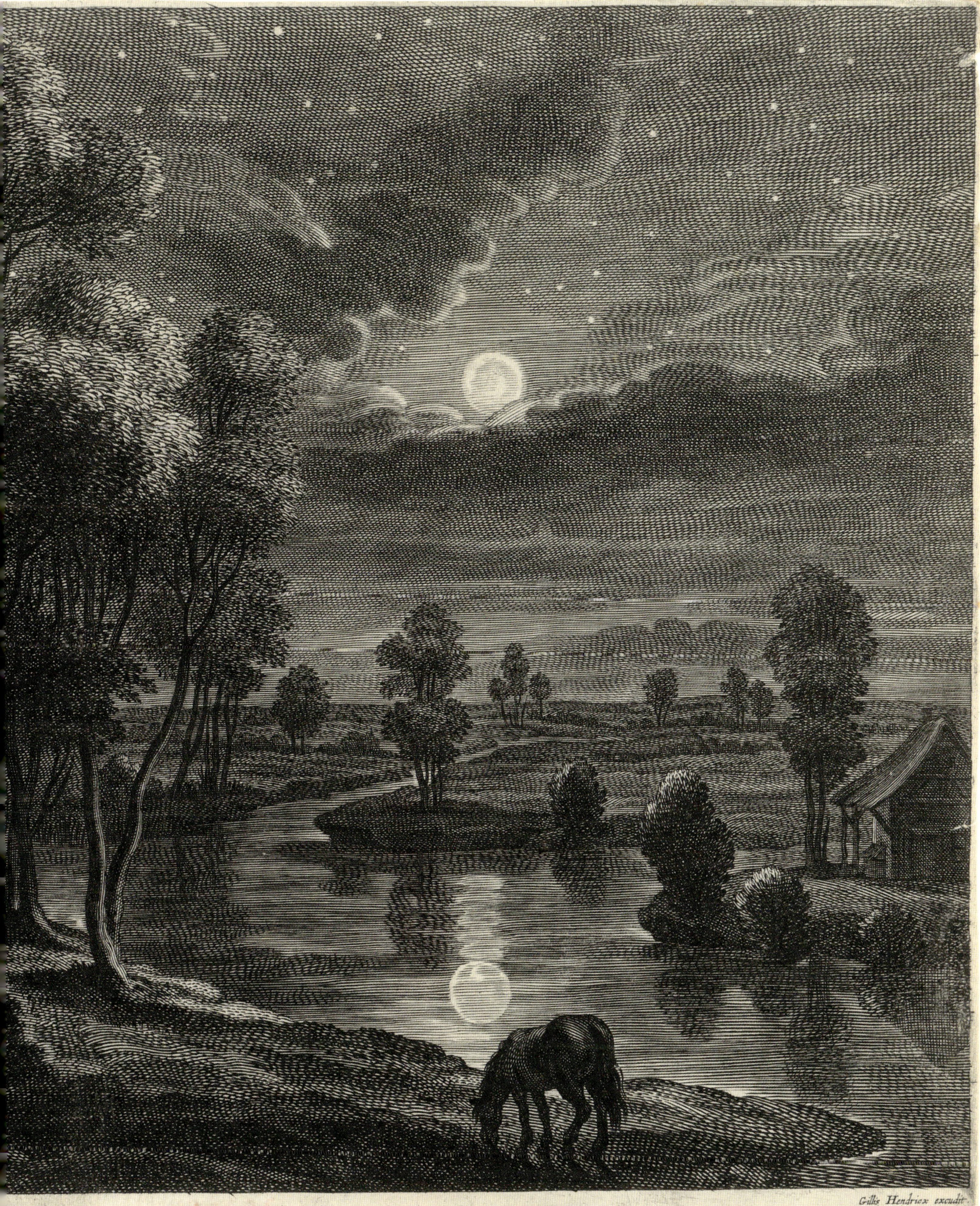
Gillis Hendricx excudit.

VIII. Antike

Ab dem 16. Jahrhundert, als das Reisen durch Europa dank verbesserter Transportwege verbreiteter wurde, galt eine Rom-Reise als Teil jeder guten Künstlerausbildung, als Muss für jede Künstlervita. Neben der antiken Architektur waren es berühmte antike Skulpturen, welche die angereisten Künstler aufsuchten und nachzeichneten. Kunstwerke der Antike verkörperten, auch aufgrund antiker und zeitgenössischer Schriften, ein künstlerisches Ideal. Beide, Hendrick Goltzius wie Peter Paul Rubens, legten sich eine Sammlung von skulpturalen Antiken zu.[1] Im Nachzeichnen wollte man sich vor Ort diesen Vorbildern annähern und die entstandenen Zeichnungen später als *ricordi* mit nach Hause nehmen. Mit solchen „Souvenirs“ konnten die Heimkehrer belegen, dass sie die Rom-Reise unternommen und sich wortwörtlich ein eigenes Bild gemacht hatten. Die Blätter mehrten zudem das Ansehen ihrer

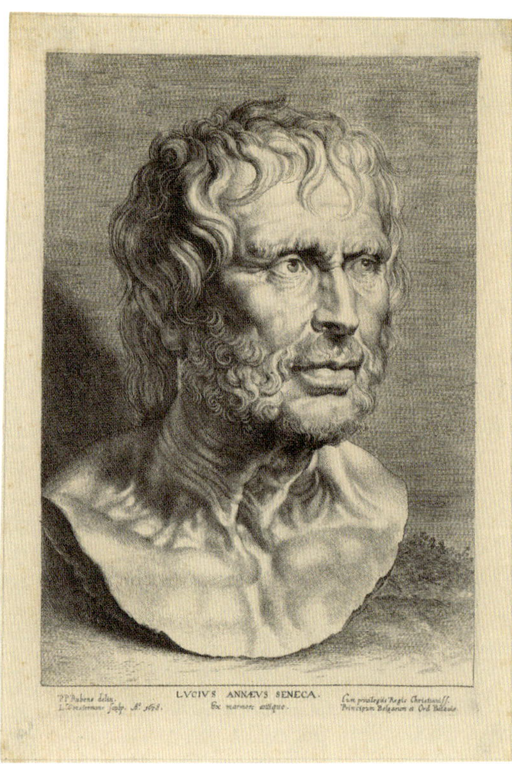

Rubens (Inventor / designer), Lucas Vorsterman I (Stecher / engraver)
Büste des Seneca / Bust of Seneca, 1638
Kupferstich / engraving SGSM, Inv. 2023:6 D

Schöpfer, weil sie von deren Gelehrsamkeit zeugten. Sowohl von Goltzius (Rom-Reise 1590/91) als auch von Rubens (Italien-Aufenthalt 1600–1608) sind Antikenzeichnungen erhalten – sie zählen bis heute zu den am meisten bewunderten Antikenzeichnungen überhaupt.[2] Ein weiterer Vorteil war, dass diese Motive in der Folge in eigenen Kompositionen verwendet werden konnten, bei Goltzius in Stichen, bei Rubens in Gemälden. Victoria Sancho Lobis resümiert:

VIII. Antiquity

From the sixteenth century on, when travel through Europe became easier and more widely practiced, a trip to Rome was a must in the training of all ambitious artists. Besides Classical architecture, many famous ancient sculptures were on display there and could be visited and drawn. Also, owing to Classical and contemporary writings, ancient Roman artworks constituted an ideal in art. Both Hendrick Goltzius and Peter Paul Rubens built collections of sculptural antiquities.[1] By drawing in situ after these works, artists wanted to approximate their models and take the resulting *ricordi* home with them later on. With such “souvenirs,” they could prove to those who had stayed behind that they had indeed taken the trip to Rome and formed a picture of it for themselves—literally. Such drawings also enhanced the reputation

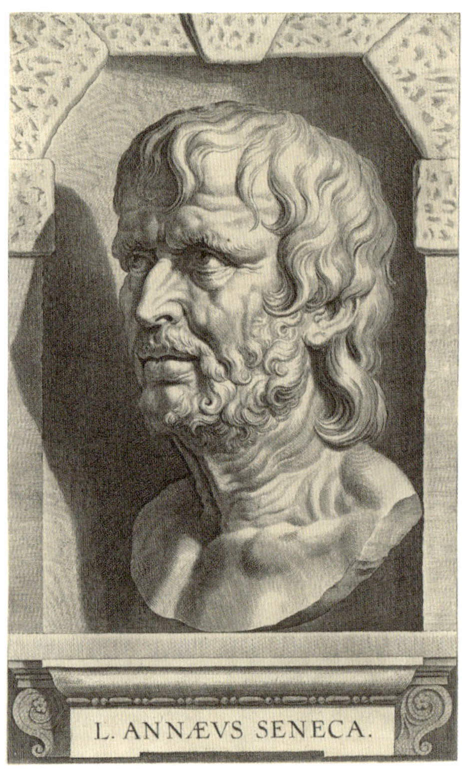

Cornelis Galle I (zugeschr. Stecher / attr. engraver),
nach / after Rubens
Büste des Seneca / Bust of Seneca, 1615
Kupferstich / engraving SGSM, Inv. 30608 D

of their creators, testifying to their erudition. Drawings after Roman sculptures are extant by both Goltzius (Rome, 1590/91) and Rubens (Italy, 1600–1608). They are among the most admired drawings after antiquities of all times.[2] A further advantage was that these motifs could be used in new compositions: in Goltzius’s case in prints, and in Rubens’s case in paintings. Victoria Sancho Lobis remarks, “In many ways Goltzius and Rubens epitomize

„In mehrererlei Hinsicht sind Goltzius und Rubens Inbegriff davon, wie niederländische Künstler danach strebten, das Studium antiker Quellen in eigene Erfindungen einzubauen."[3] Die berühmtesten ihrer Nachzeichnungen nach Antiken wurden mittels Stichen verbreitet. Zeitgenossen wie Nachwelt lobten und sammelten diese. Unter Fachleuten ist die Ansicht verbreitet, dass Rubens einige Nachzeichnungen von Goltzius kannte und sich mit ihnen messen wollte, womöglich sogar eine Mappe mit eigenhändigen Antikenzeichnungen des Kollegen besaß.[4]

Drei antike Hauptwerke arbeitete Goltzius 1592 in Stichen aus, welche allerdings aus unbekannten Gründen erst 1617, nach seinem Tod, verlegt wurden: den *Apoll vom Belvedere*, *Herkules und Telephos* sowie in einer berühmt gewordenen Rückenansicht den *Herkules Farnese* (Abb. S. 227, 225, 223). „Wir verdanken es Goltzius' Stich, dass die Rückseite der Statue genauso populär wurde wie die Vorderseite", befindet Michiel Plomp.[5] Er vertritt auch die Auffassung, dass Goltzius, im Gegensatz zu seinen Vorläufern, mit seinen Stichen nicht nur Künstler, sondern auch interessierte Laien ansprechen wollte.[6] Weil diese Blätter eine einheitliche Größe aufweisen, ist darüber gemutmaßt worden, ob Goltzius vielleicht ein Buch mit Stichen nach Antiken anvisierte. Doch die Größe der Blätter (rund 400 × 300 mm) hätte bedeutet, dass ein Prachtband vonnöten gewesen wäre, was eine enorme Investition für jeden Verleger impliziert hätte. Damit erklärt sich vielleicht, warum ein Buchprojekt nicht mehr zustande kam.[7]

Eine wichtige Neuerung der Goltzius-Stiche war die Genauigkeit, mit der er die Statuen angesehen und gezeichnet hat. Zudem waren seine Blickwinkel anders als die von Vorgängern, die meist einen höheren Standpunkt gewählt hatten und die, im Gegensatz zu Goltzius, die Skulpturen isoliert von ihrem Umfeld zeigten.[8] Das Bildnis eines zeichnenden Künstlers neben dem *Apoll* sowie die beiden Betrachter des *Herkules Farnese* hat nicht Goltzius in die Kompositionen eingefügt, sondern sie wurden vor der Drucklegung 1617 ergänzt.[9] Die Porträts haben zu der Popularität der Blätter in den folgenden Jahrhunderten enorm beigetragen.

Mit dem auf eine Episode aus Ovids antikem Dichtwerk *Metamorphosen* zurückgehenden Blatt *Pygmalion und Galatea* (1593) führt Goltzius uns vor Augen, wie geschickt und ansprechend er seine zwei Jahre zuvor in Italien erworbenen Antikenkenntnisse in seine eigenen Schöpfungen einfließen ließ (Abb. S. 229). In der Körperhaltung des Pgymalion finden sich Anlehnungen an den *Torso Belvedere*, Galatea nimmt die Haltung einer Venus pudica ein. Und doch wirken beide

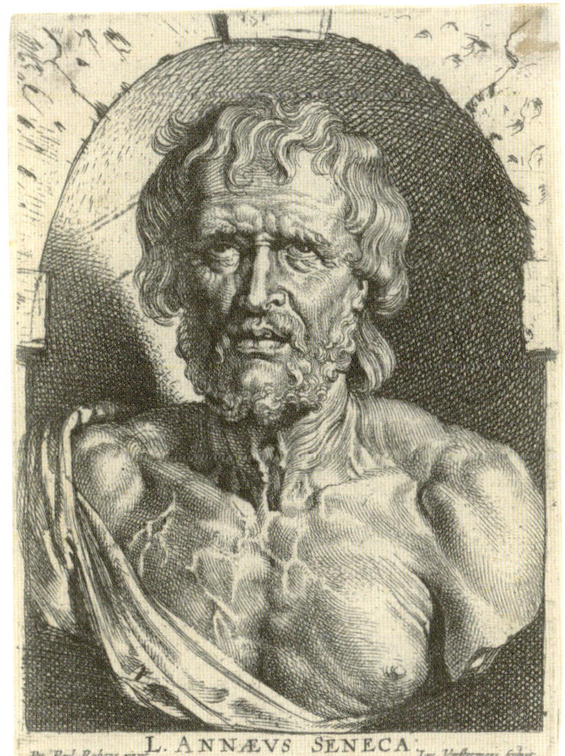

Rubens (Inventor, Radierer / designer, etcher),
Lucas Vorsterman I (Stecher / engraver)
Büste des Seneca / Bust of Seneca, ca. 1620
Radierung, Kupferstich / etching, engraving SGSM, Inv. 30595 D

how Netherlandish artists strove to incorporate study of Classical sources into their own inventions."[3] The most famous of their drawings of ancient Roman art were publicized through prints which both contemporaries and posterity praised and collected. Experts believe that Rubens was familiar with some of Goltzius's drawings of ancient artworks and may have felt challenged to outdo them, and that he may have had in his possession a portfolio of autograph drawings after Classical artworks by Goltzius.[4]

In 1592, Goltzius made engravings after three antique masterworks. For unknown reasons, however, these prints—the *Apollo Belvedere*, *Hercules and Telephos*, and a back view of the *Farnese Hercules* (figs. pp. 227, 225, 223)—were not published until 1617, after his death. "It was thanks to Goltzius's engraving that the back view of the statue became as popular as the front," Michiel Plomp believes.[5] He also thinks that Goltzius, in contrast to his predecessors, wanted to reach not only artists but also an interested lay audience.[6] Due to the fact that all three sheets have the same format, it has been speculated that Goltzius was planning a book with engravings after ancient Roman sculpture. However, the sheer size of the paper (ca. 400 × 300 mm) called for a luxury tome that would represent a financial risk for any publisher. This may explain why this book was never made.[7]

One novelty in Goltzius's prints was the precision with which he looked at and captured the statues. Moreover, the vantage point Goltzius chose differed from that of his predecessors in that it was lower and also showed the sculptures' surroundings.[8] The images of the draftsman next to the *Apollo Belvedere* and of the two admirers next to the *Farnese Hercules* were added to the plates not by Goltzius but by someone else shortly before the works were printed in 1617.[9] The inclusion of these figures greatly contributed to the popularity the prints enjoyed in the following centuries.

With the print *Pygmalion and Galatea* (1593), which depicts an episode from Ovid's Classical poem *Metamorphoses*, Goltzius demonstrated how cleverly and beautifully he was able to integrate into his own compositions the knowledge of Classical sculpture he had acquired two years earlier in Italy (fig. p. 229). The posture of Pygmalion is reminiscent of the *Belvedere Torso*, while Galatea adopts the stance of a Venus pudica. And yet neither figure looks like a stony monument, even

Figuren nicht wie steinerne Monumente, obwohl dies der Erzählung nach auf Galatea zutraf. Vielmehr ist auffällig, dass Pygmalion sich in seiner Verehrung selbst zu versteinern scheint, während Galateas Haut und Schritthaltung auf eine einsetzende Verlebendigung hindeuten. Die Altphilologin Anja Wolkenhauer hat darauf hingewiesen, dass es zudem eine Diskrepanz zwischen Ovids Geschichte, die in der Bildunterschrift paraphrasiert wird, und Goltzius' Darstellung gibt:[10] Anders als im antiken Text ist Galatea nicht aus Elfenbein gefertigt und die Werkzeuge, die Pygmalion zu ihrer Erschaffung benutzt, sind die eines Steinmetzes, nicht eines Schnitzers. Für die gelehrten Zeitgenossen waren zwei weitere Aspekte an diesem Blatt abzulesen: Goltzius thematisierte den Wettstreit der Künste und die ethische Dimension des Motivs, das als eine Warnung vor Selbstzufriedenheit verstanden wurde.[11]

Die erwähnten Moralvorstellungen im Umkreis von Goltzius wurden stark beeinflusst von neostoischem Denken, das der Künstler bereits bei seinem Lehrer Dirck Volckertsz. Coornhert (1522–1590) kennengelernt hatte und das auch in der humanistisch geprägten Bildung von Rubens eine große Rolle spielen würde.[12] Die neostoische Lehre, die sich unter anderem auf die Schriften des römischen Philosophen und Politikers Lucius Annaeus Seneca (um 4 v. Chr. – 65 n. Chr.) berief, bedeutete für beide Künstler nicht theoretisches Philosophieren, sondern war vor allem ein moralischer Handlungsfaden. Vor diesem Hintergrund erklärt sich, warum ein bestimmtes Motiv im Werk beider Künstler eine besondere Rolle spielte: *Sine Cerere et Baccho friget Venus*, zu Deutsch: Ohne Ceres und Bacchus friert Venus, oder: Ohne Speis und Trank kein Begehren.[13] Diese Auffassung war fest im neostoischen Gedankengut verwurzelt, weil es die Mäßigung der Affekte anmahnte, eine zentrale Lehre der Stoa: Das harmonische, maßhaltende Zusammenspiel dieser drei Figuren / Begehren macht ein gutes Leben aus. In den vermutlich von Jan Saenredam um 1595 ausgeführten Stichen nach Goltzius-Entwürfen sind die drei Götter zwar getrennt dargestellt, beziehen sich als Serie aber aufeinander (Abb. S. 230 f.). Die Schmuckrahmen weisen die Motive als Serie aus. Mit seinen überaus attraktiven Protagonisten sowie der Widmung der Serie an seinen Künstlerfreund Cornelis Cornelisz. van Haarlem brachte Goltzius das antike Thema in eine zeitgemäße Form. Alle drei Götter strahlen eine innere Ruhe aus, die aus ihrem Dreiklang erwächst und die für jeden Neostoiker erstrebenswert ist. Die von Saenredam erzielte technische Vollkommenheit sicherte den Blättern in den folgenden Jahrhunderten große Aufmerksamkeit an Kunstakademien, wo sie besonders oft kopiert wurden.[14]

Auch Rubens war mit neostoischen Lehren vertraut, denn sein älterer Bruder Philip (1574–1611) war Schüler des wichtigsten nordeuropäischen Verfechters dieser Ethik, des Philosophen Justus Lipsius (1547–1606).[15] Rubens zählte selbst zu den gelehrtesten Altertumsforschern seiner Zeit, was auch seine Kenntnis antiker Texte und Kunstwerke einschloss.[16] Zudem erwarb er vom englischen Gesandten in Den Haag, Sir Dudley Carleton, eine eigene Antikensammlung, die europaweit einen sehr guten Ruf genoss.[17] Zu Rubens' Lieblingsstücken zählte eine Marmorbüste in seiner Sammlung, von der man damals annahm, sie stelle Seneca dar.[18] Der antike Philosoph war der Inbegriff des stoischen Weisen, der sein Leben und Sterben nach den Maximen dieser Lehre ausgerichtet hatte. In gleich mehreren Stichen zeigte Rubens

though that is what Galatea was, according to the story. Rather, it is remarkable that Pygmalion, in his admiration for her, seems to turn into stone himself, while Galatea's skin and gait suggest she is coming alive. The Classical philologist Anja Wolkenhauer has pointed out a deviation from Ovid's story as paraphrased in the epigram and shown in Goltzius's depiction:[10] In a departure from the ancient text, Galatea is not made of ivory, and the tools Pygmalion uses to create her are not those of an ivory carver but of a stonemason. Learned contemporary viewers could discern two further aspects in Goltzius's print: He addressed the rivalry of the arts (paragone) and the moral dimension of this motif, which was understood as a warning against self-satisfaction.[11]

The abovementioned moral conceptions in Goltzius's circle were strongly influenced by Neo-Stoic thinking, with which the artist had been familiarized through his teacher Dirck Volckertsz. Coornhert (1522–1590). This ideology was also to play a great role in Rubens's humanist education.[12] Neo-Stoic teachings, based on the writings of the Roman philosopher and politician Lucius Annaeus Seneca (ca. 4 BCE–65 CE) and others, were to both artists not mere philosophical theorizing but a guide for ethical behavior. It is before this background that one specific motif especially appealed to both artists: *sine Cerere et Baccho friget Venus*, which can be translated as "Without Ceres and Bacchus, Venus grows cold." Understood more loosely: "Without food and drink there is no desire."[13] This idea was strongly rooted in Neo-Stoic conceptions because it urged a striving for affective moderation, one of the central tenets of Stoa: The harmonious, temperate interaction of these three figures / desires was what constituted a good life. The prints (probably executed by Jan Saenredam in 1595) after Goltzius's designs present the three gods—*Ceres*, *Bacchus*, and *Venus and Cupid*—separate from one another, yet the ornamental frames declare them to be a series (figs. pp. 230–231). With extremely attractive protagonists and a dedication to his artist friend Cornelis Cornelisz. van Haarlem, Goltzius found a magnificent form for this ancient theme. All three gods radiate inner calm which, as is fitting for this theme and as befits every Neo-Stoic, grows out of their triad harmony. The technical perfection Saenredam achieved in these prints secured them in the following centuries much attention in art academies, where they were often copied.[14]

Rubens, too, was familiar with Neo-Stoic ideas, because his older brother Philip (1574–1611) was a student of the philosopher Justus Lipsius (1547–1606), the most important representative of this school of ethics.[15] Rubens was one of the most respected experts in antiquity due to his intimate knowledge of the era's texts and artworks.[16] In addition, he bought a collection of ancient artworks that enjoyed excellent repute throughout Europe from Sir Dudley Carleton, British envoy to The Hague.[17] Among Rubens's favorite pieces was a marble bust in his collection that was then assumed to be of Seneca.[18] This Classical philosopher was the epitome of the Stoic wise man who had arranged his life according to the maxims of these teachings. In several prints Rubens had this bust shown from different angles. The first came from Cornelis Galle I (1576–1650), who engraved it in 1615 for the Seneca book

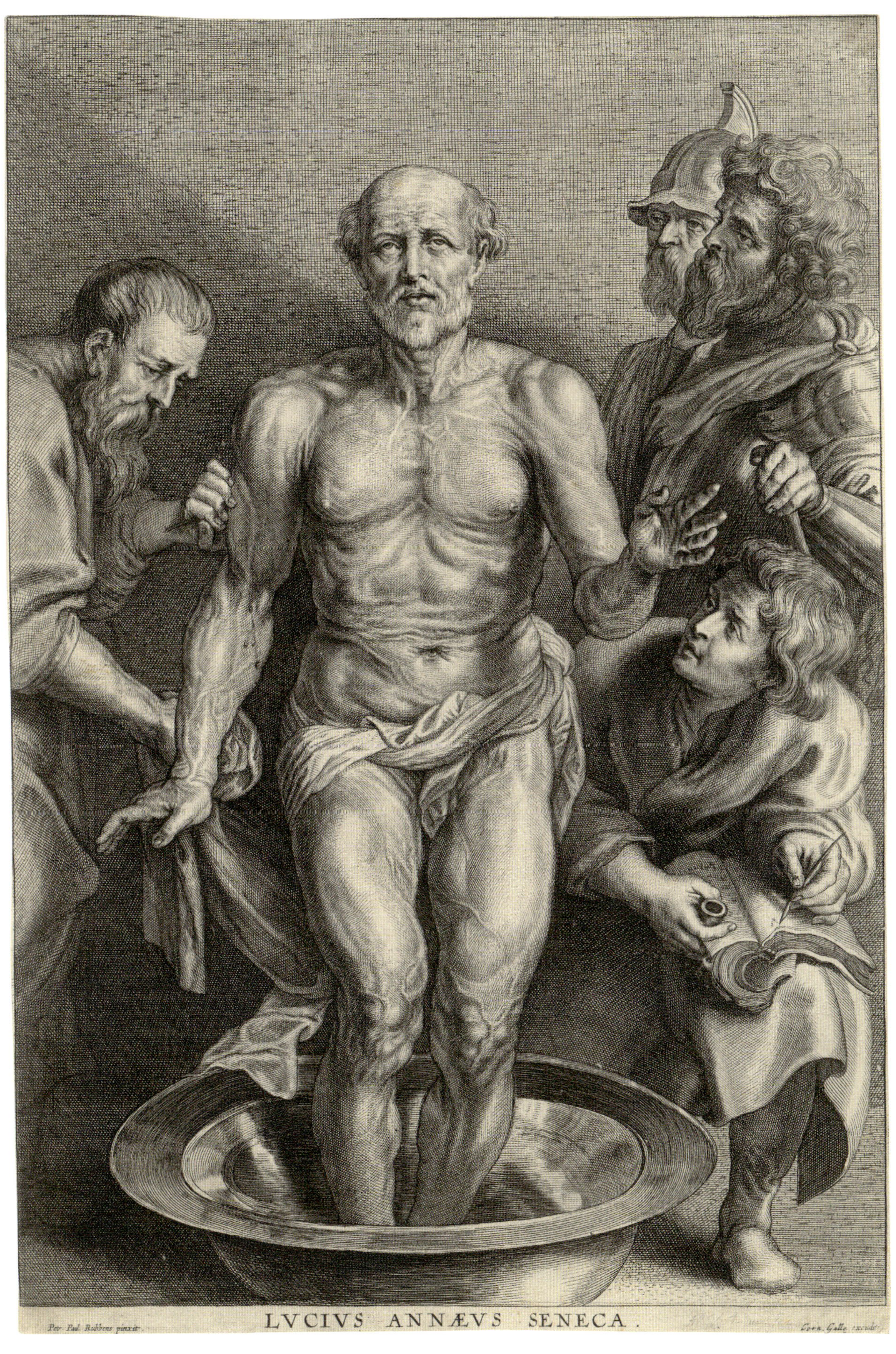

Alexander Voet II (Stecher / engraver), nach / after Rubens,
Cornelis Galle II (Verleger / publisher)
Der sterbende Seneca / The Death of Seneca, 1650–1678
Kupferstich / engraving SGSM, Inv. 30394 D

seine in Italien erworbene Büste aus unterschiedlichen Blickwinkeln. Cornelis Galle I (1576–1650) fertigte 1615 den ersten Stich als Illustration für die *Seneca*-Ausgabe von Justus Lipsius an (Abb. S. 218); Lucas Vorsterman I (1595/96–1674/75) stach das Motiv für eine Serie von zwölf Büsten und Köpfen antiker Philosophen und Kaiser, die Rubens 1638 veröffentlichte (Abb. S. 218); und schließlich ist eine kleinformatige Radierung aus der Zeit um 1620 erhalten, die in ihrer ersten Anlage Rubens selbst zugeschrieben werden kann (Abb. S. 219). Es ist eine dieser drei Radierungen, bei denen seit ihrer Entstehung darüber spekuliert wird, ob Rubens die Radiernadel selbst geführt haben könnte. Im Fall des *Seneca* sprechen Indizien dafür.[19] Vorsterman hat das Blatt mit dem Grabstichel überarbeitet und mit Rubens' und seiner eigenen Signatur versehen. Sicher ging es Rubens mit all diesen Reproduktionen nicht nur darum, seine Bewunderung für diese Antike zu zeigen. Seine Aufträge für die Stiche legen nahe, dass er gewisse Werke größeren Kreisen bekannt machen wollte – und damit sich selbst als ihren gelehrten Besitzer und kundigen Erforscher.

Höhepunkt von Rubens' Auseinandersetzung mit Seneca war sein heute in der Alten Pinakothek in München verwahrtes Gemälde *Der sterbende Seneca* (1612/13). Es zeigt die von dem Philosophen selbst gewählte Sterbeszene, ein Schreiber, dem er seine letzten Worte diktiert, ist ebenfalls im Bild zu sehen. Da es eine zentrale Lehre Senecas war, die Angst vor dem Tod zu überwinden, sollte sein eigenes Sterben als stoisches Exemplum dienen. Verfolgt von den Häschern des Kaisers Nero suchte Seneca den Freitod. Um diesen darzustellen, vereinte Rubens den Körper einer ihm bekannten Marmorstatue mit der Seneca-Büste in seinem Besitz. Den Stich nach dieser „Ikone neostoischer Philosophie", wie das Bild genannt worden ist, schuf Alexander Voet II Jahre nach Rubens' Tod zwischen 1650 und 1678 und wohl im Auftrag des damaligen Besitzers des Gemäldes (Abb. S. 221).[20] Rubens' Bewunderung für diese Skulptur wie auch für die Seneca-Büste ging aus seiner Überzeugung hervor, „dass zur höchsten Vollendung der Malerei die Kenntnis der Statuen, ja sogar die tiefe Vertrautheit mit ihnen nötig ist".[21]

Wie Goltzius war Rubens ein Meister darin, berühmte antike Statuen in seine eigenen Kompositionen so einzuflechten, dass Kenner sie zwar identifizieren konnten, sie aber innerhalb des neu geschaffenen Werks dennoch überzeugend wirkten.[22] Rubens selbst hatte in einem Manuskript über antike Statuen, das er zu veröffentlichen hoffte, erläutert, bei der motivischen Einbindung antiker Skulpturen in eigene Kompositionen müsse es Malern darum gehen, eine Wiedergabe „unter Absehung von dem, was daran Stein ist" zu erreichen.[23] Vor diesem Hintergrund transformierte er einen antiken *Kentaur, von Cupido gezähmt* in die Christusfigur einer *Ecce-homo*-Darstellung, die um 1611/12 als Gemälde das Atelier verließ und ab 1630 als Stich Verbreitung fand (Abb. S. 233).[24] Auch die alttestamentarische Geschichte der *Susanna und die beiden Alten* wusste Rubens für Antikenkenner interessant zu machen, indem er die gepeinigte Frau nach der antiken Marmorstatue der *Kauernden Venus* formte. Im Stich von Vorsterman (1620) scheint Susanna unter den grapschenden Händen der Alten zu versteinern, eine passende Reaktion für die Situation dieser Frau und eine Rückführung der Figur auf ihr skulpturales Vorbild (Abb. S. 232).

by Justus Lipsius (fig. p. 218); Lucas Vorsterman I (1595/96–1674/75) created a print as part of a series of twelve busts and heads of ancient Roman philosophers and emperors that Rubens published in 1638 (fig. p. 218); and finally there is a small-format etching from around 1620 that in its first design has traditionally been attributed to Rubens himself (fig. p. 219). This is one of three prints that has art historians speculating whether Rubens tried his hand at etching. In the case of the *Bust of Seneca*, the circumstantial evidence seems to substantiate this.[19] Vorsterman finished the print with his burin and added both Rubens's and his own signature. Certainly, with all these reproductions Rubens was not only seeking to express his admiration of the ancient bust. The fact that he commissioned these prints suggests that he wanted to make them available to a larger audience—and to make himself known as the cultured owner and erudite scholar of the bust.

The painting *The Death of Seneca* (1612/13) at the Alte Pinakothek in Munich represents the pinnacle of Rubens's admiration for Seneca. It shows the philosopher's self-chosen death scene as he dictates his last words to a scribe. As it was one of Seneca's central tenets that men were to conquer their fear of death, his own death was to serve as an example of Stoicism. Because he was persecuted by Nero's men, Seneca chose to take his own life. For his composition, Rubens combined the body of a marble sculpture he knew with the Seneca bust in his collection. The engraving after this "icon of Neo-Stoic philosophy," as the painting has been called, was made by Alexander Voet II years after Rubens's death, between 1650 and 1678, probably prompted by the wish of its owner at the time (fig. p. 221).[20] Rubens's esteem for this sculpture and the Seneca bust derived from his conviction ". . . that in order to attain the highest perfection in painting, it is necessary to understand the antiques, nay, to be so thoroughly possessed of this knowledge that it may diffuse itself everywhere."[21]

Like Goltzius, Rubens was a master at introducing famous Classical statues into his own compositions in such a manner that they could be identified by experts while still functioning convincingly within the new context.[22] Rubens himself even authored a manuscript about Classical sculpture that he hoped to publish. In it he admonished painters to take care when adopting ancient sculptures for their compositions, so that ". . . it may not in the least smell of the stone."[23] With this in mind he transformed the ancient statue *Centaur and Cupid* into the Christ in an *Ecce homo* scene which left his studio around 1611 or 1612 and was made more widely known through the print of 1630 (fig. p. 233).[24] Rubens also knew how to make the Old Testament story of *Susanna and the Elders* attractive to those familiar with ancient art, namely by painting the molested woman after an ancient marble statue of the *Crouching Venus*. In Vorsterman's engraving (1620; fig. p. 232), Susanna seems to turn to stone under the hands of the old lechers, a fitting reaction in this situation and a fascinating way of tying the figure back to her sculptural model.

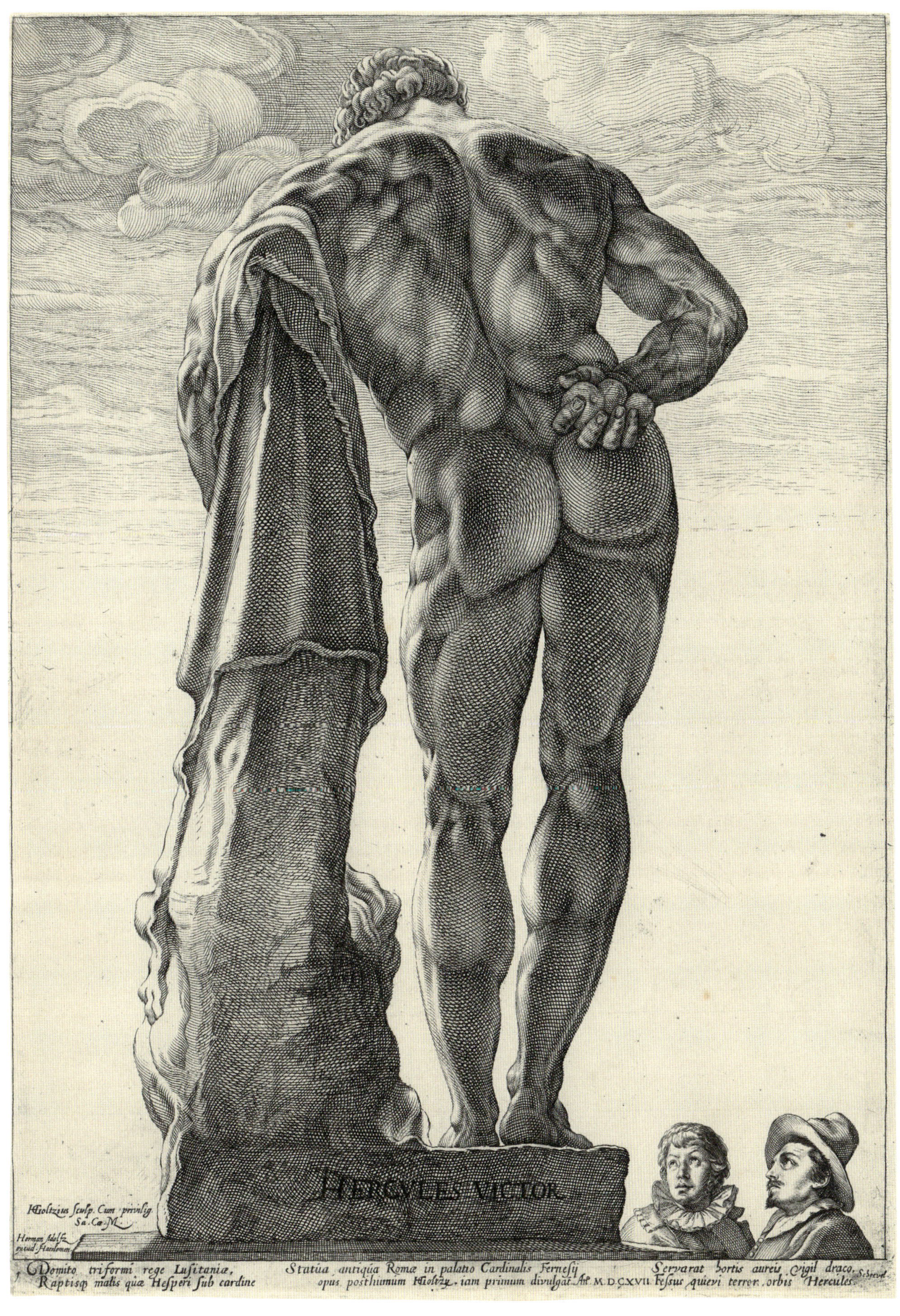

Goltzius (Inventor, Stecher / designer, engraver), Harmen Adolfsz. (Verleger / publisher)
Herkules Farnese / The Farnese Hercules, 1592/1617
Kupferstich / engraving SGSM, Inv. 30963 D

1 Für Goltzius vgl. Reznicek 1961, S. 135. Für Rubens vgl. z. B. Muller 1989, bes. S. 82–91.
2 Das größte Konvolut an Goltzius-Zeichnungen nach römischen Antiken (das sogenannte „Römische Skizzenbuch") befindet sich heute im Teylers Museum in Haarlem. Rubens-Zeichnungen nach Antiken jedoch sind verstreut in viele Sammlungen. Seine in Italien nach Antiken gefertigten Zeichnungen in: Logan/Lohse Belkin 2021, Kat. 65, 83–112, 160–164, 172–188, 190–197. – Ebenfalls Bewunderung findet das *Römische Zeichnungsbuch* (Berlin, Kupferstichkabinett) von Maarten van Heemskerck (1498–1574), auf das Goltzius und Cornelis Cornelisz. van Haarlem Zugriff hatten. Goltzius hat sich in seinen Stichen von mehreren Darstellungen inspirieren lassen. Vgl. z. B. Göttler 2020, S. 77.
3 Chicago 2019, S. 105 (Übers. der Autorin). – Für Rubens wurde dieses Vorgehen kürzlich in einer Ausstellung in Wien und Frankfurt anhand einer prägnanten Werkauswahl vorgeführt; siehe Wien/Frankfurt 2017.
4 Der Goltzius-Zeichnungsexperte Emil Reznicek spekulierte, dass es ein heute unbekanntes Konvolut von Antikenzeichnungen des Haarlemers gegeben haben könnte, welches in Rubens' Hände gelangte. Reznicek 1961, S. 202, Anm. 44, und Reznicek 1992, S. 123 f. Auffälligste Parallele sind wohl Zeichnungen nach dem *Torso Belvedere*, in denen Rubens dieselbe Ansicht und Perspektive wählte. Die Vermutung, Rubens habe eine Mappe mit Goltzius-Antikenzeichnungen besessen, wurde auch von Münster 1976, S. 138, und von Stolzenburg 2002, S. 19, übernommen.
5 Michiel Plomp, 7. Hendrick Goltzius. The Farnese Hercules, in: London 2015, S. 116 (Übers. der Autorin). Allgemein zum Werk ebd., S. 113–118.
6 Ders., 6. Hendrick Goltzius. The Apollo Belvedere, in: London 2015, S. 107–111, bes. S. 110.
7 Reznicek spekulierte: „Die Wahl des großen Formats hat hier technische Gründe: die neue, auf einem System langer, an- und abschwellender Linien basierende Stichweise erreichte nur auf großen Blättern die gewünschte Wirkung." Reznicek 1961, S. 93.
8 Eine beispielhafte Auswahl von zeitgenössischen Stichen nach dem *Apoll vom Belvedere* findet sich in dem sehr lesenswerten Aufsatz von Aurelia Brandt zu Goltzius' Antikenzeichnungen und ihre im Vergleich herausragende Qualität; siehe Brandt 2001, S. 147.
9 NHD Goltzius 2012, S. 368. Unter den Nrn. 378 und 380 Näheres zu möglichen Identitäten der Betrachter.
10 Wolkenhauer 2006, S. 115.
11 Zur Thematisierung des Paragone (Stechkunst vs. Skulptur) vgl. Karsten Müller, in: Hamburg 2002, Kat. 41, sowie Kirves 2017. Zu den zeitgenössischen moralischen Auslegungen der Geschichte (etwa durch Karel van Mander) vgl. ebenfalls Karsten Müller (wie oben) sowie Limouze 1991/92, S. 445.
12 Vgl. auch Reznicek 1961, S. 185, 188, und Weddigen 2004, S. 115 f.
13 Das Ende des 16. Jahrhunderts populär werdende Motiv leitete sich von einem Zitat aus einer Komödie des antiken Dichters Terenz ab. Zum Bildthema bei Goltzius: Larionov 2021; Viljoen 2011; Melion 2017. – Zu Rubens' Vorliebe für das Thema vgl. Renger 1981. Darin auch Verweise auf Goltzius als Vorläufer für Rubens' Bilderfindungen.
14 Vgl. NHD Goltzius 2012, 144–146, unter „Copies".
15 Justus Lipsius hatte eine textkritische Ausgabe Senecas besorgt, zu deren 1615 publizierter zweiten Ausgabe Rubens drei viel beachtete Kupferstiche beitrug (Abb. S. 218). Vgl. auch Morford 1991, bes. S. 3–13. Dank an Nils Büttner für diesen Hinweis.
16 Vgl. zum Beispiel Meulen 1994 oder kürzlich Los Angeles 2021.
17 Zu den strategischen Erwägungen Rubens', die hinter diesem Ankauf gestanden haben mögen, vgl. Büttner 2006, S. 94 f.
18 Vgl. Muller 1989, Kat. III.7, als „Pseudo-Seneca", zum Verbleib der Büste und mit weiterführender Literatur. Der Kopf ist verschollen und wird heute nicht mehr als Bildnis des Seneca angesehen, daher der Beiname „Pseudo".
19 Vgl. Renger 1975, S. 167 f., der die Argumente für und wider Rubens' aktive Beteiligung ausführt. Die anderen beiden Radierungen sind *Alte Frau mit Knabe und Kerzen*, SGSM, Inv. 30407 D, und *Die hl. Katarina*, vgl. Abb. S. 178 f. im vorliegenden Band sowie das Kapitel „Technische Experimente", S. 166–185, zur Theorie, Rubens habe selbst radiert.
20 So Konrad Renger, in: Renger/Denk 2002, S. 388. Hier auch eine Erörterung der wissenschaftlichen Positionen zur Frage, ob Rubens gegenreformatorische Ansichten im Bild umgesetzt hat.
21 Zit. nach der deutschen Übersetzung von Rubens' Manuskript „Über die Nachahmung der Statuen", in: Thielemann 2008, S. 136. Auf S. 121–125 Überlegungen zu Rubens' Faszination für Seneca.
22 Eine kurze Einführung in diese Thematik sowie umfangreiches Bildmaterial bietet Jochen Sander, in: Wien/Frankfurt 2017, S. 181–204. Zuvor ausführlicher David Jaffé mit Amanda Bradley, in: London 2005, S. 21–28, 89–112.
23 Zit. nach der deutschen Übersetzung von Rubens' Manuskript „Über die Nachahmung der Statuen", in: Thielemann 2008, S. 136.
24 Vgl. Muller 1982. Kürzlich auch Jochen Sander, in: Wien/Frankfurt 2017, S. 182, vgl. Kat. 46 und 56.

1 On Goltzius, see Reznicek 1961, p. 135. On Rubens, see, for example, Muller 1989, esp. pp. 82–91.
2 The largest group of Goltzius drawings after Roman antiquities (the so-called "Roman Sketchbook") is kept today by the Teylers Museum in Haarlem. Rubens drawings after Classical art, however, are now in various collections. See his drawings made in Italy after ancient Roman sculptures in Logan/Lohse Belkin 2021, cat. 65, 83–112, 160–164, 172–188, 190–197. – Equally admired is Maarten van Heemskerck's (1498–1574) Roman Sketchbook (Berlin, Kupferstichkabinett), which was accessible to both Goltzius and Cornelis Cornelisz. van Haarlem. Goltzius found inspiration in it in several instances (see, for example, Göttler 2020, p. 77).
3 Chicago 2019, p. 105. – In Rubens's case, this method was recently demonstrated in an exhibition in Vienna and Frankfurt with an enlightening selection of works, see Wien/Frankfurt 2017.
4 Goltzius drawings expert Emil Reznicek speculated that there may have been a group of drawings after Classical sculpture by the Haarlem master that found its way into Rubens's hands (Reznicek 1961, p. 202, n. 44, and Reznicek 1992, pp. 123–124). The most conspicuous parallel is found in the drawings after the *Belvedere Torso*, which Rubens depicted from the same angle and perspective. The hypothesis that Rubens owned a portfolio of Goltzius's drawings after ancient Roman sculptures is repeated in Münster 1976, p. 138, and Stolzenburg 2002, p. 19.
5 Michiel Plomp, 7. Hendrick Goltzius. The Farnese Hercules, in: London 2015, p. 116. For a general discussion of this work, see ibid., pp. 113–118.
6 Michiel Plomp, 6. Hendrick Goltzius. The Apollo Belvedere, in: London 2015, pp. 107–111, esp. p. 110.
7 Reznicek speculated that there were technical reasons for the choice of the large format—i.e., that the swelling lines required the space offered by a larger sheet to achieve the desired effect, see Reznicek 1961, p. 93.
8 A representative selection of historical prints after the *Apollo Belvedere* can be found in Aurelia Brandt's highly readable essay on Goltzius's drawings after ancient sculptures and how well they compared to earlier and contemporary works in terms of quality, see Brandt 2001, p. 147.
9 NHD Goltzius 2012, 368. See nos. 378 and 380 for more on the identities of these viewers.
10 Wolkenhauer 2006, p. 115.
11 On the paragone (between engraving and sculpture), see Karsten Müller, in: Hamburg 2002, cat. 41, and Kirves 2017. For historical moral interpretations of the story (for example, by Karel van Mander), see Karsten Müller, as above, and Limouze 1991/92, p. 445.
12 See also Reznicek 1961, pp. 185, 188, and Weddigen 2004, pp. 115–116.
13 The story became popular at the end of the sixteenth century and derived from a comedy by the Classical poet Terence. On the theme in Goltzius's work, see Larionov 2021; Viljoen 2011; Melion 2017. – On Rubens's predilection for the story, see Renger 1981, who cites Goltzius as an important model for the Antwerp master.
14 See NHD Goltzius 2012, 144–146, under "Copies."
15 Justus Lipsius had published a critical edition of Seneca's writings. Rubens contributed three much-noted engravings to the second edition of this work (fig. p. 218). See Morford 1991, esp. pp. 3–13. Thanks to Nils Büttner for pointing this out to me.
16 See, for example, Meulen 1994 or, more recently, Los Angeles 2021.
17 On Rubens's strategic considerations in regard to this commission, see Büttner 2006, pp. 94–95.
18 See Muller 1989, cat. III.7, regarding the later whereabouts of the bust (described as "Pseudo-Seneca") and for further literature. There is no information on the present location of the bust, which is no longer considered to be of Seneca, therefore the epithet "pseudo."
19 See Renger 1975, pp. 167–168, who goes over the arguments for and against Rubens's active involvement. The other two etchings are *Old Woman and a Boy with Candles*, SGSM, inv. 30407 D, and *St. Catherine*, see figs. pp. 178–179 in the present volume. Also see the chapter "Technical Experiments," pp. 166–185, on the theory of Rubens himself having etched.
20 Konrad Renger, in: Renger/Denk 2002, p. 388. Here also a discussion on scholarly positions regarding the question as to whether Rubens expressed opposition to the Reformation in the painting.
21 Quoted from the English translation of Rubens's manuscript "Concerning the Imitation of the Antique Statues," in: Piles 1743, pp. 86–87. See Thielemann 2008, pp. 121–125, for a discussion of Rubens's fascination with Seneca.
22 Jochen Sander offers a brief introduction to this topic, as well as many images, in Wien/Frankfurt 2017, pp. 181–204. For an earlier analysis, see David Jaffé with Amanda Bradley in London 2005, pp. 21–28, 89–112.
23 Quoted from the English translation of Rubens's manuscript "Concerning the Imitation of the Antique Statues," in: Piles 1743, p. 87.
24 See Muller 1982 and, more recently, Jochen Sander, in: Wien/Frankfurt 2017, p. 182, cat. 46, 56.

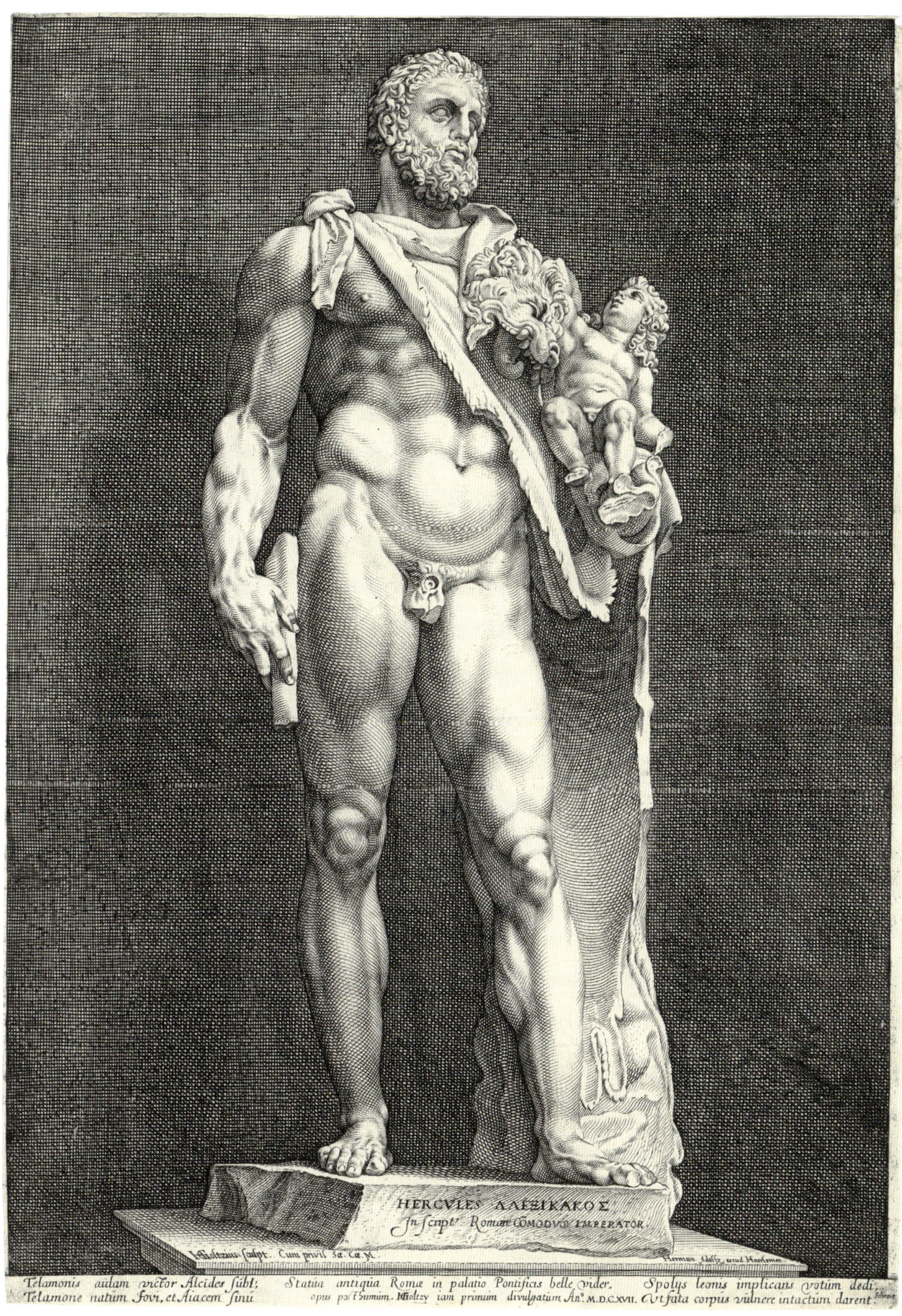

Goltzius (Inventor, Stecher / designer, engraver), Harmen Adolfsz. (Verleger / publisher)
Herkules und / Hercules and Telephos, 1592/1617
Kupferstich / engraving SGSM, Inv. 30964 D

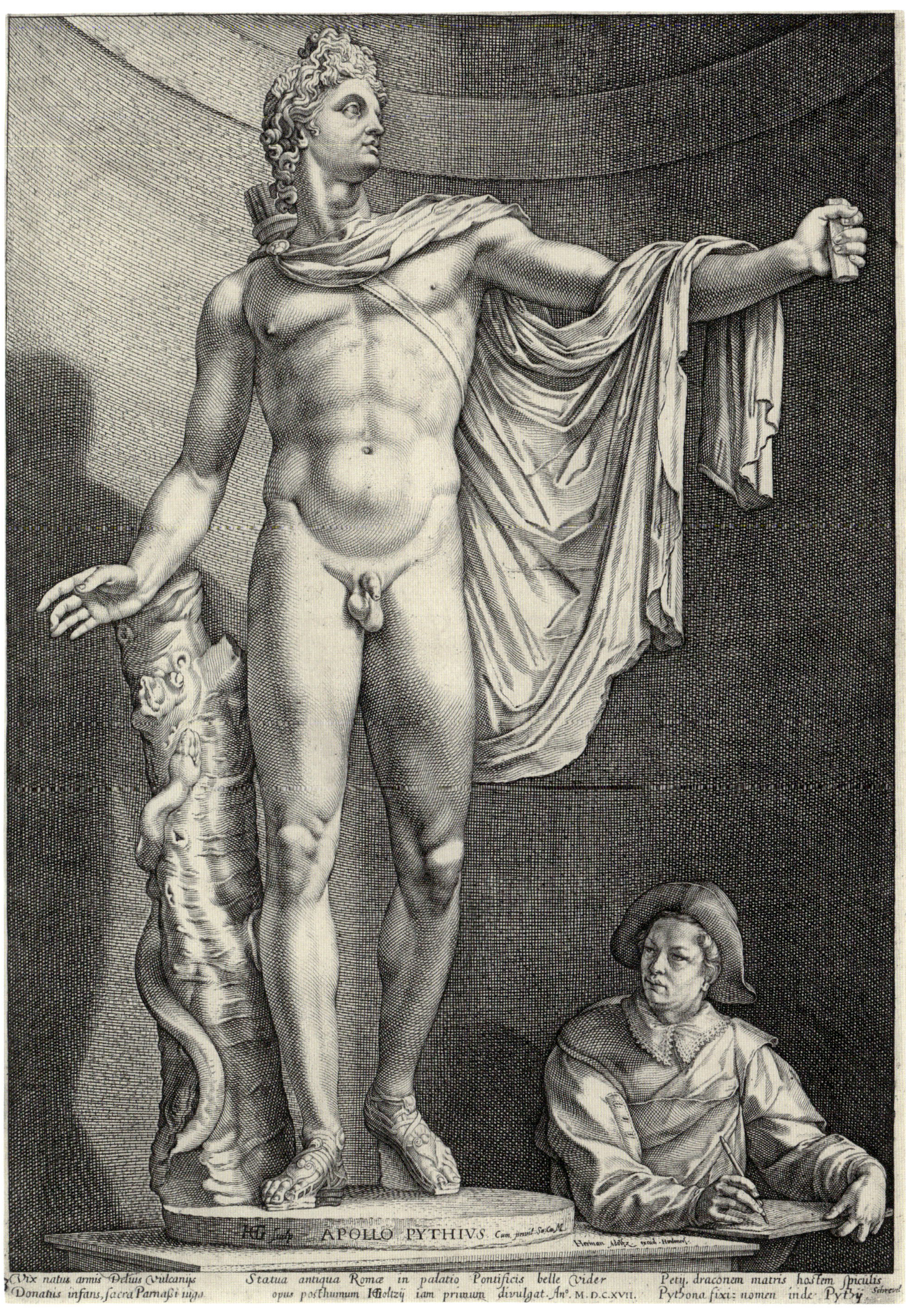

Goltzius (Inventor, Stecher / designer, engraver), Harmen Adolfsz. (Verleger / publisher)
Apoll vom Belvedere / Apollo Belvedere, 1592/1617
Kupferstich / engraving SGSM, Inv. 30965 D

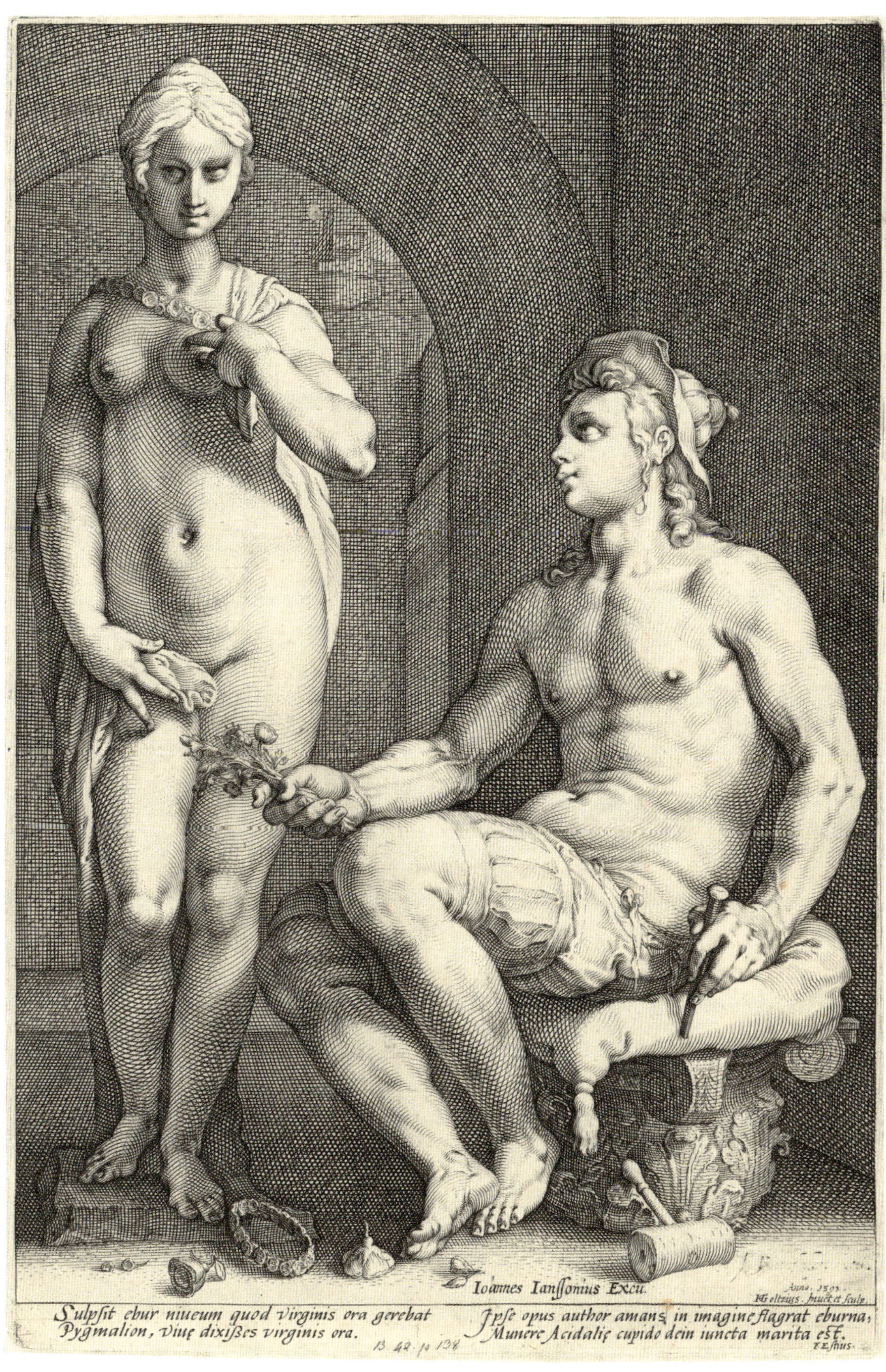

Goltzius (Inventor, Stecher / designer, engraver), Jan Janszoon I (Verleger / publisher)
Pygmalion und / and Galatea, 1593
Kupferstich / engraving SGSM, Inv. 30957 D

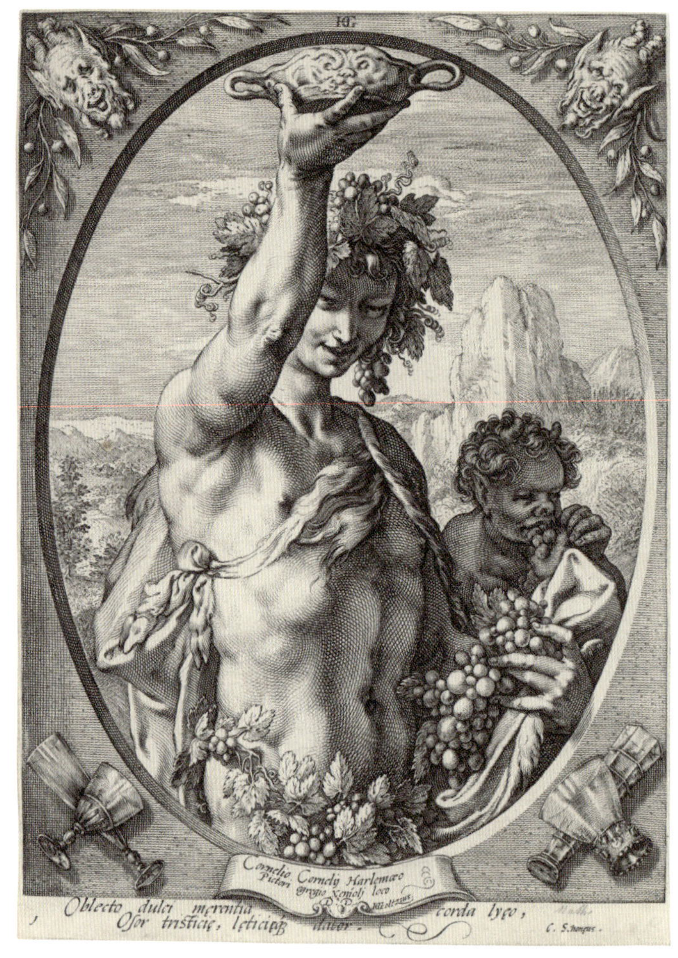
HG
Cornelio Cornelij Harlemæo
Pictori egregio Xenioli loco
Oblecto dulci merentia corda lyęo,
Osor tristicię, leticięq; dator.
C. S.tonpus.

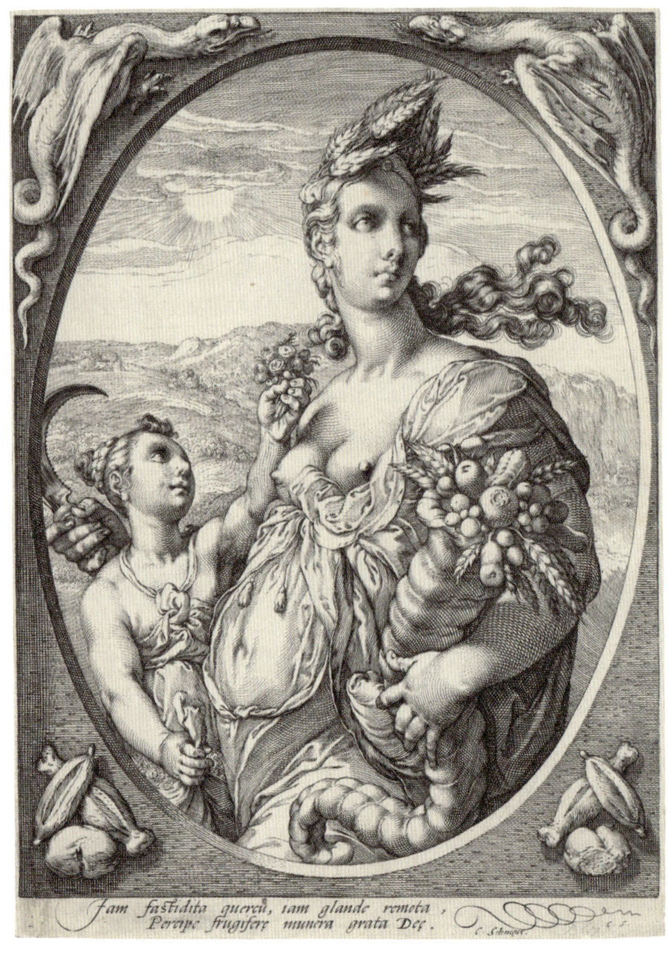
Iam fastidita quercu, iam glande remota,
Percipe frugiferę munera grata Deę.

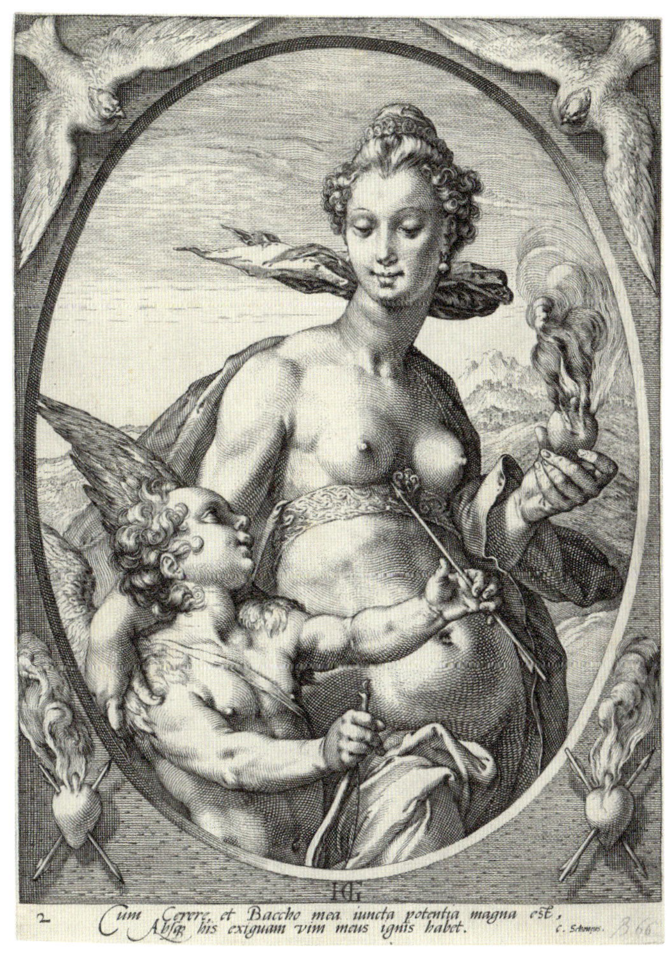

Goltzius (Inventor / designer), Jan Saenredam (Stecher / engraver)
Bacchus, Ceres, Venus und Amor / and Cupid (VON LINKS / FROM LEFT), ca. 1595
Aus der Serie / from the series *Ceres, Bacchus, Venus*, ca. 1595
Kupferstich / engraving SGSM, Inv. 31074–31076 D

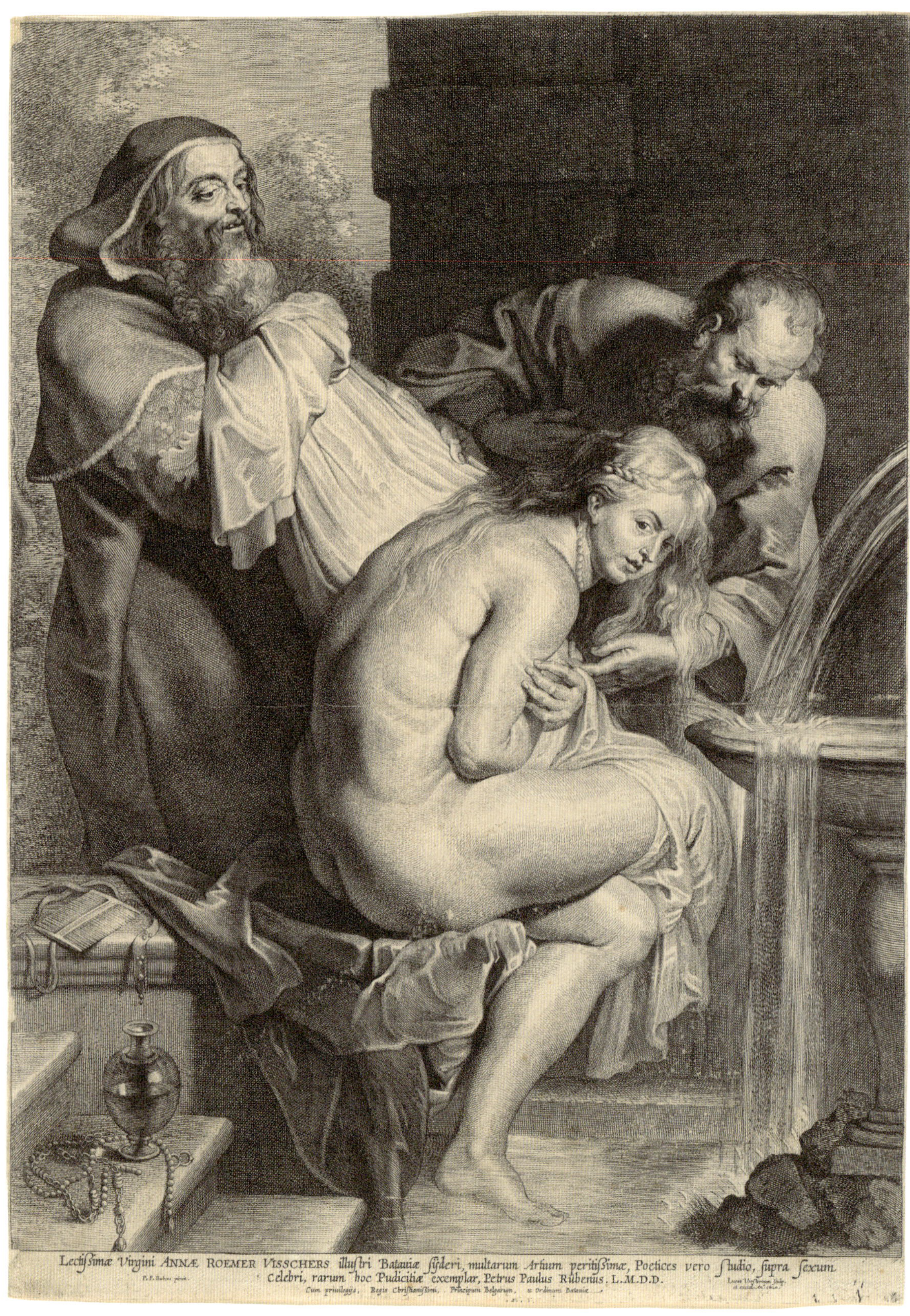

Rubens (Inventor / designer), Lucas Vorsterman I (Stecher, Verleger / engraver, publisher)
Susanna und die beiden Alten / Susanna and the Elders, 1620
Kupferstich / engraving SGSM, Inv. 30000 D

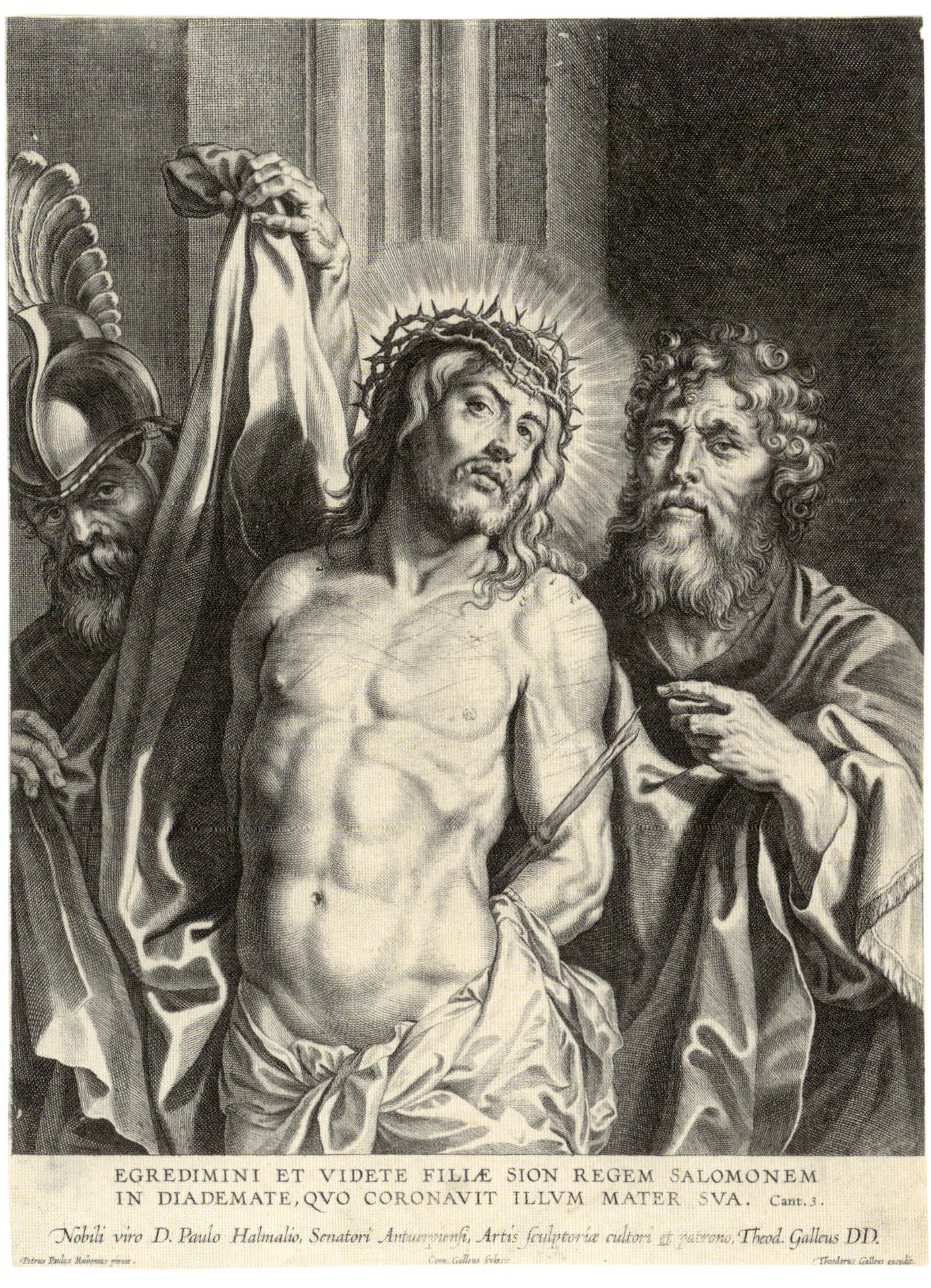

Rubens (Inventor / designer), Cornelis Galle I (Stecher / engraver), Theodoor Galle (Verleger / publisher)
Ecce homo, 1630
Kupferstich / engraving SGSM, Inv. 30089 D

IX. Vorbilder

Mit ihren Italienaufenthalten waren sowohl bei Hendrick Goltzius als auch bei Peter Paul Rubens nicht nur das Studium der Antike, sondern auch das der jüngeren italienischen Kunst verbunden. Zwar waren einige Werke von Michelangelo, Tizian und Raffael durch Stiche auch nördlich der Alpen bekannt geworden, diese waren aber von schwankender Qualität und Verlässlichkeit und konnten die Farbgebung der Originale nicht vermitteln. Zu den qualitätsvollsten Stichen nach italienischen Vorbildern, die auch in niederländische Sammlungen gelangten, gehörten Marcantonio Raimondis (1470/82–1527/34) Blätter nach Erfindungen von Raffael, die zu Beginn des 16. Jahrhunderts Furore machten, sowie etwas später Graphiken von Giorgio Ghisi (1520–1582), ebenfalls nach Raffael, für den Antwerpener Verleger Hieronymus Cock. Tizians Erfindungen erlangten eine größere Reichweite durch die Stiche von Cornelis Cort (1533–1578).

Wie bereits im Fall von Goltzius und seiner Verehrung für Albrecht Dürer und Lucas van Leyden, den großen Leitsternen der nordischen Kunst des 16. Jahrhunderts, anklang, ging es bei den Kopien nach italienischen Meistern darum, diesen zu huldigen. Durch die Verknüpfung des eigenen Namens mit dem der großen Vorläufer wurde der Anspruch öffentlich gemacht, an wem man gemessen werden wollte. Während angehende Kunststudenten große Vorbilder kopierten, um ihre eigene Technik zu verfeinern, verbreiteten namhafte Künstler wie Goltzius und Rubens ihre Kopien in der Absicht, allen zu zeigen, dass sie den Vergleich nicht scheuten, sondern suchten. Sie verbreiteten mit diesen Nachstichen gleichermaßen den Ruhm der Vorbilder wie den eigenen.

Der italienische Künstler Tizian (um 1488–1576) faszinierte Goltzius schon einige Jahre vor seiner Italienreise 1590/91. Möglich wurde diese Begegnung mit Tizian dank der Stiche von Goltzius' Landsmann Cornelis Cort, der einige Zeit für Tizian gearbeitet hatte und viele italienische Meisterwerke durch seine Stiche auch in den Niederlanden bekannt machte. Corts 1566 datiertes Blatt nach Tizians Motiv der *Hl. Magdalena* (der Italiener schuf etliche Gemäldevariationen) regte Goltzius an, die Frauenfigur 1583 in eine *Susanna* zu verwandeln (Abb. S. 240). Er stellte sie dem Thema entsprechend weniger bekleidet und nicht in einer kargen Landschaft, sondern in einem Schlossgarten dar. Goltzius konnte sich sicher sein, dass die Kunstkenner unter seinen Sammlern seine Reverenz erkennen würden. Nach seiner Rückkehr aus Italien ließ er sich außerdem von den Holzschnitten inspirieren, die nach Tizian entstanden waren.[1]

Seine Meisterkopie fertigte der Haarlemer Künstler 1592 aber nach dem Wandgemälde *Triumph der Galatea* von Raffael (1483–1520) an (Abb. S. 243). Mit diesem Blatt, das nach einer in der Villa Farnesina angefertigten Zeichnung entstand (wie in der Bildunterschrift zu lesen ist – „ibidem ab HGoltzio adnotatum", also: ebendort von Goltzius aufgezeichnet), übertraf er an Genauigkeit und Lebendigkeit den einzig bis dahin kursierenden Stich von Marcantonio Raimondi (1515/16). Susanne Pollack vermutet zudem, dass Goltzius „den Vergleich mit der Absicht anstrebte, das Publikum zu verblüffen und die

IX. Models

For both Hendrick Goltzius and Peter Paul Rubens, a stay in Italy offered an opportunity to study not only ancient artworks but also more recent Italian art. While some works by Michelangelo, Titian, and Raphael became known north of the Alps through prints, the quality and reliability of these reproductions varied, and they could not convey the colors of the originals. In terms of quality, the best prints after Italian models to reach Netherlandish collections were made by Marcantonio Raimondi (1470/82–1527/34) after inventions by Raphael, which caused quite a stir in the early sixteenth century. A little later, Giorgio Ghisi (1520–1582) created prints, also after Raphael, for the Antwerp publisher and merchant Hieronymus Cock. And Titian's inventions reached a wider audience through the prints of Cornelis Cort (1533–1578).

Goltzius made public his admiration for Italian masters in the same manner in which he expressed his veneration for Albrecht Dürer and Lucas van Leyden, the two paragons of northern sixteenth-century art: by reproducing them in print. This act was all about publicly paying homage to these precursors. By connecting his own name with those of great role models, he made clear whom he wanted to be measured against. While art students copied great models so as to refine their own technique, well-known artists like Goltzius and Rubens published their copies in order to demonstrate that they did not shy away from comparison but, on the contrary, sought it. With reproductions of famous Italian works, the artists spread their own fame as well as that of the original artists.

The Italian artist Titian (ca. 1488–1576) fascinated Goltzius even before he traveled to Italy from 1590 to 1591. Prior to this journey, Goltzius attained his knowledge of Titian's art through the prints of his compatriot Cornelis Cort, who had worked for Titian for a time and had brought fame to many Italian masterworks in the Netherlands through his prints. Cort's 1566 print after Titian's motif of *St. Mary Magdalene* (many painted versions of which exist) inspired Goltzius to adopt the female figure for his 1583 print of a *Susanna* (fig. p. 240). As befits his subject, he chose to show her more skimpily dressed and in a palace garden instead of a desert. Goltzius knew he could rely on collectors' recognizing his reference to Titian. After he returned from Italy, he also found inspiration in Titian's woodcuts.[1]

The Haarlem artist created his master reproduction in 1592 after Raphael's (1483–1520) fresco *The Triumph of Galatea* (fig. p. 243). With this print, which was based on a drawing (that, as the epigram states, was "ibidem ab HGoltzio adnotatum," or made on site by Goltzius), he outdid in terms of precision and liveliness the only other available print after the fresco, which was by Marcantonio Raimondi (1515/16). Susanne Pollack suspects that Goltzius "sought to be compared so as to stun his audience and to demonstrate the advantages of [Cornelis] Cort's technique [of the swelling line]."[2] Elizabeth McGrath was the first to point

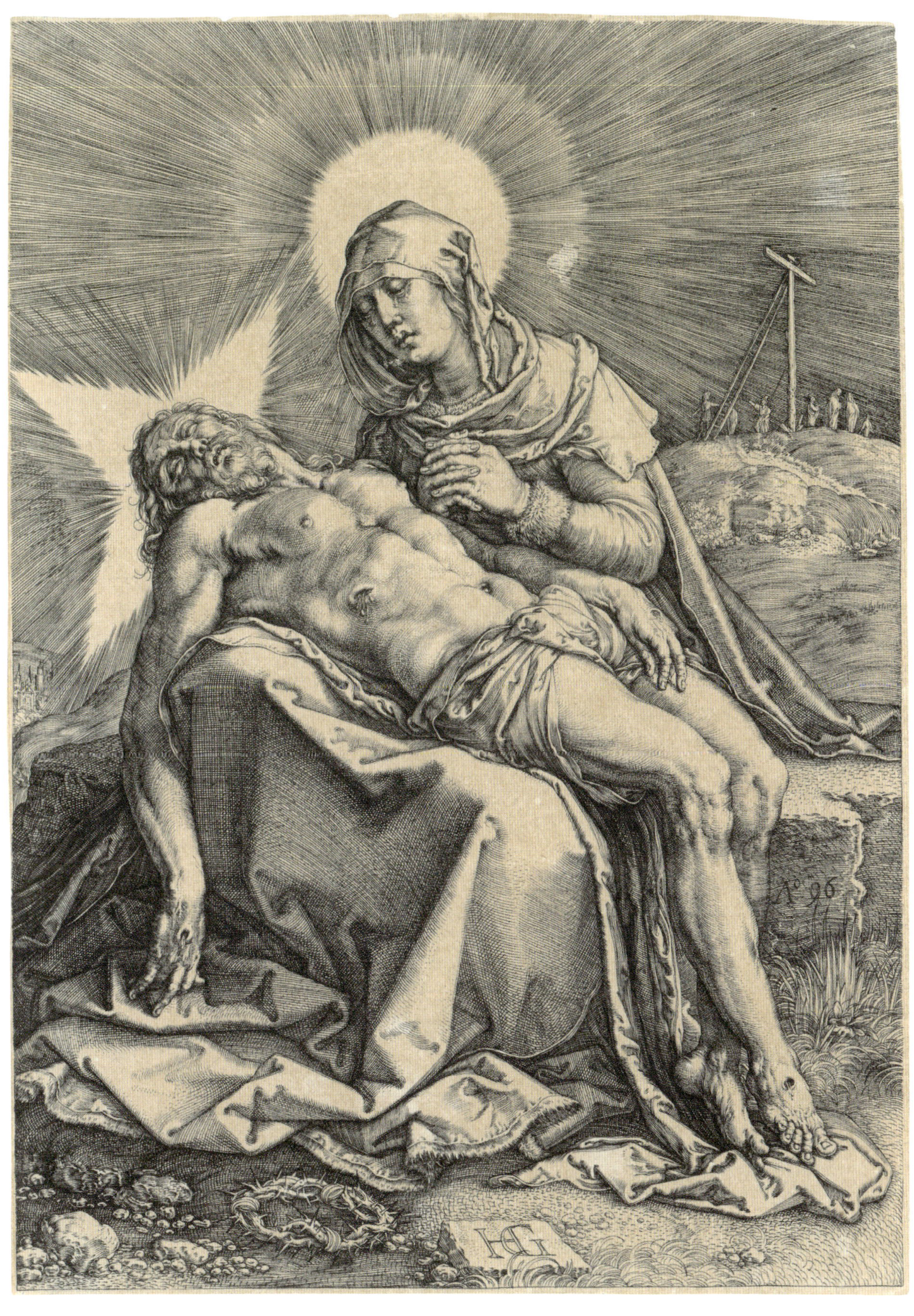

Hendrick Goltzius (Inventor, Stecher / designer, engraver)
Pietà, 1596
Kupferstich / engraving SGSM, Inv. 30918 D

Vorzüge der von ihm perfektionierten [Cornelis] Cortschen Technik [der schwellenden Linien] zu demonstrieren".[2] Auf eine Besonderheit auch der Bildlegende hat zuerst Elizabeth McGrath hingewiesen: Die Farben von Raffaels Wandgemälde sind zwar nicht in Goltzius' Stich zu sehen, werden aber von der Bildunterschrift anschaulich „ausgemalt".[3]

Ein weiteres spannendes Blatt schuf Goltzius um die Zeit seiner Arbeit an der Serie *Die Passion Christi* (1596–1598), mit der er die großen Vorbilder Albrecht Dürer und Lucas van Leyden heraufbeschwor. In Goltzius' *Pietà* (1596) zeigte der Künstler seine Variante von Michelangelos Skulptur (1498–1500) im Stechstil von Dürer (Abb. S. 235). Während der Haarlemer Künstler in den *Meisterstichen* einige Jahre zuvor italienische und nordalpine Vorbilder von Blatt zu Blatt abwechselnd zitiert hatte, führte er in diesem Werk beides zusammen. Huigen Leeflang versteht Goltzius' Blatt als ein Experiment, etwas vollkommen Neues zu schaffen: „Goltzius versuchte, eine Synthese zu erreichen zwischen der Kunst des großen Florentiners und der graphischen Kunst des Meisters aus Nürnberg."[4] Dass dieser Stich einer der letzten am Ende von Goltzius' Laufbahn als Kupferstecher war, ist wohl Ausdruck davon, dass er sich diesen Vorbildern jetzt gewachsen und vielleicht sogar ebenbürtig fühlte.

In Rom fiel Goltzius wie auch Rubens ein Künstler besonders ins Auge: Polidoro da Caravaggio (um 1499 – um 1543), der uns heute weniger geläufig ist, weil viele seiner römischen Werke der Witterung zum Opfer fielen.[5] Ihn bewunderte aber die zeitgenössische italienische Kunstliteratur in gleicher Weise, wie sie Leonardo, Raffael und Michelangelo verehrte.[6] Polidoro hatte sich auf Sgraffito-Malereien an Hausfassaden spezialisiert, von denen die meisten in Grisaille ausgeführt waren und bereits um die Jahrhundertmitte unter der Witterung litten. Goltzius kopierte gleich mehrere Motive von Polidoro, sein ehrgeizigstes Werk war die Stichfolge nach Polidoros 1527 datiertem Fries *Die Bestrafung der Niobe*, die sich aus acht Blättern (von acht Druckplatten) zusammensetzte (Abb. S. 244 f.). Polidoro wurde als hervorragender Antikenkenner geschätzt, der es verstand, dieses Wissen in eigene Kompositionen einfließen zu lassen – ein Verfahren, das zu Goltzius' und Rubens' Zeit als erstrebenswert galt. So sollte Goltzius' *Niobe*-Stich (1594), wie Karel van Mander es formulierte, die „oude Antijke wijse" (alte antike Manier) evozieren und jungen Künstlern als Lehrmaterial dienen.[7] Dass dieser über drei Meter lange Stich jedoch rein zu Ausbildungszwecken konzipiert war, ist kaum denkbar. Sicher zählt der Fries zu jenen technischen Experimenten, die auf Sammler wie Künstlerkollegen gleichermaßen Eindruck machen sollte – mit der Furchtlosigkeit, Gewandtheit und Gelehrtheit seiner Schöpfer, allen voran Hendrick Goltzius.[8]

Auch ein übergroßer Stich (rund 295 × 885 mm) von 1632 nach Leonardos *Abendmahl* (1494–1498) war als Kunstwerk alles andere als Ausdruck der Bescheidenheit seiner Schöpfer. Der Münchner Abzug trägt die Namen aller drei beteiligten Künstler (Abb. S. 246 f.): „Leonardo Da Vinci Pinxit" (Leonardo da Vinci malte es), „P. p. Rubens delineavit" (P. p. Rubens zeichnete es) sowie unter dem Plattenrand ganz rechts in Bleistift später hinzugefügt „P. Soutman sculpsit" (P. Soutman stach es).[9] Das darauf noch sichtbare Privileg bezieht sich auf Pieter Soutman (1593/1601–1657). Rubens' Name wurde mutmaßlich erst nach

out a remarkable aspect in the print's epigram: Even though the colors of Raphael's fresco are not present in Goltzius's print, the wording of the inscription "paints the picture" for its viewers in this respect.[3]

Goltzius created another fascinating print around the time he was working on the series *The Passion of Christ* (1596–1598), which paid homage to his great idols Albrecht Dürer and Lucas van Leyden. Goltzius's *Pietà* (1596) offered up his interpretation of Michelangelo's (1475–1564) famous statue (1498–1500), engraved in the style of Dürer (fig. p. 235). While a few years earlier the Haarlem artist had alternately emulated Italian or northern models in his *Masterpieces*, in this work he combined both. Huigen Leeflang interprets Goltzius's print as an experiment in creating something entirely new: ". . . Goltzius tried to bring about a synthesis between the art of the great Florentine and the graphic art of the master from Nuremberg."[4] The fact that this work was one of the last in Goltzius's career as an engraver is an indication that he felt himself to be their equal.

In Rome, one artist in particular had caught Goltzius's eye, as he would Rubens's: Polidoro da Caravaggio (ca. 1499–ca. 1543), who is today less well known because many of his Roman works, mostly frescoes, did not fare well being exposed to the elements.[5] However, there was much admiration for Polidoro in the art writing of the day; he was praised as highly as Leonardo, Raphael, and Michelangelo.[6] Polidoro had specialized in sgraffito paintings on facades, most of which he executed as grisailles. These degenerated quickly because they were extremely susceptible to the weather. Goltzius copied several motifs by Polidoro, but his most ambitious work was the composite of eight prints (from eight plates) after the 1527 frieze *The Punishment of Niobe* (fig. pp. 244–245). Polidoro was admired for being an expert on ancient art, which he cunningly adapted for his own art, a practice much admired in Goltzius's and Rubens's time. According to Karel van Mander, Goltzius's *Niobe* print (1594) was to evoke the "old ancient manner" (*oude Antijke wijse*) and to serve art students as a model.[7] Yet it is hardly conceivable that this print, which measures more than three meters when mounted, was solely meant for instruction. Rather, we can be sure that it is one of those technical experiments that was supposed to impress collectors and fellow artists in equal measure with the audacity, skill, and erudition of its creators—foremost among them Hendrick Goltzius.[8]

Similarly, the large print (ca. 295 × 885 mm) dated 1632 after Leonardo's *Last Supper* (1494–1498) was anything but an expression of the modesty of its creators. The Munich print (state II) sports the names of all three artists involved (fig. pp. 246–247): "Leonardo Da Vinci Pinxit" (painted by Leonardo da Vinci), "P. p. Rubens delineavit" (drawn by P. p. Rubens), and, below the plate on the far right and written in pencil by a later hand, "P. Soutman sculpsit" (engraved by P. Soutman).[9] The privilege in the print was Pieter Soutman's (1593/1601–1657). Rubens's name was probably added only after Soutman's death to make the print

Soutmans Tod eingefügt, um das Blatt für Käufer attraktiver zu machen.[10] Auch weil die Zeichnung von Rubens nach Leonardos berühmtem Mailänder Wandfresko verloren ging, ist an der Autorschaft von Rubens gezweifelt worden.[11] Die Figurentypen jedoch entsprechen Rubens ebenso wie die Freiheit, die sich der Vorzeichner des Stichs bei den Abänderungen von Leonardos Komposition herausgenommen hat – am auffälligsten beim schweren Vorhang hinter den Jüngern oder bei dem vor Judas liegenden Geldbeutel.[12] Die italienischen Worte der Inschrift, aus denen hervorgeht, dass der Schöpfer dieses „staunenerregenden Abendmahls", Leonardo, in den Armen des französischen Königs starb, korrespondiert mit dem Bild, das Rubens von sich selbst als Künstler pflegte.[13] Das große Format (zwei Blätter von zwei Platten) spricht dafür, dass das Werk bereits von Soutman als Verkaufserfolg eingeschätzt wurde. Die große Resonanz, die dieser Stich bei späteren Künstlern, allen voran Rembrandt, erfuhr, bestätigt das Aufgehen seines Kalküls.[14]

Vermutlich während seiner Zeit in Rubens' Werkstatt zwischen 1615/16 und 1624 fertigte Soutman eine Stichvorlage nach einer wohl nicht erhaltenen Zeichnung von Rubens an. Diese war ihrerseits eine Kopie nach Raffaels einflussreicher Komposition *Christus übergibt Petrus den Schlüssel*.[15] Raffael hatte 1515 zehn Motive für Tapisserien zur Ausschmückung der Sixtinischen Kapelle entworfen, dieses ist eines von ihnen. Innerhalb weniger Jahre verbreiteten sich gewebte Kopien nach Raffaels Zyklus an den Fürstenhöfen in ganz Europa.[16] Der Bildkanon Raffaels war Teil des visuellen Erbes, das Künstlern wie Goltzius und Rubens zur Verfügung stand, um neue Ausformungen für ihre eigenen Werke zu finden. Soutman erkannte den Marktwert dieser bekannten Komposition und fertigte nach seiner Vorlage den Stich an (Abb. S. 242). Nach Rubens' Vorbild verknüpfte Soutman seinen eigenen Namen (als Stecher, Verleger und Inhaber des Privilegs) mit dem Raffaels, dem Inventor. Wieder führte er Rubens namentlich nicht an, dessen Name wurde erst nach dem Tod Soutmans hinzugefügt.

Gleich zwei Stiche nach Bildnissen von Tizian, *Isabella d'Este* und *Kaiser Karl V.*, sind in unserer Ausstellung zu sehen (Abb. S. 241, 133). Es fällt auf, dass Rubens die beiden von Lucas Vorsterman I (1595/96–1674/75) um 1620 gestochenen Blätter selbst herausgab.[17] Offensichtlich wollte er, dass diese hochqualitativen Arbeiten mit seinem Namen in Verbindung gebracht werden. Beide Stiche entstanden nach den Gemäldekopien, die Rubens vor den Originalen für seine eigene Sammlung angefertigt hatte.[18]

Bei seinem *Bildnis des Gaspar de Guzmán* (1625) verarbeitete Rubens das einzige Mal das Werk eines Zeitgenossen in einem eigenen Stich (Abb. S. 239). Das Blatt war in mehrfacher Hinsicht für den Maler ein strategischer Coup: Guzmán (1587–1645) war der einflussreichste Politiker am Hof des spanischen Königs Philipp IV. (1605–1665) und protegierte den jungen Diego Velázquez (1599–1660), sodass dieser 1623 zum Hofmaler in Madrid berufen wurde. Bereits von Guzmáns Vorgänger, dem Herzog von Lerma, hatte Rubens sich die Erlaubnis erwirkt, ihn in einem viel beachteten Reiterbildnis zu verewigen.[19] Eine Porträtzeichnung von Velázquez diente Rubens als Vorlage für das Brustbildnis Guzmáns, das er mit einer prunkvollen allegorischen Umrahmung versah und in großem Format von Paulus Pontius stechen ließ.[20] Während die Inschriften oben sowie auf dem Sockel den

more marketable.[10] Because Rubens's drawing after Leonardo's famous Milanese fresco is lost, his authorship has been questioned in the past.[11] However, the figure types are all Rubens's, as is the freedom taken by the designer of the preparatory drawing in making changes to Leonardo's composition, most notably in the heavy background curtain behind the disciples and in the pouch of money in front of Judas.[12] The Italian words in the epigram informing us that the creator of this "Astonishing [Last] Supper," Leonardo, died in the arms of the French king mirrored the image Rubens had of himself.[13] The large format (two sheets from two plates) suggests that Soutman intended for this work to become a bestseller. The extensive resonance this print enjoyed with later artists, foremost among them Rembrandt, confirms that Soutman's plan succeeded.[14]

It was probably while he was working as an assistant in Rubens's painting studio between 1615/16 and 1624 that Soutman created a preparatory drawing after a (now lost) Rubens drawing. The latter drawing was itself a copy, namely after the influential Raphael composition *Christ's Charge to Peter*.[15] In 1515, Raphael had designed ten motifs for tapestries to adorn the Sistine Chapel, and this was one of them. Within a few years, woven copies after Raphael's series reached many courts throughout Europe.[16] The works of Raphael were even then part of a canon in European visual culture that artists like Goltzius and Rubens tapped for their own creations. Soutman recognized the market value of this famous composition and engraved it (fig. p. 242). Following Rubens's model in this regard, Soutman connected his own name (as engraver, publisher, and holder of the privilege) with that of Raphael, the designer. Once more, he did not include Rubens's name, which was added to the plate (state II) only after the engraver's death.

In our exhibition we show two prints after Titian, *Portrait of Isabella d'Este* and *Portrait of Emperor Charles V* (figs. pp. 241, 133). It is noteworthy that Rubens himself functioned as publisher for these two prints, which he had Lucas Vorsterman I (1595/96–1674/75) engrave around 1620.[17] Clearly, he wanted these high-quality works to be connected with his name. Both prints were based on painted copies Rubens had made of Titian's originals to have for his personal collection.[18]

His *Portrait of Gaspar de Guzmán* (1625) is the only instance in which Rubens worked after the drawing of a contemporary artist to produce a print (fig. p. 239). This print was a coup for the painter in several ways: Guzmán (1587–1645) was the most influential politician at the court of the Spanish King Philip IV, and was also the sponsor of young Diego Velázquez (1599–1660), whom he had made court painter in Madrid. Years earlier, Rubens had obtained permission from Guzmán's predecessor, the Duke of Lerma, to depict him in a much-noted equestrian portrait.[19] Rubens used a portrait drawing by Velázquez to conceive Guzmán's bust, which he adorned with magnificent allegorical ornamentation and had Paulus Pontius turn into a large print.[20] While the inscriptions at the top of the print and on the base of the depicted bust laud the sitter as statesman and a virtuous man, Rubens acknowledged Guzmán's protégé as the

Dargestellten überschwänglich als Staatsmann und tugendhaften Menschen loben, wies Rubens mit „Ex Archetypo Velazquez“ den Protegé Guzmáns als Quelle des Porträts aus. Seine eigene Leistung schmälerte er in einem kokettierenden Demutsgestus durch die Formulierung „ornavit“ (er schmückte aus). Zugleich aber setzte er seine Marke mit der Widmung des Stichs an den wichtigen spanischen Hofmann sowie seinem dreifachen Privileg links unten.

1 Vgl. Luijten 2004, S. 25 f.
2 Pollack 2020, S. 20.
3 McGrath 1984, S. 74. Vgl. kürzlich auch Wolkenhauer 2006, S. 337. Auf derselben Seite ihre vollständige Übersetzung der Bildunterschrift.
4 Huigen Leeflang, in: Amsterdam/New York/Toledo 2003, S. 209 (Übers. der Autorin). Er weist auch darauf hin, dass beide Künstler, Dürer und Michelangelo, von den damals maßgeblichen Biographen Giorgio Vasari und Karel van Mander als Großmeister des *disegno* beschrieben wurden.
5 Zu Rubens' Kopien nach und Überarbeitungen von Zeichnungen nach Polidoro vgl. Wood 2010, S. 70–77, sowie S. 396–402 (Nr. 90–92). Zuvor auch in München 2009, S. 64 f. Der Münchner Katalog und die Ausstellung behandelten Graphik nur am Rande.
6 So Giovanni Paolo Lomazzo in seinem 1584 erschienenen mehrbändigen *Trattato dell'arte della pittura*. Vgl. Leeflang 2012, S. 37 f., und Göttler 2020, bes. S. 70 f. und 77.
7 Mander 1604, fol. 128v: „Dese comt oock, tot een goet fundament der jonghe Schilders in Druck, waerom ick den inhoudt niet behoeve te verhalen.“
8 Uta Schmidt-Clausen weist auf folgende Besonderheit in der Bild-Text-Relation in diesem Werk hin: „Die Kupferstiche sind gegenüber dem Original seitenverkehrt, Estius' Bildgedichte aber folgen der Handlungschronologie.“ Schmidt-Clausen 2016, S. 337. Sollte dem Verleger Goltzius hier ein Fehler unterlaufen sein? Oder konnte er bei seiner humanistisch gebildeten Kundschaft einen Gefallen an dieser Diskrepanz voraussetzen?
9 In einem früheren Zustand war nicht Rubens, sondern nur Pieter Soutman genannt und auch als Verleger ausgewiesen worden. Einen solchen Abzug des früheren Zustands im Berliner Kupferstichkabinett zeigt Meier 2020a, S. 334 f. Vgl. hierzu die kluge und informative Diskussion ebd., Kat. 74.
10 So Barrett 2012, S. 48 f. Ihr folgt Meier 2020a, Kat. 74.
11 Die Frage, wann und wo Rubens die verlorene Zeichnung angefertigt hat, verhandeln Gerhard Langemeyer und Reinhard Schleier (Münster 1976, S. 160, 164). Die Autoren sehen in Rubens' Abweichungen von Leonardos Komposition bewusste Entscheidungen. Ihnen folgt Büttner 2011a, S. 126. Die Frage nach Rubens' Zeichnung, die Soutman als Vorlage nutzte, verhandelt Wood 2010, Kat. 168.
12 Die Figur des Christus (einschließlich der Handhaltungen) findet sich ganz ähnlich in Anthonis van Dycks/Rubens' Gemälden *Christus und der Gichtbrüchige* (um 1619). Münster 1976, S. 163, bildet ein van Dyck zugeschriebenes *Abendmahl* in damals spanischem Privatbesitz ab, das dieselben Typen wie in Soutmans Stich zeigt.
13 Der ungewöhnlicherweise auf Italienisch formulierte Text lautet: „la caena stupenda di Leonardo d'Avinci chi moriua nelle braccie di Rè di francia“, also: Das staunenerregende Abendmahl des Leonardo da Vinci, der in den Armen des Königs von Frankreich starb.
14 Vgl. Barrett 2012, S. 49 und hier Anm. 62.
15 Ob Rubens eine solche Kopie am Hofe von Vincenzo I. Gonzaga (1562–1612) in Mantua nach den dort befindlichen Tapisserien zeichnete, während er ebenda Hofkünstler war, oder nach anderen Vorlagen, kann nicht mit Sicherheit gesagt werden. Auch, ob Abweichungen wie die Aussparung der Landschaft im Stich auf Soutman oder Rubens zurückgehen, lässt sich nicht mehr klären. Ausführlich hierzu Wood 2006. Er erwähnt auch Hinweise auf eine verlorene Rubens-Zeichnung nach der *Schlüsselübergabe* (ebd., fig. 2 und S. 269).
16 Die Geschichte dieser Verbreitung ist im Artikel „The Story of the Raphael Cartoons“ zusammengefasst und illustriert, in: V & A, unter: <https://www.vam.ac.uk/articles/story-of-the-raphael-cartoons/#slideshow=5239394909&sli de=0> [gelesen am 9. Dezember 2023].
17 Die Zuschreibung an Vorsterman beruht auf stilkritischen Erwägungen und wurde zuletzt auch von Hans Jakob Meier in seinem Standardwerk zur Rubens-Graphik übernommen; siehe Meier 2020a, Kat. 14 und 15.
18 Für *Isabella d'Este* vermutet Jeremy Wood eine Entstehung um 1600/01 oder 1629/30. Jeremy Wood, in: München 2009, S. 61 f. und Kat. 1, bes. S. 138. Aufgrund des um 1620 entstandenen Stichs lässt sich die zweite Datierung nicht halten.
19 Nico Van Hout vermutet, Guzmán habe Rubens um einen Porträtstich gebeten, nachdem er jenen von Charles de Longueval (siehe im Kapitel „Porträts“, Abb. S. 269) gesehen hatte, den Vorsterman um 1621 schuf; vgl. hierzu Nils Büttner in diesem Katalog, S. 78 f. Der Stich für Guzmán habe, so Van Hout, dessen „militaire rol“ herausstellen sollen. Nico Van Hout, in: Antwerpen/Québec 2004, S. 58.
20 Die Zeichnung von Velázquez befindet sich in der Sammlung der École nationale supérieure des Beaux-Arts de Paris. Zur Ausdeutung von Rubens' allegorischer Gestaltung sowie dem wohl in Absprache mit Jan Gaspard Gevaerts komponierten Text siehe Meier 2020a, Kat. 30. Der Dankesbrief Guzmáns an Rubens ist erhalten. Vgl. Rooses/Ruelens 1887–1909, Bd. 3 (1900), S. 453 f., Brief CCCCVII. Auch abgedruckt, zudem kommentiert, in Meier 2020a, S. 390.

source for this portrait with the inscription “Ex Archetypo Velazquez.” He diminished his own contribution with the coquettishly modest phrase “ornavit” (ornamented by). But he also made sure to leave his mark by dedicating the print to the important Spanish courtier and by adding his privileges on the lower left.

1 See Luijten 2004, pp. 25–26.
2 Pollack 2020, p. 20.
3 McGrath 1984, p. 74, and, more recently, Wolkenhauer 2006, p. 337.
4 Huigen Leeflang, in: Amsterdam/New York/Toledo 2003, p. 209. He also points out that both artists, Dürer and Michelangelo, were described by Giorgio Vasari and Karel van Mander, the two major biographers of the time, as grand masters of *disegno*.
5 On Rubens's copies and reworkings of drawings after Polidoro, see Wood 2010, pp. 70–77, 396–402 (nos. 90–92). This topic was also dealt with earlier in München 2009, pp. 64–65. The Munich catalog and exhibition did not examine the prints in detail, however.
6 Giovanni Paolo Lomazzo in his 1584 multi-volume *Trattato dell'arte della pittura*. See Leeflang 2012, pp. 37–38, and Göttler 2020, esp. pp. 70–71 and 77.
7 Mander 1604, fol. 128v: “Dese comt oock, tot een goet fundament der jonghe Schilders in Druck, waerom ick den inhoudt niet behoeve te verhalen.”
8 Uta Schmidt-Clausen points out that in Goltzius's version, the prints are in the opposite order of the original work, while the captions describe the story in the correct chronological order. Schmidt-Clausen 2016, p. 337. Was this a mistake that the publisher Goltzius overlooked? Or did he expect his humanist customers to enjoy this discrepancy?
9 In an earlier state the print only named Pieter Soutman (as publisher as well as engraver) and not Rubens. For a copy of the earlier state in the Berlin Kupferstichkabinett, see Meier 2020a, pp. 334–335. Also see his informative discussion, cat. 74.
10 Barrett 2012, pp. 48–49. Meier 2020a, cat. 74, agrees with her.
11 Gerhard Langemeyer and Reinhard Schleier (Münster 1976, pp. 160, 164) consider the question of when and where Rubens might have seen the lost drawing. These authors interpret Rubens's deviations from Leonardo's composition as a conscious choice. Büttner 2011a, p. 126, agrees with them. Wood 2010, cat. 168, discusses the question of the Rubens drawing that Soutman used.
12 The figure of Christ (including his hands) appears in similar fashion in the paintings *Christ Healing the Paralytic* (ca. 1619; variously attributed to Anthony van Dyck and to Rubens). Münster 1976, p. 163, reproduces a *Last Supper* attributed to Van Dyck in a Spanish collection that shows the same types as in Soutman's print.
13 Strangely, the caption is in Italian and reads: “la caena stupenda di Leonardo d'Avinci chi moriua nelle braccie di Rè di francia,” namely: “The Astonishing [Last] Supper by Leonardo da Vinci, Who Died in the Arms of the King of France.”
14 See Barrett 2012, p. 49 (also see n. 62 on the same page).
15 We cannot be certain if Rubens drew a copy after such a tapestry while he was a court painter of Vincenzo I Gonzaga (1562–1612) in Mantua, or if he saw the motif elsewhere. Also, it is unclear if neglecting to depict the landscape was Rubens's or Soutman's idea. Extensively on this, see Wood 2006. He also mentions a lost Rubens drawing after *Christ's Charge to Peter* (see fig. 2 and p. 259).
16 For the story of this dissemination, see the illustrated article “The Story of the Raphael Cartoons,” V&A, accessed December 9, 2023, https://www.vam.ac.uk/articles/story-of-the-raphael-cartoons/#slideshow=5239394909&slide=0.
17 Scholars made the attribution to Vorsterman based on considerations of style, and Hans Jakob Meier agrees with this. See Meier 2020a, cat. 14, 15.
18 Jeremy Wood assumes 1600/01 or 1629/30 to be the date of *Isabella d'Este*. Jeremy Wood in: München 2009, pp. 61–62, and cat. 1, esp. p. 138. Because Vorsterman created the print around 1620, the second proposal cannot hold.
19 Nico Van Hout assumes that Guzmán asked Rubens for a portrait print after he saw that of Charles de Longueval (see the chapter “Portraits,” fig. p. 269), which Vorsterman engraved around 1621. For more on this, see Nils Büttner in the present catalog, pp. 78–79. Van Hout thinks the print for Guzmán emphasized his “militaire rol,” see Nico Van Hout, in: Antwerpen/Québec 2004, p. 58.
20 Velázquez's drawing is now in the collection of the École nationale supérieure des Beaux-Arts de Paris. For an interpretation of Rubens's allegorical iconography and the caption, composed with the help of Jan Gaspard Gevaerts, see Meier 2020a, cat. 30. Guzmán's letter of thanks to Rubens has been preserved, see Rooses/Ruelens 1887–1909, vol. 3 (1900), pp. 453–454, letter CCCCVII. Reprinted with commentary in: Meier 2020a, p. 390.

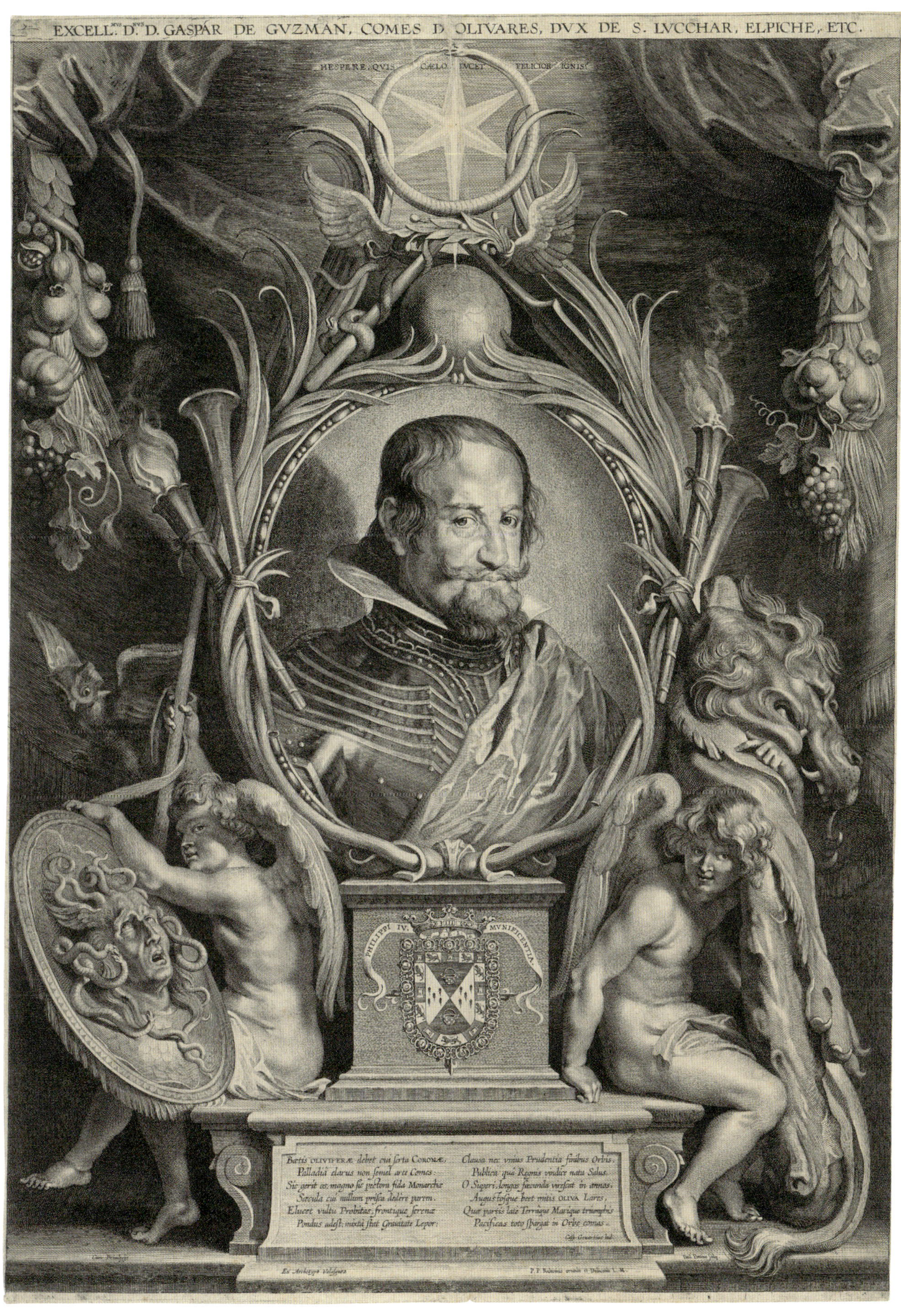

Rubens (Inventor / designer), Paulus Pontius (Stecher / engraver), nach / after Diego Velázquez
Bildnis des Gaspar de Guzmán, Graf von Olivares, Herzog von Sanlúcar /
Portrait of Gaspar de Guzmán, Count of Olivares, Duke of Sanlúcar, 1625
Kupferstich / engraving SGSM, Inv. 30309 D

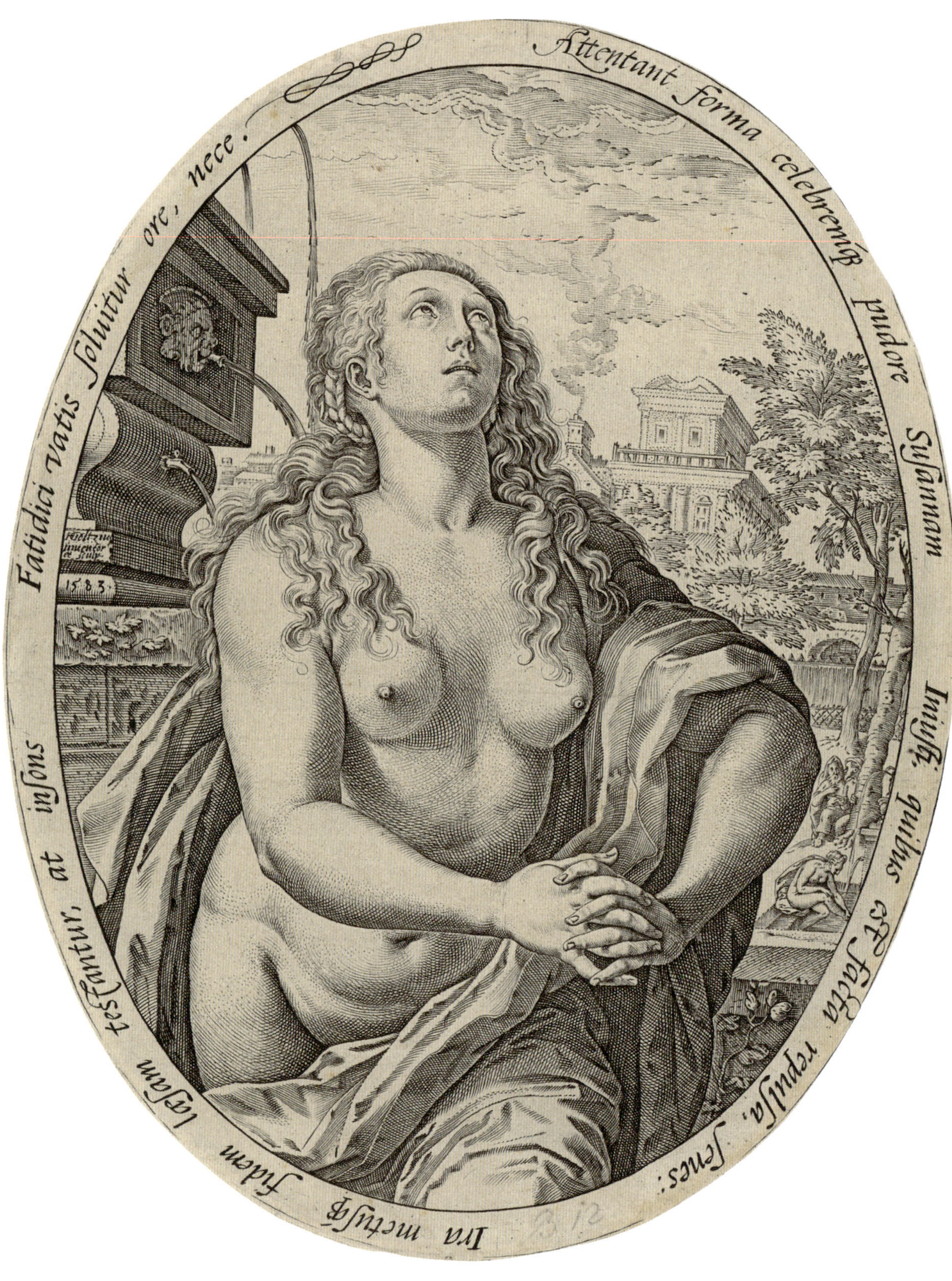

Hendrick Goltzius (Inventor, Stecher, Verleger / designer, engraver, publisher)
Susanna, 1583
Kupferstich / engraving SGSM, Inv. 30895 D

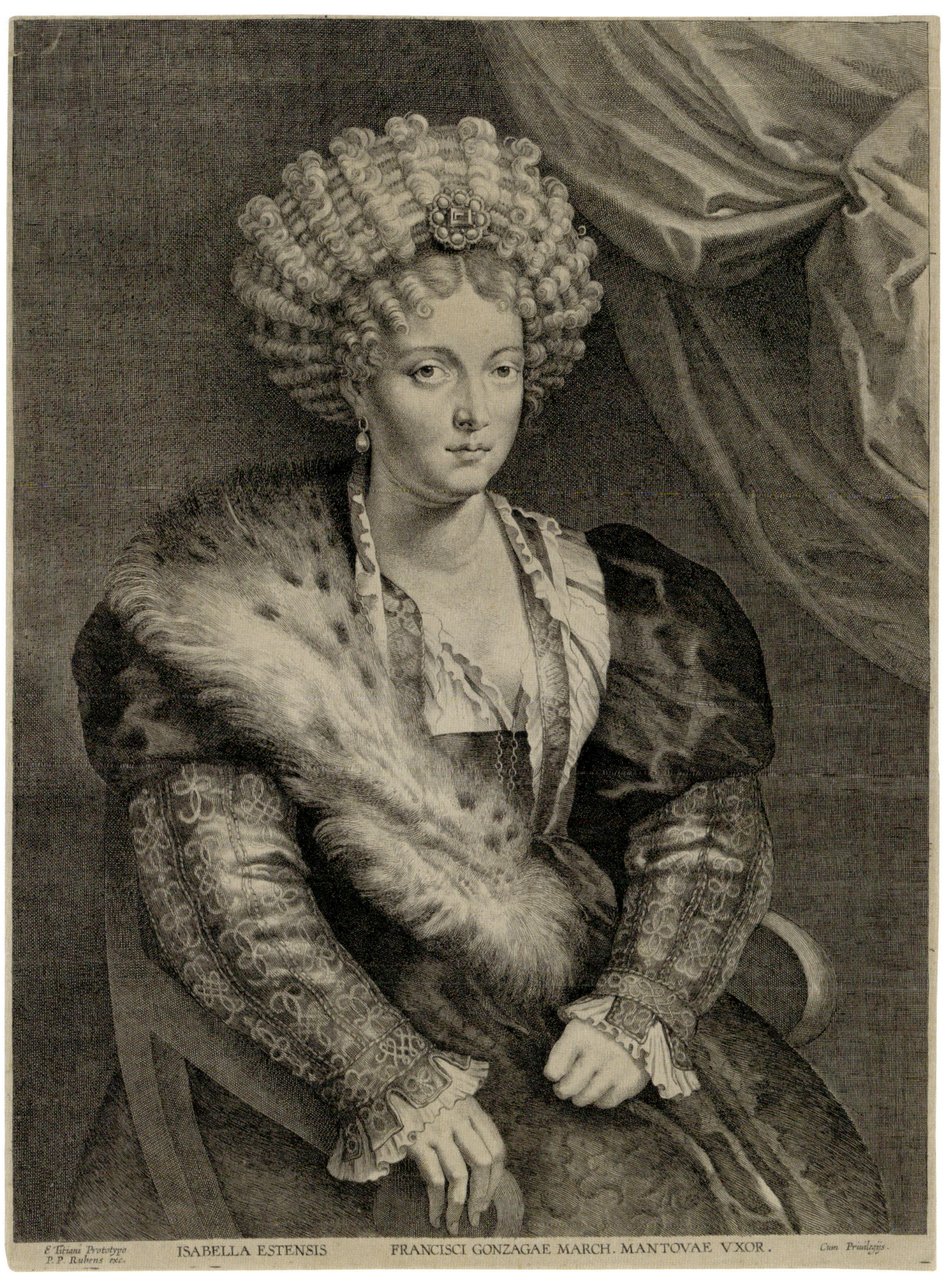

Rubens (Inventor, Verleger / designer, publisher), Lucas Vorsterman I (Stecher / engraver), nach Tizian / after Titian
Bildnis der / Portrait of Isabella d'Este, ca. 1620
Kupferstich / engraving SGSM, Inv. 138165 D

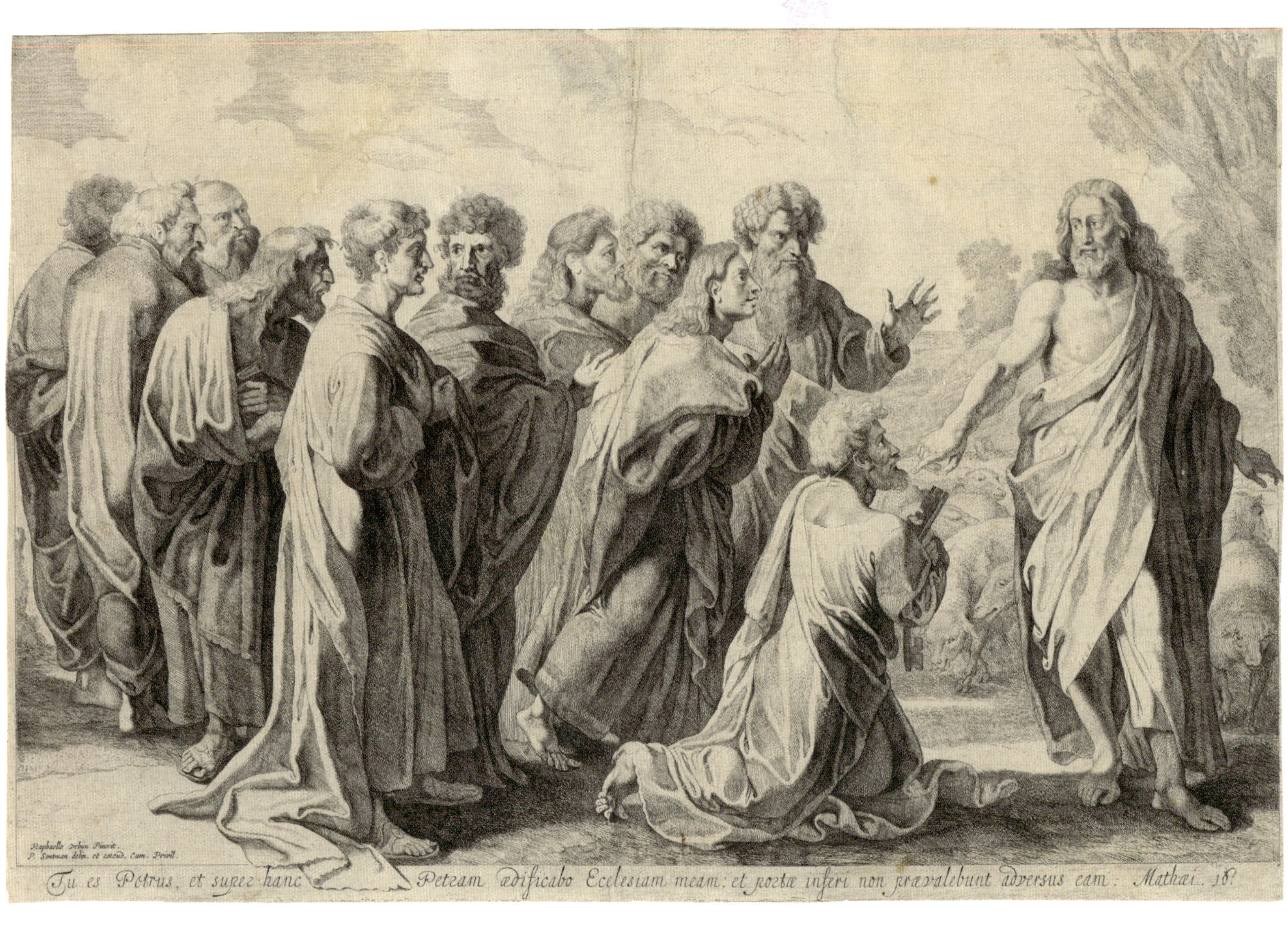

Pieter Soutman (Stecher, Radierer, Verleger / engraver, etcher, publisher), nach / after Rubens, nach Raffael / after Raphael
Christus übergibt Petrus den Schlüssel / Christ's Charge to Peter, 1632
Kupferstich, Radierung / engraving, etching, Zustand / state I SGSM, Inv. 4209 D

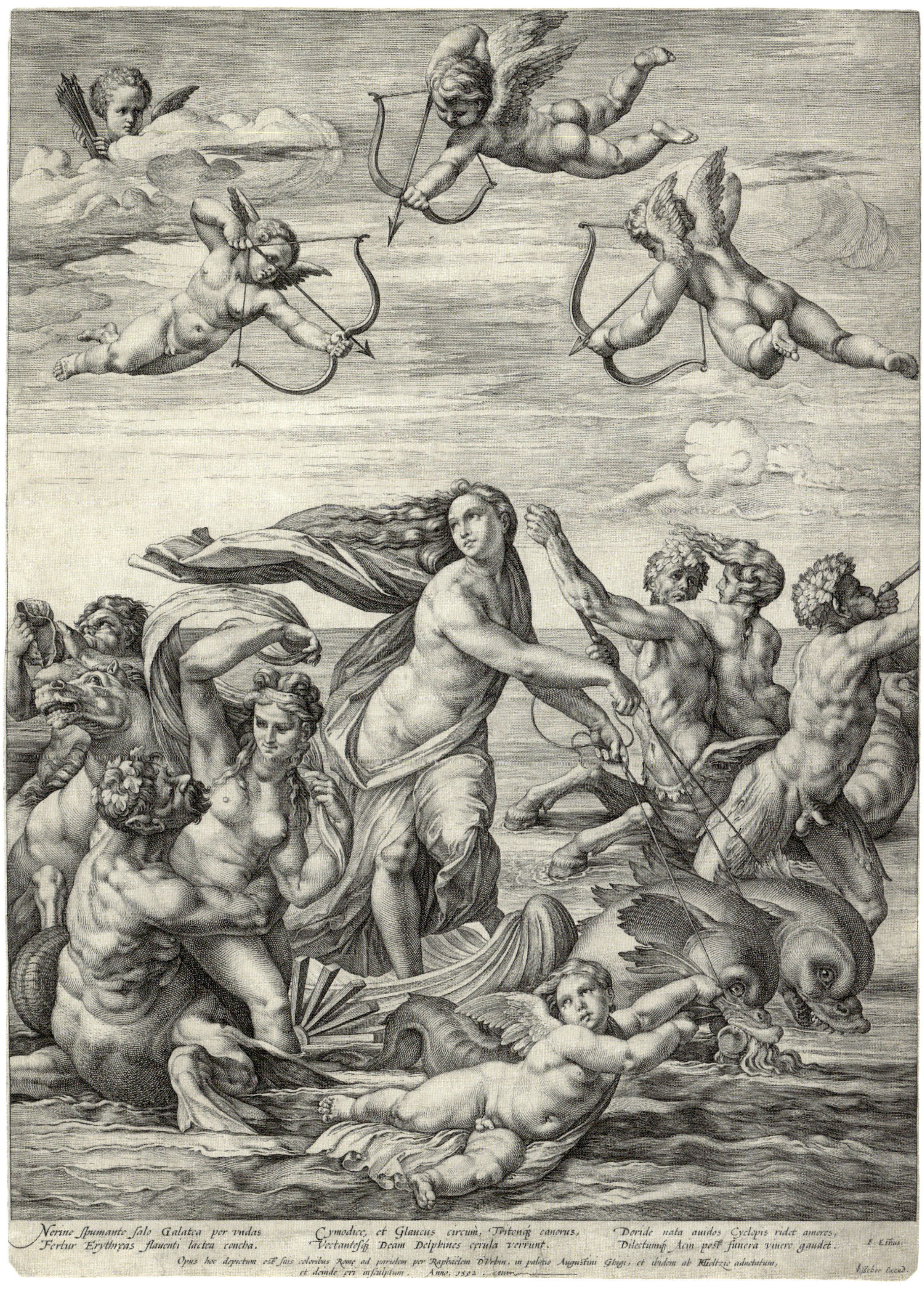

Goltzius (Zeichner, Stecher / draftsman, engraver), nach Raffael / after Raphael, Claes Jansz. Visscher (Verleger / publisher)
Triumph der Galatea / The Triumph of Galatea, 1592
Kupferstich / engraving SGSM, Inv. 1988:89 D

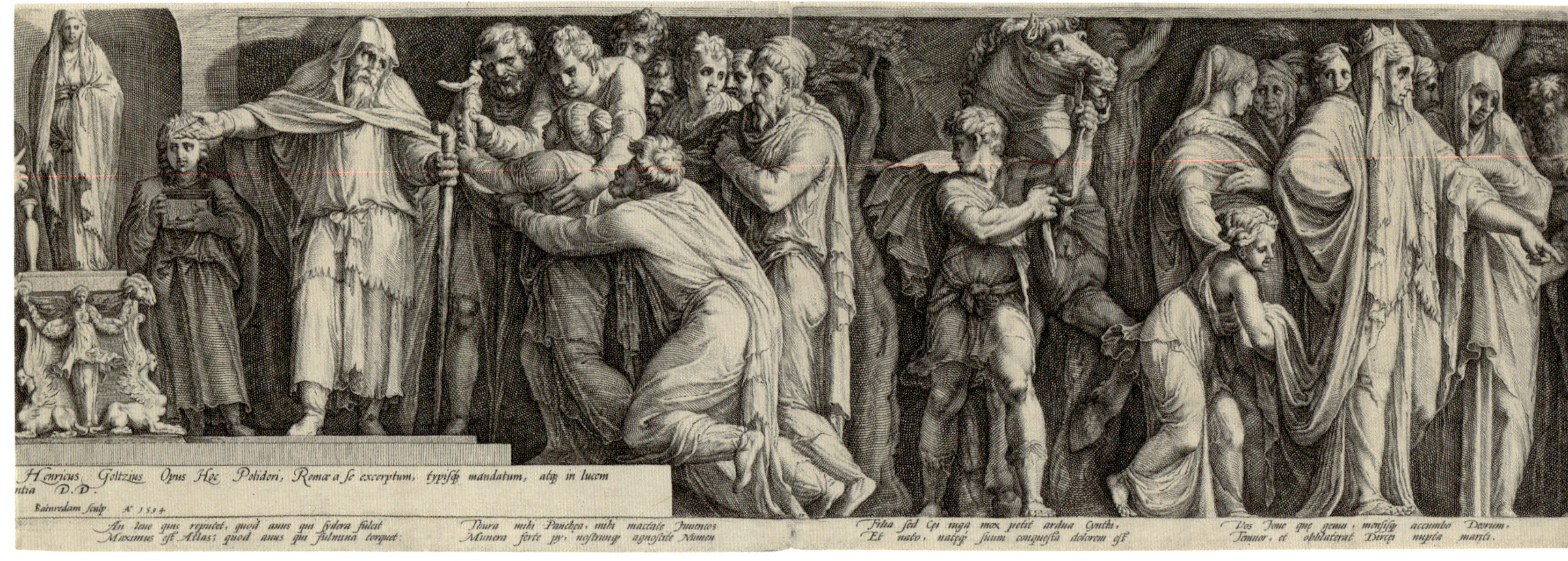

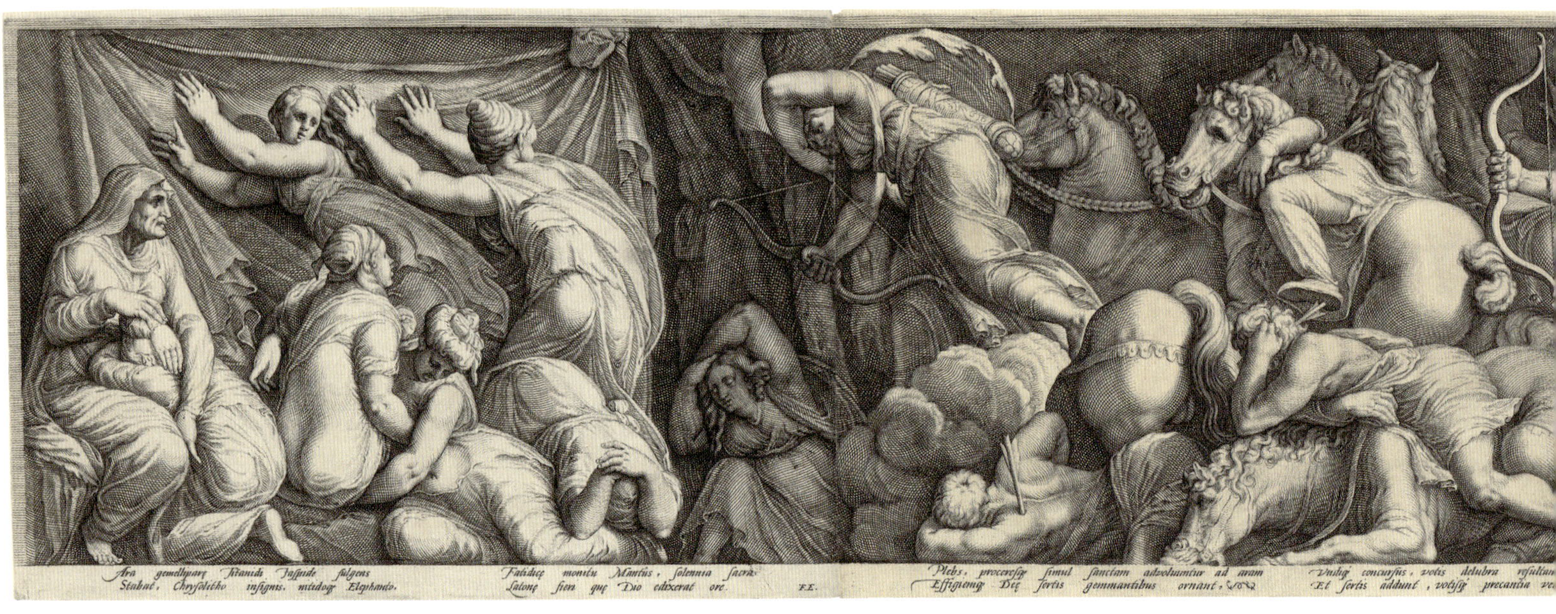

Goltzius (Zeichner / draftsman), Jan Saenredam (Stecher / engraver), nach / after Polidoro da Caravaggio, Claes Jansz. Visscher (Verleger / publisher)
Die Bestrafung der Niobe / The Punishment of Niobe, 1594 / vor / before 1680
Kupferstich / engraving SGSM, Inv. 62318 a–d D; 62319 a–d D

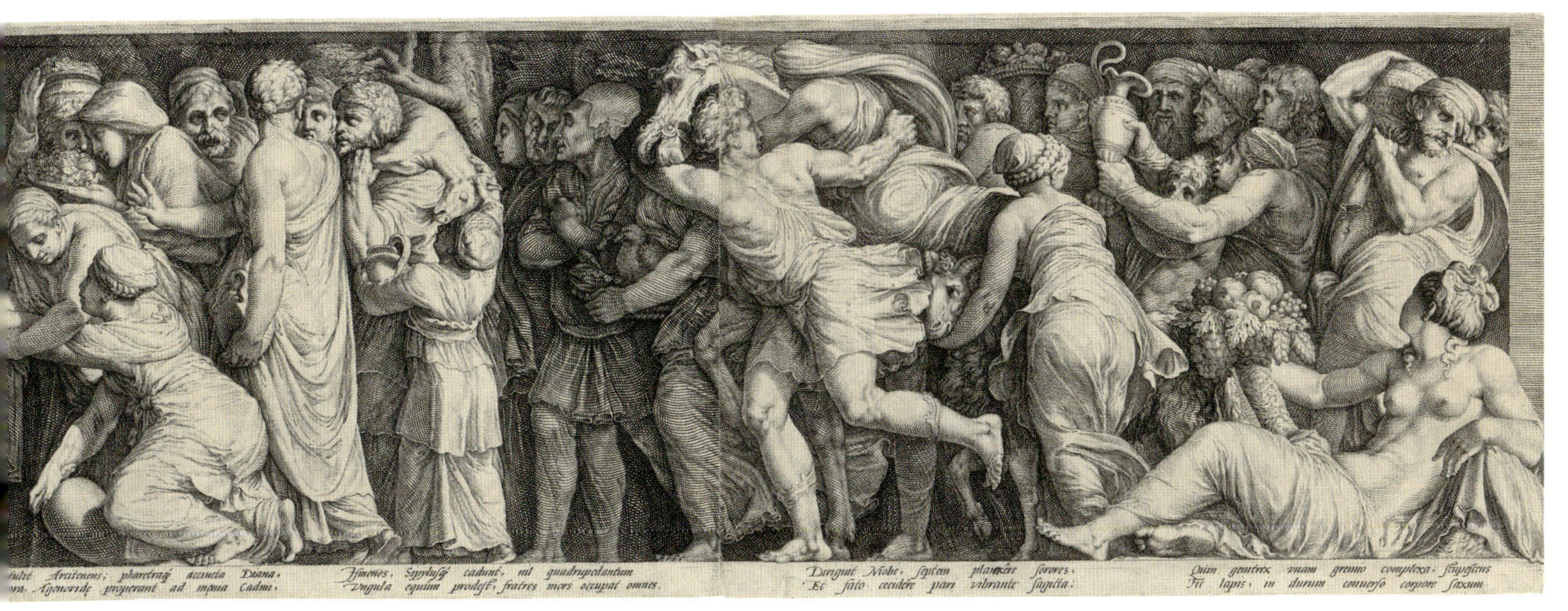
tulit Arcitenens; pharetraq accincta Diana,
Agenoride properant ad impia Cadmi,
Ismenos, Sipylusq cadunt, nil quadrupedantum
Ungula equum prodest, fratres mors occupat omnes.
Diriguit Niobe, septem planxere sorores,
Et fato cecidere pari vibrante sagitta:
Quin genitrix vnam gremio complexa, stupescens
Fit lapis, in durum conuerso corpore saxum

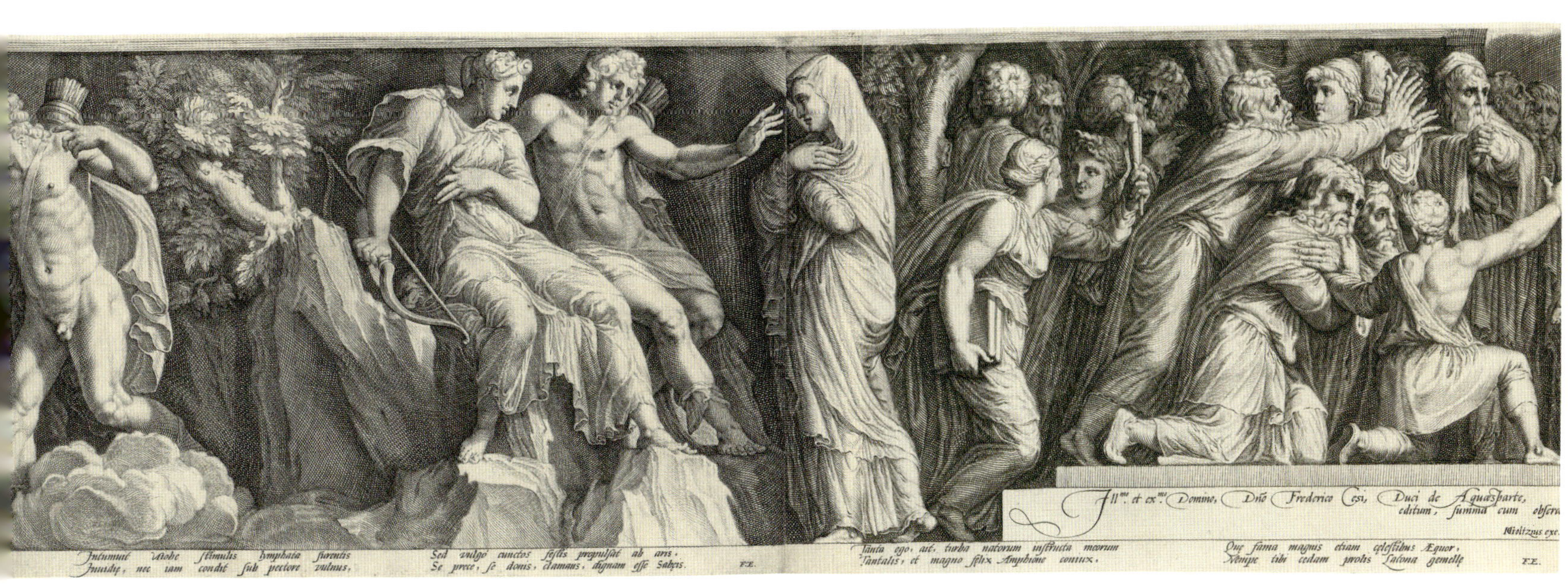
Intumuit Niobe stimulis lymphata furentis
Inuidiæ, nec iam condit sub pectore vulnus,
Sed vulgo cunctos festis propulsat ab aris,
Se prece, se donis, clamans, dignam esse Sabæis.
F.E.
Ill.me et ex.me Domino, Dño Frederico Cesi, Duci de Aguasparte,
editum, summa cum obser
Goltzius exe.
Tanta ego, ait, turba natorum instructa meorum
Tantalis, et magno felix Amphione coniux.
Quæ fama magnis etiam cœlestibus Æquor,
Nempe tibi cedam prolis Latona gemellæ
F.E.

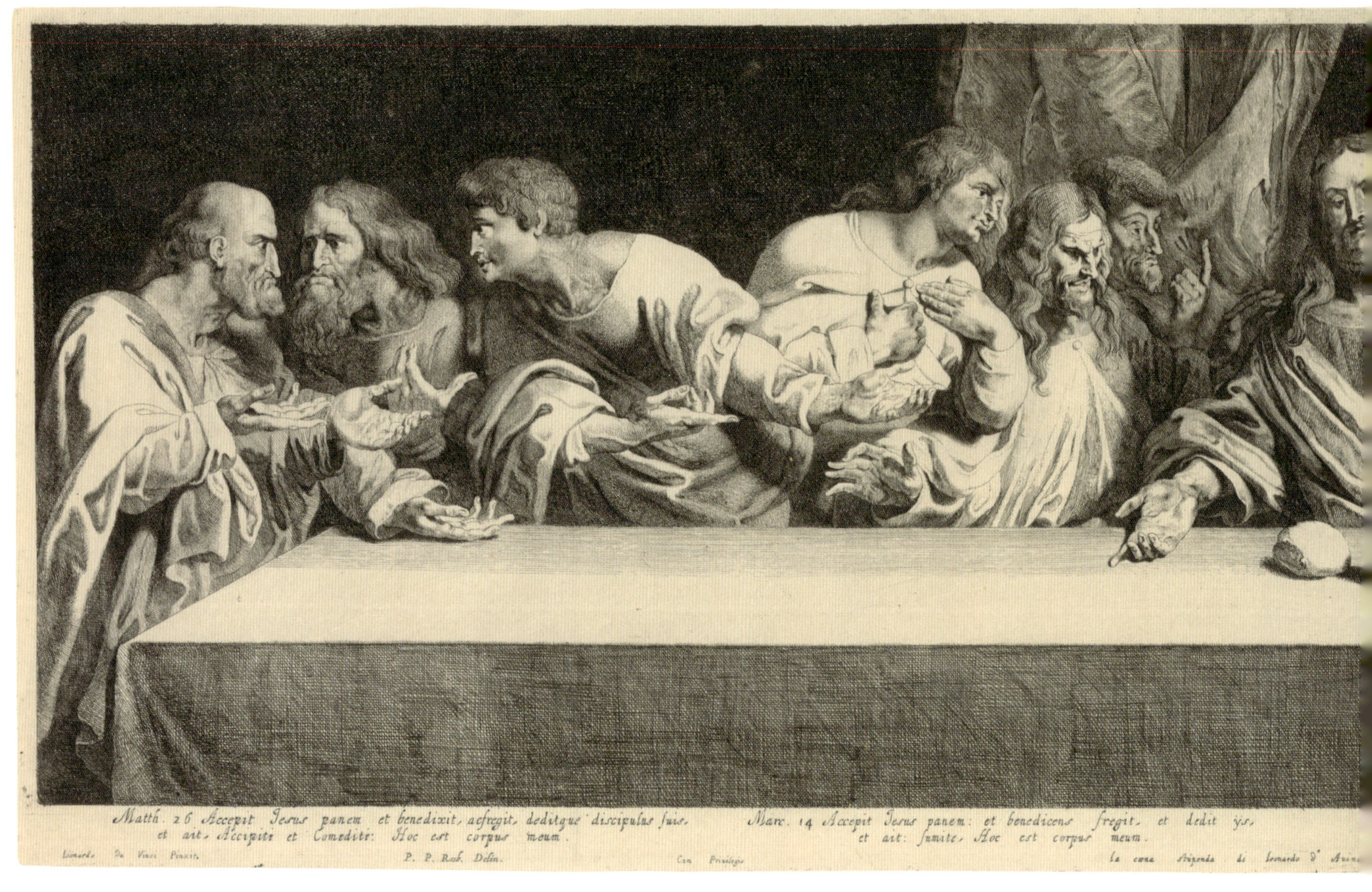

Pieter Soutman (Radierer / etcher), nach / after Rubens, nach / after Leonardo da Vinci
Das letzte Abendmahl / The Last Supper, 1632
Radierung / etching, Zustand / state II SGSM, Inv. 6715-a–b D

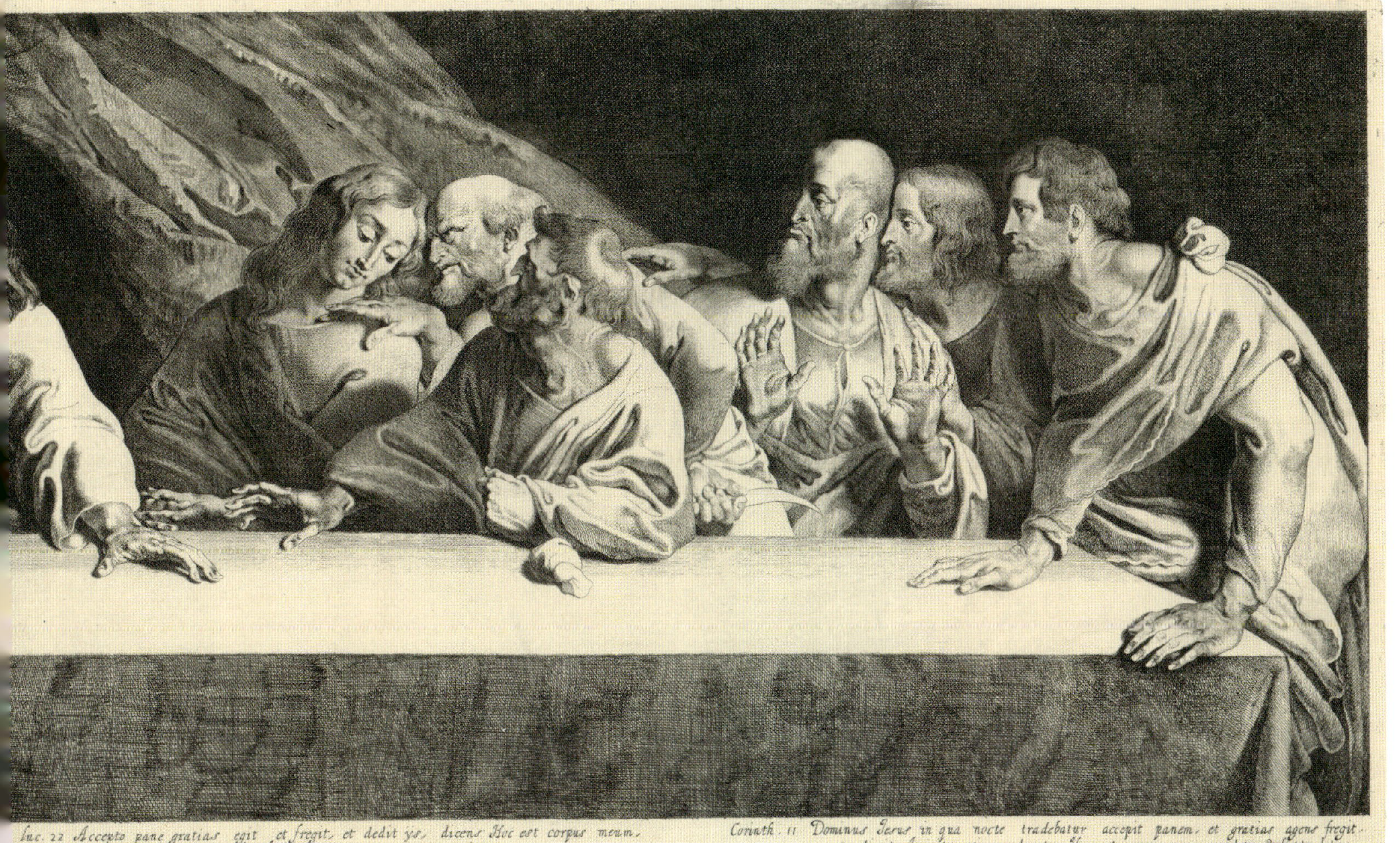
luc. 22 Accepto pane gratias egit et fregit, et dedit ys, dicens: Hoc est corpus meum,
quod pro vobis datur: hoc facite in meam commemorationem.
Corinth. 11 Dominus Jesus in qua nocte tradebatur accepit panem, et gratias agens fregit,
et dixit Accipite et manducate: Hoc est corpus meum, quod pro vobis tradetur:
hoc facite in meam commemorationem.

X. Porträts

Sowohl Hendrick Goltzius als auch Peter Paul Rubens gehörten zu den gesuchtesten und erfolgreichsten Porträtisten ihrer Zeit. Leicht hätten sie sich auf dieses Genre spezialisieren können, aber eine solche thematische Beschränkung war für beide undenkbar. Zwar finden sich in ihren informellen Zeichnungen auch Bildnisse aus dem privaten Umfeld. Der Schwerpunkt in ihren Graphiken lag jedoch auf dem, womit sie namentlich vor eine internationale Öffentlichkeit treten würden. Und hier zählte in erster Linie, wen man selbst kannte und wer einen (aner)kannte. Bildnisse von Gelehrten aus dem eigenen Umkreis zeigten, in welcher Welt der Gebildeten und Wohlhabenden die Künstler verkehrten. Wichtiger aber noch waren die Porträts von Fürsten und Politikern. Denn mit ihnen konnten die Künstler diesen Machthabern huldigen und zugleich darstellen, dass sie umgekehrt von den Potentaten geschätzt und protegiert wurden.

Beide *Bildnisse des Hendrick Goltzius* von Jacob Matham (1571–1631) erschienen erst nach dem Tod von Goltzius 1617 und 1618 (Abb. S. 13, 250). Der Stiefsohn fertigte sie – vielleicht als Todesanzeigen – nach einem Selbstbildnis an, das Goltzius gegen Ende seines Lebens gezeichnet hatte.[1] Sie unterscheiden sich jedoch stark in ihren Formaten und in der Ausschmückung, die jeweils auf Matham zurückgehen, möglicherweise, weil sie Adressaten unterschiedlichen Ranges erreichen sollten. Auf beiden Stichen benannte Matham sich als „privigenus", als Stiefsohn, was im Kontext des Stichs implizierte, dass er auch der künstlerische Erbe sei. Dies war sicher auch als Werbemaßnahme zu verstehen. Das große Blatt (442 × 298 mm; Abb. S. 13) erhebt in Format und allegorischer Ausschmückung den Anspruch, dass hier ein Künstler von Weltruhm gewürdigt wird.[2]

Die *Bildnisse des Willem van Oranje* und seiner dritten Frau *Charlotte* von Bourbon (beide 1581) entstanden sicher als Auftragsarbeiten, doch Näheres wissen wir nicht (Abb. S. 258f.). Sie sind als Pendants mit ähnlichen Schmuckrahmen angelegt. Die Szenen in Willems Rahmen feiern ihn als holländischen Moses, der sein Volk aus der Unterdrückung (der spanischen Feinde) und in die Unabhängigkeit führte. In den Niederlanden trägt er daher auch den Titel „Vater des Vaterlandes". Die Forschung geht davon aus, dass Goltzius Zeichnungen vom Königspaar anfertigen durfte, dass er also für diesen Zweck persönlich vorgelassen wurde. Dies zeigt, welch hohes Ansehen seine Kunst und er als Künstler bereits genossen, noch bevor er sich selbstständig gemacht hatte.

Als Einzelblatt und Freundschaftsgabe konzipiert, schuf Goltzius 1582 das *Bildnis des Philips Galle* (Abb. S. 249). Im Jahr seiner eigenen Geschäftsgründung gestochen, war das Blatt eine Hommage an den Älteren, wodurch der Firmengründer auch ein Licht auf sich selbst richten wollte.[3] Galle (1537–1612) war einer der ersten Verleger, von dem Goltzius Aufträge erhalten hatte, und sein Verlagshaus war Vorbild für das eigene. Goltzius zog mit diesem Stich alle damals zur Verfügung stehenden Register seiner Zunft: Er schuf das innovative Porträt eines erfolgreichen Mannes, beauftragte bei dem Staatsmann und Dichter Johann van der Does (1545–1604) eine lateinische

X. Portraits

Hendrick Goltzius and Peter Paul Rubens were among the most sought-after and successful portraitists of their times. They could have easily made a specialization of this genre, but such a narrow thematic direction was unthinkable to both artists. While there exist informal portrait drawings from their private circles, the emphasis in their prints was clearly on what they wanted a wider audience to associate with their names. And that was, above all, to show off the who's who of people they knew and who knew them. Portraits of scholars with whom they were acquainted showed that both artists moved in the worlds of the well-educated and well-established. Even more important were portraits of princes and politicians. With such official representations, artists could pay homage to men in power and simultaneously cast them as admirers and patrons of their art.

Both *Portraits of Hendrick Goltzius* by Jacob Matham (1571–1631) were published only after the subject's death, namely in 1617 and 1618 (figs. pp. 13, 250). The stepson engraved them—perhaps as a kind of obituary—after a self-portrait Goltzius had drawn toward the end of his life.[1] They differ in size and in the amount of ornamentation Matham added, perhaps with the intention of reaching different audiences. In both prints, Matham referred to himself as "privigenus," or stepson, which in the context of a print implied that he wanted to be perceived as the heir to Goltzius's artistic legacy as well. It was a kind of marketing device. In terms of both size and allegorical ornamentation, the larger of the two prints (442 × 298 mm; fig. p. 13) aims at honoring an artist who enjoyed international fame.[2]

The *Portraits of Willem van Oranje* and his third wife, *Charlotte van Oranje* (both 1581), were most certainly commissioned works, but no further details are known (figs. pp. 258–259). With their ornamental frames, they were conceived as companion pieces. The scenes in Willem's frame celebrate him as a Dutch Moses who has led his people out of submission (by the Spanish oppressor) and to independence. In Holland, he is therefore referred to as "father of the fatherland." Scholars assume that Goltzius received permission to make drawings of the couple and that he was allowed for this purpose to meet them in person. This shows that he and his art enjoyed tremendous esteem even before he became an independent printmaker and publisher.

Goltzius engraved the *Portrait of Philips Galle* (fig. p. 249), which was conceived as an individual print and a gift of friendship, in 1582, the year he set up shop. The print was an homage to his mentor—and it also helped direct attention to himself and his new firm.[3] Not only was Galle (1537–1612) one of the first publishers to commission prints from Goltzius, but his publishing house became a model for the younger man. For this print, Goltzius played all the cards available in print publishing: he created an innovative portrait of a successful man and commissioned the statesman and poet Johann van der Does (1545–1604) to author a

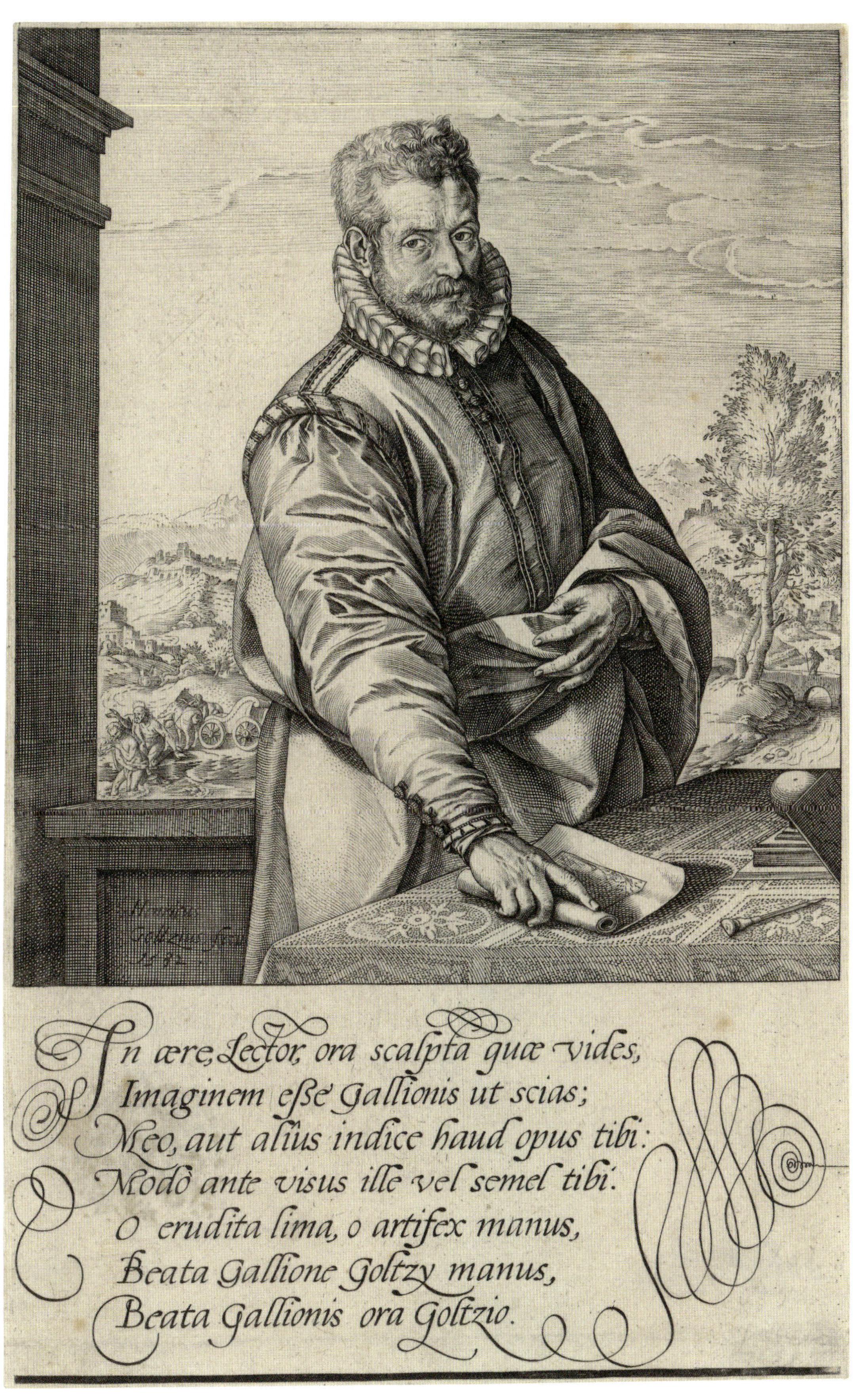

Hendrick Goltzius (Inventor, Stecher / designer, engraver)
Bildnis des / Portrait of Philips Galle, 1582
Kupferstich / engraving SGSM, Inv. 31028 D

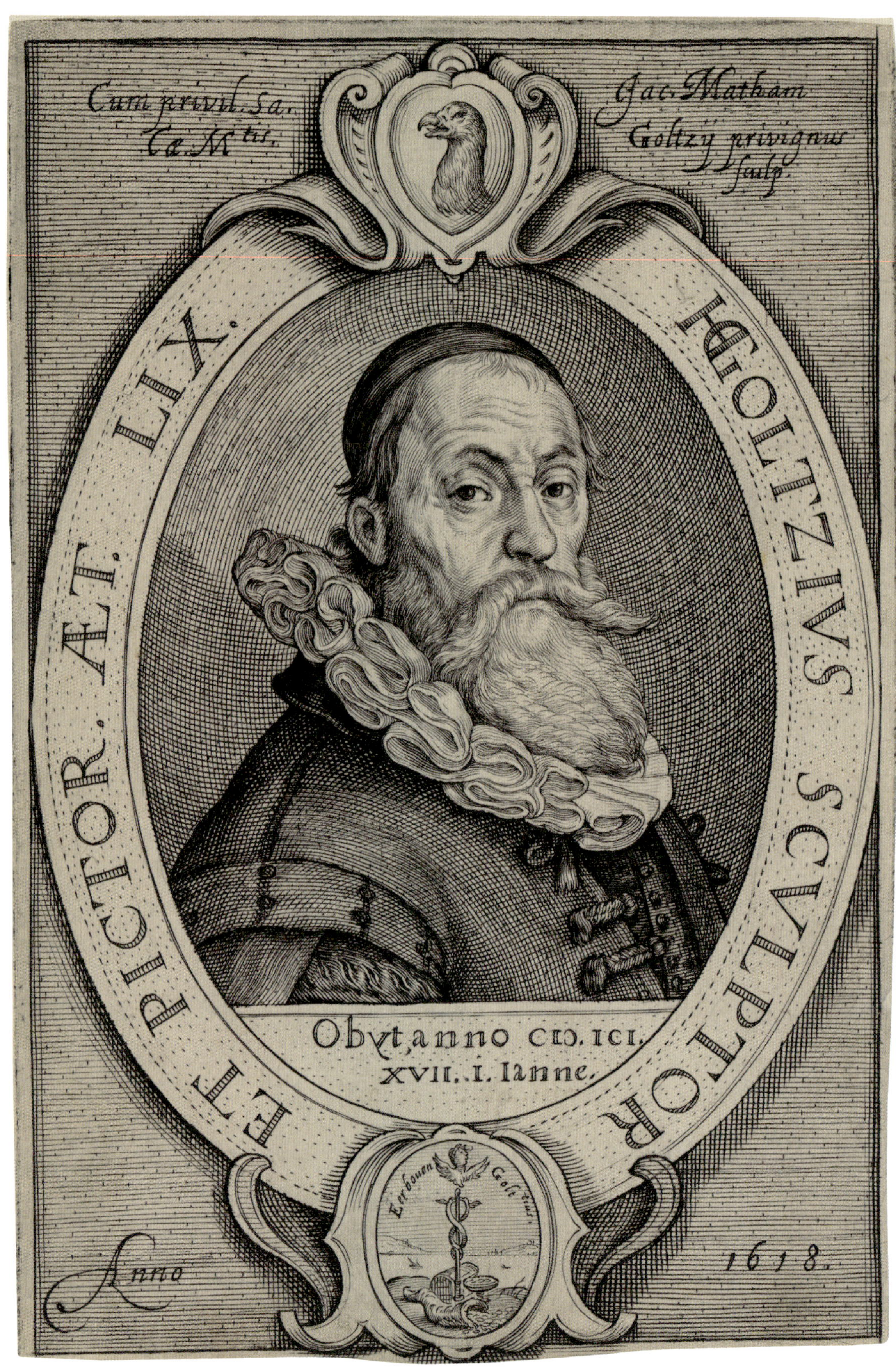

Jacob Matham (Stecher / engraver), nach / after Goltzius
Bildnis des / Portrait of Hendrick Goltzius, 1618
Kupferstich / engraving SGSM, Inv. 1909:316 D

Rubens (Inventor / designer), Paulus Pontius (Stecher, Verleger / engraver, publisher)
Selbstbildnis des / Self-Portrait of Peter Paul Rubens, 1630
Kupferstich / engraving SGSM, Inv. 101990 D

Bildunterschrift und ließ diese noch dazu von einem herausragenden (aber uns namentlich nicht bekannten) Kalligraphen ausführen.[4] Seinen eigenen Namen brachte Goltzius gleich zweimal ein: als Signatur in der Darstellung selbst und als Hingucker am Ende der Bildunterschrift – „Goltzio" –, sodass die auffällige kalligraphische Schleife rechts aus seinem Namen hervorgeht, aber vor allem auf diesen zurückweist. Diese Ausstattung des Stichs war für jeden Zeitgenossen als hochwertig erkennbar. Sie setzte den Ton für den Anspruch, dem Goltzius in Zukunft mit seinem eigenen Verlag gerecht werden wollte.

Um Freundschaftsporträts handelte es sich auch bei einem Holzschnitt mit dem *Bildnis des Gillis van Breen* sowie der Zeichnung, die diesem vorausging (Abb. S. 260 f.). Van Breen (um 1560–1602) war der einzige uns namentlich bekannte Drucker in Goltzius' Werkstatt.[5] In den Bildnissen aus Goltzius' privatem Umfeld ist er gleich mehrfach zu finden.[6] Die auf 1588 datierte lebensgroße Zeichnung (376 × 292 mm) aus dem Frankfurter Städel Museum ist Goltzius' erstes in farbiger Kreide ausgeführtes Porträt und lässt besonders im Umgang mit den Farben die unglaubliche Qualität der bald darauf in Italien entstandenen Bildnisse anklingen. Wer hätte sich nicht ein solch lebensgroßes, einfühlsames und sympathisches Bildnis von sich selbst gewünscht? Goltzius widmete eine Reihe dieser Blätter Künstlern und Freunden. Sie gehören bis heute zu den größten Schätzen in graphischen Sammlungen.

Etwa um dieselbe Zeit wie die Zeichnung fertigte Goltzius den rund halb so großen Holzschnitt (207 × 145 mm) mit dem *Bildnis des Gillis van Breen*, doch mit ganz anderem Effekt. Die Linien sind ausgeführt wie bei einer Federzeichnung, das wird deutlich in den ersten Abzügen, die den Kopf nur als flachen Abdruck vom Linienblock brachten. Die beiden braunen Tonplatten im hier gezeigten Abzug verstärken zwar die Bildtiefe, nicht aber seine Klarheit. Das Motiv wirkt wie eine späte Reminiszenz an italienische Vorbilder. Interessanterweise hat auch Goltzius, wie Jahre nach ihm Rubens, nur ein einziges Porträt als Holzschnitt angefertigt. Für beide scheint dieses Experiment reizvoll, aber letztlich nicht zufriedenstellend gewesen zu sein.

Eine Besonderheit innerhalb der Porträts sind die Bildnismedaillons, die Goltzius eine Zeitlang in Silber oder Gold anfertigte (Abb. S. 262 f.). Dabei handelte es sich in vielen Fällen um Metallanhänger, von denen eine kleine Handvoll Abzüge genommen wurde, die der Besitzer dann im Freundeskreis verteilen konnte. Solche Abzüge erkennt man daran, dass die Schrift seitenverkehrt ist. Auf dem Metall selbst war sie lesbar. Die meisten der Medaillons sind verloren, aber einige der Abzüge sind erhalten. An dieser Stelle seien zwei Bildnisse besonders hervorgehoben: das von *Hieronymus Scholiers* (1583) und jenes von *Heinrich IV.* (1592). In beiden arbeitete Goltzius mit Trompe-l'Œil-Effekten. Die Büsten der Dargestellten durchbrechen die Bildumschrift und werfen Schatten, wodurch sie noch etwas lebendiger wirken. Goltzius erreichte mit seinen Bildnismedaillons, die viele Nachahmer fanden, eine bis dahin unbekannte Qualität im Porträt.

Das *Bildnis des Frederick de Vries* (1597) stand am Ende von Goltzius' Tätigkeit als Stecher und war dazu angetan, ähnlich Sensationelles zu bieten (Abb. S. 257). Dieses Kalkül ging auf. Frederick de Vries war der Sohn eines engen Freundes, den Goltzius zusammen mit dessen Bruder als Pflegekinder bei sich aufgenommen hatte. Versehen mit dem kaiserlichen Privileg und den gelehrten Texten war das Blatt

Latin epigram which he had engraved on the plate by a superb calligrapher (unknown to us by name).[4] Goltzius included his own name twice: as a signature inside the portrait and as an eye-catcher at the end of the epigram—"Goltzio"—with a flamboyant calligraphic bow flowing from his own name while actually pointing back to it. Choosing these luxurious accoutrements for the print made it stand out. This portrait proclaimed the ambitions Goltzius had for his own publishing house.

Both the preparatory drawing and the woodcut of the *Portrait of Gillis van Breen* were conceived as portraits honoring and expressing friendship (figs. pp. 260–261). Van Breen (ca. 1560–1602) is the only printer in Goltzius's workshop we know by name.[5] His likeness appears several times in drawings Goltzius made of his private circle.[6] The life-size drawing (376 × 292 mm), dated 1588, now in the Städel Museum in Frankfurt, is the artist's first portrait in colored chalks. It foreshadows the extraordinary quality of the portraits he was to produce soon after on his Italian journey. Who would not want such a life-size, sensitive, and likable portrait of themselves? Goltzius dedicated a number of these works to artists and friends. To this day they belong to the most treasured works in any graphic art collection.

Around the same time as the drawing, Goltzius engraved the woodcut of the *Portrait of Gillis van Breen*, yet to a different effect. He drove the lines to imitate a pen drawing, as can be seen in the first prints, which render the head as a flat print from the line-block only. The two brown tone-blocks he added, which are visible in the print depicted here, contributed depth but not clarity. In this the motif appears like a belated remembrance of Italian models. It is noteworthy that Goltzius, like Rubens years later, designed only one portrait for woodcut. Both artists seem to have been tempted by the experiment, only to be disappointed by the results.

A specialty among Goltzius's portraits are the medallions he engraved for a short time in silver and gold (figs. pp. 262–263). Many of these were created as metal pendants from which a few prints could be made. These prints can be identified by their mirrored inscriptions; on the original metal pendants, the words were legible. Most of the medallions are now lost, but a few of the prints survive. Two portraits stand out in another aspect: those of *Hieronymus Scholiers* (1583) and *Henry IV* (1592). In both, Goltzius used trompe l'oeil effects. The busts of the sitters overlap the inscriptions surrounding the ovals and cast shadows on them, thus appearing even more lifelike. In his portrait medallions Goltzius was much emulated and achieved an unknown level of quality.

The *Portrait of Frederick de Vries* (1597) dates to the end of Goltzius's active time as an engraver and was intended to make its mark (fig. p. 257). In this it succeeded. Frederick de Vries was the son of a close friend of Goltzius's, and the artist had taken the boy and his brother on as foster children. Adorned with the imperial privilege and with scholarly inscriptions, the print was recognizable to anyone, according to Karsten Müller, as a "doubly distinguished commodity."[7] Countless copies helped spread its fame even faster.[8] The image offered unseen novelties not only in

für jedermann als „doppelt ausgezeichnete Handelsware“ erkennbar, so Karsten Müller.[7] Unzählige Kopien verbreiteten den Stich sofort noch schneller.[8] Das Bild bot unerhört Neues im Genre Porträt, aber auch zum Thema Allegorie. Noch nie hatte man ein solch verspieltes Kind dargestellt. Der Knabe gibt vor, ein Falkner zu sein, der Hund ersetzt ihm das Pferd, die Taube den Falken.[9] Darüber hinaus ist der Hund auch als Selbstbildnis des Goltzius verstanden worden, was aus dem Bild ein Doppelporträt machen würde.[10] Wie die Bildunterschrift erläutert, ist der Hund als Symbol der Treue, der Knabe als Personifikation der Einfachheit zu verstehen.

Ein zweites Mal nach dem oben erwähnten Medaillon hat Goltzius ein *Bildnis von Heinrich IV.* (nach 1600), dem französischen König (1553–1610), gestochen (Abb. S. 255). Dabei handelte es sich um eine Auftragsarbeit für den Pariser Verleger Paulus de la Houve, der eine Serie von Bildnissen aus dem engeren Kreis des Königs bei verschiedenen Künstlern bestellt hatte.[11] Goltzius fiel das wichtigste Werk der Serie zu. Obwohl er sich seit einigen Jahren vom Stechen zurückgezogen hatte, konnte er diesen Auftrag wohl nicht ablehnen, doch er meisterte ihn mit Bravur.[12] Nicht nur verhalf er den Texturen (wenn schon nicht dem König, der entsprechend den übrigen Werken der Serie vornehm steif wirkt) zu großer Lebendigkeit. Auch die Bildunterschrift lässt seinen Anspruch erkennen, dass dieses Bildnis herausstäche. Die Kalligraphie ist besonders aufwendig und zeigt eine extravagante Schleife, wie er sie auch im *Bildnis des Philips Galle* verwendet hatte.

Das Gemälde (Abb. S. 75), nach dem Paulus Pontius (1603–1658) 1630 das *Selbstbildnis des Peter Paul Rubens* stach (Abb. S. 251), bedeutete 1623 eine kleine Revolution in diesem Genre. Nie zuvor hatte ein Künstler sich selbst auf diese Weise porträtiert. Als der britische Thronfolger ihn drängte, ihm ein Selbstbildnis zu senden, war es dieses Gemälde, das Rubens nach England sandte.[13] Sich der Dreistigkeit seiner fast adligen Selbstinszenierung wohl bewusst, suchte er diesen Eindruck in seiner Kommunikation darüber mit einer rhetorischen Bescheidenheitsformel zu mildern: „[…] obwohl es mir unpassend schien, einem Fürsten dieses Ranges mein Porträt zu schicken. Aber er bezwang meine Bescheidenheit […].“[14] Dass er stolz auf dieses Bild war, zeigt der Stich, den er sieben Jahre später von Pontius anfertigen ließ und der sein Bildnis in der ganzen Welt bekannt machte.[15] Erste Kopien des Motivs erschienen bereits vor 1650, ungezählte weitere seither. Der in München aufbewahrte Umdruck (um 1630) weist keine Korrekturen auf, wie sie manche Probedrucke tragen (Abb. S. 12). Er erleichterte Rubens und Pontius im Produktionsprozess den Vergleich mit der Kupferplatte (und der Stichvorlage, siehe Abb. S. 82 und Nils Büttner, S. 80), mit der er seitengleich ist, und vermutlich wurde er genau für einen solchen Abgleich angefertigt.[16]

Der herausragende Stecher Jan Harmensz. Muller war zuvor für Goltzius tätig gewesen, für den er 1589 die Serie *Die Erschaffung der Welt* stach (vgl. Abb. S. 201–203 im Kapitel „Meisterdrucke“). 1615 veröffentlichte Muller die datierten und mit seinem Privileg versehenen *Bildnisse von Albrecht VII.* und *Isabella Clara Eugenia*, den Statthaltern der südlichen Niederlande (Abb. S. 264 f.). In der Bildunterschrift teilte er mit, dass seine Darstellungen auf die Gemälde des Hofmalers Peter Paul Rubens zurückgehen. Dabei sind die Steifheit von Rubens’ Kompositionen wie auch die wenig schwungvolle Ausführung Mullers wohl

the portrait genre but also in allegories. Never before had anyone depicted such a playful child. The boy plays at being a falconer, using the dog for his horse and the pigeon for the falcon.[9] Moreover, the dog has also been interpreted as a self-portrait of Goltzius, which would make the picture a double portrait.[10] As the inscription states, the dog is a symbol of fidelity, while the boy personifies simplicity.

In addition to the abovementioned portrait medallion of the French king, Goltzius engraved another *Portrait of Henry IV* (fig. p. 255) sometime after 1600. This was a commission from the Parisian publisher Paul de la Houve, who had asked various artists to create portraits of members of the king’s inner circle.[11] The most important portrait fell to Goltzius. Even though he had given up engraving a few years before, he could not decline this commission and mastered it with great style.[12] Not only did he lend much vivacity to the textures (if not to the king himself, who had to appear nobly stiff in accordance with the other works in the series), but he also made sure the inscription would match his desire that this portrait stand out. The calligraphy here is especially extravagant and sports an eccentric bow like the one we saw in the *Portrait of Philips Galle*.

The painting of 1623 (fig. p. 75) after which Paulus Pontius (1603–1658) engraved the *Self-Portrait of Peter Paul Rubens* (fig. p. 251) was a small revolution in this genre. Never before had an artist depicted himself in this way. When the British heir to the throne pushed the artist to send him a self-portrait, it was this painting that Rubens sent to England.[13] Well aware of the audacity of presenting himself like a nobleman, in his correspondence about the artwork he sought to lessen this impression with assumed rhetorical humility: “Though to me it did not seem fitting to send my portrait to a prince of such rank, he overcame my modesty.”[14] The fact that he was proud of this picture is evident in the print he had Pontius engrave seven years later, which made the portrait known to all the world.[15] Copies of the motif appeared as early as before 1650, and countless others have appeared since. The counterproof in the Munich collection (ca. 1630; fig. p. 12) has no correction marks, as some counterproofs do. During the production process, Rubens and Pontius would have compared it with the copperplate (see fig. p. 82 and Nils Büttner in the present catalog, p. 80), since like the preparatory drawing it faced in the same direction as the plate. Most likely the counterproof was pulled for this very purpose.[16]

The brilliant engraver Jan Harmensz. Muller had previously worked for Goltzius on the 1589 series *The Creation of the World* (see figs. pp. 201–203 in the chapter “Masterprints”). In 1615 Muller published the *Portraits of Albert VII* and *Isabella Clara Eugenia*, governors of the Southern Netherlands, which bore the date and his privilege (figs. pp. 264–265). In the inscription he declared that his portrayals were based on the paintings by court painter Peter Paul Rubens. The rigidity of Rubens’s compositions and the restrained execution by Muller stem from the Brussels court etiquette, which was modeled on that of Spain. In any case, these two large royal portraits (each ca. 420 × 300 mm) served as

dem vom spanischen Vorbild geprägten strengen Brüsseler Hofzeremoniell geschuldet. In jedem Fall aber erwiesen sich diese beiden mit je rund 420 × 300 mm großformatigen Regentenbildnisse als beste Propaganda nicht nur für die Dargestellten selbst, sondern auch für Rubens, denn weite Verbreitung war ihnen – in Form von Stichen – bereits aufgrund der politischen Bedeutung der Dargestellten gewiss. Obwohl der Künstler diesen Auftrag gar nicht selbst an Muller vergeben hatte, verbreitete er Rubens' Namen und folglich seinen Ruhm.[17]

Das *Bildnis des Charles de Longueval* (um 1621) ist ein politisches Porträt, dessen Entstehung in mancher Hinsicht bemerkenswert war (Abb. S. 269). Vermutlich als Auftrag der Familie entstand es kurz nach dem Tod Longuevals (1571–1621), der in einer Schlacht ums Leben kam.[18] Longueval war politisch und militärisch lange Jahre für die katholische Sache und den Kaiser des Heiligen Römischen Reichs tätig gewesen. Rubens legte seinem Stecher Lucas Vorsterman I (1595/96–1674/75) in diesem Fall aber als Stichvorlage keine Zeichnung auf Papier vor, sondern eine eigenhändige, teils kolorierte Ölskizze (Abb. S. 79). Die erhöhte Schwierigkeit, diese auf die Kupferplatte zu übertragen, sowie der starke Zeitdruck, den Memorialstich zeitnah herauszubringen, trieben Vorsterman wohl dazu, seine „vielen schlaflosen Nächte" und anderen Beschwerden in der Ölskizze zu verewigen, die als Stichvorlage diente.[19] Der Stich mit dem lebendigen Porträt und dem umfangreichen allegorischen Schmuckprogramm setzte Maßstäbe in diesem Genre und verbreitete nicht nur den Namen des Toten, sondern auch den von Vorsterman und Rubens in ganz Europa.

Immer wieder zelebrierte Rubens auch in Stichen seinen Freundes- und Bekanntenkreis. Dazu gehörten gelehrte Humanisten aus dem Patrizierstand, mit denen er sich in Antwerpen umgab oder die er auf Reisen kennengelernt hatte. So stach Paulus Pontius etwa das *Bildnis des Jan Gaspard Gevaerts* (nach 1644; Abb. S. 267), das voller Anspielungen auf die Gelehrsamkeit und den gesellschaftlichen Status des Dargestellten (1593–1666) ist.[20] Auf Erstere weisen die Studierstube, die antike Büste des Marc Aurel sowie die Worte „HISTORIOGRAPHVS, ARCHIGRAMMATEVS ANTVERPIANVS" (Historiker, Archigrammautor zu Antwerpen) in der Bildunterschrift hin;[21] auf Letzteren das Wappen oben rechts, die kostbare Kleidung sowie die an einer Kette getragene Goldmünze mit dem Bildnis von Ferdinand III., ein Geschenk des Kaisers, der Gevaerts für seine juristischen Dienste ausweislich des Textes ebenso schätzte wie der spanische König Philipp IV. Dies war die Gesellschaft, in der Rubens verkehren wollte, mehr aber noch, in der er gesehen werden wollte. Rembrandt ließ sich von Pontius' Stich zu seinem Gemälde *Aristoteles mit der Büste des Homer* (1653) anregen.[22]

Wie zuvor Goltzius versuchte sich Rubens nur ein einziges Mal im Holzschnitt an einem Porträt. Das *Bildnis eines bärtigen Mannes* (1633–1635) geht zurück auf ein Gemälde Jacopo Tintorettos, das Rubens im Ausschnitt kopiert hatte (Abb. S. 266).[23] Für den Druck fertigte der Holzschneider Christoffel Jegher (1596–1652/53) vier Farbstöcke an, sodass ein Chiaroscuro-Effekt in Braun entstand. Damit bezog sich Rubens einerseits auf italienische Holzschnitte in der Tizian-Nachfolge.[24] Andererseits setzte er sich aber auch mit einer nordischen Tradition auseinander.[25] Das Bildnis hat von dieser Synthese aus Nord und Süd nicht profitiert, es lässt den Mann steif und etwas unnahbar wirken. Dennoch veröffentlichte Rubens diesen Holzschnitt unter seiner Verlegeradresse.

excellent propaganda not only for the regents but also for Rubens: Thanks to the prints and the political significance of the sitters, their wide circulation was certain. Thus, although the artist had not himself commissioned Muller, these portraits also spread his name and consequently his fame.[17]

The *Portrait of Charles de Longueval* (ca. 1621) is a politically motivated print whose creation was remarkable in several ways (fig. p. 269). Probably commissioned by the sitter's family, Rubens designed it shortly after Longueval's (1571–1621) death in battle.[18] For many years, Longueval had been entrusted with the political and military charge of enforcing Catholicism and politically representing the Holy Roman Empire. In this specific case, Rubens gave his engraver Lucas Vorsterman I (1595/96–1674/75) a partially colored oil sketch he had created himself (fig. p. 79) rather than a preparatory drawing on paper. This made it more difficult to transfer the motif to a copperplate. In addition, the great pressure to quickly finish this commemorative likeness may have been what prompted Vorsterman to memorialize his "many nights of waking" and other complaints on the oil sketch that served as the preparatory drawing.[19] With its lively portrait and extensive allegorical ornamental design, the engraving set standards in the genre and helped spread not only the name of the deceased but also that of Vorsterman and Rubens throughout Europe.

At various times, Rubens celebrated his circle of friends and acquaintances in prints, among them learned humanist patricians whose company he enjoyed in Antwerp or whom he met on his travels. Paulus Pontius engraved his *Portrait of Jan Gaspard Gevaerts* (after 1644; fig. p. 267), which is full of allusions to that scholar's (1593–1666) erudition and social status.[20] The sitter's intellectual eminence is referenced in the setting of the study, in the ancient bust of Marcus Aurelius, and in the words "HISTORIOGRAPHVS, ARCHIGRAMMATEVS ANTVERPIANVS" (historian, author of archigrams in Antwerp) in the inscription.[21] Meanwhile, the coat of arms in the upper right corner, the expensive clothes, and the gold coin on a chain sporting the likeness of Ferdinand III—obviously a gift from the emperor—testify to Gevaerts's standing with that regent, just as he was also in King Philip IV's good graces. These were the circles Rubens wanted to have access to, the people he wanted to be seen among. Rembrandt found inspiration in Pontius's engraving for his painting *Aristotle with a Bust of Homer* (1653).[22]

Like Goltzius before him, Rubens only conceived one portrait as a woodcut. The *Portrait of a Bearded Man* (1633–1635) is based on a painting by Jacopo Tintoretto, a detail of which Rubens had copied in Italy (fig. p. 266).[23] The woodcutter Christoffel Jegher (1596–1652/53) made four tone-blocks for this print, creating a chiaroscuro effect in brown. On the one hand, Rubens let himself be inspired by the Italian woodcuts of Titian's followers.[24] On the other, he also looked to the northern tradition.[25] The *Portrait of a Bearded Man* did not profit from this synthesis of northern and southern influences; the sitter looks rigid and aloof. Nevertheless, Rubens published this woodcut under his own address.

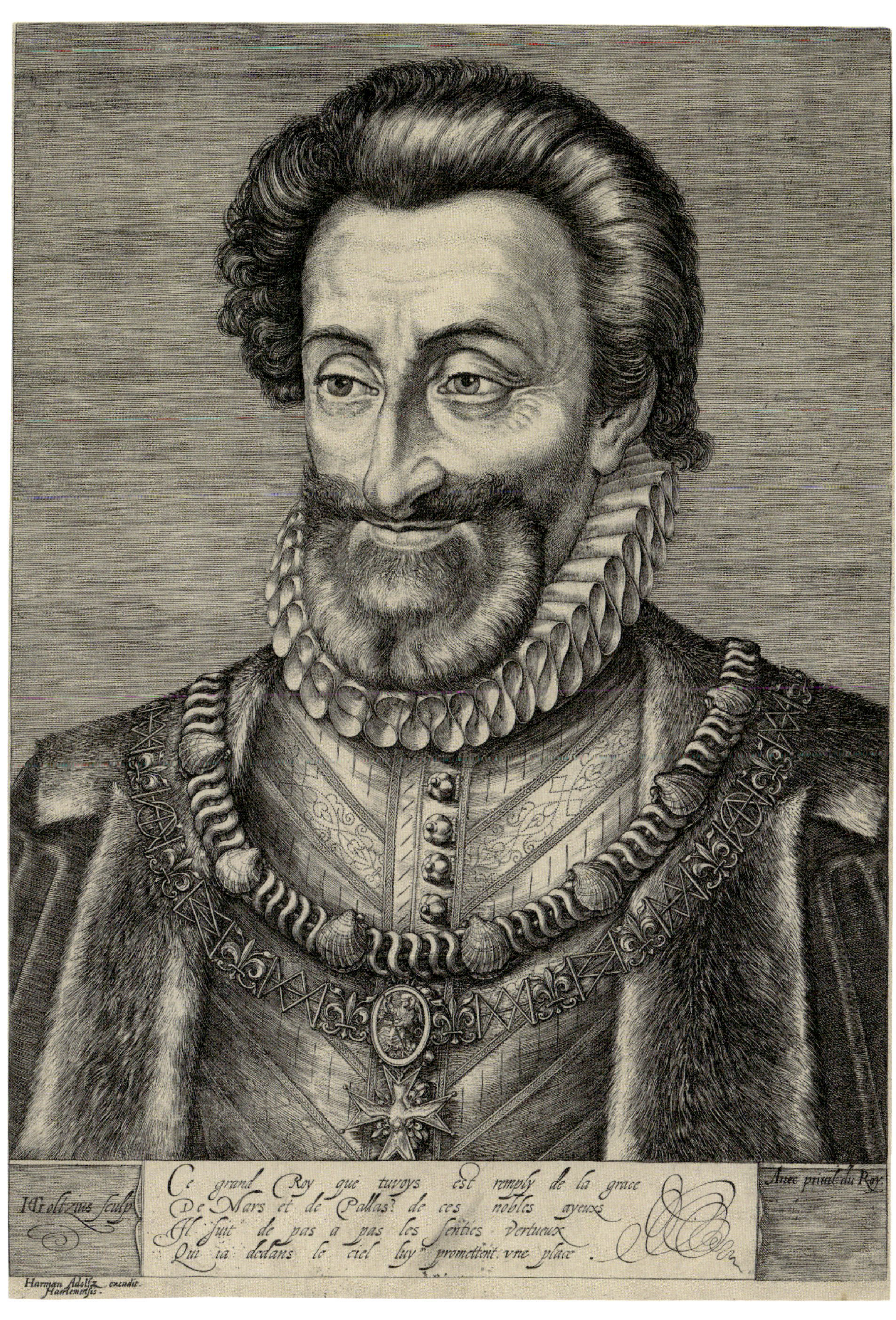

Goltzius (Inventor, Stecher / designer, engraver), Harmen Adolfsz. (Verleger / publisher)
Bildnis von Heinrich IV., König von Frankreich / Portrait of Henry IV, King of France, nach / after 1600
Kupferstich / engraving SGSM, Inv. 31026 D

1 Diese Zeichnung wird aufbewahrt in Berlin, Kupferstichkabinett, Inv. KdZ 568.

2 Zur Ausdeutung der Figuren siehe beispielsweise Limouze 1991/92, S. 440 f.

3 Darauf, dass Galles Verlagshaus Modell für Goltzius war, hat Marjolein Leesberg hingewiesen. Leesberg 2017b, S. 87. Zu diesem Stich als humanistische Freundschaftsgabe vgl. Filedt Kok 1996, S. 163 f.

4 Zu Technik und Bedeutung kalligraphischer Schriften dieser Art um 1600 vgl. Namowitz Worthen 1991/92. Zum Topos der „kunstfertigen Hand" vgl. Roettig 2002.

5 Vgl. NHD Goltzius 2012, S. lvi.

6 Tristan Weddigen hat Breens Bildnis in dem allegorischen Blatt *Tabula Cebetis* nach Goltzius identifizieren wollen (Weddigen 2004, S. 106). Zwei Porträt-Federzeichnungen Breens, gezeichnet von Goltzius, werden aufbewahrt in Amsterdam, Rijksmuseum, Inv. RPT-2000-1, und in Haarlem, Teylers Museum, Inv. N 057.

7 Karsten Müller, in: Hamburg 2002, Kat. 50.

8 In Italien erschien bereits 1599 eine von Raffaello Guidi gestochene und verlegte Kopie, vgl. SGSM, Inv. 110693 D. Eine der vielen weiteren Kopien aus dem 17. Jahrhundert im Kapitel „Nachbilder" in diesem Katalog, Abb. S. 283. Die vierte Kopie in der SGSM (Inv. 31020 D) datiert ebenfalls noch aus dem 16. Jahrhundert, siehe das Kapitel „Privilegien", Abb. S. 123.

9 In seinem Gemälde *Venus und Adonis* von 1614 (Abb. S. 293) variiert Goltzius dieses erfolgreiche Motiv links: Der Amorknabe versucht in ganz ähnlicher Weise den hier nicht ganz so freundlichen Hund als Reittier zu benutzen.

10 Das Werk wurde in der Literatur lange als *Der Hund des Goltzius* betitelt.

11 Drei andere Porträts zeigen Damen des Hofes: Maria de' Medici, die Frau Heinrichs, seine Geliebte und seine Schwester. Sie alle schauen nach rechts. Gestochen wurden die Damenbildnisse von Goltzius' Künstlerkollegen, den Brüdern Johannes und Hieronymus Wierix. Von Matham bestellte derselbe Verleger ein Bildnis des Maximilien de Béthune, Duc de Sully, das jedoch erst 1614, also Jahre nach den anderen Bildnissen, entstand. Es zeigt den engen Freund und Berater des Königs.

12 Marijn Schapelhouman vermutet, dass dieses Bildnis vielleicht Goltzius' letzter Stich überhaupt war. Vgl. Amsterdam/New York/Toledo 2003, S. 147.

13 Zu den Details des Auftrags siehe White 2007, Kat. 61. White zufolge hatte Rubens das Gemälde für den Altertumsforscher Nicolas-Claude Fabride Peiresc (1580–1637) angefertigt (Abb. 1, S. 75). Nachdem aber die Anfrage aus England kam, schickte Rubens die erste Fassung dorthin und ließ für den Freund 1628 eine Replik anfertigen (Abb. 2, S. 75). Vgl. auch Vlieghe 1987, Nr. 135. Der Stich entstand nach der Vorlage, die heute in Köln aufbewahrt wird. Vgl. Nils Büttner im vorliegenden Katalog, S. 80 sowie Abb. S. 82.

14 Brief von Rubens an Palamède de Fabri, Sieur de Valavez, 10. Januar 1625, in: Zoff 1918, S. 122.

15 Auffällig ist, dass im Stich ein Rahmen dargestellt ist. Dieser ist typengleich mit jenem, den Pontius zwei Jahre später auch den *Bildnissen von Philipp IV. von Spanien* und seiner Frau *Elisabeth von Bourbon* (beide 1632 SGSM, Inv. 30323 D und 30303 D) verlieh, die im Übrigen auch das Format mit Rubens' *Selbstbildnis* teilten. Durch die Verwendung desselben Rahmens für die königlichen Porträts wertete er sein *Selbstbildnis* nachträglich auf, wohl ein Indiz dafür, dass seine Bescheidenheit eher Floskel als Überzeugung war.

16 Vgl. Stijnman 2012, S. 321.

17 Die Frage, ob Rubens in die Auftragsvergabe an Muller involviert war oder überhaupt darüber informiert, dass seine Gemälde gestochen werden sollten, kann nach derzeitiger Quellenlage nicht beantwortet werden. Nach Abwägung verschiedener Indizien nimmt Meier das nicht an. Vgl. Meier 2020a, Kat. 3.

18 Meier 2020a, Kat. 24, erläutert ausführlich die Indizien, die für den Auftrag durch die Familie sprechen.

19 Das ganze Zitat („veel nachten waken") und die Episode bei Nico Van Hout, in: Antwerpen/Québec 2004, S. 48, 50. Mehr zu diesem Stich im Essay von Nils Büttner im vorliegenden Katalog, S. 78 ff.

20 Gevaerts war der Verfasser der Lobestexte für die Publikation von Rubens' Stichen zum Festeinzug des neuen Statthalters Ferdinand in Antwerpen 1635, die Pompa Introitus Ferdinandi. Vgl. Vlieghe 1987, Nr. 106.

21 Die Büste des Marc Aurel spielt darauf an, dass Gevaerts einen Kommentar über diesen antiken Philosophen erarbeitet hatte. Dieser wurde jedoch nicht publiziert.

22 Diese und weitere Angaben zu Rubens' Komposition bei Vlieghe 1987, Kat. 93. – Rembrandt, *Aristoteles mit der Büste des Homer*, 1653, Öl auf Leinwand, New York, The Metropolitan Museum of Art, Inv. 61.198.

23 Vgl. Meier 2020a, Kat. 64 mit Abb.

24 Vgl. Nico Van Hout, in: Antwerpen/Québec 2004, S. 26, der den Tizian-Bezug herausstellt.

25 Vgl. Renger 1975, S. 198.

1 This drawing is in the collection of the Kupferstichkabinett Berlin, inv. KdZ 568.

2 For an interpretation of the figures in the ornamentation, see Limouze 1991/92, pp. 440–441.

3 Marjolein Leesberg points out that Galle's publishing house was the model for that of Goltzius. Leesberg 2017b, p. 87. On this print as a gift among humanist friends, see Filedt Kok 1996, pp. 163–164.

4 On the technique and meaning of calligraphic writing of this kind around 1600, see Namowitz Worthen 1991/92. On the topos of the "artful hand," see Roettig 2002.

5 See NHD Goltzius 2012, p. lvi.

6 Tristan Weddigen suggested an identification of Breen's portrait in Matham's allegorical print *Tabula Cebetis*, after Goltzius (Weddigen 2004, p. 106). Two portrait pen drawings of Breen by Goltzius are in the collections of the Rijksmuseum, Amsterdam, inv. RPT-2000-1, and the Teylers Museum, Amsterdam, inv. N 057.

7 Karsten Müller, in: Hamburg 2002, cat. 50. Translation by the author.

8 In Italy, a copy engraved and published by Raffaello Guidi appeared as early as 1599 (see SGSM, inv. 110693 D). For one of the many seventeenth-century copies, see the chapter "Afterimages" in this catalog (fig. p. 283). For the fourth copy in the SGSM (inv. 31020 D), which also dates to the sixteenth century, see the chapter "Privileges" in this catalog (fig. p. 123).

9 In his painting *Venus and Adonis* (1614; fig. p. 293), Goltzius shows a variation of this motif: Cupid, on the left, attempts to mount the fierce hound in a similar fashion.

10 For some time, this print was referred to by scholars as *Goltzius's Dog*.

11 Three other portraits show ladies of the court: Henry's wife, Maria de' Medici; his mistress; and his sister. They all look to the right. The engravers of these female portraits were the brothers Johannes and Hieronymus Wierix. The same publisher commissioned Jacob Matham with the portrait of Maximilien de Béthune, duc de Sully, but this was finished only in 1614, years after the other portraits. It captures the close friend and adviser of the king.

12 Marijn Schapelhouman suggests that this portrait may have been Goltzius's very last engraving. See Amsterdam/New York/Toledo 2003, p. 147.

13 For details on this commission, see White 2007, cat. 61. According to White, Rubens had painted the portrait for his friend (fig. 1, p. 75), the Classical scholar Nicolas-Claude Fabri de Peiresc (1580–1637). After the request came from England, Rubens sent the first version there and had a replica made for his friend in 1628 (fig. 2, p. 75). See also Vlieghe 1987, cat. 135. The print was engraved after the preparatory drawing now in Cologne. See Nils Büttner in the present catalog, p. 80, and fig. p. 82.

14 Letter from Rubens to Palamède de Fabri, Sieur de Valavez, January 10, 1625, in: Magurn 1955, p. 102.

15 It is noteworthy that there is a frame depicted in the print. It is the same type as those Pontius used two years later in the *Portraits of Philip IV of Spain* and his wife *Elizabeth of Bourbon* (both 1632, SGSM, inv. 30323 D and 30303 D), which moreover are of the same size as Rubens's *Self-Portrait*. By using the same frame as for the royal portraits, the artist retroactively upgraded his *Self-Portrait*, which may be an indication that his modesty was coquetry rather than conviction.

16 See Stijnman 2012, p. 321.

17 The question as to whether Rubens was in any way involved in having these prints made after his paintings cannot be decided based on the documents we have at present. Considering the circumstantial evidence, Meier does not think this was the case. See Meier 2020a, cat. 3.

18 Meier 2020a, cat. 24, lists the evidence suggesting that the family gave the commission.

19 The full quotation ("veel nachten waken") and episode are related by Nico Van Hout, in: Antwerpen/Québec 2004, pp. 48, 50. For more on this print, see Nils Büttner, pp. 78–79, in the present catalog.

20 Gevaerts had written the laudatory texts for the *Pompa Introitus Ferdinandi*, the book that published Rubens's prints of the 1635 Triumphal Entry of the new governor Ferdinand into Antwerp. See Vlieghe 1987, no. 106.

21 The bust of Marcus Aurelius alludes to the fact that Gevaerts had authored a commentary on the ancient philosopher. This text was never published, however.

22 For this, along with further information on Rubens's composition, see Vlieghe 1987, no. 93. – Rembrandt, *Aristotle with a Bust of Homer*, 1653, oil on canvas, New York, The Metropolitan Museum of Art, inv. 61.198.

23 See Meier 2020a, cat. 64 with fig.

24 For a discussion of the connection to Titian, see Nico Van Hout, in: Antwerpen/Québec 2004, p. 26.

25 See Renger 1975, p. 198.

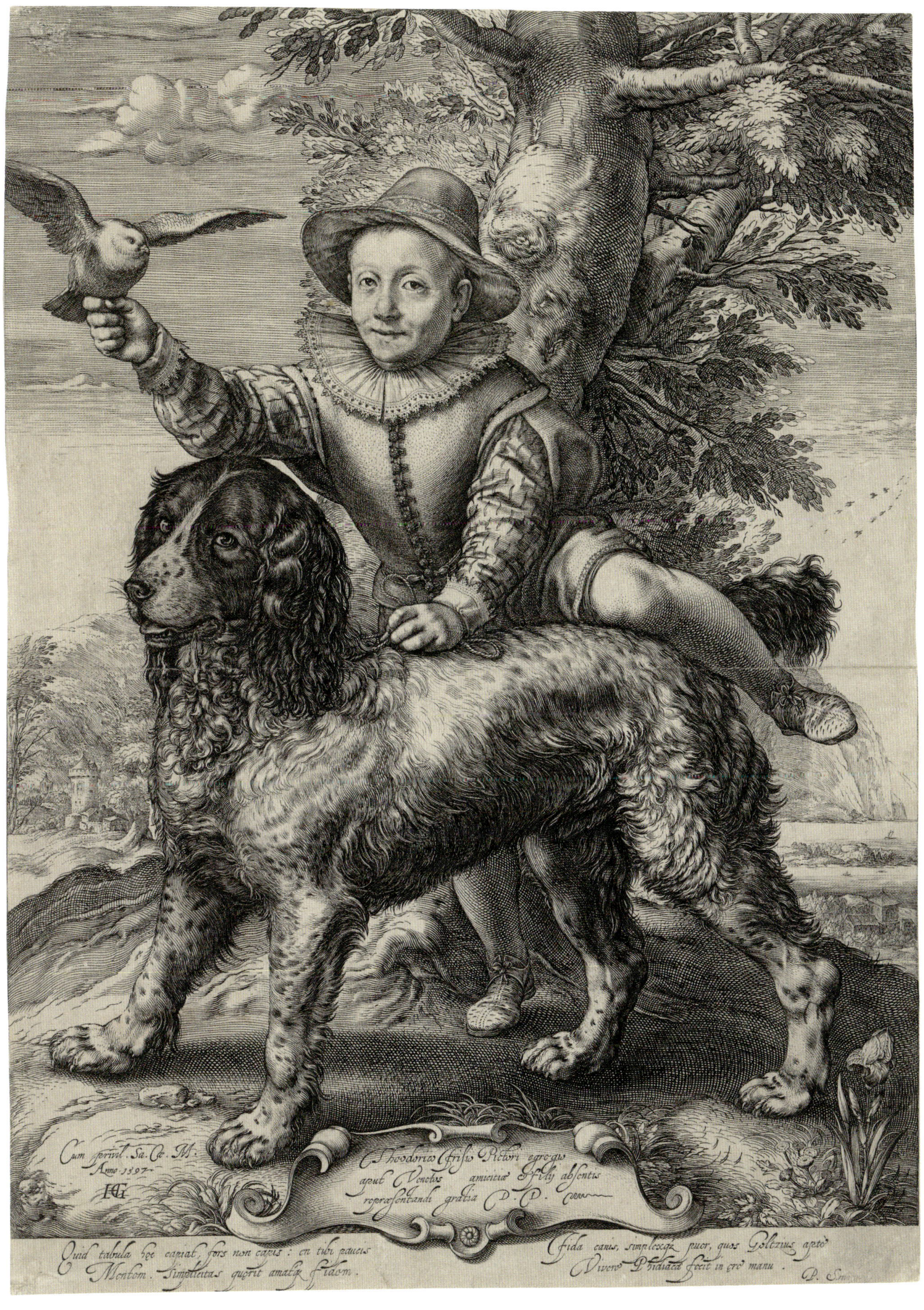

Hendrick Goltzius (Inventor, Stecher / designer, engraver)

Bildnis des Frederick de Vries (Der Hund des Goltzius) / Portrait of Frederick de Vries (Goltzius's Dog), 1597

Widmung an / dedicated to Dirck de Vries von / by Goltzius

Kupferstich / engraving SGSM, Inv. 31019 D

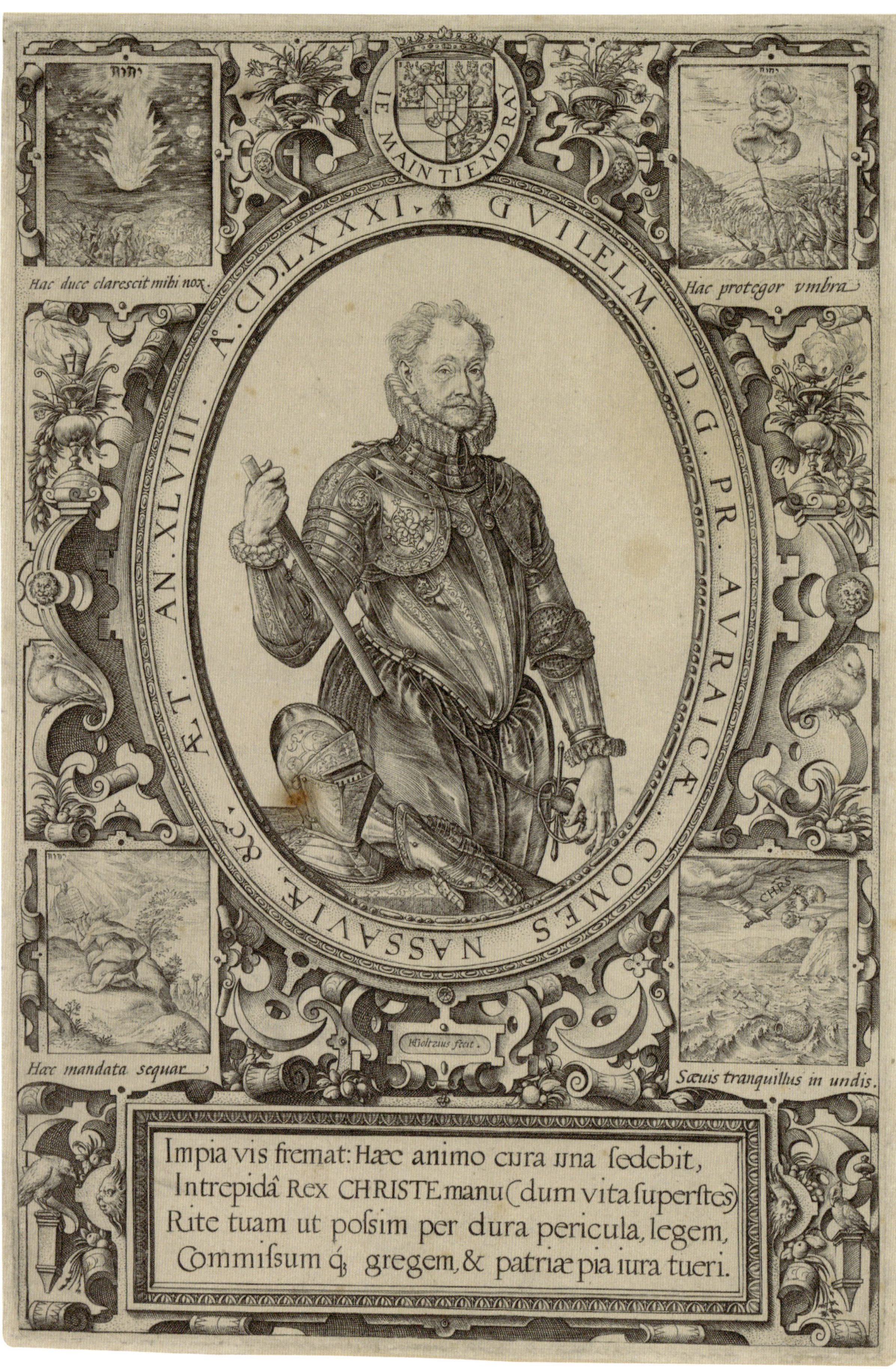

Hendrick Goltzius (Inventor, Stecher / designer, engraver)
Bildnis des / Portrait of Willem van Oranje, 1581
Kupferstich / engraving SGSM, Inv. 117288 D

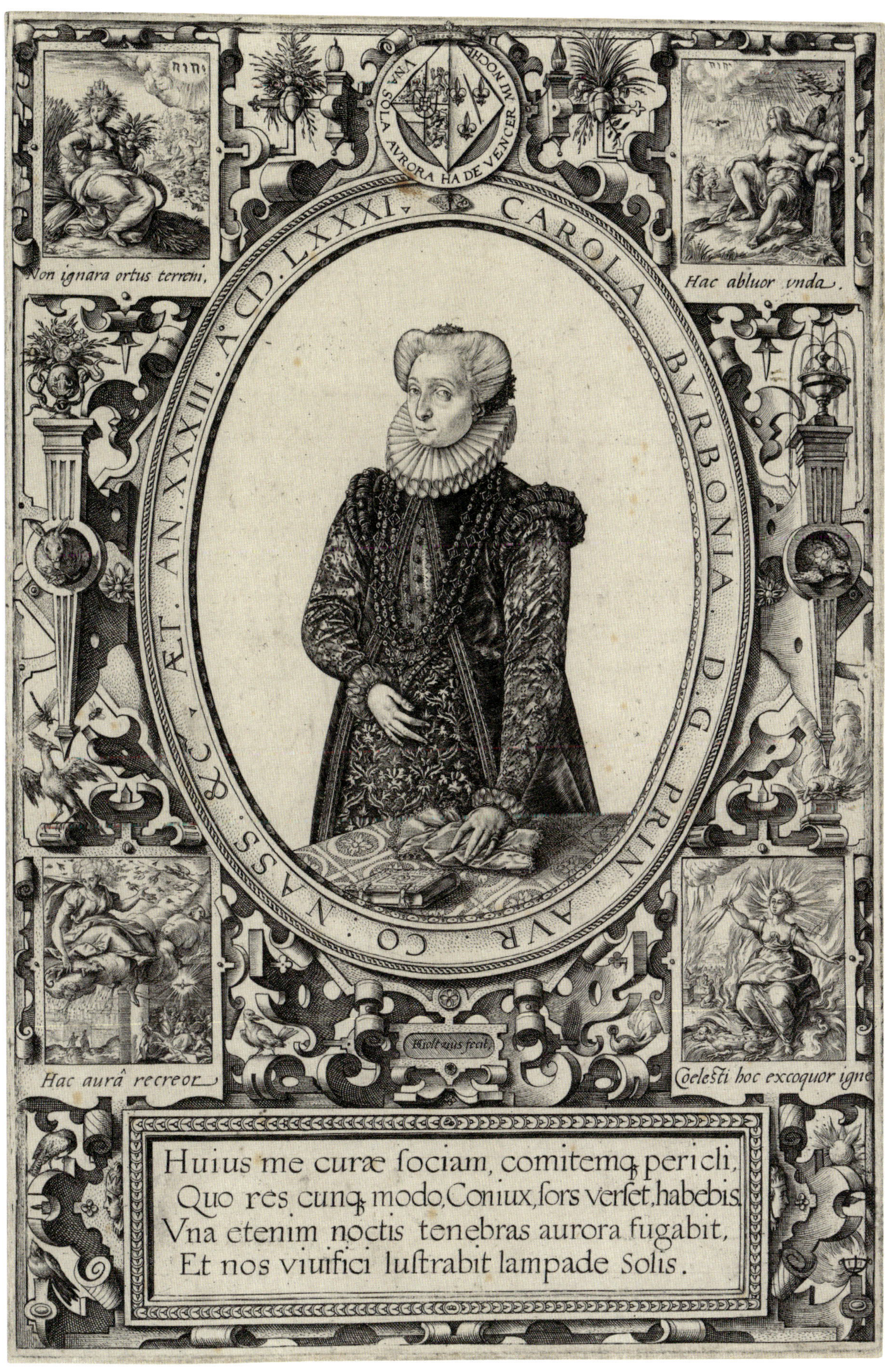

Hendrick Goltzius (Inventor, Stecher / designer, engraver)
Bildnis der / Portrait of Charlotte van Oranje, 1581
Kupferstich / engraving SGSM, Inv. 31025 D

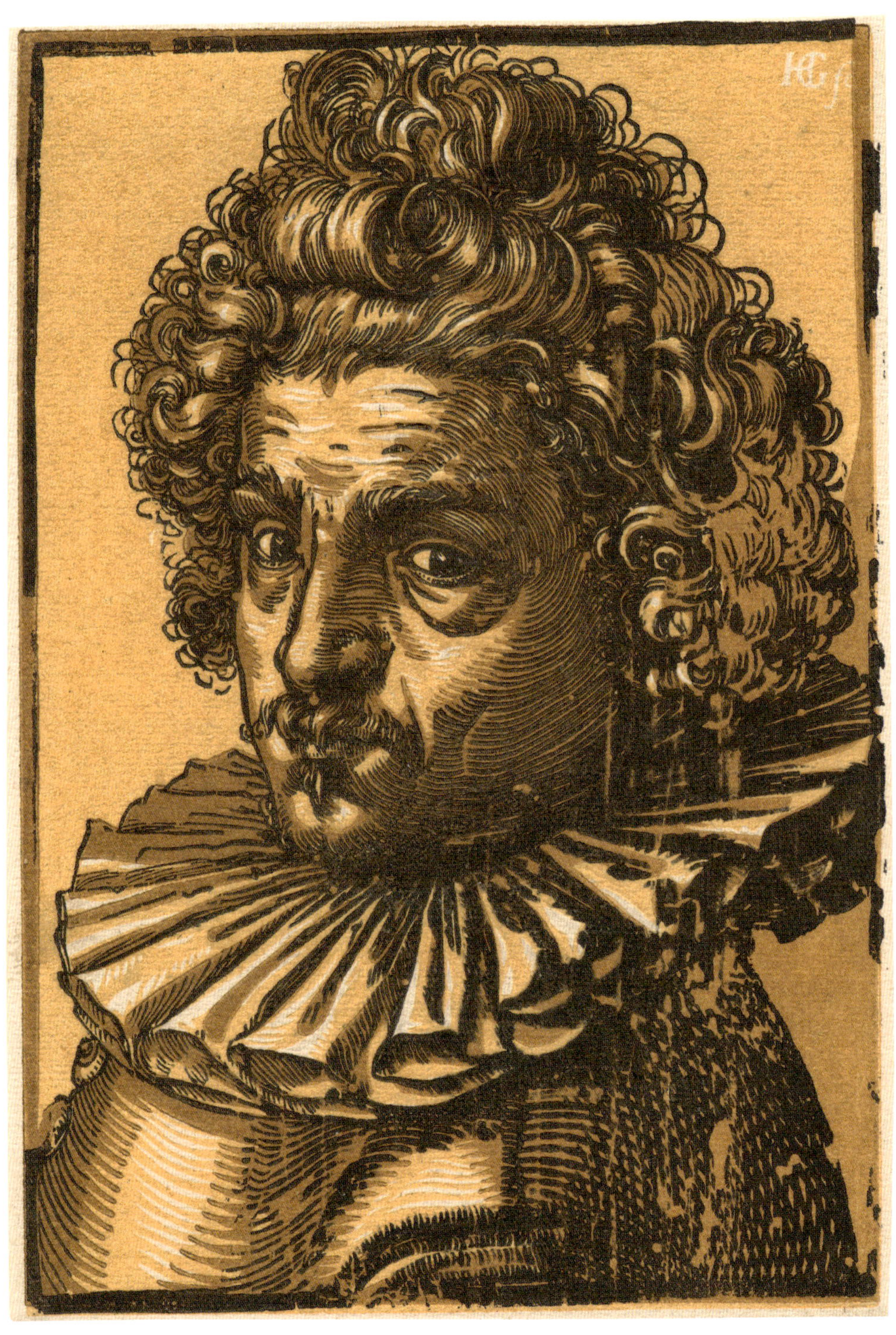

Hendrick Goltzius (Inventor, Holzschneider / designer, woodcutter)
Bildnis des / Portrait of Gillis van Breen, ca. 1588
Chiaroscuro-Holzschnitt / chiaroscuro woodcut Frankfurt am Main, Städel Museum, Inv. 3972

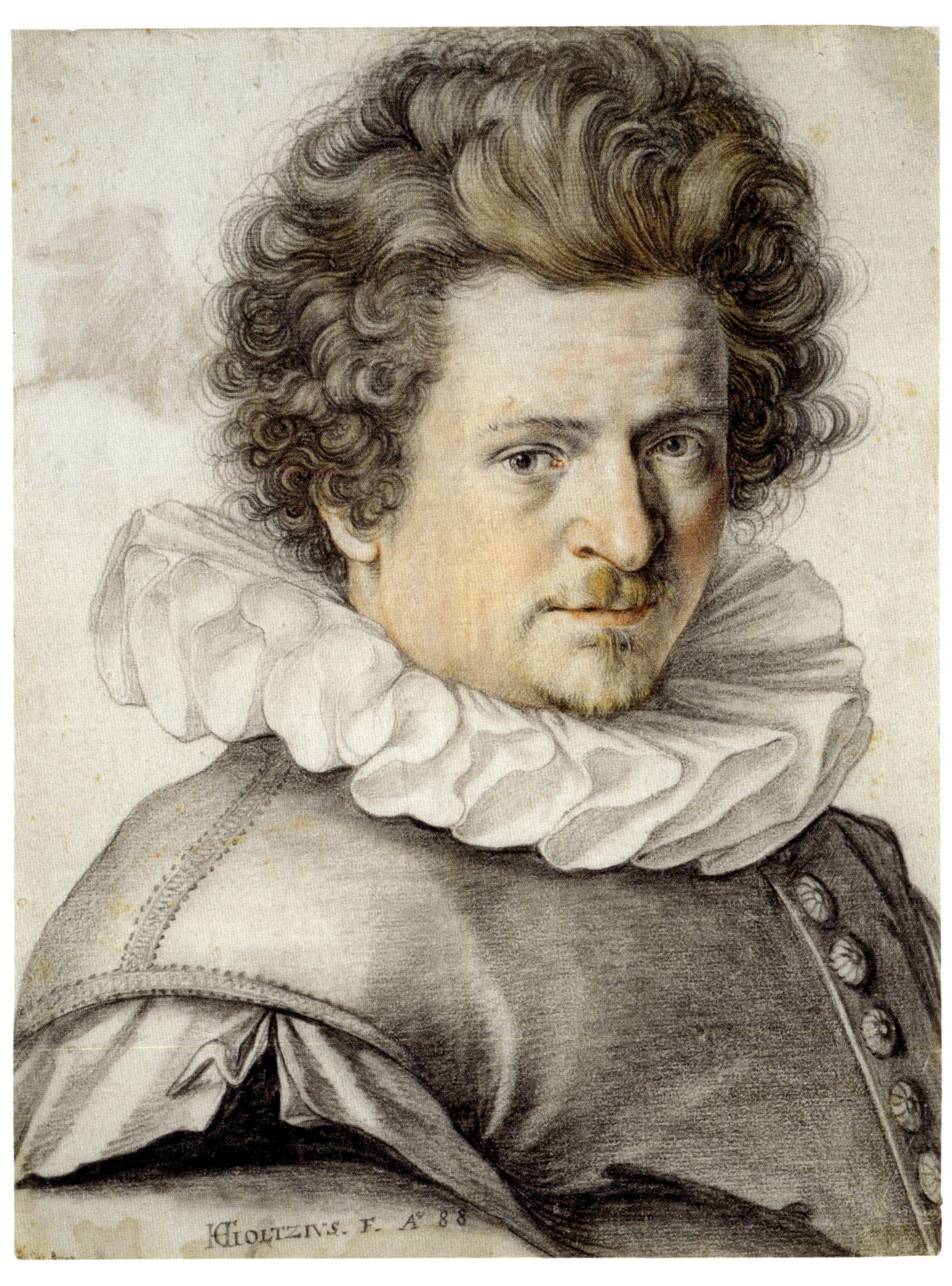

Hendrick Goltzius
Bildnis des / Portrait of Gillis van Breen, 1588
Kreide / chalk Frankfurt am Main, Städel Museum, Inv. 807 Z

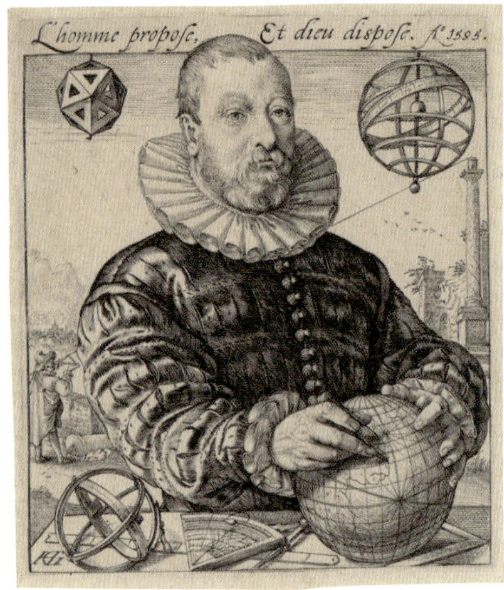

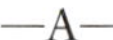

L'homme propose. Et dieu dispose. A° 1588.

BENE AGERE ET NIL TIMERE. Ætatis suæ. 30. A° 1583.
HGoltzius fecit.

40
HENRICVS. 4. D.G. REX FRANC
ORVM. & NAVARRÆ. ÆTAT

—A—

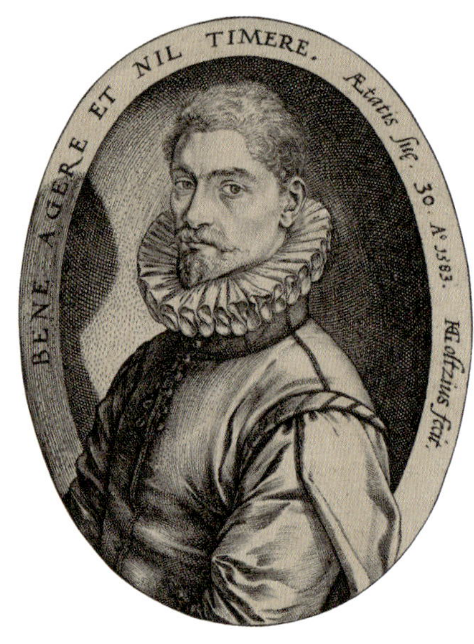

—B—

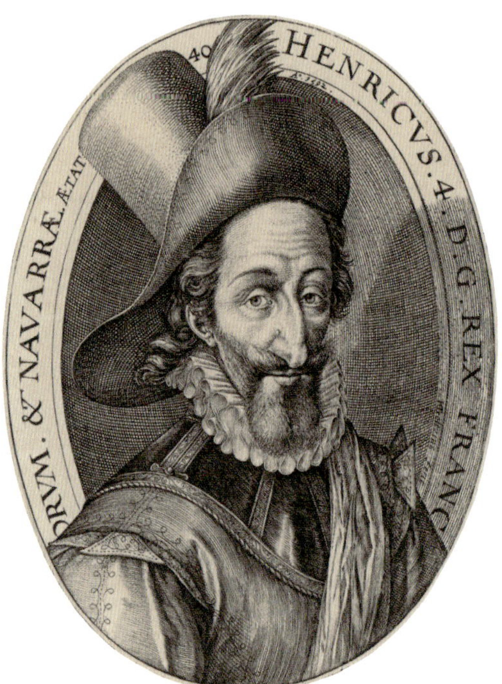

—C—

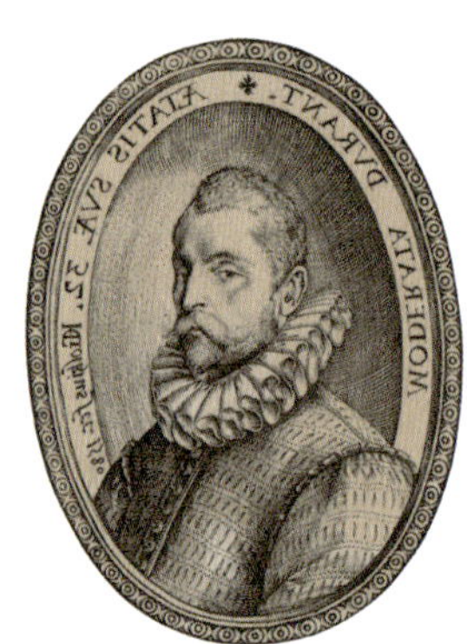

—D—

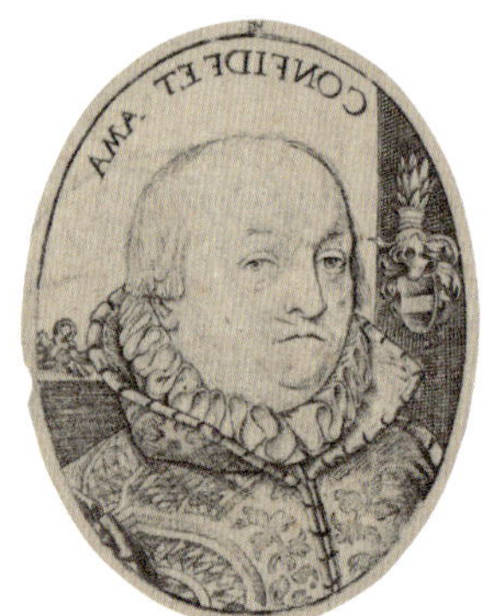

—E—

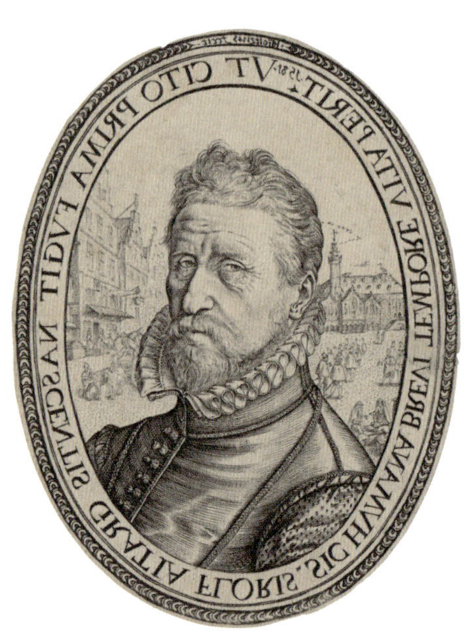

—F—

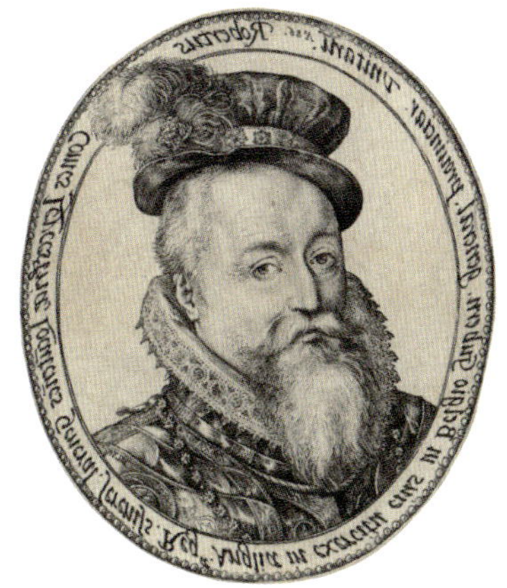

—G—

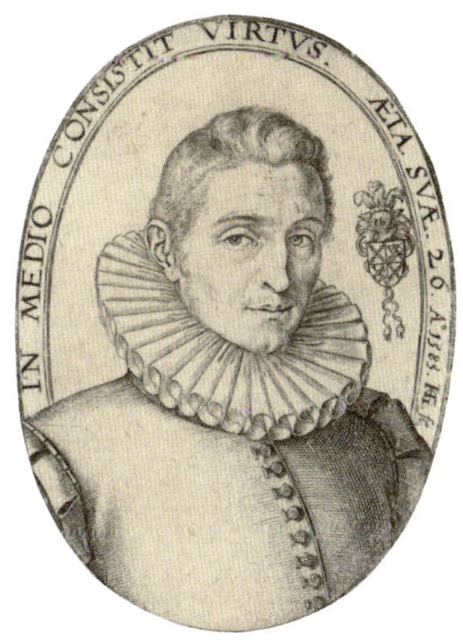

—H—

—I—

Hendrick Goltzius (Inventor, Stecher / designer, engraver)

Bildnis des / Portrait of

A— *Nicolaus Petri van Deventer*, 1595 SGSM, Inv. 1984:33 D

B— *Hieronymus Scholiers*, 1583 SGSM, Inv. 31017 D

C— *Heinrich IV., König von Frankreich / Henry IV, King of France*, 1592 SGSM, Inv. 119010 D

D— *eines Unbekannten / an Unknown Man*, 1580 SGSM, Inv. 118647 D

E— *Anton von Wildberg*, 1579 SGSM, Inv. 63022 D

F— *Allaert Fransz. Schatter*, 1581 SGSM, Inv. 173851 D

G— *Robert Dudley*, 1586 SGSM, Inv. 1988:2 D

H— *eines Unbekannten / an Unknown Man*, 1585 SGSM, Inv. 1989:6 D

I— *Hans Felbier*, 1582 SGSM, Inv. 147932 D

Alle Kupferstich / All engravings

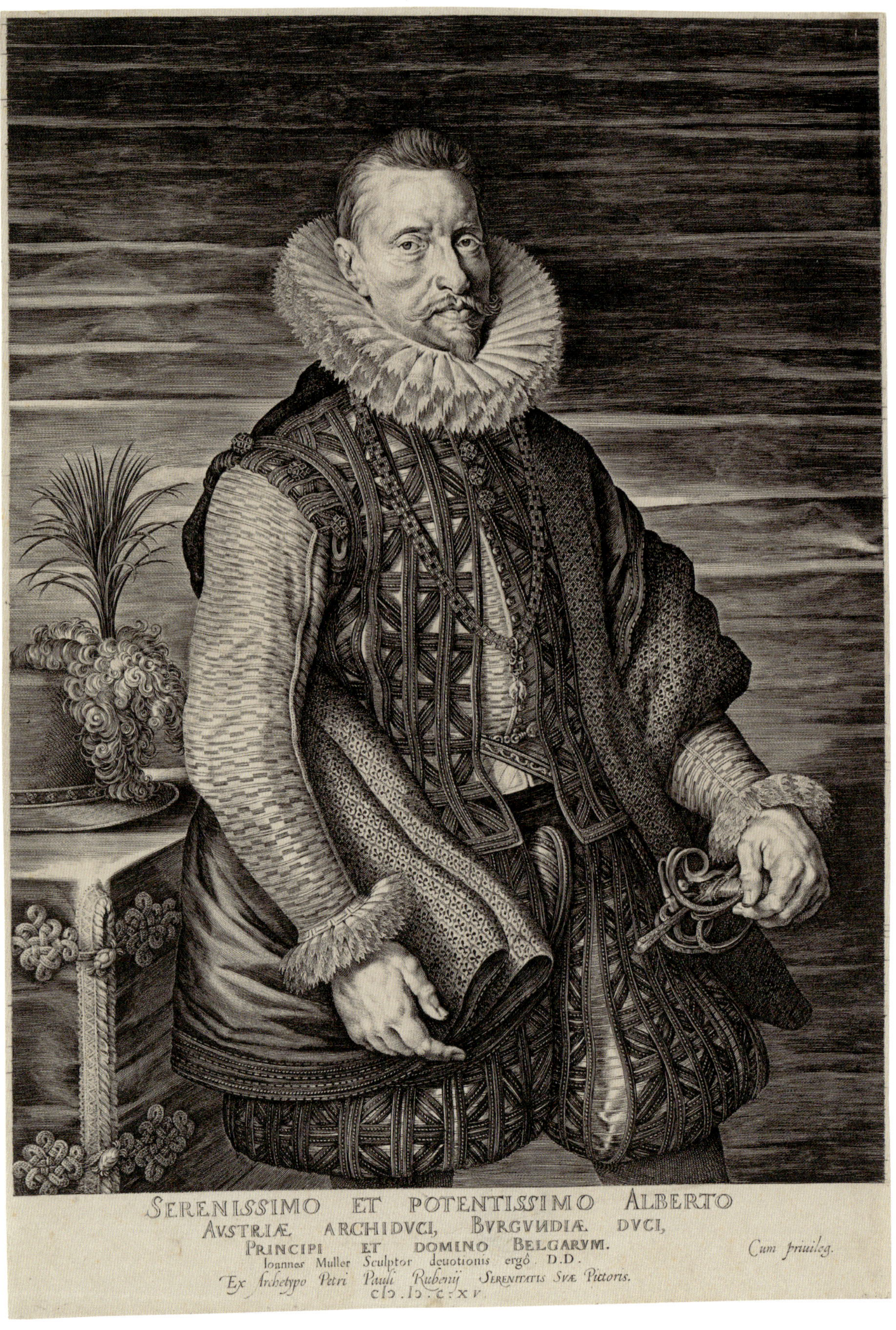

Jan Harmensz. Muller (Stecher / engraver), nach / after Rubens
Bildnis von Albrecht VII., Erzherzog von Österreich / Portrait of Albert VII, Archduke of Austria, 1615
Kupferstich / engraving SGSM, Inv. 30296 D

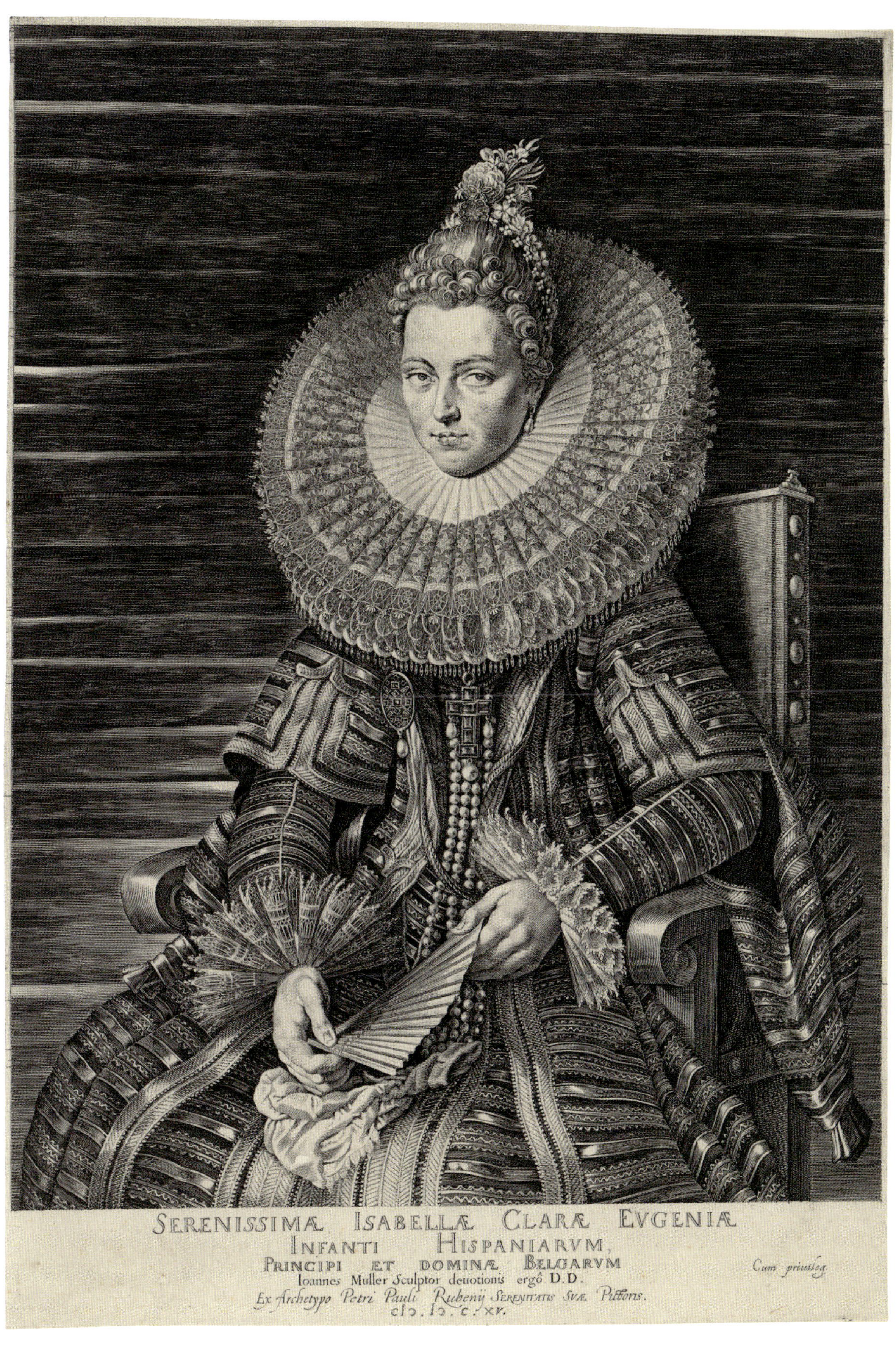

Jan Harmensz. Muller (Stecher / engraver), nach / after Rubens
Bildnis der / Portrait of Isabella Clara Eugenia, Infantin von Spanien / Infanta of Spain, 1615
Kupferstich / engraving SGSM, Inv. 30311 D

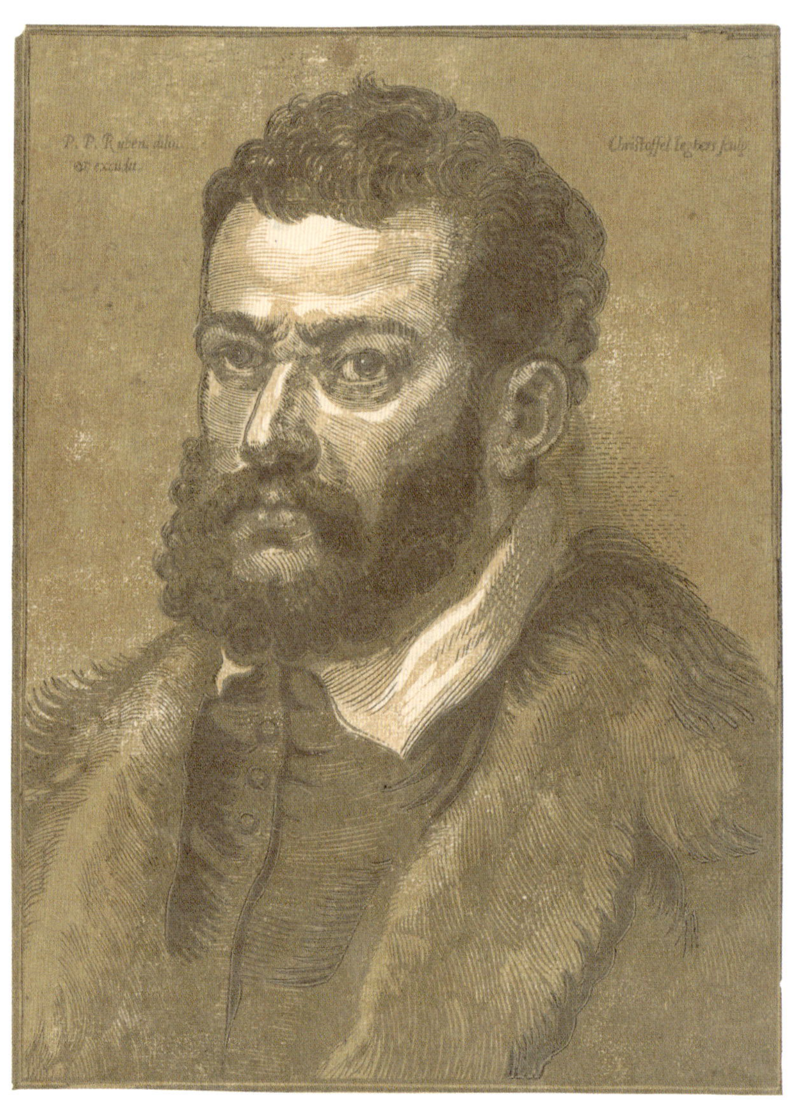

Rubens (Inventor, Zeichner, Verleger / designer, draftsman, publisher),
Christoffel Jegher (Holzschneider / woodcutter), nach / after Jacopo Tintoretto
Bildnis eines bärtigen Mannes / Portrait of a Bearded Man, 1633–1635
Chiaroscuro-Holzschnitt / chiaroscuro woodcut SGSM, Inv. 30334 D

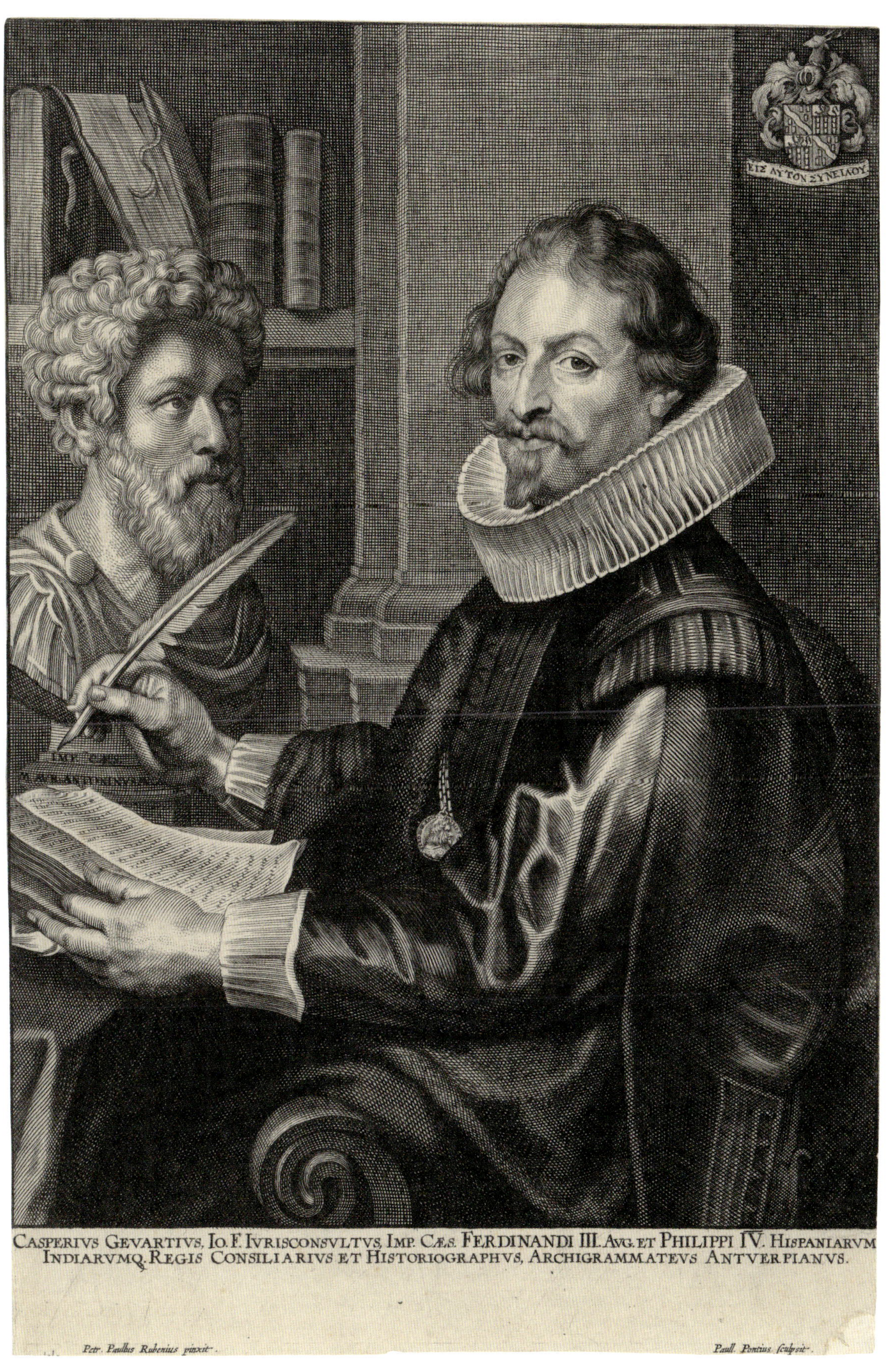

Paulus Pontius (Stecher / engraver), nach / after Rubens
Bildnis des / Portrait of Jan Gaspard Gevaerts, nach / after 1644
Kupferstich / engraving SGSM, Inv. 30308 D

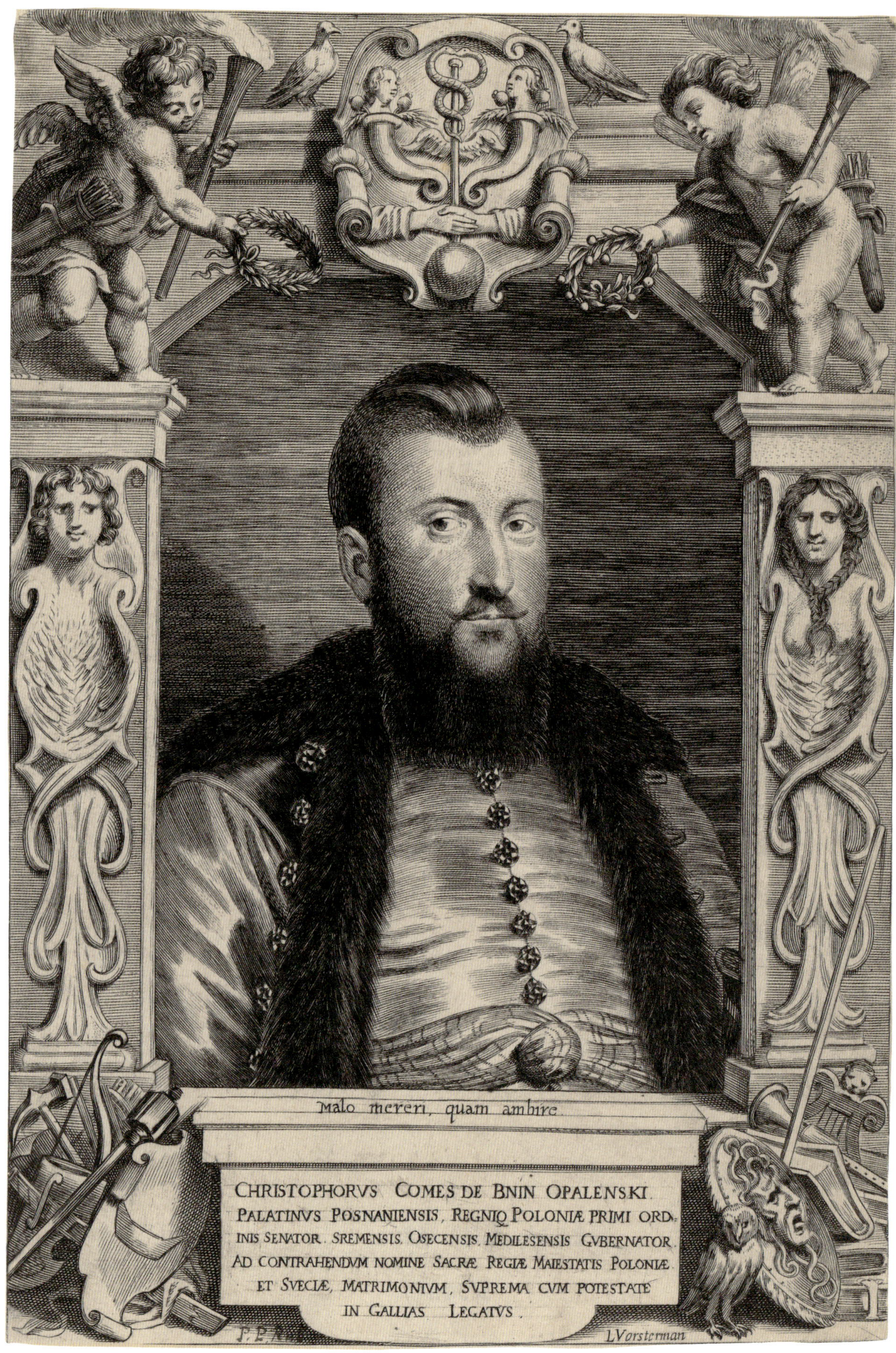

Lucas Vorsterman I (Stecher / engraver), nach / after Rubens
Bildnis des / Portrait of Christopher Opalinski, ca. 1620
Kupferstich / engraving SGSM, Inv. 38338 D

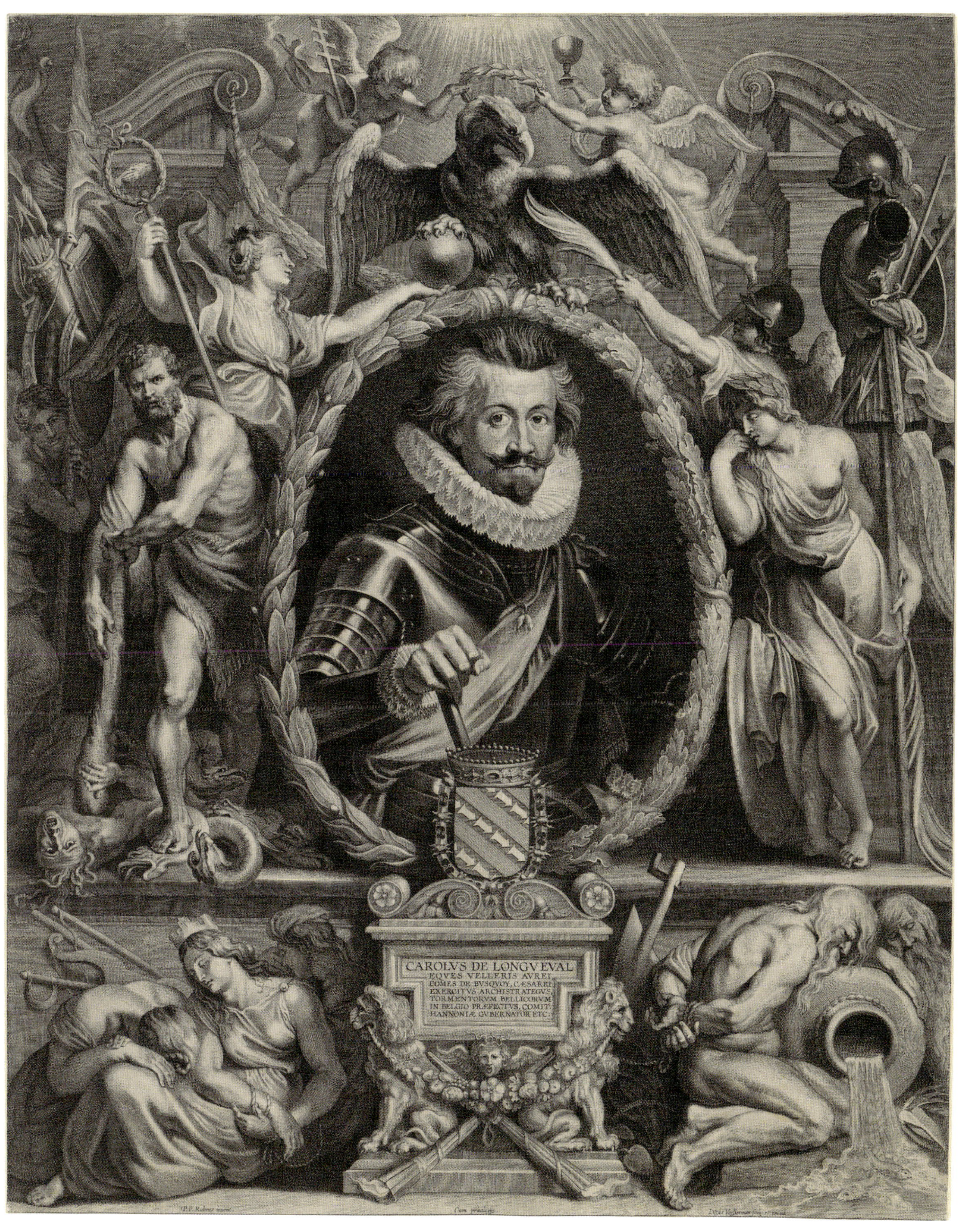

Rubens (Inventor / designer), Lucas Vorsterman I (Stecher, Verleger / engraver, publisher)
Bildnis des / Portrait of Charles de Longueval, ca. 1621
Kupferstich / engraving SGSM, Inv. 148973 D

XI. Nachbilder

Bereits die kleine Werkauswahl in diesem Kapitel macht sichtbar, dass auf den Ruhm der Goltzius- und Rubens-Graphik in ihrer jeweiligen Zeit auch der Nachruhm in späteren Jahrhunderten folgte. Zwar unterlag die Beliebtheit beider Œuvres Moden und anderen (etwa lokalen oder nationalen) Konjunkturen, die mal eine stärkere, mal eine geringere Nachfolge hervorbrachten. Aber wir können an diesen Beispielen deutlich machen, dass bis ins 19. Jahrhundert eine künstlerische Auseinandersetzung mit den jeweiligen Druckgraphiken stattfand. Bedenkenswert ist die Überlegung von Timothy Riggs, mit der „Rubens-Schule" sei für den Kupferstich zugleich ein Höhe- und Endpunkt erreicht gewesen.[1] Von nun an taten sich die innovativen und aufregenden Neuerungen in anderen Techniken auf, etwa in der Radierung, die von Anthonis van Dyck (der zeitweilig mit Rubens zusammengearbeitet hatte) und von Rembrandt zu einem eigenständigen, virtuosen und geachteten graphischen Medium entwickelt wurde. „Nachbilder" der Goltzius- und Rubens-Graphik entstanden bereits zu beider Leb- und Schaffenszeiten und finden sich ab der zweiten Hälfte des 17. bis weit in das 19. Jahrhundert. Sie zeugen von der eingangs beschriebenen Wucht, mit der ihre Neuerungen in die Geschichte der Druckgraphik einschlugen.

Im Fall von Hendrick Goltzius kopierten Nachfolger bestimmte Lieblingsmotive oder Werke zur Übung an Kunstakademien. Bei Peter Paul Rubens wurde die Druckgraphik weiter als wichtigstes Reproduktionsmedium seiner Gemälde genutzt und nach seinem Tod erschienen sehr viele Motive erstmals als Druckgraphiken.[2] Hinzu kam ab dem 18. Jahrhundert auch, dass manche Stiche nach Rubens-Gemälden ihre Sammler benannten. Damit mehrten und verewigten die Graphiken nicht nur den Ruhm des Künstlers, sondern auch dieser sammelnden Kunstliebhaber.

Auf den Kopisten Abraham Bloteling (1640–1690) geht ein Stich aus der zweiten Hälfte des 17. Jahrhunderts zurück, welcher die leeren Bildstellen von Goltzius' berühmter, fragmentarisch gebliebener *Anbetung der Hirten* (entworfen 1599, verlegt 1615, Abb. S. 188 f.) füllte und sozusagen vollendete (Abb. S. 277). Goltzius' Darstellung kommt uns heute aufgrund der Auslassungen sehr modern vor, doch vielen Zeitgenossen erschien sie wohl als unfertig. Nach Karel van Mander hatte sich Goltzius von einem Gemälde Tizians inspirieren lassen, in dem die Reflexion des Lichts auf den Gesichtern besonders eindrucksvoll war (vgl. S. 192 im Kapitel „Meisterdrucke").[3] Doch dieses Gemälde kannte Bloteling offensichtlich nicht, er ließ seiner eigenen Phantasie freien Lauf und erfand, was seiner Ansicht nach fehlte.

Eine zeitgenössische Kopie nach Goltzius' überaus erfolgreicher Komposition *Bildnis des Frederick de Vries* wurde bereits im Kapitel „Privilegien" vorgestellt (siehe Abb. S. 123). Vor 1652 ist nun ein weiterer, gespiegelter und anonymer Kupferstich zu datieren, den der Amsterdamer Verleger Claes Jansz. Visscher (1586/87–1652) in sein Sortiment aufnahm, anscheinend, weil er sich auch ein halbes Jahrhundert nach der Entstehung des Originals ein Geschäft mit dem Motiv versprach (Abb. S. 283). Visscher behielt die Widmung und die

XI. Afterimages

The small selection of works in this chapter illustrates that the fame enjoyed by Hendrick Goltzius's and Peter Paul Rubens's prints during their lifetimes was followed by yet more posthumous fame in subsequent centuries. The popularity of their works was subject to fashions and other (local or national) tastes that prompted sometimes more, sometimes fewer epigones to emulate their examples. Nevertheless, the works discussed below demonstrate that artists continued to engage with Goltzius's and Rubens's respective print oeuvres into the nineteenth century. In this regard, a remark by Timothy Riggs is worth considering: "The emergence of the 'Rubens school' of engraving marks on the one hand a perfection of engraving as a reproductive technique; on the other, it marks the end of a period of dynamic evolution in that technique."[1] From this point on, the innovative and exciting new advances occurred in other techniques—for example in etching, which Anthony van Dyck (who had for a time worked with Rubens) and Rembrandt explored and developed into an independent, dazzling, and respected graphic art. "Afterimages" of the Goltzius and Rubens prints emerged even during their lifetimes and continued to appear from the second half of the seventeenth century through to the nineteenth century. These images testify to the thrust their innovations had given to the history of prints.

In the case of Goltzius, certain epigones copied bestsellers or favorite works as exercises at the art academies. As for Rubens, engraving remained the most important reproductive technique for making his paintings known, with many of his works published for the first time as prints after his death.[2] In addition, starting in the eighteenth century many prints after Rubens named the owners of the original paintings in the inscriptions. As a result, the prints spread the fame not only of the artist but also of the proud collectors of his paintings.

In the second half of the seventeenth century, the copyist Abraham Bloteling (1640–1690) engraved a print that filled in the areas of Goltzius's famous *Adoration of the Shepherds* (designed in 1599 and published in 1615; figs. pp. 188, 189) that had been left blank, thereby completing, so to speak, Goltzius's work (fig. p. 277). The Haarlem master's print seems to us especially modern precisely because of those blank areas, but to many of his contemporaries it must have seemed unfinished. According to Karel van Mander, Goltzius was inspired by Titian's painting in which light reflections captivatingly illuminated the faces of the shepherds (see p. 192 in the chapter "Masterprints").[3] Bloteling, however, did not know this painting, so he followed his own ideas and invented what he thought was missing.

In the earlier chapter "Privileges," we presented a contemporary copy of one of Goltzius's most successful compositions, the *Portrait of Frederick de Vries* (fig. p. 123). A later copy—one of many—can be dated to before 1652. This print, a copy in reverse by an anonymous hand (fig. p. 283), was part of the stock of the

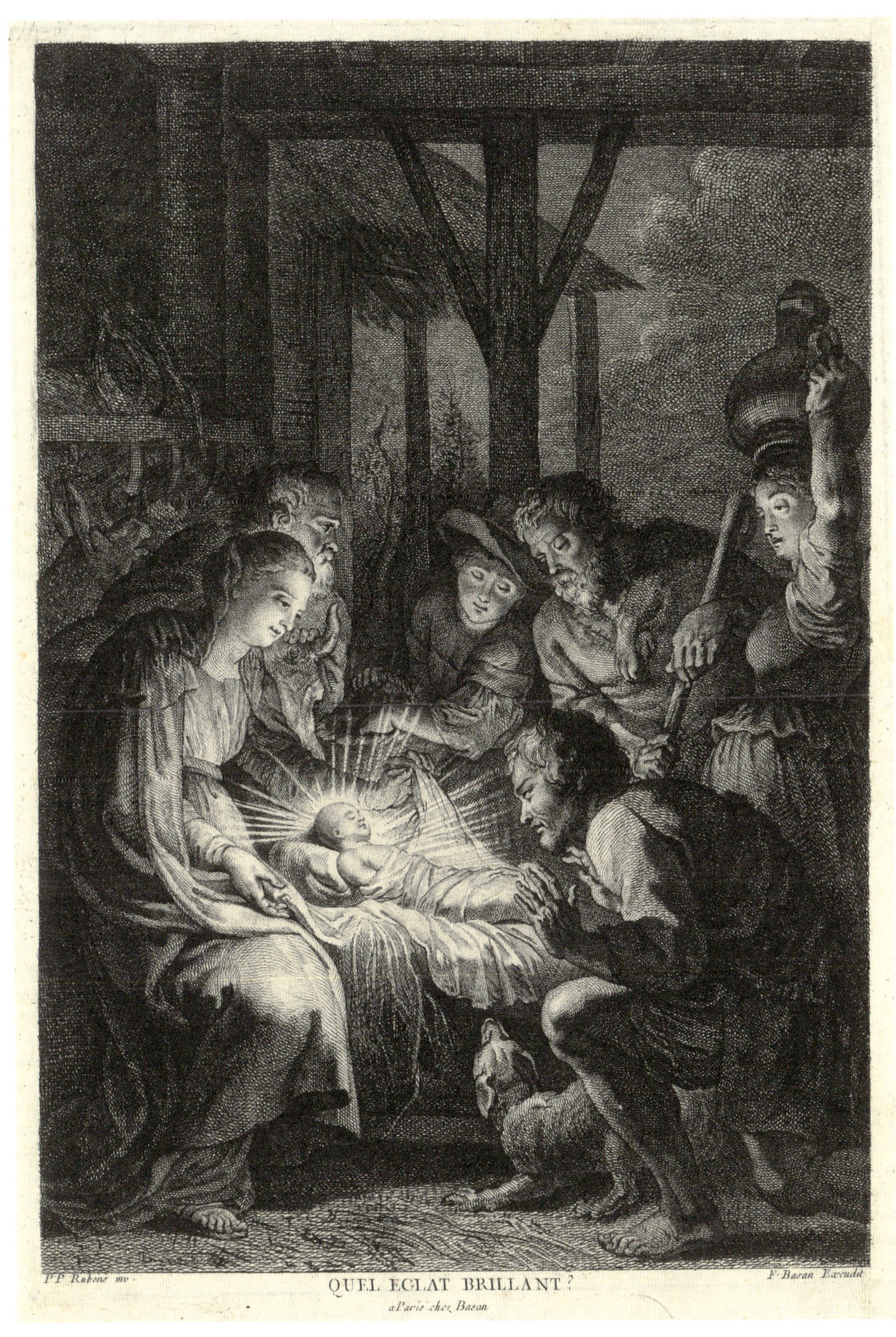

Pierre-François Basan (Stecher, Verleger / engraver, publisher), Kopie nach / copy after Theodoor Galle, nach / after Rubens
Die Anbetung der Hirten / The Adoration of the Shepherds, vor / before 1767
Kupferstich / engraving SGSM, Inv. 30048 D

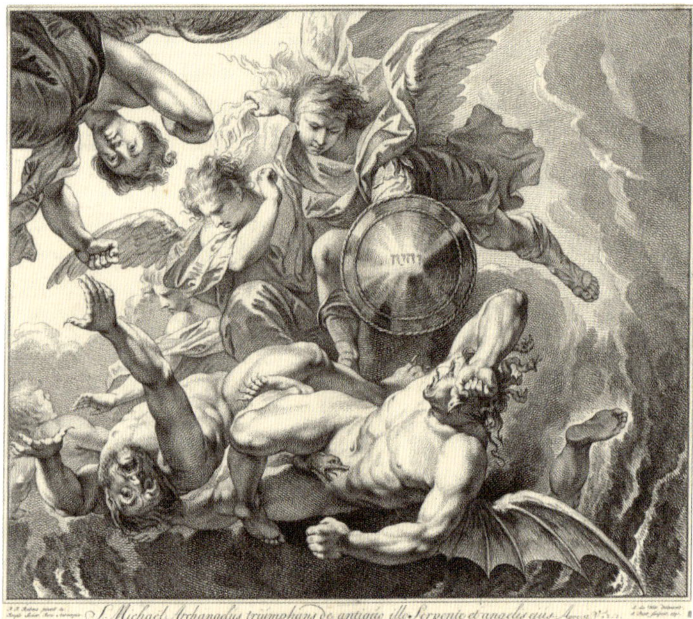

Jacob de Wit (Zeichner / draftsman),
Jan Punt (Stecher, Radierer, Verleger / engraver, etcher, publisher),
nach / after Rubens
Engelsturz / The Fall of the Rebel Angels, 1751/63
Kupferstich, Radierung / engraving, etching SGSM, Inv. 29971-a-01 D

Verszeilen unter dem Stich bei, kopierte aber nicht das Privileg. Die Qualität dieses Blatts ist deutlich schwächer als die der anderen gezeigten Kopie, es wird jedoch sein Publikum gefunden haben.

Eine 1770 datierte Farbradierung markiert vielleicht den Auftakt für die Vervielfältigung auch von Goltzius' Zeichnungen, die sich im 18. Jahrhundert größerer Anerkennung erfreuten als seine oft stärker dem Manierismus verhaftete Druckgraphik. Das beeindruckende *Bildnis einer Frau* (Abb. S. 281) nach einer farbigen Kreidezeichnung von Goltzius entstammt dem wichtigsten Publikationsprojekt des geschäftstüchtigen Graphikers und Verlegers Cornelis Ploos van Amstel (1726–1798), einer Mappe mit 46 teils farbigen Radierungen nach niederländischen Zeichnungen aus seiner umfangreichen Kunstsammlung.[4]

Auch wenn seine oft manieristisch geprägten Stiche nicht immer uneingeschränkt geschätzt wurden, stand die technische Meisterschaft von Goltzius zu allen Zeiten außer Frage. So übten sich Studenten an den Kunstakademien in Stuttgart, Dresden, Nürnberg, Wien, Basel, Paris, Rom und Amsterdam im Nachstechen von bestimmten Goltzius-Motiven.[5] Einer dieser Studenten an der Königlichen Kunstakademie in Dresden, der später selbst Lehrer werden sollte, war Christian Friedrich Stölzel (1751–1816). Ihm verdanken wir einen Nachstich (vor 1816, Abb. S. 279) nach der *Euterpe* aus Goltzius' Serie *Die neun Musen*.[6]

Dem französischen Karikaturisten Honoré Daumier (1808–1879) stand Mitte des 19. Jahrhunderts anscheinend aus Studienzeiten noch Goltzius' Stich des *Herkules Farnese* in Rückenansicht vor Augen (Abb. S. 223), als er eine böse Satire auf einen geschäftstüchtigen

Amsterdam publisher Claes Jansz. Visscher (1586/87–1652). The motif must have sold well even half a century after its first release, for it seems to have been a profitable investment for Visscher. He kept the dedication and the verses below the motif, but did not copy the privilege. The quality of this print is visibly lower than that of the other copy illustrated in this catalog (fig. p. 283), yet this copy too will have found its buyers.

A color etching dated 1770 may mark the beginning of the reproduction of Goltzius's drawings, which enjoyed great admiration in the eighteenth century—much more than his more visibly Mannerist prints. The impressive *Portrait of a Woman* (fig. p. 281), after a color chalk drawing by Goltzius, was part of the enterprising engraver and publisher Cornelis Ploos van Amstel's (1726–1798) most important publication project: a portfolio of forty-six etchings (some in color) after Dutch drawings from his own sizable collection.[4]

Even though his often Mannerist prints were not cherished equally at all times, Goltzius's technical mastery was never questioned. Art students at the academies in Stuttgart, Dresden, Nuremberg, Vienna, Basel, Paris, Rome, and Amsterdam did engraving exercises after certain Goltzius motifs.[5] Christian Friedrich Stölzel (1751–1816), a student at the Royal Art Academy in Dresden who went on to become a teacher there himself, engraved a print (before 1816; fig. p. 279) after *Euterpe* from Goltzius's series *The Nine Muses*.[6]

The French caricaturist Honoré Daumier (1808–1879) may have remembered Goltzius's famous print of the back view of the *Farnese Hercules* (fig. p. 223) from his days as an art student. The Frenchman conceived a biting satire of a successful businessman who had tried to instigate a campaign for rabies shots which he himself hoped to sell. Daumier's chalk lithograph *Un nouvel Hercule Farnèse* appeared in the satirical magazine *Le Charivari* in 1852 and showed the businessman—in anything but athletic shape—as the victor over a pack of infected dogs, viewed from the back and below as in Goltzius's print (fig. p. 285).[7] The French caricaturist satirized everything that in Goltzius's print had added to the heroic posture of the sculpture: its position on a pedestal, the view from below, and the emphatically muscular body.

Scholars have speculated as to whether Rubens had engravings made after his paintings during his stay in Italy (1600–1608), but there is no evidence to support this hypothesis.[8] The print *The Supper at Emmaus*, engraved in 1611 by Willem van Swanenburgh (1580–1612) after a Rubens painting, is the earliest known and accepted print after a picture by Rubens. There is no indication that the artist authorized or contributed to this reproduction.[9] However, this print marks the starting point of reproductions after works by the Fleming. Thanks in large measure to former students and apprentices of Pieter Soutman (1593/1601–1657), prints after Rubens paintings remained in circulation in the later seventeenth century. Scholars refer to these followers as "Rubens's school of engravers."[10] One example is Pieter van Sompel's (1600–?) copy, commissioned by Soutman, after Rubens's painting *The Supper at*

Unternehmer machte. Dieser Unternehmer hatte zu einer Kampagne gegen Tollwut aufgerufen, gegen die er ein Mittel verkaufen wollte. In der Zeitschrift *Le Charivari* erschien 1852 Daumiers Kreidelithographie *Un nouvel Hercule Farnèse*, in der dieser Unternehmer in wenig athletischer Figur als Bezwinger der infizierten Hunde gezeigt wird – wie bei Goltzius von hinten und in Untersicht (Abb. S. 285).[7] Alles, was bei Goltzius zur Steigerung des Heroischen an dieser Skulptur beitrug – die Platzierung auf dem Sockel, die Untersicht sowie die Betonung des athletischen Körperbaus –, zog der französische Karikaturist ins Lächerliche.

Es ist spekuliert worden, ob Rubens bereits in seiner italienischen Zeit (1600–1608) Stiche nach seinen Gemälden anfertigen ließ, doch dafür gibt es keine Belege.[8] So bleibt das Blatt *Christus in Emmaus*, das Willem van Swanenburgh (1580–1612) bereits 1611 nach einem Rubens-Gemälde stach, die früheste bekannte und akzeptierte Graphik nach einem Rubens-Gemälde. Es gibt kein Indiz, dass der Künstler hierfür die Zustimmung von Rubens eingeholt oder diesen am Werkprozess beteiligt hatte.[9] Aber spätestens mit dieser Graphik begann das Reproduktionswesen nach Werken des Flamen. Die Schüler von Pieter Soutman (1593/1601–1657), der zahlreiche Rubens-Stiche zu dessen Lebzeiten angefertigt hatte, taten ihr Übriges, um Rubens-Kompositionen im späteren 17. Jahrhundert präsent zu halten. In der Literatur ist daher auch die Rede von einer „Rubens'schen Stecherschule".[10] Ein Beispiel ist Pieter van Sompel (1600–?), der 1643 für Soutman eine neue Kopie nach Rubens' Gemälde *Christus in Emmaus* stach (Abb. S. 127).[11] Im Vergleich mit Goltzius, der mit wachsendem zeitlichen Abstand immer weniger für seine – dem Zeitgeschmack geschuldeten – manieristischen Formen geschätzt wurde, beobachtet Timothy Riggs für den Flamen eine stetigere Rezeption: „Rubens hatte ein Produktionssystem für eine bestimmte Art des Kupferstichs eingeführt, das so gut funktionierte, dass es von alleine lief. Der Rubens-Stil der Stiche sollte ein viel längeres Leben haben als der Goltzius-Stil."[12]

Dem Rubens-Stil und -Qualitätsanspruch entsprachen die Radierungen des Willem Panneels (1600/05–1634) weniger. Rubens stand mit diesem Maler und Radierer auf gutem Fuße und vertraute ihm während einer längeren Abwesenheit zwischen 1628 und 1630 einmal die Aufsicht über seine Zeichnungen an. Diesen Zugang nutzte Panneels, um viele dieser Zeichnungen zu kopieren und später einige Motive auch als Radierungen zu verbreiten, in denen er sich als „discipulus", als Schüler, von Rubens auswies.[13] Diese Stiche sind für uns interessant, denn sie geben mutmaßlich Rubens-Kompositionen wieder, die heute zum Teil verloren sind. Die *Madonna* (1630–1634) geht womöglich ebenfalls auf Rubens-Zeichnungen zurück (Abb. S. 289).[14]

Auch im 18. Jahrhundert erfreuten sich Rubens-Kompositionen in Stichen größter Beliebtheit, besonders seine politischen Großprojekte wurden jetzt auf diese Weise bekannt gemacht. 1710 legte der Pariser Verleger Gaspard Duchange den Medici-Zyklus mit Stichen der Brüder Jean-Baptiste (1678–1726) und Jean-Marc Nattier (1685–1766) graphisch auf.[15] Dieser Zyklus ausgefeilter politischer Propaganda, der erst seit 1793 im Louvre in Paris frei zugänglich ist, wurde damit zum ersten Mal einer breiteren Öffentlichkeit bekannt. 1720 veröffentlichte Simon Gribelin (1661–1733) seine Stiche nach den Deckengemälden,

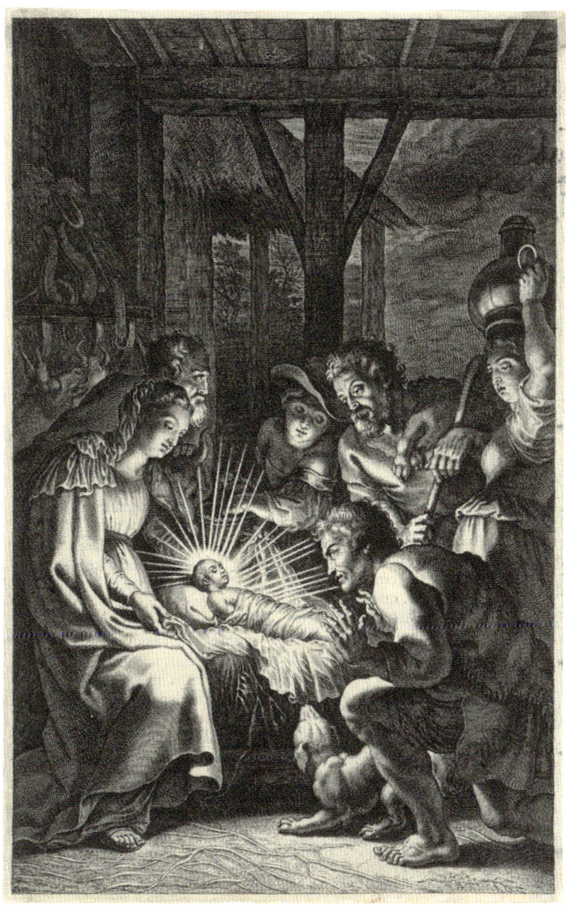

Rubens (Inventor / designer), Theodoor Galle (Stecher / engraver), Plantiniana (Verlag / publisher)
Die Anbetung der Hirten / The Adoration of the Shepherds, 1614/28
Aus / from *Breviarum Romanum*, Antwerpen 1628
Kupferstich/engraving SGSM, Inv. 30006 D

Emmaus (fig. p. 127).[11] Whereas Goltzius's Mannerist forms met with less and less appreciation as tastes changed over time, Timothy Riggs observes a more stable appreciation for the prints of the Fleming: "Rubens had set up a system for the production of a certain kind of engraving, and it worked so well it functioned by itself. The Rubens style of engraving was to have a far longer life than the Goltzius style."[12]

The etchings of Willem Panneels (1600/05–1634) do not match the Rubens style, nor do they approach the quality of his prints. The Antwerp master was fond of this painter and etcher, however, and during an absence from 1628 to 1630 entrusted Panneels with his drawings. The latter took advantage of this access and copied many of the drawings, some of which he later turned into etchings and published. He signed these prints as "discipulus," as Rubens's student.[13] These prints are of interest to us because some of them reproduce Rubens compositions which have been lost. It is assumed that the *Madonna* (1630–1634) was based on such a Rubens drawing (fig. p. 289).[14]

die Rubens 1634 bis 1636 für das Banqueting House im Whitehall Palace in London angefertigt hatte.[16] Die seit einem Brand für uns verlorenen Deckengemälde der Antwerpener Jesuitenkirche hielten gleich zwei Verleger für ein lukratives Projekt: 1735 der Nürnberger Stecher Johann Justin Preißler (1698–1771), der seine eigenen Stiche veröffentlichte,[17] und 1763 der Amsterdamer Verleger Jan Punt mit den qualitätvolleren Stichen nach Zeichnungen von Jacob de Wit (1695–1754; Abb. S. 272).[18]

Einen Stich nach Rubens' Gemälde *Der trunkene Silen* können wir auf 1701/02 datieren, denn in dieser Zeit hielt sich der Radierer und Stecher Richard van Orley II (1663–1732) am Düsseldorfer Hof auf und übersetzte dort das Gemälde (vermutlich erst in eine Zeichnung und danach) in einen Stich (Abb. S. 287). Dies ist die erste Druckgraphik nach dem Bild, welches Rubens bis zu seinem Tod im eigenen Besitz behalten hatte.[19] Wie bei anderen Gemälden auch, die er für sich zurückbehielt, ließ er zu Lebzeiten keinen Stich davon anfertigen.

Dem Wiener Stecher Quirin Mark (1753–1811) verdanken wir das im späten 18. Jahrhundert entstandene Blatt *Susanna und die beiden Alten* (Abb. S. 286). Ausweislich der Bildunterschrift hatte Mark nicht, wie sonst üblich, nach Rubens' Gemälde oder Pontius' Stich gearbeitet, sondern nach einer Rubens (zugeschriebenen) Zeichnung, welche sich damals in der Sammlung des Fürsten Gallitzin befand.[20] Rechts und links des Familienwappens der Gallitzin platzierte Mark die Bildunterschrift auf Französisch, damit ein internationales Publikum sie verstünde: „Gravé d'apres le dessein original de Rubens tiré du Cabinet de Mr le Prince de Galitzin Ministre Plenipre de Russie à la Cour Imple et Royale" (gestochen nach der Originalzeichnung von Rubens aus dem Kabinett des Prinzen von Galitzin ...). Im 18. Jahrhundert wurden viele der damals nach Rubens-Kompositionen angefertigten Stiche auf diese Weise in Verbindung mit ihren Sammlern gebracht.

Der Autor eines der ersten Werkverzeichnisse von Rubens' Druckgraphik, Pierre-François Basan (1723–1797), führt in demselben hochtrabend auch einen Stich an, den er selbst vor 1767 nach einer *Anbetung der Hirten*, einer 1614 entstandenen Buchillustration von Theodoor Galle nach Rubens, angefertigt hatte (Abb. S. 271, 273).[21] Nicht ganz unbescheiden schreibt er dort über seinen Stich, er habe ihn „dans la maniere de Rembrandt" ausgeführt. Damit war nicht die Technik gemeint, denn Basan arbeitete das Blatt als Kupferstich aus, während Rembrandt für seine Radierungen bekannt war. Vordergründig spielte Basan wohl auf Rembrandts Meisterschaft in der graphischen Darstellung von Hell-Dunkel an. Der Franzose adelte seinen eigenen Namen, indem er ihn mit den Namen der beiden großen Künstler des nordeuropäischen 17. Jahrhunderts – mit Rubens und Rembrandt – in Verbindung brachte.

In the eighteenth century, prints after Rubens compositions continued to enjoy great popularity, foremost among them political projects that were now being published for the first time. In 1710 the Parisian publisher Gaspard Duchange issued the *Medici* series in prints by the brothers Jean-Baptiste (1678–1726) and Jean-Marc Nattier (1685–1766).[15] This painted series of polished political propaganda, which was not open to the public at the Louvre in Paris until 1793, thus reached a wider public through the prints. In 1720, Simon Gribelin (1661–1733) produced engravings after the ceiling paintings Rubens had created between 1634 and 1636 for the Banqueting House at Whitehall Palace in London.[16] The ceiling paintings of the Antwerp Jesuit church, later lost in a fire, struck not one but two publishers as profitable print projects: in 1735 the Nuremberg publisher Johann Justin Preißler (1698–1771) issued his own prints,[17] followed in 1763 by the Amsterdam publisher Jan Punt with his finer engravings (fig. p. 272) after drawings by Jacob de Wit (1695–1754).[18]

We can narrow in on the years 1701 to 1702 for a print after Rubens's painting *Drunken Silenus*, because this is when the etcher and engraver Richard van Orley II (1663–1732) worked at the Düsseldorf court and transferred the painting (probably by way of a preparatory drawing after the painting) into print (fig. p. 287). This is the first print after the painting, because the picture had remained in Rubens's possession until his death in 1640.[19] Rubens did not have prints made of the paintings he retained for his own collection.

We have the Viennese engraver Quirin Mark (1753–1811) to thank for the late eighteenth-century print *Susanna and the Elders* (1784–1793; fig. p. 286). According to the print's inscription, Mark had not, as was customary, worked after Rubens's painting or Pontius's engraving, but instead after an (alleged) Rubens drawing in the collection of Prince Gallitzin.[20] Mark positioned an inscription below the motif, to the right and left of the Gallitzin family coat of arms, in French so that an international audience might understand it: "Gravé d'apres le dessein original de Rubens tiré du Cabinet de Mr le Prince de Galitzin Ministre Plenipre de Russie à la Cour Imple et Royale" (engraved after the original Rubens drawing from the Cabinet of the prince of Galitzin . . .). In the eighteenth century attention was drawn to the work's collector in this manner in many prints after Rubens compositions.

The author of the first catalogue raisonné of Rubens prints, Pierre-François Basan (1723–1797), boastfully listed in his tome one of his own prints (1767) after *The Adoration of the Shepherds*, a book illustration engraved by Theodoor Galle in 1614 after Rubens (figs. pp. 271, 273).[21] Rather immodestly, he wrote of his own print that he had executed it "dans la maniere de Rembrandt." Here Basan could not be referring to the technique, because he produced an engraving whereas Rembrandt was famous for his etchings. Rather, Basan seems to be addressing Rembrandt's mastery of light and shadow. The Frenchman thus ennobled his own name by connecting it with the names of the two great artists of seventeenth-century northern Europe: Rubens and Rembrandt.

1 Riggs 1993, S. 102.

2 Hans-Martin Kaulbach (in: Stuttgart 2021, S. 274) nennt die konkreten Zahlen: 100 Stiche unter Rubens' Aufsicht, 800 am Ende des 17. Jahrhunderts, etwa 2200 bekannt im Jahr 1873. – Vgl. hierzu auch Nils Büttner auf S. 92, Anm. 38, im vorliegenden Katalog.

3 Vgl. Mander (1604) 1916, S. 279.

4 Die Mappe führt keinen Titel, nur eine Widmungsseite. Die Radierung nach Goltzius ist Blatt Nr. 18. Vgl. Wurzbach 1910, Bd. II, S. 333f. Die Goltzius-Zeichnung befindet sich heute im Amsterdam Museum, Inv. TA 10184.

5 Zu dieser Rezeption ab dem 18. Jahrhundert vgl. Marjolein Leesberg, in: NHD Goltzius 2012, S. lxxii, sowie Leesberg 2017b, S. 90 f. Zur Rezeption zu Beginn des 17. Jahrhunderts von Goltzius' Umgang mit der Zeichenfeder und Empfehlungen, diese zu imitieren, vgl. Namowitz Worthen 1991/92, S. 278.

6 Vgl. NHD Goltzius 2012, 129–137, SGSM, Inv. 30966 D bis 30974 D. Goltzius hatte die Serie seinem Münchner Kollegen Hans Sadeler (1550–1600) gewidmet, mit dem ihn eine freundschaftliche Künstlerrivalität verband, wie im Kapitel „Widmungen" (S. 106) ausgeführt wurde.

7 Vgl. Mitchell 2013, S. 334f.

8 Hans Gerhard Evers vermutete in einem Stich der SGSM, Inv. 7914-Verlust D (zu Evers' Zeit als Inv. 7914 unter „nach Tizian" geführt und im Inventar mit dem späteren Zusatz „Villamena?" bezeichnet), den ersten Stich nach einem Rubens-Gemälde, namentlich nach seinem ersten *Vallicella*-Altarblatt. Der bei Evers abgebildete Stich wurde nach dem Zweiten Weltkrieg im Inventar als vermisst markiert. Vgl. Evers 1944, S. 118, Abb. 26; Meier 2020a, Kat. 89, S. 371, Anm. 2, erwähnt diese Vermutung, kennt jedoch wohl nicht die Abbildung. Dank an Kurt Zeitler für die Auslegung des Inventarvermerks.

9 Freilich erinnert man sich an Rubens' Reise 1612 nach Holland, die ihn neben Haarlem auch nach Leiden führte, wo Swanenburgh lebte. Zu erwägen wäre daher, dass der Stecher in Vorbereitung auf Rubens' Besuch bereits diesen Stich anfertigte. Die Adressierung von Rubens in der Bildunterschrift als „unser Apelles" wäre demnach als schmeichelnde Geste für den Gast und Schöpfer der Komposition zu verstehen. Zum Auftraggeber und weiteren Details rund um diesen Stich vgl. Meier 2020a, Kat. 1.

10 Vgl. Renger 1974a, S. 124. Auf S. 123f. eine Zusammenfassung der kritischen Rezeption der Rubens-Graphik und der Geschichte der Werkverzeichnisse derselben, die bereits 1751 mit der Publikation des Franzosen Robert Hecquet (Hecquet 1751) einsetzte.

11 Das Blatt wurde 1700 erneut von dem Amsterdamer Verleger Gerard Valck herausgegeben, der ein Schwager des oben erwähnten Abraham Bloteling war. – Soutman war 1643 wieder in Haarlem, vielleicht hatte er Zugang zu dem Gemälde, das sich in den nördlichen Niederlanden befand, und fertigte danach eine Stichvorlage für Sompel an.

12 Riggs 1993, S. 115 (Übers. der Autorin).

13 Zu diesem Konvolut von Zeichnungskopien des Willem Panneels, das heute als „Rubens Cantoor" bekannt ist und das in Kopenhagen im Kupferstich-Kabinett aufbewahrt wird, vgl. Meier 2020a, sub Kat. 82; Logan/Lohse Belkin 2022, S. 14.

14 Alternativ ist denkbar, dass Panneels das Motiv direkt nach dem Mittelteil des Gemäldes *Madonna im Blumenkranz*, um 1616–1618, München, Alte Pinakothek, Inv. 331, kopierte. Zur *Madonna im Blumenkranz* siehe Renger/Denk 2002, S. 336–341. Zu den Kopien nach diesem Gemälde im Konvolut Rubens Cantoor siehe Konrad Renger, in: Renger/Denk 2002, S. 341.

15 SGSM, Inv. 1960:1281-01 bis 24 D sowie etliche verstreute Dubletten.

16 SGSM, Inv. 30383 D bis 30385 D, 30392 D sowie die Dublette 2023:84 D.

17 SGSM, Inv. 30016 D bis 30035 D.

18 SGSM, Inv. 29971-a-01 bis 24 D.

19 Vgl. Konrad Renger, in: Renger/Denk 2002, S. 374.

20 Vgl. s. v. Mark, Quirin, in: Wurzbach 1856–1891, Bd. 16 (1876), S. 452f. – Der genannte Sammler, der russische Diplomat Dmitri Michailowitsch Golizyn/Gallitzin (1721–1793), war seit 1784 Botschafter in Wien, als welchen ihn die Bildunterschrift ausweist. Der Stich muss folglich zwischen 1784 und 1793 von Mark angefertigt worden sein. – Gallitzins Zeichnung kann nicht übereinstimmen mit jener heute noch bekannten und Pontius zugeschriebenen im Louvre, Inv. 20317, die bereits 1671 mit der Sammlung Jabach in die Pariser Bestände einging. Vgl. <https://collections.louvre.fr/en/ark:/53355/cl020110493> [gelesen am 1. Januar 2024]. In Marks Stich fehlen einige der schönen Details, die Pontius' früheren Stich auszeichneten, wie die Pergola im Hintergrund.

21 Basan 1767, S. 14, Kat 11 bis.

1 Riggs 1993, p. 102.

2 Hans-Martin Kaulbach (in: Stuttgart 2021, p. 274) cites specific numbers: one hundred prints under Rubens's supervision, eight hundred by the end of the seventeenth century, and about 2,200 in total by 1873. – See also Nils Büttner on p. 93, n. 38, in the present catalog.

3 Mander 1604, fol. 49r v34.

4 The portfolio bears no title, only a dedication page. The etching after Goltzius is no. 18. See Wurzbach 1910, vol. 2, pp. 333–334. Goltzius's drawing is now in the Amsterdam Museum, inv. TA 10184.

5 On the reception from the eighteenth century onward, see Marjolein Leesberg, in: NHD Goltzius 2012, p. lxxii, and Leesberg 2017b, pp. 90–91. On the early seventeenth-century reception of Goltzius's handling of the pen and advice on how to copy it, see Namowitz Worthen 1991/92, p. 278.

6 See NHD Goltzius 2012, 129–137. SGSM, inv. 30966 D through 30974 D. Goltzius dedicated this series to his Munich colleague Hans Sadeler (1550–1600), with whom he had a friendly artistic rivalry, as is mentioned in the chapter "Dedications" (p. 106).

7 See Mitchell 2013, pp. 334–335.

8 Hans Gerhard Evers assumed that a print in the SGSM, inv. 7914-Verlust D, was the very first print after a Rubens painting—namely, after his first Vallicella altarpiece. At the time Evers saw it, this print was stored as inv. 7914 under "after Titian"; in 1951 the addendum "Villamena?" was added to its entry in the inventory books. The print Evers reproduced was marked in the inventory books as missing after World War II. See Evers 1944, p. 118 (fig. 26); Meier 2020a, cat. 89, p. 371, n. 2, mentions this hypothesis. I am grateful to Kurt Zeitler for the interpretation of the inventory mark.

9 Rubens's trip to Holland in 1612—which took him not only to Haarlem but also to Leyden, where Swanenburgh lived—comes to mind. It might be worth considering the possibility that the engraver produced this print in anticipation of Rubens's visit. Addressing the Fleming in the inscription as "our Apelles" would have flattered the guest and creator of the composition. On the question of who commissioned the print and for further details around it, see Meier 2020a, cat. 1.

10 See Renger 1974a, p. 124. On pp. 123–124 is a synopsis of the critical reception of Rubens prints and the history of the catalogues raisonnés of prints, which started in 1751 with the publication of Frenchman Robert Hecquet (Hecquet 1751).

11 This print was reissued in 1700 by the Amsterdam publisher Gerard Valck, a brother-in-law of the abovementioned Abraham Bloteling. – By 1628, Soutman was back in Haarlem, where he may have had access to the painting and made the preparatory drawing that Sompel used for his print.

12 Riggs 1993, p. 115.

13 On this group of copies by Willem Panneels after Rubens drawings, today known as "Rubens Cantoor" and kept in the print cabinet in Copenhagen, see Meier 2020a, cat. 82; Logan/Lohse Belkin 2022, p. 14.

14 Alternatively, it is conceivable that Panneels copied the motif directly from the middle part of Rubens's painting *Madonna in a Flower Garland*. On the copies after *Madonna in a Flower Garland* (ca. 1616–1618, Munich, Alte Pinakothek, inv. 331) from the group of Rubens Cantoor drawings, see Konrad Renger, in: Renger/Denk 2002, p. 341.

15 SGSM, inv. 1960:1281-01 through 24 D, as well as several duplicates.

16 SGSM, inv. 30383 D through 30385 D, 30392 D, and duplicate inv. 2023:84 D.

17 SGSM, inv. 30016 D through 30035 D.

18 SGSM, inv. 29971-a-01 through 24 D.

19 See Konrad Renger, in: Renger/Denk 2002, p. 374.

20 See s.v. Mark, Quirin, in: Wurzbach 1856–1891, vol. 16 (1876), pp. 452–453. – The said collector, Russian diplomat Dmitri Michailowitsch Golizyn/Gallitzin (1721–1793) was ambassador to Vienna from 1784. Therefore, Mark must have made the print between 1784 and 1793. Gallitzin's drawing cannot be identical with the one still known and attributed to Pontius in the Louvre, inv. 20317, which had entered the Parisian holdings by way of the Jabach collection as early as 1671. See the Louvre's website, "Suzanne au bain surprise par les deux vieillards," <https://collections.louvre.fr/en/ark:/53355/cl020110493> [accessed on Januar 1, 2024]. Mark left out some of the beautiful details that graced Pontius's print, such as the pergola in the background.

21 Basan 1767, p. 14, cat. 11 bis.

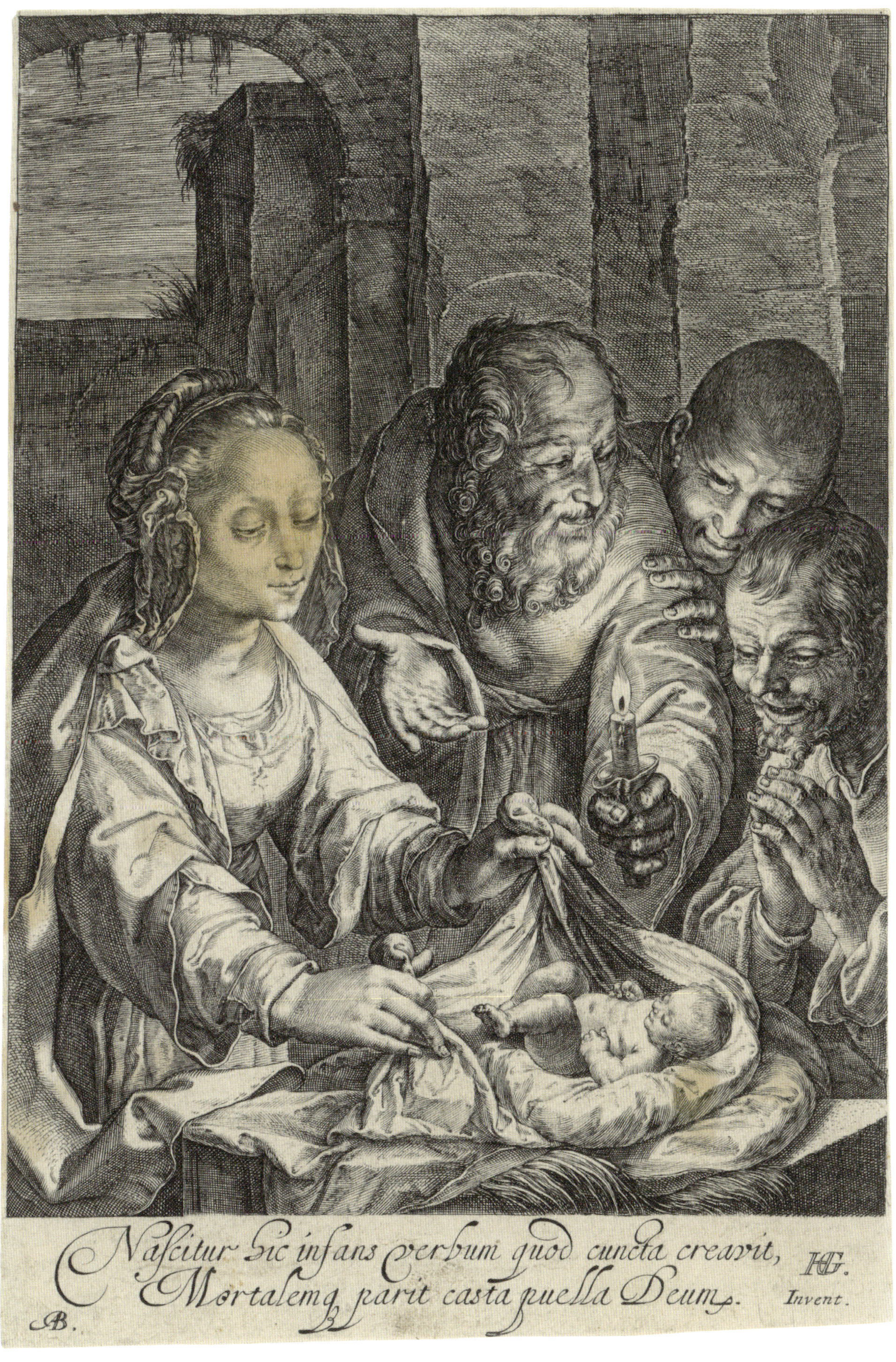

Abraham Bloteling (Stecher / engraver), nach / after Goltzius
Die Anbetung der Hirten / The Adoration of the Shepherds, 1650–1690
Kupferstich / engraving SGSM, Inv. 36901 D

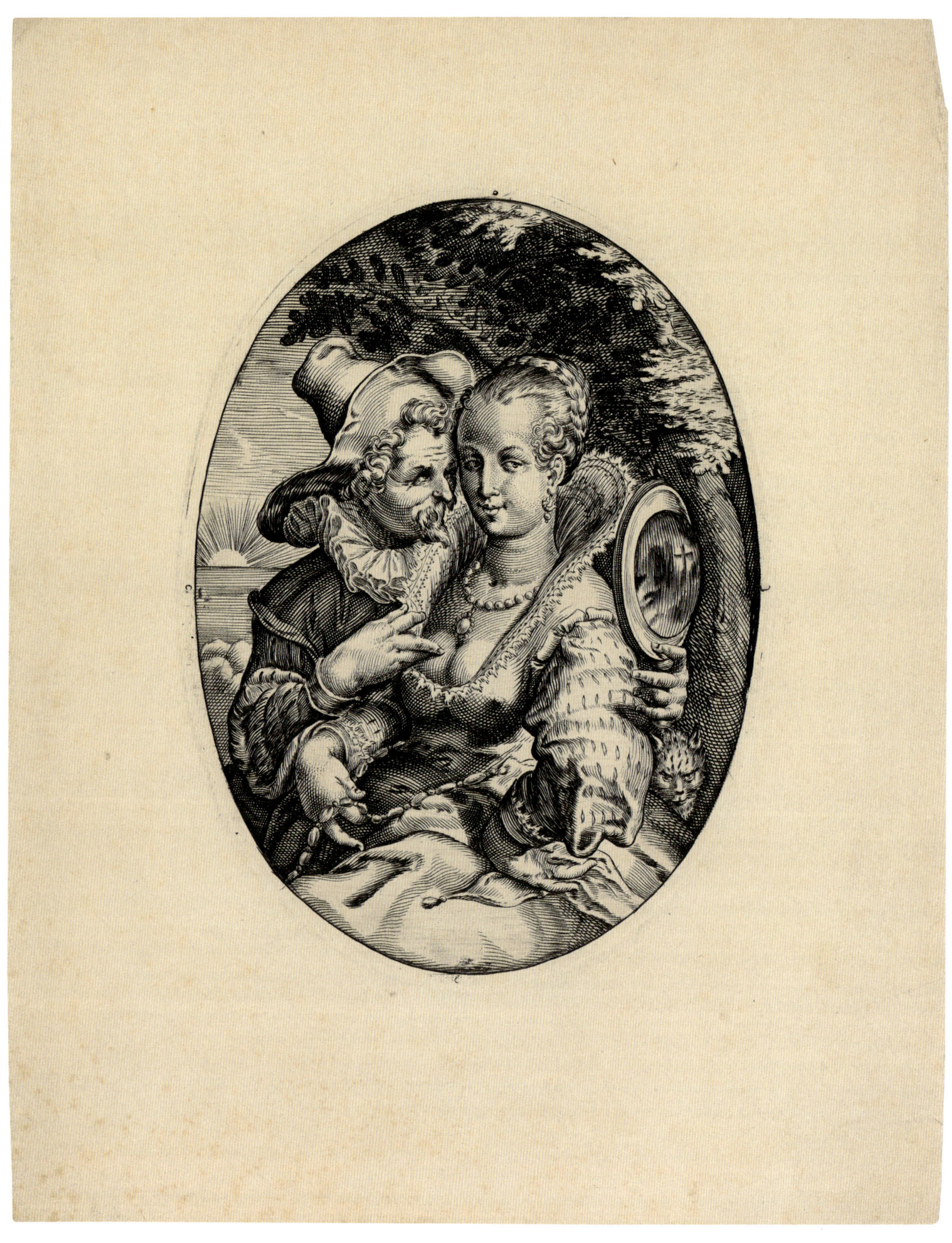

Anonymer Stecher / anonymous engraver, Kopie nach / copy after Goltzius
Der Sehsinn / Sight, 19. Jh. / 19th cent.
Aus der Serie *Die fünf Sinne* / from the series *The Five Senses*, 19. Jh. / 19th cent.
Kupferstich / engraving SGSM, Inv. 2023:25 D

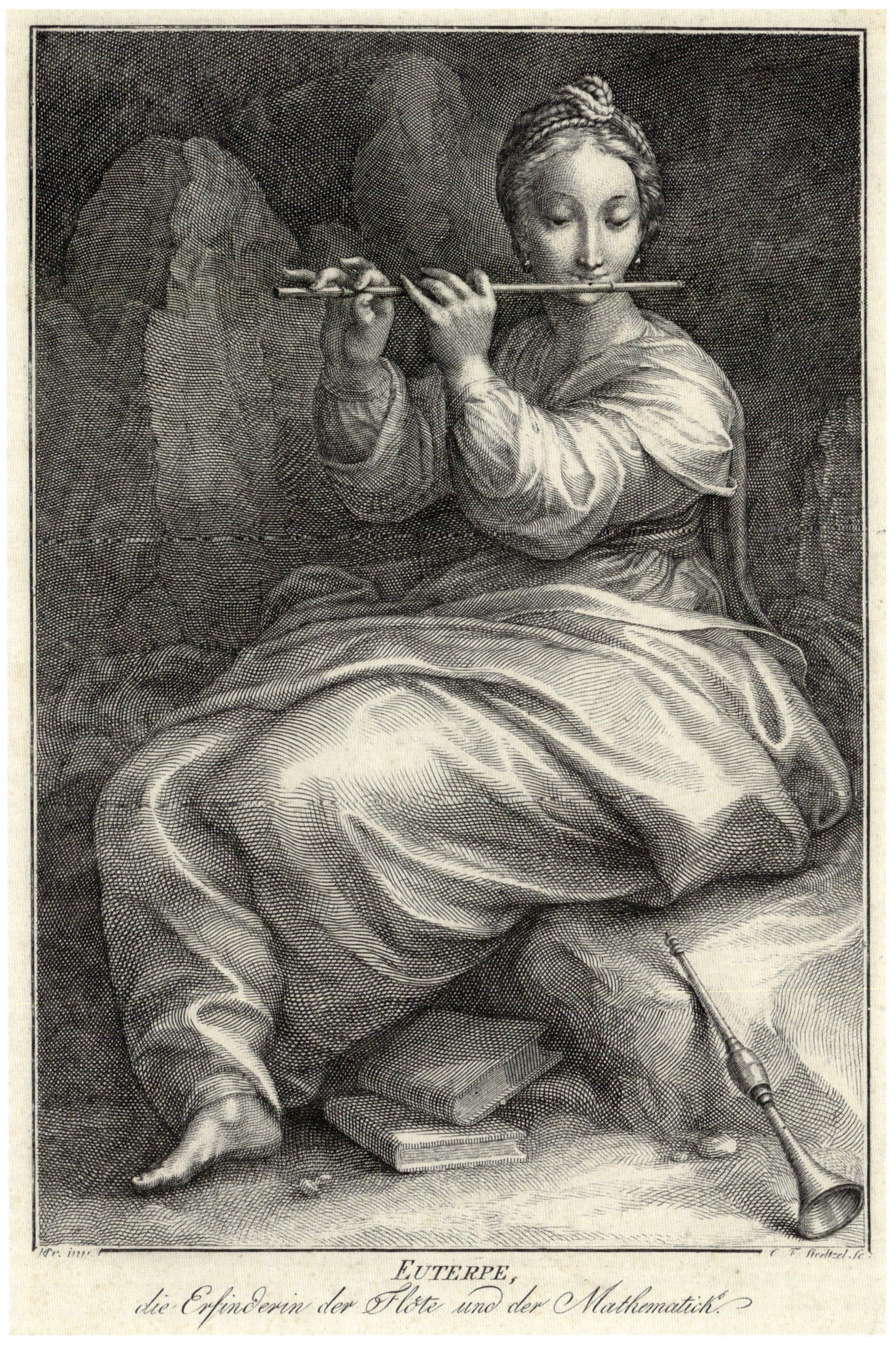

Christian Friedrich Stölzel (Stecher / engraver), Kopie nach / copy after Goltzius
Euterpe, vor / before 1816
Aus der Serie *Die neun Musen* / from the series *The Nine Muses*, 1816
Kupferstich / engraving SGSM, Inv. 2021:502 D

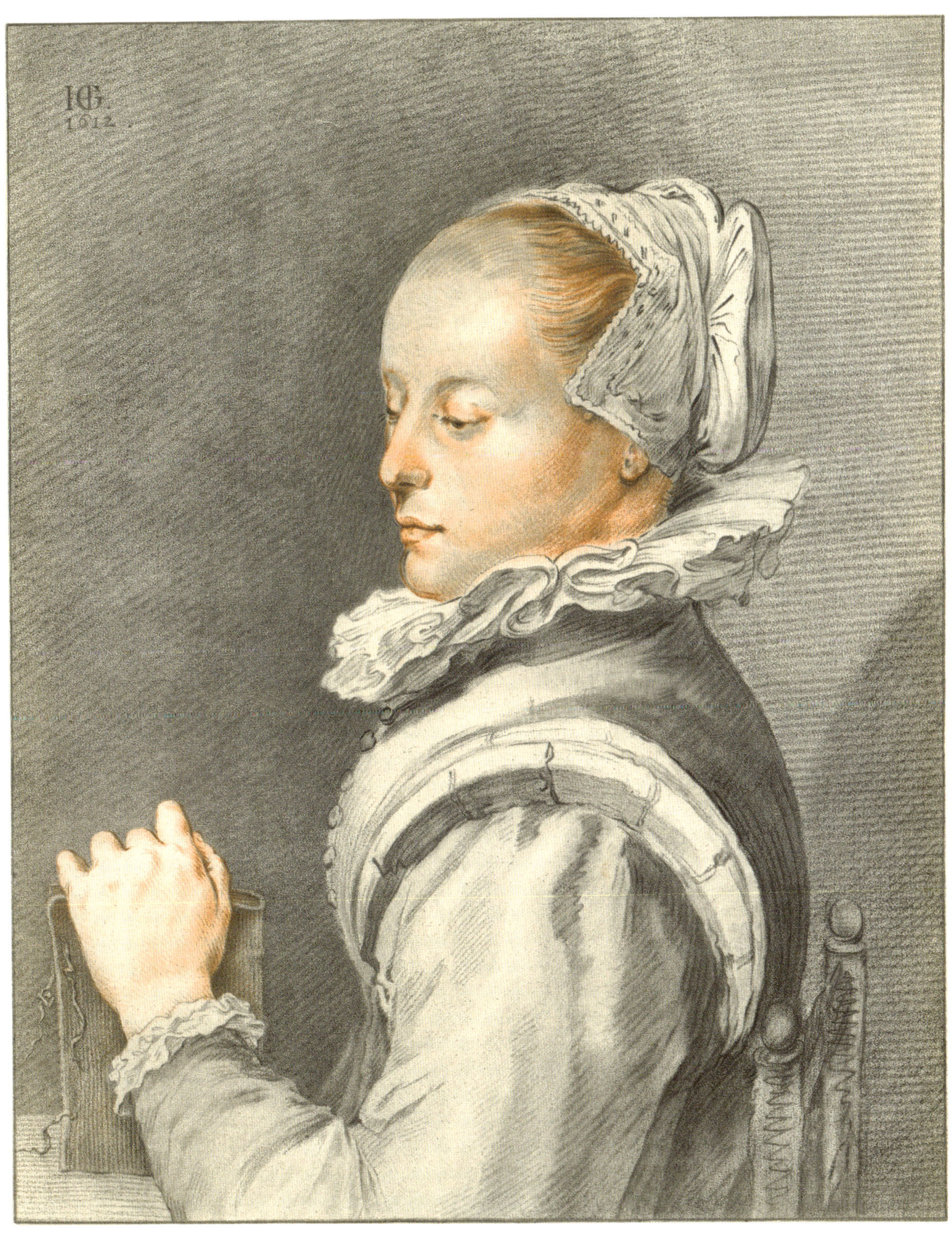

Johannes Körnlein (Radierer / etcher), Kopie nach / copy after Goltzius, Cornelis Ploos van Amstel (Verleger / publisher)
Bildnis einer Frau / Portrait of a Woman, 1770
Farbradierung / color etching SGSM, Inv. 39944 D

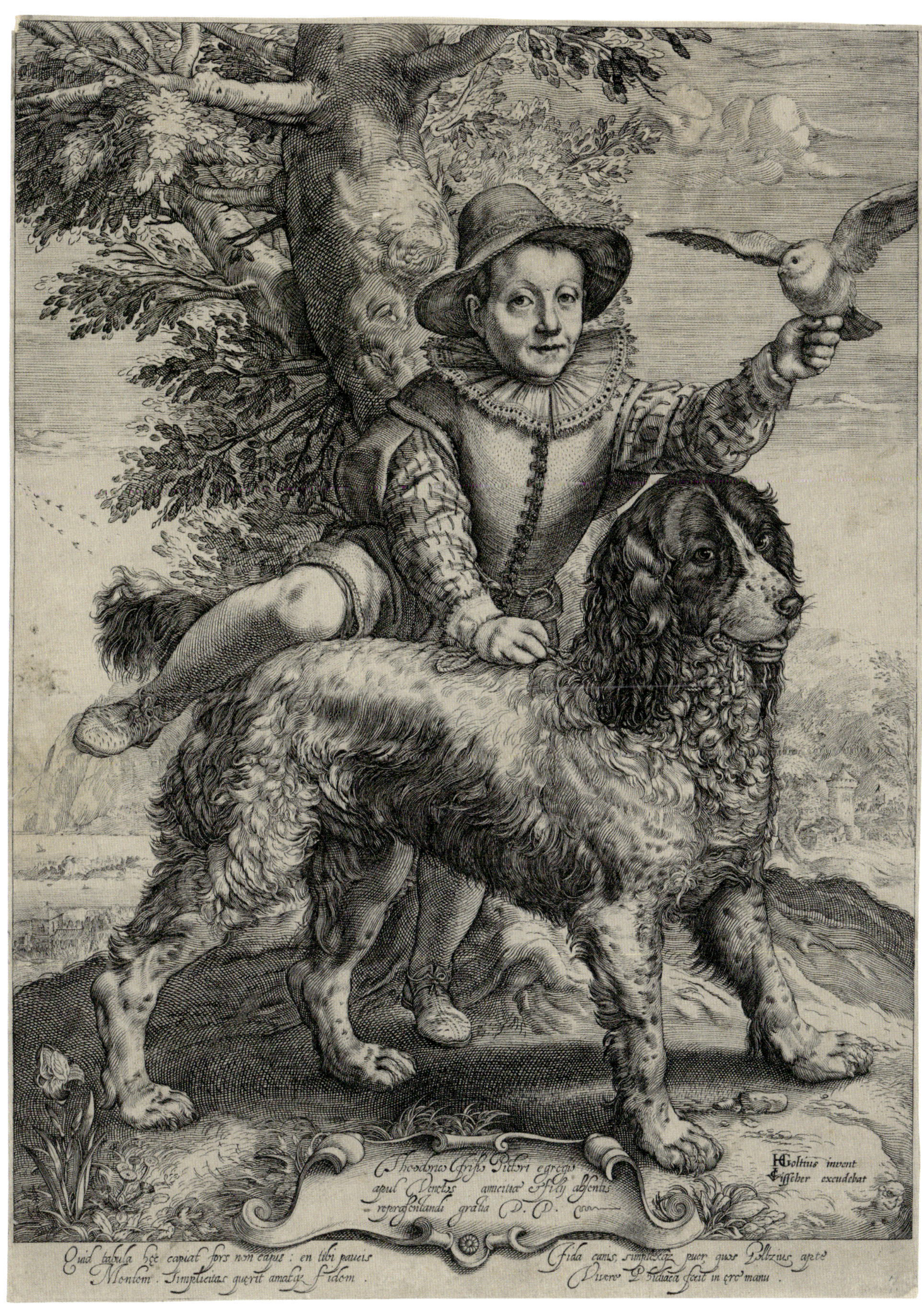

Anonymer Stecher / anonymous engraver, Kopie nach / copy after Goltzius, Claes Jansz. Visscher (Verleger / publisher)
Bildnis des Frederick de Vries (Der Hund des Goltzius) / Portrait of Frederick de Vries (Goltzius's Dog), vor / before 1652
Kupferstich / engraving SGSM, Inv. 110694 D

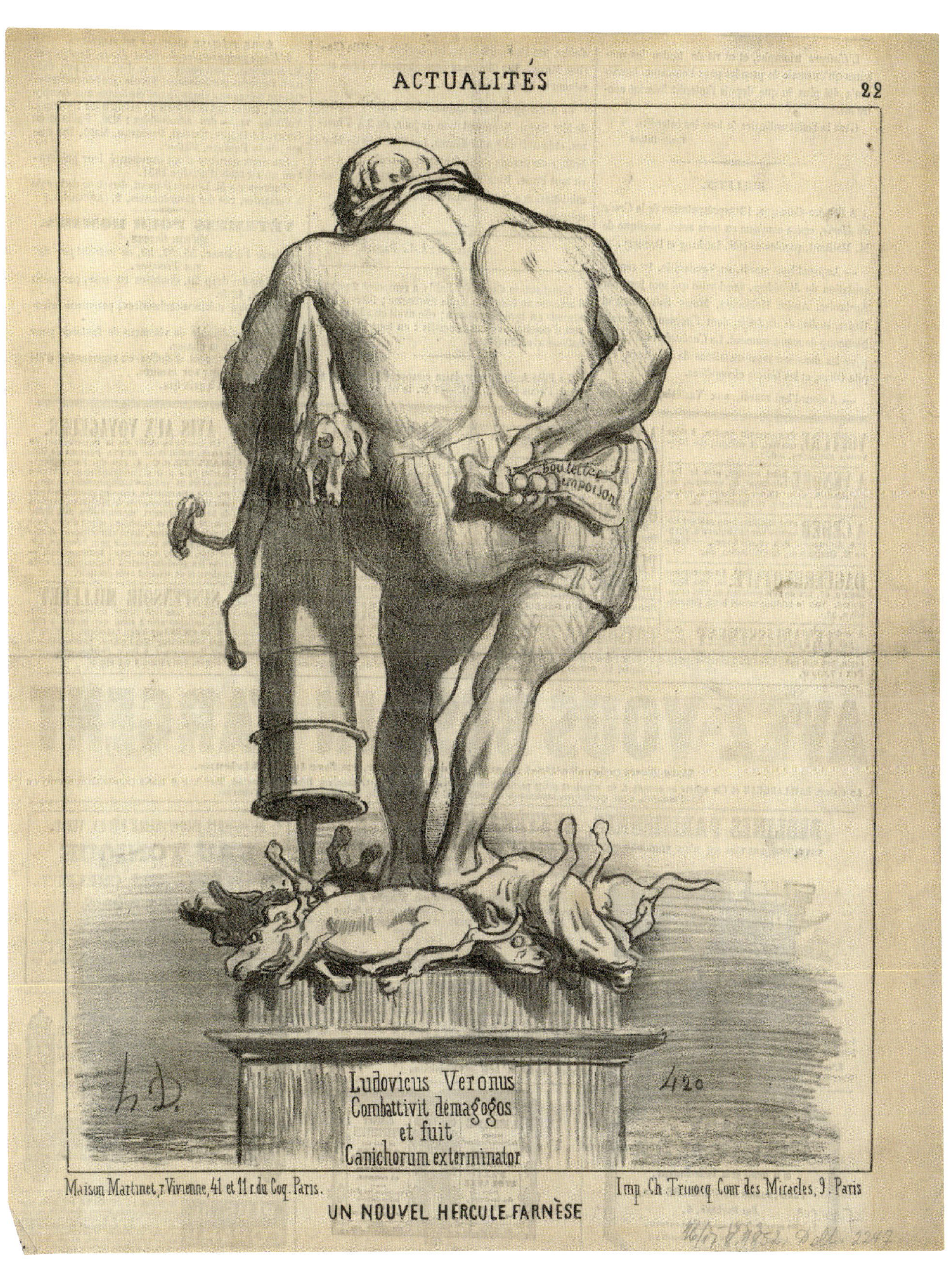

Honoré Daumier (Inventor, Lithograph / designer, lithographer)
Un nouvel Hercule Farnèse
Aus / from *Le Charivari*, August 1852
Lithographie / lithograph SGSM, Inv. GVS 3083

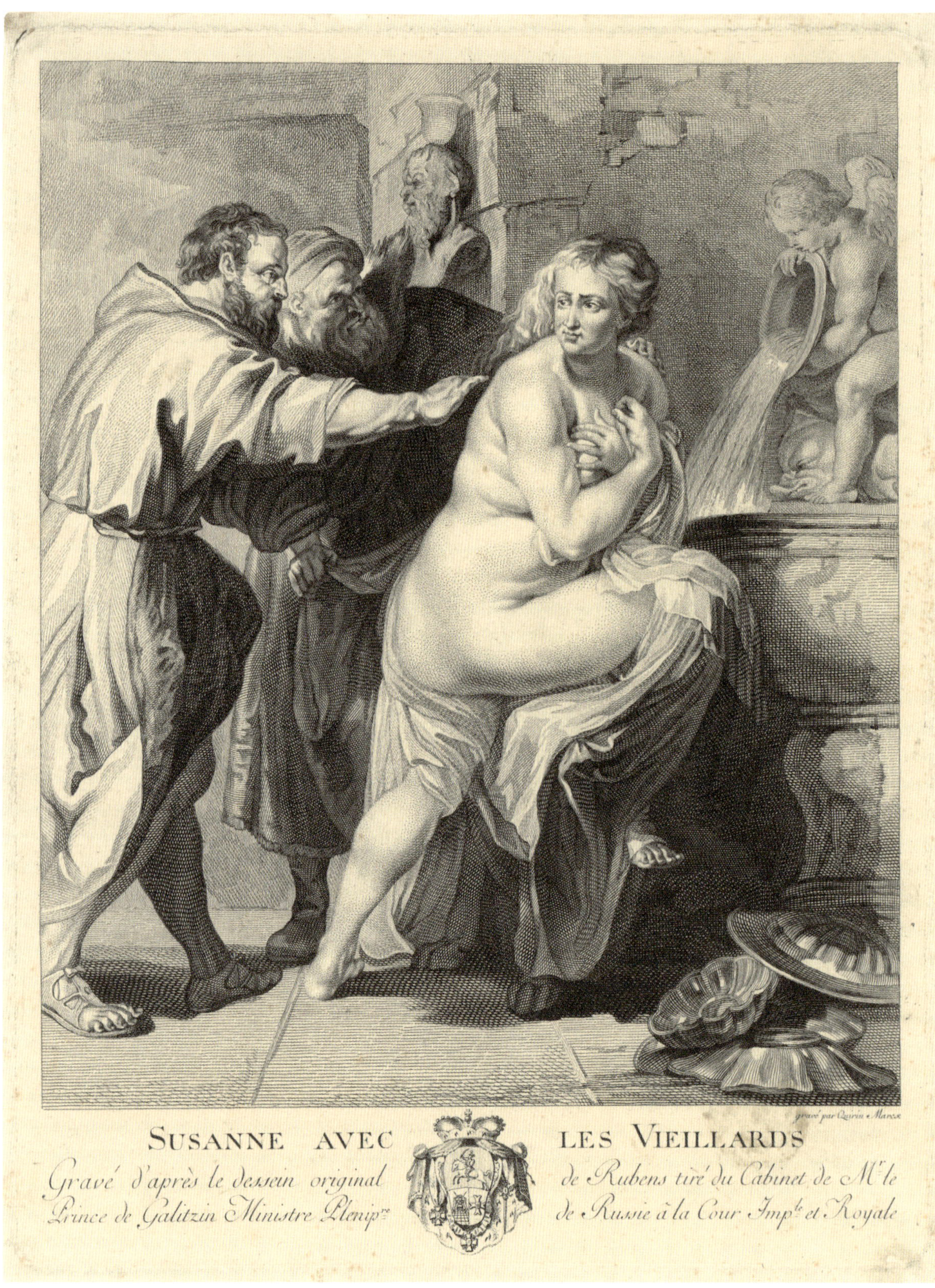

Quirin Mark (Stecher / engraver), nach / after Rubens
Susanna und die beiden Alten / Susanna and the Elders, 1784–1793
Kupferstich / engraving SGSM, Inv. 30003 D

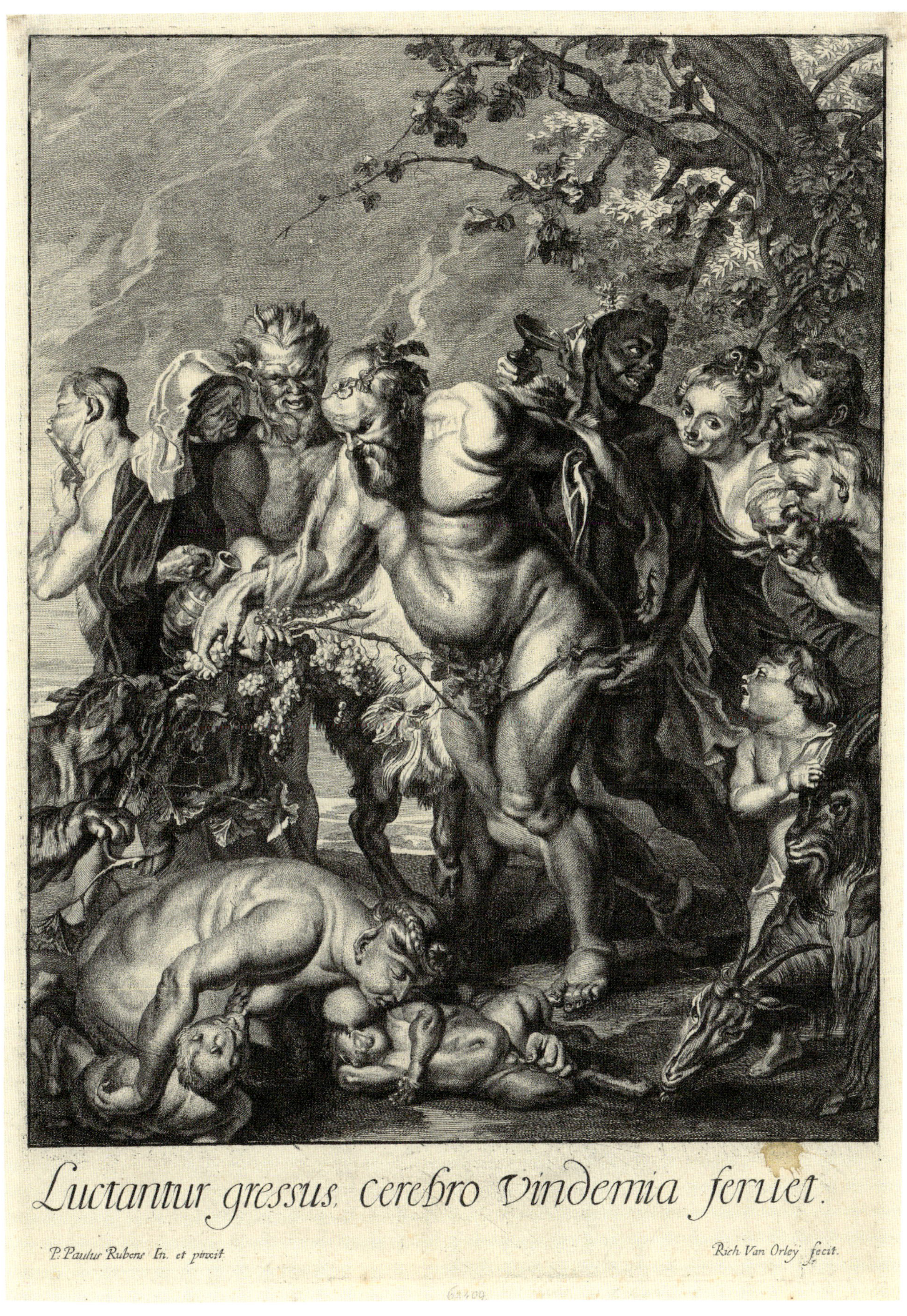

Richard van Orley II (Radierer / etcher), nach / after Rubens
Der trunkene Silen / Drunken Silenus, 1701/02
Radierung / etching SGSM, Inv. 62409 D

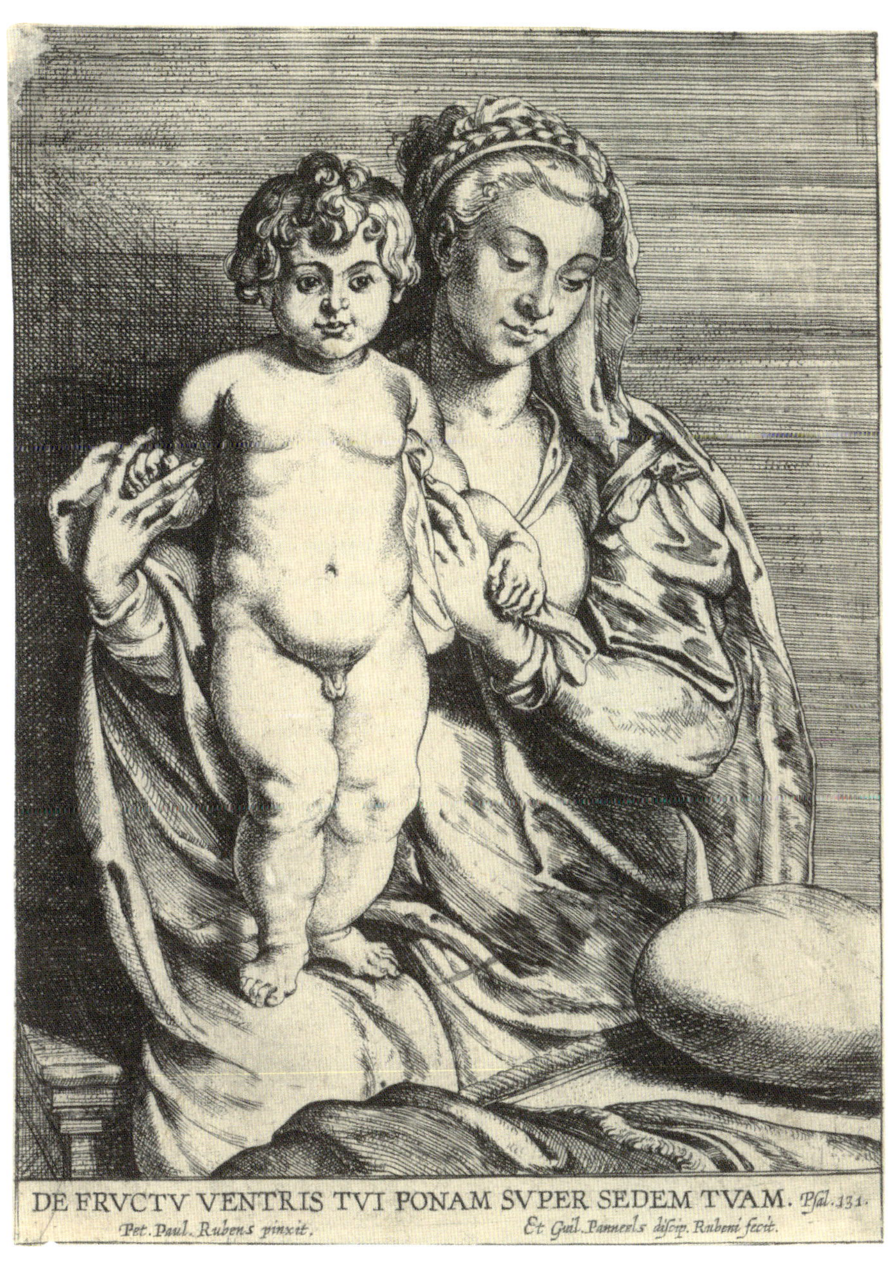

Willem Panneels (Radierer / etcher), nach / after Rubens
Madonna, 1630–1634
Radierung / etching SGSM, Inv. 30179 D

Druckgraphik von Goltzius und Rubens in der Staatlichen Graphischen Sammlung München

Die Staatliche Graphische Sammlung München verfügt über besonders qualitätsvolle Bestände an Druckgraphik von Hendrick Goltzius und Peter Paul Rubens, genauer *nach* Werken von Peter Paul Rubens. In verschiedenen Museumspräsentationen wurden zumindest Glanzlichter aus dem Goltzius-Bestand gelegentlich der Öffentlichkeit gezeigt, Rubens hingegen war in der Vergangenheit keine Schau gewidmet.[1] Beide Konvolute wurden in Hinblick auf die Ausstellung *Careers by design. Hendrick Goltzius & Peter Paul Rubens* aufgearbeitet. Diese Arbeit umfasste die Ermittlung der Werke in den Beständen, die Aufnahme aller physischen Daten in der Datenbank (Maße, Beschriftungen, Werkverzeichnisnummern, Sammlerstempel, Wasserzeichen etc.), digitale Photographien, neue Passepartouts sowie eine neue Standortvergabe. Ganz essenziell in diesem Zusammenhang war die restauratorische Bearbeitung des Bestands, die von der Kulturstiftung der Länder unterstützt wurde.

Als erstes, überaus erfreuliches Ergebnis ließ sich konstatieren, dass ein Großteil der Druckgraphiken in ganz vorzüglichem Zustand ist, das heißt, in erstklassigen, oft wie druckfrischen Abzügen vorliegt.

Die Graphik von Hendrick Goltzius genoss bereits zu seinen Lebzeiten hohes Ansehen. In den Jahrhunderten danach wurde er als Meister seines Fachs angesehen und von Künstlern wie Sammlern in besonderem Maße geschätzt. Zu diesen Sammlern zählte im 16. Jahrhundert der bayerische Herzog Albrecht V. (1528–1579), dessen Münchner Kunstkammer auch in den Graphikbeständen ihresgleichen suchte. Verbürgt ist darin eine *Apostel*-Serie des Verlegers Philips Galle (1537–1612), die von Goltzius gewesen sein könnte.[2] Der 1587 erschienene monumentale Kupferstich *Hochzeit von Amor und Psyche* (Abb. S. 172 f.) diente unmittelbar nach seinem Erscheinen als Vorlage für die beiden Deckenfresken in der Grottenhofosthalle der Münchner Residenz, mit der der Hofkünstler Friedrich Sustris (um 1540–1599) betraut war.[3] Insofern war wohl auch dieses Goltzius-Blatt in der Kunstkammer vorhanden. Albrechts kunstsinnigem Sohn Wilhelm V. (1548–1626) widmete Goltzius seine *Meisterstiche* und überstellte ihm Widmungsexemplare dieser Serie. Diese sind jedoch zusammen mit allen Beständen der Münchner Kunstkammer verloren gegangen.[4] Die heute vorhandenen Druckgraphikbestände gehen im Grundstock auf Kurfürst Karl Theodor von der Pfalz (1724–1799) zurück, der ab 1777 auch Kurfürst von Bayern war, sie kamen in den 1790er-Jahren mit der Mannheimer Zeichnungssammlung nach München.

Zeichnungen des Manieristen Goltzius sind in der Sammlung kein Schwerpunkt, heute werden noch fünf Blätter diesem Künstler zugeschrieben, während wir bei neun Werken von Kopien nach Goltzius ausgehen (Abb. S. 291).[5] Auch der Blick in die Bestände der Alten Pinakothek, wo sich einzig ein Gemälde von Hendrick Goltzius findet, unterstreicht die Vorliebe für sein druckgraphisches Werk.[6]

Prints by Goltzius and Rubens in the Staatliche Graphische Sammlung München

The Staatliche Graphische Sammlung München preserves high-quality holdings of prints by Hendrick Goltzius and Peter Paul Rubens—or, more precisely, prints *after* works by Rubens. Although highlights from the Goltzius holdings were presented to the public in a number of past shows, our collection of Rubens prints has never been exhibited.[1] Both groups of works were processed by our staff in preparation for the 2024 exhibition *Careers by design. Hendrick Goltzius & Peter Paul Rubens*. This entailed ascertaining the specific locations of works in our storage facilities, recording their physical data (measurements, inscriptions, catalogue raisonné numbers, collectors' marks, watermarks, etc.) in the museum's database, producing digital scans, mounting the prints in new mats, and assigning new locations in storage to these holdings. An essential part of this process was the conservational treatment of each work, which was made possible by a grant from the Kulturstiftung der Länder.

The first very happy result was the discovery that the majority of prints are in excellent condition. These first-class copies often appear as though they have just come off the printing press.

Prints by Hendrick Goltzius found much appreciation even during his lifetime, and he was considered a master engraver in the following centuries. As such, his work was highly esteemed by artists and collectors alike. One of these collectors in the sixteenth century was the Bavarian Duke Albert V (1528–1579), whose Munich *Kunstkammer* (chamber of wonders) was unrivaled, as were the print collections that were part of it. Records show that these included an *Apostles* series by the publisher Philips Galle (1537–1612), which may have been by Goltzius.[2] Immediately after being published in 1587, Goltzius's monumental engraving *The Wedding of Cupid and Psyche* (fig. pp. 172–173) served as the template for a project that was entrusted to the court artist Friedrich Sustris (ca. 1540–1599): two ceiling frescoes in the so-called *Grottenhofosthalle* (the eastern hall in the grotto courtyard) of Munich's royal palace, or *Residenz*.[3] Therefore, this Goltzius print was very likely also in the *Kunstkammer*. The artist dedicated his *Masterpieces* to Albert's art-loving son Wilhelm V (1548–1626) and sent him several obligatory complimentary sets of the series. These were lost, however, along with the Munich *Kunstkammer* collection.[4] The core group of prints that are now in the holdings of the SGSM came here with Karl Theodor von der Pfalz (1724–1799), who in 1777 became Elector of Bavaria. He brought the works to Munich in the 1790s, along with his collection of drawings.

Drawings by the Mannerist Goltzius were never a focus in the Munich collection. Only five drawings in the collection are accepted attributions to the master, while nine have been

Der Barockmaler Rubens ist in München mit einer der drei (neben Madrid und Wien) qualitätsvollsten Gemäldesammlungen vertreten. Spätestens ab dem 19. Jahrhundert scheint es ein Anliegen gewesen zu sein, auch eine Sammlung der Druckgraphik nach Werken von Rubens aufzubauen, die zudem für die Produktion in allen Jahrhunderten Vollständigkeit anstrebte und den Rubens-Bestand in München auch auf diesem Gebiet zu einem außergewöhnlichen machen sollte.

Wie wohl in den meisten Sammlungen gilt der Großteil der Zeichnungen, die früher Rubens zugeschrieben wurden, heute als Werke aus seinem Umkreis. Nach Publikation des jüngsten Werkverzeichnisses der Rubens-Zeichnungen bleibt der Staatlichen Graphischen Sammlung München lediglich die *Studie für das Reiterbildnis des Herzogs von Lerma* (1603; Abb. S. 292) als eigenhändige Arbeit, 16 weitere Zeichnungen dagegen sind zurückgewiesen.[7]

Nach Erfassung aller Werke in der Museumsdatenbank blicken wir auf einen Graphikbestand von über 600 Nummern bei Hendrick Goltzius und über 1200 Nummern bei Peter Paul Rubens. Mit diesen Zahlen ist München in Deutschland führend. Für die Werkverzeichnisse zu diesen beiden Künstlern im *New Hollstein* waren die Münchner Bestände von herausragender Bedeutung, wobei dafür nur der Teil Beachtung fand, der bis dahin auch bekannt war.[8] Durch unsere hauseigene Erschließung in den Jahren 2021 bis 2023 konnte der Umfang beider Konvolute nahezu verdoppelt werden. Mit dem Onlinegang dieser Bestände im Jahr 2024 wird dieser Schatz nicht nur der deutschen, sondern der weltweiten Öffentlichkeit zugänglich.

Mehr als 70 Prozent der genannten Bestände sind mit der Sammlung von Kurfürst Karl Theodor Ende des 18. Jahrhunderts nach München gekommen. Hier sind fast durchgängig keine Stempel früherer Sammler zu finden, was sicherlich bedeutet, dass die Blätter damals direkt aus dem Handel für die kurfürstliche Sammlung bezogen wurden. Ausnahmen bezüglich der Stempel in diesem frühen Bestand sind sieben Goltzius-Blätter, die zu einem unbekannten Zeitpunkt durch die Hände der Sammler- und Kunsthändlerfamilie der Mariettes in Paris gegangen sind.[9] Die übrigen Werke kamen durch Ankäufe oder Schenkungen im späten 19. und im 20. Jahrhundert hinzu.

Ein weiteres Ergebnis des Projekts ist eine überaus aufschlussreiche Liste der Verluste in den Goltzius- und Rubens-Beständen. Vorgenommen wurde ein Abgleich zwischen den aufgefundenen und den im Inventar geführten Werken beider Künstler. Die Verluste wurden in unserer Datenbank dokumentiert.[10] Aus dieser Liste ist beispielsweise zu erfahren, dass das so seltene Goltzius-Bildnis von Jan Harmensz. Muller einmal zum Bestand gehörte.[11] Und dass etliche der herausragenden Motive von Rubens in ein, zwei oder drei weiteren Abzügen vorhanden waren. Aber auch, dass vielleicht nie ein Abzug der hinreißenden *Amazonenschlacht* erworben wurde, die Lucas Vorsterman I für Rubens 1623 nach dem aus Wittelsbacher Beständen stammenden Gemälde in der Alten Pinakothek in München (Inv. 324) auf sechs Kupferplatten stach.

Im Rahmen des aktuellen Projekts konnten den Künstlern jedoch auch etwas mehr als einhundert bislang nicht erfasste Werke zugeordnet werden. Auf diese Weise fanden spektakuläre Neuzugänge statt, bei Goltzius etwa die Ergänzung von gleich zwei Abzügen von *Die venezianische Hochzeit* sowie eine seltene frühe Farbvariante seines

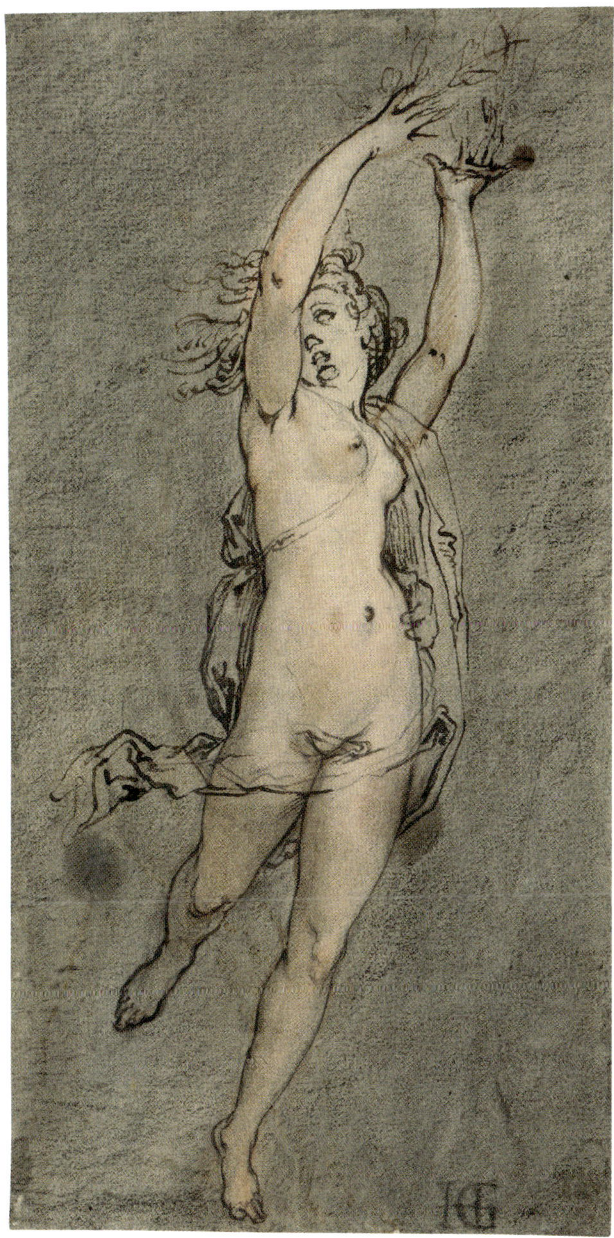

Hendrick Goltzius
Die Metamorphose der Daphne / Metamorphosis of Daphne, 1595/1600
Feder, Buntstift, Rötel, Kreide / ink, color pencil, red chalk, chalk SGSM, Inv. 21085 Z

designated as copies after him (fig. p. 291).[5] In the holdings of the Alte Pinakothek, where Munich's old master paintings are kept, there is only one accepted painting by Hendrick Goltzius (fig. p. 293). This underlines the fact that in Munich, the focus has long been on his print oeuvre.[6]

Munich, next to Madrid and Vienna, has one of the world's three outstanding painting collections by the Baroque painter Rubens. By the nineteenth century at the latest, there

Holzschnitts *Herkules erschlägt Cacus* (Abb. S. 57, 181); bei Rubens die Auffindung eines unikalen Umdrucks von Christoffel Jeghers Holzschnitt *Herkules erschlägt die Missgunst* (Abb. S. 183)[12] sowie einige wichtige, bislang nicht erfasste von Vorsterman gestochene Blätter.

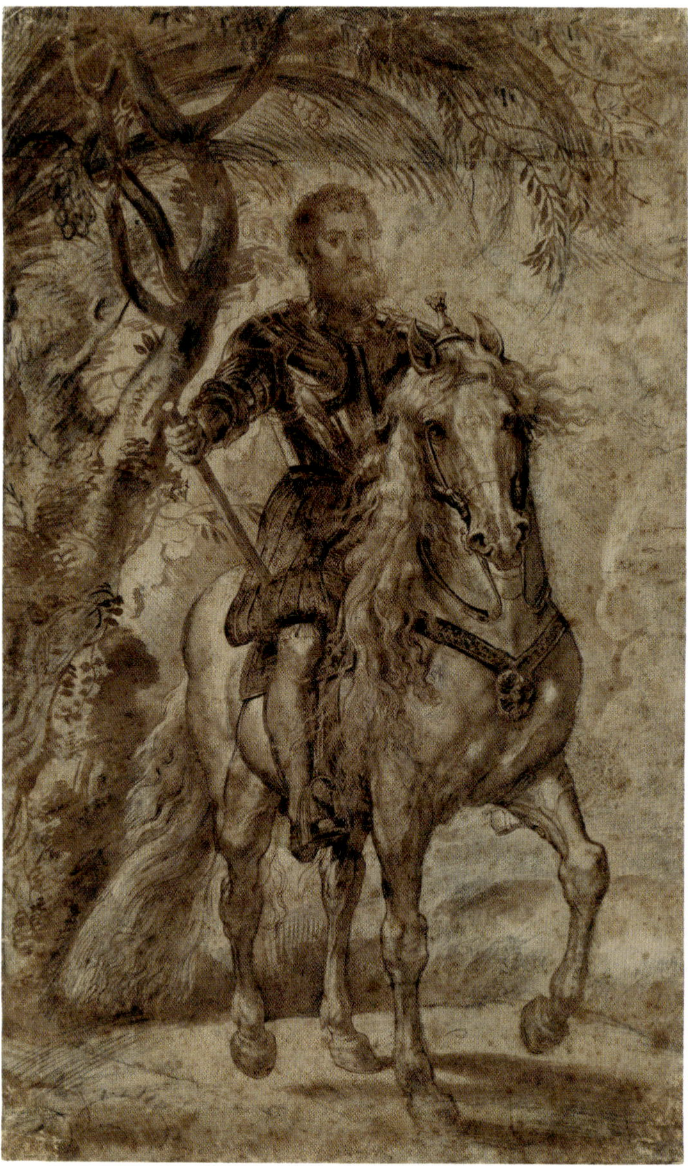

Peter Paul Rubens
Studie für das Reiterbildnis des Herzogs von Lerma / Study for the Portrait of the Duke of Lerma, 1603
Kreide, Feder, laviert, weiß gehöht / chalk, ink, wash, white highlights SGSM, Inv. 1983:84 Z

seems to have been a desire to build a worthy collection of prints after his works as well, one that would also reflect the production of prints after Rubens in subsequent centuries. The aim was for a completeness that would make the Munich Rubens collections outstanding in this medium as well.

As is probably the case in most museums, the majority of drawings formerly attributed to Rubens are today considered to be by his workshop or followers. According to the latest catalogue raisonné of Rubens drawings, the Staatliche Graphische Sammlung München has only one drawing by the master's own hand, *Study for the Portrait of the Duke of Lerma* (1603, fig. p. 292); sixteen other drawings have been rejected.[7]

After having documented all of the prints in the museum's database, we are looking at more than 600 entries by Hendrick Goltzius and more than 1,200 by Peter Paul Rubens. With these numbers, Munich stands out in all of Germany. For the compilers of the *New Hollstein* print catalogues raisonnés, our holdings in works by these two artists were of crucial importance, even before they were available in their entirety.[8] Since processing them in full and documenting them in our database from 2021 to 2023, we have been able to double the known entries. As we make these holdings available in our online database in 2024, this treasure becomes accessible not only to a German but to an international public.

The works that came to Munich with Elector Karl Theodor—which make up more than 70 per cent of the museum's holdings—are almost completely without marks of former collections. We can thus infer that they were most likely acquired directly from print merchants for the elector's collection.[9] The remaining works came into the Munich collection through acquisitions or gifts in the late nineteenth or twentieth century.

Another result of our processing project was a highly revealing list of losses in the holdings of Goltzius and Rubens prints (also documented in our database). We carried out a cross-check between the works now in the collection and those listed in the inventory books.[10] From the resulting list, we learned, for example, that the rare Goltzius portrait by Jan Harmensz. Muller was once in our collection.[11] And that many of the outstanding Rubens prints existed in one, two, or three copies. But we also discovered that there is no evidence that the riveting *Battle of the Amazons*, engraved in 1623 on six plates by Lucas Vorsterman I after the Rubens painting now at the Alte Pinakothek (inv. 324), was ever part of the Munich collections.

In the context of our project, however, we were also able to identify more than one hundred works that had not been registered before. Thus we celebrated spectacular new additions to our collection: for Goltzius, for example, two copies of *The Venetian Wedding* and a rare early color variant of his chiaroscuro woodcut *Hercules Killing Cacus* (figs. pp. 57, 181); and for Rubens a newly discovered counterproof of Christoffel Jegher's woodcut *Hercules Slaying Envy* (fig. p. 183),[12] as well as some capital prints by Vorsterman.

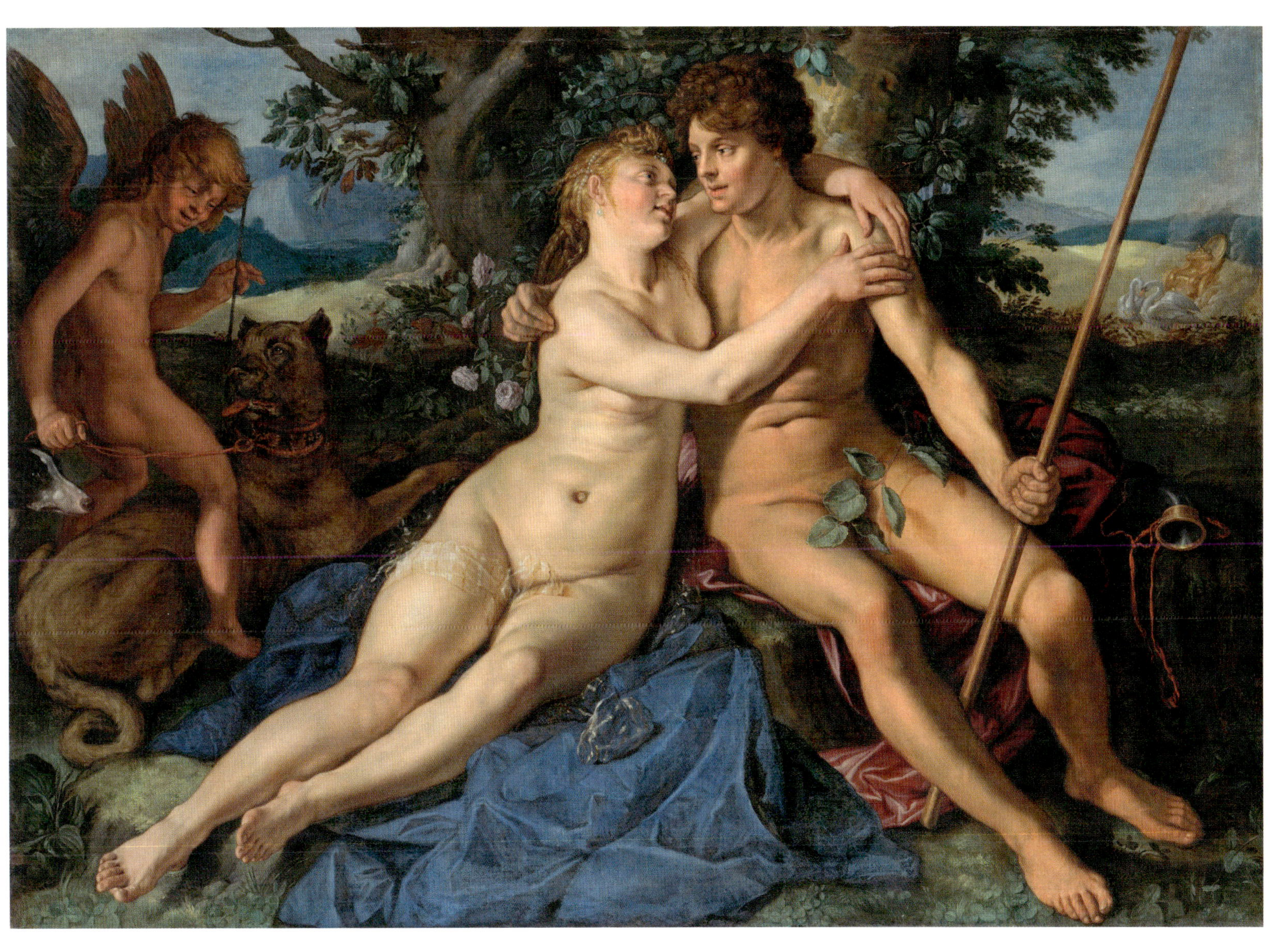

Hendrick Goltzius
Venus und Adonis / Venus and Adonis, 1614
Öl auf Leinwand / oil on canvas München, Alte Pinakothek, Inv. 5613

Besonderer Dank an meine Kollegen Birgitta Heid und Kurt Zeitler, die diese Ausführungen vorab kritisch gelesen und kommentiert haben.

1 Die Auswahl der Goltzius-Werke für die 1930 ausgerichtete Ausstellung *Druckgraphische Werke von Pieter Brueghel und Hendrick Goltzius* ist nicht überliefert. 1979 wählte Konrad Renger für die Ausstellung *Graphik der Niederlande 1508–1617. Kupferstiche und Radierungen von Lucas van Leyden bis Hendrick Goltzius* 13 Werke von Goltzius aus. 1989/90 zeigte Holm Bevers die Kabinettausstellung *Hendrick Goltzius. Druckgraphik*, zu der er ein Faltblatt verfasste. Thea Vignau-Wilberg widmete dem Manieristen 2003 die Schau *Hendrick Goltzius. Graphik* mit 24 Blättern. Vgl. München 1979, München 1989 und München 2003.

2 So eine der Vermutungen, was sich unter Nr. 51, 2b des Kunstkammer-Inventars verborgen haben könnte, das Johann Baptist Fickler 1598 anfertigte. Auch in dem Druckgraphik-Klebeband der Kunstkammer unter Nr. 58 könnte sich eine Goltzius-Serie befunden haben. Vgl. Kunstkammer 2008, sub 51 bzw. 58.

3 Die Fresken sind heute verloren. Zu ihrer Entstehung nach Goltzius' Stich vgl. Thea Vignau-Wilberg, in: München 2005, S. 134–137, sowie Kat. C1–C3.

4 Die Tatsache, dass kein Exemplar der *Meisterstiche*, die der Künstler Wilhelm V. gewidmet hatte, erhalten blieb, erklärt Peter Diemer überzeugend damit, dass die wohl in mehreren Sets vorhandenen Widmungsexemplare aus der Kunstkammer an die Hofbibliothek überstellt wurden, wo sie einer späteren Plünderung zum Opfer fielen (vgl. Diemer 2008, S. 234). Derzeit verfügt die SGSM nur über vier der sechs Motive der Serie (es fehlen die *Heimsuchung* und die *Hl. Familie*), die überdies erst im 20. Jahrhundert einzeln erworben wurden.

5 Im heute noch gültigen Werkverzeichnis von Emil Karel Josef Reznicek (Reznicek 1961 und 1993) wurden folgende fünf Blätter anerkannt: *Bildnis eines Mannes*, Inv. 1038 Z, nach einem Gemälde in der Alten Pinakothek, ist daher das einzige Werk mit explizitem Münchner Bezug; die in der Ausstellung zu sehende Stichvorzeichnung *Die sieben Tugenden*, Inv. 1043 Z (Abb. S. 158), die einzige Goltzius-Zeichnung, die einen Stempel der Mannheimer Galerie, also der Kunstsammlung von Kurfürst Karl Theodor, trägt (Lugt 620 in Schwarz); ein präpariertes Täfelchen mit Tierdarstellungen recto und verso, Inv. 1296 Z und 1297 Z; die selbstständige Zeichnung *Metamorphose der Daphne*, Inv. 21085 Z; sowie der *Junge Krieger*, eine frühe Auseinandersetzung mit der Kunst Lucas van Leydens, Inv. 41053 Z.

6 Goltzius, *Venus und Adonis*, 1614, Öl auf Leinwand, Inv. 5613. Im Bestandskatalog der Alten Pinakothek ist die Rede vom „deutlich von der Kunst des Peter Paul Rubens inspirierten Münchner Liebespaar" (München 2006, S. 148). Der Gedanke liegt nahe, dass es diese Nähe zu Rubens war, die den Erwerb des Gemäldes für die Sammlung interessant machte.

7 Anne-Marie Logan schrieb 2022 folgende zwei, bis dahin noch als eigenhändige Zeichnungen geführten Werke ab (Logan/Lohse Belkin 2022, sub Kat. 332, S. 218, Anm. 4, resp. sub Kat. 320, S. 203, Anm. 1): Inv. 2871 Z, eine *Figurenstudie für den hl. Andreas*, ein Motiv aus dem Mechelner Altar mit dem *Wunderbaren Fischzug* (1618), ein Blatt, das als Werk von Giovanni Lanfranco erworben und erst im 20. Jahrhundert Rubens zugeschrieben wurde; sowie Inv. 1981:15 Z, eine in den 1980er-Jahren erworbene *Studie zur Laurentiusmarter*. So bleibt nach Auffassung von Logan lediglich Inv. 1983:84 Z, die *Studie für das Reiterbildnis des Herzogs von Lerma*, die ebenfalls in den 1980er-Jahren erworben wurde.

8 Für Goltzius siehe NHD Goltzius 2012. Die Bände zu Rubens sind noch nicht erschienen, wurden jedoch bearbeitet von Simon Turner und werden herausgegeben von Jaco Rutgers. Beiden ein herzlicher Dank für hilfreiche Informationen vorab.

9 Vgl. die Markierungen „Lugt 1786b" verso auf Inv. 30899 D, 31015 D, 31024 D, 31028 D; „Lugt 1787 bis 1790" auf Inv. 30955 D, 31071 D, 31072 D.

10 Diese Liste wird in den kommenden Jahren im Zuge der Erfassung des Gesamtbestands der SGSM noch ergänzt werden müssen, denn bislang wurden nur die Verluste innerhalb von Werkkonvoluten, das heißt aufeinanderfolgenden Inventarnummern, erfasst. Im Inventar einzeln aufgeführte Werke von Goltzius oder Rubens sind hier noch nicht berücksichtigt.

11 Um dieses handelt es sich wohl bei der Beschreibung im Inventar „Bildnis des Hen. Goltzius Büste in Lebensgröße" unter Inv. 31030 D, in der Datenbank jetzt auffindbar unter Inv. 31030-Verlust D. Vgl. NHD Goltzius 2012, 92.

12 Goltzius, *Die venezianische Hochzeit*, Inv. 2021:492 D und Inv. 2021:493 D; siehe Abb. 4 im Beitrag von Nadine M. Orenstein, S. 57. Vermutlich war das Motiv bis ins 19. Jahrhundert bereits in einem heute verlorenen Abzug vorhanden und führte die Inventarnummer 31000 D, jetzt geführt unter Inv. 31000-Verlust D (im Inventar als „Hochzeit zu Cana"); Goltzius, *Herkules erschlägt Cacus*, Inv. 2021:1 D. Rubens, *Herkules erschlägt die Missgunst*, Inv. 2021:494 D.

I am indebted to our director, Michael Hering, and to my colleagues Birgitta Heid and Kurt Zeitler for carefully reading and commenting on an early draft of this text.

1 The checklist of Goltzius works for the 1930 show *Druckgraphische Werke von Pieter Brueghel und Hendrick Goltzius* was not preserved. In 1979 Konrad Renger selected thirteen works by Goltzius for his exhibition *Graphik der Niederlande 1508–1617. Kupferstiche und Radierungen von Lucas van Leyden bis Hendrick Goltzius*. Holm Bevers authored a leaflet (without a list of works) for his small presentation *Hendrick Goltzius. Druckgraphik* in 1989/90. In 2003, Thea Vignau-Wilberg selected twenty-four prints by the Mannerist for her show *Hendrick Goltzius. Graphik*. See München 1979, München 1989, and München 2003.

2 This is one theory as to which works were included under cat. 51, 2b of the *Kunstkammer* inventory authored by Johann Baptist Fickler in 1598. There may also have been a Goltzius series included in the *Kunstkammer*'s album of prints under cat. 58. See Kunstkammer 2008, under entries 51 and 58 respectively.

3 These frescoes are lost today. On their creation after Goltzius's print, see Thea Vignau-Wilberg, in: München 2005, pp. 134–137, and cats. C1–C3.

4 Peter Diemer convincingly explains the fact that no complimentary sets of the *Masterpieces* dedicated to Wilhelm V survive: the sets, of which there were probably several, were transferred from the *Kunstkammer* to the court library (*Hofbibliothek*), where they were later lost in a looting (see Diemer 2008, p. 234).

5 The catalogue raisonné of Goltzius drawings by Emil Karel Josef Reznicek (Reznicek 1961 and 1993), which is still definitive today, lists the following five works as by the artist's hand: *Copy After the Painted Portrait of a Palatinate Prince*, inv. 1038 Z, after a painting in the Alte Pinakothek, making this the only work with a connection to the Munich collections; the preparatory drawing *The Seven Virtues*, inv. 1043 Z (fig. p. 158), on display in the present exhibition, which is the only Goltzius drawing bearing a mark of the Mannheim gallery, i.e., the *Kunstkammer* of Elector Karl Theodor (Lugt 620 in black); a small primed tablet with sketches of animals recto and verso, inv. 1296 Z and 1297 Z; the autonomous drawing *Metamorphosis of Daphne*, inv. 21085 Z; and the *Young Warrior with Beret and Sword*, an early emulation of the art of Lucas van Leyden, inv. 41053 Z.

6 Goltzius, *Venus and Adonis*, 1614, oil on canvas, inv. 5613. The 2006 museum catalog of the Alte Pinakothek remarks that this work is "visibly inspired by the art of Peter Paul Rubens," which may be the facet that made the acquisition of the painting attractive for the Munich collections.

7 In 2022 Anne-Marie Logan rejected the attribution of the following two drawings, which had until then been considered to be by Rubens's hand (Logan/Lohse Belkin 2022, under cat. 332, p. 218, n. 4, and under cat. 320, p. 203, n. 1): inv. 2871 Z, a *Study for St. Andrew*, a motif from the Mechelen altarpiece with *The Miraculous Draught* (1618), a drawing which was acquired as a work by Giovanni Lanfranco and only in the twentieth century attributed to Rubens; and inv. 1981:15 Z, the sketch *Study for the Martyrdom of St. Lawrence*, which was acquired in the 1980s. According to Logan, that leaves us with only inv. 1983:84 Z, the *Study for the Portrait of the Duke of Lerma*, which also came into the collection in the 1980s.

8 For Goltzius, see NHD Goltzius 2012. The *New Hollstein* volumes on Rubens have not yet been released, but they were compiled by Simon Turner and edited by Jaco Rutgers, both of whom I thank for providing helpful information in advance of the publication of the volumes.

9 An exception in regard to collector's marks in this early part of the collection is a group of seven Goltzius prints that at some unknown prior moment passed through the hands of the Mariette family of collectors and art merchants in Paris. See the marks Lugt 1786b verso on inv. 30899 D, 31015 D, 31024 D, 31028 D; and Lugt 1787 through 1790 on inv. 30955 D, 31071 D, 31072 D.

10 This list will have to be completed in coming years when all the holdings of the SGSM are successively processed, because so far only losses within groups of works—i.e., as part of consecutive numbers—have been documented, not individually inventoried works by Goltzius and Rubens.

11 It is probably this portrait that the following entry in the inventory book refers to: "Bildnis des Hen. Goltzius Büste in Lebensgröße" (portrait of Hen. Goltzius life-size bust), inv. 31030 D, now listed in our database as inv. 31030-Verlust D. See NHD Goltzius 2012, 92.

12 Goltzius, *The Venetian Wedding*, inv. 2021:492 D and inv. 2021:493 D; see Nadine M. Orenstein's essay in the present catalog, p. 57, fig. 4. A print with this motif was probably in the collection in the nineteenth century and inventoried as inv. 31000 D (the inventory book entry reads "Wedding at Cana"). It can now be found under inv. 31000-Verlust D. – Goltzius, *Hercules Killing Cacus*, inv. 2021:1 D. Rubens, *Hercules Slaying Envy*, inv. 2021:494 D.

Bibliographie — Bibliography

AKL
Allgemeines Künstlerlexikon. Die Bildenden Künstler aller Zeiten und Völker, 119 Bde./vols., Leipzig etc. 1983–2023

Amsterdam/Cleveland 1992
Nancy Bialler, *Chiaroscuro Woodcuts. Hendrick Goltzius (1558–1617) and His Time* (Ausst.-Kat./exh. cat. Amsterdam, Rijksmuseum/Cleveland, The Cleveland Museum of Art), Amsterdam/Gent 1992

Amsterdam /New York/Toledo 2003
Hendrick Goltzius (1558–1617). Drawings, Prints and Paintings, hg. von/ed. Huigen Leeflang, Ger Luijten (Ausst.-Kat./exh. cat. Amsterdam, Rijksmuseum/New York, The Metropolitan Museum of Art/Toledo, OH, Toledo Museum of Art), Zwolle 2003

Antwerpen 1996
The Illustration of Books Published by the Moretuses, hg. von/ed. Dirk Imhof, Karen Lee Bowen (Ausst.-Kat./exh. cat. Antwerpen, Museum Plantin-Moretus), Antwerpen 1996 (*Publicaties van het Museum Plantin-Moretus en het Stedelijk Prentenkabinet* 36)

Antwerpen 1999
Anthony van Dyck as a Printmaker, hg. von/ed. Carl Depauw, Ger Luijten (Ausst.-Kat./exh. cat. Antwerpen, Museum Plantin-Moretus), Antwerpen 1999

Antwerpen/Québec 2004
Copyright Rubens. Rubens en de grafiek, hg. von/ed. Nico Van Hout (Ausst.-Kat./exh. cat. Antwerpen, Koninklijk Museum voor Schoone Kunsten/Québec, Musée National des Beaux-Arts du Québec), Gent/Amsterdam 2004

Antwerpen/Vienna 2007
Samson and Delilah. A Rubens Painting Returns, hg. von / ed. Hildegard Van de Velde, Johann Kräftner (Ausst.-Kat. / exh. cat. Antwerpen, Rockoxhuis/Wien, Liechtenstein Museum), Milano 2007

Arbeitsgruppe Estius 2017
Arbeitsgruppe Estius (Tübingen) unter Leitung von/led by Anja Wolkenhauer, Die übersehene Hälfte. Ein Werkstattbericht zur Erschließung der Bildepigramme in der frühneuzeitlichen Druckgraphik, in: Dessau 2017, S./pp. 108–117

Arents 2001
Prosper Arents, *De bibliotheek van Pieter Pauwel Rubens. Een reconstructie*, hg. von/ed. Frans Baudouin, Alfons K. L. Thijs, Antwerpen 2001

Arnulf 2020
Arwed Arnulf, „… auf das fleissigste in Kupfern stechen und mit artigen Epigrammatibus zieren …“. Tradition, Funktion und Produktion bildbegleitender lateinischer Versbeischriften für Kupferstiche der Goltzius-Werkstatt, in: *Verwandlung der Welt. Meisterblätter von Hendrick Goltzius* (Ausst.-Kat./exh. cat. Freiburg, Augustinermuseum/Göttingen, Kunstsammlung der Georg-August-Universität), Petersberg 2020, S./pp. 44–51

Atkins 2012
Christopher D. M. Atkins, *The Signature Style of Frans Hals. Painting, Subjectivity, and the Market in Early Modernity*, Amsterdam 2012

Balis (2001) 2023
Arnout Balis, Rubens and Inventio. The Contribution of His Theoretical Notebook [2001], in: *Thinking through Rubens*, hg. von/ed. Elizabeth McGrath, Paul van Calster, Turnhout 2023, S./pp. 122–147

Balis 1993
Arnout Balis, “Fatto da un mio discepolo”. Rubens’s Studio Practices Reviewed, in: Tokyo 1993, S./pp. 97–127

Balis 2007
Arnout Balis, Rubens and His Studio. Defining the Problem, in: Brussel 2007, S./pp. 30–51

Baroni Vannucci 1997
Alessandra Baroni Vannucci, *Jan van der Straet detto Giovanni Stradano. Flandrus Pictor et Inventor*, Milano 1997

Barrett 2012
Kerry Barrett, *Pieter Soutman. Life and Œuvre*, Amsterdam 2012 (*Occuli. Studies in the Arts of the Low Countries* 12)

Basan 1767
Pierre François Basan, *Catalogue des estampes gravées d’après P. P. Rubens*, Paris 1767

Basel 2016
Ariane Mensger, *Bestechend Gestochen. Das Unternehmen Hendrick Goltzius* (Ausst.-Kat./exh. cat. Basel, Kunstmuseum), München 2016

Baxandall 1985
Michael Baxandall, *Patterns of Intention. On the Historical Explanation of Pictures*, New Haven 1985

Bellori (1672) 2020
Giovanni Pietro Bellori. Le vite de’ pittori, scultori e architetti moderni, hg. von/ed. Fiona Healy, 13 Bde./vols., Göttingen 2020, Bd. / vol. 6: Vita di Pietro Paolo Rubens & Vita di Antonio Van Dyck, übers. von/transl. Anja Brug

Bertram 2018
Gitta Bertram, *Peter Paul Rubens as a Designer of Title Pages. Title Page Production and Design in the Beginning of the Seventeenth Century*, Heidelberg 2018

Bertram 2021
Gitta Bertram, Rez. von/rev. of Hans Jakob Meier, *Rubens und die Druckgraphik*, in: *The Burlington Magazine* 163, 2021, S./pp. 295–296.

Bertram/Büttner 2018
Gitta Bertram, Nils Büttner, *Sinnbild, Bildsinn. Rubens als Buchkünstler*, Stuttgart 2018

Biesboer 2002
Pieter Biesboer, *Collections of Paintings in Haarlem 1572–1745*, Los Angeles 2002 (*Documents for the History of Collecting. Netherlandish Inventories* 1)

Biesboer 2008
De gouden eeuw begint in Haarlem, hg. von/ed. Pieter Biesboer (Ausst.-Kat./exh. cat. Haarlem, Frans Hals Museum), Haarlem 2008

Biesboer et al. 1996
Pieter Biesboer et al., *Vlamingen in Haarlem*, Haarlem 1996

Biffis 2021
Mattia Biffis, Itinerant Matters. Rubens and the Itineraries of Painting, in: *Konsthistorisk Tidskrift/Journal of Art History* 90, 2021, S./pp. 211–230

Bleyerveld 2022
Yvonne Bleyerveld, Two Seated Monkeys. The Earliest “Pen Works” by Jacob Matham, in: *Master Drawings* 60, 1, Spring 2022, S./pp. 31–34

Boers-Goossens 1999
Marion Boers-Goossens, Een nieuwe markt voor kunst. De expansie van de Haarlemse schilderijenmarkt in de eerste helft van de zeventiende eeuw, in: *Nederlands Kunsthistorisch Jaarboek* 50, 1999, S./pp. 195–220

Boers-Goossens 2001
Marion Boers-Goossens, Schilders en de markt. Haarlem 1605–1635 (unveröff. Diss./unpublished PhD thesis), Leiden 2001

Bok 2001
Marten Jan Bok, The Rise of Amsterdam as a Cultural Center. The Market for Paintings 1580–1680, in: *Urban Achievement in Early Modern Europe*, hg. von/ed. Patrick O'Brien, Derek Keene, Cambridge 2001, S./pp. 186–209

Bonne 2022
Griet Bonne, Panoramic Ambitions. Collecting Rubens's Œuvre, in: *Reproduction 1877–1927. History of Photography* 46, 1, Feb. 2022, DOI: <10.1080/03087298.2023.2178745>

Bouchery/Wijngaert 1941
Herman F. Bouchery, Frank van den Wijngaert, *P.-P. Rubens en het Plantijnsche huis*, Antwerpen 1941

Brakensiek 2003
Stephan Brakensiek, *Vom „Theatrum mundi" zum „Cabinet des Estampes". Das Sammeln von Druckgraphik in Deutschland 1565–1821*, Hildesheim 2003

Brakensiek 2011
Stephan Brakensiek, Reproduktion und Wahrheit. Überlegungen zum Phänomen von Gleichheit und Ungleichheit bei der Wiedergabe von Kunst im Medium der Druckgraphik, in: *Totentanz Reloaded! Zum Verhältnis von Original und Reproduktion*, hg. von/ed. Stefanie Knöll, Düsseldorf 2011, S./pp. 18–36

Brandt 2001
Aurelia Brandt, Goltzius and the Antique, in: *Print Quarterly* 18, 2, June 2001, S./pp. 135–149

Braunschweig 2004
Peter Paul Rubens. Barocke Leidenschaften, hg. von/ed. Nils Büttner, Ulrich Heinen (Ausst.-Kat./exh. cat. Braunschweig, Herzog Anton Ulrich-Museum), München 2004

Breazeale 2013
William Breazeale, Goltzius's "Birth and Early Life of Christ". Transformation and Renown, in: *Passion and Virtuosity. Hendrick Goltzius and the Art of Engraving*, hg. von/ed. William Breazeale, Victoria Sancho Lobis (Ausst.-Kat./exh. cat. Sacramento, CA, Crocker Art Museum/San Diego, University of San Diego), San Diego, CA, 2013, S./pp. 13–25

Bredius 1914
A. Bredius, Bijdragen tot de levensgeschiedenis van Hendrick Goltzius, in: *Oud Holland* 32, 3, 1914, S./pp. 137–146

Briels 1976
Johannes G. Briels, *De Zuidnederlandse immigratie in Amsterdam en Haarlem omstreeks 1572–1630, met een keuze van archivalische gegevens betr. de kunstschilders = Amsterdam et Haarlem* (Diss./PhD thesis Utrecht Univ.), Utrecht 1976

Brown 2002
Christopher Brown, The Dutchness of the Golden Age, Working Paper, Amsterdam 2002 (unveröff./unpubl.)

Brussel 1998
Albrecht & Isabella 1598–1621, hg. von/ed. Luc Duerloo, Werner Thomas (Ausst.-Kat./exh. cat. Brussel, Koninklijke Musea voor Kunst en Geschiedenis), Turnhout 1998

Brussel 2007
Rubens. A Genius at Work, hg. von/ed. Joost van der Auwera, Sabine Van Sprang (Ausst.-Kat./exh. cat. Brussel, Koninklijke Musea voor Schone Kunsten van België), Tielt 2007

Bulckens 2017
Koen Bulckens, *Rubens. The Life of Christ before the Passion*, 2 Bde./vols., *The Ministry of Christ*, Bd./vol. 2, London/Turnhout 2017 (*Corpus Rubenianum Ludwig Burchard* V)

Büttner 2006
Nils Büttner, *Herr P. P. Rubens. Von der Kunst, berühmt zu werden*, Göttingen 2006 (*Rekonstruktionen der Künste* 7)

Büttner 2008
Nils Büttner, Echtheitsfragen. Kunsthistorische Überlegungen zum Begriff des Originals in der Malerei der frühen Neuzeit, in: *Echtheitskritik bei Bach. Bericht über das 5. Dortmunder Bach-Symposion 2004*, hg. von/ed. Reinmar Emans, Martin Geck, Dortmund 2008, S./pp. 9–23

Büttner 2011a
Nils Büttner, „Unzahlbare in Kupfer gebrachte Werke". Rubens-Grafik in Europa, in: *Reproduktion. Techniken und Ideen von der Antike bis heute. Eine Einführung*, hg. von/ed. Jörg Probst, Berlin 2011, S./pp. 118–133

Büttner 2011b
Nils Büttner, Peter Paul Rubens und Franciscus Junius. *Aemulatio* in Praxis und Theorie, in: Müller/Pfisterer 2011, S./pp. 319–367

Büttner 2015a
Nils Büttner, "Se ipsum expressit". Rubens's Self-Portraits as Public Statements, in: *Rubens in Private. The Master Portrays His Family/Rubens privé. De meester portretteert zijn familie*, hg. von/ed. Ben van Beneden (Ausst.-Kat./exh. cat. Antwerpen, Rubenshuis), Brussel 2015, S./pp. 39–53

Büttner 2015b
Nils Büttner, „Peter Paul Rubens, Mahler von Antorf". Joachim von Sandrarts Entwurf eines idealen Lebensbildes, in: *Aus aller Herren Länder. Die Künstler der „Teutschen Academie" von Joachim von Sandrart*, hg. von/ed. Susanne Meurer, Anna Schreurs-Morét, Lucia Simonato, Turnhout 2015, S./pp. 221–233

Büttner 2015c
Nils Büttner, *Pietro Pauolo Rubens. Eine Biographie*, Regensburg 2015 (*Regensburger Studien zur Kunstgeschichte* XXV)

Büttner 2017a
Nils Büttner, The Hands of Rubens. On Copies and Their Reception, in: *Appreciating the Traces of an Artist's Hand*, hg. von/ed. Toshiharu Nakamura, Kyoto 2017, S./pp. 41–53 (*Kyoto Studies in Art History* II)

Büttner 2017b
Nils Büttner, Rubens' Werkstattpraxis, in: *Zeitschrift für Kunsttechnologie und Konservierung* 31, 2, 2017, S./pp. 113–118

Büttner 2020
Nils Büttner, „Eine ungemeine Kunst-Schule". Ausbreitung und Nachwirkung der flämischen Malerei des 17. Jahrhunderts, in: *Wissenstransfer und Kulturimport in der Frühen Neuzeit*, hg. von/ed. Kirsten Baumann, Constanze Köster, Uta Kuhl, Petersberg 2020, S./pp. 217–229

Büttner 2023a
Nils Büttner, Rubens' Landscapes and the Dutch Republic, in: *Oud Holland* 136, 2023, S./pp. 89–102

Büttner 2023b
Nils Büttner, Michel de Marolles's Collection of Prints after Rubens, in: *The Rubenianum Quarterly*, 2023, 3, S./pp. 3–4

Chennevières/Montaiglon 1851–1860
Pierre-Jean Mariette. Abecedario de P. J. Mariette et autres notes inedites de cet amateur sur les arts et les artistes, hg. von/ed. Philippe de Chennevières, Anatole de Montaiglon, 6 Bde./vols., Paris 1851–1860

Chicago 2019
Rubens, Rembrandt, and Drawing in the Golden Age, hg. von/ed. Victoria Sancho Lobis (Ausst.-Kat./exh. cat. Chicago, The Art Institute of Chicago), New Haven/London 2019

Crawford Volk 1983
Mary Crawford Volk, On Rubens and Titian, in: *The Ringling Museum of Art Journal. Papers Presented at the International Rubens Symposium, April 1982*, Sarasota, FL, 1983, S./pp. 140–149

D'Hulst/Vandenven 1989
Roger Adolf d'Hulst, Marc Vandenven, *Rubens. The Old Testament*, London/Oxford 1989 (*Corpus Rubenianum Ludwig Burchard* III)

De Clippel 2003
Karolien De Clippel, Adriaen Brouwer. Portrait Painter. New Identifications and an Iconographic Novelty, in: *Simiolus* 30, 3/4, 2003, S./pp. 196–216

De Clippel 2006
Karolien De Clippel, Two Sides of the Same Coin? Genre Painting in North and South during the Sixteenth and Seventeenth Centuries, in: *Simiolus* 32, 1, 2006, S./pp. 17–34

De Clippel/Vermeylen 2012
Filip Vermeylen, Karolien De Clippel, Rubens and Goltzius in Dialogue. Artistic Exchanges between Antwerp and Haarlem during the Revolt, in: *De Zeventiende Eeuw* 28, 2012, S./pp. 138–160

De Marchi/Miegroet 2006
Neil De Marchi, Hans J. van Miegroet, The History of Art Markets, in: *Handbook of the Economics of Art and Culture*, hg. von/ed. Victor Ginsburgh, David Throsby, Amsterdam/Boston 2006, Bd./vol. 1, S./pp. 69–122

De Poorter/Bauduoin 2022
Nora De Poorter, Frans Bauduoin, *Rubens. Architecture and Sculpture. Rubens's House*, 2 Bde./vols., London/Turnhout 2022 (*Corpus Rubenianum Ludwig Burchard* XXII.1, 2)

De Vries 1981
Jan De Vries, *Barges and Capitalism. Passenger Transportation in the Dutch Economy, 1632–1839*, Amsterdam/Utrecht, 1981

Denhaene 1990
Godelieve Denhaene, *Lambert Lombard. Renaissance et humanisme à Liege*, Antwerpen 1990

Depauw 1996
Carl Depauw, The Realization of Illustrations in Publications by the Moretuses, in: Antwerpen 1996, S./pp. 72–73.

Dessau 2017
Hendrick Goltzius. Mythos, Macht und Menschlichkeit. Aus den Dessauer Beständen, hg. von/ed. Norbert Michels (Ausst.-Kat./exh. cat. Dessau, Anhaltische Gemäldegalerie), Petersberg 2017 (*Kataloge der Anhaltischen Gemäldegalerie Dessau* 21)

Devisscher/Vlieghe 2014
Hans Devisscher, Hans Vlieghe, *Rubens. The Life of Christ before the Passion*, 2 Bde./vols., *The Youth of Christ*, Bd./vol. 2, London/Turnhout 2014 (*Corpus Rubenianum Ludwig Burchard* V)

Diels 2009
Ann Diels, *The Shadow of Rubens. Print Publishing in 17th Century Antwerp*, London 2009

Diemer 2008
Peter Diemer, Verloren – verstreut – bewahrt. Graphik und Bücher der Kunstkammer. Aufsätze und Anhänge, in: Kunstkammer 2008, Bd./vol. 3, S./pp. 225–252

Duverger 1976
Erik Duverger, Nadere gegevens over de Antwerpse periode van Jan Porcellis, in: *Jaarboek van het Koninklijk Museum voor Schone Kunsten Antwerpen* 16, 1976, S./pp. 269–279

Eck 2008
Xander van Eck, *Clandestine Splendor. Paintings for the Catholic Church in the Dutch Republic*, Zwolle 2008 (*Studies in Netherlandish Art and Cultural History* IX)

Evanston/Chapel Hill 1993
Graven Images. The Rise of Professional Printmakers in Antwerp and Haarlem 1540–1640, hg. von /ed. Timothy Riggs, Larry Silver (Ausst.-Kat./exh. cat. Evanston, IL, Mary and Leigh Block Gallery, Northwestern University/Chapel Hill, NC, Ackland Art Museum, University of North Carolina), Evanston 1993

Evers 1944
Hans Gerhard Evers, *Rubens und sein Werk. Neue Forschungen*, Brussel 1944

Filedt Kok 1991
Jan Piet Filedt Kok, Proefdrukken uit Goltzius' atelier omstreeks 1587, in: *Bulletin van het Rijksmuseum* 39, 4, 1991, S./pp. 363–374

Filedt Kok 1991/92
Jan Piet Filedt Kok, Hendrick Goltzius. Engraver, Designer, and Publisher 1582–1600, in: Goltzius Studies 1991/92, S./pp. 159–218

Filedt Kok 1996
Jan Piet Filedt Kok, Artists Portrayed by Their Friends. Goltzius and His Circle, in: *Simiolus* 24, 2/3, 1996 (*Ten Essays for a Friend, E. de Jongh* 65), S./pp. 161–181

Filedt Kok 2014
Jan Piet Filedt Kok, Rez. von/rev. of *Hendrick Goltzius*, comp. by Marjolein Leesberg. ed. by Huigen Leeflang, Ouderkerk aan den Ijssel 2012. *The New Hollstein Dutch & Flemish Etchings, Engravings and Woodcuts 1450–1700*, in: *The Burlington Magazine* 156, 1339, 2014, S./pp. 676–677

Freedberg 1983
David Freedberg, Fame, Convention and Insight. On the Relevance of Fornenberg and Gerbier, in: *The Ringling Museum of Art Journal. Papers Presented at the International Rubens Symposium 1982*, Sarasota, FL, 1983, S./pp. 236–259

Furetière 1690
Antoine Furetière, *Dictionnaire universel, contenant généralement tous les mots François tant vieux que modernes*, Den Haag/Rotterdam 1690

Gelder 1931
Jan Gerrit van Gelder, De etsen van W. Buytewech naar Rubens, in: *Oud Holland* 48, 1931, S./pp. 49–72

Gelder 1950/51
Jan Gerrit van Gelder, Rubens in Holland in de zeventiende eeuw, in: *Nederlands Kunsthistorisch Jaarboek* 4 (1950), 1951, S./pp. 103–150

Génard 1877
Pieter Génard, *P. P. Rubens*, Antwerpen 1877

Gent 2007
Museum voor Schone Kunsten Gent. Catalogus schilderkunst, hg. von /ed. Robert Hoozee et al. (Mus.-Kat./coll. cat.), 2 Bde./vols., Gent 2007

Goltzius Studies 1991/92
Goltzius Studies. Hendrick Goltzius (1558–1617), Nederlands Kunsthistorisch Jaarboek 42/43 (1991), 1992, hg. von/ed. Reindert Falkenburg, Jan Piet Filedt Kok, Huigen Leeflang

Göttingen/Hannover/Nürnberg 1977
Rubens in der Grafik, hg. von/ed. Konrad Renger, Gerd Unverfehrt (Ausst.-Kat. / exh. cat. Göttingen, Kunstsammlung der Universität Göttingen/Hannover, Niedersächsisches Landesmuseum/Nürnberg, Stadtgeschichtliche Museen Nürnberg), Göttingen 1977

Göttler 2020
Christine Göttler, Die Lust des Zeichners. Hendrick Goltzius' Reise nach „seinem ersehnten Rom", in: Zürich 2020, S./pp. 69–87

Greenwich/Berkeley/Cincinnati 2004
Drawn by the Brush. Oil Sketches by Peter Paul Rubens, hg. von/ed. Peter C. Sutton, Marjorie E. Wieseman, Nico Van Hout (Ausst.-Kat./exh. cat. Greenwich, CT, Bruce Museum of Arts and Science/Berkeley, CA, Berkeley Art Museum/Cincinnati, OH, Cincinnati Art Museum), New Haven, CT, 2004

Grieken 2023
Joris van Grieken, Antwerp Prints 1550–1650. A Success Story, in: *Baroque Influencers. Jesuits, Rubens, and the Arts of Persuasion*, hg. von/ed. Pierre Delsaert, Esther Van Thielen (Ausst.-Kat./exh. cat. Antwerpen, Koninklijk Museum voor Schoone Kunsten), Veurne 2023, S./pp. 43–59

Gritsay/Babina 2008
Natalja I. Gritsay, Natalija P. Babina, *Seventeenth- and Eighteenth-Century Flemish Painting* (Mus.-Kat./coll. cat. St. Petersburg, State Hermitage Museum), New Haven 2008

Groenendijk 2008
Pieter Groenendijk, *Beknopt biografisch lexicon van Zuid- en Noord-Nederlandse schilders, graveurs, glasschilders, tapijtwevers et cetera van ca. 1350 tot ca. 1720*, Utrecht 2008

Haarlem/Zürich/Washington 2004
Pieter Claesz. Meester van het stilleven in de Gouden Eeuw, hg. von/ed. Pieter Biesboer (Ausst.-Kat./exh. cat. Haarlem, Frans Hals Museum/Zürich, Kunsthaus/Washington, DC, National Gallery), Haarlem 2004

Hamburg 2002
Die Masken der Schönheit. Hendrick Goltzius und das Kunstideal um 1600, hg. von/ed. Jürgen Müller, Petra Roettig (Ausst.-Kat./exh. cat. Hamburg, Kunsthalle), Hamburg 2002

Hecquet 1751
Robert Hecquet, *Catalogue des estampes gravées d'après Rubens*, Paris 1751

Held 1980
Julius S. Held, *The Oil Sketches of Peter Paul Rubens. A Critical Catalogue*, 2 Bde./vols, Published for the National Gallery of Art by Princeton Univ. Press, Princeton, NJ, 1980

Held 1986
Julius S. Held, *Rubens, Selected Drawings*, überarb./rev., Oxford/Mount Kisco, NY, 1986

Hemmer 2015
Marloes W. Hemmer, Artistic Transmission in the Low Countries. De Grebber's Creative Imitation of Rubens, in: *Jaarboek de zeventiende eeuw. Cultuur in de Nederlanden in interdisciplinair perspectief*, hg. von/ed. Werkgroep De Zeventiende Eeuw, Bd./vol. 31, 1, 2015, S./pp. 191–210

Hessels 1887
Jan Hendrik Hessels, *Abraham Ortelii et Virorum Eruditorum ad Eundem et ad Jacobum Colium Orellianum Epistulae*, Cambridge 1887

Hirschmann 1920a
Otto Hirschmann, *Hendrick Goltzius*, Leipzig 1920 (*Meister der Graphik* VII)

Hirschmann 1920b
Otto Hirschmann, Balthasar Gerbiers „Eer ende Claght"-dight ter eeren van Henricus Goltius, in: *Oud Holland* 38, 1, 1920, S./pp. 104–125

Hirschmann 1921
Otto Hirschmann, *Verzeichnis des graphischen Werks von Hendrick Goltzius 1558–1617*, Leipzig 1921

Hollstein
Friedrich Wilhelm Heinrich Hollstein, *Dutch & Flemish Etchings, Engravings and Woodcuts ca. 1450–1700*, 72 Bde./vols., Amsterdam/Rotterdam 1949–2010

Hottle 2004
Andrew D. Hottle, Commerce and Connections. Peter Paul Rubens and the Dedicated Print, in: Rubens and the Netherlands 2004, S./pp. 55–85

Houbraken 1718–1721
Arnold Houbraken, *De groote schouburgh der Nederlantsche konstschilders en schilderessen*, 3 Bde./vols., Amsterdam 1718–1721

Huvenne 2004
Paul Huvenne, Inleiding, in: Antwerpen/Québec 2004, S./pp. 8–17

Hyman 2021
Aaron Hyman, *Rubens in Repeat. The Logic of the Copy in Colonial Latin America*, Los Angeles 2021

Hymans 1892
Henri Hymans, Un voyage artistique de Rubens ignoré, in: *Bulletins de l'Academie Royale des Sciences, des Lettres et des Beaux-Arts* 24, 1892, S./pp. 402–408

Jaffé 1966
Michael Jaffé, *Van Dyck's Antwerp Sketchbook*, 2 Bde./vols., London 1966

Jaffé 1984
David Jaffé, Rubens and Australia, in: *Art and Australia* 21, 1984, S./pp. 368–373

Jaffé 1988
Rubens' Self-Portrait in Focus, hg. von/ed. David Jaffé (Ausst.-Kat./exh. cat. Canberra, Australian National Gallery), Brisbane 1988

Jaffé 2021
David Jaffé, Rubens im Werden, in: Stuttgart 2021, S./pp. 51–63

Judson/Van de Velde 1978
John R. Judson, Carl Van de Velde, *Rubens. Book Illustrations and Title-Pages*, 2 Bde./vols., Brussel/London/Philadelphia, PA, 1978 (*Corpus Rubenianum Ludwig Burchard* XXI)

Juntunen 2004
Eveliina Juntunen, Rubens, Van Mander und Goltzius. „Juno und Argus" und der kunsttheoretische Diskurs in den nördlichen Niederlanden, in: Rubens and the Netherlands 2004, S./pp. 245–269

Kaulbach 2021
Hans Martin Kaulbach, Rubens und die Druckgrafik, in: Stuttgart 2021, S./pp. 273–298

Kirves 2017
Martin Kirves, Das Skulpturale im Werk von Hendrick Goltzius, in: Dessau 2017, S./pp. 72–85

Kleinert 2014
Corina Kleinert, *Peter Paul Rubens (1577–1640) and His Landscapes. Ideas on Nature and Art*, Turnhout 2014 (*Pictura Nova* XX)

Krystof 1997
Doris Krystof, *Werben für die Kunst. Bildliche Kunsttheorie und das Rhetorische in Kupferstichen von Hendrick Goltzius* (Diss./PhD thesis Köln Univ.), Hildesheim 1997 (*Studien zur Kunstgeschichte* 107)

Kunstkammer 2008
Die Münchner Kunstkammer, hg. von/ed. Willibald Sauerländer, 3 Bde./vols., München 2008 (*Abhandlungen/Bayerische Akademie der Wissenschaften, Philosophisch-Historische Klasse* N. F. 129)

Larionov 2021
Alexey Larionov, Hendrick Goltzius, Rudolf II, and a New Proposal Regarding the Iconography and Patronage of the Hermitage "Penwerck", in: *Simiolus* 43, 1/2, 2021, S./pp. 26–39

Laurentius/Niemeijer 1980
Theo Laurentius, Jan W. Niemeijer, *Cornelis Ploos van Amstel (1726–1798), kunstverzamelaar en prentuitgever*, Assen 1980

Leeflang 2008
Huigen Leeflang, Post uit Praag. Over een teruggevonden tekening van Bartholomeus Spranger, in: *Bulletin van het Rijksmuseum* 56, 1/2, 2008, S./pp. 114–127

Leeflang 2012
Huigen Leeflang, The Roman Experiences of Hendrick Goltzius and Jacob Matham. A Comparison, in: *Ein privilegiertes Medium und die Bildkulturen Europas*, hg. von/ed. Eckhard Leuschner, München 2012, S./pp. 21–38 (*Römische Studien der Bibliotheca Hertziana* 32; *Rom und der Norden* 4)

Leeflang 2019
Huigen Leeflang, Hendrick Goltzius and the Origins of the Auricular Style or Kwab, in: *Simiolus* 41, 4, 2019, S./pp. 239–256

Leesberg 1991/92
Marjolein Leesberg, Goltzius, Karel van Manders „Mecenas groot", in: Goltzius Studies 1991/92, S./pp. 413–426

Leesberg 2015
Marjolein Leesberg, Hendrick Goltzius's Chiaroscuro Woodcuts Revisited, in: *Printing Colour 1400–1700*, hg. von/ed. Ad Stijnman, Elizabeth Savage, Leiden etc. 2015, S./pp. 163–170 (*Library of the Written Word* 41)

Leesberg 2017a
Marjolein Leesberg, Hendrick Goltzius und Cornelius Schonaeus. Goltzius … sculptor mirabilis, atque repertor, in: Dessau 2017, S./pp. 94–102

Leesberg 2017b
Marjolein Leesberg, Technische Virtuosität und ewiger Ruhm, in: Dessau 2017, S./pp. 86–92

Limouze 1991/92
Dorothy Limouze, Engraving as Imitation. Goltzius and His Contemporaries, in: Goltzius Studies 1991/92, S./pp. 439–453

Logan/Lohse Belkin 2021
Anne-Marie Logan mit/with Kristin Lohse Belkin, *The Drawings of Peter Paul Rubens 1590–1608. A Critical Catalogue*, Vol. One in Two Parts, Turnhout 2021

Logan/Lohse Belkin 2022
Anne-Marie Logan mit/with Kristin Lohse Belkin, *The Drawings of Peter Paul Rubens 1609–1620. A Critical Catalogue*, Vol. Two in Two Parts, Turnhout 2022

Lohse Belkin 2009
Kristin Lohse Belkin, *Rubens. Copies and Adaptations from Renaissance and Later Artists. German and Netherlandish Artists*, 2 Bde./vols., Turnhout 2009 (*Corpus Rubenianum Ludwig Burchard* XXVI. 1)

London 2005
Rubens. A Master in the Making, hg. von/ed. David Jaffé, Elizabeth McGrath et al. (Ausst.-Kat./exh. cat. London, National Gallery), London 2005

London 2015
Drawn from the Antique. Artists and the Classical Ideal, hg. von/ed. Adriano Aymonino, Anne Varick Lauder (Ausst.-Kat./exh. cat. London, Sir John Soan's Museum/Haarlem, Teylers Museum), London 2015

Los Angeles 2021
Rubens. Picturing Antiquity, hg. von/ed. Anne T. Woolett, Davide Gasparotto, Jeffrey Spier (Ausst.-Kat./exh. cat. Los Angeles, CA, Getty Museum), Los Angeles 2021

Luckschewitz 2020
Jakob Luckschewitz, *Radierung und Reproduktionsgrafik in der zweiten Hälfte des 19. Jahrhunderts. Die Diskussion über druckgrafische Techniken im deutschen Sprachraum*, Kiel 2020

Luijten 2004
Ger Luijten, Titiaan als rolmodel, in: Antwerpen/Québec 2004, S./pp. 18–29

Machiels 1997
Jeroom Machiels, *Privilegie, censuur en indexen in de Zuidelijke Nederlanden tot aan het begin van de 18de eeuw*, Brussel 1997

Magurn 1955
Ruth Saunders Magurn, *The Letters of Peter Paul Rubens*, Cambridge, MA, 1955

Mander (1604) 1916
Rudolf Hoecker, *Das Lehrgedicht des Karel van Mander, Text, Übersetzung und Kommentar nebst Anhang über Manders Geschichtskonstruktion und Kunsttheorie*, Den Haag 1916 (*Quellenstudien zur holländischen Kunstgeschichte* 8)

Mander (1604) 1994
H't leben van Henricus Goltzius, uitnemende schilder, platsnijder en glasschrijver van Mulbracht, in: *Karel van Mander. The Lives of the Illustrious Netherlandish and German Painters*, hg. von/ed. Hessel Miedema, übers. von/transl. Derry Cook-Radmore, 6 Bde./vols., Doornspijk 1994–1999, Text Bd./vol. 1 (1994), fol. 281v–287r

Mander (1604) 2000
Carel van Mander, *Das Leben der niederländischen und deutschen Maler (von 1400 bis ca. 1615)*, übers. von/transl. Hanns Floerke, Reprint der Erstausg./of the 1st ed. 1906, Wiesbaden 2000

Mander 1604
Karel van Mander, *Het schilder-boeck …* , Antwerpen 1604

Marnef 1996
Guido Marnef, *Antwerp in the Age of Reformation. Underground Protestantism in a Commercial Metropolis 1550–1577*, Baltimore 1996

Martin 2005
Gregory Martin, *Rubens. The Ceiling Decoration of the Banqueting Hall*, 2 Bde./vols., London/Turnhout 2005 (*Corpus Rubenianum Ludwig Burchard* XV)

Mazur-Contamine 1994
Hélène E. C. Mazur-Contamine, Goltzius' Seven Oval Chiaroscuro Woodcuts, a Reinterpretation, in: *Delineavit et Sculpsit* 12, April 1994, S./pp. 1–45

McGrath 1984
Elizabeth McGrath, Rubens's "Susanna and the Elders" and Moralizing Inscriptions on Prints, in: Vekeman/Müller-Hofstede 1984, S./pp. 73–90

McGrath 1997
Elizabeth McGrath, *Rubens. Subjects from History*, 2 Bde./vols., London 1997 (*Corpus Rubenianum Ludwig Burchard* XIII)

McGrath et al. 2022
Elizabeth McGrath et al., *Rubens. Mythological Subjects. Hercules to Olympus*, 2 Bde./vols., London/Turnhout 2022 (*Corpus Rubenianum Ludwig Burchardt* XI)

Meier 2020a
Hans Jakob Meier, *Die Kunst der Interpretation. Rubens und die Druckgraphik*, mit einem Beitrag von/with a contribution by Jeremy Wood, Berlin/München 2020

Meier 2020b
Hans Jakob Meier, Der Beitrag von Hendrick Goltzius und Agostino Carracci zum interpretierenden Kupferstich, in: Zürich 2020, S./pp. 53–68

Melion 1993
Walter S. Melion, Theory & Practice. Reproductive Engravings in the Sixteenth-Century Netherlands, in: Evanston/Chapel Hill 1993, S./pp. 47–70

Melion 2017
Walter S. Melion, The Trope of Anthropomorphosis in Hendrick Goltzius's "Venus and Cupid" (1590), "Venus, Bacchus, and Ceres" (1593), and "Portrait of Frederick de Vries" (1597), in: *Ut Pictura Amor. The Reflexive Imagery of Love in Artistic Theory and Practice 1500–1700*, hg. von/ed. Walter S. Melion, Joanna Woodall, Michael Zell, Chicago, IL, Emory University, Leiden/Boston, MA, 2017, S./pp. 158–228

Meulen 1994
Marjon van der Meulen, *Rubens. Copies after the Antique*, 3 Bde./vols., hg. von/ed. Arnout Balis, London 1994/95 (*Corpus Rubenianum Ludwig Burchard* XXIII)

Miedema 1985
Hessel Miedema, Originaliteit in de kunstenaar?, in: *Handelingen van het acht en dertigste Nederlands filologencongres gehouden te Nijmegen, 16.–17. April 1984*, Amsterdam/Maarsen 1985, S./pp. 477–492

Mitchell 2013
Alexandre G. Mitchell, Democracy and Popular Media. Classical Receptions in Nineteenth, Twentieth, and Twenty-First Century Political Cartoons. Statesmen, Mythological Figures, and Celebrated Artworks, in: *Classics in the Modern World. A "Democratic Turn"?*, hg. von/ed. Lorna Hardwick, Stephen J. Harrison, Oxford 2013, S./pp. 319–349

Monballieu 1965
Adolf E. E. Monballieu, P. P. Rubens en het „Nachtmael" voor St.-Winoksbergen (1611), in: *Jaarboek Koninklijk Museum voor Schone Kunsten Antwerpen* 1965, S./pp. 183–205

Morford 1991
Mark Morford, *Stoics and Neostoics. Rubens and the Circle of Lipsius*, Princeton, NJ, 1991

Mühlen 1998
Ilse von zur Mühlen, *Bild und Vision. Peter Paul Rubens und der „Pinsel Gottes"* (Diss./PhD thesis München Univ.), Frankfurt am Main etc. 1998

Muller 1982
Jeffrey M. Muller, Rubens's Theory and Practice of the Imitation of Art, in: *The Art Bulletin* 64, 1982, S./pp. 229–247

Muller 1989
Jeffrey M. Muller, *Rubens. The Artist as Collector*, Princeton, NJ, 1989

Müller/Pfisterer 2011
Aemulatio. Kulturen des Wettstreits in Text und Bild 1450–1620, hg. von/ed. Jan-Dirk Müller, Ulrich Pfisterer, Berlin 2011

München 1979
Konrad Renger, *Graphik der Niederlande 1508–1617. Kupferstiche und Radierungen von Lucas van Leyden bis Hendrik Goltzius* (Ausst.-Kat./exh. cat. München, Staatliche Graphische Sammlung), München 1979

München 1989
Holm Bevers, *Hendrick Goltzius. Druckgraphik* (Faltblatt/brochure, München, Staatliche Graphische Sammlung), München 1989

München 2003
Thea Vignau-Wilberg, *Hendrick Goltzius. Graphik* (Ausst.-Kat./exh. cat. München, Staatliche Graphische Sammlung), München 2003

München 2005
Thea Vignau-Wilberg, *In Europa zu Hause. Niederländer in München um 1600. Citizens of Europe. Dutch and Flemish Artists in Munich c. 1600* (Ausst.-Kat./exh. cat. München, Staatliche Graphische Sammlung), München 2005

München 2006
Marcus Dekiert, *Holländische und deutsche Malerei. Alte Pinakothek*, hg. von/ed. Bayerische Staatsgemäldesammlungen (Mus.-Kat./coll. cat. München, Alte Pinakothek), Ostfildern 2006 (*Katalog der ausgestellten Gemälde* 4)

München 2009
Rubens im Wettstreit mit Alten Meistern, hg. von/ed. Bayerische Staatsgemäldesammlungen (Ausst.-Kat./exh. cat. München, Alte Pinakothek), Ostfildern 2009

Münster 1976
Bilder nach Bildern. Druckgraphik und die Vermittlung von Kunst, hg. von/ed. Gerhard Langemeyer, Richard Schleier (Ausst.-Kat./exh. cat. Münster, Westfälisches Landesmuseum für Kunst und Kulturgeschichte), Münster 1976

Myers 1966
Mary L. Myers, Rubens and the Woodcuts of Christoffel Jegher, in: *The Metropolitan Museum of Art Bulletin* N.S. 25, 1, Summer 1966, S./pp. 7–24

Namowitz Worthen 1991/92
Amy Namowitz Worthen, *Calligraphic Inscriptions on Dutch Mannerist Prints*, in: Goltzius Studies 1991/92, S./pp. 261–306

New York 2005
Peter Paul Rubens. The Drawings, hg. von/ed. Anne-Marie Logan, Michiel Plomp (Ausst.-Kat./exh. cat. New York, The Metropolitan Museum), New Haven/London 2005

NHD Cort 2000
Manfred Sellink, *Cornelis Cort*, hg. von/ed. Huigen Leeflang, 3 Bde./vols., Rotterdam etc. 2000 (*The New Hollstein Dutch & Flemish Etchings, Engravings and Woodcuts 1450–1700*)

NHD Custos I 2022
Jörg Diefenbacher (Bearb./compiler), *Dominicus Custos*, hg. von/ed. Eckhard Leuschner, 7 Bde./vols., Ouderkerk aan den Ijssel 2022, Bd./vol. 1 (*The New Hollstein German Engravings, Etchings and Woodcuts 1450–1700*)

NHD Goltzius 2012
Marjolein Leesberg, *Hendrick Goltzius*, hg. von/ed. Huigen Leeflang, 4 Bde./vols., Ouderkerk aan den Ijssel 2012 (*The New Hollstein Dutch & Flemish Etchings, Engravings and Woodcuts 1450–1700*)

NHD Matham 2007
Léna Widerkehr (Bearb./compiler), *Jacob Matham*, 3 Bde./vols., Beitr. und Hg./contr. and ed. Huigen Leeflang, Ouderkerk aan den Ijssel 2007, Bd./vol. I (*The New Hollstein Dutch & Flemish Etchings, Engravings and Woodcuts 1450–1700*)

NHD Vorsterman I 1993
Christiaan Schuckman, *Lucas Vorsterman I*, Roosendaal/Amsterdam 1993 (*Hollstein's Dutch & Flemish Etchings, Engravings and Woodcuts 1450–1700* XLIII)

Nichols 1991/92
Lawrence W. Nichols, Hendrick Goltzius. Documents and Printed Literature Concerning His Life, in: Goltzius Studies 1991/92, S./pp. 77–120

Nichols 1992
Lawrence W. Nichols, The "Pen Works" of Hendrick Goltzius, in: *Philadelphia Museum of Art Bulletin* 88, 1992, S./pp. 4–56, 373–374

Nichols 2013
Lawrence W. Nichols, *Hendrick Goltzius (1558–1617). A Monograph and Catalogue Raisonné*, Doornspijk 2013

Oberhuber 1958
Konrad Oberhuber, *Die stilistische Entwicklung im Werk Bartholomäus Sprangers*, Wien 1958

Orenstein 2006
Nadine M. Orenstein, Sleeping Caps, City Views, and State Funerals. Privileges for Prints in the Dutch Republic 1593–1650, in: *In His Milieu. Essays on Netherlandish Art in Memory of John Michael Montias*, hg. von/ed. Amy Golahny, Mia M. Mochizuki, Lisa Vergara, Amsterdam 2006, S./pp. 313–346

Orenstein et al. 1993
Nadine M. Orenstein et al., Print Publishers in the Netherlands 1580–1620, in: *The Dawn of the Golden Age. Northern Netherlandish Art 1580–1620*, hg. von/ed. Ger Luijten et al. (Ausst.-Kat./exh. cat. Amsterdam, Rijksmuseum), Amsterdam 1993, S./pp. 167–200

Paolini 2022
Cecilia Paolini, Notizie inedite dall'Archivio Gonzaga di Mantova. I rapporti tra il duca Vincenzo e il patriziato genovese 1600–1608, in: *Rubens a Genova*, hg. von/ed. Nils Büttner, Anna Orlando (Ausst.-Kat./exh. cat. Genova, Palazzo Ducale), Milano 2022, S./pp. 332–335

Parshall 2005
Peter Parshall, Rubens and the Woodcut, Rez. von/rev. of *Peter Paul Rubens. The Drawings* by Anne-Marie Logan and Michiel C. Plomp, in: *Print Quarterly* 22, Dez./Dec. 2005, S./pp. 466–472

Peters 2009
Emily J. Peters, Systems and Swells. The Collective Lineage of Engraved Lines, 1480–1650, in: Providence/Evanston 2009, S./pp. 12–47

Piles 1699
Roger de Piles, *Abrégé de la vie des peintres, avec des réflexions sur leurs ouvrages*, Paris 1699

Piles 1743
Roger de Piles, *The Principles of Painting*, London 1743

Pollack 2020
Susanne Pollack, Schwellende Linien. Cornelis Cort, Agostino Carracci, Hendrick Goltzius und die Erweiterung gestochener Liniensysteme im 16. Jahrhundert, in: Zürich 2020, S./pp. 14–29

Porter/Béland 2004
John R. Porter, Mario Béland, Leermeester op aftstand. De invloed van Rubens op de kunst in Québec, in: Antwerpen/Québec 2004, S./pp. 156–171

Providence/Evanston 2009
The Brilliant Line. Following the Early Modern Engraver 1480–1650 (Ausst.-Kat./exh. cat. Providence, RI, Museum of Art, Rhode Island School of Design/Evanston, IL, Mary and Leigh Block Museum, Northwestern University), Providence, RI, 2009

Rabb 2011
Theodore K. Rabb, Separate Paths, in: *The Art Newspaper* XXI, 229, 2011, S./pp. 78, 83

Renger 1974a
Konrad Renger, Rubens dedit dedicavitque. Rubens' Beschäftigung mit der Reproduktionsgraphik, I. Teil. Der Kupferstich, in: *Jahrbuch der Berliner Museen* 16, 1974, S./pp. 122–175

Renger 1974b
Konrad Renger, Planänderungen in Rubensstichen, in: *Zeitschrift für Kunstgeschichte* 37, 1974, S./pp. 1–30

Renger 1975
Konrad Renger, Rubens dedit dedicavitque. Rubens' Beschäftigung mit der Reproduktionsgraphik, II. Teil. Radierung und Holzschnitt. Die Widmungen, in: *Jahrbuch der Berliner Museen* 17, 1975, S./pp. 166–213

Renger 1981
Konrad Renger, Sine Cerere et Baccho friget Venus. Zu bacchischen Themen bei Rubens, in: *Peter Paul Rubens. Werk und Nachruhm*, hg. von/ed. Zentralinstitut für Kunstgeschichte, Bayerische Staatsgemäldesammlungen, München 1981, S./pp. 105–135

Renger/Denk 2002
Konrad Renger mit/with Claudia Denk, *Flämische Malerei des Barock in der Alten Pinakothek*, München 2002

Reznicek 1961
Emil Karel Josef Reznicek, *Hendrick Goltzius als Zeichner. Mit einem beschreibenden Katalog*, 2 Bde./vols., Utrecht 1961

Reznicek 1992
Emil Karel Josef Reznicek, Rapporti fra Goltzio e Rubens, in: *Rubens dall' Italia all' Europa. Atti des convegno internazionale di studi. Padova, 24–27 maggio 1990*, hg. von/ed. Caterina Limentani Virdis, Francesca Bottacin, Vicenza 1992, S./pp. 121–129

Reznicek 1993
Emil Karel Josef Reznicek, Drawings by Hendrick Goltzius, Thirty Years Later. Supplement to the 1961 Catalogue Raisonné, in: *Master Drawings* 31, 3, 1993, S./pp. 215–278

Riggs 1993
Timothy Riggs, Graven Images. A Guide to the Exhibition, in: Evanston/Chapel Hill 1993, S./pp. 101–108

Roettig 2002
Petra Roettig, „Oh gelehrter Stichel, oh kunstfertige Hand". Über Schrift und Bild in den Kupferstichen von Hendrick Goltzius, in: Hamburg 2002, S./pp. 22–26

Rooses 1877
Max Rooses, *Titels en portretten gesneden naar P.-P. Rubens voor de Plantijnsche drukerij*, Antwerpen 1877

Rooses/Ruelens 1887–1909
Correspondance de Rubens et documents épistolaires concernant sa vie et ses oeuvres, hg. von/ed. Max Rooses, Charles Ruelens, 6 Bde./vols., Antwerpen 1887–1909

Royalton-Kisch 1989
Martin Royalton-Kisch, Dirck Barendsz. and Hendrick Goltzius, in: *Bulletin van het Rijksmuseum* 37, 1989, S./pp. 14–26

Rubens and the Netherlands 2004
Rubens and the Netherlands. Nederlands Kunsthistorisch Jaarboek 55, 2004, hg. von/ed. Jan de Jong et al., Zwolle 2006

Ruelens 1883
Charles Ruelens, La vie de Rubens par Roger de Piles, in: *Rubens-Bulletijn* II, 1883, S./p. 166

Rutgers 2019
Jaco Rutgers, Rubens's Early Involvement in Printmaking, in: *Early Rubens*, hg. von/ed. Alexandra Suda, Kirk Nickel (Ausst.-Kat./exh. cat. San Francisco, Fine Arts Museums of San Francisco, CA/Ontario, Art Gallery of Ontario), München etc. 2019, S./pp. 102–114

Rutgers 2021
Jaco Rutgers, Rubens's printmaking enterprise, Rez. von/rev. of *Die Kunst der Interpretation. Rubens und die Druckgraphik*, Hans Jakob Meier; mit einem Beitrag von Jeremy Wood, 2020, in: *Print Quarterly* 38, 1, March 2021, S./pp. 103–108

Ruyven-Zeman 2002
Zsuzsanna van Ruyven-Zeman, Portretten van hoog tot lag en van klein tot groot. De familie Wierix en Hendrick Goltzius, in: *Bulletin van het Rijksmuseum* 50, 2002, S./pp. 390–405

Sandrart 1675
Joachim von Sandrart, *L'Academia Tedesca della Architectura, Scultura & Pittura. Oder Teutsche Academie der Edlen Bau-, Bild- und Mahlerey-Künste*, Nürnberg 1675, URL: <http://ta.sandrart.net/472> [aufgerufen am 1.11.2023/accessed November 1, 2023]

Sandrart (1675) 2019
Joachim von Sandrart, The Life of Peter Paul Rubens, Painter. From "Teutsche Academie" 1675, in: *Lives of Rubens. Baglione, Sandrart, de Piles*, übers. von/transl. Kristin Belkin, London 2019, S./pp. 35–62

Schallaburg 1991
Stadtbilder in Flandern. Spuren bürgerlicher Kultur 1477–1787, hg. von/ed. Jan van der Stock (Ausst.-Kat./exh. cat. Schollach bei Melk, Renaissanceschloss Schallaburg), Brussel 1991

Schmidt-Clausen 2016
Uta Schmidt-Clausen, Bildgedichte von Franco Estius (ca. 1544–ca. 1594) nach Livius und Ovid in der Druckgraphik von Hendrick Goltzius, in: *Neulateinisches Jahrbuch. Journal of Neo-Latin Language and Literature* 18, 2016, S./pp. 307–352

Seigneur 2004
Marie-Christine Seigneur, On Counterproofs, in: *Print Quarterly* 21, 2, June 2004, S./pp. 115–127

SGSM FS 2008
Künstler zeichnen, Sammler stiften. 250 Jahre Staatliche Graphische Sammlung München, hg. von/ed. Michael Semff, Kurt Zeitler, 3 Bde./vols., Ostfildern 2008

Silver 1993a
Larry Silver, Graven Images. Reproductive Engravings as Visual Models, in: Evanston/Chapel Hill 1993, S./pp. 1–46

Silver 1993b
Larry Silver, Imitation & Emulation. Goltzius as Evolutionary Reproductive Engraver, in: Evanston/Chapel Hill 1993, pp. 71–100

Silver 2011
Larry Silver, Hendrick Goltzius Translates the Renaissance, in: Müller/Pfisterer 2011, S./pp. 277–318

Sluijter 1991
Eric Jan Sluijter, „Vertumnus en Pomona" door Hendrick Goltzius (1613) en Jan Tengnagel (1617). Constanten en contrasten in vorm en inhoud, in: *Bulletin van het Rijksmuseum* 39, 4, 1991, S./pp. 386–400

Sluijter 2005
Eric Jan Sluijter, Goltzius, Painting and Flesh. Or, Why Goltzius Began to Paint in 1600, in: *The Learned Eye. Regarding Art, Theory and the Artist's Reputation. Essays for Ernst van de Wetering*, hg. von/ed. Marieke van den Doel et al., Amsterdam 2005, S./pp. 158–177

Smet 1977
Rudolf de Smet, Een nauwkeuriger datering van Rubens' eerste reis naar Holland in 1612, in: *Jaarboek van het Koninklijk Museum voor Schone Kunsten Antwerpen*, 1977, S./pp. 199–220

Sonnabend 2018
Martin Sonnabend, Rubens kopiert Goltzius, in: *Von der Genauigkeit des Sehens. Festschrift für Anne Röver-Kann zum 75. Geburtstag*, hg. von/ed. Rebecca Duckwitz et al., Bremen 2018, S./pp. 57–64

Stadsarchief Gent 1797
Stadsarchief Gent. Notice des tableaux, dessins et estampes trouvés dans la ci-d(evant) Ecole de l'Abbaije de Baudeloo. Ceux marqués d'un K sont conformes à la note du 10 ventôse an V, trouvé au quartier de l'Abbé de Saint-Pierre, Gent 1797

Stechow 1927
Wolfgang Stechow, Zu Rubens' erster Reise nach Holland, in: *Oud Holland* 44, 1927, S./pp. 138–139

Stijnman 2012
Ad Stijnman, *Engraving and Etching 1400–2000. A History of the Development of Manual Intaglio Printmaking Processes*, London 2012

Stolzenburg 2002
Andreas Stolzenburg, Hendrick Goltzius und die Antike, in: Hamburg 2002, S./pp. 17–26

Stuttgart 2021
Becoming Famous. Peter Paul Rubens wird berühmt, hg. von/ed. Nils Büttner, Sandra-Kristin Diefenthaler (Ausst.-Kat./exh. cat. Stuttgart, Staatsgalerie), Dresden 2021

Sutton 1999
Peter Sutton, Pieter de Grebber, in: *Hollands classicisme in de zeventiende-eeuwse schilderkunst*, hg. von/ed. Albert Blankert et al. (Ausst.-Kat./exh. cat. Rotterdam, Museum Boijmans Van Beuningen/Frankfurt am Main, Städelsches Kunstinstitut), Rotterdam 1999, S./pp. 116–143

Sweertius 1613
Franciscus Sweertius, *Monumenta Sepulcralia et Inscriptiones Publicae Privataeque Ducatus Brabantiae*, Antwerpen 1613

Taylor 1998
Paul Taylor, The Glow in Late Sixteenth and Seventeenth-Century Dutch Paintings, in: *Looking Through Paintings. The Study of Painting Techniques and Materials in Support of Art Historical Research*, hg. von/ed. Erma Hermens, Baarn 1998, S./pp. 159–178 (*Leids Kunsthistorisch Jaarboek* XI)

Thielemann 2008
Andreas Thielemann, Rubens' Traktat „De imitatione statuarum", in: *Imitatio als Transformation*, hg. von/ed. Ursula Rombach, Peter Seiler, Petersberg 2008, S./pp. 95–150

Thiel-Stroman 1989a
Irene van Thiel-Stroman, De documenten over Frans Hals. Geschreven en gedrukte bronnen 1582–1679, in: *Frans Hals*, hg. von/ed. Seymour Slive (Ausst.-Kat./exh. cat. Washington, DC, National Gallery of Art/London, Royal Academy of Arts/Haarlem, Frans Hals Museum), London 1989, S./pp. 45–60

Thiel-Stroman 1989b
Irene van Thiel-Stroman, Chronologie, in: *Frans Hals*, hg. von/ed. Seymour Slive (Ausst.-Kat./exh. cat. Washington, DC, National Gallery of Art/London, Royal Academy of Arts/Haarlem, Frans Hals Museum), London 1989, S./pp. 19–22

Thiel-Stroman 2006
Irene van Thiel-Stroman, Pieter Fransz de Grebber, in: *Painting in Haarlem 1500–1850. The Collection of the Frans Hals Museum*, hg. von/ed. Neeltje Köhler, Gent/Amsterdam 2006, S./pp. 168–172

Tieze 2012
Agnes Tieze, Meisterlich kopieren. Kopieren nach dem Meister, in: *Déjà-vu? Die Kunst der Wiederholung von Dürer bis You Tube*, hg. von/ed. Ariane Mensger (Ausst.-Kat./exh. cat. Karlsruhe, Staatliche Kunsthalle), Bielefeld 2012, S./pp. 46–53

Tokyo 1993
The Flight of Lot and His Family from Sodom. Rubens and His Workshop, hg. von/ed. Toshiharu Nakamura (Ausst.-Kat./exh. cat. Tokyo, The National Museum of Western Art), Tokyo 1993

Tummers 2015
Anna Tummers, Goltzius, Rubens and Artistic Rivalry. Seventeenth Century Views on Citing and Emulating Another Artist's Work, Vortrag gehalten im/lecture delivered at the Philadelphia Museum, 17. Oktober/October 17, 2015 (unveröff./unpubl.)

Van Hout 2004
Nico Van Hout, Copyright Rubens. Cum privilegiis …, in: Antwerpen/Québec 2004, S./pp. 30–39

Van Thiel 1989
Pieter J. J. Van Thiel, Hendrick Goltzius, „Lot en zijn dochters" (1616), in: *Bulletin van het Rijksmuseum* 37, 3, 1989, S./pp. 124–140

Vekeman/Müller-Hofstede 1984
Wort und Bild in der niederländischen Kunst und Literatur des 16. und 17. Jahrhunderts, hg. von/ed. Herman Vekeman, Justus Müller-Hofstede, Erfstadt 1984

Venne 2017
Hans van de Venne, Zu den Kupferstichen von Hendrick Goltzius mit Epigrammen von Cornelius Schonaeus, in: Dessau 2017, S./pp. 103

Verhoeven 2009a
Gerrit Verhoeven, "Een divertissant somertogje". Transport Innovations and the Rise of Short-Term Pleasure Trips in the Low Countries 1600–1750, in: *Journal of Transport History* 30, 1, 2009, S./pp. 78–97

Verhoeven 2009b
Gerrit Verhoeven, *Anders reizen? Evoluties in de vroegmoderne reiservaringen van Hollandse en Brabantse elites 1600–1750*, Hilversum 2009

Vermeylen 2003
Filip Vermeylen, *Painting for the Market. Commercialization of Art in Antwerp's Golden Age*, Turnhout 2003

Vermeylen 2004
Filip Vermeylen, Antwerp Beckons. The Reasons for Rubens' Return to the Netherlands in 1608, in: *Nederlands Kunsthistorisch Jaarboek* 55, 2004, S./pp. 16–33

Vermeylen 2014
Filip Vermeylen, Greener Pastures? Capturing Artists' Migrations during the Dutch Revolt, in: *Nederlands Kunsthistorisch Jaarboek* 63, 2014, S./pp. 40–57

Viljoen 2011
Madeleine Viljoen, "To Print or Not to Print?" Hendrick Goltzius' 1595 "Sine Baccho et Cerere Friget Venus" and Engraving with Precious Metals, in: *Zeitschrift für Kunstgeschichte* 74, 2011, S./pp. 45–76

Vlieghe 1972
Hans Vlieghe, *Rubens. Saints*, 2 Bde./vols., Brussel/London/New York 1972 (*Corpus Rubenianum Ludwig Burchard* VIII.1, 2)

Vlieghe 1987
Hans Vlieghe, *Rubens. Portraits of Identified Sitters Painted in Antwerp*, London/New York 1987 (*Corpus Rubenianum Ludwig Burchard* XIX.2)

Voorhelm Schneevoogt 1873
George Voorhelm Schneevoogt, *Catalogue des estampes gravées d'après P. P. Rubens*, Haarlem 1873

Walsh 1974a
John Walsh, The Dutch Marine Painters Jan and Julius Porcellis, I. Jan's Early Career, in: *The Burlington Magazine* 116, 1974, S./pp. 653–662

Walsh 1974b
John Walsh, The Dutch Marine Painters Jan and Julius Porcellis, II. Jan's Maturity and "de jonge Porcellis", in: *The Burlington Magazine* 116, 1974, S./pp. 734–745

Wandrey 2018
Petra Wandrey, *Ehre über Gold. Die Meisterstiche von Hendrick Goltzius. Bildtheorie und Ikonografie um 1600*, Berlin 2018

Weddigen 2004
Tristan Weddigen, Italienreise als Tugendweg. Hendrick Goltzius' „Tabula Cebetis", in: *Nederlands Kunsthistorisch Jaarboek* 54 (2003), 2004, S./pp. 90–139

White 2007
Christopher White, *The Later Flemish Pictures in the Collection of Her Majesty the Queen*, London 2007

Wien 2004
Peter Paul Rubens, hg. von/ed. Klaus Albrecht Schröder, Heinz Widauer (Ausst.-Kat./exh. cat. Wien, Albertina), mit Beiträgen von/with contributions by Anne-Marie Logan et al., Wien 2004

Wien/Frankfurt 2017
Rubens. Kraft der Verwandlung, hg. von/ed. Gerlinde Gruber et al. (Ausst.-Kat./exh. cat. Wien, Kunsthistorisches Museum/Frankfurt, Städel Museum), München 2017 [English edition: *Rubens. The Power of Transformation*, hg. von/ed. Gerlinde Gruber et al. (Ausst.-Kat./exh. cat. Wien, Kunsthistorisches Museum/Frankfurt, Städel Museum), München 2017]

Wijngaert 1940
Frank van den Wijngaert, *Inventaris der Rubeniaansche prentkunst*, Antwerpen 1940

Wolkenhauer 2006
Anja Wolkenhauer, Genese und Funktion von Epigrammen in der Druckgraphik des 16. Jahrhunderts am Beispiel einiger Stiche von Hendrick Goltzius, in: *Künstler und Literat. Schrift- und Buchkultur in der europäischen Renaissance*, hg. von/ed. Bodo Guthmüller, Berndt Hamm, Andreas Tönnesmann, Wiesbaden 2006 (*Wolfenbütteler Abhandlungen zur Renaissanceforschung* 24)

Wood 2006
Jeremy Wood, Rubens and Raphael. The Designs for the Tapestries in the Sistine Chapel, in: *Munuscula Amicorum. Contributions on Rubens and His Colleagues in Honour of Hans Vlieghe*, hg. von/ed. Katlijne van Stighelen, 2 Bde./vols., Turnhout 2006, Bd./vol. 1, S./pp. 259–282

Wood 2010
Jeremy Wood, *Rubens. Copies and Adaptations from Renaissance and Later Artists*, 3 Bde./vols., *Italian Masters I. Raphael and His School*, hg. von/ed. Carl Van de Velde et al., Bd./vol. 2.1, Turnhout 2010 (*Corpus Rubenianum Ludwig Burchard* XXVI)

Wood 2020
Jeremy Wood, „In meiner Anwesenheit ausgeführt". Rubens' „Modelli" als Stichvorlagen, in: Meier 2020a, S./pp. 46–80

Wouk 2018
Edward H. Wouk, Pathosformel as Grammar. From Lambert Lombard to Aby Warburg, in: *Nederlands Kunsthistorisch Jaarboek* 68, 2018, S./pp. 100–134

Wurzbach 1856–1891
Constantin von Wurzbach, *Biographisches Lexikon des Kaisertums Österreich, enthaltend die Lebensskizzen der denkwürdigen Personen, welche 1750 bis 1850 im Kaiserstaate und in seinen Kronländern gelebt haben*, 60 Bde./vols., Wien 1856–1891

Wurzbach 1910
Alfred von Wurzbach, *Niederländisches Künstlerlexikon*, 2 Bde./vols., Wien/Leipzig 1910

Zoff 1918
Otto Zoff, *Die Briefe des P. P. Rubens*, Wien 1918

Zürich 2020
Sich kreuzende Parallelen. Agostino Carracci. Hendrick Goltzius, hg. von/ed. Susanne Pollack, Samuel Vitali (Ausst.-Kat./exh. cat. Zürich, Graphische Sammlung der ETH Zürich), Petersberg 2020 [English edition: *Crossing Parallels. Agostino Carracci. Hendrick Goltzius*, hg. von/ed. Susanne Pollack, Samuel Vitali (Ausst.-Kat./exh. cat. Zürich, Graphische Sammlung der ETH Zürich), Petersberg 2020]

Der Katalog erscheint zur Ausstellung / This catalog is published on the occasion of the exhibition

Careers by design. Hendrick Goltzius & Peter Paul Rubens

13.06.–15.09.2024 Staatliche Graphische Sammlung München in der / at the Pinakothek der Moderne, München / Munich

Direktor / Director Michael Hering
Kuratorin der Ausstellung / Exhibition Curator Nina Schleif
Datenerfassung / Data Entry Stephanie Holl, Nina Schleif
Restaurierung / Conservation Katrin Holzherr, Melanie Anderseck, Mizuho Matsunaga mit / with Cornelia Stahl, Dafne Diamante, Nadine Bretz, Ronda Hansen, Franziska Huber
Social Media & Digitalisierung / Digitization Enikö Zséller
Rahmen, Passepartouts & Aufbau / Frames, Matting, & Exhibition Installation Bernhard Eglmeier, Karl-Heinz Francota Staat, Rafael Díaz Noguero, Mizuho Matsunaga, Joe Holzner
Sekretariat & Registrarinnen / Director's Assistants & Registrars Romy Halász, Sabine Wölfel
Studiensaal / Study Hall Florian Kislinger, Rafael Díaz Noguero, Michael Graßl (†)

KATALOG / CATALOG
Herausgeberin / Editor Nina Schleif, Staatliche Graphische Sammlung München
Autoren / Authors Nils Büttner, Karolien De Clippel, Michael Hering, Nadine M. Orenstein, Nina Schleif, Filip Vermeylen
Projektmanagement Hirmer Verlag / Project Management Hirmer Publishers Jutta Allekotte, Katja Durchholz
Lektorat / Copyediting Simone Albiez (D), Rita Forbes (EN)
Übersetzung / Translation Nikolaus G. Schneider (EN–D: S./pp. 24–66), Julian Jain (D–EN: S./pp. 6–9, 14–23, 69–93, 96–109), Nina Schleif (D–EN: S./pp. 116–294)
Photothek / Rights & Reproductions Sabine Wölfel
Scans & Bildbearbeitung / Imaging Stephanie Holl, Gunnar Gustafsson
Graphik & Satz / Design & Typesetting Sarah Nöllenheidt, buero noc, Berlin
Herstellung / Production Katja Durchholz
Lithographie / Pre-press & Repro Genceller Reproline, München
Papier / Paper Gardapat Kiara, 150 g/m²
Schriften / Fonts Foglihten, Verdigris
Druck & Bindung / Printing & Binding Printer Trento s.r.l., Trento

Bestandskatalog online / Catalog of the holdings Im Rahmen der Vorbereitung dieser Ausstellung wurden die Bestände von Hendrick Goltzius und Peter Paul Rubens vollständig erschlossen und sind nun online auf der Homepage der Staatlichen Graphischen Sammlung München abrufbar. / In preparation for this exhibition, the holdings of Hendrick Goltzius and Peter Paul Rubens were identified and documented in their entirety. They can now be researched online on the homepage of the Staatliche Graphische Sammlung München.

› www.sgsm.eu/sgsm-online/ ‹

Bibliographische Information der Deutschen Nationalbibliothek Die Deutsche Nationalbibliothek verzeichnet diese Publikation in der Deutschen Nationalbibliografie; detaillierte bibliographische Daten sind im Internet über http://dnb.de abrufbar. / *Bibliographic information published by the Deutsche Nationalbibliothek* The Deutsche Nationalbibliothek lists this publication in the Deutsche Nationalbibliografie; detailed bibliographic data are available in the Internet at http://dnb.de.

www.hirmerverlag.de www.hirmerpublishers.com www.hirmerpublishers.co.uk

WWW.SGSM.EU

ISBN 978-3-7774-4352-2

PRINTED IN ITALY

STAATLICHE GRAPHISCHE SAMMLUNG MÜNCHEN

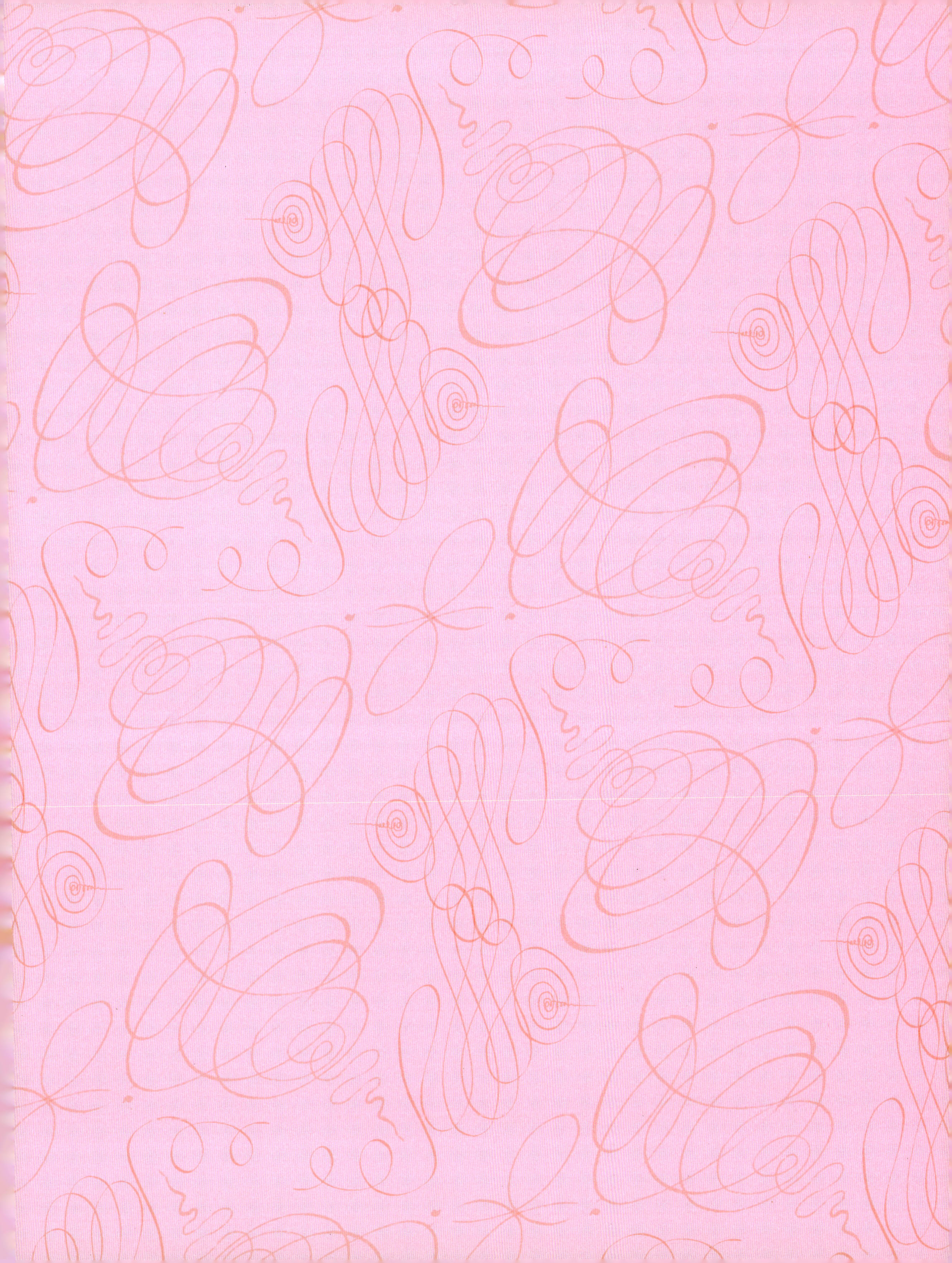

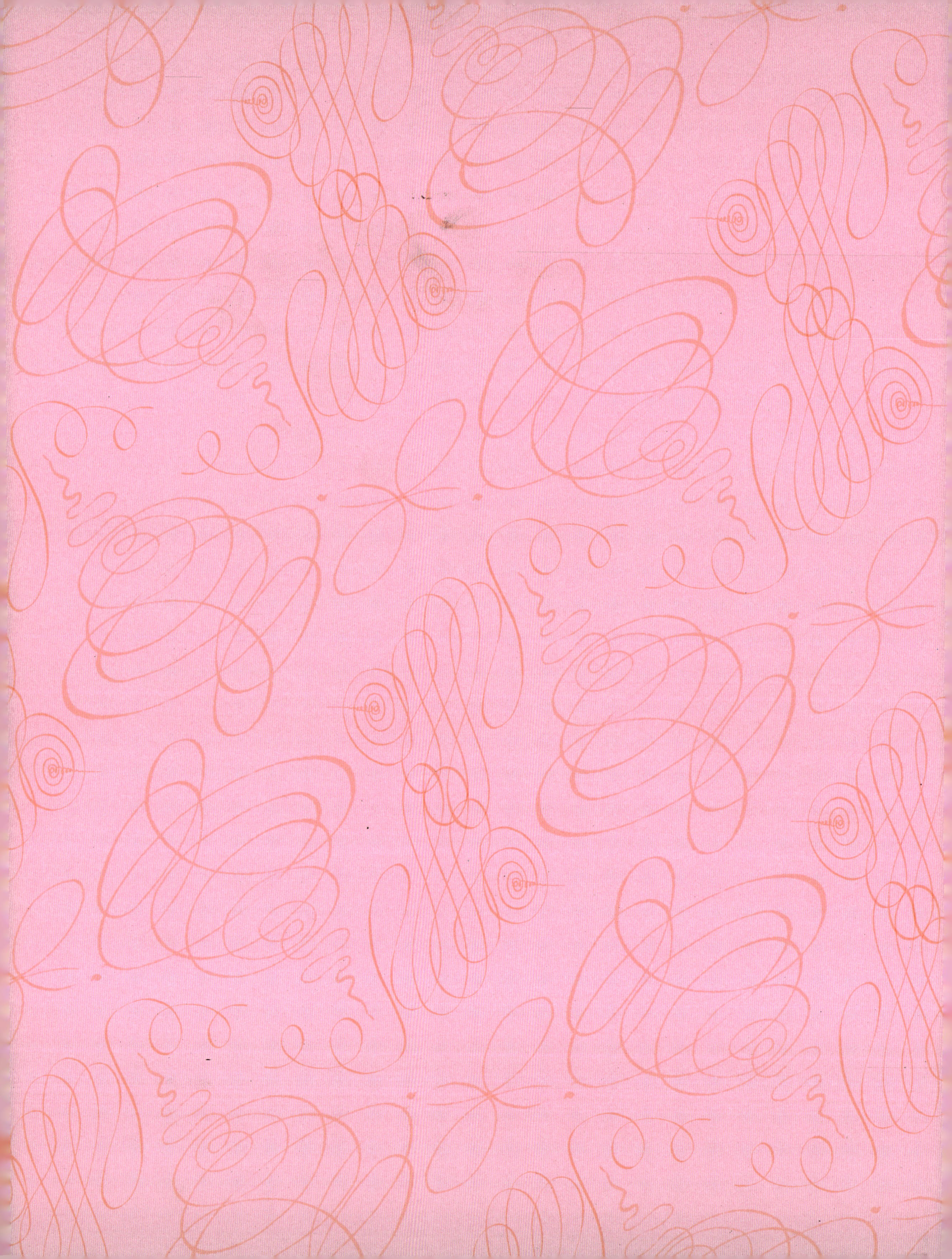